Lecture Notes in Computer Science 1298

Edited by G. Goos, J. Hartmanis and J. van Leeuwen

Springer
Berlin
Heidelberg
New York
Barcelona
Budapest
Hong Kong
London
Milan
Paris
Santa Clara
Singapore
Tokyo

Michael Hanus Jan Heering
Karl Meinke (Eds.)

Algebraic and Logic Programming

6th International Joint Conference
ALP '97 — HOA '97
Southampton, UK, September 3-5, 1997
Proceedings

Springer

Series Editors

Gerhard Goos, Karlsruhe University, Germany

Juris Hartmanis, Cornell University, NY, USA

Jan van Leeuwen, Utrecht University, The Netherlands

Volume Editors

Michael Hanus
RWTH Aachen, Forschungsgebiet Informatik II
Ahornstr. 55, D-52074 Aachen, Germany
E-mail: hanus@informatik.rwth-aachen.de

Jan Heering
CWI
P.O. Box 94079, 1090 GB Amsterdam, The Netherlands
E-mail: Jan.Heering@cwi.nl

Karl Meinke
Royal Institute of Technology/NADA
Osquars backe 2, S-100 44 Stockholm, Sweden
E-mail: karlm@nada.kth.se

Cataloging-in-Publication data applied for

Die Deutsche Bibliothek - CIP-Einheitsaufnahme

Algebraic and logic programming : 6th international joint conference ; proceedings / ALP '97 ; HOA '97, Southampton, UK, September 3 - 5, 1997. Michael Hanus ... (ed.). - Berlin ; Heidelberg ; New York ; Barcelona ; Budapest ; Hong Kong ; London ; Milan ; Paris ; Santa Clara ; Singapore ; Tokyo : Springer, 1997
(Lecture notes in computer science ; Vol. 1298)
ISBN 3-540-63459-2

CR Subject Classification (1991): D.3, F.3-4, I.2.3

ISSN 0302-9743
ISBN 3-540-63459-2 Springer-Verlag Berlin Heidelberg New York

Printed in Germany

Typesetting: Camera-ready by author
SPIN 10546333 06/3142 – 5 4 3 2 1 0 Printed on acid-free paper

Preface

This volume contains the proceedings of the *Sixth International Conference on Algebraic and Logic Programming* (ALP'97) and the *Third International Workshop on Higher-Order Algebra, Logic and Term Rewriting* (HOA'97), held in Southampton (Great Britain) during September 3–5, 1997. The conference ALP'97 was preceded by meetings in Gaussig (1988), Nancy (1990), Volterra (1992), Madrid (1994), and Aachen (1996). The proceedings of these conferences have been published by Springer-Verlag, as Lecture Notes in Computer Science volumes 343, 463, 632, 850, and 1139, respectively. The workshop HOA'97 was preceded by meetings in Amsterdam (1993) and Paderborn (1995). The proceedings of these workshops have also been published as Lecture Notes in Computer Science volumes 816 and 1074 respectively.

The ALP conference aims at strengthening the connections between algebraic techniques and logic programming. On the one hand, logic programming has been very successful during the last two decades, and many efforts have been made to enhance its expressive power and efficiency, including in particular the emergence of constraint logic programming. On the other hand, concepts such as functions, types, equational theories, and modularity are particularly well handled in an algebraic framework. As during the previous conferences, ALP promotes the cross-fertilizing exchange of ideas and experiences among researchers from the algebraic and logic programming communities.

The HOA workshop aims to provide an overview of current research, and to suggest new research directions, in the area of higher-order methods. These are now widely applied in declarative programming languages, as well as in software and hardware specification and verification. The scope of the workshop includes higher-order aspects of: algebra, logic and model theory, term rewriting, specification and verification languages, computational logic and theorem proving, and also system implementations and case studies.

On this occasion, ALP'97 and HOA'97 were held jointly, allowing contributors and participants to exploit the overlap in these subject areas. ALP'97 and HOA'97 were also held concurrently with the Ninth International Symposium on Programming Languages, Implementations, Logics, and Programs (PLILP'97).

The joint ALP'97/HOA'97 Program Committee met electronically during the final week of May, 1997. There was an email discussion of those papers for which there was a significant disagreement about the judgement. Finally, the combined Program Committees selected 18 papers from 31 submissions.

We would like to thank all the members of the Program Committee and all the referees for their careful work in the reviewing and selection process.

The ALP'97 and HOA'97 conferences were organised in cooperation with the British Computer Society, the Association of Logic Programming, the European Association for Programming Languages and Systems, Compulog Net (the ESPRIT Network of Excellence in Computational Logic), and the European Association for Computer Science Logic (EACSL).

Finally, we express our gratitude to all members of the local Organizing Committee for their help in organizing a successful event.

Aachen
Amsterdam
Stockholm
June 1997

Michael Hanus
Jan Heering
Karl Meinke
Proceedings Editors

ALP'97 Program Committee Co-Chairs

M. Hanus (Germany)
K. Meinke (Sweden)

Program Committee

F. Benhamou (France)
F. Fages (France)
M. Haveraaen (Norway)
J.W. Klop (Netherlands)
G. Nadathur (USA)
P. Stuckey (Australia)
S. Thompson (Great Britain)
J. Tiuryn (Poland)
M. Wirsing (Germany)
D. De Schreye (Belgium)
I. Guessarian (France)
S. Hölldobler (Germany)
A. Middeldorp (Japan)
C. Palamidessi (Italy)
R. Stärk (Switzerland)
J.V. Tucker (Great Britain)
A. Voronkov (Sweden)

HOA'97 Program Committee Co-Chairs

J. Heering (Netherlands)
K. Meinke (Sweden)
B. Möller (Germany)
T. Nipkow (Germany)

Program Committee

D. Dougherty (USA)
A. Felty (USA)
M. Gordon (Great Britain)
G. Dowek (France)
J. Field (USA)

Local Organization

H. Glaser and P. Hartel

List of Referees

C. Baral, K. Van Belleghem, M. Bialasik, M. Carlsson, P. Cenciarelli, A. Degtyarev, U. Furbach, B. Gramlich, K. Hanna, J. Harland, J. Hodas, S. Kahrs, A. Knapp, P. Kosiuczenko, V. Kriaučiukas, A. Leitsch, M. Leuschel, M. Marchiori, T. Melham, D. Miller, E. Moggi, M. Okada, V. van Oostrom, P.C. Ölveczky, D. Plump, C. Prehofer, F. van Raamsdonk, G. Richard, H. Søndergaard, G. Stålmarck, C. Urban, H. Vandecasteele, E. Visser, H. Zantema.

Table of Contents

Functional and Logic Programming

Higher-Order Methods

Term Rewriting

Types

Lambda-Calculus

Theorem Proving Methods

Safe Folding/Unfolding with Conditional Narrowing*

M. Alpuente[1] and M. Falaschi[2] and G. Moreno[3] and G. Vidal[1]

[1] DSIC, Universidad Politécnica de Valencia, Camino de Vera s/n, Apdo. 22012, 46020 Valencia, Spain. e.mail:{alpuente,gvidal}@dsic.upv.es.
[2] Dipartimento di Matematica e Informatica, Università di Udine, Via delle Scienze 206, 33100 Udine, Italy. e.mail:falaschi@dimi.uniud.it.
[3] Departamento de Informática, Universidad de Castilla-La Mancha, Campus Universitario s/n, 02071 Albacete, Spain. e.mail:Gmoreno@info-ab.uclm.es.

Abstract. Functional logic languages with a complete operational semantics are based on narrowing, a generalization of term rewriting where unification replaces matching. In this paper, we study the semantic properties of a general transformation technique called *unfolding* in the context of functional logic languages. Unfolding a program is defined as the application of narrowing steps to the calls in the program rules in some appropriate form. We show that, unlike the case of pure logic or pure functional programs, where unfolding is correct w.r.t. practically all available semantics, unrestricted unfolding using narrowing does not preserve program meaning, even when we consider the weakest notion of semantics the program can be given. We single out the conditions which guarantee that an equivalent program w.r.t. the semantics of computed answers is produced. Then, we study the combination of this technique with a *folding* transformation rule in the case of innermost conditional narrowing, and prove that the resulting transformation still preserves the computed answer semantics of the initial program, under the usual conditions for the completeness of innermost conditional narrowing. We also discuss a relationship between unfold/fold transformations and partial evaluation of functional logic programs.

1 Introduction

The problem of integration of functional and logic programming is an important challenge for research in declarative programming (see [15] for a recent survey). A functional logic program can be seen as a Conditional Term Rewriting System (CTRS for short), i.e. a set of conditional equations where the equation in the conclusion is implicitly oriented from left to right. Functional logic languages obtain the power of logic variables, automatic search and constraint solving from logic programming. From functional programming, they obtain the expressivity of functions and types, and a more efficient evaluation mechanism thanks to

* This work has been partially supported by CICYT under grant TIC 95-0433-C03-03 and by HCM project CONSOLE.

the deterministic reduction of functional expressions [14, 15]. The operational semantics is usually based on some variant of narrowing, an execution mechanism which consists of the instantiation of goal variables followed by a reduction step on the instantiated goal. The standard declarative semantics of a program $\mathcal{E}$ is given by the least Herbrand $\mathcal{E}$-model of the program, i.e. the set of all ground equations which hold in the underlying theory [17].

The folding and unfolding transformations, which were first introduced by Burstall and Darlington in [7] for functional programs, are the most basic and powerful techniques for a framework to transform programs. Unfolding is essentially the replacement of a call by its body, with appropriate substitutions. Folding is the inverse transformation, the replacement of some piece of code by an equivalent function call. For functional programs, folding and unfolding steps involve only pattern matching. The fold/unfold transformation approach was first adapted to logic programs by Tamaki and Sato [28] by replacing matching with unification in the transformation rules. A lot of literature has been devoted to proving the correctness of unfold/fold systems w.r.t. the various semantics proposed for functional programs [7, 20], logic programs [18, 25, 27, 28], and constraint logic programs [12]. However, to the best of our knowledge, these techniques have not been studied for functional logic programs so far.

The purpose of this paper is to consider unfold/fold transformations which preserve the semantics of computed answer substitutions of functional logic programs. This type of program behavior is naturally observed by the programmers. However, for the sake of simplicity, most often logic program transformation techniques are only proved correct w.r.t. the declarative semantics of ground logical consequences. We first show what are the problems with naïve extensions of these transformation rules to functional logic programs, considering unrestricted narrowing as the language operational semantics.

Then we show a non standard and extremely useful relationship of partial evaluation with unfolding. We show that a slightly modified transformation (*generalized unfolding*) can be formulated in terms of partial evaluation. As a consequence, the conditions to ensure completeness of the partial evaluation process (defined in [4]) can be used to formalize a sufficient condition for the completeness of unfolding w.r.t. the computed answers for unrestricted narrowing. Note that this is different from the case of pure logic programming, where no applicability condition is required to produce an equivalent program.

The definition of a folding transformation for unrestricted narrowing requires conditions which are too strong to preserve computed answers. For this reason and in order to study the typical properties of a more efficient narrowing strategy, we have defined a folding rule directly for innermost narrowing and have instantiated the general unfolding definition to this case. We have then proved that the unfolding/folding transformation preserve the computed answers under the usual conditions for the completeness of innermost conditional narrowing. In our formulation, unfolding allows the expansion of a single innermost call of a program rule at each step, and hence can be 'selectively' applied. This allows us to see the techniques of unfolding/folding as a base for the definition of a framework for the transformation of programs, in which heuristics or automatic transformation processes might be combined. Finally, as an example application of the unfolding technique we have defined a semantics modelling computed answers which consists of a (possibly infinite) set of unconditional rules, computed as the limit of the unfolding expansions of the initial program.

In the literature, we found only three explicit formulations of fold/unfold rules for functional logic programs, which are based on some form of narrowing. In [8], Darlington and Pull showed how instantiation (an operation of the Burstall/Darlington framework which introduces an instance of an existing equation) can be embedded into unfolding steps to get the ability (of narrowing) to deal with logical variables by means of unification. Similarly, folding steps are regarded as narrowing steps against the reversed equations. However, in this paper we show that folding steps require the ability to generalize (or "deinstantiate") calls rather than instantiating them, which is similar to the case of logic programming and unlike what is done by narrowing or SLD–resolution steps. No claim is made in [8] for any sort of completeness of the transformations and, indeed, some restrictions for the application of the rules are necessary to obtain it [11, 20]. Another closely related approach is that of [11], which formulates a rewrite-based technique for the synthesis of functional programs which makes use of the rule of instantiation. However, there, the manipulations induced to allow folding/unfolding are often more complex than simple instantiation and involve auxiliary function definition and induction. Finally, the forward closures of [9] produce a kind of unfolding of program rules which is used to formulate conditions for the termination of the program.

This paper is organized as follows. Section 2 formalizes the conditional narrowing semantics we focus on. In Section 3, we formalize the notion of unfolding for functional logic programs using conditional narrowing, give the conditions for the soundness and completeness of the transformation w.r.t. the set of ground equational consequences and show the relationship with partial evaluation. Then, we state and prove the soundness and completeness properties for a generalized unfolding technique w.r.t. computed answers. Section 4 introduces a transformation method which combines folding and unfolding for an efficient (call-by-value) evaluation strategy: innermost narrowing. As an application of the innermost unfolding transformation, in Section 5, we define a semantics based on unfolding which is able to characterize the answer substitutions computed by innermost narrowing syntactically. Section 6 concludes the paper and outlines some directions for future research. More details and missing proofs can be found in [1].

2 Semantics of Functional Logic Programs

An equational Horn theory $\mathcal{E}$ consists of a finite set of equational Horn clauses of the form $(\lambda = \rho) \Leftarrow C$, where the condition C is a (possibly empty) sequence $e_1, \ldots, e_n$, $n \geq 0$, of equations. A Conditional Term Rewriting System (CTRS for short) is a pair $(\Sigma, \mathcal{R})$, where $\mathcal{R}$ is a finite set of reduction (or rewrite) rule schemes of the form $(\lambda \rightarrow \rho \Leftarrow C)$, $\lambda, \rho \in \tau(\Sigma \cup V)$, $\lambda \notin V$, and

$Var(\rho) \cup Var(C) \subseteq Var(\lambda)$. We will often write just $\mathcal{R}$ instead of $(\Sigma, \mathcal{R})$. If a rewrite rule has no condition we usually write $\lambda \rightarrow \rho$. A Horn equational theory $\mathcal{E}$ which satisfies the above assumptions can be viewed as a CTRS $\mathcal{R}$, where the rules are the heads (implicitly oriented from left to right) and the conditions are the respective bodies. We assume that these assumptions hold for all theories we consider in this paper.

The computation mechanism of functional logic languages is based on narrowing, an evaluation mechanism that uses unification for parameter passing [26]. Narrowing solves equations by computing unifiers with respect to a given CTRS (which we call 'program'). $O(t)$ and $\bar{O}(t)$ denote the set of occurrences and the set of nonvariable occurrences of a term t, respectively. $t_{|u}$ is the subterm at the occurrence u of t. $t[r]_u$ is the term t with the subterm at the occurrence u replaced with r. These notions extend to sequences of equations in a natural way. We denote by $\theta_{\restriction W}$ the substitution obtained from θ by restricting its domain to W. $\widehat{\theta}$ denotes the equational representation of a substitution θ. A function symbol $f/n \in \Sigma$ is irreducible iff there is no rule $(\lambda \rightarrow \rho \Leftarrow C) \in \mathcal{R}$ such that f occurs as the outermost function symbol in λ, otherwise it is a defined function symbol. In theories where the above distinction is made, the signature Σ is partitioned as $\Sigma = \mathcal{C} \uplus \mathcal{F}$, where $\mathcal{C}$ is the set of irreducible function symbols (or constructors) and $\mathcal{F}$ is the set of defined function symbols. For CTRS $\mathcal{R}$, $r \ll \mathcal{R}$ denotes that r is a new variant of a rule in $\mathcal{R}$. For more details on term rewriting and functional logic programming consult [10, 15, 17, 19].

Given a program $\mathcal{R}$, an equational goal g conditionally narrows into a goal clause g' (in symbols[4] $g \overset{\theta}{\leadsto} g'$), iff:

1. there exists $u \in \bar{O}(g)$, a standardised apart variant $(\lambda \rightarrow \rho \Leftarrow C) \ll \mathcal{R}$ and a substitution θ such that $\theta = mgu(\{g_{|u} = \lambda\})$ and $g' = (C, g[\rho]_u)\theta$, or
2. $\theta = mgu(g)$ and $g' = true$.

A *narrowing derivation* for g in $\mathcal{R}$ is defined by $g \overset{\theta}{\leadsto}{}^* g'$ iff $\exists\theta_1, \ldots, \exists\theta_n.\ g \overset{\theta_1}{\leadsto} \ldots \overset{\theta_n}{\leadsto} g'$ and $\theta = \theta_1 \ldots \theta_n$. We say that the derivation has length n. If $n = 0$, then $\theta = \epsilon$. A successful derivation (or refutation) for g in $\mathcal{R}$ is a narrowing derivation $g \overset{\theta}{\leadsto}{}^* true$, and $\theta_{\restriction Var(g)}$ is called a computed answer substitution (c.a.s.) for g in $\mathcal{R}$. We define the *success set* of an equational goal g in the program $\mathcal{R}$ as: $\mathcal{O}_{\mathcal{R}}(g) = \{\theta_{\restriction Var(g)} \mid g \overset{\theta}{\leadsto}{}^* true,$ and $\theta_{\restriction Var(g)}$ is normalized$\}$.

Since unrestricted narrowing has quite a large search space, several strategies for controlling the selection of redexes have been devised to improve the efficiency of narrowing by getting rid of some useless derivations. A *narrowing strategy* (or *position constraint*) is any well-defined criterion which obtains a smaller search space by permitting narrowing to reduce only some chosen positions, e.g. *basic*, *innermost*, *innermost basic*, or *lazy* narrowing (see, e.g., [15]). Formally, a narrowing strategy φ is a mapping that assigns to every goal g (different from *true*) a subset $\varphi(g)$ of $\bar{O}(g)$ such that for all $u \in \varphi(g)$ the goal g is

---

[4] We sometimes write $g \overset{[u,r,\theta]}{\leadsto} g'$ or $g \overset{[u,\theta]}{\leadsto} g'$ to make the occurrence or the rule used to prove the narrowing step explicit.

narrowable at occurrence u. An important property of a narrowing strategy φ is completeness, meaning that the narrowing constrained by φ is still complete. In this context, completeness means that for every solution σ to a given set of equations g, a more general $\mathcal{E}$-unifier θ can be found by narrowing (i.e., a $\mathcal{E}$-unifier θ s.t. $\theta \leq_{\mathcal{E}} \sigma\ [Var(g)]$). It is well-known that the subscript $\mathcal{E}$ in $\theta \leq_{\mathcal{E}} \sigma$ can be dropped if we only consider completeness w.r.t. normalized substitutions. A survey of results about the completeness of narrowing strategies can be found in [15]. Unrestricted narrowing is complete, e.g., for confluent programs w.r.t. normalized substitutions.

3 Unfolding of Functional Logic Programs

In logic programming, unfolding is usually defined as the application of a resolution step to a subgoal in the body of a program clause in all possible ways. Transformation typically proceeds in a 'step-by-step' fashion: a call is unfolded, then the clause is deleted from the program and replaced by the unfolded clauses [6, 18, 25, 27, 28]. This technique is safe for the least Herbrand model semantics [28], for the semantics of computed answer substitutions [6, 18], and also preserves the finite failure [25, 27]. In this section we first introduce, mimicking the case of logic programming, a naïve unfolding transformation based on conditional narrowing.

Definition 1 Unfolding of a rule in a program. Let $\mathcal{R}$ be a program and $r \equiv (\lambda \rightarrow \rho \Leftarrow C) \ll \mathcal{R}$ be a program rule. Let $\{g \overset{\theta_i}{\leadsto} (C'_i, \rho'_i = y)\}_{i=1}^{n}$ be the set of all one-step narrowing derivations that perform an effective narrowing step for the goal $g \equiv (C, \rho = y)$ in $\mathcal{R}$. Then, $Unf_{\mathcal{R}}(r) = \{(\lambda\theta_i \rightarrow \rho'_i \Leftarrow C'_i) \mid i = 1 \ldots n\}$.

Note that the unfolding of a rule in a program never gives back the original, unfolded rule, since we have purposely left out the one-step narrowing derivations $(C, \rho = y) \overset{\theta_i}{\leadsto} true$ that could be proved if the goal $(C, \rho = y)$ syntactically unifies. This corresponds to the naïve, intuitive idea that one has in mind about how to define the unfolding operation.

Definition 2 Unfolding of a program w.r.t. a rule. Let $\mathcal{R}$ be a program and $r \in \mathcal{R}$ be a program rule. The unfolding of $\mathcal{R}$ w.r.t. r is the program:

$$Unfold(\mathcal{R}, r) = \begin{cases} (\mathcal{R} - \{r\}) \cup Unf_{\mathcal{R}}(r) & \text{if } Unf_{\mathcal{R}}(r) \neq \emptyset \\ \mathcal{R} & \text{otherwise.} \end{cases}$$

Note that, with this definition of unfolding, even the (weaker) semantics of (ground) equational consequences of the original program is not preserved by the transformation:

Example 1. Let us consider the following program $\mathcal{R} = \{\ f(c(x)) \rightarrow f(x)\ \}$. The rhs of the rule, $f(x)$, can only be narrowed to $f(y)$ with substitution $\{x/c(y)\}$. Then, we obtain the following unfolded program $\mathcal{R}' = \{\ f(c(c(y))) \rightarrow f(y)\ \}$. Now, the equation $f(c(a)) = f(a)$ is only true in the original program.

The results in this paper show that there is a close connection between the conditions for the correctness of the partial evaluation of functional logic programs (see [4]) and the correctness of the unfolding transformation. By exploiting this relation, we identify sufficient conditions that guarantee the correctness of the unfolding transformation. Namely, the transformation is always strongly sound but the properties of *confluence, decreasingness* [15], and a sort of *closedness* are necessary for completeness. The notion of closedness was introduced in [4] for the correctness of the Partial Evaluation (PE) of functional logic programs. PE is a transformation technique which, given a program $\mathcal{R}$ and a goal g, returns a partially evaluated program $\mathcal{R}'$ which gives exactly the same answers for g (and for any goal which satisfies some specific requirements, including the closedness condition) as $\mathcal{R}$ does. Roughly speaking, a term t is S-closed if 1) t is a variable, 2) t is a constructor term, or 3) t is an instance of a term $s \in S$, with $t = s\theta$, and the terms in θ are also S-closed. Intuitively, the closedness condition guarantees that all calls that might occur during the execution of g are "covered" by some program rule of $\mathcal{R}'$.

Theorem 3 Strong soundness. *Let $\mathcal{R}$ be a program and $\mathcal{R}' = Unfold(\mathcal{R}, r)$, $r \in \mathcal{R}$. Then, we have that $\mathcal{O}_{\mathcal{R}'}(g) \subseteq \mathcal{O}_{\mathcal{R}}(g)$, for any goal g.*

Theorem 4 Completeness. *Let $\mathcal{R} \equiv \{\lambda_i \to \rho_i \Leftarrow C_i\}_{i=1}^{n}$ be a confluent, left-linear and decreasing program and let $L = \{\lambda_1, \ldots, \lambda_n\}$. Let $\mathcal{R}' = Unfold(\mathcal{R}, r)$, $r \in \mathcal{R}$, and g be a goal. If $\mathcal{R}$ is L-closed, then $\mathcal{R}'$ is decreasing and L-closed, and for all $\theta \in \mathcal{O}_{\mathcal{R}}(g)$, there exists $\theta' \in \mathcal{O}_{\mathcal{R}'}(g)$ such that $\theta' \leq \theta\ [Var(g)]$.*

Roughly speaking, the condition that $\mathcal{R}$ is L-closed requires that the calls in the rhs's and in the conditions of program rules whose outermost functor is a defined function symbol not be in normal form. The extra requirement for decreasingness ensures that these calls can be finitely normalized. These conditions suffice for ensuring that the considered rule can be safely dropped from the original program in exchange for the rules that result from unfolding, without losing completeness.

In the following section, we introduce a generalized definition of unfolding which preserves completeness under less demanding conditions.

3.1 Generalized-unfolding Operation

Definition 5. Let $\mathcal{R}$ be a program and $r \equiv (\lambda \to \rho \Leftarrow C) \ll \mathcal{R}$ be a program rule. We define the generalized unfolding of r in $\mathcal{R}$ by:

$$Gen\text{-}Unf_{\mathcal{R}}(r) = Unf_{\mathcal{R}}(r) \cup \{(\lambda \to y)\theta \mid \theta = mgu(C \cup \{\rho = y\}) \not\equiv fail\}.$$

We note that the unfolding and generalized unfolding transformations coincide for the case when $mgu(C \cup \{\rho = y\}) \equiv fail$. We also note that, for unconditional rules, $mgu(\{true, \rho = y\})$ is never *fail*, which implies that unconditional rules are always reproduced in the derived program. Finally, for $r \equiv (\lambda \to \rho \Leftarrow C)$, note that if $Gen\text{-}Unf_{\mathcal{R}}(r) = \emptyset$ then there is no successful derivation starting from $(C, \rho = y)$ in $\mathcal{R}$.

The following example illustrates the previous definition and points out the difference w.r.t. Definition 2.

Example 2. Consider again the program $\mathcal{R}$ of Example 1. The generalized unfolding of the first rule of $\mathcal{R}$ is $\{f(c(x)) \rightarrow f(x),\ f(c(c(y))) \rightarrow f(y)\}$, which contains the original rule (and thus the semantics is preserved).

An unfolding transformation which would always reproduce the original unfolded rule would be trivially complete, and practically useless. This does not happen, in general, with our generalized unfolding operation. On the contrary, the use of other, seemingly equivalent, definitions of conditional narrowing, like the one that substitutes single equations by *true* as soon as they syntactically unify (instead of requiring the unification of the whole sequence [23]), would lead to generalized unfolding definitions that always reproduce the unfolded rule.

Definition 6 Generalized unfolding of a program w.r.t. a rule.
The generalized unfolding of a program $\mathcal{R}$ w.r.t. a rule is defined as:

$$\textit{Gen-Unfold}(\mathcal{R}, r) = (\mathcal{R} - \{r\}) \cup \textit{Gen-Unf}_{\mathcal{R}}(r).$$

Given a program $\mathcal{R}$ and a rule $r \in \mathcal{R}$, $\textit{Unfold}(\mathcal{R}, r)$ and $\textit{Gen-Unfold}(\mathcal{R}, r)$ do not coincide for all narrowing strategies. For unrestricted conditional narrowing, e.g., $\textit{Unfold}(\mathcal{R}, r) \subseteq \textit{Gen-Unfold}(\mathcal{R}, r)$. Therefore, $\textit{Gen-Unfold}(\mathcal{R}, r)$ is complete whenever $\textit{Unfold}(\mathcal{R}, r)$ is.

In the following, we describe and prove the strong soundness and completeness of the generalized unfolding operation under easier, weaker conditions, which rely on the properties of the PE transformation of [4]. We start by formalizing an alternative characterization of $\textit{Gen-Unfold}(\mathcal{R}, r)$ in terms of partial evaluation. Roughly speaking, the definition of the PE-based, generalized unfolding operation is based on the idea of partially evaluating the program w.r.t. the lhs's of the heads of program rules. The inspiration for this definition comes from [22].

In [4], a general framework for partial evaluation of functional logic programs is defined which is based on building partial narrowing trees for the goal and extracting the specialized definition —the resultants— from the non-failing root-to-leaf branches. Roughly speaking, a PE of a term s is obtained by building a finite narrowing tree for the goal $s = y$ (where $y \notin Var(s)$), and then constructing a resultant $(s\theta_i \rightarrow t_i \Leftarrow C_i)$ for each narrowing derivation $(s = y \overset{\theta_i}{\leadsto}{}^* C_i, t_i = y)$ of the tree. See [4] for a detailed definition.

Now we provide a generalized definition of unfolding, following [22].

Definition 7 Generalized unfolding of a rule using PE. Let $\mathcal{R}$ be a program and $r \equiv (\lambda \rightarrow \rho \Leftarrow C) \ll \mathcal{R}$ be a program rule. Let (f/n) be the outermost function symbol of λ. Let $s \equiv f(x_1, \ldots, x_n)$, with $x_i \not\equiv x_j$, for all $i \neq j$. The PE-based, generalized unfolding of r in $\mathcal{R}$, $\textit{PE-Unf}_{\mathcal{R}}(r)$, is a PE of the term s in $\mathcal{R}$ obtained by stopping the branches of the narrowing tree at the end of the first edge for all rules except r, and continuing the branches which use r one more level.

The following proposition is our key point for proving the correctness of the generalized unfolding transformation.

Proposition 8. *Let $\mathcal{R}$ be a program, and $r \equiv (f(t_1,\ldots,t_n) \rightarrow \rho \Leftarrow C) \ll \mathcal{R}$ be a program rule. Then, Gen-Unf$_\mathcal{R}(r) \cup (\mathcal{R}_r - \{r\})=$ PE-Unf$_\mathcal{R}(r)$, where $\mathcal{R}_r$ denotes the subset of rules $(f(t'_1,\ldots,t'_n) \rightarrow \rho' \Leftarrow C') \ll \mathcal{R}$. Also, Gen-Unfold$(\mathcal{R},r) = (\mathcal{R}-\{r\}) \cup$ Gen-Unf$_\mathcal{R}(r) = (\mathcal{R}-\{r\}) \cup$ PE-Unf$_\mathcal{R}(r)$.*

Now, the correctness results of the unfolding transformation directly follow from the results in [4] since the closedness, linearity and independence conditions required in [4] for the correctness of PE are automatically satisfied for the set of terms partially evaluated when producing the generalized unfolding of the program $\mathcal{R}$.

Theorem 9 Completeness. *Let $\mathcal{R}$ be a canonical program, $r \in \mathcal{R}$ be a rule, $\mathcal{R}'$ = Gen-Unfold$(\mathcal{R},r)$, and g be a goal. Then, for all $\theta \in \mathcal{O}_\mathcal{R}(g)$, there exists $\theta' \in \mathcal{O}_{\mathcal{R}'}(g)$ s.t. $\theta' \leq \theta\,[Var(g)]$.*

As a consequence of Theorem 9, generalized unfolding is complete for the semantics of the least Herbrand $\mathcal{E}$-model in canonical programs.

The strong correctness is formulated using the ultra-linearity condition [4], which means that no variable appears twice in the rhs and the condition of the rules. Ultra-linearity is quite usual in the case of unconditional programs (where it is known as *right-linearity*). For conditional programs, we plan to study whether the (weaker) conditions for the completeness of a sharing-based implementation of narrowing [16], where terms are represented by graphs and all occurrences of the same variable are shared, are sufficient to get rid of the ultra-linearity condition.

Theorem 10 Strong correctness. *Let $\mathcal{R}$ be a confluent program, $\mathcal{R}'$ = Gen-Unfold$(\mathcal{R},r)$, $r \in \mathcal{R}$, and g be a goal. Then,*

1. (STRONG SOUNDNESS) $\mathcal{O}_{\mathcal{R}'}(g) \subseteq \mathcal{O}_\mathcal{R}(g)$.
2. (STRONG COMPLETENESS) $\mathcal{O}_\mathcal{R}(g) \subseteq \mathcal{O}_{\mathcal{R}'}(g)$, *if $\mathcal{R}$ is ultralinear.*

Partial evaluation and the unfold/fold transformational approaches have been developed rather independently. Recently, their relation has been the subject of some discussion [21, 25, 27]. In essence, PE is a *strict subset* of the unfold/fold transformation in which unfolding is the only basic transformation rule. Only a limited form of implicit folding is obtained by imposing the closedness condition [25]. In return for this, lower complexity and a more detailed understanding of control are gained using the PE approach.

4 Unfolding/Folding via Innermost Narrowing

The use of efficient forms of narrowing can significantly improve the accuracy of the specialization method and increase the efficiency of the resulting program. In this section, we formalize and study the properties of a highly efficient unfold/fold transformation based on innermost conditional narrowing.

4.1 Innermost Conditional Narrowing

An *innermost* term t is an operation applied to constructor terms, i.e. $t = f(t_1, \ldots, t_k)$, where $f \in \mathcal{F}$ and, for all $i = 1, \ldots, k$, $t_i \in \tau(C \cup V)$. A CTRS is *constructor-based* (CB), if the left-hand side of each rule is an innermost term. A *constructor goal* is a goal which consists of a sequence of equations $s_i = t_i$, with $s_i, t_i \in \tau(C \cup V)$. A substitution σ is *(ground) constructor*, if $x\sigma$ is a (ground) constructor term for all $x \in Dom(\sigma)$.

A function symbol is *completely-defined* (everywhere defined), if it does not occur in any ground term in normal form, that is to say that functions are reducible on all ground terms (of an appropriate sort). $\mathcal{R}$ is said to be completely-defined (CD), if each defined function symbol is completely-defined. In a CD CTRS, the set of ground normal terms is the set of ground constructor terms $\tau(\mathcal{C})$ over $\mathcal{C}$.

Let $\varphi_{\blacktriangleleft}(g)$ be an innermost selection function, a narrowing strategy which assigns the occurrence u of an innermost subterm of g to the goal g. We formulate innermost conditional narrowing $\leadsto_{\blacktriangleleft}$ as the smallest relation satisfying:

$$(1) \quad \frac{\sigma = mgu(g) \ \wedge \ g \text{ is a constructor goal}}{g \overset{\sigma}{\leadsto}_{\blacktriangleleft} \ true}$$

$$(2) \quad \frac{u = \varphi_{\blacktriangleleft}(g) \ \wedge \ (\lambda \rightarrow \rho \Leftarrow C) \ll \mathcal{R} \ \wedge \ \sigma = mgu(\{g_{|u} = \lambda\})}{g \overset{\sigma}{\leadsto}_{\blacktriangleleft} (C, g[\rho]_u)\sigma}$$

We let $\mathcal{O}_{\mathcal{R}}^{\blacktriangleleft}(g)$ denote the *innermost success set* of g in $\mathcal{R}$, i.e., the set of all computed answer substitutions corresponding to the successful innermost conditional narrowing derivations for g in $\mathcal{R}$. Note that all answers computed by innermost conditional narrowing are normalized since they are constructor [13].

For a goal g and CB-CD, canonical program $\mathcal{R}$, innermost conditional narrowing is complete w.r.t. ground constructor solutions σ satisfying that $Var(g) \subseteq Dom(\sigma)$. This means that, given σ, there is a c.a.s. θ for $\mathcal{R} \cup \{g\}$ using $\leadsto_{\blacktriangleleft}$ such that $\theta \leq \sigma[Var(g)]$ [13].

4.2 Innermost Unfolding Transformation

Let us now formally introduce the unfolding of a program rule at one of its innermost function calls. By abuse, for a rule $r \equiv (\lambda \ \rightarrow \ \rho \Leftarrow C)$, we define $O(r) = O(C, \rho = y)$ and use it to unequivocally refer to the positions of r. We also use $r_{|u}$ and $r[t]_u$, $u \in O(r)$, with the obvious meaning.

Definition 11 Innermost unfold. Let $\mathcal{R}$ be a program and $r \equiv (\lambda \rightarrow \rho \Leftarrow C) \ll \mathcal{R}$ be a program rule. Let $u \in \bar{O}(r)$ be the occurrence of an innermost subterm of the rule r. We define the unfolding of $\mathcal{R}$ w.r.t. u and r as follows:

$$Unfold^{\blacktriangleleft}(\mathcal{R}, u, r) = (\mathcal{R} - \{r\}) \cup Unf_{\mathcal{R}}^{\blacktriangleleft}(u, r)$$

where $Unf_{\mathcal{R}}^{\blacktriangleleft}(u, r)$ is the set of unfolded rules which result from the one-step innermost narrowing derivations $\{(C, \rho = y) \overset{[u,\theta_i]}{\leadsto}_{\blacktriangleleft} g_i \mid i = 1, \ldots, n\}$ for $(C, \rho = y)$ in $\mathcal{R}$. By abuse, we omit the parameter u when it is fixed by $\varphi_{\blacktriangleleft}((C, \rho = y)) = u$.

The only difference w.r.t. the general definition is in the use of innermost narrowing instead of unrestricted narrowing to build the derived rules. For innermost narrowing, the selection of the innermost position to be narrowed is don't-care nondeterministic, hence we prefer to leave the unfolding position as a parameter of the innermost unfolding definition. Note that, for the innermost strategy, unfolding and general unfolding coincide.

The following theorem establishes the computational equivalence of a program and any of its innermost unfoldings, under the simple, standard requirements for the completeness of innermost conditional narrowing.

Theorem 12. *Let $\mathcal{R}$ be a CB-CD canonical program, $r \in \mathcal{R}$ a program rule, and $u \in \bar{O}(r)$ the occurrence of an innermost subterm of r. Let $\mathcal{R}' = Unfold^{\blacktriangleleft}(\mathcal{R}, u, r)$. Then, we have that $\mathcal{O}^{\blacktriangleleft}_{\mathcal{R}}(g) = \mathcal{O}^{\blacktriangleleft}_{\mathcal{R}'}(g)$, for any goal g.*

4.3 Innermost Folding Transformation

Now we introduce a folding transformation, which is intended to be the inverse of the unfolding operation, that is, an unfolding step followed by the corresponding folding step (and viceversa) is expected to give back the initial program. Roughly speaking, the folding operation consists of substituting a function call (*folding call*) for a definitionally equivalent set of calls (*folded calls*) together with a set of equational conditions. This operation is generally used in all transformation techniques in order to pack back unfolded rules and to detect implicitly recursive definitions. It is also used when partial evaluation techniques are recast in terms of unfold/fold transformations [25].

In the following, we introduce a folding transformation that can be seen as an extension to functional logic programs of the reversible folding of [25] for logic programs. We have chosen this form of folding since it exhibits the useful, pursued property that the answer substitutions computed by innermost narrowing are preserved through the transformation. We consider the investigation of more general definitions of folding as a matter of further research.

Let us now introduce the innermost folding operation. Note that it has two sources of nondeterminism. The first is in the choice of the folded calls; the second, is in the choice of a generalization (folding call) of the heads of the instantiated function definitions which are used to substitute the folded calls.

Definition 13 Innermost fold. Let $\mathcal{R}$ be a program. Let $\{r_1, \ldots, r_n\} \ll \mathcal{R}$ (the "folded rules") and $R_{def} \equiv \{r'_1, \ldots, r'_n\} \ll \mathcal{R}$ (the "folding rules") be two disjoint subsets of program rules (up to renaming), with $r'_i \equiv (\lambda'_i \rightarrow \rho'_i \Leftarrow C'_i)$, $i = 1, \ldots, n$. Let r be a rule[5], $u \in O(r)$ be a position of the rule r, and t be an *innermost* term such that, for all $i = 1, \ldots, n$:

1. $\theta_i = mgu(\{\lambda'_i = t\}) \not\equiv fail$,

[5] Roughly speaking, r is the "common skeleton" of the rules that are folded in the folding step. The occurrence u in r acts as the pointer to the "hole" where the folding call is let fall.

2. $r_i \equiv (\lambda \to \rho_i \Leftarrow C_i', C_i)\theta_i$ and $r[\rho_i']_u \equiv (\lambda \to \rho_i \Leftarrow C_i)$, and
3. for any rule $r' \equiv (\lambda' \to \rho' \Leftarrow C') \ll \mathcal{R}$ not in R_{def}, $mgu(\{\lambda' = t\}) \equiv fail$.

Then, we define the folding of $\{r_1, \ldots, r_n\}$ in $\mathcal{R}$ using R_{def} as follows:

$$Fold^{\blacktriangleleft}(\mathcal{R}, \{r_1, \ldots, r_n\}, R_{def}) = (\mathcal{R} - \{r_1, \ldots, r_n\}) \cup \{r_{fold}\}$$

where $r_{fold} \equiv r[t]_u$.

Intuitively, the folding operation proceeds in a contrary direction to the narrowing steps. In narrowing steps, for a given unifier of the redex and the lhs of the applied rule, a reduction step is performed on the instantiated redex, then the conditions of the unfolding rule are added to the unfolded one, and finally the narrowing substitution is applied. Here, first folded rules are "deinstantiated" (generalized). Next, one gets rid of the conditions of the applied folding rules, and, finally, a reduction step is performed against the reversed heads of the folding rules. The following example illustrates our notion of innermost folding.

Example 3. Let us consider the following CB-CD canonical program $\mathcal{R}$:

$$f(x) \to s(x) \Leftarrow h(s(x)) = 0 \;(r_1) \qquad num(y) \to y \Leftarrow h(y) = 0 \quad (r_3)$$
$$f(s(z)) \to s(s(0))) \Leftarrow z = 0 \quad (r_2) \quad num(s(s(z))) \to s(s(0)) \Leftarrow z = 0 \;(r_4)$$

Now, we can fold the rules $\{r_1, r_2\}$ of $\mathcal{R}$ w.r.t. $R_{def} \equiv \{r_3, r_4\}$ using $r \equiv (f(x) \to \Box)$ and $t \equiv num(s(x))$, obtaining the resulting program:

$$\mathcal{R}' = \{ \quad f(x) \to num(s(x)) \quad (r_{fold})$$
$$num(y) \to y \Leftarrow h(y) = 0 \quad (r_3)$$
$$num(s(s(z))) \to s(s(0)) \Leftarrow z = 0 \;(r_4) \quad \}.$$

The above definition requires two applicability conditions for a folding step: (1) the set of folded rules and the set of folding rules are disjoint (up to renaming) and (2) the term t which replaces the folded calls is innermost. Note that the latter requirement is novel as it arises for the first time in the functional logic context, and it is a key point for proving the *reversibility* property that a folded program can be unfolded back by an innermost step.

The following lemma formalizes the reversibility condition, by showing how folding steps can be undone by appropriate innermost unfolding steps. This allows us to prove, in Theorem 15, the total correctness of the transformation.

Lemma 14 Reversibility. *Let $\mathcal{R}$ be a CB-CD, canonical program. If $\mathcal{R}' = Fold^{\blacktriangleleft}(\mathcal{R}, \{r_1, \ldots, r_n\}, R_{def})$, then there exists an occurrence $u \in \bar{O}(r_{fold})$ of an innermost term s.t. $\mathcal{R} = Unfold^{\blacktriangleleft}(\mathcal{R}', u, r_{fold})$ (up to renaming), where r_{fold} is the new rule introduced in $\mathcal{R}'$ by the innermost folding step.*

Example 4. Consider again the folded program $\mathcal{R}'$ of Example 3. If we unfold the rule r_{fold} of $\mathcal{R}'$ w.r.t. the occurrence of the innermost function call $num(s(x))$, then we get back the initial program $\mathcal{R}$.

Theorem 15 Strong correctness. *Let $\mathcal{R}$ be a CB-CD, canonical program and $\mathcal{R}' = Fold^{\blacktriangleleft}(\mathcal{R}, \{r_1, \ldots, r_n\}, R_{def})$ be a folding of $\{r_1, \ldots, r_n\}$ in $\mathcal{R}$ using R_{def}. Then, we have that $\mathcal{O}^{\blacktriangleleft}_{\mathcal{R}}(g) = \mathcal{O}^{\blacktriangleleft}_{\mathcal{R}'}(g)$, for any equational goal g.*

Theorem 12 and Theorem 15 show that it is possible to define a program transformation strategy based on our innermost unfold/fold rules preserving computed answer substitutions, which is outside the scope of this paper.

As an application of the innermost unfolding transformation, in the following section, we define a semantics based on unfolding which is able to characterize the answer substitutions computed by innermost narrowing syntactically.

5 A Semantics Modelling Computed Answers

The operational semantics of a program is a mapping from the set of programs to a set of program denotations which, given a program $\mathcal{R}$, returns a set of 'results' of the computations in $\mathcal{R}$. In this section, we formalize a *nonground* operational semantics for functional logic programs which is defined in terms of the set of all 'values' that functional expressions can compute. This semantics fully characterizes the c.a.s.'s computed by innermost conditional narrowing and it admits an alternative characterization in terms of innermost unfolding.

5.1 Operational Semantics

The following definitions are auxiliary. An equation of the form $x = y$, $x, y \in V$ is called a *trivial* equation. A *flat* equation is an equation of the form $f(x_1, \ldots, x_n) = x_{n+1}$ or $x_n = x_{n+1}$, where $x_i \not\equiv x_j$ for all $i \neq j$. Any goal g can be transformed into an equivalent one, *flat*(g), which is flat [5].

Definition 16. Let $\mathcal{R}$ be a program. Then,

$$\mathcal{O}^{\blacktriangleleft}(\mathcal{R}) = \{(f(x_1, \ldots, x_n) = x_{n+1})\theta \mid f(x_1, \ldots, x_n) = x_{n+1} \overset{\theta\,*}{\leadsto}_{\blacktriangleleft} \mathit{true} \text{ in } \mathcal{R}, \text{ and } (f/n) \in \Sigma \}.$$

The following theorem asserts that the computed answer substitutions of any (possibly conjunctive) goal g can be derived from $\mathcal{O}^{\blacktriangleleft}(\mathcal{R})$ (i.e. from the observable behaviour of single equations), by unification of the equations in the goal with the equations in the denotation. We note that this property is a kind of AND-compositionality which does not hold for unrestricted conditional narrowing [3]. We assume that the equations in the denotation are renamed apart. Equations in the goal have to be flattened first, i.e. subterms have to be unnested so that the term structure is directly accessible to unification.

Definition 17. Let g be a goal. We define the function *split* : *Goal* $\rightarrow$ *Goal* $\times$ *Goal* by *split*$(g) = (g_1, g_2)$, where all trivial equations of g are in g_2, and g_1 contains the other, non-trivial, equations of g.

Theorem 18. *Let $\mathcal{R}$ be a CB-CD canonical program and let g be a goal. Let split(flat(g)) $= (g_1, g_2)$. Then θ is a computed answer substitution for g in $\mathcal{R}$ iff there exists $C \equiv (e_1, \ldots, e_m) \ll \mathcal{O}^{\blacktriangleleft}(\mathcal{R})$ such that $\theta' = mgu(g_1, C)$ and $\theta = (\theta' \Uparrow mgu(g_2))\ [Var(g)]$.*

Theorem 18 shows that $\mathcal{O}^{\blacktriangleleft}(\mathcal{R})$ is a fully abstract semantics w.r.t. computed answer substitutions, i.e. two programs $\mathcal{R}_1$ and $\mathcal{R}_2$ with $\mathcal{O}^{\blacktriangleleft}(\mathcal{R}_1) = \mathcal{O}^{\blacktriangleleft}(\mathcal{R}_2)$ (up to renaming) cannot produce different computed answers. Moreover, $\mathcal{O}^{\blacktriangleleft}(\mathcal{R})$ can be viewed as a (possibly infinite) set of 'unit' clauses, and the computed answer substitutions for g in $\mathcal{R}$ can be determined by 'executing' *flat*(g) in the program $\mathcal{O}^{\blacktriangleleft}(\mathcal{R})$ by syntactic unification, as if the equality symbol were an ordinary predicate. We note that in [2] a similar operational semantics was defined for basic conditional narrowing.

5.2 Unfolding Semantics

Now we introduce an unfolding semantics for functional logic programs, based on the unfolding transformation we have defined in Section 4.2. First, we define the unfolding of a program as follows.

Definition 19 Unfolding of a program. The unfolding of a program $\mathcal{R}$ is the program obtained by unfolding the rules of $\mathcal{R}$ w.r.t. $\mathcal{R}$. Formally,

$$Unfold^{\blacktriangleleft}(\mathcal{R}) = \bigcup_{r \in \mathcal{R}} \{Unf^{\blacktriangleleft}_{\mathcal{R}}(r) \mid r \in \mathcal{R}\}.$$

Now, the repeated application of unfolding leads to a sequence of equivalent programs which is inductively defined as follows.

Definition 20. The sequence:

$$\mathcal{R}^0 = \mathcal{R}$$
$$\mathcal{R}^{i+1} = Unfold^{\blacktriangleleft}(\mathcal{R}^i),\ i \geq 0$$

is called the innermost unfolding sequence starting from $\mathcal{R}$.

We notice that, as an immediate consequence of Theorem 12, we have that $\mathcal{O}^{\blacktriangleleft}(\mathcal{R}^i) = \mathcal{O}^{\blacktriangleleft}(\mathcal{R}^{i+1})$, $i \geq 0$, for CB-CD, canonical programs.

The unfolding semantics of a program is defined as the limit of the (top-down) unfolding process described in Definition 19. Let us now formally define the *unfolding semantics* $\mathcal{U}^{\blacktriangleleft}(\mathcal{R})$ of a program $\mathcal{R}$. The main point of this definition is in compelling the rhs's of the equations in the denotation to be constructor terms. Let Φ_C be the set of identical equations $c(x_1, \ldots, x_n) = c(x_1, \ldots, x_n)$, for each $c/n \in C$.

Definition 21. Let $\mathcal{R}$ be a program. Then,

$$\mathcal{U}^{\blacktriangleleft}(\mathcal{R}) = \Phi_C \cup \bigcup_{i \in \omega} \{(s = d) \mid (s \rightarrow d \Leftarrow) \in \mathcal{R}^i \text{ and } d \in \tau(C \cup V)\}$$

where $\mathcal{R}^0, \mathcal{R}^1, \ldots$ is the innermost unfolding sequence starting from $\mathcal{R}$.

The following theorem is the main result of this section and it formalizes the intuitive claim that, since the unfolding rule preserves the observable properties, we have found out a useful alternative characterization of the computed answers semantics $\mathcal{O}^{\blacktriangleleft}(\mathcal{R})$ in terms of unfolding.

Theorem 22. *Let $\mathcal{R}$ be a CB-CD canonical program. Then,* $\mathcal{U}^{\blacktriangleleft}(\mathcal{R}) = \mathcal{O}^{\blacktriangleleft}(\mathcal{R})$.

6 Conclusions and Further Research

In this paper, we have considered the correctness of the unfold/fold transformations in relation to some standard semantics of functional logic programs, namely, unrestricted conditional narrowing and innermost conditional narrowing. We have taken on the systematic study of program transformations for unrestricted narrowing because it brings to light some common problems caused by the basic mechanism and not tied to the intricacies of any particular strategy. We have ascertained and exemplified general conditions that guarantee that the meaning of the program is not modified by the transformation. These conditions cover many practical cases and are easy to check, since they are mostly syntactical and do not depend on the final program, but only on the initial one.

Future investigation concerns the study of unfolding techniques based on more elaborated narrowing strategies. As logic programming unfold/fold suggests, constructor computed answer substitutions are easier to preserve by transformed programs. Since lazy narrowing only computes solutions of this kind, we hope that stronger results may be obtained with this strategy when used as operational semantics in unfold/fold transformations. The definition of a framework for combining folding and unfolding with new, useful transformation techniques is subject of ongoing research.

References

1. M. Alpuente, M. Falaschi, G. Moreno, and G. Vidal. Safe Folding/Unfolding with Conditional Narrowing. Technical Report DSIC-II/3/97, DSIC, UPV, 1997.
2. M. Alpuente, M. Falaschi, M.J. Ramis, and G. Vidal. A Compositional Semantics for Conditional Term Rewriting Systems. In H.E. Bal, editor, *Proc. of 6th Int'l Conf. on Computer Languages, ICCL'94*, pages 171–182. IEEE, New York, 1994.
3. M. Alpuente, M. Falaschi, and G. Vidal. A Compositional Semantic Basis for the Analysis of Equational Horn Programs. *Theoretical Computer Science*, 165(1):97–131, 1996.
4. M. Alpuente, M. Falaschi, and G. Vidal. Partial Evaluation of Functional Logic Programs. Technical Report DSIC-II/33/96, DSIC, UPV, 1996. Short version in *Proc. of ESOP'96*, Springer LNCS 1058, pages 45-61. Also available from URL: http://www.dsic.upv.es/users/elp/papers.html.
5. P. Bosco, E. Giovannetti, and C. Moiso. Narrowing vs. SLD-resolution. *Theoretical Computer Science*, 59:3–23, 1988.
6. A. Bossi and N. Cocco. Basic Transformation Operations which preserve Computed Answer Substitutions of Logic Programs. *Journal of Logic Programming*, 16:47–87, 1993.
7. R.M. Burstall and J. Darlington. A Transformation System for Developing Recursive Programs. *Journal of the ACM*, 24(1):44–67, 1977.
8. J. Darlington and H. Pull. A Program Development Methodology Based on a Unified Approach to Execution and Transformation. In D. Bjørner, A.P. Ershov, and N.D. Jones, editors, *Proc. of the Int'l Workshop on Partial Evaluation and Mixed Computation*, pages 117–131. North-Holland, Amsterdam, 1988.

9. N. Dershowitz. Termination of Rewriting. *Journal of Symbolic Computation*, 3(1&2):69–115, 1987.
10. N. Dershowitz and J.-P. Jouannaud. Rewrite Systems. In J. van Leeuwen, editor, *Handbook of Theoretical Computer Science*, volume B: Formal Models and Semantics, pages 243–320. Elsevier, Amsterdam, 1990.
11. N. Dershowitz and U. Reddy. Deductive and Inductive Synthesis of Equational Programs. *Journal of Symbolic Computation*, 15:467–494, 1993.
12. S. Etalle and M. Gabbrielli. Modular Transformations of CLP Programs. In *Proc. of 12th Int'l Conf. on Logic Programming.* The MIT Press, 1995.
13. L. Fribourg. SLOG: a logic programming language interpreter based on clausal superposition and rewriting. In *Proc. of Second IEEE Int'l Symp. on Logic Programming*, pages 172–185. IEEE, New York, 1985.
14. M. Hanus. Efficient Implementation of Narrowing and Rewriting. In *Proc. Int'l Workshop on Processing Declarative Knowledge*, pages 344–365. Springer LNAI 567, 1991.
15. M. Hanus. The Integration of Functions into Logic Programming: From Theory to Practice. *Journal of Logic Programming*, 19&20:583–628, 1994.
16. M. Hanus. On Extra Variables in (Equational) Logic Programming. In *Proc. of 20th Int'l Conf. on Logic Programming*, pages 665–678. The MIT Press, 1995.
17. S. Hölldobler. *Foundations of Equational Logic Programming.* Springer LNAI 353, 1989.
18. T. Kawamura and T. Kanamori. Preservation of Stronger Equivalence in Unfold/Fold Logic Programming Transformation. In *Proc. Int'l Conf. on Fifth Generation Computer Systems*, pages 413–422. ICOT, 1988.
19. J.W. Klop. Term Rewriting Systems. In S. Abramsky, D. Gabbay, and T. Maibaum, editors, *Handbook of Logic in Computer Science*, volume I, pages 1–112. Oxford University Press, 1992.
20. L. Kott. Unfold/fold program transformation. In M. Nivat and J.C. Reynolds, editors, *Algebraic methods in semantics*, chapter 12, pages 411–434. Cambridge University Press, 1985.
21. M. Leuschel, D. De Schreye, and A. de Waal. A Conceptual Embedding of Folding into Partial Deduction: Towards a Maximal Integration. In M. Maher, editor, *Proc. of the Joint International Conference and Symposium on Logic Programming JICSLP'96*, pages 319–332. The MIT Press, Cambridge, MA, 1996.
22. J.W. Lloyd and J.C. Shepherdson. Partial Evaluation in Logic Programming. *Journal of Logic Programming*, 11:217–242, 1991.
23. A. Middeldorp and E. Hamoen. Completeness Results for Basic Narrowing. *Applicable Algebra in Engineering, Communication and Computing*, 5:213–253, 1994.
24. A. Middeldorp, S. Okui, and T. Ida. Lazy Narrowing: Strong Completeness and Eager Variable Elimination. *Theoretical Computer Science*, 167(1,2):95–130, 1996.
25. A. Pettorossi and M. Proietti. Transformation of Logic Programs: Foundations and Techniques. *Journal of Logic Programming*, 19,20:261–320, 1994.
26. U.S. Reddy. Narrowing as the Operational Semantics of Functional Languages. In *Proc. of 2nd Int'l Symp. on Logic Programming*, pages 138–151. IEEE, 1985.
27. H. Seki. Unfold/fold Transformation of General Logic Programs for the Well-Founded Semantics. *Journal of Logic Programming*, 16(1&2):5–23, 1993.
28. H. Tamaki and T. Sato. Unfold/Fold Transformations of Logic Programs. In *Proc. of 2nd Int'l Conf. on Logic Programming*, pages 127–139, 1984.

Optimal Non-deterministic Functional Logic Computations *

Sergio Antoy

Portland State University

Abstract. We show that non-determinism simplifies coding certain problems into programs. We define a non-confluent, but well-behaved class of rewrite systems for supporting non-deterministic computations in functional logic programming. We show the benefits of using this class on a few examples. We define a narrowing strategy for this class of systems and prove that our strategy is sound, complete, and optimal, modulo non-deterministic choices, for appropriate definitions of these concepts. We compare our strategy with related work and show that our overall approach is fully compatible with the current proposal of a universal, broad-based functional logic language.

1 Introduction

Curry [4], a recently proposed, general-purpose, broad-based functional logic language, offers lazy evaluation, higher order functions, non-deterministic choices, and a unified computation model which integrates narrowing and residuation. *Curry* models functions by the defined operations of a constructor-based, almost orthogonal, term rewriting system (*CAT*). Non-determinism occurs typically in three situations: when variables are instantiated during a narrowing step; when certain arguments of a non-inductively sequential function, e.g., the *parallel or*, are selected for evaluations; and when an alternative of a *choice* operator, a device to encapsulate non-deterministic computations, is selected for execution. This careful combination of features ensures true functionality, i.e., the application of a function to a tuple of arguments yields at most one value. This condition simplifies declarative, non-backtrackable I/O, but, we will show shortly, it sacrifices the expressive power of the language.

Non-determinism and expressiveness are key ingredients of functional logic programming. The contribution of this note is the discovery of the existence of a class of rewrite systems that are more non-deterministic and expressive than *CAT*s without loss of the properties that make *CAT*s appealing for *Curry*. Our approach has the following features: (1) it is compatible with the unified computation model for functional and logic programming based on narrowing and residuation [8]; (2) it is compatible with the mechanism, the *choice* operator, that has been proposed to encapsulate non-deterministic computations [4]; (3) it is sound, depending on an implementation option, with respect to either the call-time or the evaluation-time semantics that may be adopted for non-deterministic computations [10]; (4) on deterministic computations it is as efficient as the best currently known strategy [2] and on inherently non-deterministic computations it has the potential to be superior.

* This work has been supported in part by the NSF grant CCR-9406751.

This paper is organized as follows. We show in a few examples, in Section 2, some limitations of *CAT*s for expressing simple non-deterministic computations. Then, after some preliminaries in Section 3, we define in Section 4 a new class of rewrite systems and re-program our examples using this class. In Section 5 we define a narrowing strategy for the new class of systems. In the following Sections 6 and 7 we prove that our strategy is sound, complete, and optimal. In Sections 8 and 9 we briefly compare our approach with related work and we offer our conclusions.

2 Motivation

This section presents three small examples of computations that are not conveniently coded using *CAT*s. The first example, rather benign, proposes a simple abstraction that has to be coded in a less clear, natural, and expressive form than it is commonly stated. The second example, more compelling, shows that traditional logic programmers must give up some convenient, familiar programming techniques when functions become available. An attempt to adapt a couple of well-typed, pure Prolog predicates to functional logic programming gives rise to several problems whose solutions require more convoluted code. The third example presents two computations, conceptually very similar, that should both succeed—however, one may fail.

The common root of these difficulties is non-determinism. Functions modeled by *CAT*s are too deterministic for these problems. The ability to handle non-determinism is a major asset of logic programming, perhaps the single most important factor of its success. A consequence of overly limiting non-determinism is that programs for the problems that we discuss must be coded in a less natural, expressive, and declarative form than a high-level, declarative language would lead us to expect. We will show later that by adopting a new class of rewrite systems we gain back all the expressiveness and declarativeness needed for these problems without any loss of soundness, completeness, and/or efficiency.

Example 1. Consider an abstraction dealing with family relationships: There are people, parents, and a person's attribute, having blue eyes. Since *parent* is not a function, the standard functional logic approach to its definition is to cast parenthood as a binary predicate.

```
parent Alice  Beth   = true
parent Fred   Beth   = true
parent Carol  Dianna = true
...
blue_eyed Alice = true
```

With this program, a goal to find out whether *Beth* has a blue-eyed *parent* is

```
(parent x Beth) && (blue_eyed x)
```

where `&&` is *Curry*'s predefined sequential conjunction operator.

There are several mildly undesirable aspects of this program:

- it is not clear from a program equation whether the first argument of *parent* is the parent or the child, e.g., whether *Alice* is a parent of *Beth* or vice versa.
- *parent* is a function less completely defined than it should, e.g., *parent Carol Beth*, is undefined even though we may know that its value is *false*.
- the goal is clumsy and verbose, it is not a natural formalization of the way one would state it: "Is there a blue-eyed parent of Beth?"

Example 2. Consider a program that computes permutations of a list. A naive translation of the standard Prolog approach, e.g., see [12, p. 38], would be

```
permute []      [] = true
permute (x:xs) y   = (permute xs ys) && (insert x ys y)

insert x xs         (x : xs) = true
insert x (y : ys)   (y : z)  = insert x ys z
```

Unfortunately, the above program is incorrect in *Curry* for three independent reasons.

- In the second equation of *permute* the symbol *ys* is an extra variable [7,13], i.e., it occurs in the right hand side of the equation, but not in the left hand side.
- Both equations of *insert* are not left-linear, i.e., some variable, e.g., x in the first equation, occurs twice in the left hand side.
- The equations of *insert* create a non-trivial critical pair, i.e., there exists a unifier of the left hand sides of the two equations that does not unify the right hand sides.

Example 3. To keep small the size of this example, we consider an abstract problem. Suppose that *ok* is a unary function that, for all arguments, evaluates to *true* and *double* is a function of a natural number that doubles its argument.

```
ok _ = true

double 0     = 0
double (s x) = s (s (double x))
```

Evaluating whether the "*double* of some expression t is *ok*", i.e., solving the goal

```
ok (double t)
```

succeeds regardless of t, i.e., even if t is undefined.

Suppose now that we extend our program with a mechanism to halve numbers. We call it "mechanism," rather than function, because halving odd numbers rounds non-deterministically. Even numbers are halved as usual. Following the standard practice, we code *half* as a predicate.

```
half 0         0     = true
half (s 0)     0     = true
half (s 0)     (s 0) = true
half (s (s x)) (s y) = half x y
```

Now, if we want to find out whether the "*half* of some expression t is *ok*", we must solve the goal

```
(half t x) && (ok x)
```

which requires to evaluate t and consequently is unnecessarily inefficient and may even fail if t cannot be evaluated to a natural. However, we have shown that the analogous computation for *double* always succeeds.

3 Preliminaries

A *narrowing step*, or *step* for short, of a term t is a two-part computation. *Part one* is an instantiation of t, i.e., the application of a substitution to t. *Part two* is a rewrite step, i.e., the application of a rule to a subterm of t. The substitution in part one of a narrowing step is a constructor substitution, and can be the identity. In this case, part one *has no effect* on the term and we consider it only for uniformity. This is consistent with the viewpoint that narrowing generalizes rewriting. It is convenient to consider steps in which part two *has no effect* on a term as well, i.e., there is no rewriting. These steps, called *degenerate*, are not intended to be performed during the execution of a program. We consider them only as a device to prove some results. A non-degenerate narrowing step is denoted $(p, l \to r, \sigma)$. Its application is denoted $t \rightsquigarrow_{(p,l \to r,\sigma)} t'$, were t' is obtained from $\sigma(t)$ by contracting the subterm at p using rule $l \to r$. A degenerate narrowing step is denoted $(=, =, \sigma)$. Its application to a term t yields $\sigma(t)$.

In a step $t \rightsquigarrow_{(p,l \to r,\sigma)} t'$, σ is a substitution, rather than the traditional unifier, that makes $t_{|p}$ an instance of l. A most general substitution σ makes a term t an instance of a rule's left hand side l is denoted with $t \lhd l$. In this case, the domain of $t \lhd l$ is contained in the set of the variables of t and over these variables $t \lhd l$ is equal to $mgu(t, l)$, a most general unifier of t and l. Note that "$\lhd$" is not a commutative function.

The *composition* $\sigma_1 \circ \sigma_2$ of substitutions σ_1 and σ_2 is defined for all terms t as $(\sigma_1 \circ \sigma_2)(t) = \sigma_2(\sigma_1(t))$. A substitution σ is *idempotent* iff $\sigma \circ \sigma = \sigma$. A most general unifier of a narrowing step is an idempotent substitution. Two substitutions σ_1 and σ_2 are *unifiable* iff there exists a substitution σ such that $\sigma_1 \circ \sigma = \sigma_2 \circ \sigma$. For a discussion of properties of substitutions and unifications used in this paper, see, e.g., [5].

4 Overlapping Inductively Sequential Systems

Below we reformulate at a higher level of abstraction the notion of definitional tree originally proposed in [1]. We assume that defined operations are not "totally undefined." Symbols of this kind are generally regarded as constructors in constructor based systems.

Definition 4. A *pattern* is a term of the form $f(t_1, \ldots, t_n)$, where f is a defined operation and, for all $i = 1, \ldots, n$, t_i is a constructor term. A *definitional tree* of an operation f is a non-empty set $\mathcal{T}$ of linear patterns partially ordered by subsumption and having the following properties up to renaming of variables.

- [leaves property] The maximal elements, referred to as the *leaves*, of $\mathcal{T}$ are all and only variants of the left hand sides of the rules defining f. Non-maximal elements are referred to as *branches*.
- [root property] The minimum element, referred to as the *root*, of $\mathcal{T}$ is $f(X_1, \ldots, X_n)$, where $X_1, \ldots, X_n$ are new, distinct variables.
- [parent property] If π is a pattern of $\mathcal{T}$ different from the root, there exists in $\mathcal{T}$ a unique pattern π' strictly preceding π such that there exists no other pattern strictly between π and π'. π' is referred to as the *parent* of π and π as a *child* of π'.
- [induction property] All the children of a same parent differ from each other only at the position, referred to as *inductive*, of a variable of their parent.

There exist operations with no definitional tree, and operations with more than one definitional tree, examples are in [1]. The existence of a definitional tree of an operation is decidable. In most practical situations, computing a definitional tree of an operation is a simple task. An operation is called ***inductively sequential*** if it has a definitional tree. A rewrite system is called ***inductively sequential*** if all its operations are inductively sequential. It follows from the definition that inductively sequential systems are left linear. So far, inductive sequentiality has been studied only for non-overlapping systems [1,2]. In the following, we extend this study to overlapping systems.

The next result shows that the left hand sides of the rules of an inductively sequential rewrite program overlap only if they are ***variants*** (of each other), i.e., one can be obtained from the other by a renaming of variables. The converse obviously holds for any program. This property of overlapping left hand sides is stronger than that of weakly orthogonal rewrite systems. By contrast, in inductively sequential systems there are no specific restrictions on the right hand sides beside those of general rewrite systems.

Proposition 5. *Let f be an inductively sequential operation and $l \to r$ and $l' \to r'$ defining rules of f. If l and l' overlap, then l and l' are variants.*

Proposition 5 suggests to group together all the equations whose left hand sides are variants and to code the left hand side only once with alternative choices for the right hand sides. We revisit our introductory examples using overlapping inductively sequential systems.

Example 6. (Example 1 revisited) Only the definition of *parent* changes.

```
parent Beth   = Alice | Fred
parent Dianna = Carol
...
blue_eyed Alice = true
```

and the goal is

```
blue_eyed (parent Beth)
```

All the mildly annoying, syntactical problems discussed earlier disappear.

Example 7. (Example 2 revisited) The definitions of both *permute* and *insert* change. *Insert* non-deterministically inserts its first argument, an element, into its second argument, a list of elements, either at the head or anywhere but the head. For the second choice we introduce a new operation, *tail_insert*, that implicitly ensures that the second argument of *insert* is a non-empty list. We will further discuss this example in Section 8.

```
permute []        = []
permute (x : xs) = insert x (permute xs)
insert x xs =  (x : xs) | tail_insert x xs
tail_insert x (y : ys) = (y : insert x ys)
```

Example 8. (Example 3 revisited) The definition of *half* changes as follows.

```
half 0           = 0
half (s 0)       = 0 | s 0
half (s (s x)) = half x
```

The goal becomes

```
ok (half t)
```

and its behavior with respect to evaluation, efficiency, and termination becomes identical to the analogous goal involving *double*.

5 Narrowing

In this section we define a narrowing strategy, which we call **I***nductively* **S***equential* **N***arrowing* **S***trategy*, or *INS* for short, for possibly overlapping, inductively sequential rewrite systems. In following sections we prove that *INS* is sound, complete, and optimal. *INS* coincide with the **N***eeded* **N***arrowing Strategy* [2], *NN* for short, on non-overlapping systems, but has some relevant differences in general due its larger domain. *NN* has strong normalization properties. In particular:

- *NN* is hyper-normalizing on ground terms, i.e., if a ground term is reducible to a data term, then there exists no derivation that computes an infinite number of *NN* steps,
- *NN* is optimal in the number of steps, provided that the common subterms of a term are shared,
- *NN* only performs steps that are needed to compute root-stable terms, this property is more fundamental than normalization, since it allows us to compute infinitary normal forms [13].

However, *INS* shares only a weaker form of the last property with *NN*. The first two properties do not hold as shown by the following overlapping, inductively sequential rewrite program

```
f = f | 0
```
(1)

INS computes, among others, the derivation $f \rightarrow f \rightarrow \cdots$. We will argue later that this difference originates from non-determinism and that inherently non-deterministic computations performed by *NN* are in practice similar to, if not less efficient than, those computed by *INS*.

Throughout the rest of the paper, we make the following assumptions:

- Every rewrite system that we discuss is inductively sequential, possibly overlapping.
- Definitional trees are fixed. We choose a tree for every defined operation once and for all and we use it for all our claims. The choice of the tree does not affect a claim.

Lemma 9. *Let $t = f(t_1, \ldots, t_k)$ be an operation-rooted term and $\mathcal{T}$ a definitional tree of f. There exists a pattern in $\mathcal{T}$ that unifies with t.*

Definition 10. Let $t = f(t_1, \ldots, t_k)$ be an operation-rooted term, $\mathcal{T}$ the fixed definitional tree of f, and π a maximal pattern of $\mathcal{T}$ that unifies with t. *INS*(t) is the set of all and only the triples of the form (p, R, σ), where p is a position, R is a rule, and σ is a substitution such that:

$$(p, R, \sigma) = \begin{cases} (\Lambda, R, t \lhd l) & \text{if } \pi \text{ is a } \textit{leaf} \text{ of } \mathcal{T}, \text{ where} \\ & \quad R = l \rightarrow r \text{ is a variant of a rule} \\ & \quad \text{such that } l = \pi; \\ (q \cdot q', R, \eta \circ \eta') & \text{if } \pi \text{ is a } \textit{branch} \text{ of } \mathcal{T}, \text{ where} \\ & \quad q \text{ is the inductive position of } \pi, \\ & \quad \eta = t \lhd \pi, \text{ and} \\ & \quad (q', R, \eta') \in \textit{INS}(\eta(t_{|q})). \end{cases} \tag{2}$$

If t is not operation-rooted, then a triple $s = (p, R, \sigma)$ is in *INS*(t) iff $s \in$ *INS*(t') for some maximal operation-rooted subterm t' of t.

Lemma 11. *If t is a term such that $s = (p, R, \sigma) \in \mathrm{INS}(t)$, then*
- *s is a narrowing step of t,*
- *σ is a constructor substitution.*

The substitution of a step computed by *INS* is not the restriction of a most general unifier. This is different from most narrowing strategies, the major exception being Needed Narrowing. The "extra" substitution computed by *INS* ensures that future steps of a derivation are necessary. This claim will be proved later. The following simple example clarifies this point.

Example 12. Consider the inductively sequential, non-overlapping program

```
0 <= _         = true
(s _) <= 0     = false
(s x) <= (s y) = x <= y
0 + x          = x
(s x) + y = s (x + y)
```

INS computes the step $\bar{s} = (2, 0 + z \to z, \{x \mapsto s\ x', y \mapsto 0\})$ on the term $x \leq y + y$. Without instantiating x in the substitution of $\bar{s}$, the step is still possible, but it could become superfluous depending on later steps. E.g., one could compute

$$x \leq y + y \leadsto_{\{y \mapsto 0\}} x \leq 0 \leadsto_{\{x \mapsto 0\}} true$$

where the first step is useless. However, including $\{x \mapsto s\ x'\}$ in $\bar{s}$ prevents this derivation.

Lemma 13. *Let t be a term and $s = (p, R, \sigma) \in \mathrm{INS}(t)$ and $s' = (p', R', \sigma') \in \mathrm{INS}(t)$.*
- *σ (and σ') is of the form $\{v_1 \mapsto t_1, \ldots v_n \mapsto t_n\}$, where for all i in $1, \ldots, n$, t_i is a linear term whose set of variables is disjoint from the set of variables of t_j, for $j \neq i$ and j in $1, \ldots, n$;*
- *σ and σ' unify iff, for any variable v in the domains of both σ and σ', $\sigma(v)$ and $\sigma'(v)$ unify.*

6 Soundness and Completeness

Proposed notions of soundness and completeness of a calculus with non-deterministic functions [6,10] have not yet obtained a universal consensus. In this paper we take the following approach. A term rewriting system defines *all and only* the allowed steps of a computation, but it does not say which of the generally many steps that are allowed in term should be performed. The selection of a step is the job of a strategy. Since not every step selection policy is useful, a good strategy should guarantee that all and only the results of a computation are reached and that time and space resources are not unnecessarily consumed.

In constructor based system, constructors define data, whereas operations define computations. Thus, a term t is a *computation* and if $t \xrightarrow{*} u$ and u is a normal form, i.e., it cannot be further rewritten, then u is a *result* or *value* of t. In constructor based system, as in most functional programming languages, only normal forms that do not contain operations are interesting or legal and we refer to them as *data terms*.

The notions of soundness and completeness arise in computations performed with incomplete information, i.e., in terms containing uninstantiated variables. Narrowing has the potential to fill in the missing information necessary to compute results. We stipulate, as usual, that a variable of sort S stands for all and only the ground data terms of sort S and we consider only well-typed instantiations of a variables. Thus, if t is a computation with incomplete information, i.e., a term with uninstantiated variables, the results of t are all and only the elements of the set of data terms rewritten from $\sigma(t)$, when $\sigma(t)$ is ground and σ is a ground constructor substitution whose domain is the set of variables of t. The soundness and completeness of a narrowing strategy are thus defined as the properties of the strategy to compute only and all, respectively, the results of a term. A differing viewpoint is discussed in Section 8.

In practice, things are slightly more complicated. When we compute with incomplete information, we care not only for the results, but also, and perhaps even more, for the substitutions, called *computed answers*, that allow us to compute the results. For example, the result of the computation $0 \leq x$, where "$\leq$" is the usual relational operator on the naturals defined in Example 12, are the data term *true* and the computed answer set $\{\{x \mapsto 0\}, \{x \mapsto s\ 0\}, \ldots\}$. Infinite sets of computed answers are not unusual and dealing with them is unconvenient at best, thus we relax the requirement that values and computed answers must be ground. This, for example, allows us to represent the result of the above computation, in *Curry*'s *computed expression* notation, as $\{\}\,[]\,$*true*. The following definitions capture the intuition that we just discussed.

Definition 14. A narrowing strategy S is *sound* iff for any derivation $t \stackrel{*}{\leadsto}_\sigma u$ computed by S, $\sigma(t) \stackrel{*}{\to} u$. A narrowing strategy S is *complete* iff for any derivation $\sigma(t) \stackrel{*}{\to} u$, where u is a data term and σ is a constructor substitution, there exists a derivation $t \stackrel{*}{\leadsto}_{\sigma'} u'$ computed by S such that $\sigma' \leq \sigma$ and $u' \leq u$.

Next we prove the soundness and completeness of *INS*. In passing, we observe that rewriting is unaffected by incomplete information.

Proposition 15. *If* $t \stackrel{*}{\to} u$, *then, for any substitution* σ, $\sigma(t) \stackrel{*}{\to} \sigma(u)$.

Theorem 16. *If* INS *computes a narrowing derivation* $A : t \stackrel{*}{\leadsto}_\sigma u$, *where* u *is a data term, then* $\sigma(t) \stackrel{*}{\to} u$.

The proof of completeness requires a few auxiliary lemmas that shed some light on the ideas of Definitional Tree and Inductively Sequential Narrowing. Lemma 20 is an extension to narrowing of the *Parallel Moves Lemma* [9]. Lemma 22 shows that a pattern is an abstraction of the set of rules that can narrow a term that unifies with the pattern. Lemmas 23 and 24 address the persistence of a step computed by *INS* in a term t after t undergoes respectively an instantiation or another narrowing step. These properties are crucial since a necessary step of t remains necessary if t is further instantiated or another step is performed on t, provided that these operations are compatible with the necessary step. Lemma 26 shows that a step computed by

INS must be performed, eventually, to reach a certain class of constructor-rooted terms. These computations are more fundamental than needed computations [11]. Theorem 27 shows that any derivation that narrows a term at the root must perform a step computed by *INS* on t. Its proof further shows that *INS* lays the foundations for a sequence of steps that must be performed to compute a root-stable form. Although *INS* does not compute a minimal (most general) unifier for a step, it computes a minimal unifier for this sequence of steps. Theorem 29 addresses the relationship between any derivation to a data term and the *INS* step implicitly performed by this derivation. Corollary 30 shows that if a term t is narrowable to a data term, then there exists an *INS* derivation that computes a similar term. Termination is a relevant aspect of the proof. Finally, Corollary 31 proves the completeness of *INS*.

It is well-known that a set of disjoint redexes in a term can be contracted simultaneously [9]. We generalize this notion to a sets of narrowing step. In addition to the disjointness of redexes, we also require the unifiability of the substitutions of the steps.

Definition 17. If $S = \{(p_i, l_i \to r_i, \sigma_i)\}_{i=1,\ldots,n}$ is a set of narrowing steps of a term t such that σ is an upper bound of the set of substitutions $\{\sigma_i\}_{i=1,\ldots,n}$, and for all distinct i and j in $1,\ldots,n$, $\sigma_i(t)_{|p_i}$ and $\sigma_j(t)_{|p_j}$ are disjoint redexes, then $t' = \sigma(t)[\sigma(r_1),\ldots,\sigma(r_n)]_{|p_1,\ldots,p_n}$ is well defined and independent of the order in which the redexes are contracted. We call $t \rightsquigarrow t'$ a *narrowing multistep*.

Likewise, we generalize to narrowing the notion of descendant [9], which is of paramount importance for investigating the derivation space of a term. Separating the two parts of a narrowing step pays off here.

Definition 18. Let t be a term and $s_1 = (p_1, R_1, \sigma_1)$ and $s_2 = (p_2, R_2, \sigma_2)$ possibly degenerate narrowing steps of t. Steps s_1 and s_2 are *compatible* iff σ_1 and σ_2 unify and if $p_1 = p_2$ then $R_1 = R_2$. If s_1 and s_2 are compatible, $t \rightsquigarrow_{s_1} t_1$, and σ is a most general unifier of σ_1 and σ_2 restricted to the variables of t_1, then the set of descendants of s_2 by s_1, denoted $s_2 \backslash s_1$, is defined as follows.

$$s_2\backslash s_1 = \begin{cases} \{(=,=,\sigma)\} & \text{if } p_1 = p_2 \\ \{(p_2, R_2, \sigma)\} & \text{if } p_1 \not\leq p_2 \\ \{(p_1 \cdot p \cdot q, R_2, \sigma) \mid r_{1|p} = x\} & \text{if } s_1 \text{ is not degenerate,} \\ & R_1 = l_1 \to r_1, \\ & p_2 = p_1 \cdot p' \cdot q, \text{ and} \\ & l_{1|p'} = x \text{ is a variable} \end{cases} \tag{3}$$

The notions of descendant of either a step or multistep by either a multistep or a derivation are defined as for rewriting using Equation 3. The descendants of a term t by a narrowing step (p, R, σ) is defined as the descendant of $\sigma(t)$ by the rewrite step at p.

The above definition is a conservative extension of the definition of descendant (residual) for rewriting in orthogonal systems. Narrowing in inductively sequential systems adds two new dimensions to the problem: instantiations and distinct right hand sides of a same left hand side. Compatibility of steps, which always holds for rewriting in orthogonal systems, ensures (see Lemma 20) that after a narrowing step

s_1 of a term t we can perform what remains to be done of a narrowing step s_2 of t. The major novelty in our discussion is when two steps differ only in their substitutions. If, after doing one step, we want to catch up with the other step, we may have to further instantiate the term without any rewriting. This situation is consistent and natural with our viewpoint that a narrowing step is a two-part computation.

Example 19. Consider the program that defines addition and multiplication on the naturals in unary representation

```
0 + x       = x
(s x) + y = s (x + y)
0 * x       = 0
(s x) * y = y + x * y
```

and the term $t = y + x * y$. Given the following steps of t (only the substitution is indicated in the steps)

$$y + x * y \rightsquigarrow_{s_1=\{y\mapsto 0\}} x * 0$$
$$y + x * y \rightsquigarrow_{s_2=\{x\mapsto 0\}} y + 0$$

the step $x * 0 \rightsquigarrow_{\{x\mapsto 0\}} 0$ is a descendant of s_2 by s_1 whereas $x * 0 \rightsquigarrow_{\{x\mapsto s\ z\}} 0 + z * 0$ is not.

Lemma 20. *If* $t \rightsquigarrow_{s_1} t_1$ *and* $t \rightsquigarrow_{s_2} t_2$ *are compatible steps, then*
- *there exist narrowing steps* $t_1 \rightsquigarrow_{s_2\backslash s_1} u$ *and* $t_2 \rightsquigarrow_{s_1\backslash s_2} v$;
- $u = v$;
- $t \rightsquigarrow_{s_1} t_1 \rightsquigarrow_{s_2\backslash s_1} u$ *and* $t \rightsquigarrow_{s_2} t_2 \rightsquigarrow_{s_1\backslash s_2} v$ *compute the same substitution;*
- *for every step* s *of* t *compatible with both* s_1 *and* s_2, $s\backslash(s_2\backslash s_1) = s\backslash(s_1\backslash s_2)$.

Example 21. Consider the functions *half* and *double* defined in Example 8. The diagram of Fig. 1, where f is a binary function whose rules are irrelevant, illustrates Lemma 20. Let $t = f\ (half\ u)\ (double\ u)$. The top left step narrows t at position 1, whereas the top right step narrows t at position 2. Each bottom step is the descendant of the step at the opposite side of the diagram.

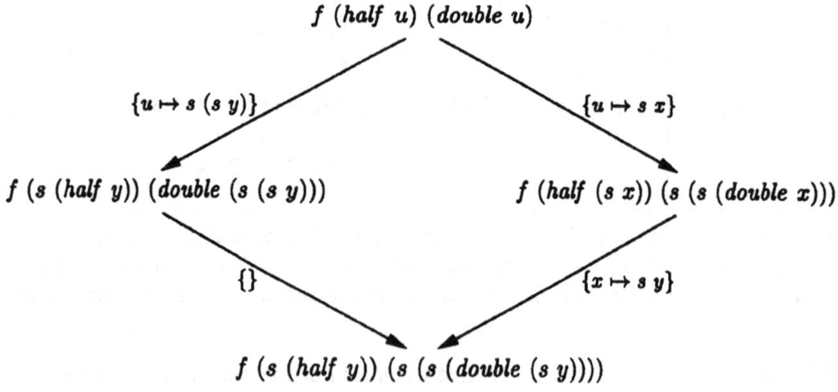

Fig. 1. Pictorial representation of the Parallel Narrowing Moves Lemma. An arrow represents a narrowing step and its label shows the step's substitution.

Lemma 22. *Let t be an operation rooted term, $\mathcal{T}$ the fixed definitional tree of the root of t, π a maximal pattern of $\mathcal{T}$ that unifies with t, and $\eta = t \lhd \pi$. If $l \to r$ is a rule applied to narrow a descendant of $\eta(t)$, then $\pi \leq l$.*

Lemma 23. *Let t be a term such that $s = (p, R, \eta) \in$ INS(t), and σ an idempotent substitution whose domain is contained in the set of the variables of t. If σ and η are unifiable, then there exists a substitution σ' such that $(p, R, \sigma') \in$ INS$(\sigma(t))$.*

Lemma 24. *Let t be a term, $t \leadsto_{s_1} t_1$ any narrowing step, $t \leadsto_{s_2} t_2$ a narrowing step compatible with s_1 computed by* INS *on t, and $s_3 = s_2 \backslash s_1$. If s_3 is not degenerate, then $s_3 \in$ INS(t_1).*

Definition 25. We say that a narrowing step $(p, l \to r, \sigma)$ is *root-needed* for an operation-rooted term t iff in any narrowing derivation $t \overset{+}{\leadsto}_\eta u$, where u is constructor-rooted and $\eta \geq \sigma$, a descendant of $t_{|p}$ is narrowed.

Lemma 26. INS *computes only root-needed steps.*

INS does not compute every root-needed step of a term, but if an operation-rooted term t can be narrowed to a constructor-rooted term, then *INS* always computes a step of t. If a term t is narrowable, but not to a data term, then *INS* may fail to compute any step. This property is a blessing in disguise. For example, consider

```
f = 0
g 0 = 0
h 0 0 = 0
```

and the term $t = h\ (g\ (s\ 0))\ f$. For some definitional tree of h, e.g., $\{h\ x_1\ y_1,\ h\ 0\ y_2,\ h\ 0\ 0\}$, *INS* does not compute any step on t, although t is narrowable (reducible) at position 2. However, t cannot be narrowed (reduced) to a data term. The early failure of *INS* saves performing useless steps.

Lemma 26 shows that *INS* computes only root-needed steps. We now prove a somewhat complementary result roughly equivalent to the fact that *INS* computes all the steps necessary to reach a data term. Because narrowing in non-confluent systems is more general than rewriting in strongly sequential systems, our formulation takes a different form and is broken into several results.

Theorem 27. *Let t be an operation-rooted term and $A : t \overset{+}{\leadsto}_{\eta'} t'$ a derivation that performs a step at the root.* INS *computes a step $s = (q, R, \eta)$ on t such that $\eta \leq \eta'$.*

The proof of previous theorem associates a step computed by *INS* to any derivation that narrows an operation-rooted term to a constructor-rooted term. Next we formally define this step.

Definition 28. Let t be an operation-rooted term and $A : t = t_0 \leadsto_{s_1} t_1 \leadsto_{s_2} \cdots \leadsto_{s_n} t_n$ a derivation that performs a step at the root. For all i in $1, \ldots, n$, let $s_i = (p_i, l_i \to r_i, \sigma_i)$ and let k be the minimum index such that $p_k = \Lambda$. We define the step s *associated* to A as follows. If t and l_k unify, then $s = (\Lambda, l_k \to r_k, t \lhd l_k)$, else we define s by structural induction on t as follows. The base case of the definition is vacuous. Ind. case of the definition: There exists a non-empty set S of patterns of the fixed definitional tree of the root of t that unify with t. Let π be a maximal pattern in S, $\sigma = t \lhd \pi$, and $\pi < l_k$. Let p be the inductive position of π. Since $t_{|p}$ is operation-rooted and $t_{k-1|p}$ is constructor-rooted, A defines a derivation, which we denote $A_{|p}$, of $t_{|p}$ to a constructor-rooted term. By induction, let $(p', l \to r, \tau)$ be the step associated to $A_{|p}$. The proof of Theorem 27 shows that σ and τ unify. Hence, by Lemma 23, there exists a substitution σ' such that $(p', l \to r, \sigma') \in INS(\sigma(t_{|p}))$. We define $s = (p \cdot p', l \to r, \sigma \circ \sigma')$.

Theorem 29. *Let $A = A_1; A_2; \ldots A_n$ be a narrowing derivation of a term t_0 to a data term t_n, and let B_0 be the step associated to A. There exists a commutative diagram (arrows stand for narrowing multisteps)*

$$\begin{array}{ccccccc}
t_0 & \xrightarrow{A_1} & t_1 & \xrightarrow{A_2} & \cdots & \xrightarrow{A_n} & t_n \\
\downarrow{\scriptstyle B_0} & & \downarrow{\scriptstyle B_1} & & & & \downarrow{\scriptstyle B_n} \\
t'_0 & \xrightarrow{A'_1} & t'_1 & \xrightarrow{A'_2} & \cdots & \xrightarrow{A'_n} & t'_n
\end{array}$$

where $A'_{i+1} = A_{i+1} \backslash B_i$ and $B_{i+1} = B_i \backslash A_{i+1}$, for $i = 0, \ldots, n-1$, and the substitution of step B_n is a permutation.

Corollary 30. *Let $A : t \overset{+}{\rightsquigarrow}_{\sigma} u$ a narrowing derivation of a term t to a data term u.* INS *computes a narrowing derivation $B : t \overset{+}{\rightsquigarrow}_{\sigma'} u'$ such that $\sigma' \leq \sigma$ and $u' \leq u$.*

Corollary 31. *If $A : \sigma(t) \overset{*}{\to} u$, where u is a data term and σ is a constructor substitution, then* INS *computes a narrowing derivation $B : t \overset{*}{\rightsquigarrow}_{\sigma'} u$ with $\sigma' \leq \sigma$ and $u' \leq u$.*

7 Optimality

Strategies are intended to avoid or minimize unnecessary computations. When non-determinism is involved, the notion of what is or is not necessary becomes subtle. Often, we use non-determinism when we do not know how to make the "right" steps and we cannot expect the narrowing *strategy* to choose for us. Thus, a realistic measure of the quality of a strategy should discount unnecessary work which is performed only because of a wrong non-deterministic choice.

INS makes three kinds of non-deterministic choices in the computation of a step of a term t: (0) a maximal operation-rooted subterm t' of t; (1) a maximal pattern π that unifies with t' in the fixed definitional tree of the root of t', and (2) when π is leaf, a rule whose left hand side is a variant of π. We refer to these choices as *type-0*, *type-1*, and *type-2* choices, respectively. Type-0 choices are *don't care* choices whereas the other choices are *don't know* choices. Type-2 choices originate from overlapping rules whereas type-1 choices occur in non-overlapping systems too, e.g., the strongly sequential ones. The following results show that according to this viewpoint *INS* does not waste a single step, though it may still make "wrong" choices.

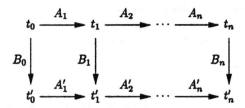

Lemma 32. *Let $s_1 = (p_1, l_1 \to r_1, \sigma_1)$ and $s_2 = (p_2, l_2 \to r_2, \sigma_2)$ be narrowing steps computed by* INS *on some operation-rooted term t. If s_1 and s_2 differ for a type-1 choice, then σ_1 and σ_2 are independent.*

Theorem 33. *Let $A_1 : t \overset{+}{\leadsto}_{\sigma_1} t_1$ and $A_2 : t \overset{+}{\leadsto}_{\sigma_2} t_2$ be narrowing derivations computed by* INS. *If A_1 and A_2 differ for a type-1 choice in some step, then σ_1 and σ_2 are independent.*

Corollary 34. *A narrowing derivation to a data term computed by* INS *performs only unavoidable steps, modulo non-deterministic choices.*

Example 35. The previous result, does not imply that *INS* computes "the best" derivation. Referring to the operation defined in display (1), both the following derivations satisfy Corollary 34.

$$f \to 0$$
$$f \to f \to 0$$

This fact is not surprising. It is obvious *a posteriori* that the second derivation makes an inappropriate type-2 choice to minimize the number of steps of the derivation. This is not a specific problem of *INS*. It is well-known [9] that even when the rewrite system does not allow type-2 choices, a derivation that makes only unavoidable steps may not minimize their number.

8 Related Work

INS has similarities with both Needed Narrowing [2] and CRWL [6]. The class of rewrite systems to which *INS* can be applied is wider than the class to which *NN* can be applied. *NN* is limited to confluent systems and consequently does not support the kind of non-deterministic computations discussed in Section 2. By contrast, CRWL does not place any specific limitation on rewrite systems. This "in-between" position of *INS* is an asset for the reasons discussed next.

Needed Narrowing is optimal in the number of steps of a derivations, but is likely to be less efficient than *INS* on inherently non-deterministic computations. For example, suppose that we want to solve the N-queen problem with the well-known technique of trial and error. With limited non-determinism, we would follow the standard functional programming approach, e.g., see [3, p. 133–134], which employs list comprehensions and higher order functions. This approach lazily generates permutations, stores them in a structure, and then tests the generated permutations one after another. By contrast, an inductively sequential program, see Example 7, does not require the explicit potential generation of all the permutations nor a structure to hold them nor higher order functions to process this structure. This approach simplifies the programming task and does not incur the cost of explicitly building and later garbage collecting the structure that holds the permutations. We dare to argue that inductively sequential programs would be welcome in functional programming, if this paradigm were equipped for backtracking and non-deterministic choices.

The lack of restrictions placed by CRWL on rewriting systems is not always advantageous. CRWL does not guarantee that computed answers are independent or that every performed step is unavoidable modulo non-deterministic choices. Furthermore, pattern matching for functions defined by not left-linear rules may become computationally expensive. From a software design perspective, programs in CRWL can be poorly structured. E.g., referring to Example 7 the following definition of *insert*, accepted by CRWL, is not inductively sequential.

```
insert x xs       = (x : xs)
insert x (y : ys) = (y : insert x ys)
```

According to this program, the need to evaluate or instantiate the second argument of *insert* depends on the non-deterministic selection of a rule, rather than on the definition of a function. Reasoning about laziness becomes difficult in this situation. By contrast, the definitions of functions in inductively sequential programs are well-understood and familiar. They are exactly the first order Haskell programs except, possibly, for allowing multiple choices of right hand side expressions. Inductive sequentiality imposes on the definition of functions restrictions weaker than those of functional programming, yet we have shown that it provides considerable benefits.

The notion of soundness that we have proposed differs from that adopted in [6]. CRWL adopts what is referred to as *call-time* choice for non-deterministic computations [10]. By contrast, we have adopted an *evaluation-time* choice. Intuitively, the first freezes at the time of a call the non-deterministic choices that will be made to evaluate the arguments of the call, whereas the second does not. Both approaches are plausible and defensible and we defer any decision on their appropriateness to another arena. However, we observe that evaluation-time choice is more natural when semantics are based on rewriting. The call-time choice approach is sound only if some rewrite steps, legal according to the rewrite semantics, are actually prohibited. From a purely computational and implementative point of view, our approach effortlessly supports call-time choice if the common subterms of a term are shared. Sharing would have no negative effects on our strategy completeness, whose definition for call-time choice differs, and would strengthen its optimality by ensuring derivations of minimum length modulo type-2 non-deterministic choices.

9 Conclusion

We have defined a novel class of programs, modeled by possibly overlapping inductively sequential rewrite systems, which simplifies coding non-deterministic functional logic computations. Our approach has been driven by *Curry*, a universal functional logic language currently discussed by researchers in this field, and has been inspired by CRWL, a rewriting logic for declarative programming. We have shown the existence of a sound, complete, and optimal narrowing strategy for inductively sequential programs.

The unified computation model proposed for *Curry* is based on definitional trees. Thus, it can be applied to inductively sequential programs, whether or not overlapping, without any change. When multiple results of non-deterministic computations are not acceptable, the *choice* operator already provided in *Curry* can be used, explicitly or implicitly, to prune the solution space. An implementation option, based on sharing common subterms of a term, accommodates either call-time or evaluation-time choice as the semantics of non-deterministic computations. Deterministic computations are performed by our strategy as efficiently as theoretically possible. In particular, inductively sequential narrowing is a conservative extension of needed narrowing. Inherently non-deterministic computations are performed more efficiently than needed narrowing computations, since it is no longer necessary to cast non-deterministic algorithms into deterministic ones.

Acknowledgments

This paper would not have been possible without the fruits of my long lasting collaboration with R. Echahed and M. Hanus on narrowing strategies. I also owe to the ideas and explanations of P. López Fraguas, M. Rodríguez-Artalejo, and others on the *Curry* mailing list.

Note

The full version of this paper, which includes all the proofs, is available at URL `www.cs.pdx.edu/~antoy/publications.html`.

References

1. S. Antoy. Definitional trees. In *Proc. of the 4th Intl. Conf. on Algebraic and Logic Programming*, pages 143–157. Springer LNCS 632, 1992.
2. S. Antoy, R. Echahed, and M. Hanus. A needed narrowing strategy. In *Proc. 21st ACM Symposium on Principles of Programming Languages*, pages 268–279, Portland, 1994. Full versions at URL `www.cs.pdx.edu/~antoy/publications.html`.
3. R. Bird and P. Wadler. *Introduction to Functional Programming*. Prentice Hall, New York, NY, 1988.
4. Curry: An integrated functional logic language. M. Hanus (ed.), Draft Dec. 5, 1996.
5. E. Eder. Properties of substitutions and unifications. *Journal of Symbolic Computation*, 1:31–46, 1985.
6. J. C. González Moreno, F. J. López Fraguas, M. T. Hortalá González, and M. Rodríguez Artalejo. A rewriting logic for declarative programming. In *ESOP' 96*, Linköping, Sweden, April, 1996. LNCS 1058, Extended version TR DIA 95/5.
7. M. Hanus. On extra variables in (equational) logic programming. In *Proc. Twelfth International Conference on Logic Programming*, pages 665–679. MIT Press, 1995.
8. M. Hanus. A unified computation model for functional logic programming. In *Proc. 24th ACM Symposium on Principles of Programming Languages*, pages 80–93, Paris, 1997.
9. G. Huet and J.-J. Lévy. Computations in orthogonal term rewriting systems. In J.-L. Lassez and G. Plotkin, editors, *Computational logic: essays in honour of Alan Robinson*. MIT Press, Cambridge, MA, 1991. Previous version: Call by need computations in non-ambiguous linear term rewriting systems, Technical Report 359, INRIA, Le Chesnay, France, 1979.
10. H. Hussmann. Nondeterministic algebraic specifications and nonconfluent rewriting. *J. of Logic Programming*, 12:237–255, 1992.
11. A. Middeldorp. Call by need computations to root-stable form. In *Proc. 24th ACM Symposium on Principles of Programming Languages*, pages 94–105, Paris, 1997.
12. R. A. O'Keefe. *The Craft of Prolog*. The MIT Press, Cambridge, MA, 1990.
13. T. Suzuki, A. Middeldorp, and T. Ida. Level-confluence of conditional rewrite systems with extra variables in right-hand sides. In *6th International Conference on Rewriting Techniques and Applications*, pages 179–193, Kaiserslautern, 1995. Lecture Notes in Computer Science 914.

A Semantic Basis for Termination Analysis of Logic Programs and Its Realization Using Symbolic Norm Constraints

Michael Codish Cohavit Taboch

Department of Mathematics and Computer Science
Ben-Gurion University of the Negev
Beer-Sheba, Israel
{codish,taboch}@cs.bgu.ac.il

Abstract. This paper presents a declarative semantics which exhibits the termination properties of a logic program. The semantics associates a program with its *binary unfoldings* — a possibly infinite set of binary clauses. Termination of a program P and goal G is indicated by the absence of an infinite chain in the binary unfoldings of P starting with G. The main contribution is a formal semantic basis for the termination analysis of logic programs which facilitates both design and implementation. As an implementation vehicle we propose a simple meta-interpreter for binary unfoldings and the use of an abstract domain based on symbolic norm constraints. Many of the recently proposed termination analyses for logic programs can be expressed concisely within our approach. To demonstrate our approach we have reformulated the analysis originally described in [13]. The implementation uses a standard library for linear equations over the reals. The combination of binary unfoldings and a constraint solver is shown to significantly simplify the design of the analysis.

1 Introduction

This paper provides a declarative (fixed-point) semantics which captures termination properties of logic programs. Several semantic definitions for logic programs have been proposed to better capture a variety of different notions of observables: the standard minimal model semantics models logical consequences, the c-semantics and the s-semantics [9] model correct and computed answers respectively, the semantic definition of [10] models the notion of call patterns, etc. In this paper we prove that the definition of [10] is suitable to model also the termination properties of programs. This provides a formal semantic basis for the analysis of termination of logic programs based on abstract interpretation [6].

We study the universal termination of logic programs executed by means of *LD-resolution*, which consists of SLD-resolution combined with Prolog's leftmost selection rule. By universal termination we refer to the termination of all computations of a given atomic initial goal with the leftmost selection rule. This corresponds to the finiteness of the corresponding SLD tree. The results can easily be generalized to consider any local selection rule and non-atomic initial goals.

Our semantics, similar to the definition of [10] is based on the notion of binary unfoldings and is shown to correspond to the closure of a binary relation on the calls selected in a computation. Non-termination for a specific goal implies the existence of a corresponding infinite chain in this binary relation. Consequently, the semantics of binary unfoldings provides a basis for the analysis of termination using the techniques of abstract interpretation: it captures the termination properties while abstracting away from other details present in an operational semantics such as those based on SLD trees. This is the main contribution of the paper.

To demonstrate the use of our approach we describe a termination analysis based on the ideas, originally introduced in [13]. The analysis is presented as an abstraction of the binary unfoldings semantics over an abstract domain of *symbolic norms* as described in [13, 16, 1]. Since this domain does not satisfy the ascending chain condition, a finite analysis is guaranteed by applying a suitable widening technique [7]. One possibility is to introduce an additional layer of abstraction based on monotonicity constraints as described in [13, 15]. Another possibility is to apply polyhedral approximations as described in [16] with a precise widening method [8] as in [1]. Both of these approaches are easily integrated into our proposed semantic foundation and easily implemented in a suitable constraint language. Termination of a program and a given query is determined using a simple test applied on the results of the semantic based analysis, also formulated as a query to the constraint solver. This is a sufficient condition for termination, which means that if the result is positive the query will surely terminate. We have implemented the termination analysis based on monotonicity constraints using the constraint libraries of SICStus Prolog version 3.

2 Preliminaries

In the following we assume a familiarity with the standard definitions and notation for logic programs [14] and abstract interpretation [6]. We assume a first order language with a fixed vocabulary of predicate symbols, function symbols and variables denoted Π, Σ and $\mathcal{V}$. We let $T(\Sigma, \mathcal{V})$ denote the set of terms constructed using symbols from Σ and variables from $\mathcal{V}$; *Atom* denotes the set of atoms constructed using predicate symbols from Π and terms from $T(\Sigma, \mathcal{V})$. A goal is a finite sequence of atoms. The set of goals is denoted by $Atom^*$. The empty goal is denoted by *true*. Substitutions and their operations are defined as usual. The most general unifier of syntactic objects s_1 and s_2 is denoted $mgu(s_1, s_2)$. A syntactic object s_1 is less instantiated than a syntactic object s_2 denoted $s_1 \leq s_2$ if there exists a substitution θ such that $s_2 = s_1\theta$.

A clause is an object of the form $head \leftarrow body$ where *head* is an atom and *body* is a goal. If *body* consists of at most one atom then the clause is said to be binary. The set of binary clauses is denoted $\Im$. A binary clause can be viewed as a relation "$\leftarrow$" on $Atom \times Atom \cup \{true\}$. An *identity clause* is a binary clause of the form $p(\bar{x}) \leftarrow p(\bar{x})$ where $\bar{x}$ denotes a tuple of distinct variables. Identity clauses play a technical role in the definition of the fixed point semantics presented below. These clauses are identities with respect to the operation of unfolding. Namely, unfolding a clause C with an identity clause gives back the clause C. We denote by *id* the set of identity clauses over the given alphabet.

A *variable renaming* is a substitution that is a bijection on $\mathcal{V}$. Two syntactic objects t_1 and t_2 are *equivalent up to renaming* if $t_1\rho = t_2$ for some variable renaming ρ. Given an equivalence class X of syntactic objects and a finite set of variables V, it is always possible to find a representative x of X that contains no variables from V. For a syntactic object s and a set of equivalence classes of objects I, we denote by $\langle c_1, \ldots, c_n \rangle \ll_s I$ that $c_1, \ldots, c_n$ are representatives of elements of I renamed apart from s and from each other. Note that for $n = 0$ (the empty tuple) $\langle\,\rangle \ll_s I$ holds vacuously for any I and s (in particular if $I = \emptyset$). In the discussion that follows, we will be concerned with sets of binary clauses modulo renaming. For simplicity of exposition, we will abuse notation and assume that a (binary) clause represents its equivalence class.

3 Operational semantics

The operational semantics for logic programs is formalized as usual in terms of a transition relation on goals. A pair in the relation corresponds to the reduction of a goal with a renamed clause from the program.

Definition 1. (LD-resolution) Let P be a logic program. An LD-resolution step for P is the smallest relation $\leadsto_P \subseteq Atom^* \times Atom^*$ such that $G \leadsto_P G'$ if and only if

1. $G = \langle a_1, \ldots, a_k \rangle$,
2. $h \leftarrow b_1, \ldots, b_n \ll_G P$,
3. $\vartheta = mgu(a_1, h)$, and
4. $G' = \langle b_1, \ldots, b_n, a_2, \ldots, a_k \rangle\vartheta$.

We sometimes write $G \overset{\vartheta}{\leadsto}_P G'$ to indicate explicitly the substitution ϑ associated with the resolution step.

Definition 2. (LD-derivation) Let P be a logic program and G_0 an initial goal. An LD-derivation of P and G_0 is a (finite or infinite) sequence of goals $G_0, G_1, \ldots$ consecutively related by LD-resolution steps. If $G_0 \overset{\vartheta_1}{\leadsto}_P G_1 \ldots \overset{\vartheta_n}{\leadsto}_P G_n$ is a derivation and $\vartheta = \vartheta_1 \circ \cdots \circ \vartheta_n$ then we write $G_0 \overset{\vartheta}{\leadsto}{}^*_P G_n$. If there is an infinite derivation of the form $G_0 \overset{\vartheta_1}{\leadsto}_P G_1 \ldots \overset{\vartheta_n}{\leadsto}_P G_n \ldots$ then we say that G_0 is non-terminating with P.

The following is an operational definition for the notions of calls and answers.

Definition 3. (calls and answers) Let P be a program and G_0 be a goal. We say that A is a call in a derivation of G_0 with P if and only if $G_0 \leadsto^*_P \langle A, \ldots \rangle$. We denote by $calls_P(G_0)$ the set of calls in the computations of G_0 with P. We say that $G_0\theta$ is an answer for G_0 with P if $G_0 \overset{\theta}{\leadsto}{}^*_P$ *true*. The set of answers for G_0 with P are denoted $ans_P(G_0)$.

The calls-to relation specifies the dependencies between calls in a computation and serves as a convenient link between the operational and denotational semantics with regards to observing termination.

Definition 4. (calls-to relation) Let P be a program and G_0 be a goal. We say that there is a call from a to b (denoted by $a \overset{P,G_0}{\hookrightarrow} b$) in a computation of G_0 with P if $a \in \mathit{calls}_P(G_0)$ and $b \in \mathit{calls}_P(a)$. When clear from the context we write $a \hookrightarrow b$. We sometimes write $a \overset{\vartheta}{\hookrightarrow} b$ to emphasize that ϑ is the substitution associated with a corresponding derivation from $\langle a \rangle$ to $\langle b, \ldots \rangle$ in the above relation.

The following lemma relates the termination of a goal with a property of the calls-to relation.

Lemma 5. (observing termination in the calls-to relation)
Let P be a program and G_0 be a goal. Then, there is an infinite derivation for G_0 in P if and only if there is an infinite chain in the calls-to relation.

Proof. ($\Leftarrow$) Immediate by the definition of the calls-to relation. ($\Rightarrow$) We prove by induction that for every n, there is a chain $a_0 \hookrightarrow \cdots \hookrightarrow a_n$ starting from G_0 such that a_n has an infinite derivation with P.
base: By assumption G_0 is atomic and has an infinite derivation.
step: Assume the existence of a chain $a_0 \hookrightarrow \cdots \hookrightarrow a_k$ starting from G_0 such that a_k has an infinite derivation $\delta = g_0, g_1, g_2, \ldots$, with P where $g_0 = \langle a_k \rangle$. We show that there exists an atom a_{k+1} such that $a_k \hookrightarrow a_{k+1}$ which has an infinite derivation with P. Let $g_1 = \langle b_1, \ldots, b_m \rangle$ and let b_i be the first atom in g_1 which has an infinite derivation. Such an atom must exist because δ is infinite. It follows that there must be a subsequent state $\langle b'_i \ldots, b'_m \rangle$ in δ (which is an instance of $\langle b_i, \ldots, b_m \rangle$) and such that b'_i has an infinite derivation. The atom we are looking for is $a_{k+1} = b'_i$.

4 Denotational Semantics

As a basis for termination analysis, we adopt a simplification of the goal independent semantics for call patterns defined in [10]. The definition is given as the fixed point of an operator T_P^β over the domain of *binary clauses*. Intuitively, a binary clause $a \leftarrow b$ specifies that a call to a in a computation implies a subsequent call to b. A clause of the form $a \leftarrow \mathit{true}$ is a fact, and indicates a success pattern. We refer to this semantics as defining the set of *binary unfoldings* of a program. Given a set of binary clauses X, $T_P^\beta(X)$ is constructed as follows: for each clause $h \leftarrow b_1, \ldots, b_m \in P$ we unfold prefixes of the body to obtain new binary clauses in three possible ways: (1) we unfold $b_1, \ldots, b_{i-1}$ with facts of the form $h_j \leftarrow \mathit{true}$ $(1 \leq j \leq i-1)$ from X to obtain a corresponding instance of $h \leftarrow b_i$; (2) we unfold $b_1, \ldots, b_{i-1}$ with facts from X and b_i with a binary clause $h_i \leftarrow b$, which is not a fact ($b \neq \mathit{true}$), to obtain a corresponding instance of $h \leftarrow b$; and (3) we unfold $b_1, \ldots, b_m$ with facts from X to obtain a corresponding instance of h. We refer the reader to [10] for more details regarding to the following definition.

Definition 6. (binary unfoldings semantics $T_P^\beta : \Im \to \Im$)

$$T_P^\beta(X) = \left\{ (h \leftarrow b)\vartheta \,\middle|\, \begin{array}{l} C = h \leftarrow b_1, \ldots, b_m \in P, \; 1 \leq i \leq m, \\ (h_j \leftarrow true)_{j=1}^{i-1} \ll_C X, \\ h_i \leftarrow b \ll_C X \cup id, \; i < m \Rightarrow b \neq true \\ \vartheta = mgu(\langle b_1, \ldots, b_i \rangle, \langle h_1, \ldots, h_i \rangle) \end{array} \right\}$$

$$bin\_unf(P) = lfp(T_P^\beta)$$

Example 1 The following table illustrates a program P (on the left) with its (finite) set of binary unfoldings (on the right):

$p(X, Y) \leftarrow$	$p(A, B) \leftarrow q(A).$	$p(A, B) \leftarrow r(A).$
$\quad q(X), r(Y), p(X, Y).$	$p(a, A) \leftarrow r(A).$	$p(a, b) \leftarrow p(a, b).$
$p(X, Y) \leftarrow$	$p(a, b) \leftarrow q(a).$	$p(a, b) \leftarrow r(a).$
$\quad r(X), r(Y).$	$p(a, b) \leftarrow r(b).$	$p(b, A) \leftarrow r(A).$
$q(a).$	$q(a) \leftarrow true.$	$r(b) \leftarrow true.$
$r(b).$	$p(b, b) \leftarrow true.$	

Figure 1 illustrates a simple Prolog interpreter which computes the binary unfoldings of a program P, if there are finitely many of them. This interpreter provides the basis for the bottom-up evaluation of the abstract semantics for termination analysis defined in the next sections.

```
iterate ← tp_beta, fail.
iterate ← retract(flag),
     iterate.
iterate.

cond_assert(F) ←
     in_database(F), !.
cond_assert(F) ←
     assert(F),
     cond_assert(flag).

in_database(G) ←
     functor(G, N, A),
     functor(B, N, A), call(B),
     variant(B, G), !.
```

```
tp_beta ←
     user_clause(Head, Body),
     solve(Head, Body).

solve(Head, [ ]) ←
     cond_assert(fact(Head)).
solve(Head, [B|Bs]) ←
     cond_assert(bin(Head, B)),
     fact(B),
     solve(Head, Bs).
solve(Head, [B|_]) ←
     bin(B, C),
     cond_assert(bin(Head, C)).
```

Fig. 1. Prolog interpreter for binary unfoldings

The interpreter assumes that each clause $h \leftarrow b_1, \ldots, b_n$ in P is represented as a fact of the form $user\_clause(h, [b_1, \ldots, b_n])$. The interpreter can be divided conceptually into two components. On the right, the predicate **tp_beta/0** provides the "logic" and the inner loop of the algorithm which for each $user\_clause(Head,$

Body) in P uses the binary unfoldings derived so far to derive new ones. Each time a new fact F is derived it is asserted to the Prolog database as an atom of the form $fact(F)$. Binary clauses are asserted as atoms of the form $bin(H, B)$. The predicate `cond_assert/1` asserts a derived object if it is new — namely not equivalent to any of those derived so far. The control component, on the left, invokes iterations of `tp_beta` until no new unfoldings are derived. When a new unfolding is asserted to the Prolog database, a *flag* is raised (unless the flag has already been raised). Iteration terminates when *retract(flag)* fails in the second clause indicating that nothing new was asserted in the previous iteration. Bottom-up evaluation is initiated by the query `?- iterate` which leaves the result of the evaluation in the Prolog database.

In [10] and similarly in [3] the authors show that the binary unfoldings of a program provide a goal independent representation of its success and call patterns.

Proposition 7. (observing calls and answers)
Let P be a program and G an atomic goal. Then, the computed answers for G with P and the calls that arise in the computations of G with P are characterized respectively by :

1. $$ans_P(G) = \left\{ G\vartheta \,\middle|\, \begin{array}{l} h \leftarrow true \in bin\_unf(P), \\ \vartheta = mgu(G, h) \end{array} \right\}$$
2. $$calls_P(G) = \left\{ b\vartheta \,\middle|\, \begin{array}{l} h \leftarrow b \in bin\_unf(P), \\ \vartheta = mgu(G, h) \end{array} \right\}.$$

Example 2 Consider again the program P from Example 1 and the initial goal $p(X, b)$. Observe that:

$$calls_P(p(X,b)) = \left\{ q(X), r(X), r(b), p(a,b), q(a), r(a), r(b) \right\}; \textit{ and}$$

$$ans_P(p(X,b)) = \left\{ p(b,b) \right\}.$$

This paper illustrates that binary unfoldings exhibit not only the calls and answers of a program but also its termination properties. This motivates the use of binary unfoldings as a semantic basis for termination analysis.

Theorem 8. (observing termination)
Let P be a program and G_0 be a goal. Then G_0 is non-terminating for P if and only if G_0 is non-terminating for $bin\_unf(P)$.

Proof. By Lemma 5 it is sufficient to show that there is an infinite chain in the calls-to relation for G_0 with P if and only if there is an infinite chain in the calls-to relation for G_0 with $bin\_unf(P)$. We show that in fact the calls-to relations for G_0 with P and with $bin\_unf(P)$ are identical: By Proposition 7 (2) it follows that for any goal G, $calls_P(G) = calls_{bin\_unf(P)}(G)$. This implies by Definition 4 that

$$a \overset{P,G_0}{\hookrightarrow} b \;\Leftrightarrow\; a \overset{\mathrm{bin\_unf(P)},G_0}{\hookrightarrow} b.$$

Example 3 Consider the program P from Example 1 which is non-terminating for the initial query $p(X, b)$. The calls-to relation contains the infinite chain $p(X, b) \hookrightarrow p(a, b) \hookrightarrow p(a, b) \hookrightarrow p(a, b) \hookrightarrow \ldots$ which can be observed in the binary unfoldings through the clause $p(a, b) \leftarrow p(a, b)$.

5 Abstract Interpretation

Termination analysis is based on descriptions of the binary unfoldings of a program called ***abstract binary unfoldings***. To determine that a goal G does not have an infinite computation with $bin\_unf(P)$, the analysis derives a (finite) set of abstract binary unfoldings which approximates the (possibly infinite) set of binary unfoldings which can occur in the computations with G. A sufficient condition for termination determines that none of the elements in this set can represent an infinite subcomputation of corresponding concrete binary clauses.

We introduce an abstract domain for termination analysis based on the use of constraint logic programs with linear arithmetic constraints. For termination analysis we need two types of information: (1) information about the size of terms (and how they decrease in a loop); and information about how "instantiated" terms are. This is to ensure a decrease over a well founded domain. It is not sufficient to show that a term decreases in size because this can still enable an infinite decreasing chain. However if we also know that a term is sufficiently instantiated then termination can be proven.

Recall, that logic programs in our setting are constructed as a first order language involving predicate and function symbols from Π and Σ and variables from $\mathcal{V}$. To formalize termination analysis we introduce ***symbolic norm constraint logic programs*** (CLP(SN)).

Definition 9. (CLP(SN) — symbolic norm constraints) CLP(SN) is the set of constraint logic programs with predicate symbols from $\Pi' = \Pi \cup \{=, \leq /2, < /2\}$, non-negative integers and addition $\Sigma' = \mathcal{N} \cup \{+/2\}$ and variables from $\mathcal{V}$, where $=, \leq /2, < /2$, $\mathcal{N}$ and $+$ are given their natural interpretation over the positive integer numbers.

Syntactic objects are CLP(SN) clauses of the form $h \leftarrow \mu, b_1, \ldots, b_n$ where μ is a conjunction of constraints, and $b_1, \ldots, b_n$ are atoms with predicate symbols from Π. If $n = 0$ the object is called a *constrained atom*. If $n \leq 1$ the object is a *constrained binary clause*. The underlying constraint structure is associated with the natural notions of entailment, solutions, instantiation, conjunction, projection, etc. For Example the set of instances of a constrained atom $\pi = p \leftarrow \mu$ denoted $[\pi]$, is the set of constrained atoms of the form $(p)\vartheta$ such that ϑ is a *solution* of μ. Namely, ϑ is a ground substitution which satisfies the constraint μ. A syntactic CLP(SN) object s_1 is less instantiated than an object s_2, denoted $s_1 \preceq s_2$ if $[s_1] \supseteq [s_2]$ and $s_1 \equiv s_2$ if $s_1 \preceq s_2$ and $s_2 \preceq s_1$. The sets of CLP(SN) binary clauses and CLP(SN) atoms modulo this notion of equivalence are denoted $\Im_{SN}$ and $Atom_{SN}$ respectively.

Intuitively, an abstract (constrained) object π describes the set of concrete objects with terms, the sizes of which, satisfy the constraints in π. For example a constrained atom of the form $p(A, B, C) \leftarrow \{A < B, C = B + 1\}$ describes a concrete atom $p(t_1, t_2, t_3)$ if the size of t_1 is less than the size of t_2 and the size of t_3 is equal to the size of t_2 plus 1.

For (abstract) atoms $a = p(t_1, \ldots, t_n)$ and $a' = p(s_1, \ldots, s_n)$ we often write $a = a'$ as an abbreviation for the conjunction of equations $\bigwedge_{i=1}^{n} (t_i = s_i)$.

The formal definition of the abstract domain is parameterized by the choice of a *symbolic norm* (e.g. as in [13]) which gives an interpretation to the notion of the "*size of a term*". Symbolic norms are similar to semi-linear norms as defined in [2], but variables are mapped to variables. For a term t containing a variable X with size $X + 1$, it means that the size of any instance of t is 1 plus the size of the term bound to X.

Definition 10. (symbolic norm)
A symbolic norm is a function $\|\cdot\| : T(\Sigma, \mathcal{V}) \rightarrow T(\Sigma', \mathcal{V})$ such that

$$\|t\| = \begin{cases} c + \sum_{i=0}^{n} a_i \|t_i\| & \text{if } t = f(t_1, \ldots, t_n) \\ t & \text{if } t \text{ is a variable} \end{cases}$$

where c and $a_1, \ldots, a_n$ are constants depending only on f/n.

Symbolic norms can be applied to an arbitrary syntactic object s simply by replacing the terms occurring in s by their sizes. The result of applying term-size norm (where $a_1, \ldots, a_n = 1, c = n$) on program clauses is demonstrated in Example 4 below.

Our abstract domain is constructed from constrained binary clauses. We introduce a description relation $\propto \subseteq \mathfrak{I}_{SN} \times \mathfrak{I}$ which specifies when a constrained binary clause describes a corresponding concrete object.

Definition 11. (description relation) A constrained (abstract) binary clause $\beta = a \leftarrow \mu, b$ describes a concrete binary clause $c = a' \leftarrow b'$, denoted $\beta \propto c$ if $\beta \preceq \|c\|$. This is equivalent to saying that the set of equations induced by $a = \|a'\|$ and $b = \|b'\|$ has a solution which implies μ.

Our abstract domain is the power set of (equivalence classes of) CLP(SN) binary clauses: $(2^{\mathfrak{I}_{SN}}, \subseteq)$.

Definition 12. (abstraction and concretization)

$\alpha : 2^{\mathfrak{I}} \rightarrow 2^{\mathfrak{I}_{SN}}$ $\qquad\qquad$ $\gamma : 2^{\mathfrak{I}_{SN}} \rightarrow 2^{\mathfrak{I}}$

$\alpha(I) = \{\, \|a \leftarrow b\| \mid a \leftarrow b \in I \,\}$ $\qquad$ $\gamma(\mathcal{I}) = \{\, a \leftarrow b \mid \beta \in \mathcal{I}, \beta \propto a \leftarrow b \,\}$

Lemma 13. $(2^{\mathfrak{I}}, \alpha, 2^{\mathfrak{I}_{SN}}, \gamma)$ *is a Galois insertion.*

Example 4 The following clauses illustrate a logic program for addition and multiplication (on the left) and its term-size abstraction (on the right).

$add(0, Y, Y).$	$add(0, Y, Y).$
$add(s(X), Y, s(Z)) \leftarrow$ $\quad add(X, Y, Z).$	$add(X + 1, Y, Z + 1) \leftarrow$ $\quad add(X, Y, Z).$
$mult(0, Y, 0).$	$mult(0, Y, 0).$
$mult(s(X), Y, Z) \leftarrow$ $\quad mult(X, Y, W), add(W, Y, Z).$	$mult(X + 1, Y, Z) \leftarrow$ $\quad mult(X, Y, W), add(W, Y, Z).$

CLP(SN) programs can be given a semantics in any of the standard techniques, for example as shown in [11] or in [12]. The notion of a resolution step (Definition 1) lifts naturally for constraint programs by replacing the unification by constraint conjunctions. Likewise, for termination analysis we generalize the binary unfoldings semantics of Definition 6 for CLP(SN) using standard techniques which basically involve replacing the unification operation with constraint conjunction.

Definition 14. (abstract binary unfoldings semantics $T_P^\alpha : \Im_{SN} \to \Im_{SN}$)

$$T_P^\alpha(\mathcal{I}) = \left\{ \|h\| \leftarrow \mu, b \;\middle|\; \begin{array}{l} C = h \leftarrow b_1, \ldots, b_m \in P,\ 1 \leq i \leq m, \\ \langle a_j \leftarrow \mu_j \rangle_{j=1}^{i-1} \ll_C \mathcal{I}, \\ a_i \leftarrow \mu_i, b \ll_C X \cup id,\ i < m \Rightarrow b \neq true \\ \mu = \bigwedge_{j=1}^{i} (\mu_j \wedge \{\|b_j\| = a_j\}) \end{array} \right\}$$

$$bin\_unf^\alpha(P) = lfp(T_P^\alpha)$$

The correctness of the operator in Definition 14, namely, that for any program P, $lfp(T_P^\alpha) \propto lfp(T_P^\beta)$, follows by showing that $\mathcal{I} \propto I \;\Rightarrow T_P^\alpha(\mathcal{I}) \propto T_P^\beta(I)$. This is a straightforward consequence of the following theorem.

Theorem 15. *Let a_1 and a_2 be concrete atoms such that $\theta = mgu(a_1, a_2)$. Let $\pi_1 = p_1 \leftarrow \mu_1$ and $\pi_2 = p_2 \leftarrow \mu_2$ be abstract atoms such that $\pi_1 \propto a_1$ and $\pi_2 \propto a_2$ and let $\pi_3 = p_1 \leftarrow \{p_1 = p_2\} \wedge \mu_1 \wedge \mu_2$. Then, $\pi_3 \propto a_1\theta$.*

The proof relies on the following lemmata:

Lemma 16. (most general common instance) *Let $\pi = a \leftarrow \mu$ and $\pi' = a' \leftarrow \mu'$ be constrained atoms. Then $a \leftarrow \{a = a'\} \wedge \mu \wedge \mu'$ is the most general common instance of π and π'.*

Lemma 17. (monotonicity of $\|\cdot\|$) *Let $\|\cdot\|$ be a symbolic norm and let a_1 and a_2 be (concrete) atoms. Then, $a_1 \leq a_2 \;\Rightarrow\; \|a_1\| \preceq \|a_2\|$.*

Proof. (of Theorem 15) Assume the premise of the theorem. By Lemma 17 we have $\pi_1 \preceq \|a_1\| \preceq \|a_1\theta\|$ and $\pi_2 \preceq \|a_2\| \preceq \|a_2\theta\|$ which implies that π_1 and π_2 have $\|a_1\theta\|$ as a common instance (because $a_1\theta = a_2\theta$). However, by Lemma 16, π_3 is the most general common instance of π_1 and π_2 so, $\pi_3 \preceq \|a_1\theta\|$ which by Definition 11 implies that $\pi_3 \propto a_1\theta$.

The abstract domain of symbolic norms does not satisfy the ascending chain condition, and hence the least fixed point of Definition 14 is not guaranteed to be finitely computable. To obtain a finite analysis we need to apply a further abstraction or a widening operator. There are a variety of different abstractions and widening strategies commonly used in termination analyses which can be applied to provide finite approximations of the binary unfoldings of a program. For example, in [1] the authors show how to implement an analysis based on polyhedra using a standard constraint solver. Another simple approach which turns out to be powerful is described in [13] where the authors use disjunctions of monotonicity constraints (which are conjunctions of constraints of the form $X \leq Y$, $X < Y$ and $X = Y$) between argument positions. Using either method, our semantic based analysis produces a finite set of abstract binary unfoldings for a given program. Both of the methods integrate into our semantic basis and are easily implemented using constraint logic programming technology.

The method adapted from [13] (originally defined using weighted graphs) restricts constrained abstract binary clauses to exclude natural number constants and arithmetic addition (+/2). As a result we get constrained syntactic objects which describe relations between pairs of argument positions. The semantic objects are sets of constrained atoms of this simple form viewed as disjunctions. The least upper bound is set union. For example, the constrained atom $add(X+1, Y, Z+1) \leftarrow \{X \leq Y, X \leq Z, Y = Z\}$ is abstracted to $add(A, B, C) \leftarrow \{A \leq C, B < C\}$. The new list of constraints is obtained by testing for entailment on the corresponding argument positions.

The method of polyhedral approximations as described in [16] and implemented in [1], can also be used for termination analysis. The least upper bound of two constrained syntactic objects is their convex hull, which can be expressed as a set of inequalities. Implementing a finite analysis over this domain requires a widening operator as described in [1].

In addition to the information on term sizes, we require also information about instantiation of terms in binary unfoldings of a program. We recall the notion of *instantiated enough* with respect to a symbolic norm which is closely related to that of rigidity (see for example [2]). In our context this means that the corresponding symbolic norm is ground.

Definition 18. [13] **(instantiated enough)** A term t is instantiated enough with respect to a symbolic norm $||\cdot||$ if $||t||$ is an integer (i.e does not contain variables).

Example 5 The list of variables $[X_1, X_2, X_3]$ is instantiated enough with respect to the list length symbolic norm since $||[X_1, X_2, X_3]||_{ListLength} = 3$ however it is not instantiated enough with respect to the term size norm since $||[X_1, X_2, X_3]||_{TermSize} = X_1 + X_2 + X_3 + 6$

Several papers (e.g. [4, 11]) show how to express instantiation dependencies relative to a norm function. In this paper we apply a fixed interpretation — that of groundness analysis — of the abstract domain *Prop* [5] to the symbolic norm abstraction of a given program. We apply the groundness analysis described in [3] to the CLP(SN) program obtained as $||P||$ to determine argument positions of P which are instantiated enough with respect to a given symbolic norm.

6 A Sufficient Condition for Termination

Termination analysis for the initial goal G_0 with the program P is based on a finite approximation of the binary unfoldings semantics. Let us denote $\mathcal{B} =$

bin_unf$^\alpha(P)$, the finite set of constrained binary clauses which approximates the binary unfoldings of P. For any initial call description (a constrained atom with instantiation information), $\mathcal{B}$ determines a corresponding finite set $\mathcal{C}$ of constrained atoms describing the calls that arise in the computations of G_0 (the abstract version of Proposition 7).

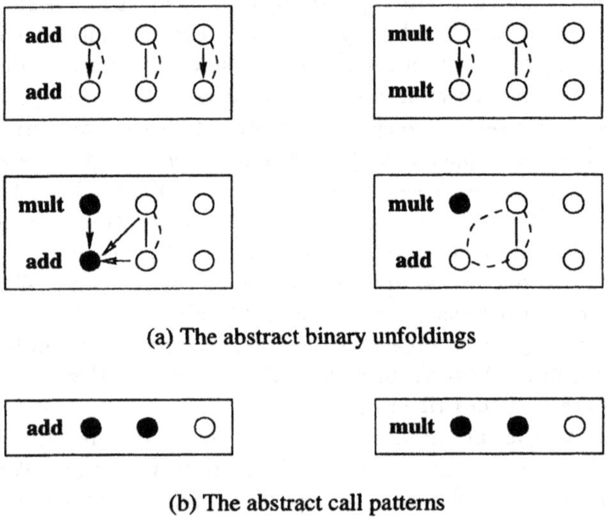

Fig. 2. Abstract binary unfoldings and call patterns for add-mult

Example 6 Figure 2 (a) depicts the abstract binary clauses for the add-mult program of Example 4 (the facts are not indicated). Each binary clause is illustrated as a graph in which the nodes are the argument positions of the head (upper) and the body (lower). The argument positions which are instantiated enough are colored in black. The dashed lines indicate instantiation dependencies between argument positions. The monotonicity constraints between argument positions X and Y are described by: a black edge if $X = Y$, a black arrow if $X < Y$ and a white arrow if $X \leq Y$ (arrows point towards the smaller position). Figure 2 (b) depicts the abstract call patterns for the initial goal $mult(A, B, C)$ in which A and B are integer inputs (instantiated enough).

A sufficient condition for termination is justified as follows: Assume that G_0 and P have an infinite derivation. Then there must be an infinite derivation for G_0 using binary unfoldings of P of the form:

$$\delta = \langle a_1 \rangle \rightarrow \langle a_2 \rangle \rightarrow \cdots$$

Since $\mathcal{C}$ is finite, δ must contain an infinite subchain

$$\delta' = \langle a_{i_1} \rangle \rightarrow^* \langle a_{i_2} \rangle \rightarrow^* \langle a_{i_3} \rangle \cdots$$

of atoms described by a single constrained atom $\pi \in \mathcal{C}$. Since the binary unfoldings of P are closed under unfolding each pair of atoms (not necessarily consecutive) in δ' correspond to a single step using some binary unfolding of P. Since $\mathcal{B}$ is finite, there is an infinite subchain of δ' which can be described as a derivation

$$\delta'' = \langle c_1 \rangle \xrightarrow{b_1} \langle c_2 \rangle \xrightarrow{b_2} \langle c_3 \rangle \cdots$$

in $bin\_unf(P)$ where each b_i is a binary unfolding of P described by the same element $\beta \in \mathcal{B}$. Moreover, by similar reasoning we can assume that the CLP(SN) derivation of π and β is of the form

$$\langle \pi \rangle \xrightarrow{\beta} \langle \pi \rangle \xrightarrow{\beta} \langle \pi \rangle \xrightarrow{\beta} \cdots$$

This observation provides the basis for a sufficient condition for termination. To prove termination we have to show that no pair π and β can describe an infinite sequence of concrete calls. Moreover, it is sufficient to check those pairs of π and β for which a single (abstract) resolution step is of the form $\langle \pi \rangle \xrightarrow{\beta} \langle \pi \rangle$. Namely, the call pattern π and the body of β are equivalent (have equivalent monotonicity constraints and instantiation dependencies) under the resolution step.

Intuitively, we will show that if the condition on each such $\beta \in \mathcal{B}$ and $\pi \in \mathcal{C}$ holds, then they cannot describe an infinite derivation like δ''.

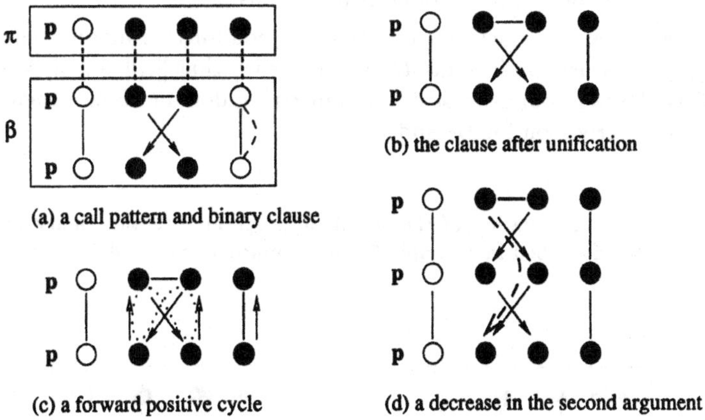

Fig. 3. A sufficient condition for termination

Figure 3 (a) depicts a call pattern π (with four arguments) and a recursive constrained binary clause β. The matching of arguments in π and the head of β are indicated by dotted edges. Figure 3 (b) depicts the instance of β after the unification with π. Note that the fourth argument in β became instantiated enough under the unification. As a consequence the call π and the body of β are now identical. The figure also illustrates the close relationship between our approach using constraints and the query mapping pairs approach of [13] based on weighted graphs.

A sufficient condition for termination (on every π and β) is that some (instantiated enough) argument position is positive and strictly decreasing in the derivation. Hence, the derivation cannot be infinite. This condition can be detected in π and β as follows: after unifying π with the head of β we add constraints of the form $h_i \leq b_i$ for each argument position i where the corresponding arguments are instantiated enough in the head and in the body (Figure 3 (c)). If as a result we get an inconsistent set of constraints, this implies that at least for one argument position i, $h_i > b_i$ after some number of resolution steps. The inconsistency is a result of adding the additional constraints that created a "forward positive cycle" (as defined in [13]) in the constraint graph. This cycle contains only black nodes and at least one black arrow. Figure 3 (d) illustrates the decrease in the size of an argument position implied by this cycle, which can occur in one or more derivation steps. Traversing the cycle from a body argument position to the corresponding head argument position can be viewed as traversing from the body argument position to the same position in the head of the next pair in the chain. This can be done a finite number of times until reaching the same position we started with. Since along the cycle we pass only through positions which are smaller or equal to the previous and at least through one position which is strictly smaller we get a strict decrease in some argument position within a finite number of derivation steps.

As a result we get a derivation (δ'') which contains an infinite sequence of terms $t_1, t_2, \ldots$ which are instantiated enough, such that $||t_1|| > ||t_2|| > \ldots$. This contradicts the well foundedness of the underlying domain. Hence there cannot be an infinite derivation for G_0 and P.

Example 7 The termination of the add-mult program with the binary unfoldings and call patterns described in Example 6 is determined in Figure 4.

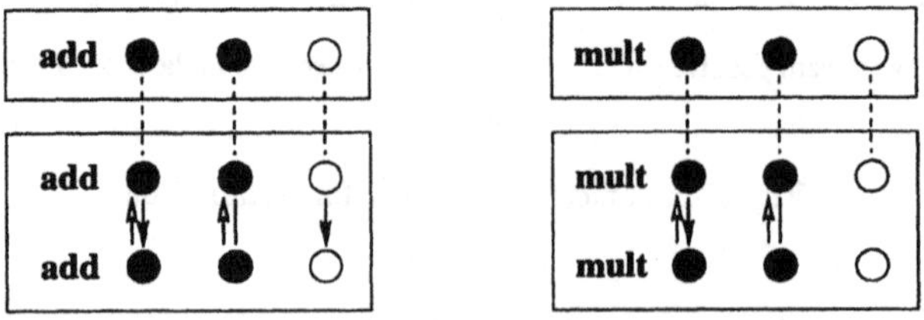

Fig. 4. Termination condition for add-mult

The figure contains the recursive binary clauses with their corresponding call patterns. When adding the constraints $h_i \leq b_i$ on the first and second argument positions which are instantiated enough, we get an inconsistent set of constraints, and indeed the relation between the first argument in the head and body shows the decrease.

7 An Implementation

We have implemented a termination analyzer based on the meta-interpreter of Figure 1 (enhanced for constraints). The implementation is written in SICStus Prolog (version 3) using the constraint solver library over the reals CLP(R). Since the $CLP(SN)$ domain consists of non-negative integers, a constraint of the form $X \geq 0$ is added for each variable X.

The widening step (for monotonicity constraints) is implemented by testing each pair of argument positions X and Y in the abstract binary clause to check if one of the constraints $X < Y$, $X \leq Y$ or $X = Y$ is entailed. To test if a constraint c is entailed by a set of constraints C it is sufficient to determine the inconsistency of $C \wedge \neg c$. The condition on binary unfoldings and a call description (i.e. the existence of a forward positive cycle) is tested using the constraint solver by adding the constraints between body and head arguments of the clause, which are instantiated enough, and testing for constraint inconsistency (see Figure 3 (c)). The analysis which determines instantiation dependencies is implemented using the approach described in [3] (for logic programs) and using the interpreter of Figure 1 to obtain the corresponding information on the instantiation of terms in the binary unfoldings.

8 Conclusions

We show that the binary unfoldings semantics, previously introduced in [10], makes termination observable in a goal independent way. This is the main contribution of the paper and suggests the use of the semantics as a basis for termination analysis. To substantiate this claim we illustrate an abstract semantics based on the notion of symbolic norms to provide for the termination analysis of logic programs. The resulting analysis is quite similar to that defined in [13]. However we find that the use of constraints in the description of the analysis simplifies both the formalization of the analysis as well as of its implementation. The termination analysis has been fully implemented in SICStus Prolog.

References

1. F. Benoy and A. King. Inferring argument size relationships with CLP(R). In *Sixth International Workshop on Logic Program Synthesis and Transformation (LOPSTR'96)*, 1996.
2. A. Bossi, N. Cocco, and M. Fabris. Proving Termination of Logic Programs by Exploiting Term Properties. In S. Abramsky and T. Maibaum, editors, *Proc. TAPSOFT'91*, volume 494 of *Lecture Notes in Computer Science*, pages 153–180. Springer-Verlag, Berlin, 1991.

3. M. Codish and B. Demoen. Analysing logic programs using "prop"-ositional logic programs and a magic wand. *The Journal of Logic Programming*, 25(3):249–274, December 1995.
4. M. Codish, M. Falaschi, and K. Marriott. Suspension analyses for concurrent logic programs. *ACM Transactions on Programming Languages and Systems*, 16(3):649–686, May 1994.
5. A. Cortesi, G. Filé, and W. Winsborough. *Prop* revisited: Propositional formula as abstract domain for groundness analysis. In *Proceedings, Sixth Annual IEEE Symposium on Logic in Computer Science*, pages 322–327, Amsterdam, The Netherlands, July 15–18 1991. IEEE Computer Society Press.
6. P. Cousot and R. Cousot. Abstract interpretation: A unified lattice model for static analysis of programs by construction or approximation of fixpoints. In *Proceedings of the Fourth ACM Symposium on Principles of Programming Languages*, pages 238–252, Jan. 1977.
7. P. Cousot and R. Cousot. Comparing the Galois Connection and Widening/Narrowing Approaches to Abstract Interpretation. In M. Bruynooghe and M. Wirsing, editors, *Proc. of PLILP'92*, volume 631 of *Lecture Notes in Computer Science*, pages 269–295. Springer-Verlag, Berlin, 1992.
8. P. Cousot and N. Halbwachs. Automatic discovery of linear restraints among variables of a program. In *Proceedings of the Fifth Annual ACM Symposium on Principles of Programming Languages*, pages 84–96, Jan. 1978.
9. M. Falaschi, G. Levi, M. Martelli, and C. Palamidessi. Declarative modeling of the operational behavior of logic languages. *Theoretical Computer Science*, 69(3):289–318, 1989.
10. M. Gabbrielli and R. Giacobazzi. Goal independency and call patterns in the analysis of logic programs. In *Proceedings of the ACM Symposium on Applied Computing*. ACM Press, 1994.
11. R. Giacobazzi, S. K. Debray, and G. Levi. Generalized semantics and abstract interpretation for constraint logic programs. *Journal of Logic Programming*, 25(3):191–247, Dec. 1995.
12. J. Jaffar and M. J. Maher. Constraint logic programming: A survey. *The Journal of Logic Programming*, 19 & 20:503–582, May 1994.
13. N. Lindenstrauss and Y. Sagiv. Automatic termination analysis of logic programs. Technical report, Hebrew University, 1996. To appear in Proceedings ICLP97.
14. J. Lloyd. *Foundations of Logic Programming*. Springer-Verlag, 2nd edition, 1987.
15. Y. Sagiv. A termination test for logic programs. In V. Saraswat and K. Ueda, editors, *Logic Programming, Proceedings of the 1991 International Symposium*, pages 518–532, San Diego, USA, 1991. The MIT Press.
16. A. van Gelder. Deriving constraints among argument sizes in logic programs. *Annals of Mathematics and Artificial Intelligence*, 3, 1991.

Parallelizing Functional Programs by Generalization

Alfons Geser[1]* and Sergei Gorlatch[2]**

[1] Wilhelm-Schickard-Institut für Informatik, University, Sand 13, D-72076 Tübingen
[2] University of Passau, D–94030 Passau, Germany. email: gorlatch@fmi.uni-passau.de

Abstract. List homomorphisms are functions that are parallelizable using the divide-and-conquer paradigm. We study the problem of finding a homomorphic representation of a given function, based on the Bird-Meertens theory of lists. A previous work proved that to each pair of *leftward* and *rightward* sequential representations of a function, based on cons- and snoc-lists, respectively, there is also a representation as a homomorphism. Our contribution is a *mechanizable method* to extract the homomorphism representation from a pair of sequential representations. The method is decomposed to a generalization problem and an inductive claim, both solvable by term rewriting techniques. To solve the former we present a sound generalization procedure which yields the required representation, and terminates under reasonable assumptions. We illustrate the method and the procedure by the parallelization of the *scan*-function (parallel prefix). The inductive claim is provable automatically.

1 Introduction

This paper addresses the problem of deriving correct parallel programs from functional specifications. It builds upon a rich body of research done in the framework of the Bird-Meertens formalism (BMF) [3, 19]. Parallelism is tackled in BMF via the notion of *homomorphism* which captures a data-parallel form of the divide-and-conquer (DC) paradigm. A classification of the DC forms suitable for static parallelization is proposed in [13].

To use homomorphisms in the design of parallel programs, two tasks must be solved: (1) *Extraction*: for a given function find its representation as a homomorphism or adjust/customize it to a homomorphic form. (2) *Implementation*: for different classes of homomorphisms, find an efficient way of implementing them on parallel machines. For both tasks, we aim at a systematic approach which would lead to a practically relevant parallel programming methodology [11, 12, 13]. A systematic extraction method, proposed in [12], proceeds by generalizing two sequential representations of the function: on the cons and snoc lists.

* Partially supported by grant Ku 996/3-1 of the DFG within the Schwerpunkt Deduktion at the University of Tübingen.

** Partially supported by the DFG project RecuR2 and by the DAAD exchange programs ARC and PROCOPE.

This so-called CS-method (CS for "Cons and Snoc") has proven to be powerful enough for a class of *almost-homomorphisms* which include famous problems like maximum segment sum and parsing the multi-bracket languages as examples.

This paper makes a further step in solving the extraction problem. Our contributions are, first, a precise formulation of the CS-approach to the extraction problem via term generalization and, second, a generalization procedure within the Bird-Meertens theory of lists, to be used in the CS-method. We propose a new, mechanizable algorithm of generalization based on term rewriting, with the desirable properties of soundness, reliability and termination.

The paper is structured as follows. Section 2 introduces the BMF notation and the notion of homomorphism. Section 3 introduces the notion of generalization and formulates the CS method of homomorphism extraction, in the generalization framework. In Section 4, we derive a generalization calculus for the theory of lists, based on term rewriting. Section 5 shows how to apply the generalization calculus to CS-generalization and derives a terminating, deterministic procedure, i.e. an algorithm, for generalization. Section 6 summarizes the results and outlines future work.

The presentation is illustrated by a running example – the *scan* function, also known as the parallel prefix [4]. For this practically relevant function, we first demonstrate the non-triviality of the extraction problem, then we show how the CS-method works for it and, finally, we apply the proposed generalization algorithm which successfully extracts the homomorphic form of scan.

The full version of the paper, with proofs of all claims, is [7].

2 BMF and Homomorphisms

We restrict ourselves to non-empty lists, which are constructed starting from singletons $[a]$ via list concatenation $+\!\!+$. The BMF expressions are built using functional composition denoted by $\circ$, and two second-order functions

$\mathit{map}\, f$ *map* of unary function f, i.e. $\mathit{map}\, f\, [x_1, \cdots, x_n] \;=\; [f x_1, \cdots, f x_n]$;

$\mathit{red}\,(\odot)$ *reduce* over a binary associative operation $\odot$,
$\mathit{red}(\odot)\,[x_1, \cdots, x_n] \;=\; x_1 \odot x_2 \odot \cdots \odot x_n.$

Definition 1. A list function h is a *homomorphism* iff there exists a binary associative *combine operator* $\circledast$, such that for all lists x and y:

$$h\,(x +\!\!+ y) = h\,(x) \;\circledast\; h\,(y) \tag{1}$$

hence, the value of h on a list depends in a particular way (using $\circledast$) on the values of h on the pieces of the list. The computations of $h(x)$ and $h(y)$ in (1) are independent and can be carried out in parallel.

Theorem 2 Bird [3]. *Function h is a homomorphism iff there exists a binary associative combine operator $\circledast$ such that*

$$h = \mathit{red}\,(\circledast) \;\circ\; (\mathit{map}\, f) \tag{2}$$

where f is defined by $f\,(a) \;=\; h\,([a])$.

The theorem provides a standard parallelization pattern for all homomorphisms as a composition of two stages. The first stage in (2), *map*, is fully parallel; the parallelization of the second, reduction stage has been studied in [11]. Loosely speaking, a function is a homomorphism iff it is well parallelizable.

Example 1 Scan as a Homomorphism. Our illustrating example in the paper is the *scan*-function which, for associative $\odot$ and a list, computes "prefix sums". On a list of 4 elements, e.g., it acts as follows:

$$scan\,(\odot)\,[a,b,c,d] = [a,\ (a \odot b),\ (a \odot b \odot c),\ (a \odot b \odot c \odot d)]$$

Function *scan* has a surprisingly wide area of applications, including evaluation of polynomials, searching, etc. [4]; its parallelization has been extensively studied and meanwhile belongs to the folklore of parallel computing.

Function *scan* is a homomorphism with combine operator $\circledast$:

$$\begin{aligned} scan\,(\odot)\,(x +\!\!+\, y) &= S_1 \circledast S_2 = S_1 +\!\!+ (map\,((last\ S_1) \odot)\ S_2), \\ \text{where } S_1 &= scan\,(\odot)\,x\,,\ S_2 = scan\,(\odot)\,y. \end{aligned} \tag{3}$$

Here, so-called sectioning is exploited in that we fix one argument of $\odot$ and obtain the unary function $((last\ S_1) \odot)$, which can be *map*ped.

Whereas the desired parallel (homomorphic) representations use list concatenation, more traditional sequential functional programming is based on the constructors cons and snoc. We use the following notation:

- $\cdot\!:$ for cons, which attaches an element at the front of the list,
- $:\!\cdot$ for snoc, which attaches the element at the list's end.

Our goal is to use sequential representations of a given function to extract its parallel homomorphic representation.

Definition 3. List function h is called *leftwards* (*lw*) iff there exists a binary operation $\oplus$ such that $h\,(a \cdot\!: y) = a \oplus h(y)$ for all elements a and lists y. Dually, function h is *rightwards* (*rw*) iff, for some $\otimes$, $h\,(y :\!\cdot\, a) = h(y) \otimes a$.

Note that $\oplus$ and $\otimes$ may be non-associative, so many functions are either *lw* or *rw* or both. The following theorem combines the so-called second and third homomorphism theorems considered folk theorems in the BMF community.

Theorem 4. *A function on lists is a homomorphism iff it is both leftwards and rightwards.*

Unfortunately, as pointed out in [2, 9], the theorem does not provide a method to construct the homomorphic representation of a function from its leftwards and rightwards definitions. The *extraction task* can be thus formulated as finding the combine operation $\circledast$ from operations $\oplus$ and/or $\otimes$.

We start by imposing an additional restriction on the leftwards and rightwards functions.

Definition 5. Function h is called *left-homomorphic* (*lh*) iff there exists $\circledast$ such that, for arbitrary list x and element a, the following holds: $h\,(a \cdot\!\!: y) = h\,([a]) \circledast h\,(y)$. The definition of a *right-homomorphic* (*rh*) function is dual.

Evidently, every *lh* (*rh*) function is also *lw* (*rw*, resp.), but not vice versa.

For a given function f, defined on elements, and operation $\oplus$, there is a unique $\circledast$-*lh* function h, such that $h\,([a]) = f\,(a)$ for arbitrary a; we denote this function by $lh\,(f, \circledast)$; similarly, notation $rh\,(f, \circledast)$ is introduced. We also write $hom\,(f, \circledast)$ for the unique $\circledast$-homomorphic function h, such that $h\,([a]) = f\,(a)$, for all a.

Theorem 6. *If* $h = \hom\,(f, \circledast)$, *then* h *is both* lh *and* rh, *moreover* $h = lh(f, \circledast) = rh\,(f, \circledast)$. *Vice versa, if* $h = lh(f, \circledast)$ *or* $h = rh\,(f, \circledast)$, *where* $\circledast$ *is associative, then* $h = \hom\,(f, \circledast)$.

In [10], we prove a slightly stronger proposition.

Theorem 6 suggests a possible way to find a homomorphic representation: construct a **cons** definition of the function in the *lh* format (or, dually, find an *rh* representation on **snoc** lists) and prove that the combine operation is associative. Sometimes this simple method works (e.g., for the function which yields the length of a list [12]), but already for *scan* it does not.

Example 1 Continued; extraction for Scan. Let us try the same simple method on the *scan* function introduced in Example 1. The sequential **cons** definition of *scan* is as follows:

$$scan\,(\odot)\,(a \cdot\!\!: y) \;=\; a \cdot\!\!: \;(map\,(a \odot)\,(scan\,(\odot)\,y)) \tag{4}$$

Representation (4) does not match the *lh* format because a is used where only $scan\,[a]$ is allowed. Since $scan\,[a] = [a]$, there are different possibilities to express a via $scan\,(\odot)\,[a]$, e.g., $a = head\,(scan\,(\odot)\,[a])$ or $a = last\,(scan\,(\odot)\,[a])$. Unfortunately, each of possible terms for $\circledast$ obtained from (4), for instance: $head\,(u) \;\circledast\; (map\,(last\,(u) \odot)\,v)$, defines a non-associative operation! We run into a similar problem for a **cons** definition [12].

We believe to have shown that the problem to extract a homomorphism is nontrivial. For the *scan* function, it even led to errors in published parallel algorithms and required a formal correctness proof [17].

3 CS Method: Extraction by Generalization

Let us assume that function h is a homomorphism, i.e., (1) holds, and t_H denotes a term over u and v that defines $\circledast$:

$$u \circledast v \leftrightarrow t_H \tag{5}$$

The following two terms, built from t_H by substitutions: $t_L = t_H.\{u \mapsto h([a]), v \mapsto h(y)\}$ and $t_R = t_H.\{u \mapsto h(x), v \mapsto h([b])\}$, are semantically equal variants to all cons and snoc representations, respectively, of function h:

$$t_B \circledast h(y) \leftrightarrow t_C \qquad (6)$$

$$h(x) \circledast t'_B \leftrightarrow t_S \ . \qquad (7)$$

The homomorphism extraction problem is formally specified as follows:

Given: A cons definition $h(a \cdot\!: y) \leftrightarrow t_C, h([a]) \leftrightarrow t_B$ and a snoc definition $h(x :\!\cdot\, b) \leftrightarrow t_S, h([b]) \leftrightarrow t'_B$ for the same function h on lists.
Wanted: A definition $u \circledast v \leftrightarrow t_H$, such that $h(x +\!\!+\, y) \leftrightarrow h(x) \circledast h(y)$.

We intend to apply the framework of generalization for this problem.

Definition 7. A term t_G is called a *generalizer* of terms t_1 and t_2 in the equational theory E if there are substitutions σ_1 and σ_2 such that $t_G.\sigma_1 \leftrightarrow^*_E t_1$ and $t_G.\sigma_2 \leftrightarrow^*_E t_2$. Here, $\leftrightarrow^*_E$ denotes the semantic equality (conversion relation) in the equational theory E.

Obviously, there is always a (most general) generalizer: a variable, x_0, since $x_0.\sigma_1 = t_1$ and $x_0.\sigma_2 = t_2$ where $\sigma_1 =_{\text{def}} \{x_0 \mapsto t_1\}$ and $\sigma_2 =_{\text{def}} \{x_0 \mapsto t_2\}$. So it is obvious that people prefer the *most special* generalizer, provided there is one. In this respect, generalization is the dual to *unification* and is sometimes also called "anti-unification" [14]. Plotkin has closely studied the special-case relation between terms [18]. In the case where E is empty, there are most general syntactic unifiers and most special syntactic generalizers.

In contrast to unification, properties and methods for generalization for non-empty E are hardly known. A few generalization methods have been exercised for use in inductive theorem proving, i.e., the systematic construction of a term rewriting system of counting functions on the basis of an effective enumeration of elements [16, 20]. For our purpose to extract homomorphisms one can do simpler. There is no need to adapt the given equational theory, nor to introduce new functions. We start from [5, 15], where a *resolvant* presentation of the equational theory to get a generalization algorithm is used; our generalization calculus differs basically by the use of rewrite derivations instead of conversions.

The generalization applied to (6) and (7), should yield t_H of (5) – the wanted piece of the definition of h as a homomorphism.

Figure 1(a) illustrates the relations between the terms t_H, t_C, t_S, t_L, and t_R. Dotted arrows indicate substitutions, solid arrows indicate conversion steps. Each substitution is applied to *two* terms – this is a simultaneous generalization problem. In order to work with the established notion of generalizer, we introduce a fresh binary function symbol, $\rightharpoonup$, and model pairs (s, t) of terms as terms $s \rightharpoonup t$, called *rule terms*. With this encoding we get the view of Figure 1(b).

Theorem 8 [7]. *Let E be the theory of lists and let $t'_B = t_B.\{a \mapsto b\}$. If two rule terms, $t_B \circledast h(y) \rightharpoonup t_C$ and $h(x) \circledast t'_B \rightharpoonup t_S$, have an E-generalizer, $u \circledast v \rightharpoonup t_H$, w.r.t. $\sigma_1 = \{u \mapsto t_B, v \mapsto h(y)\}$ and $\sigma_2 = \{u \mapsto h(x), v \mapsto t'_B\}$,*

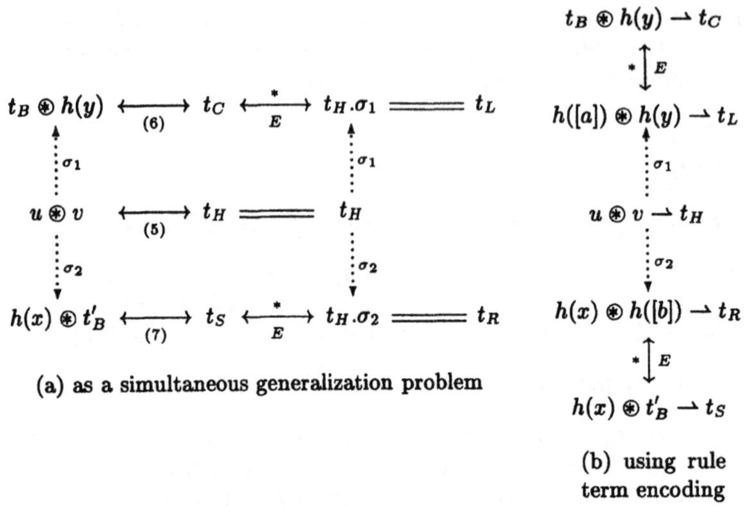

Fig. 1. The relationships of the terms after a successful CS-Generalization; here: $\sigma_1 = \{u \mapsto t_B, v \mapsto h(y)\}$, $\sigma_2 = \{u \mapsto h(x), v \mapsto t'_B\}$.

and the operation ⊛ thus defined is associative, then: (1) The cons, snoc, *and* $+\!\!+$ *definitions define the same function h. (2) Function h is lh and rh, with* $f(a) = t_B$. *(3) Function h is a homomorphism with ⊛ as combine operation.*

For the proof we only remark that (1) follows immediately from Theorem 9. The generalization in Theorem 8 is called the *CS-generalization* in the theory of lists E. We can now summarize our considerations as the following method of finding the combine operation which proceeds in two steps.

CS-Method:

1. A successful CS-generalization, applied to the rule terms $t_B \circledast h(y) \rightharpoonup t_C$ and $h(x) \circledast t'_B \rightharpoonup t_S$, yields a rule term $u \circledast v \rightharpoonup t_H$.
2. If associativity of ⊛ defined by t_H can be proven inductively then, by Theorem 8, ⊛ is the desired combine operator.

Example 1 Continued. For *scan*, the corresponding rule terms are:

$$[a] \circledast \mathit{scan}\,(\odot)\, y \rightharpoonup a \;\cdot\!: (\mathit{map}\,(a\,\odot)\,(\mathit{scan}\,(\odot)\, y))$$
$$\mathit{scan}\,(\odot)\, x \circledast [b] \rightharpoonup (\mathit{scan}\,(\odot)\, x) \;:\!\cdot\; (\mathit{last}\,(\mathit{scan}\,(\odot)\, x) \odot b)$$

Their CS-generalization yields $u \circledast v \rightharpoonup u +\!\!+ \mathit{map}\,(\mathit{last}\,(u) \odot)\, v$. One can prove that the operation ⊛ thus defined

$$u \circledast v \leftrightarrow u +\!\!+ \mathit{map}\,(\mathit{last}\,(u) \odot)\, v \qquad (8)$$

is associative, so *scan* is a homomorphism with $f(a) = [a]$ and ⊛ defined by (8).

In practice, it is advisable to present t_C in the *lw* format and t_S in the *rw* format, which would simplify the necessary generalization. Moreover, a difficulty in writing either an *rw* or an *lw* definition of a function is a good indicator that the function might not be a homomorphism.

4 Expressing the CS Method in Term Rewriting

To apply the CS method practically, the generalization step of the method must be mechanized, i.e., an algorithm is required that yields the most special generalizer of two terms. We will adopt term rewriting methods for this step, so let us first embed a fragment of Bird-Meertens theory of lists in term rewriting theory.

To have a simple technical apparatus, we henceforth restrict ourselves to first-order terms whence we suppress higher order parameters, and consider a fixed associative operation $\odot$. This renders it necessary to express a fragment of the theory of lists by first-order functions and term rewriting rules. In our running example we replace $scan\,(\odot)\,x$ by $scn(x)$, and $map\,(a\odot)\,(x)$ by $mp(a,x)$.

Moreover from now on we use rewrite rules $f(t_1,\ldots,t_n) \to t_0$ instead of conversion rules $f(t_1,\ldots,t_n) \leftrightarrow t_0$ in order to account for oriented replacement, i.e. rewriting: A rewrite rule may be used to replace a term t of the form $C[f(t_1,\ldots,t_n)]$ by t' of the form $C[t_0]$, a fact expressed by $t \to t'$. By $C[t]$ we indicate that t appears in the context C. If R is a system of such rewrite rules, then one writes $t \to_R t'$ for the application of a rule from R somewhere in t, yielding a term t'. Relation $\leftrightarrow_R^*$ is the equivalence closure of $\to_R$, i.e. the smallest binary relation on terms that contains $\to_R$ and is reflexive, symmetric, and transitive.

To be able to reason in the rewriting framework, we have to fix a few term rewriting systems: The term rewriting system R, the conversion relation $\leftrightarrow_R$ of which will be the "semantic equality", and term rewriting systems R_{cons}, R_{snoc}, and R_{conc} for the three versions of definitions of h.

We start with the oriented associativity rules of $\odot$ and $+\!\!+$:

$$a \odot (b \odot c) \to (a \odot b) \odot c \qquad (A_\odot)$$

$$x +\!\!+ (y +\!\!+ z) \to (x +\!\!+ y) +\!\!+ z \qquad (A_+)$$

The symbols $\cdot\!:$ and $:\!\cdot$ and their defining rules

$$a \cdot\!: y \to [a] +\!\!+ y \qquad \text{and} \qquad x :\!\cdot b \to x +\!\!+ [b]$$

will not appear explicitly in our method. Rather we replace throughout $t \cdot\!: t'$ and $t :\!\cdot t'$ by $[t] +\!\!+ t'$ and $t +\!\!+ [t']$, respectively.

To keep things simple, let us assume that h is not mutually recursive, i.e. that the call relation does not contain cycles of length greater than one. Next we assume given a term rewriting system, R_{base}, to contain suitable rules for the functions that are called by h. We may by an inductive argument assume that all auxiliary functions are homomorphisms themselves and that the extraction is already done for them. In other words, each function h' called by h is given by means of [.] and $+\!\!+$, and the right hand side of its definition does not use x and y unless in $h'(x)$ and $h'(y)$ respectively. (For functions in more than one parameter, we assume that parallelization is done for the last parameter, which is a list.)

Given a term rewriting system R_{base} and terms t_B, t_C, t_S, t_H, we define a term rewriting system R to describe the conversion relation, $\leftrightarrow_R^*$, that will serve as the "semantic equality", $\leftrightarrow_E^*$; and three term rewriting systems, R_{cons}, R_{snoc}, and R_{conc}, for reasoning about the **cons**, **snoc**, and $+\!\!+$ definitions of h, respectively:

$$\begin{aligned}
R &= A_\odot \cup A_+ \cup R_{base}\\
R_0 &= R \cup \{h([a]) \to t_B,\ h(x +\!\!+ y) \to h(x) \circledast h(y)\}\\
R_{cons} &= R_0 \cup \{t_B \circledast h(y) \to t_C\}\\
R_{snoc} &= R_0 \cup \{h(x) \circledast t'_B \to t_S\}\\
R_{conc} &= R_0 \cup \{u \circledast v \to t_H\}
\end{aligned}$$

Here, $t'_B = t_B.\{a \mapsto b\}$ is just the term t_B, where a is renamed by b.

Example 1 Continued. In our example, scn calls the functions mp and $last$. So, R_{base} becomes

$$last[a] \to a \tag{9}$$
$$last(x +\!\!+ y) \to last\, y \tag{10}$$
$$mp(a, [b]) \to [a \odot b] \tag{11}$$
$$mp(a, x +\!\!+ y) \to mp(a, x) +\!\!+ mp(a, y) \tag{12}$$

Next we get $t_B = [a]$, and accordingly, $t'_B = [b]$, next $t_C = [a] +\!\!+ mp(a, scn(y))$, and $t_S = scn(x) +\!\!+ [last(scn(x)) \odot b]$.

$$\begin{aligned}
R_0 &= R \cup \left\{\begin{array}{c} scn([a]) \to [a] \\ scn(x +\!\!+ y) \to scn(x) \circledast scn(y) \end{array}\right.\\
R_{cons} &= R_0 \cup \{[a] \circledast scn(y) \to [a] +\!\!+ mp(a, scn(y))\}\\
R_{snoc} &= R_0 \cup \{scn(x) \circledast [b] \to scn(x) +\!\!+ [last(scn(x)) \odot b]\}
\end{aligned}$$

What we want is t_H such that R_{conc} defines the same function h as do R_{cons} and R_{snoc}. This is speaking about an inductively valid equation.

A ground term is a term that does not contain any (free) variable. The inductive theory of a term rewriting system, R, is the set of all formal equations $s \leftrightarrow t$ between terms such that $s.\sigma \leftrightarrow_R^* t.\sigma$ holds for all substitutions σ such that $s.\sigma$ and $t.\sigma$ are ground. A term rewriting system R' is called a *conservative extension* of R if every equation $s \leftrightarrow t$ in the inductive theory of R', where s and t are terms over the signature of R, is already in the inductive theory of R. See, e.g., [1] for an introduction to inductive theorem proving based on rewriting.

Theorem 9 Reliability [7]. *Let the term rewriting systems R, R_{cons}, R_{snoc}, and R_{conc} be defined as above. If the two rule terms $t_B \circledast h(y) \rightharpoonup t_C$ and $h(x) \circledast t'_B \rightharpoonup t_S$ have a R-generalizer, $u \circledast v \rightharpoonup t_H$, w.r.t. the substitutions $\sigma_1 = \{u \mapsto t_B, v \mapsto h(y)\}$ and $\sigma_2 = \{u \mapsto h(x), v \mapsto t'_B\}$, then the following properties hold:*

1. *The conversion relations $\leftrightarrow^*_{R_{cons}}$ and $\leftrightarrow^*_{R_{snoc}}$ are included in the conversion relation $\leftrightarrow^*_{R_{conc}}$.*
2. *If $\circledast$ is associative in the inductive theory of R_{conc} then R_{conc} is a conservative extension of R.*
3. *If $\circledast$ is associative in the inductive theory of R_{conc} then the inductive theories of R_{cons}, R_{snoc}, and R_{conc} coincide.*

In other words, a generalizer of a certain shape and an inductive proof provide a solution to the homomorphism extraction problem. The inductive proof of associativity of $\circledast$ may be carried out by a mechanized inductive theorem prover.

Example 1 Continued. In our *scn* example, we have used the semi-automatic inductive prover TIP [6, 8] to produce a proof of associativity of $\circledast$ based on the lemmas

$$last(mp(a,x)) \to a \odot last\, x \qquad \text{and} \qquad mp(a, mp(b,x)) \to mp(a \odot b, x)$$

and, in turn, a proof of each lemma. The three proofs are obtained by rewriting induction, without any user interaction.

This leaves to solve the generalization problem. Following a good custom, we introduce our algorithm by means of a calculus. As the objects of the calculus we keep triples $(\sigma_1, \sigma_2, t_0)$, maintaining the invariant that t_0 is a generalizer of t_1 and t_2 via the substitutions σ_1 and σ_2, respectively. Starting from the triple $(\{x_0 \mapsto t_1\}, \{x_0 \mapsto t_2\}, x_0)$, where x_0 is the most general generalizer, we successively apply inference rules to specialize, until no more inference rule applies.

The basic idea is to repeat, as long as possible, the following step: Extract a common row of σ_1 and σ_2 and move it to t_0. Every such step, while preserving the generalization property of t_0, adds more speciality to it, until finally t_0 is maximally special.

Figure 2 and 3 show the two inference rules which we will use. The formula $t \xrightarrow[R]{\varepsilon}{}^* t'$ means that t rewrites in zero or more steps to t' where every rewrite step takes place at the root position, ε, of t. For substitutions $\sigma = \{x_1 \mapsto s_1, \ldots, x_m \mapsto s_m\}$, $\tau = \{y_1 \mapsto t_1, \ldots, y_n \mapsto t_n\}$ for which $x_i \neq y_j$ for all i, j, their disjoint union is defined by $\sigma \| \tau = \{x_1 \mapsto s_1, \ldots, x_m \mapsto s_m, y_1 \mapsto t_1, \ldots, y_n \mapsto t_n\}$.

The "ancestor decomposition" rule in Figure 2 acts as follows. First a common variable, x_i, in the domain of the two substitutions is selected. If u_i shares its root function symbol, f, with v_i then the ancestor decomposition rule is applicable with void rewrite derivations, $f(u'_1, \ldots, u'_m) = u_i$ and $f(v'_1, \ldots, v'_m) =$

If $f(u'_1,\dots,u'_m) \xrightarrow[R]{\varepsilon}{}^{*} u_i$ and $f(v'_1,\dots,v'_m) \xrightarrow[R]{\varepsilon}{}^{*} v_i$ then (13)

$$\frac{\sigma_1\|\{x_i \mapsto u_i\} \qquad \sigma_2\|\{x_i \mapsto v_i\} \qquad t_0}{\sigma_1\|\tau_1 \qquad \sigma_2\|\tau_2 \qquad t_0.\{x_i \mapsto f(x'_1,\dots,x'_m)\}}$$

where $\tau_1 = \{x'_1 \mapsto u'_1,\dots,x'_m \mapsto u'_m\}$ and $\tau_2 = \{x'_1 \mapsto v'_1,\dots,x'_m \mapsto v'_m\}$.

Fig. 2. "Ancestor Decomposition" rule

$$\frac{\sigma_1\|\{x_i \mapsto u, x_j \mapsto u\} \qquad \sigma_2\|\{x_i \mapsto v, x_j \mapsto v\} \qquad t_0}{\sigma_1\|\{x_i \mapsto u\} \qquad \sigma_2\|\{x_i \mapsto v\} \qquad t_0.\{x_j \mapsto x_i\}}$$

Fig. 3. "Agreement" rule

v_i. The common function symbol is broken down, by splitting the mapping $x_i \mapsto f(u'_1,\dots,u'_m)$ to $x_i \mapsto f(x'_1,\dots,x'_m)$ and $x'_j \mapsto u'_j$ where x'_j are fresh variables for each argument position, j, of f. Likewise $x_i \mapsto f(v'_1,\dots,v'_m)$ is split to $x_i \mapsto f(x'_1,\dots,x'_m)$ and $x'_j \mapsto v'_j$. Their common part, $x_i \mapsto f(x'_1,\dots,x'_m)$, can now be transferred to t_0.

A term t such that $t \xrightarrow[R]{\varepsilon}{}^{*} t'$ is called an *ancestor* of t'. To enable conversion by R rules, we furthermore allow that u_i or v_i are replaced by some ancestor thereof. In other words, we allow non-void rewrite derivations in Condition (13).

The "agreement" rule in Figure 3 acts as follows. The mappings $x_i \mapsto u$ and $x_j \mapsto u$ with common right hand sides in the first substitution can be split into $x_j \mapsto x_i$ and $x_i \mapsto u$. If moreover $x_i \mapsto v$ and $x_j \mapsto v$ in the second substitution, then likewise $x_j \mapsto x_i$ and $x_i \mapsto v$ can be split there. The common part, $x_j \mapsto x_i$, of the two can be transferred to t_0.

Occasionally we will justify an application of the ancestor decomposition rule by a remark of the form "AncDec for f; $t \xrightarrow[R]{\varepsilon}{}^{*} t'$", or just "AncDec for f" if the rewrite derivation $t \xrightarrow[R]{\varepsilon}{}^{*} t'$ is void, i.e. $t = t'$. To justify an application of the agreement rule we will put a remark like "Agr for x_i, x_j".

It is fairly easy to prove that our calculus is sound in the following sense:

Theorem 10 Soundness. *For every inference step* $(\sigma_1, \sigma_2, t_0) \vdash (\sigma'_1, \sigma'_2, t'_0)$, *we have* $t_0.\sigma_1 \leftarrow^*_R t'_0.\sigma'_1$ *and* $t_0.\sigma_2 \leftarrow^*_R t'_0.\sigma'_2$.

Corollary 11. *If* t_0 *is a generalizer of* t_1 *and* t_2 *w.r.t. the term rewriting system* R, *and* $(\sigma_1, \sigma_2, t_0) \vdash (\sigma'_1, \sigma'_2, t'_0)$ *is an inference step, then* t'_0 *is a more special generalizer of* t_1 *and* t_2 *w.r.t.* R.

Example 1 Continued. Now let us study our *scn* example to see how our calculus operates. Here we have

$$t_1 = ([a] \circledast scn(y) \rightharpoonup [a] + mp(a, scn(y)))$$
$$t_2 = (scn(x) \circledast [b] \rightharpoonup scn(x) + [last(scn(x)) \odot b])$$

A derivation is listed in Figure 4.

5 A Generalization Algorithm

To turn our generalization calculus into an algorithm, one has to decide on a rule application strategy, and prove its termination. We adopt the strategy to prefer the "agreement" rule, and to choose the smallest index i for which an inference rule applies. If only the "ancestor decomposition" rule applies, we branch for every pair of justifying rewrites. Certainly, the complexity may become exponential this way, but experience shows that branching is harmless: Rarely is there more than one branch.

To be on the safe side, we replace Condition (13) of the ancestor decomposition rule by:

$$f(u'_1,\ldots,u'_m) \xrightarrow[R]{\varepsilon}{}^{X} u_i, \quad f(v'_1,\ldots,v'_m) \xrightarrow[R]{\varepsilon}{}^{Y} v_i, \quad X+Y \leq 1 \tag{14}$$

Here $t \xrightarrow[R]{\varepsilon}{}^{X} t'$ means that t rewrites in exactly X steps to t' where each step takes place at the root position, ε, of t. We call the resulting calculus the ***restricted generalization calculus.***

In the restricted generalization calculus, as opposed to the unrestricted, the ancestor decomposition rule is finitely branching, and its applicable instances are computable, provided that R contains no *erasing* rules, i.e. rules $l \to r$ where l contains a variable not in r. For instance, Rule (10) is erasing: it has x on its left, but not on its right hand side.

Condition (14) is not as hard in practice as it may seem. Observe, for instance, that the derivations in Example 2 and in Figure 4 each are within the restricted generalization calculus. The restricted generalization calculus is not complete for the simple fact that many function definitions need recursion and so an unbounded number of steps in the ancestor decomposition rule.

Even in the restricted generalization calculus there are non-terminating derivations.

Example 2. Let s be the successor and p the predecessor on integers, together with the rewrite rules

$$p(s(x)) \to x \qquad s(p(x)) \to x \ .$$

Then we get the infinite derivation

$$\begin{array}{ll} & (\{x \mapsto s(0)\}, \{x \mapsto p(p(0))\}, x) \\ \vdash & (\{x' \mapsto s(s(0))\}, \{x' \mapsto p(0)\}, p(x')) \\ \vdash & (\{x'' \mapsto s(0)\}, \{x'' \mapsto p(p(0))\}, s(p(x''))) \\ \vdash & \ldots \end{array}$$

$$\{x_0 \mapsto t_1\} \qquad \{x_0 \mapsto t_2\} \qquad x_0$$

$\vdash$ (AncDec for $\rightharpoonup$)

$$\left\{\begin{array}{c} x_1 \mapsto [a] \circledast scn(y) \\ x_2 \mapsto [a] +\!\!+ \\ \qquad mp(a, scn(y))) \end{array}\right\} \qquad \left\{\begin{array}{c} x_1 \mapsto scn(x) \circledast [b] \\ x_2 \mapsto scn(x) +\!\!+ \\ \qquad [last(scn(x)) \odot b] \end{array}\right\} \qquad x_1 \rightharpoonup x_2$$

$\vdash$ (AncDec for $\circledast$)

$$\left\{\begin{array}{c} x_3 \mapsto [a] \\ x_4 \mapsto scn(y) \\ x_2 \mapsto [a] +\!\!+ \\ \qquad mp(a, scn(y))) \end{array}\right\} \qquad \left\{\begin{array}{c} x_3 \mapsto scn(x) \\ x_4 \mapsto [b] \\ x_2 \mapsto scn(x) +\!\!+ \\ \qquad [last(scn(x)) \odot b] \end{array}\right\} \qquad x_3 \circledast x_4 \rightharpoonup x_2$$

$\vdash$ AncDec for $+\!\!+$)

$$\left\{\begin{array}{c} x_3 \mapsto [a] \\ x_4 \mapsto scn(y) \\ x_5 \mapsto [a] \\ x_6 \mapsto mp(a, scn(y))) \end{array}\right\} \qquad \left\{\begin{array}{c} x_3 \mapsto scn(x) \\ x_4 \mapsto [b] \\ x_5 \mapsto scn(x) \\ x_6 \mapsto [last(scn(x)) \odot b] \end{array}\right\} \qquad x_3 \circledast x_4 \rightharpoonup x_5 +\!\!+ x_6$$

$\vdash$ Agr for x_3, x_5)

$$\left\{\begin{array}{c} x_3 \mapsto [a] \\ x_4 \mapsto scn(y) \\ x_6 \mapsto mp(a, scn(y))) \end{array}\right\} \qquad \left\{\begin{array}{c} x_3 \mapsto scn(x) \\ x_4 \mapsto [b] \\ x_6 \mapsto [last(scn(x)) \odot b] \end{array}\right\} \qquad x_3 \circledast x_4 \rightharpoonup x_3 +\!\!+ x_6$$

$\vdash$ (AncDec for mp; $mp(last(scn(x)), [b]) \xrightarrow[(11)]{\varepsilon} [last(scn(x)) \odot b]$)

$$\left\{\begin{array}{c} x_3 \mapsto [a] \\ x_4 \mapsto scn(y) \\ x_7 \mapsto a \\ x_8 \mapsto scn(y) \end{array}\right\} \qquad \left\{\begin{array}{c} x_3 \mapsto scn(x) \\ x_4 \mapsto [b] \\ x_7 \mapsto last(scn(x)) \\ x_8 \mapsto [b] \end{array}\right\} \qquad x_3 \circledast x_4 \rightharpoonup x_3 +\!\!+ mp(x_7, x_8)$$

$\vdash$ (Agr for x_4, x_8)

$$\left\{\begin{array}{c} x_3 \mapsto [a] \\ x_4 \mapsto scn(y) \\ x_7 \mapsto a \end{array}\right\} \qquad \left\{\begin{array}{c} x_3 \mapsto scn(x) \\ x_4 \mapsto [b] \\ x_7 \mapsto last(scn(x)) \end{array}\right\} \qquad x_3 \circledast x_4 \rightharpoonup x_3 +\!\!+ mp(x_7, x_4)$$

$\vdash$ (AncDec for mp; $last([a]) \xrightarrow[(9)]{\varepsilon} a$)

$$\left\{\begin{array}{c} x_3 \mapsto [a] \\ x_4 \mapsto scn(y) \\ x_9 \mapsto [a] \end{array}\right\} \qquad \left\{\begin{array}{c} x_3 \mapsto scn(x) \\ x_4 \mapsto [b] \\ x_9 \mapsto scn(x) \end{array}\right\} \qquad x_3 \circledast x_4 \rightharpoonup x_3 +\!\!+ mp(last(x_9), x_4)$$

$\vdash$ (Agr for x_3, x_9)

$$\left\{\begin{array}{c} x_3 \mapsto [a] \\ x_4 \mapsto scn(y) \end{array}\right\} \qquad \left\{\begin{array}{c} x_3 \mapsto scn(x) \\ x_4 \mapsto [b] \end{array}\right\} \qquad x_3 \circledast x_4 \rightharpoonup x_3 +\!\!+ mp(last(x_3), x_4)$$

Fig. 4. **A successful derivation for** ***scn***

The standard way to get finiteness of derivations, and so termination of the procedure, is to take care that derivations $(\sigma_1^1, \sigma_2^1, t_0^1) \vdash (\sigma_1^2, \sigma_2^2, t_0^2) \vdash \cdots$ satisfy $(\sigma_1^i, \sigma_2^i, t_0^i) \succ (\sigma_1^{i+1}, \sigma_2^{i+1}, t_0^{i+1})$ for an appropriate well-founded order $\succ$ on triples.

In term rewriting, finiteness of rewrite derivations is ensured by the requirement $l > r$ for every rule $l \to r$ in R, where $>$ is a suitable *termination order*: a well-founded order on terms that is closed under contexts and substitution applications. The knowledge $l > r$ however is useless for our purposes since we need to apply rules in their *reverse direction.* It is not realistic to require $r > l$ instead; this property is usually violated. For instance $l = last[a]$, $r = a$ does not satisfy $l > r$ for any termination order since no term can be greater than a superterm.

Now we observe that not only do we apply the rule in the reverse direction, but also strip the top symbol off the left hand side. Stripping off the top symbol can be considered a decrease, provided that the reverse rule application does not harm it.

Definition 12. Let $>$ be an order on pairs of terms. A term rewriting system R is called *reversely guarded by* $>$ if for every rewrite rule $f(l_1, \ldots, l_m) \to r$ in R, both $(r, f(x_1, \ldots, x_m)) > (l_j, x_j)$ and $(f(x_1, \ldots, x_m), r) > (x_j, l_j)$ hold for all $1 \leq j \leq n$.

Theorem 13 Termination [7]. *Let $>$ be a well-founded order on pairs of terms, closed under substitution application, that extends the component-wise subterm order. If R is reversely guarded by $>$ then the restricted generalization calculus admits no infinite derivations.*

A term rewriting system that contains erasing rules is not reversely guarded. The term rewriting system R for our *scn* function is therefore *not* reversely guarded. As we argued for Condition (14), it is sensible to exclude erasing rules for computability reasons.

Example 1 Continued. The term rewriting system $R\backslash\{(10)\}$ is reversely guarded. To prove this, assign each function symbol, f, its weight, a non-negative integer, $\#f$. The weight $\#t$ of a term t is defined to be the sum of all weights of function symbols in t. Now a relation $>$ on pairs of terms is defined as follows.

$(t_1, t_2) > (t_1', t_2')$, if
every variable occurs in (t_1, t_2) at least as often as in (t_1', t_2'), and
$\#t_1 + \#t_2 > \#t_1' + \#t_2'$

It is straightforward to show that $>$ is a well-founded order, closed under substitution application, and that $>$ contains the component-wise subterm relation.

To show reverse guardedness, we show $\#r + 2\#f > \#l$ for every rule $l \to r$ where the root symbol on the left is f. The weight assignment $\#last = 2$ and $\#f = 1$ for all f else obviously does the job. Here is the reasoning for Rule (9):

$$\#r + 2\#f = 0 + 2 \cdot 2 > 2 + 1 = \#l$$

So every derivation in the restricted generalization calculus that refuses to use Rule (10) is finite: We obtain an algorithm that computes a finite set of generalizers.

6 Conclusion

Extraction of a homomorphism from a **cons** and a **snoc** definition of a function on lists is a systematic, powerful technique for designing parallel programs. Its advantage over the direct, intuition-based construction of a parallel solution is even more clearly visible for more complex problems than scan, e.g., so-called almost homomorphisms [12], which are not considered here because of lack of space.

We have successfully applied two techniques from the area of term rewriting, *generalization* and *rewriting induction*, to attack the nontrivial, intriguing extraction problem. If the rules for **cons** and **snoc** are encoded in terms then each generalizer of a certain form encodes the definition of the homomorphism. This, provided that an associativity result can be proven inductively, e.g., by an automated inductive theorem prover. We prove reliability of this method to extract a homomorphism.

We have introduced a very simple sound calculus for generalization of terms. We impose a strategy and a sensible restriction on the calculus, under which we obtain a terminating, deterministic procedure. There is an exponential upper bound in worst-case time complexity, but the algorithm appears to perform almost linearly in practice.

Our work is, to the best of our knowledge, the very first successful mechanization of the homomorphism extraction problem. We can imagine improvements of the calculus, such as rewriting modulo associativity or a more powerful ancestor decomposition rule which is able to "jump" over a number of non-top rewrite steps, together with an appropriately weakened application condition. Of course, the next step to do is an implementation of the algorithm.

Acknowledgements. Thanks to Chris Lengauer and to the four anonymous referees for helpful remarks.

References

1. Leo Bachmair. *Canonical Equational Proofs.* Research Notes in Theoretical Computer Science. Wiley and Sons, 1989.
2. D. Barnard, J. Schmeiser, and D. Skillicorn. Deriving associative operators for language recognition. *Bulletin of EATCS*, 43:131–139, 1991.
3. R. S. Bird. Lectures on constructive functional programming. In M. Broy, editor, *Constructive Methods in Computing Science*, NATO ASI Series F: Computer and Systems Sciences. Vol. 55, pages 151–216. Springer Verlag, 1988.
4. G. Blelloch. Scans as primitive parallel operations. *IEEE Trans. on Computers*, 38(11):1526–1538, November 1989.

5. Hubert Comon, Marianne Haberstrau, and Jean-Pierre Jouannaud. Syntacticness, cycle-syntacticness, and shallow theories. *Inform. and Computation*, 111:154–191, 1994.
6. Ulrich Fraus and Heinrich Hußmann. Term induction proofs by a generalization of narrowing. In C. Rattray and R. G. Clark, editors, *The Unified Computation Laboratory — Unifying Frameworks, Theories and Tools*, Oxford, UK, 1992. Clarendon Press.
7. A. Geser and S. Gorlatch. Parallelizing functional programs by term rewriting. Technical Report MIP-9709, Universität Passau, April 1997. Available from http://brahms.fmi.uni-passau.de/cl/papers/GesGor97a.html.
8. Alfons Geser. Mechanized inductive proof of properties of a simple code optimizer. In Peter D. Mosses, Mogens Nielsen, and Michael I. Schwartzbach, editors, *Proc. 6th Theory and Practice in Software Development (TAPSOFT)*, LNCS 915, pages 605–619. Springer, 1995.
9. J. Gibbons. The third homomorphism theorem. *J. Fun. Programming*, 6(4):657–665, 1996.
10. S. Gorlatch. Constructing list homomorphisms. Technical Report MIP-9512, Universität Passau, August 1995.
11. S. Gorlatch. Systematic efficient parallelization of scan and other list homomorphisms. In L. Bouge, P. Fraigniaud, A. Mignotte, and Y. Robert, editors, *Euro-Par'96. Parallel Processing*, Lecture Notes in Computer Science 1124, pages 401–408. Springer-Verlag, 1996.
12. S. Gorlatch. Systematic extraction and implementation of divide-and-conquer parallelism. In H. Kuchen and D. Swierstra, editors, *Programming languages: Implementation, Logics and Programs*, Lecture Notes in Computer Science 1140, pages 274–288. Springer-Verlag, 1996.
13. S. Gorlatch and H. Bischof. Formal derivation of divide-and-conquer programs: A case study in the multidimensional FFT's. In D. Mery, editor, *Formal Methods for Parallel Programming: Theory and Applications. Workshop at IPPS'97*, pages 80–94, 1997.
14. B. Heinz. Lemma discovery by anti-unification of regular sorts. Technical Report 94-21, TU Berlin, May 1994.
15. Jean-Pierre Jouannaud. Syntactic theories. In B. Rovan, editor, *Mathematical Foundations of Computer Science*, pages 15–25, Banská Bystrica, 1990. LNCS 452.
16. Steffen Lange. Towards a set of inference rules for solving divergence in Knuth-Bendix completion. In Klaus P. Jantke, editor, *Proc. Analogical and Inductive Inference*, pages 305–316. LNCS 397, 1989.
17. J. O'Donnell. A correctness proof of parallel scan. *Parallel Processing Letters*, 4(3):329–338, 1994.
18. Gordon D. Plotkin. Lattice-theoretic properties of subsumption. Technical Report Memo MIP-R-77, Univ. Edinburgh, UK, 1970.
19. D. Skillicorn. *Foundations of Parallel Programming*. Cambridge Univ. Press, 1994.
20. Muffy Thomas and Phil Watson. Solving divergence in Knuth-Bendix completion by enriching signatures. *Theoretical Computer Science*, 112(1):145–185, 1993.

Higher-Order Equational Unification via Explicit Substitutions

Claude Kirchner, Christophe Ringeissen

INRIA-Lorraine & CRIN-CNRS
615, rue du Jardin Botanique, BP 101, F-54602 Villers-lès-Nancy Cedex France
e-mail: {Claude.Kirchner,Christophe.Ringeissen}@loria.fr
Web: http://www.loria.fr/equipe/protheo.html

Abstract. We show how to reduce the unification problem modulo $\beta\eta$-conversion and a first-order equational theory E, into a first-order unification problem in a union of two non-disjoint equational theories including E and a calculus of explicit substitutions. A rule-based unification procedure in this combined theory is described and may be viewed as an extension of the one initially designed by G. Dowek, T. Hardin and C. Kirchner for performing unification of simply typed λ-terms in a first-order setting via the $\lambda\sigma$-calculus of explicit substitutions. Additional rules are used to deal with the interaction between E and $\lambda\sigma$.

1 Introduction

Unification modulo an equational theory plays an important rôle in automated deduction and in logic programming systems. For example, λProlog [NM88] is based on higher-order unification, ie. unification modulo the $\beta\eta$-conversion. In order to design more expressive higher-order logic programming systems enhanced with a first-order equational theory E, one should consider higher-order E-unification, ie. unification modulo $=_{\beta\eta}$ and $=_E$. The problem of combining λ-calculi with first-order equational theories was initied in [BT88] and the higher-order E-unification problem has been already successfully studied [QW96, NQ91, Sny90] by extending the techniques developed [Hue75] for unification of simply typed λ-terms. On the side of functional programming languages implementations, the operation of substitution (issued from β-reduction) is expensive and explicit substitutions aim at controlling this operation. The internalization of the substitution-calculus was originally introduced for describing the implementation of λ-calculi and led to the design of several calculi among which the $\lambda\sigma$-calculus based on a first-order rewrite system [ACCL91]. Recently, G. Dowek, T. Hardin and C. Kirchner [DHK95] have shown how to reduce the higher-order unification problem into a first-order unification problem modulo a first-order theory of explicit substitutions. A natural extension is now to express higher-order E-unification as a first-order combination problem. So, in this paper, we show how to perform higher-order E-unification thanks to the use of explicit substitutions and to the related first-order rewrite system $\lambda\sigma$. The theory $\lambda\sigma E$ of interest is defined as the combined equational theory $=_{\lambda\sigma(E)\cup E}$ where $\lambda\sigma(E)$ is a $\lambda\sigma$-calculus integrating the first-order equational theory E and its function symbols.

It is a non-disjoint combination of first-order equational theories. Therefore, we cannot reuse the well-known techniques developed for combining unification algorithms in the union of signature-disjoint theories [BS96], and those developed in [DKR94] for some specific non-disjoint unions of theories cannot be applied to this particular case.

Thus, we are designing in this work a complete $\lambda\sigma E$-unification procedure starting from the simple algorithm developed in [DHK95]. This leads to additional transformation rules for dealing with E and with the interaction between E and $\lambda\sigma$. For sake of simplicity, we assume that E is *regular* (left- and right-hand side of each axiom contain the same variables) and *collapse-free* (no variable as left- or right-hand side of axioms). But this work could be generalized to arbitrary theories E at the cost of more complicated rules (and proofs). Following the rule-based approach developed for unification [JK91], our unification procedure may be viewed as a set of transformation rules together with a given strategy. The interest of this unification procedure lies in the result that a higher-order E-unification problem can be translated into a first-order $\lambda\sigma E$-unification problem and solutions of the latter remain in the image of the translation. Hence, we show how to reduce higher-order E-unification into first-order equational unification.

The paper is organized as follows. Section 2 introduces the main concepts and notations concerning the first-order equational theory, whereas Section 3 recalls the basic notions related to higher-order E-unification. The $\lambda\sigma(E)$-calculus is presented in Section 4, and the connection between $\lambda\sigma E$-unification and higher-order E-unification is stated in Section 5. A $\lambda\sigma E$-unification procedure is given in Section 6. A complete version of this paper can be found in [KR97].

2 First-order equational theory

Let $\mathcal{X}$ be a denumerable set of (meta) variables and K be a finite set of basic types. As usual, the set of simple types is obtained from K by closure under the arrow $\rightarrow$, and $\rightarrow$ is assumed to be right-associative. We assume that $\mathcal{F} = \cup_{n\geq 0}\mathcal{F}_n$ is a set of first-order function symbols where $\mathcal{F}_n$ denotes the set of function symbols f of type $A_1 \rightarrow \ldots \rightarrow A_n \rightarrow B$ such that $A_1, \ldots, A_n, B$ are basic types. Let E be a set of axioms where left-hand sides and right-hand sides are in $\mathcal{T}(\mathcal{F}, \mathcal{X})$, the set of first-order terms built over function symbols in $\mathcal{F}$ and variables in $\mathcal{X}$. Typical examples are commutative symbols or associative-commutative symbols. In this paper, first-order terms are denoted by $(f\ t_1 \ldots t_n)$ instead of $f(t_1, \ldots, t_n)$ in order to be coherent with the standard notation of application in λ-calculus (but it is just a matter of taste). The top-symbol of $t = (f\ t_1 \ldots t_n)$ is $t(\epsilon) = f$. A E-unification problem (or equivalently an E-equational system) P is a conjunction of E-equations $s =^?_E t$ such that $s, t \in \mathcal{T}(\mathcal{F}, \mathcal{X})$. The set of (meta) variables occurring in a term t (resp. a E-unification problem P) is denoted by $\mathcal{V}(t)$ (resp. $\mathcal{V}(P)$).

A *grafting* is an endomorphism μ of first-order terms (i.e. a first-order substitution) such that finitely many variables (called the domain of μ) are not mapped to themselves. The domain (resp. the range) of μ is denoted by $\mathcal{D}om(\mu)$ (resp.

$\mathcal{R}an(\mu)$). To each grafting $\mu = \{x_1 \mapsto t_1, \ldots, x_l \mapsto t_l\}$, one can naturally associate a unification problem denoted by $\hat{\mu} = (x_1 =^? t_1 \wedge \cdots \wedge x_l =^? t_l)$ which is in solved form provided that μ is idempotent wrt. the composition operation. The application of μ to a unification problem P (resp. a term t) is written $P\mu$ (resp. $t\mu$). The E-subsumption ordering $\leq_E^V$ on graftings is defined by: $\mu \leq_E^V \phi$ if there exists a grafting φ such that $\forall x \in V,\ x\mu\varphi =_E x\phi$. An *identification* ξ on $V \subset \mathcal{X}$ is an idempotent grafting such that $\mathcal{D}om(\xi)$ and $\mathcal{R}an(\xi)$ are included in V (in that case, $\hat{\xi}$ corresponds to a conjunction of equations between variables). The set of identifications on V is denoted by ID_V. The set of E-unifiers $\mathcal{U}_E(P, V)$ of P wrt. *frozen variables* in V is the set of all graftings μ such that $\forall x \in V,\ x\mu = x$ and $s\mu =_E t\mu$ for any equation $s =_E^? t$ in P. $\mathcal{U}_E(P)$ simply denotes $\mathcal{U}_E(P, \emptyset)$. A complete set of E-unifiers $\mathcal{CSU}_E(P)$ or more generally $\mathcal{CSU}_E(P, V)$ is defined as usual according to $\leq_E^{\mathcal{V}(P)}$.

Let $\mathcal{F}'$ be a superset of $\mathcal{F}$ and $\overline{\mathcal{F}} = \mathcal{F}' \backslash \mathcal{F}$. A $\mathcal{F}$-term (resp. $\overline{\mathcal{F}}$-term) in $\mathcal{T}(\mathcal{F}', \mathcal{X})$ is a term such that its top-symbol is in $\mathcal{F}$ (resp. $\overline{\mathcal{F}}$). An alien subterm u of a $\mathcal{F}$-term t (resp. alien subterm t of a $\overline{\mathcal{F}}$-term u) is a $\overline{\mathcal{F}}$-subterm of t (resp. $\mathcal{F}$-subterm of u) such that all its superterms are $\mathcal{F}$-terms (resp. $\overline{\mathcal{F}}$-terms). A $\mathcal{F}$-term t (resp. $\overline{\mathcal{F}}$-term u) may also be denoted by $t\langle u_1 \ \ldots \ u_m\rangle$ where $u_1, \ldots, u_m$ are all alien subterms of t (resp. $u\lfloor t_1 \ \ldots \ t_m\rfloor$ where $t_1, \ldots, t_m$ are all alien subterms of u).

3 Typed λ-calculus in de Bruijn notation

The syntax of simply typed λ-calculus using de Bruijn indices is:

$$\begin{array}{ll} \textbf{Types} & A ::= K \mid A \to B \\ \textbf{Contexts} & \Gamma ::= nil \mid A.\Gamma \\ \textbf{Terms} & a ::= \mathtt{n} \mid X \mid (a\ b) \mid (f\ a_1 \ldots a_n) \mid \lambda_A.a \end{array}$$

where $X \in \mathcal{X}$ and $f \in \mathcal{F}_n$. The set of **Terms** is denoted by $\Lambda_{DB}(\mathcal{F}, \mathcal{X})$. The typing rules are:

$(var1)$ $$A.\Gamma \vdash \mathtt{1} : A$$

$(var+)$ $$\frac{\Gamma \vdash \mathtt{n} : B}{A.\Gamma \vdash (\mathtt{n+1}) : B}$$

$(lambda)$ $$\frac{A.\Gamma \vdash b : B}{\Gamma \vdash \lambda_A.b : A \to B}$$

(app) $$\frac{\Gamma \vdash a : A \to B \quad \Gamma \vdash b : A}{\Gamma \vdash (a\ b) : B}$$

$(appF)$ $$\frac{\Gamma \vdash a_1 : A_1 \ \ldots \ \Gamma \vdash a_n : A_n}{\Gamma \vdash (f\ a_1 \ldots a_n) : B} \text{ if } f : A_1 \to \ldots \to A_n \to B \in \mathcal{F}_n$$

$(Metavar)$ $$\Gamma \vdash X : T_X$$

In a calculus with meta-variables, to each meta-variable X we associate a unique type T_X. This type is imposed to be independent of the context where it appears. We assume that for each type T there is an infinite set of variables X such that $T_X = T$. Let us now recall some technicalities which are needed to define β and η-reductions in a λ-calculus with a de Bruijn notation. This is a simple extension of [DHK95] which takes into account additional functional constants in $\mathcal{F}$. The *λ-height* of an occurrence u in a term a is the number of λ's at prefix occurrences of u, written $|u|$. Let u be an occurrence of a de Bruijn number p in a given term a. If $\mathtt{p} \leq |u|$, then p is said *bound* in a, otherwise it is a *free* number of a. The term a^+, called *lift* of a, is obtained from a by incrementing the free numbers occurring in a. The substitution by b at the λ-height $(n-1)$ in a, written $\{\mathtt{n}/b\}a$ is defined by induction as follows:

$$\begin{array}{lll}
\{\mathtt{n}/b\}(a_1\ a_2) & = (\{\mathtt{n}/b\}a_1\ \{\mathtt{n}/b\}a_2) & \\
\{\mathtt{n}/b\}(f\ a_1 \ldots a_k) & = (f\ \{\mathtt{n}/b\}a_1 \ldots \{\mathtt{n}/b\}a_k) & (\text{if } f \in \mathcal{F}_k) \\
\{\mathtt{n}/b\}X & = X & \\
\{\mathtt{n}/b\}\,\lambda a & = \lambda\,(\{\mathtt{n+1}/b^+\}a) & \\
\{\mathtt{n}/b\}\mathtt{m} & = \mathtt{m}-1 \text{ if } m > n & (\mathtt{m} \in FV(a)) \\
 & \quad b \quad\ \text{if } m = n & (\mathtt{m} \text{ bound by the Beta-redex } \lambda) \\
 & \quad \mathtt{m} \quad \text{if } m < n & (\mathtt{m} \in BV(a))
\end{array}$$

The β-reduction and η-reduction are respectively defined by:

$$(\beta)\ \ ((\lambda\, a)\ b) \ \rightarrow\ \{\mathtt{1}/b\}a$$

$$(\eta)\ \ \lambda\,(a\ \mathtt{1}) \ \rightarrow b \text{ if there exists } b \in \Lambda_{DB}(\mathcal{F},\mathcal{X}) \text{ such that } a = b^+$$

The equivalence relation $=_{\beta\eta E}$ is $(\longleftrightarrow_E \cup \longleftrightarrow_\beta \cup \longleftrightarrow_\eta)^*$. A valuation θ from $\mathcal{X}$ to $\Lambda_{DB}(\mathcal{F},\mathcal{X})$ is denoted by $\{X_1/a_1,\ldots,X_n/a_n\}$ and uniquely extends to a *$\mathcal{X}$-substitution* $\bar{\theta}$ defined by:

1. $\bar{\theta}(X) = \theta(X)$,
2. $\bar{\theta}(\mathtt{n}) = \mathtt{n}$,
3. $\bar{\theta}((a_1\ a_2)) = (\bar{\theta}(a_1)\ \bar{\theta}(a_2))$,
4. $\bar{\theta}((f\ a_1 \ldots a_k)) = (f\ \bar{\theta}(a_1)\ldots\bar{\theta}(a_k))$ if $f \in \mathcal{F}_k$,
5. $\bar{\theta}(\lambda a) = \lambda(\bar{\theta}^+(a))$ where $\theta^+ = \{X_1/a_1^+,\ldots,X_n/a_n^+\}$ if $\theta = \{X_1/a_1,\ldots,X_n/a_n\}$.

As usual, the notations θ and $\bar{\theta}$ are identified. We can now define a solution of a higher-order E-equation $a \stackrel{?}{=}_{\beta\eta E} b$ as a substitution θ such that $\theta(a) =_{\beta\eta E} \theta(b)$.

4 Typed $\lambda\sigma$-calculus

The rewrite system $\boldsymbol{\lambda\sigma}$ (resp. σ) as presented in [DHK95] defines a rewrite relation on a first-order many-sorted term-generated structure $\mathcal{T}_{\lambda\sigma}(\mathcal{X})$ where a sort is either a pair (Context,Type) denoted by $\Gamma \vdash A$ or a pair (Context, Context) denoted by $\Gamma \vdash \Gamma'$. The first kind of elements are `terms` whereas the second ones are `substitutions`. We assume that there is no `substitution` variable in $\mathcal{X}$ and so only *substitution-closed* terms are considered. Any meta-variable $X \in \mathcal{X}$ has a unique sort $\Gamma_X \vdash T_X$. The rewrite system $\boldsymbol{\lambda\sigma}$ has been proved weakly normalizing and confluent on substitution-closed terms. In our context, we need to introduce a new (conditional) rewrite system $\boldsymbol{\lambda\sigma(E)}$ defined on $\mathcal{T}_{\lambda\sigma}(\mathcal{F}, \mathcal{X})$ (see Figure 1 and Figure 2). The rewrite system $\boldsymbol{\sigma(E)}$ is $\boldsymbol{\lambda\sigma(E)}$ without **Beta** and **Eta**.

Beta	$(\lambda a)b$	$\to a[b.id]$
App	$(a\ b)[s]$	$\to (a[s]\ b[s])$
VarCons	$1[a.s]$	$\to a$
Id	$a[id]$	$\to a$
Abs	$(\lambda a)[s]$	$\to \lambda(a[1.(s \circ \uparrow)])$
Clos	$(a[s])[t]$	$\to a[s \circ t]$
IdL	$id \circ s$	$\to s$
ShiftCons	$\uparrow \circ (a.s)$	$\to s$
AssEnv	$(s_1 \circ s_2) \circ s_3$	$\to s_1 \circ (s_2 \circ s_3)$
MapEnv	$(a.s) \circ t$	$\to a[t].(s \circ t)$
IdR	$s \circ id$	$\to s$
VarShift	$1.\uparrow$	$\to id$
SconsE	$1[s].(\uparrow \circ s')$	$\to s$ if $s =_E s'$
AppF	$\forall f \in \mathcal{F}_n : \quad (f\ a_1 \dots a_n)[s]$	$\to (f\ a_1[s] \dots a_n[s])$
Eta	$\lambda(a\ 1)$	$\to b$ if $a =_{\sigma(E)} b[\uparrow]$

Fig. 1. The $\boldsymbol{\lambda\sigma(E)}$-term rewriting system

Proposition 1. [KR97] $\boldsymbol{\lambda\sigma(E)}$ is weakly normalizing and confluent on substitution-closed terms.

The $\lambda\sigma(E)$-normal form of a term t is $t{\downarrow}_{\lambda\sigma(E)}$ and $=_{\lambda\sigma E}$ is $(\leftrightarrow_E \cup \leftrightarrow_{\lambda\sigma(E)})^*$.

Proposition 2. $\forall s, t \in \mathcal{T}_{\lambda\sigma}(\mathcal{F}, \mathcal{X}), s =_{\lambda\sigma E} t \iff (s{\downarrow}_{\lambda\sigma(E)}) =_E (t{\downarrow}_{\lambda\sigma(E)})$.

From now on, a $\lambda\sigma(E)$-normal form is simply called normal form. The same result holds with the notion of *long* normal form instead of normal form.

Definition 3. (η-long normal form) Let a be a term of type $A_1 \to \dots \to A_n \to B$ in the context Γ and in $\lambda\sigma(E)$-normal form. The η-long normal form of a, written a', is defined by:

$1_{A.\Gamma\vdash A}$	:	$\rightharpoonup A.\Gamma \vdash A$
$(\_\,\_)_{\Gamma\vdash A\to B,\Gamma\vdash A}$	$: \Gamma \vdash A \to B \;\; \Gamma \vdash A$	$\rightharpoonup \Gamma \vdash B$
$(f\_\ldots\_)_{\Gamma\vdash A_1,\ldots,\Gamma\vdash A_n}$	$: \Gamma \vdash A_1 \ldots \Gamma \vdash A_n$	$\rightharpoonup \Gamma \vdash B$ if $f : A_1 \to \ldots \to A_n \to B \in \mathcal{F}_n$
$(\lambda\,\_)_{A.\Gamma\vdash B}$	$: A.\Gamma \vdash B$	$\rightharpoonup \Gamma \vdash A \to B$
$\_[\_]_{\Gamma'\vdash A,\Gamma\vdash\Gamma'}$	$: \Gamma' \vdash A \;\; \Gamma \vdash \Gamma'$	$\rightharpoonup \Gamma \vdash A$
$id_{\Gamma\vdash\Gamma}$	:	$\rightharpoonup \Gamma \vdash \Gamma$
$\uparrow_{A.\Gamma\vdash\Gamma}$	:	$\rightharpoonup A.\Gamma \vdash \Gamma$
$\_\cdot\_{}_{\Gamma\vdash A,\Gamma\vdash\Gamma'}$	$: \Gamma \vdash A \;\; \Gamma \vdash \Gamma'$	$\rightharpoonup \Gamma \vdash A.\Gamma'$
$\_\circ\_{}_{\Gamma\vdash\Gamma'',\Gamma''\vdash\Gamma'}$	$: \Gamma \vdash \Gamma'' \;\; \Gamma'' \vdash \Gamma'$	$\rightharpoonup \Gamma \vdash \Gamma'$

Fig. 2. Disambiguated many-sorted signature of $\mathcal{T}_{\lambda\sigma}(\mathcal{F}, \mathcal{X})$

1. If $a = \lambda_C b$ then $a' = \lambda_C b'$.
2. If $a = (\mathbf{k}\ b_1 \ldots b_p)$ then $a' = \lambda_{A_1} \ldots \lambda_{A_n}(\mathbf{k+n}\ c_1 \ldots c_p\ \mathbf{n}' \ldots \mathbf{1}')$, where c_i is the η-long normal form of the normal form of $b_i[\uparrow^n]$.
3. If $a = (f\ a_1 \ldots a_n)$ where $f \in \mathcal{F}$, then $a' = (f\ a'_1 \ldots a'_n)$.
4. If $a = (X[s]\ b_1 \ldots b_p)$ then $a' = \lambda_{A_1} \ldots \lambda_{A_n}(X[s']\ c_1 \ldots c_p\ \mathbf{n}' \ldots \mathbf{1}')$, where c_i is the η-long normal form of the normal form of $b_i[\uparrow^n]$ and if $s = d_1 ... d_q.\uparrow^k$ then $s' = e_1 ... e_q.\uparrow^{k+n}$ where e_i is the η-long normal form of the normal form of $d_i[\uparrow^n]$.

The *long normal form* is the η-long normal form of its normal form.

5 Application to higher-order E-unification

Given a simply-typed λ-calculus $\Lambda_{DB}(\mathcal{F}, \mathcal{X})$ using de Bruijn notation, a term a in $\Lambda_{DB}(\mathcal{F}, \mathcal{X})$ can be transformed into a term in $\mathcal{T}_{\lambda\sigma}(\mathcal{F}, \mathcal{X})$ according to the mapping defined below. This transformation is called *pre-cooking.*

Definition 4. Let $a \in \Lambda_{DB}(\mathcal{F}, \mathcal{X})$ such that $\Gamma \vdash a : A$ (i.e. a is of type A in the context Γ). The pre-cooking is the mapping $\Lambda_{DB}(\mathcal{F}, \mathcal{X}) \to \mathcal{T}_{\lambda\sigma}(\mathcal{F}, \mathcal{X}) : a \mapsto a_F = F(a, 0)$, where the sort of a_F is $\Gamma \vdash A$ and $F(a, n)$ is inductively defined by:
1) $F((\lambda a), n) = \lambda(F(a, n+1))$,
2) $F((a\ b), n) = (F(a, n)\ F(b, n))$,
3) $F(\mathbf{k}, n) = 1[\uparrow^{k-1}]$,
4) $F(X, n) = X[\uparrow^n]$.

Proposition 5. Let a, b be terms in $\Lambda_{DB}(\mathcal{F}, \mathcal{X})$.

1. If $a \longrightarrow_\beta b$, then $a_F \overset{*}{\longrightarrow}_{\lambda\sigma(E)} b_F$.
2. If $a \longrightarrow_\eta b$, then $a_F \overset{*}{\longrightarrow}_{\lambda\sigma(E)} b_F$.
3. If a is $\beta\eta$-normal then a_F is $\lambda\sigma(E)$-normal.

4. $a =_E b$ if and only if $a_F =_E b_F$.
5. $a =_{\beta\eta E} b$ if and only if $a_F =_{\lambda\sigma E} b_F$.

One should be aware that higher-order unification relies on a notion of substitution (denoted by $\{X/N\}$) that includes the manipulation of de Bruijn indices whereas in first-order unification the notion of grafting (denoted by $\{X \mapsto M\}$) simply replaces the occurrences of variables by terms.

Proposition 6. Let a, b be terms in $\Lambda_{DB}(\mathcal{F}, \mathcal{X})$. There exist terms $N_1, \ldots, N_p$ such that $\{X_1/N_1, \ldots, X_p/N_p\}(a) =_{\beta\eta E} \{X_1/N_1, \ldots, X_p/N_p\}(b)$ if and only if there exist terms $M_1, \ldots, M_p$ *in the image of the pre-cooking translation* such that $a_F\{X_1 \mapsto M_1, \ldots, X_p \mapsto M_p\} =_{\lambda\sigma E} b_F\{X_1 \mapsto M_1, \ldots, X_p \mapsto M_p\}$.

Proof. Follows Proposition 5 and the fact [DHK95] that

$$(\{X_1/N_1, \ldots, X_p/N_p\}(a))_F = a_F\{X_1 \mapsto (N_1)_F, \ldots, X_p \mapsto (N_p)_F\}.$$

As a direct corollary, if the problem $a =^?_{\beta\eta E} b$ has a solution, then the problem $a_F =^?_{\lambda\sigma E} b_F$ also has a solution. Conversely, using the results of the next section, we show that if $a_F =^?_{\lambda\sigma E} b_F$ has a solution, then it also has a solution in the image of the pre-cooking translation. The construction of such a solution is based on a notion called *Γ-stability* in [DHK95], which can be reused without any change. Finally, the connection between higher-order E-unification and a first-order unification integrating E-unification is stated as follows:

Theorem 7. *Let $a =^?_{\beta\eta E} b$ be a higher-order unification problem in $\Lambda_{DB}(\mathcal{F}, \mathcal{X})$. The first-order unification problem $a_F =^?_{\lambda\sigma E} b_F$ has a solution if and only if the higher-order unification problem $a =^?_{\beta\eta E} b$ has a solution. Thus, $\lambda\sigma E$-unification is undecidable. Furthermore, any solution of $a =^?_{\beta\eta E} b$ can be obtained from $a_F =^?_{\lambda\sigma E} b_F$ by applying the $\lambda\sigma E$-unification procedure (Section 6) followed by the "Back to λ-calculus" process described in [DHK95].*

6 $\lambda\sigma E$-Unification procedure

The unification procedure is described as a set of transformation rules together with a given strategy. The application of transformation rules mainly depends on the form of top-symbols occurring in the two members of an equation. If both top-symbols are constructors in $\lambda\sigma$, then we apply the decomposition rules developed for $\lambda\sigma$ which are still correct in this context. Otherwise, if both top-symbols are in E, then we use the well-known notion of variable-abstraction [BS96] to purify the equation. The pure equation will be solved thanks to the E-unification algorithm. It is also possible to have a theory clash between a constructor in $\lambda\sigma$ and a function symbol in E. In this case, the process fails since E is assumed to be collapse-free. Finally, we should also consider "explosion" rules to solve the *flex-rigid* case. These rules aim at performing a step towards a solution and so introduce the non-determinism.

Let us now formalize this unification procedure. The reader is assumed to be familiar with the rule-based description of unification algorithms [JK91]. Starting from a unification problem with *well-sorted* equations (ie. the left- and right-hand sides are well-sorted and have the same sort), the idea is to apply rules until a "solved form" is reached. The only equations that are not treated by our rules are of the form:

$$X[a_1 \ldots a_p . \uparrow^n] =^?_{\lambda\sigma E} Y[a'_1 \ldots a'_{p'} . \uparrow^{n'}].$$

As in λ-calculus, such equations, called *flexible-flexible* always have solutions. Thus, we should use an adequate notion of solved form.

Definition 8. A system P is a *$\lambda\sigma E$-solved form* if all its meta-variables are of atomic type and it is a conjunction of non trivial equations of the forms:

Solved: $X =^?_{\lambda\sigma E} a$ where the variable X does not appear anywhere else in P and a is in long normal form. Such an equation is said to be *solved in* P, and the variable X is also said solved.

Flex-flex: $X[a_1 \ldots a_p . \uparrow^n] =^?_{\lambda\sigma E} Y[a'_1 \ldots a'_{p'} . \uparrow^{n'}]$, where $X[a_1 \ldots a_p . \uparrow^n]$ and $Y[a'_1 \ldots a'_{p'} . \uparrow^{n'}]$ are long normal terms, and the equation is not solved.

Lemma 9. Any $\lambda\sigma E$-solved form has $\lambda\sigma E$-unifiers.

Proof. The key point is to verify that a flex-flex $\lambda\sigma E$-equation always has a solution. The proof is the same as the one developed for a flex-flex $\lambda\sigma$-equation and does not depend on terms occurring in the substitutions $a_1 \ldots a_p . \uparrow^n$ and $a'_1 \ldots a'_{p'} . \uparrow^{n'}$.

6.1 Transformation rules

We consider the transformation rules developed in [DHK95] for $\lambda\sigma$-unification (**$\lambda\sigma$-Unif**, see Figure 3) together with some additional rules for dealing with the equational theory E (**E-Unif**, see Figure 4). Let **$\lambda\sigma E$-Unif** be the union of these two sets of transformation rules. We shall now prove the following results:

- The **$\lambda\sigma E$-Unif** normal forms of equation systems are $\lambda\sigma E$-solved forms,
- The application of each rule in **$\lambda\sigma E$-Unif** preserves the set of unifiers,

First, we must check that the **$\lambda\sigma E$-Unif** transformation rules do not introduce ill-sorted terms:

Lemma 10. The transformation by the rules in **$\lambda\sigma E$-Unif** of a well-sorted equation[1] gives rise only to well-sorted equations, or to the unsatisfiable unification problem $\mathbb{F}$.

Proof. This follows from a rule by rule analysis of the transformation.

[1] A well-sorted equation $s =^? t$ is also denoted by $(s =^? t)^{\Gamma \vdash A}$ or $(s =^? t)^{\Gamma}$, where $\Gamma \vdash A$ is the sort of s and t.

Lemma 11. Any $\lambda\sigma E$-solved problem is normalized for $\boldsymbol{\lambda\sigma E}$**-Unif**. Conversely, if a system P is a conjunction of equations irreducible by the rules of $\boldsymbol{\lambda\sigma E}$**-Unif**, then it is a $\lambda\sigma E$-solved form.

Proof. It is clear that any solved form is in normal form for $\boldsymbol{\lambda\sigma E}$**-Unif**. Conversely, given a non solved system P, let us show that it is reducible by $\boldsymbol{\lambda\sigma E}$**-Unif**. Since P is not a solved form, it contains an equation $s =^?_{\lambda\sigma E} t$ that is neither solved nor flexible-flexible.
The first possibility is to have an equation of the form $X =^?_{\lambda\sigma E} t$, where X appears somewhere else in P, in which case **Replace** applies.
If s or t are not in long normal form, then we apply the rule **Normalize**.
The cases where s and t are long normal terms without top-symbols in $\mathcal{F}$ are taken into account by $\boldsymbol{\lambda\sigma}$**-Unif**. The other cases where s or t has a top-symbol in $\mathcal{F}$ are summarized in the following table. We use the result of [Río93] to describe the form of the terms in long normal form and assume that $f, g \in \mathcal{F}$, and $\mathbf{b} = b_1, \ldots, b_q$ and $\mathbf{c} = c_1, \ldots, c_s$ consist both in at least one element.

$s =^?_{\lambda\sigma E} t$	λb	$(\mathbf{n}\ \mathbf{b})$	$(f\ \mathbf{b})$	$(X[s]\ \mathbf{b})$ or $(X\ \mathbf{b})$	$X[s]$	X
$(g\ \mathbf{c})$	***E*-Conflict**	***E*-Conflict**	**E-Solve** or ***E*-Dec**	**Exp-$\boldsymbol{\lambda}$**	***E*-Exp**	**Replace** or ***E*-Exp**

Lemma 12. Any rule $\mathbf{r}$ in $\boldsymbol{\lambda\sigma E}$**-Unif** is correct and complete i.e.:

$$P \overset{\mathbf{r}}{\twoheadrightarrow} P' \Rightarrow \mathcal{U}_{\lambda\sigma E}(P) = \mathcal{U}_{\lambda\sigma E}(P').$$

Proof. Let us check the completeness (the inclusion $\subseteq$) for all the rules:
Normalize: clear.
Dec-$\boldsymbol{\lambda}$, **Dec-App**, **Dec-Fail**: Since $\lambda_A, \mathtt{1}, \ldots, \mathtt{n}$ are constructors, the result follows.
Exp-$\boldsymbol{\lambda}$: The proof is as for $\boldsymbol{\lambda\sigma}$ alone.
Exp-App: Since by hypothesis $X[a_1 \ldots a_p . \uparrow^n] =^?_{\lambda\sigma E} (\mathtt{m}\ b_1\ \ldots\ b_q)$ is unifiable by μ, the unifier should be such that $\mu(X) = (\mathtt{r}\ c_1 \ldots c_s)$ since E is collapse-free. Then the rest of the proof is as for $\boldsymbol{\lambda\sigma}$ alone.
Replace: The proof works as usual in the first-order case.
***E*-Dec**: Solutions are obviously preserved since new variables are existentially quantified.
***E*-Conflict**: See Lemma 13 and use the fact that $\lambda, \mathtt{1}, \ldots, \mathtt{n}$ are constructors.
***E*-Solve**: See Lemma 14.
***E*-Exp**: Let μ be a unifier of $X[a_1 \ldots a_p . \uparrow^n] =^?_{\lambda\sigma E} (f\ b_1\ \ldots\ b_q)$. There are two possible cases.

If $\mu(X) = (g\ c_1 \ldots c_s)$, then

$$\begin{array}{ll} (g\ c_1 \ldots c_s)[a'_1 \ldots a'_p . \uparrow^n] & =^?_{\lambda\sigma E} (f\ b'_1\ \ldots\ b'_q) \Leftrightarrow \\ (g\ c_1[a'_1 \ldots a'_p . \uparrow^n] \ldots c_s[a'_1 \ldots a'_p . \uparrow^n]) & =^?_{\lambda\sigma E} (f\ b'_1\ \ldots\ b'_q) \end{array}$$

and μ is clearly a solution of $\exists H_1, \ldots, H_k,\ X =^?_{\lambda\sigma E} (g\ H_1\ \ldots\ H_k)$.

If $\mu(X) = (\mathtt{r}\ c_1 \ldots c_s)$, then it verifies

$$\begin{array}{ll}(\mathtt{r}\ c_1 \ldots c_s)[a'_1 \ldots a'_p . \uparrow^n] & =^?_{\lambda\sigma E} (f\ b'_1\ \ldots\ b'_q) \Leftrightarrow \\ (\mathtt{r}[a'_1 \ldots a'_p . \uparrow^n] \ldots) & =^?_{\lambda\sigma E} (f\ b'_1\ \ldots\ b'_q) \Leftrightarrow \\ (1[\uparrow^{r-1} \circ (a'_1 \ldots a'_p . \uparrow^n)] \ldots) & =^?_{\lambda\sigma E} (f\ b'_1\ \ldots\ b'_q).\end{array}$$

If $r \leq p$, then the equation becomes:

$$\begin{array}{ll}(1[a'_r \ldots a'_p . \uparrow^n] \ldots) & =^?_{\lambda\sigma E} (f\ b'_1\ \ldots\ b'_q) \Leftrightarrow \\ (a'_r\ c_1[a'_1 \ldots a'_p . \uparrow^n] \ldots) & =^?_{\lambda\sigma E} (f\ b'_1\ \ldots\ b'_q).\end{array}$$

In this case, the long normal form of $(a'_r\ c_1[a'_1 \ldots a'_p . \uparrow^n] \ldots)$ must be a $\mathcal{F}$-term since E is collapse-free. Otherwise, $r > p$ and it becomes $(1[\uparrow^{n+(r-p)}] \ldots) =^?_{\lambda\sigma E} (f\ b'_1\ \ldots\ b'_q)$. This would contradict the fact that E is collapse-free. So in all the cases, the grafting μ is a solution of the result of **E-Exp**. Notice that the case $r > p$ always leads to a failure. This corresponds to the imitation transformation in the higher-order unification algorithm.

Lemma 13. Let s be a $\mathcal{F}$-term and let t be a term in $\lambda\sigma(E)$-normal form. If $s =_{\lambda\sigma E} t$, then t is a $\mathcal{F}$-term.

Proof. If $s =_{\lambda\sigma E} t$, then $s{\downarrow_{\lambda\sigma(E)}} =_E t$ since t is $\lambda\sigma(E)$-normal, and $s{\downarrow_{\lambda\sigma(E)}}$ is still a $\mathcal{F}$-term. Since E is collapse-free, t is also a $\mathcal{F}$-term.

Lemma 14. Let P^Γ_E be a $\lambda\sigma E$-unification problem built over terms in $\mathcal{T}(\mathcal{F}, \mathcal{X})$ and ϕ a grafting in $\lambda\sigma(E)$-normal form. If $\phi \in \mathcal{U}_{\lambda\sigma E}(P^\Gamma_E)$, then there exists a grafting μ such that:

- $\mathcal{R}an(\mu) \in \mathcal{T}(\mathcal{F}, \mathcal{X})$,
- $\mu \in \mathcal{CSU}_E(P^\Gamma_E)$,
- $\mu \leq_E^{\mathcal{V}(P^\Gamma_E)} \phi$,
- $\forall x \in \mathcal{V}(P^\Gamma_E)$, $x\phi(\epsilon) \in \{1, \ldots, \mathtt{n}\}^2 \Rightarrow x\mu \in \mathcal{X}$.

For proving this lemma, we need to introduce some definitions borrowed from the combination of first-order equational theories. Let π be a mapping from $\mathcal{T}_{\lambda\sigma}(\mathcal{F}, \mathcal{X})$ onto "new" variables such that $\pi(x) = x$ for any $x \in \mathcal{X}$ and $\pi(s) = \pi(t)$ if and only if $s =_{\lambda\sigma E} t$ for any terms $s, t \in \mathcal{T}_{\lambda\sigma}(\mathcal{F}, \mathcal{X})$. Given a term t, t^π is defined as follows: $x^\pi = x$, $t\langle u_1\ \ldots\ u_m\rangle^\pi = t\langle \pi(u_1)\ \ldots\ \pi(u_m)\rangle$, and $u\lfloor t_1\ \ldots\ t_m\rfloor^\pi = \pi(u\lfloor t_1\ \ldots\ t_m\rfloor)$. The grafting ϕ^π is $\{x \mapsto (x\phi)^\pi\}_{x \in \mathcal{D}om(\phi)}$. Hence, $\phi^\pi \leq_E^{\mathcal{X}} \phi$ by definition.

Lemma 15. Let s and t be two terms in $\mathcal{T}(\mathcal{F}, \mathcal{X})$ and ϕ a grafting in $\lambda\sigma(E)$-normal form. Then $s\phi =_{\lambda\sigma E} t\phi \Longleftrightarrow s\phi^\pi =_E t\phi^\pi$.

Proof. We have $s\phi =_{\lambda\sigma E} t\phi \Longleftrightarrow s\phi = (s\phi{\downarrow_{\lambda\sigma(E)}}) =_E (t\phi{\downarrow_{\lambda\sigma(E)}}) = t\phi$. Then, since E is only built over $\mathcal{F}$, we have $s \longleftrightarrow_E t$ iff $s^\pi \overset{*}{\longleftrightarrow}_E t^\pi$ for any $s, t \in \mathcal{T}_{\lambda\sigma}(\mathcal{F}, \mathcal{X})$. Finally, we easily prove by induction on the length of equational proofs that $s\phi =_E t\phi \Longleftrightarrow s\phi^\pi =_E t\phi^\pi$.

Therefore, ϕ^π is obviously an instance of a most general E-unifier μ satisfying Lemma 14.

[2] By abuse of notation, $(\mathtt{n}\ \mathbf{b})(\epsilon) = \mathtt{n}$

Dec-λ $P \wedge \lambda_A a =^?_{\lambda\sigma E} \lambda_A b$
$\rightarrow$
$P \wedge a =^?_{\lambda\sigma E} b$

Dec-App $P \wedge (\mathtt{n}\ a_1 \ \ldots \ a_p) =^?_{\lambda\sigma E} (\mathtt{n}\ b_1 \ \ldots \ b_p)$
$\rightarrow$
$P \wedge (\bigwedge_{i=1..p} a_i =^?_{\lambda\sigma E} b_i)$

Dec-Fail $P \wedge (\mathtt{n}\ a_1 \ \ldots \ a_p) =^?_{\lambda\sigma E} (\mathtt{m}\ b_1 \ \ldots \ b_q)$
$\rightarrow$
$\mathbb{F}$
if $n \neq m$

Exp-λ P
$\rightarrow$
$\exists Y : (A.\Gamma \vdash B),\ \ P \wedge X =^?_{\lambda\sigma E} \lambda_A Y$
if $(X : \Gamma \vdash A \rightarrow B) \in \mathcal{V}(P), Y \notin \mathcal{V}(P)$,
and X is not a solved variable

Exp-App $P \wedge X[a_1 \ldots a_p . \uparrow^n] =^?_{\lambda\sigma E} (\mathtt{m}\ b_1 \ \ldots \ b_q)$
$\rightarrow$
$P \wedge X[a_1 \ldots a_p . \uparrow^n] =^?_{\lambda\sigma E} (\mathtt{m}\ b_1 \ \ldots \ b_q)$
$\wedge \bigvee_{r \in R_p \cup R_i} \exists H_1, \ldots, H_k,\ X =^?_{\lambda\sigma E} (\mathtt{r}\ H_1 \ \ldots \ H_k)$
if X has an atomic type and is not solved
where $H_1, \ldots, H_k$ are variables of appropriate types, not occurring in P, with the contexts $\Gamma_{H_i} = \Gamma_X$, R_p is the subset of $\{1, \ldots, p\}$ such that $(\mathtt{r}\ H_1 \ \ldots \ H_k)$ has the right type, $R_i =$ if $m \geq n+1$ then $\{m-n+p\}$ else $\emptyset$

Replace $P \wedge X =^?_{\lambda\sigma E} a$
$\rightarrow$
$P\{X \mapsto a\} \wedge X =^?_{\lambda\sigma E} a$
if $X \in \mathcal{V}(P), X \notin \mathcal{V}(a)$ and $a \in \mathcal{X} \Rightarrow a \in \mathcal{V}(P)$

Normalize $P \wedge a =^?_{\lambda\sigma E} b$
$\rightarrow$
$P \wedge a' =^?_{\lambda\sigma E} b'$
if a or b is not in long normal form
where a' (resp. b') is the long normal form of a (resp. b) if a (resp. b) is not a solved variable and a (resp. b) otherwise

Fig. 3. **λσ-Unif**, the basic rules for unification in $\lambda\sigma$

E-Dec $P \wedge (s\langle u_1 \ \ldots \ u_m\rangle =^?_{\lambda\sigma E} t\langle u_{m+1} \ \ldots \ u_{m+n}\rangle)^\Gamma$
$\rightarrow$
$\exists V_1 \ \ldots \ V_{m+n},\ P \wedge (s\langle V_1 \ \ldots \ V_m\rangle =^?_{\lambda\sigma E} t\langle V_{m+1} \ \ldots \ V_{m+n}\rangle)^\Gamma$
$\wedge \bigwedge_{k=1}^{m+n} V_k =^?_{\lambda\sigma E} u_k$
$\wedge \bigwedge_{\{i \mid u_i(\epsilon)=\mathbf{n}\}} M_E(V_i)$
where $V_i : \Gamma \vdash T_{u_i}$

E-Dec $P \wedge (X =^?_{\lambda\sigma E} s\langle u_1 \ \ldots \ u_m\rangle)^\Gamma$
$\rightarrow$
$\exists V_1 \ \ldots \ V_m,\ P \wedge (X =^?_{\lambda\sigma E} s\langle V_1 \ \ldots \ V_m\rangle)^\Gamma$
$\wedge \bigwedge_{k=1}^{m} V_k =^?_{\lambda\sigma E} u_k$
$\wedge \bigwedge_{\{i \mid u_i(\epsilon)=\mathbf{n}\}} M_E(V_i)$
if $X \in \mathcal{V}(s\langle u_1 \ \ldots \ u_m\rangle)$
where $V_i : \Gamma \vdash T_{u_i}$

E-Conflict $P \wedge s\langle u_1 \ \ldots \ u_m\rangle =^?_{\lambda\sigma E} t$
$\rightarrow$
$\mathbb{F}$
if $t(\epsilon) = \mathbf{n}$

E-Solve $P \wedge P_E^\Gamma \wedge \bigwedge_{V \in VS} M_E(V)$
$\rightarrow$
$\bigvee_{\xi \in ID_{VS}} \bigvee_{\mu \in CSU_E(P_E\xi, VS)} P \wedge (\hat{\mu} \wedge \hat{\xi})_E^\Gamma \wedge \bigwedge_{V \in VS} M_E(V)$
if P_E^Γ is not in solved form

E-Exp $P \wedge X[a_1 \ldots a_p . \uparrow^n] =^?_{\lambda\sigma E} (f\ b_1 \ \ldots \ b_q)$
$\rightarrow$
$P \wedge X[a_1 \ldots a_p . \uparrow^n] =^?_{\lambda\sigma E} (f\ b_1 \ \ldots \ b_q)$
$\wedge (\bigvee_{g \in \mathcal{F}} \exists H_1, \ldots, H_k,\ X =^?_{\lambda\sigma E} (g\ H_1 \ \ldots \ H_k)$
$\vee \bigvee_{r \in R_p} \exists H_1, \ldots, H_k,\ X =^?_{\lambda\sigma E} (\mathbf{r}\ H_1 \ \ldots \ H_k))$
if X has an atomic type and is not solved, $f \in \mathcal{F}$
where $H_1, \ldots, H_k$ are variables of appropriate types, not occurring in P, with the contexts $\Gamma_{H_i} = \Gamma_X$, R_p is the subset of $\{1, \ldots, p\}$ such that $(\mathbf{r}\ H_1 \ \ldots \ H_k)$ has the right type

Fig. 4. ***E*-Unif**, additional rules for unification in $\lambda\sigma E$

6.2 A complete strategy

The repeated application of rules in **$\lambda\sigma E$-Unif** is not terminating for any strategy. One could try for instance to apply as long as possible **Exp-λ**... The strategy described next makes each application of an explosion rule immediately followed by **Replace**. In this context, ***E*-Solve** may be also viewed as an explosion rule since E is assumed to be finitary but not necessarily unitary. However, the transformation rule **Replace** must be applied more carefully than in the $\lambda\sigma$-case since aliens could be created. Thus, we consider a new replacement rule which is applicable only on some unification problems.

NewReplace $P \wedge X =^?_{\lambda\sigma E} a$

$\mapsto\!\!\!\to$

$P\{X \mapsto a\} \wedge X =^?_{\lambda\sigma E} a$

if $X \in \mathcal{V}(P), X \notin \mathcal{V}(a)$ and $a \in \mathcal{X} \Rightarrow a \in \mathcal{V}(P)$ and ($a \notin \mathcal{X}$ and a is not a $\mathcal{F}$-term) implies that X does not occur in a non-solved equation of P directly under a function symbol of $\mathcal{F}$.

If this rule cannot be applied, then either an explosion rule or ***E*-Solve** or a decomposition rule succeeds. We are thus proving the completeness of a particular class **$\lambda\sigma E$-UnifReplace** of strategies which are built on any *fair* application of the following rules or group of rules:

Normalize or **Dec-λ** or **Dec-App** or **Dec-Fail** or **NewReplace** or
Exp-λR = (**Exp-λ;Replace**) or
Exp-AppR = (**Exp-App;Replace**) or
***E*-Dec** or ***E*-Conflict** or
E*-ExpR** = (E*-Exp;Replace**) or
E*-SolveR** = (E*-Solve;NewReplace***)

These rules are assumed to be applied in a *fair* way on the problem to be solved, which means that in a disjunction of systems, none of the disjuncts is left forever without applying transformation rules on it.

Some application of rules are followed by **Replace** or **NewReplace**. In this case, the replacement only concerns the just introduced equations.

Theorem 16. *The rules in* **$\lambda\sigma E$-Unif** *describe a correct and complete $\lambda\sigma E$-unification procedure in the sense that, given a $\lambda\sigma E$-unification problem P:*

- *if* **$\lambda\sigma E$-Unif** *leads in a finite number of steps to a disjunction of systems having one of its disjuncts solved, then the problem P is $\lambda\sigma E$-unifiable and a solution to P is the solution constructed by taking into account flex-flex equations [DHK95],*
- *P has a unifier μ then the strategy* **$\lambda\sigma E$-UnifReplace** *leads in a finite number of steps to a disjunction of systems such that one disjunct is solved and has μ as a unifier.*

Example 1. Let $E = \{(*\ x\ y) = (*\ y\ x)\}$ and $\lambda yx.(*\ x\ y) =^?_{\beta\eta E} \lambda yx.(*\ y\ (F\ x))$. The pre-cooking transformation leads to $\lambda\lambda(*\ 1\ 2) =^?_{\lambda\sigma E} \lambda\lambda(*\ 2\ (F[\uparrow^2]\ 1))$. Applying the decomposition rule **Dec-λ**, we get $(*\ 1\ 2) =^?_{\lambda\sigma E} (*\ 2\ (F[\uparrow^2]\ 1))$. Then we can use ***E*-Dec** (where $s\langle 1,2\rangle = (*\ 1\ 2)$ and $s\langle a,b\rangle = (*\ a\ b)$) to purify this equation by adding new existentially quantified variables a, b, V and we obtain the following unification problem: $(*\ a\ b) =^?_{\lambda\sigma E} (*\ b\ V) \wedge M_E(a) \wedge M_E(b) \wedge a =^?_{\lambda\sigma E} 1 \wedge b =^?_{\lambda\sigma E} 2 \wedge V =^?_{\lambda\sigma E} (F[\uparrow^2]\ 1)$ such that a, b must be frozen (ie. non-instantiated) in the commutative theory E. The E-unification algorithm (rule ***E*-Solve**) applied on the first equation yields $V =^?_{\lambda\sigma E} a \wedge a =^?_{\lambda\sigma E} 1 \wedge b =^?_{\lambda\sigma E} 2 \wedge V =^?_{\lambda\sigma E} (F[\uparrow^2]\ 1)$ (Note that the identification $a =^?_{\lambda\sigma E} b$ leads to a failure). Then, we can replace V and a by their respective values and we obtain the equation $(F[\uparrow^2]\ 1) =^?_{\lambda\sigma E} 1$ that is solved by exclusively using transformation rules developed for $\lambda\sigma$-unification, yielding $F =^?_{\lambda\sigma E} \lambda 1$. Back to λ-calculus, this corresponds to the solution $F =^?_{\beta\eta E} \lambda x.x$.

7 Conclusion

We have considered in this paper the case where E is a regular and collapse-free theory (including Commutativity (C) and Associativity-Commutativity (AC)). This leads to a very natural $\lambda\sigma E$-unification procedure with many possible failures cases (conflicts have no solution). Thus, this unification procedure is very simple. The call of the E-unification algorithm is restricted as much as possible, and an origin of non-determinism is avoided. More generally, when E is not collapse-free, a conflict is solved thanks to the following rule

***E*-Conflict** $P \wedge (s\langle u_1 \ldots u_m\rangle =^?_{\lambda\sigma E} u_{m+1})^\Gamma$

$$\begin{array}{l}
\twoheadrightarrow \\
\exists V_1 \ldots V_{m+1},\ P \wedge (s\langle V_1 \ldots V_m\rangle =^?_{\lambda\sigma E} V_{m+1})^\Gamma \\
\qquad\qquad \wedge \bigwedge_{k=1}^{m+1} V_k =^?_{\lambda\sigma E} u_k \\
\qquad\qquad \wedge \bigwedge_{\{i \mid u_i(\epsilon)\in\{\lambda_A, \mathrm{n}\}\}} M_E(V_i) \\
\text{if } u_{m+1}(\epsilon) = \mathrm{n} \\
\text{where } V_i : \Gamma \vdash T_{u_i}
\end{array}$$

but at the cost of more non-determinism. Moreover, in the general case, we have to deal with a $\lambda\sigma$-calculus integrating an *arbitrary* disjoint first-order equational theory E. In this more general setting, proving confluence and weak normalization of the related $\lambda\sigma(E)$-calculus remains an open problem. A possible way to tackle this problem consists in using a calculus of explicit substitutions based on a left-linear rewrite system [Muñ, Pag]. It would also be interesting to study particular cases where the unification procedure can be turned into a terminating algorithm. For instance, we could consider second-order E-matching and higher-order E-unification of patterns provided that the appropriate solving tool is available for E.

Acknowledgements: We would like to thank Gilles Dowek, Thérèse Hardin and Bruno Pagano for many fruitful discussions.

References

[ACCL91] M. Abadi, L. Cardelli, P.-L. Curien, and J.-J. Lévy. Explicit substitutions. *Journal of Functional Programming*, 1(4):375–416, 1991.

[BS96] F. Baader and K. U. Schulz. Unification in the union of disjoint equational theories: Combining decision procedures. *Journal of Symbolic Computation*, 21(2):211–243, February 1996.

[BT88] V. Breazu-Tannen. Combining algebra and higher-order types. In *Proceedings, Third Annual Symposium on Logic in Computer Science*, pages 82–90, Edinburgh, Scotland, 5–8 July 1988. IEEE Computer Society.

[DHK95] G. Dowek, T. Hardin, and C. Kirchner. Higher-order unification via explicit substitutions, extended abstract. In D. Kozen, editor, *Proceedings of LICS'95*, pages 366–374, San Diego, June 1995.

[DKR94] E. Domenjoud, F. Klay, and C. Ringeissen. Combination techniques for non-disjoint equational theories. In A. Bundy, editor, *Proceedings 12th International Conference on Automated Deduction, Nancy (France)*, volume 814 of *Lecture Notes in Artificial Intelligence*, pages 267–281. Springer-Verlag, June/July 1994.

[Hue75] G. Huet. A unification algorithm for typed lambda calculus. *Theoretical Computer Science*, 1(1):27–57, 1975.

[JK91] J.-P. Jouannaud and C. Kirchner. Solving equations in abstract algebras: a rule-based survey of unification. In J.-L. Lassez and G. Plotkin, editors, *Computational Logic. Essays in honor of Alan Robinson*, chapter 8, pages 257–321. The MIT press, Cambridge (MA, USA), 1991.

[KR97] C. Kirchner and C. Ringeissen. Higher-Order Equational Unification via Explicit Substitutions. Research report, CRIN, 1997.

[Muñ] C. Muñoz. A left linear variant of $\lambda\sigma$. Manuscript.

[NM88] G. Nadathur and D. Miller. An overview of λ PROLOG. In R. A. Kowalski and K. A. Bowen, editors, *Proceedings of the Fifth International Conference and Symposium on Logic Programming*, pages 810–827, Seatle, 1988. ALP, IEEE, The MIT Press.

[NQ91] T. Nipkow and Z. Qian. Modular higher-order E-unification. In R. V. Book, editor, *Proceedings 4th Conference on Rewriting Techniques and Applications, Como (Italy)*, volume 488 of *Lecture Notes in Computer Science*, pages 200–214. Springer-Verlag, 1991.

[Pag] B. Pagano. Extensions of lambda-calculi with explicit substitutions preserving the church-rosser's property. Manuscript.

[QW96] Z. Qian and K. Wang. Modular higher-order equational preunification. *Journal of Symbolic Computation*, 22(4):401–424, October 1996.

[Río93] A. Ríos. *Contributions à l'étude des λ-calculs avec des substitutions explicites*. Thèse de Doctorat d'Université, U. Paris VII, 1993.

[Sny90] W. Snyder. Higher-order E-unification. In M. E. Stickel, editor, *Proceedings 10th International Conference on Automated Deduction, Kaiserslautern (Germany)*, volume 449 of *Lecture Notes in Computer Science*, pages 573–587, July 1990.

Parameterised Higher–Order Algebraic Specifications

L. J. Steggles

Department of Computer Science, University of Newcastle upon Tyne,
Newcastle upon Tyne, NE1 7RU.
email: L.J.Steggles@ncl.ac.uk

Abstract. Motivated by the need to address the issue of specification in the large and the problems of specifying a full function space we consider extending the theory of parameterised algebraic specifications to the higher–order case. We develop the notion of a higher–order abstract parameterised data type and a parameterised higher–order equational specification. Due to the nature of the higher–order initial model we cannot extend the results for the first–order free functor semantics to the higher–order case and thus we present a concrete construction of a functor which we take to be the semantics of a parameterised higher–order equational specification. We demonstrate the theory we develop by considering a detailed specification case study of a second–order abstract parameterised data type for convolution.

1 Introduction.

In recent years there has been increasing interest in higher–order algebraic methods. Research has centred around developing and investigating the fundamental theory of higher–order algebra (see for example the papers Möller [1987], Möller et al [1988], Meinke [1992, 1995] and Kosiuczenko and Meinke [1995]) and applying the methods to small benchmark case studies (see for example Meinke and Steggles [1994, 1996] and Steggles [1995]). This work has shown that higher–order algebra provides a natural and expressive formal framework in which to model and reason about computing systems. However, in order for higher–order algebra to be accepted as a practical formal method further research is needed into the issues of specification in the large, such as modular design, specification reuse and machine assistance.

In this paper we begin to address these issues by formulating a theory for *parameterised higher–order algebraic specifications*. A parameterised specification is a specification which contains a distinguished formal parameter part, the structure and semantics of which are left open. Thus a formal parameter acts as a place holder allowing suitable actual parameters to be substituted into the specification. Parameterised specifications allow generic data types to be specified facilitating the reuse of specifications and provide a simple mechanism for structuring specifications. For an introduction to parameterised (first–order) specifications we suggest Thatcher et al [1978], Ehrig and Mahr [1985] and Wirsing [1990].

Further motivation for a theory of parameterised higher–order specifications is provided by the problems encountered when trying to specify a full stream space such as $[\mathbf{N} \to \mathbf{N}]$. The simple approach used in Meinke and Steggles [1994, 1996] is based on the method of diagrams; a stream constant $\hat{a}$ is included in the signature for each $a : \mathbf{N} \to \mathbf{N}$ and the equational diagram of the function space is then added to the equational specification. However, this approach results in an uncountable equational specification and thus excludes the possibility of encoding the specification onto a machine. One possible way around this problem is to use a parameterised specification in which the function space is a parameter. This approach is demonstrated in the case study presented in Section 5.

In this paper we consider extending the first–order theory of parameterised specifications based on a free functor semantics (see for example Thatcher et al [1978], Ehrig et al [1984] and Ehrig and Mahr [1985]) to the higher–order case. We begin by generalizing the notion of a (higher–order) abstract data type to a *(higher–order) abstract parameterised data type* (APDT). An APDT is a 3–tuple consisting of: a tuple of higher–order equational specifications, referred to as the *multiple formal parameter specification*, which specifies the parameterised part of the abstract data type; a higher–order equational specification, referred to as the *target specification*, which extends the formal parameter specifications; and an isomorphism class of functors which define how to map actual parameters to target data types. In order to specify APDTs we define the notion of a *parameterised higher–order equational specification* (or simply parameterised specification). A parameterised higher–order equational specification is a pair consisting of a multiple formal parameter specification and a target specification which extends the formal parameter specifications. We consider how to construct an APDT to represent the intended semantics of a parameterised specification. Following the usual first–order approach (see for example Ehrig and Mahr [1985]) we use the *A–quotient term algebra* construction to extend actual parameter algebras to target algebras. However, unlike in the first–order case, it turns out that in the higher–order case the A–quotient term algebra is not necessarily a *free construction*, due to the nature of the higher–order initial model. Thus it cannot be extended to a *free functor* which can be used as the basis of the semantics of a parameterised specification. We overcome this problem by giving a concrete construction of a functor based on the A–quotient term algebra which we argue represents the intended semantics of a parameterised specification. In particular, we note that this new functor respects the first–order free functor semantics. We conclude by considering what it means for a parameterised specification to *correctly* specify an APDT.

We demonstrate the theory of parameterised higher–order specifications we have developed by considering a detailed case study of the specification of a second–order APDT for convolution in which the set of streams is parameterised. We construct a parameterised second–order equational specification which we prove correctly specifies the APDT of convolution. This case study demonstrates how parameterised higher–order specifications overcome the problem of requiring an infinite number of stream constants to specify a full stream space.

The paper is structured as follows. In Section 2 we begin with a brief introduction to higher–order algebra and by recalling some basic definitions and results of category theory. In Section 3 we introduce the notion of a higher–order abstract parameterised data type (APDT). In Section 4 we define the syntax and semantics of parameterised higher–order specifications and consider what it means for a parameterised higher–order equational specification to *correctly* specify a higher–order APDT. In Section 5 we demonstrate the ideas introduced in the preceding sections by considering a detailed case study of the specification of a second–order APDT for convolution. Finally, in Section 6 we discuss the theory of parameterised higher–order equational specifications we have presented.

2 Preliminaries.

In this section we briefly introduce the theory of higher–order algebra which we take from Meinke [1992] and present some basic definitions and results of category theory which are required to formulate the theory of parameterised specifications.

We begin by fixing our notation for many–sorted first–order universal algebra which is taken from Meinke and Tucker [1993].

A *many-sorted signature* (S, Σ) denoted by Σ consists of a non–empty set S, the elements of which are *sorts*, and an $S^* \times S$–indexed family $\langle \Sigma_{w,s} \mid w \in S^*,\ s \in S \rangle$ of sets of symbols. We usually refer to Σ as an *S–sorted signature.* An *S–sorted Σ algebra* is an ordered pair (A, Σ^A), consisting of an S–indexed family $A = \langle A_s \mid s \in S \rangle$ of *carrier sets* A_s and an $S^* \times S$–indexed family $\Sigma^A = \langle \Sigma^A_{w,s} \mid w \in S^*,\ s \in S \rangle$ of sets of constants and algebraic operations which interpret the symbols of the signature Σ. As usual, we allow A to denote both a Σ algebra and its S–indexed family of carrier sets. We assume that the reader is familiar with basic universal algebraic constructions and results.

The theory of higher–order universal algebra can be developed within the framework of many–sorted first–order universal algebra (see Meinke [1992]). We begin by defining notations for higher–order types.

2.1 Definition. By a *type basis* $\mathcal{B}$ we mean a non-empty set. The (finite) *type hierarchy* $H(\mathcal{B})$ generated by $\mathcal{B}$ is the set $H(\mathcal{B}) = \bigcup_{n \in \omega} H_n(\mathcal{B})$ of formal expressions defined inductively by $H_0(\mathcal{B}) = \mathcal{B}$, and

$$H_{n+1}(\mathcal{B}) = H_n(\mathcal{B}) \cup \{\ (\sigma \times \tau), (\sigma \to \tau) \mid \sigma, \tau \in H_n(\mathcal{B})\ \}.$$

Each $\tau \in \mathcal{B}$ is termed a *basic type*, each $(\sigma \times \tau) \in H(\mathcal{B})$ is termed a *product type* and each $(\sigma \to \tau) \in H(\mathcal{B})$ is termed a *function type.* □

We can assign an *order* $O(\tau) \in \mathbf{N}$ to each type $\tau \in H(\mathcal{B})$ inductively as follows. For each basic type $\tau \in \mathcal{B}$ define $O(\tau) = 0$. For any types $\sigma, \tau \in H(\mathcal{B})$ define $O(\sigma \times \tau) = sup\{O(\sigma), O(\tau)\}$, $\quad O(\sigma \to \tau) = sup\{O(\sigma) + 1, O(\tau)\}$.

2.2 Definition. A *type structure* S over a type basis $\mathcal{B}$ is a subset $S \subseteq H(\mathcal{B})$

which is closed under subtypes in the sense that for any types $\sigma, \tau \in H(\mathcal{B})$, if $(\sigma \times \tau) \in S$ or $(\sigma \rightarrow \tau) \in S$ then both $\sigma \in S$ and $\tau \in S$. We say that S is a *basic type structure* if, and only if, $S \subseteq \mathcal{B}$. A type structure $S \subseteq H(\mathcal{B})$ is said to be an *nth–order type structure* if, and only if, the order of each type $\tau \in S$ is strictly less than n. We say that S is an *ω–order type structure* if, and only if, there is no such $n \in \mathbf{N}$. □

In a *higher–order signature* Σ we take a type structure S as the sort set and include distinguished projection and evaluation function symbols.

2.3 Definition. Let $S \subseteq H(\mathcal{B})$ be a type structure over a type basis $\mathcal{B}$. An *S-typed signature* Σ is an S-sorted signature such that:
(i) for each product type $(\sigma \times \tau) \in S$ we have two unary *projection operation symbols* $proj^{(\sigma\times\tau),1} \in \Sigma_{(\sigma\times\tau),\sigma}$ and $proj^{(\sigma\times\tau),2} \in \Sigma_{(\sigma\times\tau),\tau}$;
(ii) for each function type $(\sigma \rightarrow \tau) \in S$ we have a binary *evaluation operation symbol* $eval^{(\sigma\rightarrow\tau)} \in \Sigma_{(\sigma\rightarrow\tau)\ \sigma,\tau}$. □

An S-typed signature Σ is also termed an *nth–order signature* when S is an nth–order type structure and $\mathcal{L}(\Sigma, X)$ is said to be an *nth–order language*. When the types σ and τ are clear we let $proj^1$ and $proj^2$ denote the projection operation symbols $proj^{(\sigma\times\tau),1}$ and $proj^{(\sigma\times\tau),2}$ respectively.

In the sequel let S be a type structure over a type basis $\mathcal{B}$, Σ be an S-typed signature and let X be an S-indexed family of sets of variables. Next we introduce the intended interpretations of a higher–order signature.

2.4 Definition. Let A be an S-sorted Σ algebra. We say that A is an *S-typed Σ algebra* if, and only if, for each product type $(\sigma \times \tau) \in S$ we have $A_{(\sigma\times\tau)} \subseteq A_\sigma \times A_\tau$, and for each function type $(\sigma \rightarrow \tau) \in S$ we have $A_{(\sigma\rightarrow\tau)} \subseteq [A_\sigma \rightarrow A_\tau]$, i.e. $A_{(\sigma\rightarrow\tau)}$ is a subset of the set of all (total) functions from A_σ to A_τ. Furthermore, for each product type $(\sigma \times \tau) \in S$ the operations

$$proj_A^{(\sigma\times\tau),1} : A_{(\sigma\times\tau)} \rightarrow A_\sigma, \quad proj_A^{(\sigma\times\tau),2} : A_{(\sigma\times\tau)} \rightarrow A_\tau,$$

are the standard *first* and *second projection operations*; and for each function type $(\sigma \rightarrow \tau) \in S$ the operation $eval_A^{(\sigma\rightarrow\tau)} : A_{(\sigma\rightarrow\tau)} \times A_\sigma \rightarrow A_\tau$ is the standard *evaluation operation*.

We let $Alg_{typ}(\Sigma)$ denote the class of all S-typed Σ algebras. Given any set $\Phi \subseteq \mathcal{L}(\Sigma, X)$ of Σ formulas we let $Alg_{typ}(\Sigma, \Phi)$ denote the class of all S-typed Σ algebras which are models of Φ. □

An S-typed Σ algebra is also termed an *nth–order Σ algebra* when Σ is an nth–order signature. When S is a basic type structure an S-typed Σ algebra is just an S-sorted Σ algebra. Given any S-typed Σ algebra A and any function type $(\sigma \rightarrow \tau) \in S$ we may write $a(n)$ as an abbreviation for $eval_A^{(\sigma\rightarrow\tau)}(a, n)$, for any $a \in A_{(\sigma\rightarrow\tau)}$ and $n \in A_\sigma$.

From the viewpoint both of algebra and specification theory we are mainly concerned with the structure of higher-order algebras up to isomorphism. This structure can be characterised by a set of first-order sentences as follows.

2.5 Definition. The set $\mathbf{Ext} = \mathbf{Ext}_{\Sigma}$ of *extensionality sentences* over Σ is the set of all Σ sentences of the form

$$\forall x\ \forall y\ (proj^1(x) = proj^1(y)\ \wedge\ proj^2(x) = proj^2(y) \Rightarrow x = y),$$

for each product type $(\sigma \times \tau) \in S$ and variables $x, y \in X_{(\sigma\times\tau)}$, and

$$\forall x\ \forall y\ (\forall z\ (eval^{(\sigma\to\tau)}(x,z) = eval^{(\sigma\to\tau)}(y,z)) \Rightarrow x = y),$$

for each function type $(\sigma \to \tau) \in S$ and variables $x, y \in X_{(\sigma\to\tau)}$ and $z \in X_{\sigma}$.

We say that a Σ algebra A is *extensional* if, and only if, $A \models \mathbf{Ext}$. We let $Alg_{Ext}(\Sigma)$ denote the class $Alg(\Sigma, \mathbf{Ext})$ of all extensional Σ algebras and $Alg_{Ext}(\Sigma, \Phi)$ denote the class $Alg(\Sigma, \mathbf{Ext} \cup \Phi)$, for any set $\Phi \subseteq \mathcal{L}(\Sigma, X)$. □

It is straightforward to show that a Σ algebra A is isomorphic to an S-typed Σ algebra if, and only if, A is extensional (see Meinke [1992]).

We are interested in specifying higher-order algebras or classes of higher-order algebras by means of higher-order formulas, i.e. many-sorted first-order formulas over a higher-order signature Σ. By a higher-order equation over Σ and X we mean a formula of the form

$$t = t',$$

where $t, t' \in T(\Sigma, X)_{\tau}$, for some type $\tau \in S$. We let $Eqn(\Sigma, X)$ denote the set of all higher-order equations over Σ and X. An equation $t = t' \in Eqn(\Sigma, X)$ is said to be *ground* if, and only if, t and t' have no free variables. Given any Σ algebra A, we have the usual notion of truth for an equation under an assignment $\alpha : X \to A$, and the usual validity relation $\models$ on an equation or set of equations. An *equational theory* E over Σ and X is a set of equations $E \subseteq Eqn(\Sigma, X)$.

Let E be an equational theory over Σ and X. The *extensional equational class* $Alg_{Ext}(\Sigma, E)$ can be shown to be an *extensional variety*, i.e. a class of extensional Σ algebras closed under the formation of extensional homomorphic images, extensional subalgebras and direct products. In general $Alg_{Ext}(\Sigma, E)$ does not admit an initial algebra. However, by a basic result of higher-order universal algebra (see Meinke [1992]) $Alg_{Ext}(\Sigma, E)$ admits an algebra $I_{Ext}(\Sigma, E)$ which is initial in the subclass $Min_{Ext}(\Sigma, E)$ of all minimal extensional Σ algebras which are models of E. Thus $I_{Ext}(\Sigma, E)$ is initial in a weaker, but nontrivial sense and unique up to isomorphism. We refer to $I_{Ext}(\Sigma, E)$ as the *higher-order initial model* and use it as the appropriate higher-order initial algebra semantics of the pair $Spec = (\Sigma, E)$ viewed as a higher-order equational specification.

Higher-order initial models can be concretely constructed from syntax using a *higher-order equational calculus*. This calculus extends the many-sorted first-order equational calculus with additional inference rules for higher types and contains an infinitary inference rule.

2.6 Definition. *Higher-order equational logic* extends the rules of first-order equational logic (see Meinke and Tucker [1993]) as follows.
(i) For each product type $(\sigma \times \tau) \in S$ and any terms $t_0, t_1 \in T(\Sigma, X)_{(\sigma\times\tau)}$,

$$\frac{proj^1(t_0) = proj^1(t_1), \quad proj^2(t_0) = proj^2(t_1)}{t_0 = t_1}$$

is a *projection* rule.
(ii) For each function type $(\sigma \to \tau) \in S$, any terms $t_0, t_1 \in T(\Sigma, X)_{(\sigma\to\tau)}$ and any variable symbol $x \in X_\sigma$ not occurring in t_0 or t_1,

$$\frac{eval^{(\sigma\to\tau)}(t_0, x) = eval^{(\sigma\to\tau)}(t_1, x)}{t_0 = t_1}$$

is an (finitary) *evaluation* rule.
(iii) For each function type $(\sigma \to \tau) \in S$ and any terms $t_0, t_1 \in T(\Sigma, X)_{(\sigma\to\tau)}$,

$$\frac{\langle eval^{(\sigma\to\tau)}(t_0, t) = eval^{(\sigma\to\tau)}(t_1, t) \mid t \in T(\Sigma)_\sigma \rangle}{t_0 = t_1}$$

is an (infinitary) *ω-evaluation rule.* □

We let $\vdash_\omega$ denote the inference relation between equational theories $E \subseteq Eqn(\Sigma, X)$ and equations $e \in Eqn(\Sigma, X)$, defined by $E \vdash_\omega e$ if, and only if, there exists an (infinitary) proof of e from E using the inference rules of higher-order equational logic. Clearly, if $E \vdash_\omega e$ then $A \models e$, for every minimal extensional Σ, E algebra A. We note that the finitary higher-order equational calculus obtained by omitting inference rule (iii) is complete with respect to extensional models (see Meinke [1992]). Define the extensional Σ congruence $\equiv^{E,\omega} = \langle \equiv_\tau^{E,\omega} \mid \tau \in S \rangle$ on the term algebra $T(\Sigma)$ by $t \equiv_\tau^{E,\omega} t' \Leftrightarrow E \vdash_\omega t = t'$, for each type $\tau \in S$ and any terms $t, t' \in T(\Sigma)_\tau$. Factoring $T(\Sigma)$ by the congruence $\equiv^{E,\omega}$ gives a concrete construction of the higher-order initial model $I_{Ext}(\Sigma, E)$.

2.7 Theorem. *Let Σ be an S-typed signature. Let $E \subseteq Eqn(\Sigma, X)$ be any equational theory over Σ. Then $T(\Sigma)/\equiv^{E,\omega} \cong I_{Ext}(\Sigma, E)$. Thus $T(\Sigma)/\equiv^{E,\omega}$ is initial in the class $Min_{Ext}(\Sigma, E)$ of all minimal extensional models of E.*

Proof. See Meinke [1992]. □

Next we introduce the basic definitions and results of category theory needed in the sequel. For a comprehensive introduction to category theory we suggest MacLane [1971] and Barr and Wells [1990]. We begin by recalling the definition of a category.

2.8 Definition. A *category* **C** consists of: a class of *objects* $|\mathbf{C}|$; for any objects $A, B \in |\mathbf{C}|$, a set of *morphisms* $\mathbf{C}(A, B)$ (when no ambiguity arises we write $f : A \to B \in \mathbf{C}$ or simply $f : A \to B$ to denote that $f \in \mathbf{C}(A, B)$); and a family of ***composition operations***

$$\circ_{\mathbf{C}} = \langle \circ_{\mathbf{C}}^{A,B,C} : \mathbf{C}(B,C) \times \mathbf{C}(A,B) \to \mathbf{C}(A,C) \mid A,B,C \in |\mathbf{C}| \rangle,$$

(when the category $\mathbf{C}$ and objects $A, B, C \in |\mathbf{C}|$ are clear we write $\circ_{\mathbf{C}}$ or simply $\circ$ to denote $\circ_{\mathbf{C}}^{A,B,C}$). A category must also satisfy the following conditions:
(1) composition is ***associative***, i.e. for all morphisms $f : A \to B$, $g : B \to C$, $h : C \to D \in \mathbf{C}$, we have $(h \circ g) \circ f = h \circ (g \circ f)$.
(2) for each object $A \in |\mathbf{C}|$ there exists an ***identity morphism*** $id_A \in \mathbf{C}(A, A)$ satisfying $f \circ id_A = f$ and $id_A \circ g = g$, for all $f : A \to B$, $g : B \to A \in \mathbf{C}$. □

Let us illustrate the above definition with a simple example.

2.9 Example. Given a higher–order algebraic specification $Spec = (\Sigma, \Phi)$ we can define a category $\mathbf{Cat}(Spec)$ as follows. Define the objects of $\mathbf{Cat}(Spec)$ to be all the extensional Σ algebras which are models of Φ, i.e. $|\mathbf{Cat}(Spec)| = Alg_{Ext}(\Sigma, \Phi)$, and define the morphisms to be all homomorphisms between the objects of $\mathbf{Cat}(Spec)$. The composition operation is simply defined to be the normal composition of homomorphisms and the identity morphism $id_A : A \to A \in \mathbf{Cat}(Spec)$, for each object $A \in |\mathbf{Cat}(Spec)|$, is the identity homomorphism. Clearly, $\mathbf{Cat}(Spec)$ is a well defined category. The isomorphisms in $\mathbf{Cat}(Spec)$ are exactly the bijective homomorphisms. □

Next we recall the definition of a *functor* between two categories.

2.10 Definition. Let $\mathbf{C}$ and $\mathbf{C}'$ be two categories. By a *functor* $F : \mathbf{C} \to \mathbf{C}'$ we mean a mapping which assigns to each object $A \in |\mathbf{C}|$ an object $F(A) \in |\mathbf{C}'|$ and to each morphism $g : A \to B \in \mathbf{C}$ a morphism $F(g) : F(A) \to F(B) \in \mathbf{C}'$ such that the following two conditions hold.
(i) For any morphisms $f : B \to C, g : A \to B \in \mathbf{C}$ we have $F(f \circ g) = F(f) \circ F(g)$.
(ii) For each object $A \in |\mathbf{C}|$ we have $F(id_A) = id_{F(A)}$. □

Let $\mathbf{C}$ be any category then the ***identity functor*** $Id_{\mathbf{C}} : \mathbf{C} \to \mathbf{C}$ is defined by $Id_{\mathbf{C}}(A) = A$ and $Id_{\mathbf{C}}(f) = f$, for each object $A \in |\mathbf{C}|$ and each morphism $f : A \to B \in \mathbf{C}$. The relationship between two functors may be characterised by a family of morphisms referred to as a natural transformation.

2.11 Definition. Let $\mathbf{C}$ and $\mathbf{C}'$ be two categories, and let $F, G : \mathbf{C} \to \mathbf{C}'$ be two functors. Then a family of morphisms

$$u = \langle u(A) : F(A) \to G(A) \mid A \in |\mathbf{C}| \rangle$$

in $\mathbf{C}'$ is said to be a ***natural transformation***, denoted $u : F \to G$, if, and only if, for each morphism $f : A \to B \in \mathbf{C}$ we have $u(B) \circ F(f) = G(f) \circ u(A)$. A natural transformation $u : F \to G$ is said to be a ***natural isomorphism***, denoted $u : F \cong G$, if and only if, each morphism $u(A) \in u$ is an isomorphism. We let

$Iso(F) = \{G : \mathbf{C} \to \mathbf{C}' \mid G \cong F\}$ denote the class of functors isomorphic to a functor $F : \mathbf{C} \to \mathbf{C}'$. □

The concept of a free algebra found in universal algebra can be generalized to a *free construction* in category theory as follows.

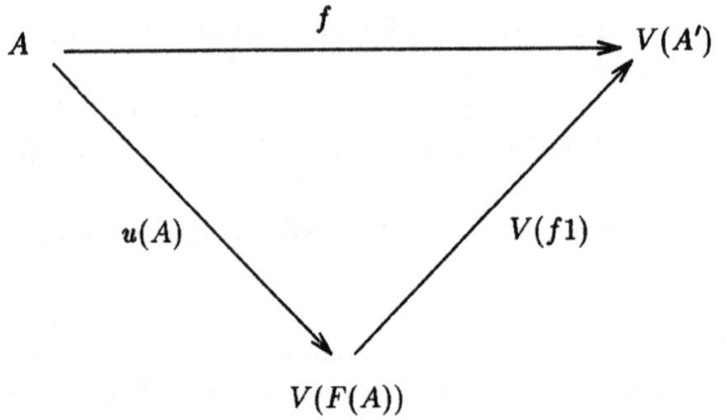

Fig. 1. Commutative diagram for free construction.

2.12 Definition. Let $\mathbf{C}$ and $\mathbf{C}'$ be any two categories, $V : \mathbf{C}' \to \mathbf{C}$ be any functor and $A \in |\mathbf{C}|$. Then $F(A) \in |\mathbf{C}'|$ is said to be a *free construction over A with respect to V* if, and only if, there exists a morphism $u(A) : A \to V(F(A)) \in \mathbf{C}$, called the *universal morphism*, which satisfies the following *universal property*: for each object $A' \in |\mathbf{C}'|$ and each morphism $f : A \to V(A') \in \mathbf{C}$ there exists a unique morphism $f1 : F(A) \to A' \in \mathbf{C}'$ such that $V(f1) \circ u(A) = f$. That is the diagram in Figure 1 commutes. □

Note that the free construction $F(A)$ and the universal morphism $u(A) : A \to V(F(A))$ are uniquely determined up to isomorphism. If a free construction $F(A)$ over A with respect to V exists for all objects $A \in |\mathbf{C}|$ we can extend it to a *free functor* as follows.

2.13 Lemma. *Let $F : |\mathbf{C}| \to |\mathbf{C}'|$ be a mapping such that for each object $A \in |\mathbf{C}|$, $F(A) \in |\mathbf{C}'|$ is a free construction over A with respect to a given functor $V : \mathbf{C}' \to \mathbf{C}$. Then we can extend F to a functor $F : \mathbf{C} \to \mathbf{C}'$, called a free functor with respect to V, by defining F on the morphisms of $\mathbf{C}$ as follows. For each morphism $h : A \to B \in \mathbf{C}$ define $F(h) : F(A) \to F(B) \in \mathbf{C}'$ to be the unique morphism such that $u(B) \circ h = V(F(h)) \circ u(A)$.*

Proof. See Ehrig and Mahr [1985]. □

Note that free functors are uniquely determined upto isomorphism and are closed under composition.

3 Abstract Parameterised Higher–Order Data Types.

In algebraic specification a data type is modelled by an algebra, that is a collection of data sets with some associated operations defined on them. An abstract data type can then be naturally defined as an isomorphism class of algebras, i.e. a class of algebras which differ only in their concrete representation of data. In this section we generalize these concepts to the parameterised case following the approach of Thatcher et al [1978] and Ehrig et al [1984]. We define a parameterised data type to be essentially a functor from the category of actual parameter algebras to the category of target algebras. An abstract parameterised data type then naturally corresponds to an isomorphism class of functors.

Before being able to formulate the definition of an abstract parameterised data type we need a few technical definitions.

3.1 Definition. A *multiple formal parameter specification*

$$Spec^{(P1,\ldots,Pn)} = (Spec^{P1}, \ldots, Spec^{Pn})$$

is an n-tuple of higher–order equational specifications, for some $n \in \mathbf{N}$. For each $1 \leq i \leq n$ the higher–order equational specification $Spec^{Pi} = ((S_{Pi}, \Sigma^{Pi}), E^{Pi})$ is referred to as a *formal parameter specification*. For convenience we define

$$S_P = S_{P1} \cup \cdots \cup S_{Pn}, \ \Sigma^P = \Sigma^{P1} \cup \cdots \cup \Sigma^{Pn}, \ E^P = E^{P1} \cup \cdots \cup E^{Pn}. \qquad \square$$

By the very nature of formal parameter specifications they will in general lack the necessary generating symbols needed to ensure their initial algebra semantics is meaningful. Thus we choose to use the loose semantics of the formal parameter specifications and define the category $\mathbf{Pcat}(Spec^{(P1,\ldots,Pn)})$.

3.2 Definition. Let $Spec^{(P1,\ldots,Pn)} = (Spec^{P1}, \ldots, Spec^{Pn})$ be a multiple formal parameter specification. Then we define the category $\mathbf{Pcat}(Spec^{(P1,\ldots,Pn)})$ as follows.

Define the objects of $\mathbf{Pcat}(Spec^{(P1,\ldots,Pn)})$ to be all n–tuples

$$(A(1), \ldots, A(n)) \in (Alg_{Ext}(Spec^{P1}) \times \cdots \times Alg_{Ext}(Spec^{Pn})),$$

such that for any $1 \leq i, j \leq n$ and any $\tau \in S_{Pi} \cap S_{Pj}$ we have $A(i)_\tau = A(j)_\tau$, and for any $w \in (S_{Pi} \cap S_{Pj})^*$, $\tau \in S_{Pi} \cap S_{Pj}$ and any $f \in \Sigma^{Pi}_{w,\tau} \cap \Sigma^{Pj}_{w,\tau}$ we have $f_{A(i)} = f_{A(j)}$. We define the set of morphisms $\mathbf{Pcat}(Spec^{(P1,\ldots,Pn)})(A, B)$, for objects $A = (A(1), \ldots, A(n)), B = (B(1), \ldots, B(n)) \in |\mathbf{Pcat}(Spec^{(P1,\ldots,Pn)})|$, to consist of all n-tuples $f = (f^1, \ldots, f^n)$ such that
(i) for each $1 \leq i \leq n$, $f^i : A(i) \to B(i)$ is a surjective homomorphism, and
(ii) for any $1 \leq i, j \leq n$ and any $\tau \in S_{Pi} \cap S_{Pj}$ we have $f^i_\tau = f^j_\tau$.

Finally, we define the composition operation $\circ_{\mathbf{Pcat}(Spec^{(P1,\ldots,Pn)})}$ to be simply the pointwise application of the ordinary composition operation on functions. It is straightforward to check that $\mathbf{Pcat}(Spec^{(P1,\ldots,Pn)})$ is a well defined category.

Note that if $n = 0$ then $\mathbf{Pcat}(Spec^{(P1,\ldots,Pn)})$ is taken to be a unit category. □

We refer to each object $A \in |\mathbf{Pcat}(Spec^{(P1,\ldots,Pn)})|$ as an *actual parameter*. Note that since we do not insist that the formal parameter specifications are disjoint we have had to ensure that the objects and morphisms of $\mathbf{Pcat}(Spec^{(P1,\ldots,Pn)})$ are comprised of consistent actual parameter algebras respectively epimorphisms. We restrict the morphisms of $\mathbf{Pcat}(Spec^{(P1,\ldots,Pn)})$ to being epimorphisms since the property of surjectivity is needed to prove a number of technical results in the higher–order case (see Lemma 4.5).

We may now define the concept of an abstract parameterised data type.

3.3 Definition. A *(higher–order) abstract parameterised data type* (APDT)

$$APDT = (Spec^{(MP1,\ldots,MPn)}, Spec^{MT}, Iso(M))$$

is a 3–tuple consisting of:
(i) a *multiple formal parameter specification* $Spec^{(MP1,\ldots,MPn)} = (Spec^{MP1}, \ldots, Spec^{MPn})$;
(ii) a *target specification* $Spec^{MT} = (\Sigma^{MT}, E^{MT})$, which extends each formal parameter specification $Spec^{MPi} = (\Sigma^{MPi}, E^{MPi})$, i.e. $S_{MPi} \subseteq S_{MT}$, $\Sigma^{MPi} \subseteq \Sigma^{MT}$ and $E^{MPi} \subseteq E^{MT}$;
(iii) an isomorphism class of functors $Iso(M)$, where

$$M : \mathbf{Pcat}(Spec^{(MP1,\ldots,MPn)}) \rightarrow \mathbf{Cat}(Spec^{MT}),$$

is a functor referred to as the *model functor*. □

Clearly an APDT generalizes the notion of an abstract data type since if the multiple formal parameter specification is empty then the model functor is from a one object category and simply picks out an isomorphism class of target algebras. The axioms in the formal parameter and target specifications are used to simplify the definition of the model functor for an APDT.

The above ideas are illustrated in Section 5 where a second–order abstract parameterised data type $APDT(Conv)$ for convolution is presented.

4 Parameterised Higher–Order Specifications.

In this section we consider how to specify APDTs and develop a theory of parameterised higher–order equational specifications based on the standard first–order theory (see for example Thatcher et al [1978], Ehrig et al [1984] and Ehrig and Mahr [1985]). We begin by introducing the syntax of parameterised higher–order equational specifications. We then consider how to construct the intended semantics of a parameterised higher–order equational specification. We conclude the section by considering what it means for a parameterised specification to *correctly* specify an APDT.

4.1 Definition. A *parameterised higher-order equational specification*

$$PSpec = (Spec^{(P1,\ldots,Pn)}, Spec^T)$$

is an ordered pair consisting of a *multiple formal parameter specification*

$$Spec^{(P1,\ldots,Pn)} = (Spec^{P1}, \ldots, Spec^{Pn}),$$

and a *target specification* $Spec^T = ((S_T, \Sigma^T), E^T)$ which extends the formal parameter specifications, i.e. for each formal parameter specification $Spec^{Pi} = ((S_{Pi}, \Sigma^{Pi}), E^{Pi})$ we have $S_{Pi} \subseteq S_T$, $\Sigma^{Pi} \subseteq \Sigma^T$, $E^{Pi} \subseteq E^T$. □

In the sequel we refer to parameterised higher-order equational specifications as simply parameterised specifications. Also we will often denote parameterised specifications by names such as *String(Data)*, *Stack(Datau)* and *Stream(Datau)*. In this notation the names in brackets are the formal parameter specifications (e.g. *Data* and *Datau*) and, in a slight abuse of notation, the whole name is the target specification.

The above definitions and ideas are illustrated in Section 5 where a parameterised second-order equational specification *Conv(Time, Ring, Stream)* for convolution is presented.

Recall that given any multiple formal parameter specification $Spec^{(P1,\ldots,Pn)} = (Spec^{P1}, \ldots, Spec^{Pn})$ we define $((S_P, \Sigma^P), E^P)$ to be the union of the formal parameter specifications (see Definition 3.1). We now consider how to construct an APDT which represents the intended meaning (semantics) of a parameterised specification. We begin by considering how to extend an actual parameter $A \in |\mathbf{Pcat}(Spec^{(P1,\ldots,Pn)})|$ to a target algebra $F_{PSpec}(A) \in |\mathbf{Cat}(Spec^T)|$. Following the first-order approach we define the (higher-order) A-quotient term algebra construction as follows.

4.2 Definition. Let $PSpec = (Spec^{(P1,\ldots,Pn)}, Spec^T)$ be a parameterised specification and let $A = (A(1), \ldots, A(n)) \in |\mathbf{Pcat}(Spec^{(P1,\ldots,Pn)})|$ be an actual parameter. Then we have the following definitions.
(i) Let $\overline{A}$ be the S_P-typed Σ^P algebra defined as follows. For each $1 \leq i \leq n$ and each $\tau \in S_{Pi}$ define the carrier set $\overline{A}_\tau = A(i)_\tau$, and for each $w \in S^*_{Pi}$, $\tau \in S_{Pi}$ and each $f \in \Sigma^{Pi}_{w,\tau}$ define $f_{\overline{A}} = f_{A(i)}$. Clearly $\overline{A}$ is a well defined higher-order algebra by definition of the objects of $\mathbf{Pcat}(Spec^{(P1,\ldots,Pn)})$.
(ii) Define the S_P-typed signature $\Sigma^P[A]$ by $\Sigma^P[A]_{\lambda,\tau} = \Sigma^P_{\lambda,\tau} \cup \{\overline{a} \mid a \in \overline{A}_\tau\}$, for each $\tau \in S_P$, and $\Sigma^P[A]_{w,\tau} = \Sigma^P_{w,\tau}$, for each $w \in S^+_P$ and $\tau \in S_P$.
(iii) Let $Eqn[A] = Eqn_{\overline{A}}(\Sigma^P[A])$ be the ground equational diagram defined by

$$Eqn[A] = \{t = t' \mid t, t' \in T(\Sigma^P[A])_\tau, \tau \in S_P \text{ and } t_{\overline{A}} = t'_{\overline{A}}\},$$

where $\overline{A}$ denotes both itself and the $\Sigma^P[A]$ extension of $\overline{A}$ defined by distinguishing a constant $\overline{a}_{\overline{A}} = a$, for each type $\tau \in S_P$ and each $a \in \overline{A}_\tau$.
(iv) Define the higher-order equational specification

$$Spec^T[A] = Spec^T \cup (\Sigma^P[A], Eqn[A]).$$

We refer to $Spec^T[A]$ as the *A–enlargement* of $Spec^T$.
(v) Finally, we define the S_T–typed Σ^T algebra

$$F_{PSpec}(A) = V_A(I_{Ext}(Spec^T[A])),$$

where $V_A : \mathbf{Cat}(Spec^T[A]) \to \mathbf{Cat}(Spec^T)$ is the forgetful functor. We refer to $F_{PSpec}(A)$ as the (higher–order) *A–quotient term algebra.* □

For a first–order parameterised specification $PSpec = (Spec^{(P1,\ldots,Pn)}, Spec^T)$ and any actual parameter $A \in |\mathbf{Pcat}(Spec^{(P1,\ldots,Pn)})|$ the A–quotient term algebra can be shown to be a free construction over A with respect to the forgetful functor $V : \mathbf{Cat}(Spec^T) \to \mathbf{Pcat}(Spec^{(P1,\ldots,Pn)})$. So by Lemma 2.13 it can be extended to a free functor which can be used to define the semantics of *PSpec* (see Ehrig and Mahr [1985]). However, it turns out that in the higher–order case the A–quotient term algebra is not necessarily a free construction due to the higher–order initial model being initial only in the class of all minimal models satisfying a higher–order equational specification. Thus the (higher–order) A–quotient term algebra construction cannot automatically be extended to a free functor. To overcome this problem we give a concrete construction of a functor

$$F_{PSpec} : \mathbf{Pcat}(Spec^{(P1,\ldots,Pn)}) \to \mathbf{Cat}(Spec^T),$$

for a parameterised higher–order specification $PSpec = (Spec^{(P1,\ldots,Pn)}, Spec^T)$ which is based on the natural A–quotient term algebra construction. We claim this functor represents the intended semantics of a higher–order parameterised specification despite not necessarily being a free functor. This claim is supported by the fact that this new functor preserves the first–order free functor semantics.

In the following let $PSpec = (Spec^{(P1,\ldots,Pn)}, Spec^T)$ be a parameterised specification, let $A = (A(1), \ldots, A(n)), B = (B(1), \ldots, B(n)) \in |\mathbf{Pcat}(Spec^{(P1,\ldots,Pn)})|$ and let $f = (f^1, \ldots, f^n) : A \to B \in \mathbf{Pcat}(Spec^{(P1,\ldots,Pn)})$. For any $A \in |\mathbf{Pcat}(Spec^{(P1,\ldots,Pn)})|$ define the S_T–typed signature $\Sigma^T[A]$ by $\Sigma^T[A] = \Sigma^T \cup \Sigma^P[A]$. We begin by considering how to extend a morphism $f : A \to B \in \mathbf{Pcat}(Spec^{(P1,\ldots,Pn)})$ to a mapping between $\Sigma^T[A]$ and $\Sigma^T[B]$ terms.

4.3 Definition. Let $X = \langle X_\tau \mid \tau \in S_T \rangle$ be an S_T–indexed family of sets of variables. Define the S_T–indexed family of mappings

$$\alpha(f) = \langle \alpha(f)_\tau : T(\Sigma^T[A], X)_\tau \to T(\Sigma^T[B], X)_\tau \mid \tau \in S_T \rangle,$$

as follows.
(i) For each type $\tau \in S_T$ and each variable $x \in X_\tau$ define $\alpha(f)_\tau(x) = x$.
(ii) For each $1 \le i \le n$, each $\tau \in S_{Pi}$ and each $a \in A(i)_\tau$ define $\alpha(f)_\tau(\overline{a}) = \overline{f^i_\tau(a)}$.
(iii) For each type $\tau \in S_T$ and each constant symbol $c \in \Sigma^T_{\lambda,\tau}$ define $\alpha(f)_\tau(c) = c$.
(iv) For each $w = \tau(1)\ldots\tau(m) \in S_T^+$, $\tau \in S_T$, each function symbol $h \in \Sigma^T_{w,\tau}$ and any terms $t_1 \in T(\Sigma^T[A], X)_{\tau(1)}, \ldots, t_m \in T(\Sigma^T[A], X)_{\tau(m)}$ define

$$\alpha(f)_\tau(h(t_1, \ldots, t_m)) = h(\alpha(f)_{\tau(1)}(t_1), \ldots, \alpha(f)_{\tau(m)}(t_m)).$$ □

We need the following technical results about the term mapping $\alpha(f)$.

4.4 Lemma. *For any $1 \leq i \leq n$, any type $\tau \in S_{Pi}$ and any term $t \in T(\Sigma^P[A])_\tau$ we have*

$$\alpha(f)_\tau(t)_{\overline{B}} = f^i_\tau(t_{\overline{A}}).$$

Proof. By induction on the construction of terms. □

4.5 Lemma. *For any type $\tau \in S_T$ and any terms $t, t' \in T(\Sigma^T[A], X)_\tau$,*

$$E^T \cup Eqn[A] \vdash_\omega t = t' \implies E^T \cup Eqn[B] \vdash_\omega \alpha(f)_\tau(t) = \alpha(f)_\tau(t').$$

Proof. Let $\tau \in S_T$ and $t, t' \in T(\Sigma^T[A], X)_\tau$, and suppose that

$$E^T \cup Eqn[A] \vdash_\omega t = t'. \tag{1}$$

Then we show that $E^T \cup Eqn[B] \vdash_\omega \alpha(f)_\tau(t) = \alpha(f)_\tau(t')$, by induction on the construction of higher-order equational proofs.

Basis. We have three cases to consider.
(i) Suppose $t = t' \in Eqn[A]$, for some $1 \leq i \leq n$, $\tau \in S_{Pi}$ and terms $t, t' \in T(\Sigma^P[A])_\tau$. Then by definition of $Eqn[A]$, $f^i_\tau(t_{\overline{A}}) = f^i_\tau(t'_{\overline{A}})$ and so by Lemma 4.4, $\alpha(f)_\tau(t)_{\overline{B}} = \alpha(f)_\tau(t')_{\overline{B}}$. Since t and t' are ground terms we can easily show that $\alpha(f)_\tau(t)$ and $\alpha(f)_\tau(t')$ are ground terms. So by definition of $Eqn[B]$ we have $\alpha(f)_\tau(t) = \alpha(f)_\tau(t') \in Eqn[B]$ and thus $E^T \cup Eqn[B] \vdash_\omega \alpha(f)_\tau(t) = \alpha(f)_\tau(t')$.
(ii) Let $\tau \in S_T$, let $t, t' \in T(\Sigma^T, X)_\tau$ and suppose that $t = t' \in E^T$. Then since t and t' are terms over just Σ^T and X we can easily show that $\alpha(f)_\tau(t) = t$ and $\alpha(f)_\tau(t') = t'$. Thus it follows that $E^T \cup Eqn[B] \vdash_\omega \alpha(f)_\tau(t) = \alpha(f)_\tau(t')$.
(iii) Suppose that (1) was derived by reflexivity, i.e. t and t' are identical terms. Then it follows by reflexivity that $E^T \cup Eqn[B] \vdash_\omega \alpha(f)_\tau(t) = \alpha(f)_\tau(t')$.

Induction step. We have six cases to consider corresponding to the symmetry, transitivity, substitution, projection, evaluation and ω–evaluation rules. We only present a proof for the ω–evaluation rule since the proofs for the remaining rules are straightforward or follow along similar lines.

Suppose $\tau = (\sigma \to \sigma')$, for some $\sigma, \sigma' \in S_T$ and that (1) was derived by the ω–evaluation rule. Then it follows that for each $t_0 \in T(\Sigma^T[A])_\sigma$

$$E^T \cup Eqn[A] \vdash_\omega t(t_0) = t'(t_0).$$

So by the induction hypothesis and the definition of $\alpha(f)$

$$E^T \cup Eqn[B] \vdash_\omega \alpha(f)_{(\sigma\to\sigma')}(t)(\alpha(f)_\sigma(t_0)) = \alpha(f)_{(\sigma\to\sigma')}(t')(\alpha(f)_\sigma(t_0)), \tag{2}$$

for each $t_0 \in T(\Sigma^T[A])_\sigma$. Since by definition of $\mathbf{Pcat}(Spec^{(P1,\ldots,Pn)})$ we know f^i is an epimorphism, for $1 \leq i \leq n$, we can easily show that $\alpha(f)$ is a surjective family of mappings. So it follows that for each term $t_1 \in T(\Sigma^T[B])_\sigma$ there exists a term $t_2 \in T(\Sigma^T[A])_\sigma$ such that $t_1 = \alpha(f)_\sigma(t_2)$. Thus by (2) and the

ω–evaluation rule we have $E^T \cup Eqn[B] \vdash_\omega \alpha(f)_{(\sigma\to\sigma')}(t) = \alpha(f)_{(\sigma\to\sigma')}(t')$. □

We now use the A–quotient term algebra construction and the term mapping $\alpha(f)$ to define the functor F_{PSpec} as follows.

4.6 Definition. The functor $F_{PSpec} : \mathbf{Pcat}(Spec^{(P1,\ldots,Pn)}) \to \mathbf{Cat}(Spec^T)$ is defined as follows.
(i) For each $A \in |\mathbf{Pcat}(Spec^{(P1,\ldots,Pn)})|$ define $F_{PSpec}(A) = V_A(I_{Ext}(Spec^T[A]))$;
(ii) For each $f : A \to B \in \mathbf{Pcat}(Spec^{(P1,\ldots,Pn)})$ define the morphism $F_{PSpec}(f)$: $F_{PSpec}(A) \to F_{PSpec}(B)$ by $F_{PSpec}(f)_\tau([t]) = [\alpha(f)_\tau(t)]$ for each type $\tau \in S_T$ and each term $t \in T(\Sigma^T[A])_\tau$. □

4.7 Proposition. *For any parameterised specification $PSpec = (Spec^{(P1,\ldots,Pn)}, Spec^T)$ we have that $F_{PSpec} : \mathbf{Pcat}(Spec^{(P1,\ldots,Pn)}) \to \mathbf{Cat}(Spec^T)$ is a well defined functor.*

Proof. Clearly, by the definition of the A–quotient term algebra $F_{PSpec}(A) \in |\mathbf{Cat}(Spec^T)|$, for each actual parameter $A \in |\mathbf{Pcat}(Spec^{(P1,\ldots,Pn)})|$. For any morphism $f : A \to B \in \mathbf{Pcat}(Spec^{(P1,\ldots,Pn)})$ we have by Lemma 4.5 that $F_{PSpec}(f) : F_{PSpec}(A) \to F_{PSpec}(B)$ is well defined and clearly by the definition of $\alpha(f)$ we know $F_{PSpec}(f)$ is a homomorphism. Thus it follows that $F_{PSpec}(f) : F_{PSpec}(A) \to F_{PSpec}(B) \in \mathbf{Cat}(Spec^T)$. Finally, we need to show that F_{PSpec} satisfies conditions (i) and (ii) of Definition 2.10. This is straightforward to do and is left as an exercise for the reader. □

We use the functor F_{PSpec} to define an abstract parameterised data type which we take to be the semantics of a parameterised specification.

4.8 Definition. The *semantics* of a parameterised specification

$$PSpec = (Spec^{(P1,\ldots,Pn)}, Spec^T)$$

is the abstract parameterised data type

$$APDT(PSpec) = (Spec^{(P1,\ldots,Pn)}, Spec^T, Iso(F_{PSpec})),$$

where F_{PSpec} is the functor defined in Definition 4.6. □

We conclude this section by defining what it means for a parameterised specification to correctly specify an abstract parameterised data type.

4.9 Definition. Let $APDT = (Spec^{(MP1,\ldots,MPn)}, Spec^{MT}, Iso(M))$ be an abstract parameterised data type and let $PSpec = (Spec^{(P1,\ldots,Pn)}, Spec^T)$ be a parameterised specification. We say that $PSpec$ is a *correct* parameterised specification of $APDT$ if, and only if, $Spec^{(MP1,\ldots,MPn)} \subseteq Spec^{(P1,\ldots,Pn)}$, $Spec^{MT} \subseteq Spec^T$, and

$$U^T \circ F_{PSpec} \cong M \circ U^{(P1,\ldots Pn)},$$

that is the diagram in Figure 2 commutes up to natural isomorphism, where U^T and $U^{(P1,\ldots Pn)}$ are the corresponding forgetful functors. □

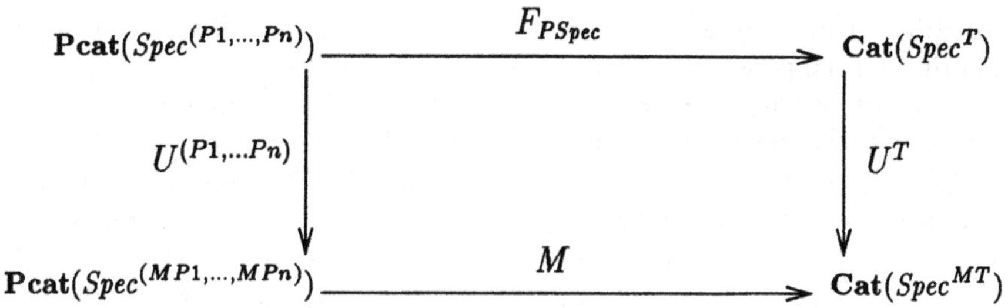

Fig. 2. Commutative diagram for correctness.

5 Specification Case Study: Convolution.

In the preceding sections we developed a theory of parameterised higher–order algebraic specifications. We now demonstrate this theory by considering a detailed case study of the specification of an APDT for convolution in which the stream space is parameterised. This case study is important because it demonstrates how parameterised specifications can be used to overcome the problem of requiring an uncountable specification to specify a full stream space (see Meinke and Steggles [1994, 1996]). We begin by defining a second–order APDT $APDT(Conv)$ for convolution. We then present a parameterised second–order equational specification $Conv(Time, Ring, Stream)$ and conclude by showing that $Conv(Time, Ring, Stream)$ is a *correct* parameterised specification of $APDT(Conv)$.

Recall the definition of the convolution function (see for example Meinke and Steggles [1994]). Let $\mathbf{R} = (\mathbf{R}; 0, 1; -, +, \times)$ denote a ring with unity and let $n \in \mathbf{N}$ be some arbitrarily chosen but fixed non-zero natural number. We can view convolution of sample size n over $\mathbf{R}$ as a stream transformer (second–order function) $conv^n : \mathbf{R}^n \times [\mathbf{N} \to \mathbf{R}] \to [\mathbf{N} \to \mathbf{R}]$, defined for each $(w_1, \ldots, w_n) \in \mathbf{R}^n$, $a \in [\mathbf{N} \to \mathbf{R}]$ and $t \in \mathbf{N}$ by

$$conv^n(w_1, \ldots, w_n, a)(t) = (a(t) \times w_1) + \cdots + (a(t+n-1) \times w_n).$$

We can generalize this definition from the natural numbers as time to any set $\mathbf{T}$ with a next time unary operation $tick : \mathbf{T} \to \mathbf{T}$.

We begin by defining an abstract parameterised data type for convolution.

5.1 Definition. Define the abstract parameterised data type

$$APDT(Conv) = ((Time, Ring, Stream), MConv, Iso(CV))$$

as follows.

Multiple Parameter Specification. Let $TRS = (Time, Ring, Stream)$ be a multiple formal parameter specification defined as follows.
(a) Define the formal parameter specification $Time = (\Sigma^{Time}, \emptyset)$, where $S_{Time} = \{time\}$ is a basic type structure and Σ^{Time} is an S_{Time}-typed signature defined by $\Sigma^{Time}_{time,time} = \{tick\}$, and for all other $w \in S^*_{Time}$, $\tau \in S_{Time}$, $\Sigma^{Time}_{w,\tau} = \emptyset$.
(b) Define the formal parameter specification $Ring = (\Sigma^{Ring}, E^{Ring})$, where $S_{Ring} = \{ring\}$ is a basic type structure and Σ^{Ring} is an S_{Ring}-typed signature defined by $\Sigma^{Ring}_{\lambda,ring} = \{0, 1\}$, $\Sigma^{Ring}_{ring,ring} = \{-\}$, $\Sigma^{Ring}_{ring\ ring,ring} = \{+, \times\}$, and for all other $w \in S^*_{Ring}$, $\tau \in S_{Ring}$, $\Sigma^{Ring}_{w,\tau} = \emptyset$. Let X be an infinite set of variables and $x, y, z \in X$. The first-order equational theory E^{Ring} of rings with unity consists of the following equations over Σ^{Ring} and X.

$$x + y = y + x, \tag{1}$$

$$x + (y + z) = (x + y) + z, \quad x \times (y \times z) = (x \times y) \times z, \tag{2,3}$$

$$x + 0 = x, \quad x + (-x) = 0, \tag{4,5}$$

$$x \times 1 = x, \ 1 \times x = x, \tag{6,7}$$

$$x \times (y + z) = (x \times y) + (x \times z), \quad (x + y) \times z = (x \times z) + (y \times z). \tag{8,9}$$

(c) Define the formal parameter specification $Stream = (\Sigma^{Stream}, \emptyset)$, where we have $S_{Stream} = \{time, ring, (time \to ring)\}$ is a type structure over the type basis $B = \{time, ring\}$ and Σ^{Stream} is a second-order S_{Stream}-typed signature defined by $\Sigma^{Stream}_{(time \to ring)\ time,ring} = \{eval\}$, and for all other $w \in S^*_{Stream}$, $\tau \in S_{Stream}$, $\Sigma^{Stream}_{w,\tau} = \emptyset$.

Target Specification. Define the target specification

$$MConv = (\Sigma^{Conv}, E^{Ring}),$$

where $\Sigma^{Conv} = \Sigma^{Time} \cup \Sigma^{Ring} \cup \Sigma^{Stream} \cup \Sigma^{Bdy}$ and Σ^{Bdy} is an S_{Stream}-sorted signature defined by $\Sigma^{Bdy}_{ring^n\ (time \to ring),(time \to ring)} = \{conv^n\}$, and for all other $w \in S^*_{Stream}$, $\tau \in S_{Stream}$, $\Sigma^{Bdy}_{w,\tau} = \emptyset$.

Model Functor. Define the model functor $CV : \mathbf{Pcat}(TRS) \to \mathbf{Cat}(MConv)$ as follows.
(i) For each actual parameter $A = (A^T, A^R, A^S) \in |\mathbf{Pcat}(TRS)|$ define $CV(A)$ to be the S_{Stream}-typed Σ^{Conv} algebra with carrier sets

$$CV(A)_{time} = A^T_{time}, \ CV(A)_{ring} = A^R_{ring}.$$

To define the carrier set $CV(A)_{(time \to ring)}$ we first ensure that the elements of $A^S_{(time \to ring)}$ are actual functions (since A^S is an extensional algebra) and then close up under the application of the function $conv^n_{CV(A)}$ (defined below). Define $CV(A)_{(time \to ring)} = \bigcup_{i \in \mathbf{N}} U(A)^i$, where

$$U(A)^0 = \{f : A^S_{time} \to A^S_{ring} \mid \text{exists } a \in A^S_{(time \to ring)} \text{ such that}$$

$$\text{for all } t \in A^S_{time} \text{ we have } (f(t) = eval_{A^S}(a, t))\},$$

and for any $i \in \mathbf{N}$,

$$U(A)^{i+1} = U(A)^i \cup$$

$$\{conv^n_{CV(A)}(w_1, \ldots, w_n, a) \mid w_1, \ldots, w_n \in CV(A)_{ring},\ a \in U(A)^i\}.$$

Note that by definition of $U(A)^0$ we know that for each $a \in U(A)^0$ there exists a unique element of $A^S_{(time \to ring)}$, denoted $\hat{a}$, such that $a(t) = eval_{A^S}(\hat{a}, t)$, for each $t \in A^S_{time}$. Define the constants and operations of $CV(A)$ by $0_{CV(A)} = 0_{A^R}$, $1_{CV(A)} = 1_{A^R}$, $tick_{CV(A)} = tick_{A^T}$, $-_{CV(A)} = -_{A^R}$, $+_{CV(A)} = +_{A^R}$, $\times_{CV(A)} = \times_{A^R}$. Define $eval_{CV(A)}(a, t) = a(t)$, for any $a \in CV(A)_{(time \to ring)}$ and any $t \in CV(A)_{time}$. For any $w_1, \ldots, w_n \in CV(A)_{ring}$, $a \in CV(A)_{(time \to ring)}$ and $t \in CV(A)_{time}$ define

$$conv^n_{CV(A)}(w_1, \ldots, w_n, a)(t) = (w_n \times_{\overline{A}} a(tick^{n-1}_{\overline{A}}(t))) +_{\overline{A}} \cdots +_{\overline{A}} (w_1 \times_{\overline{A}} a(t))$$

where $tick^0(t) = t$ and for any $m \in \mathbf{N}$, $tick^{m+1}(t) = tick(tick^m(t))$.
(ii) For any objects $A = (A^T, A^R, A^S), B = (B^T, B^R, B^S) \in |\mathbf{Pcat}(TRS)|$ and each morphism $f = (f^T, f^R, f^S) : A \to B \in \mathbf{Pcat}(TRS)$, define the morphism $CV(f) : CV(A) \to CV(B)$ on each $t \in CV(A)_{time}$ and $x \in CV(A)_{ring}$ by

$$CV(f)_{time}(t) = f^T_{time}(t),\ CV(f)_{ring}(x) = f^R_{ring}(x).$$

Define $CV(f)_{(time \to ring)} : CV(A)_{(time \to ring)} \to CV(B)_{(time \to ring)}$ by

$$CV(f)_{(time \to ring)}(a)(t) = eval_{B^S}(f^S_{(time \to ring)}(\hat{a}), t),$$

for each $a \in U(A)^0$ and $t \in CV(B)_{time}$, and

$$CV(f)_{(time \to ring)}(a) =$$

$$conv^n_{CV(B)}(CV(f)_{ring}(w_1), \ldots, CV(f)_{ring}(w_n), CV(f)_{(time \to ring)}(b)),$$

for each $a \in U(A)^{k+1}$, $k \in \mathbf{N}$, such that $a \notin U(A)^k$ and for some $w_1, \ldots, w_n \in CV(A)_{ring}$, $b \in U(A)^k$ we have $a = conv^n_{CV(A)}(w_1, \ldots, w_n, b)$. □

We need to show that $APDT(Conv)$ is a well defined APDT. We begin by proving that for any morphism $f : A \to B \in \mathbf{Pcat}(TRS)$ that $CV(f) : CV(A) \to CV(B)$ is a well defined morphism in $\mathbf{Cat}(MConv)$. In the sequel we let $CV(f)$ denote the function $CV(f)_\tau$ when the type $\tau \in S_{Stream}$ is clear.

5.2 Proposition. *For any morphism $f : A \to B \in$ **Pcat**(TRS) we have that $CV(f) : CV(A) \to CV(B)$ is a well defined morphism in* **Cat**$(Conv)$.

Proof. Let $f = (f^T, f^R, f^S) : A \to B \in$ **Pcat**(TRS). Clearly since f^T and f^R are well defined it follows that $CV(f)_{time}$ and $CV(f)_{ring}$ are well defined. We begin by assuming that $CV(f)_{(time \to ring)}$ is well defined and showing that $CV(f)$ is a homomorphism. We then prove that $CV(f)_{(time \to ring)}$ is well defined.

We only show that $conv^n$ satisfies the homomorphism condition since the proofs for the remaining functions is routine. We need to show that

$$CV(f)(conv^n_{CV(A)}(w_1, \ldots, w_n, a)) =$$
$$conv^n_{CV(B)}(CV(f)(w_1), \ldots, CV(f)(w_n), CV(f)(a)),$$

for any $w_1, \ldots, w_n \in CV(A)_{ring}$ and $a \in CV_{(time \to ring)}$. We do this by showing that for each $t \in CV(A)_{time}$

$$CV(f)(conv^n_{CV(A)}(w_1, \ldots, w_n, a))(CV(f)(t)) =$$
$$conv^n_{CV(B)}(CV(f)(w_1), \ldots, CV(f)(w_n), CV(f)(a))(CV(f)(t)),$$

from which (using the definition of $CV(f)$, the fact that f^T is surjective and the extensionality of $CV(B)$) the result follows.

It remains to prove that $CV(f) : CV(A) \to CV(B)$ is well defined on each $a \in U(A)^i$, $i \in \mathbf{N}$. This is straightforward to do by induction on $i \in \mathbf{N}$. □

We may now show that $APDT(Conv)$ is a well defined APDT.

5.3 Proposition. *The abstract parameterised data type*

$$APDT(Conv) = ((Time, Ring, Stream), MConv, Iso(CV))$$

is well defined.

Proof. Clearly the formal parameter specifications *Time*, *Ring* and *Stream* are subspecifications of *MConv*. Thus it only remains to show that CV is a well defined functor.

For each object $A \in |$**Pcat**$(TRS)|$ we have by definition that $CV(A) \in |$**Cat**$(MConv)|$ and by Proposition 5.2 we know

$$CV(f) : CV(A) \to CV(B) \in \mathbf{Cat}(MConv),$$

for each morphism $f : A \to B \in$ **Pcat**(TRS). It only remains to show that CV satisfies conditions (i) and (ii) of Definition 2.10. This is straightforward to do and is left as an exercise for the reader. □

Next we present a parameterised specification *Conv*(*Time*, *Ring*, *Stream*) which we show to be a correct specification of the abstract parameterised data type $APDT(Conv)$.

5.4 Definition. Define the parameterised second–order specification

$$Conv(Time, Ring, Stream)$$

as follows.

Multiple Parameter Specification. Let $TRS = (Time, Ring, Stream)$ be the multiple formal parameter specification defined as in Definition 5.1.

Target Specification. Define the target specification

$$Conv(TRS) = (\Sigma^{Conv}, E^{Conv}),$$

where Σ^{Conv} is defined as in Definition 5.1. Let X be an S_{Stream}–indexed family of sets of variables and let $w_1, \ldots, w_n \in X_{ring}$, $s \in X_{(time \to ring)}$ and $t \in X_{time}$. Then define the second–order equational theory $E^{Conv} \subseteq Eqn(\Sigma^{Conv}, X)$ to consist of the first–order equations in E^{Ring} (see Definition 5.1) and the following second–order equation

$$conv^n(w_1, \ldots, w_n, s)(t) = (w_n \times s(tick^{n-1}(t))) + \cdots + (w_1 \times s(t)). \qquad (10)$$

Clearly $Conv(TRS)$ is a well defined parameterised specification. □

Using Definition 4.8 we can construct an abstract parameterised data type

$$APDT(Conv(TRS)) = (TRS, Conv(TRS), Iso(F)),$$

which represents the intended semantics of $Conv(TRS)$. It remains to prove that $Conv(TRS)$ is a correct parameterised specification of the abstract parameterised data type $APDT(Conv)$. According to Definition 4.9 we need to show that $CV \circ Id \cong U \circ F$, where $Id : \mathbf{Pcat}(TRS) \to \mathbf{Pcat}(TRS)$ it the identity functor and $U : \mathbf{Cat}(Conv(TRS)) \to \mathbf{Cat}(MConv)$ is the corresponding forgetful functor. In the remainder of this section we let CV and F denote both themselves and the functors $CV \circ Id$ respectively $U \circ F$. For any $A \in |\mathbf{Pcat}(TRS)|$ we let $CV(A)$ denote both itself and the extension of $CV(A)$ to a $\Sigma^{Conv}[A]$ algebra by distinguishing a constant $\overline{a}_{CV(A)} = a$, for each $a \in \overline{A}_\tau$, $\tau \in \{time, ring\}$, and defining $\overline{a}_{CV(A)}(t) = eval_{\overline{A}}(a, t)$, for each $a \in \overline{A}_{(time \to ring)}$ and $t \in \overline{A}_{time}$.

We begin by defining a family of morphisms which we will show to be a natural isomorphism between F and CV.

5.5 Definition. Define the family of morphisms

$$Crt = \langle\ Crt(A) : F(A) \to CV(A) \mid A \in |\mathbf{Pcat}(TRS)|\ \rangle,$$

for each actual parameter $A \in |\mathbf{Pcat}(TRS)|$, each type $\tau \in S_{Stream}$ and each term $t \in T(\Sigma^{Conv}[A])_\tau$ by $Crt(A)_\tau([t]) = t_{CV(A)}$. □

Next we show that for each actual parameter $A \in |\mathbf{Pcat}(TRS)|$ the morphism $Crt(A) : F(A) \to CV(A)$ is well defined in $\mathbf{Cat}(MConv)$.

5.6 Proposition. *For each actual parameter $A \in |\mathbf{Pcat}(TRS)|$ we have that $Crt(A) : F(A) \to CV(A)$ is a well defined morphism in $\mathbf{Cat}(MConv)$.*

Proof. Let $A \in |\mathbf{Pcat}(TRS)|$. Then we begin by showing that $Crt(A)$ is a well defined function. Let $t, t' \in T(\Sigma^{Conv}[A])_\tau$, for some $\tau \in S_{Stream}$, and suppose $[t] = [t']$. Then according to the definition of $Crt(A)$ we must show that $CV(A) \models t = t'$. Now by the initial assumption and the definition of $F(A)$ we know

$$E^{Conv} \cup Eqn[A] \vdash_\omega t = t'. \qquad (1)$$

Since it is straightforward to show that $CV(A)$ is a $\Sigma^{Conv}[A]$ minimal algebra and that $CV(A) \models E^{Conv} \cup Eqn[A]$, it follows by (1) above and the soundness of $\vdash_\omega$ with respect to minimal extensional algebras that $CV(A) \models t = t'$.

To see that $Crt(A)$ is a homomorphism consider any $w = \tau(1)\ldots\tau(m) \in S^*_{Stream}$, any type $\tau \in S_{Stream}$, any symbol $h \in \Sigma^{Conv}_{w,\tau}$ and any terms $t_1 \in T(\Sigma^{Conv}[A])_{\tau(1)}, \ldots, t_m \in T(\Sigma^{Conv}[A])_{\tau(m)}$. Then by definition of $F(A)$,

$$Crt(A)_\tau(h_{F(A)}([t_1], \ldots, [t_m])) = Crt(A)_\tau([h(t_1, \ldots, t_m)]),$$

and by definition of $Crt(A)$,

$$= h(t_1, \ldots, t_m)_{CV(A)} = h_{CV(A)}(Crt(A)_{\tau(1)}([t_1]), \ldots, Crt(A)_{\tau(m)}([t_m])). \quad \square$$

For any morphism $f : A \to B \in \mathbf{Pcat}(TRS)$ recall the definition of the term mapping $\alpha(f) : T(\Sigma^{Conv}[A], X) \to T(\Sigma^{Conv}[B], X)$ (see Definition 4.3). Before being able to show that Crt is a natural transformation we need the following technical result.

5.7 Lemma. *For any type $\tau \in S_{Stream}$, any morphism $f : A \to B \in \mathbf{Pcat}(TRS)$ and any term $t \in T(\Sigma^{Conv}[A])_\tau$ we have*

$$\alpha(f)_\tau(t)_{CV(B)} = CV(f)_\tau(t_{CV(A)}).$$

Proof. By induction on the complexity of terms. $\square$

We may now show that Crt is a natural transformation.

5.8 Proposition. *The family of morphisms*

$$Crt = \langle\ Crt(A) : F(A) \to CV(A) \mid A \in |\mathbf{Pcat}(TRS)|\ \rangle,$$

is a natural transformation.

Proof. By Proposition 5.6 we know that $Crt(A) \in \mathbf{Cat}(MConv)$, for each $A \in |\mathbf{Pcat}(TRS)|$. Thus it only remains to show that for each morphism f :

$A \to B \in \mathbf{Pcat}(TRS)$ that $Crt(B) \circ F(f) = CV(f) \circ Crt(A)$. This is straightforward to do and is left as an exercise for the reader. □

We can now prove that the parameterised specification $Conv(TRS)$ is a correct specification of the abstract parameterised data type $APDT(Conv)$.

5.9 Correctness Theorem. *The parameterised specification $Conv(TRS)$ correctly specifies the abstract parameterised data type $APDT(Conv)$.*

Proof. Clearly $MConv$ is a subspecification of $Conv(TRS)$ so according to Definition 4.9 it only remains to show that $F \cong CV$. By Proposition 5.8 above we know $Crt = \langle\ Crt(A) : F(A) \to CV(A) \mid A \in |\mathbf{Pcat}(TRS)|\ \rangle$ is a natural transformation in $\mathbf{Cat}(MConv)$. Thus it suffices to show that for each actual parameter $A = (A^T, A^R, A^S) \in |\mathbf{Pcat}(TRS)|$ the homomorphism

$$Crt(A) : F(A) \to CV(A),$$

is an isomorphism, i.e. injective and surjective.

Since we can easily show that $CV(A)$ is a minimal $\Sigma^{Conv}[A]$ algebra, it follows by definition that $Crt(A)$ is surjective. To prove that $Crt(A)$ is injective we must show that for any type $\tau \in S_{Stream}$ and any terms $t, t' \in T(\Sigma^{Conv}[A])_\tau$ that

$$Crt(A)_\tau([t]) = Crt(A)_\tau([t']) \Longrightarrow [t] = [t'].$$

We have three possible cases to consider.

(i) Suppose $t, t' \in T(\Sigma^{Conv}[A])_{time}$ and $Crt(A)_{time}([t]) = Crt(A)_{time}([t'])$. Then by the definition of $Crt(A)$ we have $t_{CV(A)} = t'_{CV(A)}$. Since $T(\Sigma^{Conv}[A])_{time} = T((\Sigma^{Conv} - \Sigma^{Bdy})[A])_{time}$ and we can easily show that $CV(A)|_{\Sigma^{Time}} = A^T$ it follows by the definition of $Eqn[A]$ that $E^{Conv} \cup Eqn[A] \vdash t = t'$. Thus by the definition of $F(A)$ we have $[t] = [t']$.

(ii) Suppose $t, t' \in T(\Sigma^{Conv}[A])_{ring}$ and $Crt(A)_{ring}([t]) = Crt(A)_{ring}([t'])$. Then for each term $t^0 \in T(\Sigma^{Conv}[A])_{ring}$ we can show that

$$E^{Conv} \cup Eqn[A] \vdash t^0 = \overline{t^0_{CV(A)}}, \tag{1}$$

by induction on the construction of terms. Since by assumption $Crt(A)_{ring}([t]) = Crt(A)_{ring}([t'])$ it follows by the definition of $Crt(A)$ that $t_{CV(A)} = t'_{CV(A)}$. So using fact (1) above and transitivity we have $E^{Conv} \cup Eqn[A] \vdash t = t'$. Thus by the definition of $F(A)$ we have $[t] = [t']$.

(iii) Finally, suppose $t, t' \in T(\Sigma^{Conv}[A])_{(time \to ring)}$ and

$$Crt(A)_{(time \to ring)}([t]) = Crt(A)_{(time \to ring)}([t']).$$

Then by definition of $Crt(A)$ we have $t_{CV(A)} = t'_{CV(A)}$ and thus

$$t(t_1)_{CV(A)} = t'(t_1)_{CV(A)},$$

for each $t_1 \in T(\Sigma^{Conv}[A])_{time}$. So using fact (1) proved above in case (ii) we have $E^{Conv} \cup Eqn[A] \vdash_\omega t(t_1) = t'(t_1)$, and thus by the ω–evaluation rule and the definition of $F(A)$ it follows that $[t] = [t']$. □

6 Concluding Remarks.

In this paper we have developed a theory of parameterised higher–order equational specifications. We took as our starting point a simple first–order theory of parameterised specifications based on a free functor semantics (see for example Thatcher et al [1978], Ehrig et al [1984] and Ehrig and Mahr [1985]) and attempted to extend this to the higher–order case. However, it turned out that due to the nature of the higher–order initial model a number of key results for the free functor semantics fail to hold in the higher–order case. In particular, since the the higher–order initial model is only initial in the class of all minimal models of a specification the so called A–quotient term algebra construction is not necessarily a free construction. Thus it cannot be extended to a free functor which can be taken as the semantics of a parameterised specification. To overcome this problem we defined a concrete construction of a functor, based on the natural A–quotient term algebra construction, which we take to represent the intended semantics of a parameterised higher–order equational specification. We saw that this approach preserved the first–order free functor semantics.

We demonstrated the theory we developed by considering a detailed case study of the specification of a second–order APDT for convolution in which the stream space is parameterised. This case study was important because it demonstrated how parameterised specifications can be used to overcome the problem of requiring an uncountable specification to specify a full function space (see Meinke and Steggles [1994, 1996]).

Much further work is needed to consolidate the theory of parameterised higher–order equational specifications we have presented. For example a theory of *parameter passing* (i.e. substituting suitable actual specifications for formal parameter specifications) needs to be developed for the higher–order case (see for example Ehrig et al [1984] and Ehrig and Mahr [1985] for an introduction to the first–order theory). In future work we also plan to consider extending parameterised higher–order specifications with requirement specifications and constraints (see for example Burstall and Goguen [1980] and Ehrig [1981]).

Acknowledgements.
It is a pleasure to thank K. Meinke and B. Möller for their helpful comments and advice during the preparation of this paper. We would also like to thank the Engineering and Physical Sciences Research Council for their financial support.

7 References.

M. Barr and C. Wells. *Category Theory for Computing Science.* International Series in Computer Science, Prentice–Hall, 1990.

R. M. Burstall and J. A. Goguen. The semantics of CLEAR, a specification language. *Proc. of 1979 Copenhagen Winter School on Abstract Software Specifications*, LNCS 86, pages 292–332, Springer–Verlag, 1980.

H. Ehrig, H-J. Kreowski, J. W. Thatcher, E. Wagner and J. Wright. Parameter

Passing in Algebraic Specification Languages. *Theoretical Computing Science*, 28:45–81, 1984.
H. Ehrig and B. Mahr. *Fundamentals of Algebraic Specification 1 – Equations and Initial Semantics.* EATCS Monographs on Theoretical Computer Science 6, Springer-Verlag, Berlin, 1985.
H. Ehrig. Algebraic theory of parameterized specifications with requirements. *Proceedings of 1981 Colloquium on Trees in Algebra and Programming*, LNCS 112, pages 1–24, Springer–Verlag, 1981.
P. Kosiuczenko and K. Meinke. On the Power of Higher–Order Algebraic Specification Methods. *Information and Computation*, 124(1):85–101, 1995.
S. MacLane. *Categories for the Working Mathematician.* Springer–Verlag, 1971.
K. Meinke and J.V. Tucker. Universal algebra. In: S. Abramsky, D. Gabbay and T.S.E. Maibaum, (eds) *Handbook of Logic in Computer Science*, Volume I, pages 189–412. Oxford University Press, Oxford, 1993.
K. Meinke and L. J. Steggles. Specification and Verification in Higher Order Algebra: A Case Study of Convolution. In: J. Heering, K. Meinke, B. Möller and T. Nipkow (eds), *Proc. of HOA '93: An Int. Workshop on Higher Order Algebra, Logic and Term Rewriting*, LNCS 816, pages 189–222, Springer–Verlag, 1994.
K. Meinke and L. J. Steggles. Correctness of Dataflow and Systolic Algorithms: Case Studies in Higher–Order Algebra. Technical Report No. 559, Department of Computer Science, University of Newcastle, 1996.
K. Meinke. Universal algebra in higher types. *Theoretical Computer Science*, 100:385–417, 1992.
K. Meinke. A completeness theorem for the expressive power of higher–order algebraic specifications. Technical Report CSR–13–95, Department of Computer Science, University of Wales, Swansea, 1995.
B. Möller, A. Tarlecki and M. Wirsing. Algebraic specifications of reachable higher–order algebras. In: D. Sannella and A. Tarlecki (eds), *Recent Trends in Data Type Specification*, LNCS 332, pages 154–169, Springer-Verlag, 1988.
B. Möller. Higher–order algebraic specifications. Fakultät für Mathematik und Informatik, Technische Universität München, Habilitationsschrift, 1987.
L. J. Steggles. *Extensions of Higher–Order Algebra: Fundamental Theory and Case Studies.* Ph.D. Thesis, University of Wales, Swansea, 1995.
J. W. Thatcher, E. G. Wagner and J. B. Wright. Data type specification: parameterization and the power of specification techniques. *SIGACT 10th Annual Symposium on the Theory of Computing*, San Diego, 1978. Also in: *ACM Transactions on Programming Languages and Systems*, 4:711–773, 1982.
M. Wirsing. Algebraic specification. In: J. van Leeuwen (ed) *Handbook of Theoretical Computer Science*, Vol. B, North Holland, Amsterdam, 1990.

Higher-Order Lazy Narrowing Calculus: A Computation Model for a Higher-Order Functional Logic Language

Taro Suzuki, Koji Nakagawa and Tetsuo Ida
Institute of Information Sciences and Electronics
University of Tsukuba
{taro, nakoji, ida}@score.is.tsukuba.ac.jp

1 Introduction

Experiences with functional programming revealed that higher-order concept leads to powerful and succinct programming. Functional logic programming, an approach to integrate functional and logic programming, would naturally be expected to incorporate the notion of higher-order-ness. Little has been investigated how to incorporate higher-order-ness in functional logic programming.

In this paper we present a computation model for a higher-order functional and logic programming. Although investigations of computation models for higher-order functional logic languages are under way[13, 9, 8, 20, 22], implemented functional logic languages like K-LEAF[6] and Babel[18] among others, are all based on first-order models of computation. First-order narrowing has been used as basic computation mechanism.

The lack of higher-order-ness is exemplified by the following prototypical program

$$\begin{array}{ll} \mathrm{map}(F, []) & \to [] \\ \mathrm{map}(F, [X \mid Xs]) & \to [F(X) \mid \mathrm{map}(F, Xs)] \end{array}$$

written in a language of term rewriting. The symbols that start with capital letters denote variables. Due to the higher-order term $F(X)$, a goal that requires the second rule cannot be solved by ordinary first-order narrowing.

This difficulty can be overcome by the use of applicative rewrite systems. By writing a program in applicative systems we can partially realize higher-order programming. In an applicative rewrite system the above example can be written as

$$\begin{array}{ll} \mathrm{map}\ F\ [] & \to [] \\ \mathrm{map}\ F\ [X \mid Xs] & \to [F\ X \mid \mathrm{map}\ F\ Xs] \end{array}$$

where term $t_1 t_2 \cdots t_n \equiv ((\cdots(t_1\ t_2)\cdots)\ t_n)$ is an abbreviation of a first-order term $\mathrm{ap}(\mathrm{ap}(\cdots \mathrm{ap}(t_1, t_2), \cdots), t_n)$.

Then, with appropriate extension of first-order rewriting, we can solve a goal like

$$\mathrm{map}\ F\ [0,(\mathrm{succ}\ 0)] = Z,$$

which is actually a first-order equation

$$\mathrm{ap}(\mathrm{ap}(\mathrm{map},F),\mathrm{ap}(\mathrm{ap}(\mathrm{cons},0),\mathrm{ap}(\mathrm{ap}(\mathrm{cons},\mathrm{ap}(\mathrm{succ},0)),[])))=Z$$

where map, succ, cons, 0 and [] are regarded as constants.

Although the use of applicative systems is a step towards higher-order programming, an important feature pertaining to higher-order programming is missing. Namely, we cannot handle anonymous functions with bound variables, *i.e.* λ-terms.

Higher-order narrowing with higher-order rewrite systems would be one direction for realizing a higher-order functional logic programming. However, as observed by Prehofer[22], simply-minded higher-order narrowing is highly non-deterministic. Prehofer's higher-order narrowing calculus LN successfully reduces some degree of non-determinism, but still a more efficient higher-order narrowing calculus is desired for a functional logic programming language. Hanus and Prehofer proposed a calculus for needed narrowing LNT, which deals with higher-order narrowing systematically[9]. Those works are based on higher-order rewriting, where β-reduction is an implicit operation.

On the other hand, first-order narrowing has been studied extensively (see [7] for survey). Several narrowing methods have been proposed for reducing search space of narrowing [11, 2, 15, 5, 10]. So once we can relate (restricted class of) higher-order narrowing and first-order narrowing, we can exploit the techniques of improving efficiency of first-order narrowing in order to improve the efficiency of higher-order narrowing.

In this paper we propose a higher-order lazy narrowing calculus, to be called HLNC, that is based on the first-order lazy narrowing calculus LNC[17]for which strong completeness and deterministic version of the calculus have been developed.

The organization of the rest of the paper is as follows. In Section 2 we introduce basic concepts of rewriting, notation and conventions to be used in the paper. In Section 3 we introduce a TRS_λ, an abstract higher-order functional logic program. In Section 4 we give a first-order narrowing calculus on which our higher-order narrowing calculus is based. In Section 5 we present HLNC together with the completeness theorem. In Section 6, we summarize our main results and their advantage, then discuss a future research theme.

2 Preliminary

We first introduce typed terms. Let Γ be the set of all types. Γ is generated from a set of base types (denoted by α) using a function type constructor $\rightarrow$. Let $\mathcal{V}$ be a set of typed variables, i.e. $\cup_{\tau\in\Gamma}\mathcal{V}_\tau$ and $\mathcal{F}$ a set of typed constants, i.e. $\cup_{\tau\in\Gamma}\mathcal{F}_\tau$, where $\mathcal{V}_\tau \cap \mathcal{V}_{\tau'} = \emptyset$ and $\mathcal{F}_\tau \cap \mathcal{F}_{\tau'} = \emptyset$ for $\tau \neq \tau'$. The set $\mathcal{V}$ is divided into the set of free variables $\mathcal{FV}$ and the set of bound variables $\mathcal{BV}$. The set $\mathcal{F}$ is divided into the set of defined function symbols $\mathcal{F}_D$ and the set of constructor symbols $\mathcal{F}_C$.

Let $\mathcal{T}(\mathcal{F},\mathcal{V})$ be a set of simply-typed λ-terms over a typed signature $\mathcal{F}$ and $\mathcal{V}$. Namely, $\mathcal{T}(\mathcal{F},\mathcal{V})$ is generated by the following grammar.

$$t ::= X|x|f|t_1t_2|\lambda x.t$$

where $X \in \mathcal{FV}, x \in \mathcal{BV}, f \in \mathcal{F}$ and $t_1, t_2 \in \mathcal{T}(\mathcal{F}, \mathcal{V})$.

A term of the form $(V\, \mathbf{s_n})$, where $n \geq 1$ and $V \in \mathcal{FV}$, is called *flex* term. Here $\mathbf{s_n}$ denotes $s_1 \cdots s_n$. A term that does not contain a flex term or a β-redex is called *β-free* term. A β-free term is a term that will never be β-reducible whatever substitutions are applied to it. A term t is linear if the same variable does not occur more than once in t. For a term t of the form $at_1 \cdots t_n$, where $a \in \mathcal{F}$, a is called root, and denoted by root(t). By $\mathcal{V}ar(t)$, we denote a set of free variables in a term t.

We adopt the following convention for symbols. Bound variables are denoted by x, y and z and free variables by X, Y, F and H. F and H are reserved for higher-order variables. f denotes a defined function symbol, g a function symbol (either defined or constructor), and c a constructor symbol.

Readers are referred to [17] for other notations, conventions and basic properties of rewriting that are used in this paper.

3 TRS_λ: Rewrite system with λ-terms

We define a restricted higher-order rewrite system to be called TRS_λ, with which we can avoid higher-order unification for the selection of rewrite rules.

Definition 1. (TRS_λ) A pair of terms $l, r \in \mathcal{T}(\mathcal{F}, \mathcal{V})$, denoted by $l \to r$, that satisfies the following conditions is called a rewrite rule:

- l and r are of base type,
- $\mathcal{V}ar(l) \supseteq \mathcal{V}ar(r)$,
- root$(l) \in \mathcal{F}_D$

A TRS_λ is a set of rewrite rules $l \to r$.

A reduction relation $\to_{\mathcal{R}}$ induced by a TRS_λ $\mathcal{R}$ is defined as follows:

$s \to_{\mathcal{R}} t$ iff there exists a position p, a substitution θ,
and a rewrite rule $l \to r \in \mathcal{R}$ such that $s|_p = l\theta$ and $t = s[r\theta]_p$,
where syntactic equality is assumed in modulo α-conversion.

A TRS_λ is called *β-free* if $\forall l \to r \in \mathcal{R}$, l is β-free. Note that abstractions are allowed in the proper subterms of the left-hand side of a rewrite rule of a TRS_λ as well as in the right-hand side. When we treat rewriting by a TRS_λ, we omit types and regard the TRS_λ as an untyped rewrite system.

The β-reduction is given by the relation induced by the following (infinite) set of rewrite rules.

$$\mathcal{R}_\beta = \{\ (\lambda x.t)\, X \to t[x := X] \ \mid\ t \in \mathcal{T}(\mathcal{F}, \mathcal{V})\} \tag{1}$$

where w.l.o.g. we assume that $(\lambda x.t)X$ is linear. A meta notation $s[x := t]$ denotes a term obtained by replacing all free occurrences of x in s by t. As in the lambda calculus, α-conversion of terms are performed implicitly. Reduction relation $\rightarrow_{\mathcal{R}_\beta}$ are defined as in $\rightarrow_{\mathcal{R}}$. The β-normal form of t is denoted by $t\downarrow_\beta$. A term t is called *outermost irreducible* if $\mathrm{root}(t) \notin \mathcal{F}_D$ or t is not a β-redex.

We are going to use a combined system $\mathcal{R} \cup \mathcal{R}_\beta$ as an abstract functional logic program. The combined system is not confluent in general even if $\mathcal{R}$ is confluent, as Klop's well-known counter example revealed [12].

Müller showed that a combined system of the β-reduction and a left-linear confluent applicative term rewriting system, where every left-hand side of its rewrite rule contains no flex term, is confluent on a subset of terms that is closed under some operations including the β-reduction[19]. Following Müller's observations in the proof of his theorem, we also can obtain the following confluence result for the combined system of $\mathcal{R} \cup \mathcal{R}_\beta$ over the set of terms $\mathcal{T}(\mathcal{F}, \mathcal{V})$.

Theorem 2. *Let $\mathcal{R}$ be a left-linear, β-free and confluent TRS_λ. $\rightarrow_{\mathcal{R}\cup\mathcal{R}_\beta}$ is confluent on $\mathcal{T}(\mathcal{F}, \mathcal{V})$.* □

Note that with TRS_λ we treat higher-order terms by applying β-reduction explicitly. Pattern matching in the selection of a rewrite rule involves no implicit β-reduction. Thus TRS_λ is not a higher-order rewrite system such as HRS of Nipkow[21], for example.

Furthermore, we can treat a TRS_λ as a first-order rewrite system by restricting terms to long η-normal forms and by viewing abstraction $\lambda x.s$ as a root-constructor term $\lambda x(s)$, application $(\lambda x.s)t$ as $\mathrm{ap}(\lambda x(s), t)$ and first-order terms $f\,t_1 \cdots t_n$ of long η-normal form as $f(t_1, \cdots, t_n)$. Here, a long η-normal form is defined as follows.

Definition 3. Let $\mathcal{T}_\eta$ be a set of well-typed terms, generated by the following grammar.
Let $t, t_1, \cdots, t_n \in \mathcal{T}_\eta$.

$$
\begin{array}{rrl}
t ::= & g\,t_1 \cdots t_n \mid & (n \geq 0) \\
& x\,t_1 \cdots t_n \mid & (n \geq 0) \\
& X\,t_1 \cdots t_n \mid & (n \geq 0) \\
& \lambda x_1 \cdots x_n.t \mid & (n \geq 1) \\
& (\lambda x_1 \cdots x_n.t)\,t_1 \cdots t_m & (n \geq m \geq 0, n \geq 1)
\end{array}
$$

subjected to the following conditions:

- Terms $g\,t_1 \cdots t_n$, $x\,t_1 \cdots t_n$ and $X\,t_1 \cdots t_n (n \geq 1)$ are of base type.
- The term t in $\lambda x_1 \cdots x_n.t$ is of base type and is not of the form $X x_1 \cdots x_n$.

A term in $\mathcal{T}_\eta$ is called *long η-normal form*. This definition of long η-normal form is different from usual long η-normal form, in that we exclude abstractions that are η-equivalent to a higher-order variable. An abstraction $\lambda x_1 \cdots x_n.X x_1 \cdots x_n$ is written only as X.

4 First-order Lazy Narrowing Calculus

Once we have defined a TRS_λ, we will use a first-order narrowing calculus called LNC(Lazy Narrowing Calculus)[17] as our base calculus for a functional logic language. LNC is presented as an inference system that manipulates a sequence of equations called goal. Below an equation is written as $s \approx t$. $s \simeq t$ denotes either $s \approx t$ or $t \approx s$.

Definition 4. (LNC) Let $\mathcal{R}$ be a TRS. The calculus LNC consists of the following five inference rules:

- *outermost narrowing* [o]

$$\frac{f(s_1, \cdots, s_n) \simeq t, E}{s_1 \approx l_1, \cdots, s_n \approx l_n, r \approx t, E}$$

  if there exists a fresh variant $f(l_1, \cdots, l_n) \to r$ of a rewrite rule in $\mathcal{R}$.

- *imitation* [i]

$$\frac{f(s_1, \cdots, s_n) \simeq X, E}{s_1 \approx X_1, \cdots, s_n \approx X_n, E}$$

  if $\theta = \{X \mapsto f(X_1, \cdots, X_n)\}$ with $X_1, \cdots, X_n$ fresh variables.

- *decomposition* [d]

$$\frac{f(s_1, \cdots, s_n) \simeq f(t_1, \cdots, t_n), E}{s_1 \approx t_1, \cdots, s_n \approx t_n, E}$$

- *variable elimination* [v]

$$\frac{s \simeq X, E}{E\theta}$$

  if $X \notin \mathcal{V}ar(s)$ and $\theta = \{X \mapsto s\}$.

- *removal of trivial equations* [t]

$$\frac{X \approx X, E}{E}$$

A derivation by using the inference rules from an initial goal G to an empty goal $\Box$ is written as $G \Rightarrow_\sigma^* \Box$. The substitution σ is obtained by composing substitutions formed in each step of the derivation. $\sigma\restriction_{\mathcal{V}ar(G)}$ is called LNC-solution of G.

Theorem 5. (Completeness of LNC) *Let $\mathcal{R}$ be a confluent TRS and G a goal. For every normalized solution θ of G there exists an LNC-derivation $G \Rightarrow_\sigma^* \Box$ such that $\sigma \leq \theta[\mathcal{V}ar(G)]$.* □

There are two sources of non-determinism in LNC: the choice of the inference rule, and the choice of the rewrite rule in the case of the inference rule [o]. Non-determinism in the choice of the inference rule except for parameter passing equations (see below for the definition) is entirely resolved if we solve equations to obtain strict solutions, and take $\mathcal{R}$ to be a left-linear confluent system.

Definition 6. Let $\mathcal{R}$ be a TRS and G a goal. A substitution θ is called *strict solution* of G if for every equation $s \approx t$ in G there exists a closed constructor term u such that $s\theta \rightarrow^*_{\mathcal{R}} u$ and $t\theta \rightarrow^*_{\mathcal{R}} u$.

Based on the above observations a strictly solving LNC[16], written as LNC$_s$, is given in Definition 7. There are two kinds of equations in LNC$_s$: one that is a descendant of equations of an initial goal, and the other generated in the inference rule [o] by equating parameters. The former equations are called *strict equations*, and the latter equations *parameter passing equations* denoted by $s \asymp t$.

The inference rules of LNC$_s$ are grouped into two: those that operate on strict equations and those that operate on parameter passing equations.

Definition 7. **(LNC$_s$)** Let $\mathcal{R}$ be a TRS. The calculus LNC$_s$ consists of the following inference rules:

Inference rules on strict equations

- *outermost narrowing* [o]

$$\frac{f(s_1,\cdots,s_n) \approx t, E}{s_1 \asymp l_1,\ldots,s_n \asymp l_n, r \approx t, E} \text{ and } \frac{t \approx f(s_1,\cdots,s_n), E}{s_1 \asymp l_1,\ldots,s_n \asymp l_n, r \approx t, E} \quad \text{root}(t) \notin \mathcal{F}_D$$

  if there exists a fresh variant $f(l_1,\cdots,l_n) \rightarrow r$ of a rewrite rule in $\mathcal{R}$.

- *imitation* [i]

$$\frac{c(s_1,\cdots,s_m) \simeq X, E}{(s_1 \approx X_1,\ldots,s_m \approx X_m, E)\theta}$$

  if $X \in \mathcal{V}ar(c(s_1,\cdots,s_m))$ or $c(s_1,\cdots,s_m) \notin \mathcal{T}(\mathcal{F}_C,\mathcal{V})$ and $\theta = \{X \mapsto c(X_1,\cdots,X_m)\}$ with $X_1,\cdots,X_m$ fresh variables.

- *decomposition* [d]

$$\frac{c(s_1,\cdots,s_n) \approx c(t_1,\cdots,t_n), E}{s_1 \approx t_1,\ldots,s_n \approx t_n, E}$$

- *variable elimination* [v]

$$\frac{s \approx X, E}{E\theta} \text{ and } \frac{X \approx s, E}{E\theta} \quad s \notin \mathcal{V}$$

  if $X \notin \mathcal{V}ar(s)$, $s \in \mathcal{T}(\mathcal{F}_C,\mathcal{V})$, and $\theta = \{X \mapsto s\}$.

- *removal of trivial equation* [t]

$$\frac{X \approx X, E}{E}$$

Inference rules on parameter passing equations

- *outermost narrowing* [o]$_\asymp$

$$\frac{f(s_1,\cdots,s_n) \asymp t, E}{s_1 \asymp l_1,\ldots,s_n \asymp l_n, r \asymp t, E} \quad t \notin \mathcal{V}$$

  if there exists a fresh variant $f(l_1,\cdots,l_n) \rightarrow r$ of a rewrite rule in $\mathcal{R}$.

- *decomposition* $[d]_{\asymp}$

$$\frac{f(s_1,\cdots,s_n) \asymp f(t_1,\cdots,t_n), E}{s_1 \asymp t_1,\ldots,s_n \asymp t_n, E}$$

- *variable elimination* $[v]_{\asymp}$

$$\frac{s \asymp X, E}{E\theta} \text{ and } \frac{X \asymp s, E}{E\theta} \quad s \notin \mathcal{V}$$

if $\theta = \{X \mapsto s\}$.

Theorem 8. (Completeness of LNC$_s$) *Let $\mathcal{R}$ be a left-linear confluent TRS and G a goal. For every normalized strict solution θ of G there exists an LNC$_s$-derivation $G \Rightarrow^*_\sigma \Box$ such that $\sigma \leq \theta[\mathcal{V}ar(G)]$.* □

This theorem derives from Theorem 22 in [16] for an orthogonal constructor-based system. Extension to left-linear system is based on the result of Suzuki[24].

5 Higher-order Lazy Narrowing Calculus

We are now ready to present a higher-order lazy narrowing calculus HLNC. For the investigation of its completeness, we present HLNC in two stages. In Subsection 5.1 we present basic HLNC and then in Subsection 5.2 we present HLNC.

5.1 BHLNC

Since we use the results of the previous sections, we require that TRS_λ is β-free, left-linear, and confluent in order to ensure the completeness of HLNC.

We often see these restrictions in the discussion of a computation model for functional logic languages. An orthogonal constructor-based system of which many functional logic programs fall into this category is an obvious example of a TRS_λ.

As for goals, we require that each side of an equation is a long η-normal form of the same type. This requirement makes the inference rules simpler. With this requirement we will easily see that $\mathcal{T}_\eta$ is closed under the HLNC-derivation. In the sequel basic HLNC is abbreviated as BHLNC.

Definition 9. (BHLNC) The calculus BHLNC consists of the following inference rules:

Inference rules on strict equations

- *outermost narrowing* $[o]$

$$\frac{f(s_1,\cdots,s_n) \approx t, E}{s_1 \asymp l_1,\ldots,s_n \asymp l_n, r \approx t, E} \text{ and } \frac{t \approx f(s_1,\cdots,s_n), E}{s_1 \asymp l_1,\ldots,s_n \asymp l_n, r \approx t, E}$$

if t is outermost irreducible and there exists a fresh variant $f(l_1,\cdots,l_n) \to r$ of a rewrite rule in $\mathcal{R}$.

- *outermost β-reduction* $[o\beta]$

$$\frac{(\lambda \mathbf{x}_n.u)\, \mathbf{s}_n \approx t, E}{u[\mathbf{x}_n := \mathbf{s}_n] \approx t, E} \text{ and } \frac{t \approx (\lambda \mathbf{x}_n.u)\, \mathbf{s}_n, E}{u[\mathbf{x}_n := \mathbf{s}_n] \approx t, E} \; t \text{ is outermost irreducible}$$

- *outermost narrowing on flex terms* $[ov]$

$$\frac{F\, \mathbf{s}_n \approx t, E}{(u[\mathbf{x}_n := \mathbf{s}_n] \approx t, E)\theta} \text{ and } \frac{t \approx F\, \mathbf{s}_n, E}{(u[\mathbf{x}_n := \mathbf{s}_n] \approx t, E)\theta} \; t \text{ is not flex}$$

if $n \geq 1$, t is outermost irreducible, $\theta = \{F \mapsto \lambda \mathbf{x}_n.u\}$, and $\lambda \mathbf{x}_n.u$ is an appropriate closed long $\eta\mathcal{R}\beta$-normal form[1].
- *imitation* $[i]$

$$\frac{c(s_1, \cdots, s_m) \simeq X, E}{(s_1 \approx X_1, \ldots, s_m \approx X_m, E)\theta}$$

if $X \in \mathcal{V}ar(c(s_1, \cdots, s_m))$ or $c(s_1, \cdots, s_m) \notin \mathcal{T}(\mathcal{F}_C, \mathcal{V})$ and $\theta = \{X \mapsto c(X_1, \cdots, X_m)\}$ with $X_1, \cdots, X_m$ fresh variables.
- *decomposition* $[d]$

$$\frac{c(s_1, \cdots, s_n) \approx c(t_1, \cdots, t_n), E}{s_1 \approx t_1, \ldots, s_n \approx t_n, E} \text{ and } \frac{x\, \mathbf{s}_n \approx x\, \mathbf{t}_n, E}{s_1 \approx t_1, \ldots, s_n \approx t_n, E}$$

$$\text{and } \frac{\lambda \mathbf{x}_n.s \approx \lambda \mathbf{x}_n.t, E}{s \approx t, E}$$

- *variable elimination* $[v]$

$$\frac{s \approx X, E}{E\theta} \text{ and } \frac{X \approx s, E}{E\theta} \; s \notin \mathcal{V}$$

if $\theta = \{X \mapsto s\}$, $X \notin \mathcal{V}ar(s)$, and $s \in \mathcal{T}(\mathcal{F}_C, \mathcal{V})$.
- *removal of trivial equation* $[t]$

$$\frac{X \approx X, E}{E}$$

Inference rules on parameter passing equations

- *outermost narrowing* $[o]_{\asymp}$

$$\frac{f(s_1, \cdots, s_n) \asymp t, E}{s_1 \asymp l_1, \ldots, s_n \asymp l_n, r \asymp t, E} \; t \notin \mathcal{V}$$

if there exists a fresh variant $f(l_1, \cdots, l_n) \to r$ of a rewrite rule in $\mathcal{R}$.
- *outermost β-reduction* $[o\beta]_{\asymp}$

$$\frac{(\lambda \mathbf{x}_n.u)\, \mathbf{s}_n \asymp t, E}{u[\mathbf{x}_n := \mathbf{s}_n] \asymp t, E} \; t \notin \mathcal{V}$$

[1] long η- and $\mathcal{R}_\beta \cup \mathcal{R}$-normal form is abbreviated as long $\eta\mathcal{R}\beta$-normal form.

- *outermost narrowing on flex terms* $[ov]_{\asymp}$

$$\frac{F\,\mathbf{s}_n \asymp t, E}{(u[\mathbf{x}_n := \mathbf{s}_n] \asymp t, E)\theta}\; t \notin \mathcal{V}$$

if $n \geq 1$, $\theta = \{F \mapsto \lambda\mathbf{x}_n.u\}$ and $\lambda\mathbf{x}_n.u$ is an appropriate fresh closed long $\eta R\beta$-normal form.

- *decomposition* $[d]_{\asymp}$

$$\frac{f(s_1,\cdots,s_n) \asymp f(t_1,\cdots,t_n), E}{s_1 \asymp t_1,\ldots,s_n \asymp t_n, E} \text{ and } \frac{x\,\mathbf{s}_n \asymp x\,\mathbf{t}_n, E}{s_1 \asymp t_1,\ldots,s_n \asymp t_n, E}$$

$$\text{and } \frac{\lambda\mathbf{x}_n.s \asymp \lambda\mathbf{x}_n.t, E}{s \asymp t, E}$$

- *variable elimination* $[v]_{\asymp}$

$$\frac{s \asymp X, E}{E\theta} \text{ and } \frac{X \asymp s, E}{E\theta}\; s \notin \mathcal{V}$$

if $\theta = \{X \mapsto s\}$.

Remarks:

- In $[ov]$ and $[ov]_{\asymp}$, how to choose u in $\lambda\mathbf{x}_n.u$ is unspecified. The selection of an appropriate u is discussed separately in the following subsection.
- In $[v]$, occur check is not necessary, since the left-hand side of a parameter passing equation is a fresh variable.
- There is no rule of *removal of a trivial equation for parameter passing equations* since $\mathcal{R}$ is left-linear and the right-hand side of a parameter passing equation contains only fresh variables.

It takes a considerable amount of work to formally discuss the correspondence between the inference rules of LNC_s and of BHLNC. The most of the discussion, however, follows the line of the formulation of NCA[20]. The only differences are the inference rules $[o\beta]$ and $[o\beta]_{\asymp}$. As space is limited, we briefly discuss the inference rules $[o\beta]$ and $[o\beta]_{\asymp}$ for treating the β-reduction. These inference rules are equal to so-called n step *weak head* β-reductions of the one side of an equation, i.e. only the root positions are contracted in these β-reductions. Such reduction derivations are always possible because every $(\mathcal{R} \cup \mathcal{R}_\beta)$-rewrite derivation starting from a β-redex can be simulated by a derivation such that (possibly zero) inner $(\mathcal{R} \cup \mathcal{R}_\beta)$-rewrite steps follow a (possibly empty) head β-reduction derivation. It is formally given in Lemma 11. On the other hand, in the application of $[o]$ of LNC_s to the β-redex in a goal we may choose the rewrite rule whose left-hand side is an instance of the β-redex; this LNC_s-step does not correspond to the BHLNC-step by $[o\beta]$. Such LNC_s-steps can be replaced with another LNC_s-steps that employ the rewrite rules whose left-hand side is more general than the original one. It is formally given in Lemma 10.

From these observations we can easily see that the undesirable LNC_s derivations are excluded. Hence we can relate desirable LNC_s-derivations with BHLNC-derivations with $[o\beta]$. The formal statement is given by Proposition 12. We will omit the full proofs of the lemmas and the proposition.

Lemma 10. *Let $\mathcal{R}$ be a left-linear confluent (first order) TRS and G a goal. Suppose we have an* LNC$_s$*-derivation $G \Rightarrow^*_\sigma \Box$ such that [o] is applied to G with a variant $l \to r$ of a rewrite rule in $\mathcal{R}$. For any* LNC$_s$*-step $G \Rightarrow_{[o]} G'$ with a rewrite rule $l' \to r'$ such that a substitution τ satisfies $l'\tau = l$ and $r'\tau = r$, there exists an* LNC$_s$*-derivation $G' \Rightarrow^*_{\sigma'} \Box$ such that $\sigma \leq \sigma'$ $[\mathcal{V}ar(G)]$.*

PROOF. The proof is done by a so-called lifting lemma. $\Box$

Lemma 11. *For any rewrite derivation $s \to^*_{\mathcal{R} \cup \mathcal{R}_\beta} t$ starting from s of the form $(\lambda x.M)N_1 \cdots N_k$ $(k > 0)$, there exists a derivation $s \to^*_{\mathcal{R}_\beta} s' \to^*_{\mathcal{R} \cup \mathcal{R}_\beta} t$, where only the root positions are contracted in the first subderivation $s \to^*_{\mathcal{R}_\beta} s'$.*

PROOF. Similar to the proof of Lemma 11.4.6 in [3]. $\Box$

Proposition 12. *Let $\mathcal{R}$ be a β-free left-linear confluent TRS_λ, S a goal of the form $(\lambda \mathbf{x}_n.M)\mathbf{s}_n \simeq t, E$ $(n > 0)$, and θ a $(\mathcal{R} \cup \mathcal{R}_\beta)$-normalized solution of S. There exists a BHLNC-step $S \Rightarrow_{[o\beta]} S'$ and a $(\mathcal{R} \cup \mathcal{R}_\beta)$-normalized solution σ of S' such that $\sigma \leq \theta$ $[\mathcal{V}ar(S)]$.*

PROOF. By Lemmas 10 and 11. $\Box$

Theorem 13. **(Completeness of BHLNC)** *Let $\mathcal{R}$ be a left-linear, β-free and confluent TRS_λ, and G a goal. For every long $\eta\mathcal{R}\beta$-normalized strict solution θ of G there exists a BHLNC-derivation $G \Rightarrow^*_\sigma \Box$ such that $\sigma \leq \theta[\mathcal{V}ar(G)]$.* $\Box$

5.2 HLNC

Although BHLNC enjoys the completeness it will not be useful as a calculus unless it is provided with an effective procedure to find an appropriate term u in $[ov]$ and $[ov]_\asymp$. In general term u is not uniquely determined, and moreover search for u involves do-not-know non-determinism. We will next discuss how to reduce the search space of u. The search space for u is reduced by observing the structures of the right-hand side term t of the processed equation $F\,\mathbf{s}_n \simeq t$ and of parameters of a rewrite rule to be used to rewrite the term $F\,\mathbf{s}_n$.

Definition 14. **(HLNC)** The calculus HLNC consists of the following inference rules and the inference rules of BHLNC excluding $[ov]$ and $[ov]_\asymp$:

- *outermost narrowing on flex terms with imitation binding* $[ovi]$

$$\frac{F\,\mathbf{s}_n \approx t, E}{(g(H_1\,\mathbf{s}_n, \cdots, H_m\,\mathbf{s}_n) \approx t, E)\theta} \text{ and } \frac{t \approx F\,\mathbf{s}_n, E}{(g(H_1\,\mathbf{s}_n, \cdots, H_m\,\mathbf{s}_n) \approx t, E)\theta}\ t \text{ is not flex}$$

  if $1 \leq n$, t is outermost irreducible, $\theta = \{F \mapsto \lambda \mathbf{x}_n.g(H_1\,\mathbf{x}_n, \cdots, H_m\,\mathbf{x}_n)\}$.

- *outermost narrowing on flex terms with projection binding* $[ovp]$

$$\frac{F\,\mathbf{s}_n \approx t, E}{(s_i\,(H_1\,\mathbf{s}_n) \cdots (H_m\,\mathbf{s}_n) \approx t, E)\theta} \text{ and } \frac{t \approx F\,\mathbf{s}_n, E}{(s_i\,(H_1\,\mathbf{s}_n) \cdots (H_m\,\mathbf{s}_n) \approx t, E)\theta}\ t \text{ is not flex}$$

  if $1 \leq n$, $1 \leq i \leq n$, t is outermost irreducible, $\theta = \{F \mapsto \lambda \mathbf{x}_n.x_i\,(H_1\,\mathbf{x}_n) \cdots (H_m\,\mathbf{x}_n)\}$.

- *outermost narrowing on flex terms with imitation binding* $[ovi]_{\asymp}$

$$\frac{F\,\mathbf{s}_n \asymp t, E}{(g(H_1\,\mathbf{s}_n, \cdots, H_m\,\mathbf{s}_n) \asymp t, E)\theta}\ t \notin \mathcal{V}$$

if $1 \leq n$, $\theta = \{F \mapsto \lambda \mathbf{x}_n.g(H_1\,\mathbf{x}_n, \cdots, H_m\,\mathbf{x}_n)\}$.

- *outermost narrowing on flex terms with projection binding* $[ovp]_{\asymp}$

$$\frac{F\,\mathbf{s}_n \asymp t, E}{(s_i\,(H_1\,\mathbf{s}_n)\cdots(H_m\,\mathbf{s}_n) \asymp t, E)\theta}\ t \notin \mathcal{V}$$

if $1 \leq n$, $1 \leq i \leq n$, $\theta = \{F \mapsto \lambda \mathbf{x}_n.x_i\,(H_1\,\mathbf{x}_n)\cdots(H_m\,\mathbf{x}_n)\}$.

The following theorem is crucial in order to justify our calculus HLNC, and is the main result of the paper. We sketch the proof because the description of its rigorous proof is beyond the scope of the present paper.

Theorem 15. (Completeness of HLNC) *Let $\mathcal{R}$ be a left-linear, β-free and confluent TRS_λ, and G a goal. For every long $\eta\mathcal{R}\beta$-normalized strict solution θ of G there exists an HLNC-derivation $G \Rightarrow^*_\sigma \square$ such that $\sigma \leq_\beta \theta[\mathcal{V}ar(G)]$.*
Proof Sketch. Given an non-empty BHLNC derivation $\Pi{:}\,G \Rightarrow^*_\theta \square$, we construct a BHLNC derivation $\Pi'{:}\,G' \Rightarrow^*_{\theta'} \square$, with an HLNC step $G \Rightarrow_{[\alpha'],\sigma_1} G'$. Applications of this construction process repeatedly to the obtained BHLNC derivations eventually yield an HLNC derivation $G \Rightarrow_{[\alpha'],\sigma_1} G' \Rightarrow^*_{\sigma_2} \square$ provided there exists a complexity measure of BHLNC derivations monotonously decreasing during this process (see the Figure 1).

$$\begin{array}{llll}
\Pi: & G & \Rightarrow_{[\alpha],\theta_1} G_1 \Rightarrow^*_{\theta_2} & \square \\
 & \Downarrow_{[\alpha'],\sigma_1} & & \\
\Pi': & G' & \Rightarrow^*_{\theta'} & \square \\
 & \Downarrow^*_{\sigma_2} & & \\
 & \square & &
\end{array}$$

Fig.1. Transformation of BHLNC derivations

The complexity $|\Pi|$ of a BHLNC derivation $\Pi{:}\,G \Rightarrow^*_\theta \square$ is defined as the pair $(M(\Pi), \#(\Pi))$, where $M(\Pi)$ is the multiset $\{|X\theta| \mid X \in \mathcal{V}ar(G)\}$ and $\#(\Pi)$ is the length of Π. Here $|t|$ is the *size* of long $\eta\beta$-normal forms defined as follows:

$$\begin{array}{ll}
|x| = 1 & x \in \mathcal{BV} \\
|f(s_1, \cdots, s_n)| = 1 + |s_1| + \cdots + |s_n| & n \geq 0 \\
|F(s_1, \cdots, s_n)| = 1 & F \in \mathcal{V}, n \geq 0 \\
|\lambda x.s| = |s| &
\end{array}$$

We define a (strict) partial order $\gg$ on BHLNC derivations by $\Pi_1 \gg \Pi_2$ if $|\Pi_1|\ \mathrm{lex}(>_{mul}, >)\ |\Pi_2|$.

In the figure 1, we show $\Pi \gg \Pi'$ for any application of the inference rule $[\alpha]$ in the first step of Π. In the case $[\alpha]$ is one of the inference rules other than $[ov]$ and $[ov]_{\asymp}$, we immediately obtain a BHLNC derivation Π' by taking $[\alpha] = [\alpha']$. It is not difficult to show that $M(\Pi) \geq M(\Pi')$ and $\#(\Pi) > \#(\Pi')$. Only the difficult cases are where $[\alpha]$ is $[ov]$ or $[ov]_{\asymp}$. Consider the following BHLNC derivation Π:

$$F\,x \approx \mathrm{d}(0) \Rightarrow_{[ov],\theta_1=\{F\mapsto\lambda x.d(0)\}} \mathrm{d}(0) \approx \mathrm{d}(0) \Rightarrow_{[d]} 0 \approx 0 \Rightarrow_{[d]} \Box.$$

Application of $[ovi]$ to the initial goal yields

$$F\,x \approx \mathrm{d}(0) \Rightarrow_{[ovi],\sigma_1=\{F\mapsto\lambda x.d(H\,x)\}} \mathrm{d}(H\,x) \approx \mathrm{d}(0).$$

The BHLNC derivation Π' starting from the goal obtained by the application of $[ovi]$ is obtained as follows:

$$\mathrm{d}(H\,x) \approx \mathrm{d}(0) \Rightarrow_{[d]} H\,x \approx 0 \Rightarrow_{[ov],\theta_1'=\{H\mapsto\lambda x.0\}} 0 \approx 0 \Rightarrow_{[d]} \Box.$$

The relationship between the subderivation of Π starting from the second goal and Π' is very clear: the same inference rules are applied to the same equations as far as a head variable introduced by $[ovi]$ does not appear in the root position of the one side of the equation. When the head variable occurs in the root position as $H\,x \approx 0$, a substitution for H is provided by $[ov]$ then the equation $0 \approx 0$ is obtained, which corresponds to the equation in Π. Furthermore, the term bound to H is the subterm 0, plus a binder λx, of the term $\lambda x.d(0)$ bound to F, thus $M(\Pi) > M(\Pi')$. As the result of the considerable amount of formal arguments, we learn that it is always the case, thereby, the construction process of HLNC derivations works as desired. □

The following example illustrates how goals are solved by HLNC. This example shows that HLNC can solve a higher-order unification problem. Let G be a goal $\mathrm{c}(\lambda x.F\,x) \approx \mathrm{c}(\lambda x.\mathrm{d}(0))$. G is solved by HLNC as follows.

$$\begin{aligned}&\mathrm{c}(\lambda x.F\,x) \approx \mathrm{c}(\lambda x.\mathrm{d}(0))\\ &\Rightarrow_{[d]} \lambda x.F\,x \approx \lambda x.\mathrm{d}(0) \Rightarrow_{[d]} F\,x \approx \mathrm{d}(0) \Rightarrow_{[ovi],\theta_1=\{F\mapsto\lambda x.d(H\,x)\}} \mathrm{d}(H\,x) \approx \mathrm{d}(0)\\ &\Rightarrow_{[d]} H\,x \approx 0 \Rightarrow_{[ovi],\theta_2=\{H\mapsto\lambda x.0\}} 0 \approx 0 \Rightarrow_{[d]} \Box\end{aligned}$$

A solution of G is $(\theta{\downarrow_\beta})\restriction_{\mathcal{V}ar(G)} = ((\theta_1\theta_2){\downarrow_\beta})\restriction_{\mathcal{V}ar(G)} = \{F \mapsto \lambda x.\mathrm{d}((\lambda x.0)\,0)\}{\downarrow_\beta} = \{F \mapsto \lambda x.\mathrm{d}(0)\}$.

6 Concluding Remarks

We have presented a higher-order lazy narrowing calculus HLNC as a computation model of a functional logic programming language. HLNC enjoys the completeness with respect to normalized solutions for a left-linear, β-free and confluent TRS_λ. HLNC is based on a first-order lazy narrowing calculus LNC that incorporates a rewriting strategy usually called lazy evaluation in functional programming. HLNC automatically inherits those properties that eliminate certain non-determinism inherent in general narrowing. This is done by the establishment of relationship between higher-order narrowing calculi and first-order narrowing calculi. Now we can exploit the techniques of improving efficiency of first-order narrowing in order to improve the efficiency of higher-order narrowing. It produces much advantages over higher-order narrowing based on higher-order rewriting because first-order narrowing is studied more extensively.

The relationship between first-order narrowing and higher-order narrowing in our framework relies on the introduction of $\mathcal{R}_\beta$, a first-order TRS embodying β-reduction. Another expression of β-reduction in the form of a first-order rewrite system is *explicit substitution*[1, 4]. The most desirable one is λv[4] proposed by Benaissa et al. since the calculus of λv is presented by a simple orthogonal TRS. However, λv is not confluent on open terms, i.e. the terms not correspond to classical λ-terms. The confluent property of the combined system $\mathcal{R} \cup \lambda v$ on closed terms, the terms of classical λ-calculus, is still unclear, though we expect it would be difficult to show its confluence.

HLNC applies β-reductions to β-redexes in the goals explicitly. Any HLNC step involves no implicit β-reduction. This property is preferable from the computational aspect. Consider the following TRS.

$$\begin{array}{l} \mathrm{if}(\mathrm{true}, X, Y) \to X \\ \mathrm{if}(\mathrm{false}, X, Y) \to Y \end{array}$$

Let Σ be a complicated λ-term whose normalization involves many β-reduction steps. We have an HLNC step issuing from the equation $\mathrm{if}(\mathrm{false}, \Sigma, \lambda x.x) \approx x$:

$$\begin{array}{l} \mathrm{if}(\mathrm{false}, \Sigma, \lambda x.x) \approx x \Rightarrow_{[o]} \mathrm{false} \asymp \mathrm{false}, \Sigma \asymp X, \lambda x.x \asymp Y, Y \approx x \Rightarrow_{[d]_\times} \\ \Sigma \asymp X, \lambda x.x \asymp Y, Y \approx x \Rightarrow_{[v]_\times, \{X \mapsto \Sigma\}} \lambda x.x \asymp Y, Y \approx x \Rightarrow_{[v]_\times, \{Y \mapsto \lambda x.x\}} \\ \lambda x.x \approx x \Rightarrow_{[o\beta]} x \approx x \Rightarrow_{[d]} \Box \end{array}$$

The discard of Σ is guaranteed by operational semantics of HLNC. Thus HLNC gives implementors a strict specification how and when β-redexes should be reduced. As long as the system is implemented correctly, the β-redexes are computed only when they are necessary. By contrast, the higher-order narrowing applying β-reductions implicitly does not specify when β-redexes are reduced. It leaves implementors how and when β-redexes should be reduced.

Our development of higher-order narrowing calculus is still under way. For instance, the lack of higher-order patterns in the left-hand side of rewrite rules causes a problem in writing interesting programs demonstrated in [22]. We conjecture that we can relax the condition of β-free for TRS_λ, such that higher-order patterns are allowed in the left-hand side of rewrite rules. We expect that a technique developed by Qian *et al.* to treat higher-order pattern unification by modular first-order unification can be exploited[23, 14].

References

1. M. Abadi, L. Cardelli, P.-L. Curien, and J.-J. Lévy. Explicit Substitutions. Technical Report 54, Digital Systems Research Center, February 1990.
2. S. Antoy, R. Echahed, and M. Hanus. A Needed Narrowing Strategy. In *Proc. of 21st ACM Symposium on Principles of Programming Languages*, pages 268–279, Portland, 1994.

3. P.H. Barendregt. *The Lambda Calculus (revised edition)*. North-Holland, 1984.
4. Z.-E.-A. Benaissa, D. Briaud, P. Lescanne, and J. Rouyer-Degli. λv, A Calculus of Explicit Substitutions Which Preserves Strong Normalization. Technical Report 2477, INRIA, Lorraine, January 1995.
5. A. Bockmayr, S. Krischer, and A. Werner. Narrowing Strategies for Arbitrary Canonical Systems. *Fundamenta Informaticae*, 24(1,2):125–155, 1995.
6. E. Giovannetti, G. Levi, C. Moiso, and C. Palamidessi. Kernel-LEAF: A logic plus functional language. *Journal of Computer and System Sciences*, 42(2):139–185, 1991.
7. M. Hanus. The Integration of Functions into Logic Programming: From Theory to Practice. *Journal of Logic Programming*, 19,20:583–628, 1994.
8. M. Hanus, H. Kuchen, and J. J. Moreno-Navarro. Curry: A Truly Functional Logic Language. In *Proc. of ILPS'95 Workshop on Visions for the Future of Logic Programming*, pages 95–107, 1995.
9. M. Hanus and C. Prehofer. Higher-order narrowing with definitional trees. In *Proceedings of Seventh International Conference on Rewrite Techniques and Applications, Lecture Notes in Computer Science 1103*, pages 138–152, 1996.
10. T. Ida and K. Nakahara. Leftmost Outside-In Narrowing Calculi. *Journal of Functional Programming*, 7(2), 1997. To appear.
11. T. Ida and S. Okui. Outside-In Conditional Narrowing. *IEICE Transactions on Information and Systems*, E77-D(6):631–641, 1994.
12. J. W. Klop. *Combinatory Reduction Systems*. Mathematical Centre Tracts Nr. 127, CWI, Amsterdam, 1980. PhD Thesis.
13. H. Kuchen. Higher Order BABEL. In S. Breitinger, H. Kröger, and R. Loogen, editors, *Proc. of 5th International Workshop on Functional and Logic Programming*, page XII, 1996.
14. J. Liu and Z. Qian. Using First-Order Narrowing to Solve Goals of Higher-Order Patterns. In *Proc. of Fuji International Workshop on Functional and Logic Programming*, pages 92–105, July 1995.
15. A. Middeldorp and E. Hamoen. Completeness Results for Basic Narrowing . *Applicable Algebra in Engineering, Communication and Computing*, 5:213–253, 1994.
16. A. Middeldorp and S. Okui. A Deterministic Lazy Narrowing Calculus. In *Fuji International Workshop on Functional and Logic Programming*, pages 104–118. World Scientific, 1995.
17. A. Middeldorp, S. Okui, and T. Ida. Lazy Narrowing: Strong Completeness and Eager Variable Elimination. *Theoretical Computer Science*, 167:95–130, 1996.
18. J. J. Moreno-Navarro and M. Rodríguez-Artalejo. Logic Programming with Functions and Predicates: The Language BABEL. *Journal of Logic Programming*, 12:191–223, 1992.
19. F. Müller. Confluence of the lambda calculus with left-linear algebraic rewriting. *Information Processing Letters*, 41:293–299, 1992.
20. K. Nakahara, A. Middeldorp, and T. Ida. A Complete Narrowing Calculus for Higher-Order Functional Logic Programming. In *Proc. of the 7th Programming Languages Implementation and Logic Programming*, Lecture Notes in Computer Sciences 982, pages 99–114, 1995.
21. T. Nipkow. Higher-order critical pairs. In *Proc. Sixth Annual IEEE Symposium on Logic in Computer Science*, pages 342–349, 1991.
22. C. Prehofer. *Solving Higher-Order Equations: From Logic to Programming*. PhD thesis, Technischen Universität München, 1995.

23. Z. Qian. Linear Unification of Higher-Order Patterns. In *Proc. of Theory and Practice of Software Development*, Lecture Notes in Computer Sciences 668, pages 391–405. Springer Verlag, 1993.
24. T. Suzuki. Standardization theorem revisited. In *Proceedings of Fifth International Conference on Algebraic and Logic Programming, Lecture Notes in Computer Science 1139*, pages 122–134, 1996.

On Composable Properties of Term Rewriting Systems

Takahito Aoto and Yoshihito Toyama

School of Information Science, JAIST
Tatsunokuchi, Ishikawa 923-12, Japan
{aoto, toyama}@jaist.ac.jp

Abstract. A property of term rewriting system (TRS, for short) is said to be composable if it is preserved under unions. We present composable properties of TRSs on the base of modularity results for direct sums of TRSs. We propose a decomposition by a naive sort attachment, and show that modular properties for direct sums of TRSs are τ-composable for a naive sort attachment τ. Here, a decomposition of a TRS $\mathcal{R}$ is a pair $\langle \mathcal{R}_1, \mathcal{R}_2 \rangle$ of (not necessary disjoint) subsets of $\mathcal{R}$ such that $\mathcal{R} = \mathcal{R}_1 \cup \mathcal{R}_2$; and for a naive sort attachment τ a property ϕ of TRSs is said to be τ-composable if for any TRS $\mathcal{R}$ such that τ is consistent with $\mathcal{R}$, $\phi(\mathcal{R}_1) \wedge \phi(\mathcal{R}_2)$ implies $\phi(\mathcal{R})$, where $\langle \mathcal{R}_1, \mathcal{R}_2 \rangle$ is the decomposition of $\mathcal{R}$ by τ.

1 Introduction

A decomposition of a term rewriting system (TRS, for short) $\mathcal{R}$ is a pair $\langle \mathcal{R}_1, \mathcal{R}_2 \rangle$ of (not necessary disjoint) subsets of $\mathcal{R}$ such that $\mathcal{R} = \mathcal{R}_1 \cup \mathcal{R}_2$. In this paper, we propose a *decomposition by a naive sort attachment*, and present *τ-composable properties* for a naive sort attachment τ. Here, for a naive sort attachment τ a property ϕ of TRSs is said to be τ-composable if for any TRS $\mathcal{R}$ such that τ is consistent with $\mathcal{R}$, $\phi(\mathcal{R}_1) \wedge \phi(\mathcal{R}_2)$ implies $\phi(\mathcal{R})$, where $\langle \mathcal{R}_1, \mathcal{R}_2 \rangle$ is the decomposition of $\mathcal{R}$ by τ.

A property of TRSs is said to be *composable* if it is preserved under unions. Composable properties, in particular, preserved under non-disjoint unions have been studied by several authors; see [10] [11].

The key idea of our composability result is a top-down labelling—a particular mapping from terms to terms, which is applied top-down. Using this labelling, we show that properties that are modular for direct sums are τ-composable for a naive sort attachment τ. Here, a property of TRSs is said be *modular (for a particular kind of disjoint unions)* if it is preserved under (for such kind of) disjoint unions; and a disjoint union of TRSs is called a *direct sum* when the sets of function symbols that appear in those TRSs are disjoint. Modularity for direct sums were studied in e.g. [3] [6] [7] [8] [12] [13] [14] [15]. Thus, on the base of these modularity results, we uniformly obtain composability results for decompositions by a naive sort attachment.

The τ-composability of a property for a naive sort attachment τ can be also obtained by the persistency of the property. Here, a property ϕ of TRSs is said to be *persistent* if for any TRS $\mathcal{R}$ and a sort attachment τ consistent with $\mathcal{R}$ it holds that $\phi(\mathcal{R}^\tau)$ if and only if $\phi(\mathcal{R})$, where $\mathcal{R}^\tau$ is the many-sorted TRS induced from $\mathcal{R}$ and τ. It was shown in [17] that for component-closed properties their persistency implies their modularity for direct sums of TRSs. For several properties, their persistency has been proved by modifying the proofs of their modularity for direct sums of TRSs; see [1] [17]. Whether the modularity for direct sums of TRSs implies the persistency (uniformly for component-closed properties) is still a conjecture, and once the conjecture is solved affirmatively the result in this paper will be subsumed. Note, however, that for component-closed properties their persistency coincides with their modularity for direct sums of many-sorted TRSs [16].

The rest of this paper is organized as follows. To introduce a notion of a decomposition by a naive sort attachment, we need a notion of sort attachment and of sort elimination. For this, we review many-sorted term rewriting in section 2. In section 3, we develop a top-down labelling technique and show that how reductions are preserved under the top-down labelling. In section 4, we give various composability results together with some examples.

2 Preliminaries

Our language is given by a set $\mathcal{S}$ of sorts (denoted by $X, Y, Z, \ldots$), a set $\mathcal{V}$ of variables (denoted by $x, y, z, \ldots$), and a set $\mathcal{F}$ of function symbols (denoted by $f, g, h, \ldots$). Each variable is given with its sort; we assume that there are countably infinite variables of sort X for each sort $X \in \mathcal{S}$. Similarly, each function symbol is given with the sorts of its arguments and the sort of its output. We write $f : X_1 \times \cdots \times X_n \to Y$ if f takes n arguments of sorts $X_1, \ldots, X_n$ respectively to a value of sort Y.

With such language, one can build up terms (of sort X) in a usual way: (1) a variable of sort X is a term of sort X; (2) if $f : X_1 \times \cdots \times X_n \to X$ is a function symbol and $t_1, \ldots, t_n$ are terms of sort $X_1, \ldots, X_n$ respectively, then $f(t_1, \ldots, t_n)$ is a term of sort X. Let $\mathcal{T}$ (and $\mathcal{T}^X$) denote the set of terms (of sort X, respectively). We also write "$t : X$" to indicate that $t \in \mathcal{T}^X$. Syntactical equality is denoted by $\equiv$. $\mathcal{V}(t)$ is the set of variables that appear in a term t.

For each sort X, let $\Box^X$ be a special constant—called a *hole*—of sort X. A *context* is a term possibly containing holes. The set of contexts is denoted by $\mathcal{C}$. We write $C : X_1 \times \cdots \times X_n \to X$ when $C \in \mathcal{C}$ has the sort X (as a term) and has n holes $\Box^{X_1}, \ldots, \Box^{X_n}$ from left to right in it. If $C : X_1 \times \cdots \times X_n \to Y$ and $t_1 : X_1, \ldots, t_n : X_n$ then $C[t_1, \ldots, t_n]$ is the term obtained from C by replacing holes with $t_1, \ldots, t_n$ from left to right. A context C is written as $C[\,]$ when C contains precisely one hole. A term t is said to be a *subterm* of s ($t \trianglelefteq s$, in symbol) if $s \equiv C[t]$ for some context $C[\,]$.

A *substitution* σ is a mapping from $\mathcal{V}$ to $\mathcal{T}$ such that x and $\sigma(x)$ have the same sort. A substitution is extended to a homomorphism from $\mathcal{T}$ to $\mathcal{T}$ in an obvious way. For a substitution σ and a term t, we customarily write $t\sigma$ instead of $\sigma(t)$.

A *(many-sorted) rewrite rule* is a pair $\langle l, r\rangle$ of terms such that (1) l and r have the same sort, (2) $l \notin \mathcal{V}$, (3) $\mathcal{V}(r) \subseteq \mathcal{V}(l)$. We conventionally write $l \to r$ instead of $\langle l, r\rangle$. A rewrite rule $l \to r$ is *collapsing* if $r \in \mathcal{V}$; it is *duplicating* if r contains more occurrences of some variable than l does. A *many-sorted term rewriting system* (*STRS*, for short) is a set of rewrite rules. A STRS is said to be *non-collapsing* (*non-duplicating*) if it contains no collapsing (resp. duplicating) rules. For $\mathcal{T}' \subseteq \mathcal{T}$, a STRS $\{l \to r \in \mathcal{R} \mid l, r \in \mathcal{T}'\}$ is denoted by $\mathcal{R}\restriction\mathcal{T}'$.

Given a STRS $\mathcal{R}$, a term s reduces to a term t ($s \to_{\mathcal{R}} t$, in symbol) when $s \equiv C[l\sigma]$ and $t \equiv C[r\sigma]$ for some $C[\,] \in \mathcal{C}$, $l \to r \in \mathcal{R}$ and substitution σ. We call $s \to_{\mathcal{R}} t$ a *rewrite step* (or a *reduction*). The *redex* of this rewrite step is $l\sigma$. The term t is called a *reduct* of the term s. One can readily check that s and t have the same sort whenever $s \to_{\mathcal{R}} t$. The transitive reflexive closure and the transitive reflexive symmetric closure of $\to_{\mathcal{R}}$ are denoted by $\xrightarrow{*}_{\mathcal{R}}$ and $\xleftrightarrow{*}_{\mathcal{R}}$, respectively. Henceforth, the subscript $_{\mathcal{R}}$ will be omitted when $\mathcal{R}$ is obvious from the context.

When $\mathcal{S} = \{*\}$, a STRS is called a TRS. Given an arbitrary STRS $\mathcal{R}$, by identifying each sort with $*$, we obviously obtain a TRS $\Theta(\mathcal{R})$—called the underlying TRS of $\mathcal{R}$.

Let $\mathcal{F}$ and $\mathcal{V}$ be sets of function symbols and variables, respectively, on a trivial set $\{*\}$ of sorts. Terms built from this language are called *unsorted terms*. Let $\mathcal{S}$ be another set of sorts. A *sort attachment* τ *on* $\mathcal{S}$ is a mapping from $\mathcal{F} \cup \mathcal{V}$ to the set $\mathcal{S}^*$ of finite sequences of elements from $\mathcal{S}$ such that $\tau(x) \in \mathcal{S}$ for any $x \in \mathcal{V}$ and $\tau(f) \in \mathcal{S}^{n+1}$ for any n-ary function symbol $f \in \mathcal{F}$. We write $\tau(f) = X_1 \times \cdots \times X_n \to Y$ instead of $\tau(f) = X_1, \ldots, X_n, Y$. Given a TRS $\mathcal{R}$, a sort attachment τ is said to be *consistent with* $\mathcal{R}$ if for any $l \to r \in \mathcal{R}$ there exists $Y \in \mathcal{S}$ such that $\vdash_\tau l : Y$ and $\vdash_\tau r : Y$ are provable in the following inference system:

$$\frac{\tau(x) = X}{\vdash_\tau x : X} \tag{1}$$

$$\frac{\tau(f) = X_1 \times \cdots \times X_n \to Y \quad \vdash_\tau t_1 : X_1 \quad \cdots \quad \vdash_\tau t_n : X_n}{\vdash_\tau f(t_1, \ldots, t_n) : Y.} \tag{2}$$

From a given TRS $\mathcal{R}$ and a sort attachment τ consistent with $\mathcal{R}$, by regarding each function symbol f to be of sort $\tau(f)$, and each variable x to be of sort $\tau(x)$, we get a STRS $\mathcal{R}^\tau$—called a STRS induced from $\mathcal{R}$ and τ. Note that $\mathcal{R}^\tau$ acts on $\mathcal{T}^\tau = \{t \in \mathcal{T} \mid \vdash_\tau t : X \text{ for some } X \in \mathcal{S}\}$, i.e. $s, t \in \mathcal{T}^\tau$ whenever $s \to_{\mathcal{R}^\tau} t$. Elements of $\mathcal{T}^\tau$ are called *well-sorted terms*. Clearly, $\mathcal{T}^\tau \subseteq \mathcal{T}$. For a fixed τ, we put $\mathcal{F}^Y = \{f \in \mathcal{F} \mid \tau(f) = X_1 \times \cdots \times X_n \to Y \text{ for some } X_1, \ldots, X_n \in \mathcal{S}\ \}$ and $\mathcal{T}^Y = \{t \in \mathcal{T} \mid \vdash_\tau t : Y\}$ for each $Y \in \mathcal{S}$. We also write $f : X_1 \times \cdots \times X_n \to Y$ instead of $\tau(f) = X_1 \times \cdots \times X_n \to Y$ when τ is obvious from the context.

3 Decomposition by a naive sort attachment

Using the notions presented in the previous section, we now define a decomposition by a naive sort attachment.

Definition 1. 1. A sort attachment τ on $\mathcal{S}$ is said to be *naive* when $\mathcal{S} = \{0,1,2\}$ and for any $f \in \mathcal{F}$ we have either
- $\tau(f) = 0 \times \cdots \times 0 \to 0$,
- $\tau(f) = X_1 \times \cdots \times X_n \to 1$ with $X_1, \ldots, X_n \in \{0,1\}$ or
- $\tau(f) = Y_1 \times \cdots \times Y_n \to 2$ with $Y_1, \ldots, Y_n \in \{0,2\}$.

2. Let $\mathcal{R}$ be a TRS and τ a naive sort attachment consistent with $\mathcal{R}$. Suppose that $\mathcal{R}_X = \Theta(\mathcal{R}^\tau \restriction (\mathcal{T}^0 \cup \mathcal{T}^X))$ for each $X \in \{1,2\}$. Then a pair $\langle \mathcal{R}_1, \mathcal{R}_2 \rangle$ of TRSs is said to be a *decomposition of* $\mathcal{R}$ *by* τ.
3. A pair $\langle \mathcal{R}_1, \mathcal{R}_2 \rangle$ of TRSs is said to be a *decomposition of* $\mathcal{R}$ *by a naive sort attachment* if there exists a naive sort attachment τ consistent with $\mathcal{R}$ such that $\langle \mathcal{R}_1, \mathcal{R}_2 \rangle$ is a decomposition of $\mathcal{R}$ by τ.

Our theorems (Theorem 12~17) are consequences of the preservation of reductions under a top-down labelling. So, our first aim is to develop a top-down labelling technique. To this end, we fix a TRS $\mathcal{R}$ on the terms built from a set $\mathcal{F}$ of function symbols and a set $\mathcal{V}$ of variables (on a trivial set $\{*\}$ of sorts). Moreover, we put $\mathcal{S} = \{0,1,2\}$ and assume that τ is a naive sort attachment on $\mathcal{S}$ consistent with $\mathcal{R}$. It should be clear from the definition that well-sorted terms of sort 0 contain neither function symbols from $\mathcal{F}^1$ nor those from $\mathcal{F}^2$, and that well-sorted terms of sort 1 contain no function symbols from $\mathcal{F}^2$ and vice versa.

In the sequel, we need the following notation. For $C \in \mathcal{C}$, we write $C : X_1 \times \cdots \times X_n \to Y$ if $\vdash_\tau C[\Box^{X_1}, \ldots, \Box^{X_n}] : Y$ is derivable by rules (1), (2) with an additional rule:

$$\frac{X \in \mathcal{S}}{\vdash_\tau \Box^X : X.} \tag{3}$$

Definition 2. 1. The *top sort* of a term $t \in \mathcal{T}$ is defined by

$$\operatorname{top}(t) = \begin{cases} \tau(t) & \text{if } t \in \mathcal{V}, \\ Y & \text{if } t \equiv f(t_1, \ldots, t_n) \text{ with } \tau(f) = X_1 \times \cdots \times X_n \to Y. \end{cases}$$

2. Let $t \equiv C[t_1, \ldots, t_n] \in \mathcal{T}$ $(n \geq 0)$ be a term with $C \not\equiv \Box$. We write $t \equiv C[\![t_1, \ldots, t_n]\!]$ if (1) $C : X_1 \times \cdots \times X_n \to Y$, and (2) $\operatorname{top}(t_i) \neq X_i$ for $i = 1, \ldots, n$. If this is the case, terms $t_1, \ldots, t_n$ are called the *principal* subterms of t. Clearly, a term t is uniquely written as $C[\![t_1, \ldots, t_n]\!]$ for some $C \in \mathcal{C}$ and terms $t_1, \ldots, t_n$.
3. The *rank* of a term $t \in \mathcal{T}$ is defined by

$$\operatorname{rank}(t) = \begin{cases} 1 & \text{if } t \in \mathcal{T}^\tau, \\ 1 + max\{\operatorname{rank}(t_i) \mid 1 \leq i \leq n\} & \text{if } t \equiv C[\![t_1, \ldots, t_n]\!] \text{ with } n \geq 1. \end{cases}$$

Example 1. Let $\mathcal{F} = \{f, g, a, b, c, F\}$ and

$$\tau \begin{cases} f : 0 \times 1 \to 1 \\ g : 0 \to 1 \\ a, b, c : 0 \\ F : 0 \times 0 \to 2. \end{cases}$$

Then $f(b, g(a)) \in \mathcal{T}^1$, $\mathrm{top}(f(a,b)) = 1$ and $\mathrm{top}(F(c, f(a,b))) = 2$. Also, $F(c, f(a,b)) \equiv C[\![f(a,b)]\!]$ is a term of rank 3 where $C \equiv F(c, \Box) : 0 \to 2$.

Definition 3. 1. A rewrite step $s \to t$ is said to be *inner* (written as $s \to^i t$) if

$$s \equiv C[\![s_1, \ldots, C'[l\sigma], \ldots, s_n]\!] \to C[s_1, \ldots, C'[r\sigma], \ldots, s_n] \equiv t$$

for some terms $s_1, \ldots, s_n$, a substitution σ, $l \to r \in \mathcal{R}$, and $C' \in \mathcal{C}$; otherwise it is *outer* (written as $s \to^o t$).

2. A rewrite step $s \to^o t$ is said to be *destructive* if $\mathrm{top}(s) \neq \mathrm{top}(t)$.

The following lemma shows that a destructive rewrite step occurs only when the applied rule is collapsing, and that the reduct of a destructive rewrite step results from one of the principal subterms.

Lemma 4. *A rewrite step $s \to^o t$ is destructive if and only if $t \equiv \sigma(x)$ and $s \equiv C[\![s_1, \ldots, \sigma(x), \ldots, s_n]\!]$ for some terms $s_1, \ldots, s_n$, a substitution σ, and $C \in \mathcal{C}$ such that $C[s_1, \ldots, \Box, \ldots, s_n] \equiv C'\sigma$ for some $C'[x] \to x \in \mathcal{R}$.*

Proof. ($\Leftarrow$) Suppose $\mathrm{top}(s) = \mathrm{top}(t)$. Then, since $C' \not\equiv \Box$ by the definition of rewrite rules, $\mathrm{top}(C'[x]) = \mathrm{top}(C'[x]\sigma) = \mathrm{top}(\sigma(x))$. Also, by consistency, $\mathrm{top}(x) = \mathrm{top}(C'[x])$, so $\mathrm{top}(x) = \mathrm{top}(t)$. But then, t can not be principal, since $C[s_1, \ldots, \Box, \ldots, s_n] \equiv C'\sigma : \mathrm{top}(x) \to \mathrm{top}(s)$. ($\Rightarrow$) Suppose $\mathrm{top}(s) \neq \mathrm{top}(t)$. By consistency, the rewrite step $s \to_{\mathcal{R}} t$ is an application of a collapsing rule, and the redex of the rewrite step is s. Let the rule be $C'[x] \to x$, and suppose $s \equiv C'[x]\sigma$ and $t \equiv \sigma(x)$. Since $C[s_1, \ldots, \Box, \ldots, s_n] : \mathrm{top}(x) \to \mathrm{top}(s)$, it suffices to show $\mathrm{top}(x) \neq \mathrm{top}(t)$. But $\mathrm{top}(x) = \mathrm{top}(C'[x])$ by consistency, and $\mathrm{top}(C'[x]) = \mathrm{top}(C'[x]\sigma) = \mathrm{top}(s)$ since $C' \not\equiv \Box$. Hence $\mathrm{top}(x) = \mathrm{top}(s) \neq \mathrm{top}(t)$. $\Box$

The next lemma is proved in a straightforward way; it analyzes the structure of a rewrite step. We write $t \equiv C\langle\!\langle t_1, \ldots, t_n\rangle\!\rangle$ when either $t \equiv C[\![t_1, \ldots, t_n]\!]$ or $C \equiv \Box$ and $t \equiv t_1$.

Lemma 5. *1. If $s \to^o t$ then*

$$\begin{cases} s \equiv C[\![s_1, \ldots, s_n]\!], \\ t \equiv C'\langle\!\langle s_{i_1}, \ldots, s_{i_m}\rangle\!\rangle, \qquad \text{where } i_1, \ldots, i_m \in \{1, \ldots, n\} \end{cases}$$

for some $C, C', s_1, \ldots, s_n$, and either

(a) $n = m = 0$ and $s, t \in \mathcal{T}^\tau$;

(b) $n \neq 0$, $s \to^o t$ is destructive, $C' \equiv \Box$ and $t \equiv s_j$ for some $1 \leq j \leq n$; or

(c) $n \neq 0$, $s \to^o t$ is not destructive and $t \equiv C'[\![s_{i_1}, \ldots, s_{i_m}]\!]$.

2. If $s \to^i t$ then

$$\begin{cases} s \equiv C[\![s_1, \ldots, s_j, \ldots, s_n]\!], \\ t \equiv C[s_1, \ldots, t_j, \ldots, s_n] \text{ and} \\ s_j \to t_j \end{cases}$$

for some $C, s_1, \ldots, s_n, t_j$, and either

(a) $t \equiv C[\![s_1, \ldots, t_j, \ldots, s_n]\!]$; or

(b) $s_j \to t_j$ *is destructive,* t_j *is a principal subterm of* s_j,

$$\begin{cases} t_j \equiv C'[\![u_1, \ldots, u_l]\!], \\ t \equiv C''[\![s_1, \ldots, u_1, \ldots, u_l, \ldots, s_n]\!] \end{cases}$$

and $C'' \equiv C[\Box, \ldots, C', \ldots, \Box]$ *for some* $C', u_1, \ldots, u_l$.

The following lemma can be proved without any difficulties.

Lemma 6. *Suppose that* $C[\![s_1, \ldots, s_n]\!] \to^o C'\langle\!\langle s_{i_1}, \ldots, s_{i_m}\rangle\!\rangle$ *and* $C : X_1 \times \cdots \times X_n \to Y$. *Then for any* $t_1, \ldots, t_n$ *such that* $X_i = X_j \wedge s_i \equiv s_j$ *implies* $t_i \equiv t_j$ *(for any* $1 \leq i, j \leq n$*), we have a rewrite step* $C[t_1, \ldots, t_n] \to^o C'[t_{i_1}, \ldots, t_{i_m}]$.

Before presenting the actual definition of our top-down labelling, we explain the idea of the top-down labelling. Note that our function symbols are divided into the three categories: $\mathcal{F}^0$, $\mathcal{F}^1$ and $\mathcal{F}^2$. By our labelling, the function symbols from $\mathcal{F}^1$ or $\mathcal{F}^2$ remain unlabelled, and the function symbols from $\mathcal{F}^0$ are labelled with 1 or 2.

Suppose a function symbol from $\mathcal{F}^0$ occurs in a term. It is not hard to observe that every term can be uniquely partitioned by well-sorted parts. If the function symbol occurs in a well-sorted part of top sort 1 or 2, then we label the function symbol with 1 or 2, respectively. The difficult case is when the function symbol belongs to a well-sorted part of top sort 0. In this case, all symbols in a well-sorted part of top sort 0 are uniformly labelled with 1 or 2, according to with which well-sorted part of top sort 1 or 2 the well-sorted part of sort 0 might be connected.

To explain the last case more precisely, suppose $t \equiv C[\![t_1, \ldots, t_n]\!]$ is a subterm of a term s and C is a well-sorted part in s. Let us call the "connection" from the position of t_i (in s) and the position of t (in s) a X_i–Y connection when $C : X_1 \times \cdots \times X_n \to Y$. So, in each well-sorted parts in a term, there are connections from the positions of its principal subterms to its root position. Now, observe that for any term t with a top sort X, its principal subterm t_i can be lifted (by a destructive rewrite step) only when t_i is placed at the hole of sort X. Thus, only X–X connections possibly eliminated (for $X \in \{0, 1, 2\}$). We have to label a well-sorted part of top sort 0 with 1 or 2 beforehand for the case it is used as a part of a well-sorted part of top sort 1 or 2. Therefore, we decide the label of a well-sorted part C of top sort 0 as follows. Starting from the root position of C, we follow up connections in each well-sorted parts above it; on the way, we skip 0–0, 1–1 and 2–2 connections, and if we eventually encounter a 0–X ($X = 1$ or 2) connection then we decide the label X. Figure 1 is an example of the labelling—the function symbols from $\mathcal{F}^0$ placed in white parts will be labelled with 1, and those placed in black parts will be labelled with 2. There, we consider function symbols $\mathcal{F}^0 = \{d : 0 \times 0 \to 0, e : 0 \to 0, a : 0\}$, $\mathcal{F}^1 = \{f : 0 \times 1 \to 1, g : 1 \times 1 \to 1, h : 0 \to 1, k : 1 \to 1, b : 1\}$, $\mathcal{F}^2 = \{E : 0 \times 2 \to 2, F : 2 \times 2 \to 2, G : 0 \to 2, H : 2 \to 2, A : 2\}$ and a term $f(e(E(a, H(d(x, e(g(k(a), b)))))), h(F(H(H(e(y))), G(e(g(h(e(A)), k(k(a))))))))$.

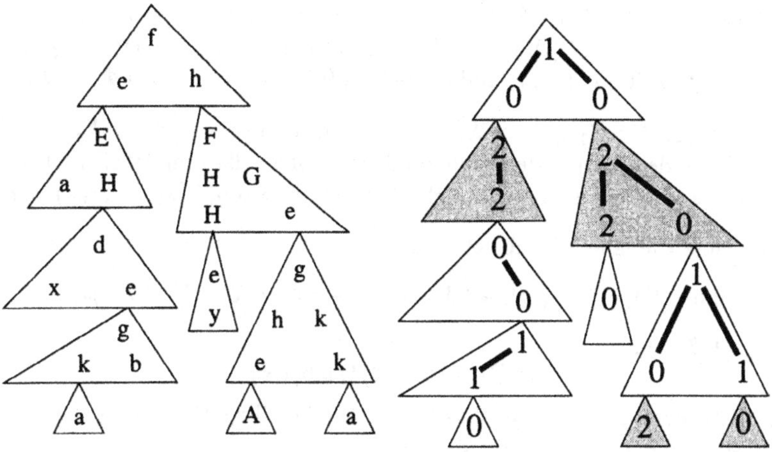

Fig. 1. The labelling of a term

Now, we present these considerations in a formal way. The set of labelled function symbols is introduced like this. For each $f \in \mathcal{F}^0$ and $X \in \{1,2\}$, f_X is a new function symbol—f labelled with X. For $X \in \{1,2\}$, let $\mathrm{lab}_X(\mathcal{F}^0) = \{f_X \mid f \in \mathcal{F}^0\}$. Elements of the set $\bigcup_{X\in\{1,2\}} \mathrm{lab}_X(\mathcal{F}^0)$ are called *labelled symbols*; we assume that these are fresh function symbols, i.e. $\mathrm{lab}_1(\mathcal{F}^0)$, $\mathrm{lab}_2(\mathcal{F}^0)$ and $\mathcal{F}$ are mutually disjoint. And finally, let $\mathrm{lab}(\mathcal{F}) = \bigcup_{X\in\{1,2\}}(\mathrm{lab}_X(\mathcal{F}^0) \cup \mathcal{F}^X)$.

Terms built from $\mathrm{lab}(\mathcal{F})$ and $\mathcal{V}$ are called *labelled terms*; those from $\mathcal{F}$ and $\mathcal{V}$ are *unlabelled*. For a term t and $X \in \{1,2\}$, $\mathrm{lab}_X(t)$ is the term obtained from t by labelling all symbols in $\mathcal{F}^0$ with X. This convention is also adapted for contexts.

Example 2. In Example 1, $\mathrm{lab}_1(\mathcal{F}^0) = \{a_1, b_1, c_1\}$ and $\mathrm{lab}_2(\mathcal{F}^0) = \{a_2, b_2, c_2\}$. We also have $\mathrm{lab}_1(f(g(a),c)) \equiv f(g(a_1),c_1)$ and $\mathrm{lab}_2(F(c,g(b))) \equiv F(c_2,g(b_2))$.

Two kinds of top-down labelling ∇_1 and ∇_2 are defined simultaneously as follows:

Definition 7. Let t be an unlabelled term such that $t \equiv C[\![t_1,\ldots,t_n]\!]$ with $C : X_1 \times \cdots \times X_n \to Y$. Labelled terms $\nabla_X t$ $(X \in \{1,2\})$ are defined by

$$\nabla_X t \equiv \begin{cases} \mathrm{lab}_X(C)[\nabla_X t_1,\ldots,\nabla_X t_n] & \text{if } Y \in \{0,X\}, \\ \mathrm{lab}_Y(C)[\Phi_1 t_1,\ldots,\Phi_n t_n] & \text{otherwise,} \end{cases}$$

where $\Phi_j = \nabla_Y$ if $X_j = 0$, and $\Phi_j = \nabla_X$ otherwise i.e. $X_j = Y$ (thus it makes a Y–Y connection).

Example 3. In Example 1, we have $\nabla_1(a) \equiv a_1$ and $\nabla_2(F(a,f(b,c))) \equiv F(a_2,f(b_1,c_2))$.

Lemma 8. *Suppose that $C[\![s_1,\ldots,s_n]\!] \to^o s_j$ is a destructive rewrite step. If $\nabla_X(C[\![s_1,\ldots,s_n]\!]) \equiv C^*[\Phi_1 s_1,\ldots,\Phi_n s_n]$, where $\Phi_1,\ldots,\Phi_n \in \{\nabla_1,\nabla_2\}$, $C^* \equiv \mathrm{lab}_{\mathrm{top}(C)}C$ if $\mathrm{top}(C) \in \{1,2\}$, and $C^* \equiv \mathrm{lab}_X(C)$ otherwise, then $\Phi_j = \nabla_X$.*

Proof. Suppose $C : X_1 \times \cdots \times X_n \to Y$. Then it suffices to show $X_j = Y$. By Lemma 4, the destructive step is an application of a collapsing rule. Let the rule be $C'[x] \to x$. But then, $X_j = \mathrm{top}(x) = \mathrm{top}(C'[x]) = \mathrm{top}(C[\![s_1,\ldots,s_n]\!]) = Y$. □

We define the labelled TRS of $\mathcal{R}$ like this:

$$\mathrm{lab}_X(\mathcal{R}) = \{\mathrm{lab}_X(l) \to \mathrm{lab}_X(r) \mid l \to r \in \Theta(\mathcal{R}^\tau \restriction (\mathcal{T}^0 \cup \mathcal{T}^X))\}$$

for $X \in \{1,2\}$, and

$$\mathrm{lab}(\mathcal{R}) = \mathrm{lab}_1(\mathcal{R}) \cup \mathrm{lab}_2(\mathcal{R}).$$

Then, in Lemma 9, it will be shown that the labelling ∇_1 and ∇_2 map every rewrite step of $\mathcal{R}$ to that of $\mathrm{lab}(\mathcal{R})$.

Example 4. Let

$$\mathcal{R}\begin{cases} f(x,y) \to x & (r1)\\ f(x,y) \to f(x,g(y)) & (r2)\\ g(x) \to h(x) & (r3)\\ F(g(x),x) \to F(x,g(x)) & (r4)\\ F(h(x),x) \to F(x,h(x)) & (r5), \end{cases} \qquad \tau\begin{cases} f : 1 \times 0 \to 1\\ g : 0 \to 0\\ h : 0 \to 0\\ F : 0 \times 0 \to 2. \end{cases}$$

Then τ is consistent with $\mathcal{R}$, and we have

$$\mathrm{lab}(\mathcal{R})\begin{cases} f(x,y) \to x\\ f(x,y) \to f(x,g_1(x))\\ g_1(x) \to h_1(x)\\ g_2(x) \to h_2(x)\\ F(g_2(x),x) \to F(x,g_2(x))\\ F(h_2(x),x) \to F(x,h_2(x)). \end{cases}$$

Lemma 9. *For any $X \in \{1,2\}$, we have $s \to_{\mathcal{R}} t$ if and only if $\nabla_X s \to_{\mathrm{lab}(\mathcal{R})} \nabla_X t$.*

Proof. (⇐) It suffices to erase all labels. (⇒) We suppose $s \to_{\mathcal{R}} t$ and show that for any $X \in \{1,2\}$, $\nabla_X s \to_{\mathrm{lab}(\mathcal{R})} \nabla_X t$. Our proof proceeds by induction on the rank of s. Base step is obvious. Suppose that $\mathrm{rank}(s) > 1$. We distinguish all possible cases according to Lemma 5:

1. $s \to^o t$. Then $s \equiv C[\![s_1,\ldots,s_n]\!]$ and $t \equiv C'\langle\!\langle s_{i_1},\ldots,s_{i_m}\rangle\!\rangle$ $(i_1,\ldots,i_m \in \{1,\ldots,n\})$ for some $C, C', s_1,\ldots,s_n$. But then, on the base of Lemma 6 and Lemma 8, one can easily show that $\nabla_X s \to_{\mathrm{lab}(\mathcal{R})} \nabla_X t$.
2. $s \to^i t$. Then $s \equiv C[\![s_1,\ldots,s_j,\ldots,s_n]\!]$, $t \equiv C[s_1,\ldots,t_j,\ldots,s_n]$ and $s_j \to t_j$ for some $C, s_1,\ldots,s_n,t_j$. If $t \equiv C[\![s_1,\ldots,t_j,\ldots,s_n]\!]$, then $\nabla_X s \to_{\mathrm{lab}(\mathcal{R})} \nabla_X t$ immediately follows from induction hypothesis. Otherwise, suppose $s_j \to t_j$ is destructive, t_j is a principal subterm of s_j, $t_j \equiv C'[\![u_1,\ldots,u_l]\!]$, $t \equiv C''[\![s_1,\ldots,u_1,\ldots,u_l,\ldots,s_n]\!]$ and $C'' \equiv C[\square,\ldots,C',\ldots,\square]$ for some $C', u_1,\ldots,u_l$.

(a) $\text{top}(C) \in \{0, X\}$.

$$\begin{aligned}\nabla_X s &\equiv \text{lab}_X(C)[\nabla_X s_1, \ldots, \nabla_X s_n] \\ \nabla_X t &\equiv \text{lab}_X(C'')[\nabla_X s_1, \ldots, \nabla_X u_1, \ldots, \nabla_X u_l, \ldots, \nabla_X s_n] \\ &\equiv \text{lab}_X(C)[\nabla_X s_1, \ldots, \text{lab}_X(C')[\nabla_X u_1, \ldots, \nabla_X u_l], \ldots, \nabla_X s_n] \\ &\equiv \text{lab}_X(C)[\nabla_X s_1, \ldots, \nabla_X t_j, \ldots, \nabla_X s_n].\end{aligned}$$

Hence, $\nabla_X s \to_{\text{lab}(\mathcal{R})} \nabla_X t$ by the induction hypothesis.

(b) $\text{top}(C) = Z \notin \{0, X\}$. Let $C : X_1 \times \cdots \times X_n \to Z$. Then,

$$\begin{aligned}\nabla_X s &\equiv \text{lab}_Z(C)[\Phi_1 s_1, \ldots, \Phi_n s_n], \\ \nabla_X t &\equiv \text{lab}_Z(C'')[\Phi_1 s_1, \ldots, \Phi'_1 u_1, \ldots, \Phi'_l u_l, \ldots, \Phi_n s_n] \\ &\equiv \text{lab}_Z(C)[\Phi_1 s_1, \ldots, \text{lab}_Z(C')[\Phi'_1 u_1, \ldots, \Phi'_l u_l], \ldots, \Phi_n s_n].\end{aligned}$$

i. $\text{top}(C') = 0$. Then $C' : 0 \times \cdots \times 0 \to 0$, and hence $\Phi'_i = \Phi_j$ for all $i = 1, \ldots, l$. Also, $X_j = \text{top}(C') = 0$, so $\Phi_j = \nabla_Z$. Therefore,

$$\begin{aligned}\nabla_X t &\equiv \text{lab}_Z(C)[\Phi_1 s_1, \ldots, \text{lab}_Z(C')[\nabla_Z u_1, \ldots, \nabla_Z u_l], \ldots, \Phi_n s_n] \\ &\equiv \text{lab}_Z(C)[\Phi_1 s_1, \ldots, \Phi_j(C'[u_1, \ldots, u_l]), \ldots, \Phi_n s_n] \\ &\equiv \text{lab}_Z(C)[\Phi_1 s_1, \ldots, \Phi_j t_j, \ldots, \Phi_n s_n].\end{aligned}$$

ii. $\text{top}(C') = Z$. Then $C' : Y_1 \times \cdots \times Y_l \to Z$, $C'' : X_1 \times \cdots \times X_{j-1} \times Y_1 \times \cdots \times Y_l \times X_{j+1} \times \cdots \times X_n \to Z$, $X_j = Z$, and $\Phi_j = \nabla_X$. Therefore,

$$\begin{aligned}\nabla_X t &\equiv \text{lab}_Z(C)[\Phi_1 s_1, \ldots, \text{lab}_Z(C')[\Phi'_1 u_1, \ldots, \Phi'_l u_l], \ldots, \Phi_n s_n] \\ &\equiv \text{lab}_Z(C)[\Phi_1 s_1, \ldots, \nabla_X(C'[u_1, \ldots, u_l]), \ldots, \Phi_n s_n] \\ &\equiv \text{lab}_Z(C)[\Phi_1 s_1, \ldots, \Phi_j t_j, \ldots, \Phi_n s_n].\end{aligned}$$

Hence in both cases, $\nabla_X s \to_{\text{lab}(\mathcal{R})} \nabla_X t$ follows from the induction hypothesis.

□

4 Composable properties

For a property ϕ of TRSs and a TRS $\mathcal{R}$, we write $\phi(\mathcal{R})$ when ϕ holds for $\mathcal{R}$.

Definition 10. Let ϕ be a property of TRSs. Then, for a given naive sort attachment τ, the property ϕ is said to be *τ-composable* if for any TRS $\mathcal{R}$ such that τ is consistent with $\mathcal{R}$, $\phi(\mathcal{R}_1) \wedge \phi(\mathcal{R}_2)$ implies $\phi(\mathcal{R})$, where $\langle \mathcal{R}_1, \mathcal{R}_2 \rangle$ is the decomposition of $\mathcal{R}$ by τ.

Proposition 11. *Let ϕ be a property of TRSs, $\mathcal{R}$ a TRS, τ a naive sort attachment consistent with $\mathcal{R}$ and $\langle \mathcal{R}_1, \mathcal{R}_2 \rangle$ the decomposition of $\mathcal{R}$ by τ. If*

1. *ϕ is preserved under the union of* $\text{lab}_1(\mathcal{R})$ *and* $\text{lab}_2(\mathcal{R})$, *and*
2. *$\phi(\text{lab}(\mathcal{R}))$ implies $\phi(\mathcal{R})$,*

then $\phi(\mathcal{R}_1) \wedge \phi(\mathcal{R}_2)$ implies $\phi(\mathcal{R})$.

Proof. Suppose that $\phi(\mathcal{R}_1) \wedge \phi(\mathcal{R}_2)$. Then, since $\mathrm{lab}_X(\mathcal{R})$ is a renaming of $\mathcal{R}_X$ ($X \in \{1,2\}$), we have $\phi(\mathrm{lab}_1(\mathcal{R}))\wedge\phi(\mathrm{lab}_2(\mathcal{R}))$. This implies $\phi(\mathrm{lab}_1(\mathcal{R})\cup\mathrm{lab}_2(\mathcal{R}))$ by the first assumption; hence $\phi(\mathrm{lab}(\mathcal{R}))$ by definition. Therefore, $\phi(\mathcal{R})$ by the second assumption. □

We are now going to give various composable properties on the base of modularity results for direct sums of TRSs. For this, let us review some basic properties of TRSs.

A term t is said to be *terminating* if there is no infinite sequence $t \to_{\mathcal{R}} t_1 \to_{\mathcal{R}} t_2 \to_{\mathcal{R}} t_3 \to_{\mathcal{R}} \cdots$ of terms starting from t. $\mathcal{R}$ is *terminating* if every term is terminating. Terms t_1 and t_2 are said to be *joinable* if there exists some term s such that $t_1 \overset{*}{\to}_{\mathcal{R}} s \overset{*}{\leftarrow}_{\mathcal{R}} t_2$. A term t is said to be *confluent* (*locally confluent*) if terms t_1 and t_2 are joinable whenever $t_1 \overset{*}{\leftarrow}_{\mathcal{R}} t \overset{*}{\to}_{\mathcal{R}} t_2$ (whenever $t_1 \leftarrow_{\mathcal{R}} t \to_{\mathcal{R}} t_2$, respectively). $\mathcal{R}$ is confluent (locally confluent) if every term is confluent (locally confluent, respectively). A term s is *normal form* if there is no term t such that $s \to_{\mathcal{R}} t$. $\mathcal{R}$ has *unique normal forms* (or is *UN*) if $s \overset{*}{\leftrightarrow}_{\mathcal{R}} t$ implies $s \equiv t$ for any normal forms s and t; $\mathcal{R}$ has *unique normal forms with respect to reduction* (or is $UN^{\to}$) if $t_1 \overset{*}{\leftarrow}_{\mathcal{R}} s \overset{*}{\to}_{\mathcal{R}} t_2$ implies $t_1 \equiv t_2$ for any term s and normal forms t_1 and t_2; $\mathcal{R}$ has the *normal form property* (or is *NF*) if $s \overset{*}{\leftrightarrow}_{\mathcal{R}} t$ implies $s \overset{*}{\to}_{\mathcal{R}} t$ for any term s and a normal form t. For the relation between these properties, we refer the reader to [7].

We first show sufficient conditions for the composability of termination.

Theorem 12. *Let $\mathcal{R}$ be a TRS and $\langle\mathcal{R}_1,\mathcal{R}_2\rangle$ a decomposition of $\mathcal{R}$ by a naive sort attachment. Suppose that either one of the following conditions are satisfied:*

1. *$\mathcal{R}$ is non-collapsing;*
2. *$\mathcal{R}$ is non-duplicating;*
3. *one of $\mathcal{R}_1$ or $\mathcal{R}_2$ is non-collapsing and non-duplicating.*

Then, $\mathcal{R}$ is terminating whenever $\mathcal{R}_1$ and $\mathcal{R}_2$ are terminating.

Proof. Let τ be a naive sort attachment consistent with $\mathcal{R}$ such that $\mathcal{R}_X = \Theta(\mathcal{R}^\tau{\restriction}(\mathcal{T}^0 \cup \mathcal{T}^X))$ for each $X \in \{1,2\}$. It suffices to show that conditions 1, 2 of Proposition 11 are satisfied. Since $\mathrm{lab}_X(\mathcal{R})$ is a renaming of $\mathcal{R}_X$, $\mathrm{lab}_1(\mathcal{R})$ and $\mathrm{lab}_2(\mathcal{R})$ are terminating TRSs. By definition, the sets of function symbols that appear in $\mathrm{lab}_1(\mathcal{R})$ and $\mathrm{lab}_2(\mathcal{R})$ are disjoint. Also, it is clear that if $\mathcal{R}$ is non-collapsing (non-duplicating) then $\mathrm{lab}(\mathcal{R}) = \mathrm{lab}_1(\mathcal{R}) \cup \mathrm{lab}_2(\mathcal{R})$ is also non-collapsing (non-duplicating, respectively); and if $\mathcal{R}_X$ is non-collapsing and non-duplicating then so is $\mathrm{lab}(\mathcal{R}_X)$. Therefore, by the modularity of the termination for direct sums of TRSs [8][12], $\mathrm{lab}(\mathcal{R})$ is terminating whenever $\mathrm{lab}_1(\mathcal{R})$ and $\mathrm{lab}_2(\mathcal{R})$ are terminating. To show the condition 2, suppose that $\mathcal{R}$ is not terminating, i.e. there exists an infinite sequence $t \to_{\mathcal{R}} t_1 \to_{\mathcal{R}} t_2 \to_{\mathcal{R}} t_3 \to_{\mathcal{R}} \cdots$. Then, by Lemma 9, $\nabla_1 t \to_{\mathrm{lab}(\mathcal{R})} \nabla_1 t_1 \to_{\mathrm{lab}(\mathcal{R})} \nabla_1 t_2 \to_{\mathrm{lab}(\mathcal{R})} \nabla_1 t_3 \to_{\mathrm{lab}(\mathcal{R})} \cdots$. Thus, $\mathrm{lab}(\mathcal{R})$ is not terminating. □

Theorem 12 with condition 1 or 2 captures an application of the persistency of termination; see [17].

To the contrary, confluence is a τ-composable property for a naive sort attachment τ.

Theorem 13. *For any naive sort attachment τ, confluence is τ-composable.*

Proof. We again show that conditions 1, 2 of Proposition 11 are satisfied. For the condition 1, let us mention only the modularity of the confluence for direct sums of TRSs [14]. To show the condition 2, suppose that lab($\mathcal{R}$) is confluent and $t_1 \overset{*}{\leftarrow}_{\mathcal{R}} t \overset{*}{\rightarrow}_{\mathcal{R}} t_2$. Then, by Lemma 9, $\nabla_1 t_1 \overset{*}{\leftarrow}_{\mathsf{lab}(\mathcal{R})} \nabla_1 t \overset{*}{\rightarrow}_{\mathsf{lab}(\mathcal{R})} \nabla_1 t_2$. By the assumption, $\nabla_1 t_1 \overset{*}{\rightarrow}_{\mathsf{lab}(\mathcal{R})} s \overset{*}{\leftarrow}_{\mathsf{lab}(\mathcal{R})} \nabla_1 t_2$. Erasing labels, we clearly have $t_1 \overset{*}{\rightarrow}_{\mathcal{R}} s' \overset{*}{\leftarrow}_{\mathcal{R}} t_2$ for some s'. Hence, $\mathcal{R}$ is confluent. Thus, confluence of lab($\mathcal{R}$) implies that of $\mathcal{R}$. □

Theorem 13 captures an application of the persistency of confluence; see [1].

A rewrite rule $l \rightarrow r$ is said to be *left-linear* if every variable occurs at most once in l. A TRS is left-linear if all rules are left-linear. For left-linear TRSs, we obtain other conditions for the composability of termination.

A TRS $\mathcal{R}$ is said to be *consistent with respect to reduction* (*r-consistent*, for short) if there exists no term t such that $x \overset{*}{\leftarrow}_{\mathsf{lab}(\mathcal{R})} t \overset{*}{\rightarrow}_{\mathsf{lab}(\mathcal{R})} y$ for distinct variables x and y.

Theorem 14. *Let $\mathcal{R}$ be a TRS and $\langle \mathcal{R}_1, \mathcal{R}_2 \rangle$ a decomposition of $\mathcal{R}$ by a naive sort attachment. Suppose that either one of the following conditions are satisfied:*

1. *$\mathcal{R}$ is left-linear and r-consistent;*
2. *one of $\mathcal{R}_1$ or $\mathcal{R}_2$ is left-linear and confluent, and the other is non-collapsing.*

Then, $\mathcal{R}$ is terminating whenever $\mathcal{R}_1$ and $\mathcal{R}_2$ are terminating.

Proof. We again show that conditions 1, 2 of Proposition 11 are satisfied. For the condition 1, we only show that r-consistency of $\mathcal{R}$ implies that of lab($\mathcal{R}$); then the condition easily follows from the modularity of the termination for direct sums of TRSs [13] [15]. If lab($\mathcal{R}$) is not r-consistent, then there exists a labelled term t and distinct variables x and y such that $x \overset{*}{\leftarrow}_{\mathsf{lab}(\mathcal{R})} t \overset{*}{\rightarrow}_{\mathsf{lab}(\mathcal{R})} y$. Erasing labels, $x \overset{*}{\leftarrow}_{\mathcal{R}} t' \overset{*}{\rightarrow}_{\mathcal{R}} y$ for some t'. Thus, $\mathcal{R}$ is not r-consistent. The condition 2 can be shown similarly to the proof of Theorem 12. □

We next examine τ-composable properties related to normal forms for a naive sort attachment τ. For this, a lemma below, which easily follows from Lemma 9, is useful.

Lemma 15. *For any $X \in \{1, 2\}$, a term s is a normal form if and only if $\nabla_X s$ is a normal form.*

Theorem 16. *For any naive sort attachment τ, UN is τ-composable.*

Proof. We again show that conditions 1, 2 of Proposition 11 are satisfied. For the condition 1, let us mention only the modularity of the UN for direct sums of TRSs [7]. To show the condition 2, suppose that lab($\mathcal{R}$) is UN and $s \overset{*}{\leftrightarrow}_{\mathcal{R}} t$ for normal forms s and t. Then $\nabla_1 s$ and $\nabla_1 t$ are normal forms by Lemma 15 and $\nabla_1 s \overset{*}{\leftrightarrow}_{\mathsf{lab}(\mathcal{R})} \nabla_1 t$ by Lemma 9. Hence $\nabla_1 s \equiv \nabla_1 t$ by the assumption. Erasing labels, we clearly have $s \equiv t$. □

Theorem 17. *Let $\mathcal{R}$ be a left-linear TRS and $\langle \mathcal{R}_1, \mathcal{R}_2 \rangle$ a decomposition of $\mathcal{R}$ by a naive sort attachment. Then, $\mathcal{R}$ is $UN^{\rightarrow}$ (NF) whenever $\mathcal{R}_1$ and $\mathcal{R}_2$ are $UN^{\rightarrow}$ (NF, respectively).*

Proof. We again show that conditions 1, 2 of Proposition 11 are satisfied. For the condition 1, let us mention only the modularity of the $\mathrm{UN}^{\rightarrow}$and NF for direct sums of left-linear TRSs [6][9] and the fact that the left-linearity of $\mathcal{R}$ implies that of lab($\mathcal{R}$). The condition 2 for $\mathrm{UN}^{\rightarrow}$: Suppose that lab($\mathcal{R}$) is $\mathrm{UN}^{\rightarrow}$and $t_1 \overset{*}{\leftarrow}_{\mathcal{R}} s \overset{*}{\rightarrow}_{\mathcal{R}} t_2$. with t_1, t_2 normal forms. Then $\nabla_1 t_1, \nabla t_2$ are normal forms by Lemma 15 and $\nabla_1 t_1 \overset{*}{\leftarrow}_{\mathsf{lab}(\mathcal{R})} \nabla_1 s \overset{*}{\rightarrow}_{\mathsf{lab}(\mathcal{R})} \nabla_1 t_2$ by Lemma 9. Hence $\nabla t_1 \equiv \nabla t_2$ by the assumption. Erasing labels, we have $t_1 \equiv t_2$. The condition 2 for NF: Suppose that lab($\mathcal{R}$) is NF and $s \overset{*}{\leftrightarrow}_{\mathcal{R}} t$ with t normal forms. Then $\nabla_1 t$ is a normal from by Lemma 15 and $\nabla_1 s \overset{*}{\leftrightarrow}_{\mathsf{lab}(\mathcal{R})} \nabla_1 t$ by Lemma 9. Hence $\nabla_1 s \overset{*}{\rightarrow}_{\mathsf{lab}(\mathcal{R})} \nabla_1 t$ by the assumption. Erasing labels, we have $s \overset{*}{\rightarrow}_{\mathcal{R}} t$. □

One can obtain similar τ-composability results for a naive sort attachment τ, on the base of other modularity results for direct sums of TRSs (e.g. [3], [6]), although we will not mention them further.

We end this section with some examples.

Example 5. Let

$$\mathcal{R}\begin{cases} f(x, g(b, a, y)) \rightarrow f(x, g(c, y, y)) & (r1) \\ f(x, y) \rightarrow y & (r2) \\ a \rightarrow b & (r3) \\ F(c, x) \rightarrow F(a, x) & (r4), \end{cases} \qquad \tau\begin{cases} f : 0 \times 1 \rightarrow 1 \\ g : 0 \times 0 \times 0 \rightarrow 1 \\ a, b, c : 0 \\ F : 0 \times 0 \rightarrow 2. \end{cases}$$

Note that one can not directly use the recursive path ordering to show the termination of $\mathcal{R}$ because of $(r1)$, nor the lexicographic path ordering because of $(r1), (r3), (r4)$.

It is easy to see that τ is consistent with $\mathcal{R}$. The decomposition of $\mathcal{R}$ by τ is the pair of $\mathcal{R}_1 = \{(r1), (r2), (r3)\}$ and $\mathcal{R}_2 = \{(r3), (r4)\}$.

- Put $a > b > c$. Then $\mathcal{R}_1$ is terminating by the lexicographic path ordering.
- Put $c > a > b$. Then, $\mathcal{R}_2$ is terminating by the lexicographic path ordering.
- $\mathcal{R}_2$ is non-collapsing and non-duplicating.

Hence, by Theorem 12, we conclude that $\mathcal{R}$ is terminating.

Example 6. In Example 4, observe that well known results, e.g. those appearing in [4], [5] or [14], are not directly helpful to infer the confluence of $\mathcal{R}$. The decomposition of $\mathcal{R}$ by τ is the pair of $\mathcal{R}_1 = \{(r1), (r2), (r3)\}$ and $\mathcal{R}_2 = \{(r3), (r4), (r5)\}$.

- Since $\mathcal{R}_1$ is orthogonal, it is confluent.
- Since $\mathcal{R}_2$ is terminating and its critical pairs are joinable, it is confluent [5].

Hence, by Theorem 13, we conclude that $\mathcal{R}$ is confluent.

Example 7. Let

$$\mathcal{R}\begin{cases} f(g(x,a,b)) \to x & (r1) \\ g(f(h(c,d)),x,y) \to h(e(x),e(y)) & (r2) \\ e(a) \to c & (r3) \\ e(b) \to d & (r4) \\ F(a,x,x) \to F(x,e(x),e(x)) & (r5), \end{cases} \qquad \tau\begin{cases} f : 1 \to 1 \\ g : 1 \times 0 \times 0 \to 1 \\ h : 0 \times 0 \to 1 \\ a, b, c, d : 0 \\ e : 0 \to 0 \\ F : 0 \times 0 \times 0 \to 2. \end{cases}$$

It is easy to see that τ is consistent with $\mathcal{R}$. The decomposition of $\mathcal{R}$ by τ is the pair of $\mathcal{R}_1 = \{(r1), (r2), (r3), (r4)\}$ and $\mathcal{R}_2 = \{(r3), (r4), (r5)\}$.

- Put $g > h > e > c, d$. Then $\mathcal{R}_1$ is terminating by the lexicographic path ordering.
- If $\mathcal{R}_2$ is not terminating, then it is easy to see that the rewrite rule (r5) should be used infinitely many times. Observe that the only term that has the reduct a is a itself, so these rewrite steps by (r5) must be of the form $F(a,a,a) \to_{\mathcal{R}_2} F(a,e(a),e(a))$. But since $F(a,e(a),e(a))$ is terminating, there is no such infinite reduction sequence. Thus $\mathcal{R}_2$ is terminating.
- $\mathcal{R}_1$ is left-linear and parallel closed; hence confluent [4].
- $\mathcal{R}_2$ is non-collapsing.

Hence, by Theorem 14, we conclude that $\mathcal{R}$ is terminating.

Remark. We now compare our work and composability results in [11].

Firstly, let us recall definitions in [11]. Let $\mathcal{R}_1$ and $\mathcal{R}_2$ be two TRSs and suppose that for $i \in \{1,2\}$ $\mathcal{F}_i$ is the set of function symbols in $\mathcal{R}_i$. Put $\mathcal{D}_i = \{\mathrm{root}(l) \mid l \to r \in \mathcal{R}_i\}$, $\mathcal{C}_i = \mathcal{F}_i \backslash \mathcal{D}_i$, $\mathcal{B} = \mathcal{F}_1 \cap \mathcal{F}_2$, $\mathcal{Q} = \{l \to r \in \mathcal{R}_1 \cup \mathcal{R}_2 \mid root(l) \in \mathcal{D}_1 \cap \mathcal{D}_2\}$ and $\mathcal{A}_i = \mathcal{F}_i \backslash \mathcal{B}$ $(i \in \{1,2\})$. Then $\mathcal{R}_1$ and $\mathcal{R}_2$ are said to be composable if (1) $\mathcal{C}_1 \cap \mathcal{D}_2 = \mathcal{C}_2 \cap \mathcal{D}_1 = \emptyset$, and (2) $\mathcal{Q} \subseteq \mathcal{R}_1 \cap \mathcal{R}_2$. Also, $\mathcal{R}_i$ is said to be layer-preserving if for any $l \to r \in \mathcal{R}_i$, $\mathrm{root}(l) \in \mathcal{A}_i$ implies $\mathrm{root}(r) \in \mathcal{A}_i$ $(i \in \{1,2\})$.

Now, Theorem 4.3.5 in [11] says that for any two composable layer-preserving confluent TRSs $\mathcal{R}_1$ and $\mathcal{R}_2$, their union is confluent. We claim that this result can not applied to Example 6. In Example 6, $\mathcal{D}_1 = \{f, g\}$, $\mathcal{C}_1 = \{h\}$, $\mathcal{D}_2 = \{F, g\}$ and $\mathcal{C}_2 = \{h\}$; hence $\mathcal{Q} = \{(r3)\}$, $\mathcal{B} = \{g, h\}$, $\mathcal{A}_1 = \{f\}$ and $\mathcal{A}_2 = \{F\}$. Thus, our system is composable. But $\mathcal{R}_1$ is not layer-preserving because of $(r1)$.

Next, Theorem 5.3.8 in [11] says that for any two composable terminating TRSs $\mathcal{R}_1$ and $\mathcal{R}_2$, their union is terminating if either

1. both $\mathcal{R}_1$ and $\mathcal{R}_2$ are layer-preserving;
2. both $\mathcal{R}_1$ and $\mathcal{R}_2$ are non-duplicating; or
3. one of $\mathcal{R}_1$ and $\mathcal{R}_2$ is both layer-preserving and non-duplicating.

We claim that this result can not applied to Example 7. In our example, $\mathcal{D}_1 = \{f, g, e\}$, $\mathcal{C}_1 = \{h, a, b, c, d\}$, $\mathcal{D}_2 = \{F, e\}$ and $\mathcal{C}_2 = \{a, b, c, d\}$; hence $\mathcal{Q} = \{(r3), (r4)\}$, $\mathcal{B} = \{a, b, c, d, e\}$, $\mathcal{A}_1 = \{f, g, h\}$ and $\mathcal{A}_2 = \{F\}$. Thus, our system is composable. But none of the conditions is satisfied, because of $(r1)$ and $(r5)$.

Remark. One can show the termination of $\mathcal{R}$ in Example 5 or 7 by using the semantic labelling technique[18]. However, unlike the case of the semantic labelling, it is decidable whether for a given finite TRS our method can be used; for, the number of naive sort attachments are finite, so we can get all possible decompositions by checking consistency.

Example 8. Let

$$\mathcal{R}\begin{cases} f(a) \to f(b) & (r1) \\ f(b) \to f(b) & (r2) \\ a \to c & (r3) \\ F(x) \to G(F(x), F(a)) & (r4), \end{cases} \qquad \tau\begin{cases} f : 0 \to 1 \\ a, b, c : 0 \\ F : 0 \to 2 \\ G : 2 \times 2 \to 2. \end{cases}$$

It is easy to see that τ is consistent with $\mathcal{R}$. The decomposition of $\mathcal{R}$ by τ is the pair of $\mathcal{R}_1 = \{(r1), (r2), (r3)\}$ and $\mathcal{R}_2 = \{(r3), (r4)\}$.

- Since rewrite steps of $\mathcal{R}_1$ can not change the number of occurrences of f in terms, nontrivial $\overset{*}{\leftrightarrow}_{\mathcal{R}_1}$-equivalence classes are of form $\{f^n(a), f^n(b), f^n(c)\}$ for some $n(> 0)$ or $\{a, c\}$. Therefore, every $\overset{*}{\leftrightarrow}_{\mathcal{R}_1}$-equivalence class has a unique normal form in it. Thus, $\mathcal{R}_1$ is UN.
- Since $\mathcal{R}_2$ is orthogonal, it is confluent; hence it is UN.

Therefore, by Theorem 16, we conclude that $\mathcal{R}$ is UN.

5 Concluding remarks

We have proposed a decomposition by a naive sort attachment, and have shown that modular properties for direct sums are τ-composable for a naive sort attachment τ. Thus, we have presented conditions under which properties such as termination, confluence, etc., are τ-composable for a naive sort attachment τ.

Our composition does not impose the disjointness condition. Among the composability results for non-disjoint TRSs, our result is based on a sort attachment, while results in [11] are based on syntactical conditions and those in [10] are based on the constructor discipline.

Acknowledgments

The authors are grateful to Aart Middeldorp and Bernhard Gramlich for their careful comments. Thanks are due to referees for lots of valuable comments.

References

1. T. Aoto and Y. Toyama. Persistency of confluence. Research Report IS-RR-96-0009F, School of Information Science, JAIST, 1996.
2. T. Aoto and Y. Toyama. Top-down labelling and modularity of term rewriting systems. Research Report IS-RR-96-0023F, School of Information Science, JAIST, 1996.
3. B. Gramlich. Abstract relations between restricted termination and confluence properties of rewrite systems. *Fundamenta Informaticae*, 24:285–296, 1995.
4. G. Huet. Confluent reductions: abstract properties and applications to term rewriting systems. *Journal of Association for Computing Machinery*, 27(4):797–821, 1980.
5. D. E. Knuth and P. B. Bendix. Simple word problems in universal algebras. In J. Leech, editor, *Computational problems in abstract algebra*, pages 263–297. Pergamon Press, 1970.
6. M. Marchiori. On the modularity of normal forms in rewriting. *Journal of Symbolic Computation*, 22:143–154, 1996.
7. A. Middeldorp. Modular aspects of properties of term rewriting systems related to normal forms. In *Proc. of the 3rd International Conference on Rewriting Techniques and Applications, Lecture Notes in Computer Science 355*, pages 263–277, 1989.
8. A. Middeldorp. A sufficient condition for the termination of the direct sum of term rewriting systems. In *Proc. of the 4th annual IEEE Symposium on Logic in Computer Science*, pages 396–401, 1989.
9. A. Middeldorp. *Modular properties of term rewriting systems*. PhD thesis, Vrije Universiteit, Amsterdam, 1990.
10. A. Middeldorp and Y. Toyama. Completeness of combinations of constructor systems. *Journal of Symbolic Computation*, 15(3):331–348, 1993.
11. E. Ohlebusch. *Modular Properties of Composable Term Rewriting Systems*. PhD thesis, Universitaet Bielefeld, 1994.
12. M. Rusinowitch. On termination of the direct sum of term rewriting systems. *Information Processing Letters*, 26:65–70, 1987.
13. M. Schmidt-Schauß, M. Marchiori, and S. E. Panitz. Modular termination of r-consistent and left-linear term rewriting systems. *Theoretical Computer Science*, 149:361–374, 1995.
14. Y. Toyama. On the Church-Rosser property for the direct sum of term rewriting systems. *Journal of Association for Computing Machinery*, 34(1):128–143, 1987.
15. Y. Toyama, J. W. Klop, and H. P. Barendregt. Termination for direct sums of left-linear complete term rewriting systems. *Journal of Association for Computing Machinery*, 42:1275–1304, 1995.
16. J. van de Pol. Modularity in many-sorted term rewriting systems. Master's thesis, Utrecht University, 1992.
17. H. Zantema. Termination of term rewriting: interpretation and type elimination. *Journal of Symbolic Computation*, 17:23–50, 1994.
18. H. Zantema. Termination of term rewriting by semantic labelling. *Fundamenta Informaticae*, 24:89–105, 1995.

Needed Reductions with Context-Sensitive Rewriting*

Salvador Lucas

Departamento de Sistemas Informáticos y Computación
Universidad Politécnica de Valencia
Camino de Vera s/n, E-46071 Valencia, Spain.
e.mail: slucas@dsic.upv.es
URL: http://www.dsic.upv.es/users/elp/slucas.html

Abstract. Computing with functional programs involves reduction of terms to normal form. When considering non-terminating programs, this is achieved by using some special, *normalizing* strategy which obtains the normal form whenever it exists. *Context-sensitive rewriting* can improve termination and also avoid useless reductions by imposing fixed, syntactic restrictions on the replacements. In this paper, we analyze the efficiency of context-sensitive computations with respect to the notion of *needed* reduction. As context-sensitive rewriting is complete in performing reductions to a root-stable form, we base our investigation on Middeldorp's theory of root-necessary reductions which is a generalization of Huet and Lévy's theory of (sequential) needed reductions to reductions leading to root-stable form both in sequential and parallel executions.

Keywords: functional programming, needed reductions, replacement restrictions, strategies, term rewriting systems.

1 Introduction

In *context-sensitive rewriting* (*csr*) [8], the evaluation of the arguments of a function call $f(t_1, \ldots, t_k)$ is restricted to some fixed argument positions of f which we denote as $\mu(f)$, and is forbidden for the others. The mapping $\mu : \Sigma \to \mathcal{P}(\mathbb{N})$ is called the *replacement map*. For example, by defining $\mu(\texttt{if}) = \{1\}$, we avoid reductions in second and third arguments of an input expression `if(and(true,false),s(0)+s(0),0+s(0))`. They do not make sense until the condition `and(true,false)` has been evaluated. The restrictions given by μ on arguments of function calls naturally extend to occurrences of terms. By imposing such replacement restrictions, we can also lose useful steps. Given a Term Rewriting System (TRS), $\mathcal{R}$, we have shown how to automatically compute the *canonical* replacement map $\mu_{\mathcal{R}}^{com}$ for $\mathcal{R}$. The replacement map $\mu_{\mathcal{R}}^{com}$ is proven to be the most restrictive one which is still able to achieve completeness in reductions leading to a root-stable form (i.e., a term which cannot be reduced to a

* This work has been partially supported by CICYT under grant TIC 95-0433-C03-03.

redex) of the input term. We have shown how to fully evaluate a term (obtaining a constructor term or value) by using a less restrictive replacement map $\mu_{\mathcal{R}}^{\mathcal{B}}$ [8].

In this paper, we are interested in how to effectively perform such computations, rather than in just ensuring the *possibility* of having them. Thus, we want to define (normalizing) context-sensitive strategies which use the replacement restrictions efficiently. To formalize 'efficiency', we consider a suitable notion of neededness of the context-sensitive computations.

When considering orthogonal TRSs, Huet and Lévy's theory of *needed redexes* gives us a precise definition of what a needed reduction step is [4]. Middeldorp argues that reduction to root-stable form, and the corresponding notion of *root-needed redex* is even a more fundamental notion than other neededness notions, since root-needed normalization provides a unified framework to analyze reductions leading to a finite normal form (i.e., it includes Huet and Lévy's theory) and also reductions leading to an infinite normal form for which Huet and Lévy's theory does not apply [12]. He also generalizes Sekar and Ramakrishnan's work on necessary sets of redexes [14] from constructor-based TRSs to root-necessary sets of redexes in general TRSs. Thus the notion of root-necessary reduction, which applies in parallel strategies, is also available.

In this work, we prove that, given an orthogonal TRS $\mathcal{R}$, every non-root-stable term t has a *replacing* root-needed redex when considering the replacement map $\mu_{\mathcal{R}}^{com}$. Hence, by imposing replacement restrictions, we still make root-needed computations possible. We also show how to find the replacing root-needed redexes of a non-root-stable term. This is the basis for the definition of optimal root-normalizing *cs*-strategies and hence optimal evaluation *cs*-strategies.

We define the concept of μ-restricted strategy $\mathbb{F}^{\mu}$ for a given TRS, replacement map μ and rewriting strategy $\mathbb{F}$. We analyze the root-normalization properties of the μ-restriction of the usual strategies (parallel outermost, leftmost-outermost, etc.). We show that they are usually improved in some aspect. We also define two classes of TRSs for which we prove that the restricted strategies have normalizing properties, while the unrestricted ones do not. We define the *strongly replacing-independent* TRSs for which *every cs*-strategy is root-normalizing. We define the *μ-left-normal* TRSs, a superset of left-normal TRSs [13] for which the μ-restricted leftmost-outermost strategy is also root-normalizing. We also extend these results to perform finite, efficient normalization and evaluation.

In Section 2, we give some preliminary definitions. Section 3 recalls the basic concepts of *csr* and characterizes the *strongly replacing-independent* and *μ-left-normal* TRSs. Section 4 compares context-sensitive computations and root-needed reductions. Section 5 defines the concept of restricted strategy and illustrates the definition of root-normalizing and normalizing *cs*-strategies. Section 6 summarizes conclusions and outlines to future work.

2 Preliminaries

Let us first introduce the main notations used in the paper. For full definitions we refer to [2, 6]. Denote a countable set of variables as V. By Σ we denote a signature: a set of function symbols $\{\mathtt{f}, \mathtt{g}, \ldots\}$, each of which has a fixed arity given by a function $ar : \Sigma \to \mathbb{N}$. By $\mathcal{T}(\Sigma, V)$ we denote the set of terms. A k-tuple $t_1, \ldots, t_k$ of terms is denoted as $\tilde{t}$, where k will be clarified from the context. Given a term t, $Var(t)$ is the set of variable symbols in t.

Terms are viewed as labelled trees in the usual way. Occurrences $u, v, \ldots$ are represented by chains of positive natural numbers used to address subterms of t. Denote as $O(t)$ the set of occurrences of a term t. If u is an occurrence, and W is a set of occurrences, $u.W$ denotes the set of occurrences $\{u.v \mid v \in W\}$. Occurrences are ordered by the standard prefix ordering: $u \leq v$ iff $\exists w$ such that $v = u.w$. We use the total ordering $\leq_L$: $\epsilon \leq_L u$; if $u = i.u'$, $v = j.v'$, $u \leq_L v \Leftrightarrow i < j \vee (i = j \wedge u' \leq_L v')$. A linear term is a term having no multiple occurrences of the same variable. The subterm at occurrence u of t is $t|_u$. $t[s]_u$ is the term t with the subterm at the occurrence u replaced with s. The symbol labelling the root of t is $root(t)$. The set of symbols from Σ appearing in t is $\Sigma(t) = \{f \in \Sigma \mid \exists u \in O(t).\, root(t|_u) = f\}$. Given $T \subseteq \mathcal{T}(\Sigma, V)$, we define $\Sigma(T) = \cup_{t \in T} \Sigma(t)$. The set of nonvariable occurrences in a term t is $O_\Sigma(t) = \{u \in O(t) \mid root(t|_u) \in \Sigma\}$. The variable occurrences are $O_V(t) = O(t) \backslash O_\Sigma(t)$.

We refer to any term C, which is the same as t everywhere except below u, i.e. $\exists s$ such that $C[s]_u = t$, as the *context* within the replacement occurs. Roughly speaking, a context is a term C with a 'hole' at a specific occurrence u.

A rewrite rule is an ordered pair (l, r), written $l \to r$, with $l, r \in \mathcal{T}(\Sigma, V)$, $l \notin V$ and $Var(r) \subseteq Var(l)$. The left-hand side (*lhs*) of the rule is l and r is the right-hand side (*rhs*). A TRS is a pair $\mathcal{R} = (\Sigma, R)$, where R is a set of rewrite rules. The set of *lhs*'s of $\mathcal{R}$ is $L(\mathcal{R})$. An instance $\sigma(l)$ of a *lhs* $l \in L(\mathcal{R})$ is a redex. Given a term t, denote as $O_\mathcal{R}(t)$ the set of redex occurrences in t, $O_\mathcal{R}(t) = \{u \in O(t) \mid \exists l \in L(\mathcal{R}).\, t|_u = \sigma(l)\}$. A TRS $\mathcal{R}$ is *left linear*, if $\forall l \in L(\mathcal{R})$, l is a linear term. Two rules $l \to r$ and $l' \to r'$ *overlap*, if there is a non-variable occurrence $u \in O_\Sigma(l)$ and a most general unifier σ such that $\sigma(l|_u) = \sigma(l')$. In this case, the pair $\langle \sigma(l)[\sigma(r')]_u, \sigma(r) \rangle$ is called a critical pair. A critical pair $\langle \sigma(l)[\sigma(r')]_u, \sigma(r) \rangle$ with $u = \epsilon$ is an overlay. A critical pair $\langle t, s \rangle$ is trivial if $t = s$. A TRS is almost non-ambiguous if all its critical pairs are trivial overlays. A TRS is non-ambiguous, if there are no overlapping *lhs*'s (trivial overlap in the same *lhs* is not considered). A left-linear, almost non-ambiguous TRS is called almost orthogonal. A left-linear, non-ambiguous TRS is called orthogonal.

Given a TRS $\mathcal{R} = (\Sigma, R)$, a term t rewrites to a term s (at the occurrence u), written $t \overset{u}{\to}_\mathcal{R} s$ (or just $t \to s$), if $t|_u = \sigma(l)$ and $s = t[\sigma(r)]_u$, for some rule $l \to r \in R$, $u \in O(t)$ and substitution σ. A term t is root-stable (also said head-normal form), if there is no derivation $t = t_1 \to t_2 \to \cdots$ which reduces the root of a term t_i, $i \geq 1$. A term t is a normal form if $O_\mathcal{R}(t) = \emptyset$. A term t is weakly normalizing if there exists a normal form $\bar{t}$ such that $t \to^* \bar{t}$. A term t is strongly normalizing if there exists no infinite rewrite sequences $t = t_1 \to t_2 \to \cdots$. A TRS $\mathcal{R}$ is weakly normalizing if every term is weakly normalizing. $\mathcal{R}$ is terminating (strongly normalizing) if every term is strongly normalizing.

$\mathbb{N}_k$ is an initial segment $\{1, 2, \ldots k\}$ of the set of positive numbers, where $\mathbb{N}_0 = \emptyset$. $\mathcal{P}(\mathbb{N})$ is the powerset of natural numbers.

3 Context-sensitive rewriting

A mapping $\mu : \Sigma \to \mathcal{P}(\mathbb{N})$ is a *replacement map* (or Σ-map) for the signature Σ iff for all $f \in \Sigma$. $\mu(f) \subseteq \mathbb{N}_{ar(f)}$. Thus, $\mu(f)$ are the *argument* positions which can be reduced for each $f \in \Sigma$ [8]. The ordering $\subseteq$ on $\mathcal{P}(\mathbb{N})$ extends pointwise to an ordering $\sqsubseteq$ on M_Σ, the set of all Σ-maps: $\mu \sqsubseteq \mu'$ if for all $f \in \Sigma$, $\mu(f) \subseteq \mu'(f)$. Then, $(M_\Sigma, \sqsubseteq, \mu_\bot, \mu_\top, \sqcup, \sqcap)$ is a complete lattice where $\mu_\bot(f) = \emptyset$, $\mu_\top(f) = \mathbb{N}_{ar(f)}$, $(\mu \sqcup \mu')(f) = \mu(f) \cup \mu'(f)$ and $(\mu \sqcap \mu')(f) = \mu(f) \cap \mu'(f)$ for all $f \in \Sigma$. Thus, $\mu \sqsubseteq \mu'$ means that μ considers less positions than μ' for reduction.

The set of μ*-replacing* occurrences $O^\mu(t)$ of t is defined by: $O^\mu(x) = \{\epsilon\}$ if $x \in V$, $O^\mu(f(t_1, \ldots, t_k)) = \{\epsilon\} \cup \bigcup_{i \in \mu(f)} i.O^\mu(t_i)$. Denote as $\widetilde{O^\mu}(t) = O(t) \backslash O^\mu(t)$, the set of *non-replacing* occurrences. Denote as $Var^\mu(t)$ the set of *replacing variables* of a term t, i.e. $x \in Var^\mu(t) \Leftrightarrow \exists u \in O^\mu(t).\ t|_u = x$. Also, $\widetilde{Var^\mu}(t) = Var(t) \backslash Var^\mu(t)$.

In *csr*, we rewrite *replacing* occurrences: a term t μ-rewrites to s, written $t \stackrel{u}{\hookrightarrow}_{\mathcal{R}(\mu)} s$ (or just $t \hookrightarrow s$), if $t \stackrel{u}{\to}_{\mathcal{R}} s$ and $u \in O^\mu(t)$. The set of *replacing redexes* is $O^\mu_{\mathcal{R}}(t) = O_{\mathcal{R}}(t) \cap O^\mu(t)$. The usual computational properties for terms t and TRSs $\mathcal{R}$ in rewriting (normal form, weak normalization, termination, etc) defined in terms of $O_{\mathcal{R}}(t)$ and $\to_{\mathcal{R}}$, generalize to *csr* (μ-normal form, weak μ-normalization, μ-termination, etc) using $O^\mu_{\mathcal{R}}(t)$ and $\hookrightarrow_{\mathcal{R}(\mu)}$.

Note that for the (top) Σ-map $\mu_\top$, $O^{\mu_\top}(t) = O(t)$. This is to say that, given a TRS $\mathcal{R}$, *csr* for $\mu_\top$ and unrestricted rewriting coincide, i.e. $\hookrightarrow_{\mathcal{R}(\mu_\top)} = \to_{\mathcal{R}}$.

A term t is μ*-compatible* ($\mathsf{comp}_\mu(t)$), if the non-replacing occurrences of t are variables: $\mathsf{comp}_\mu(t)$ iff $\widetilde{O^\mu}(t) \subseteq O_V(t)$. Equivalently, if any non-variable occurrence of t is a replacing occurrence: $\mathsf{comp}_\mu(t)$ iff $O_\Sigma(t) \subseteq O^\mu(t)$. comp is extended to sets of terms: $\mathsf{comp}_\mu(T) \Leftrightarrow \forall t \in T.\mathsf{comp}_\mu(t)$.

Given a term t, we can associate a *minimum* $\Sigma(t)$-map μ_t ensuring that t is compatible: if $t \in V$, then $\mu_t = \mu_\bot$. If $t = f(t_1, \ldots, t_k)$, we define the auxiliary $\Sigma(t)$-map μ^ϵ_t to be $\mu^\epsilon_t(f) = \{i \mid t_i \notin V,\ 1 \leq i \leq ar(f)\}$ and $\mu^\epsilon_t(g) = \emptyset$ for all $g \neq f$. Then $\mu_t = \mu^\epsilon_t \sqcup \mu_{t_1} \sqcup \cdots \sqcup \mu_{t_k}$. For instance, given the term $t = \mathtt{first}(0, \mathtt{x})$, we have $\mu_t(\mathtt{first}) = \{1\}$. Since $\mu_{\mathtt{s(x)}}(\mathtt{s}) = \emptyset$ and $\mu_{\mathtt{y::z}}(::) = \emptyset$, for $t' = \mathtt{first}(\mathtt{s}(\mathtt{x}), \mathtt{y} :: \mathtt{z})$, we get $\mu_{t'}(\mathtt{s}) = \mu_{t'}(::) = \emptyset$ and $\mu_{t'}(\mathtt{first}) = \{1, 2\}$. Given a set of terms $T \subseteq \mathcal{T}(\Sigma, V)$, $\mu_T = \sqcup_{t \in T} \mu_t$, is the minimum replacement map which makes T compatible.

Given a TRS $\mathcal{R} = (\Sigma, R)$ the *canonical* replacement map $\mu^{com}_{\mathcal{R}}$ of $\mathcal{R}$, is $\mu^{com}_{\mathcal{R}} = \mu_{L(\mathcal{R})}$. Note that $\mu^{com}_{\mathcal{R}}$ makes compatible each *lhs* of $\mathcal{R}$.

Example 3.1 *Let us consider the TRS $\mathcal{R}$ which is mainly borrowed from [12].*

$\mathtt{primes} \to \mathtt{sieve}(\mathtt{from}(\mathtt{s}(\mathtt{s}(0))))$ $\qquad$ $\mathtt{if}(\mathtt{true}, \mathtt{x}, \mathtt{y}) \to \mathtt{x}$
$\mathtt{from}(\mathtt{x}) \to \mathtt{x} :: \mathtt{from}(\mathtt{s}(\mathtt{x}))$ $\qquad$ $\mathtt{if}(\mathtt{false}, \mathtt{x}, \mathtt{y}) \to \mathtt{y}$
$\mathtt{sel}(0, \mathtt{x} :: \mathtt{y}) \to \mathtt{x}$ $\qquad$ $0 + \mathtt{x} \to \mathtt{x}$
$\mathtt{sel}(\mathtt{s}(\mathtt{x}), \mathtt{y} :: \mathtt{z}) \to \mathtt{sel}(\mathtt{x}, \mathtt{z})$ $\qquad$ $\mathtt{s}(\mathtt{x}) + \mathtt{y} \to \mathtt{s}(\mathtt{x} + \mathtt{y})$
$\mathtt{sieve}(\mathtt{x} :: \mathtt{y}) \to \mathtt{x} :: \mathtt{sieve}(\mathtt{filter}(\mathtt{x}, \mathtt{y}))$
$\mathtt{filter}(\mathtt{x}, \mathtt{y} :: \mathtt{z}) \to \mathtt{if}(\mathtt{x}|\mathtt{y}, \mathtt{filter}(\mathtt{x}, \mathtt{z}), \mathtt{y} :: \mathtt{filter}(\mathtt{x}, \mathtt{z}))$

Assume that $|$ *is a built-in predicate and* $x|y$ *means* x divides y. *We have*

$\mu_{\mathcal{R}}^{com}(f) = \emptyset$ *for all* $f \in \{\mathtt{0}, \mathtt{s}, [], ::, \mathtt{primes}, \mathtt{from}\}$, $\mu_{\mathcal{R}}^{com}(+) = \mu_{\mathcal{R}}^{com}(\mathtt{sieve}) = \mu_{\mathcal{R}}^{com}(\mathtt{if}) = \{1\}$, $\mu_{\mathcal{R}}^{com}(\mathtt{filter}) = \{2\}$ *and* $\mu_{\mathcal{R}}^{com}(\mathtt{sel}) = \{1,2\}$.

The following theorem illustrates the relevance of the replacement map $\mu_{\mathcal{R}}^{com}$. It expresses that *csr* is complete when computing root-stable terms.

Theorem 3.2 ([8]) *Let* $\mathcal{R} = (\Sigma, R)$ *be an almost orthogonal TRS and* μ *be a* Σ*-map such that* $\mu_{\mathcal{R}}^{com} \sqsubseteq \mu$. *Let* t *be a term and* $s = f(\tilde{s})$ *be a root-stable term. If* $t \to^* s$, *there exists a root-stable term* $s' = f(\widetilde{s'})$ *such that* $t \hookrightarrow^* s'$, *and* $s' \to^* s$.

Example 3.3 *Let* $\mathcal{R}$ *be as in Example 3.1. Then,* `primes` *computes the (infinite) list of prime numbers. We obtain the second one by evaluating* `sel(1,primes)` *(we use* n *as an abbreviate of* $\mathtt{s}^n(\mathtt{0})$*). We use* $\mu_{\mathcal{R}}^{com}$.

$$\begin{array}{l}
\underline{\mathtt{sel(1,\underline{primes})}} \hookrightarrow \mathtt{sel(1,sieve(\underline{from(2)}))} \\
\quad \hookrightarrow \underline{\mathtt{sel(1,\underline{sieve(2::from(3))})}} \\
\quad \hookrightarrow \underline{\mathtt{sel(1,2::sieve(filter(2,from(3))))}} \\
\quad \hookrightarrow \mathtt{sel(0,sieve(filter(2,\underline{from(3)})))} \\
\quad \hookrightarrow \mathtt{sel(0,sieve(\underline{filter(2,3::from(4))}))} \\
\quad \hookrightarrow \mathtt{sel(0,sieve(if(\underline{2|3},filter(x,z),3::filter(2,from(4)))))} \\
\quad \hookrightarrow \mathtt{sel(0,sieve(\underline{if(false,filter(x,z),3::filter(2,from(4}))))) \\
\quad \hookrightarrow \mathtt{sel(0,\underline{sieve(3::filter(2,from(4)))})} \\
\quad \hookrightarrow \underline{\mathtt{sel(0,3::filter(2,from(4)))}} \\
\quad \hookrightarrow \mathtt{3}
\end{array}$$

Given $\mathcal{R} = (\Sigma, R)$, we can consider the signature Σ as the disjoint union $\Sigma = \mathcal{C} \uplus \mathcal{F}$ of symbols $c \in \mathcal{C}$, called *constructors*, having no associated rule, and symbols $f \in \mathcal{F}$, called *defined functions*, which are defined by some rule $f(\tilde{l}) \to r \in R$. Any TRS can be presented in this way by taking $\mathcal{F} = \{root(l) \mid l \to r \in R\}$ and $\mathcal{C} = \Sigma \backslash \mathcal{F}$. Constructor terms (*values*) are denoted $\delta \in \mathcal{T}(\mathcal{C}, V)$. Note that no constructor discipline is assumed.

Regarding normalization of terms, if we restrict ourselves to values, *csr* is powerful enough to compute them. Given a set $\mathcal{B} \subseteq \mathcal{C}$, the replacement map $\mu_{\mathcal{R}}^{\mathcal{B}}$ is $\mu_{\mathcal{R}}^{\mathcal{B}} = \mu_{\mathcal{R}}^{com} \sqcup \mu_{\mathcal{B}}$, where $\mu_{\mathcal{B}}(c) = \mathbb{N}_{ar(c)}$ for all $c \in \mathcal{B}$, and $\mu_{\mathcal{B}}(f) = \emptyset$ if $f \notin \mathcal{B}$.

Theorem 3.4 ([8]) *Let* $\mathcal{R} = (\Sigma, R) = (\mathcal{C} \uplus \mathcal{F}, R)$ *be a left-linear TRS,* $\mathcal{B} \subseteq \mathcal{C}$ *and* μ *be a* Σ*-map such that* $\mu_{\mathcal{R}}^{\mathcal{B}} \sqsubseteq \mu$. *Let* $t \in \mathcal{T}(\Sigma, V)$, *and* $\delta \in \mathcal{T}(\mathcal{B}, V)$. *Then,* $t \to^* \delta$ *iff* $t \hookrightarrow^* \delta$.

For instance, since the value of `sel(1,primes)` is a natural number (this can be deduced from the type which is usually associated with the symbol functions, see [8]), we define $\mathcal{B} = \{\mathtt{0}, \mathtt{s}\}$. Then, we have[2]: $\mu_{\mathcal{R}}^{\mathcal{B}}(::) = \mu_{\mathcal{R}}^{\mathcal{B}}(\mathtt{from}) = \emptyset$, $\mu_{\mathcal{R}}^{\mathcal{B}}(\mathtt{s}) = \mu_{\mathcal{R}}^{\mathcal{B}}(+) = \mu_{\mathcal{R}}^{\mathcal{B}}(\mathtt{sieve}) = \mu_{\mathcal{R}}^{\mathcal{B}}(\mathtt{if}) = \{1\}$, $\mu_{\mathcal{R}}^{\mathcal{B}}(\mathtt{filter}) = \{2\}$, $\mu_{\mathcal{R}}^{\mathcal{B}}(\mathtt{sel}) = \{1,2\}$. In general, we are not able to compute arbitrary normal forms.

[2] Note that, in Example 3.3, we were able to compute the value by simply using $\mu_{\mathcal{R}}^{com}$. However, this is due to the particular definition of this TRS. For instance, by changing the `primes`-rule to $\mathtt{primes} \to \mathtt{from(s(0)+s(0))}$ in the TRS of Example 3.1 we really do need to use $\mu_{\mathcal{R}}^{\mathcal{B}}$ to compute the value.

Example 3.5 *Let us consider the TRS:*

$\mathtt{h(0)} \to \mathtt{0}$ $\qquad$ $\mathtt{g(0,x)} \to \mathtt{0}$

$\mathtt{h(s(0))} \to \mathtt{0}$

Let $\mu(\mathtt{g}) = \mu(\mathtt{h}) = \mu(\mathtt{s}) = \{1\}$. $\mathtt{g(s(0),h(0))}$ *is a* μ*-normal form, but it is not a normal form, since* $\mathtt{g(s(0),}\underline{\mathtt{h(0)}}\mathtt{)} \to \mathtt{g(s(0),0)}$. *Note that* $\mathtt{g(s(0),0)} \notin \mathcal{T}(\mathcal{C}, V)$.

Of course, when we speak about *completeness*, we mean that *csr* is able to compute interesting information (root-stable forms, values) using a non-trivial replacement map μ, i.e., $\mu \sqsubset \mu_\top$. Otherwise, the discussion is meaningless, because if $\mu = \mu_\top$, *csr* and unrestricted rewriting coincide.

3.1 Strongly replacing-independent and μ-left-normal TRSs

In this section, we introduce the class of *strongly replacing-independent* TRSs, for which we will prove that any $\mu^{com}_{\mathcal{R}}$-reduction is needed, and the *μ-left-normal* TRSs for which we prove that the (restricted) leftmost-outermost strategy is optimal and root-normalizing. We start with some preparatory definitions and properties: A term t is strongly μ-compatible ($\mathsf{scomp}_\mu(t)$) if every (and only) variable occurrences are non-replacing: $\mathsf{scomp}_\mu(t)$ iff $\widetilde{O^\mu}(t) = O_V(t)$. Alternatively $\mathsf{scomp}_\mu(t)$ iff $O_\Sigma(t) = O^\mu(t)$. Clearly $\mathsf{scomp}_\mu(t) \Rightarrow \mathsf{comp}_\mu(t)$. We extend the definition to sets of terms $T \subseteq \mathcal{T}(\Sigma, V)$: $\mathsf{scomp}_\mu(T) \Leftrightarrow \forall t \in T.\mathsf{scomp}_\mu(t)$. If $\mathsf{scomp}_\mu(T)$, we say that T is a strongly compatible set.

There are terms having *no* replacement map μ satisfying $\mathsf{scomp}_\mu(t)$. For instance, there is no replacement map which makes $\mathtt{f(f(x,a),y)}$ strongly compatible. Given a term t, only μ_t which can make t strongly compatible.

Proposition 3.6 *Let* $t \in \mathcal{T}(\Sigma, V)$ *and* μ *be a* $\Sigma(t)$*-map. Then,* $\mathsf{scomp}_\mu(t) \Rightarrow \mu = \mu_t$.

This proposition justifies that we do not make μ explicit in speaking about strongly compatible terms.

Also note a crucial difference between the extension of the properties comp and scomp from terms to sets of terms: A set T of terms which verifies $\mathsf{comp}_{\mu_t}(t)$ for each $t \in T$, immediately satisfies $\mathsf{comp}_{\mu_T}(T)$, where $\mu_T = \sqcup_{t \in T} \mu_t$. However, this is not the case with scomp.

Example 3.7 *Let* $t = \mathtt{first(0,x)}$ *and* $t' = \mathtt{first(s(x),y::z)}$. *Each term* t *and* t' *is strongly compatible w.r.t.* μ_t *and* $\mu_{t'}$*, respectively. However, the set* $\{t, t'\}$ *is not strongly compatible w.r.t.* $\mu_t \sqcup \mu_{t'}$.

The unique (if any) $\Sigma(T)$-map μ which makes a set T strongly compatible is μ_T. However, we note that replacement restrictions for symbols in $\Sigma \backslash \Sigma(T)$ can be freely established without damaging the strong compatibility of T. We assume this fact in the remainder of our exposition with no explicit mention.

Definition 3.8 (strongly replacing-independent TRS) *A TRS* $\mathcal{R}$ *is* strongly replacing-independent, *if* $L(\mathcal{R})$ *is a strongly compatible set of terms.*

Note that, if $\mathcal{R}$ is strongly replacing-independent, the canonical replacement map $\mu_{\mathcal{R}}^{com}$ is the only one which satisfies the property. Thus, $\mu_{\mathcal{R}}^{com}$ is the *intended* replacement map when dealing with strongly replacing-independent TRSs. An equivalent characterization is: $\mathcal{R}$ is strongly replacing-independent iff, for all $l \in L(\mathcal{R})$, we have $Var^{\mu_{\mathcal{R}}^{com}}(l) = \emptyset$. The TRS in Example 3.1 is strongly replacing-independent. The interesting property of these TRSs is that every replacing redex in non-root-stable terms is root-needed, as we show below.

Left-normal TRSs are well-known from [13] because the leftmost-outermost reduction strategy is normalizing for this class of TRSs. A TRS is left-normal if, in each *lhs* of the TRS, the function symbols *precede* the variable symbols when considering the ordering $\leq_L$. We generalize this notion.

Definition 3.9 (μ-left-normal TRS) *Given a replacement map μ, a TRS $\mathcal{R}$ is* μ-left-normal *if, for each $l \in L(\mathcal{R})$, there exists $u_l \in O(l)$ such that, for all $u \in O^\mu(l)$, $u \leq_L u_l \Rightarrow u \in O_\Sigma(l)$ and $u >_L u_l \Rightarrow u \in O_V(l)$.*

The if-rules or the sieve-rule of $\mathcal{R}$ in Example 3.1 are left-normal. Nevertheless, $\mathcal{R}$ is not left-normal due to the filter-rule and sel-rules. Any strongly replacing-independent TRS is $\mu_{\mathcal{R}}^{com}$-left-normal (we just take $u_l = max_{\leq_L}(O(l))$ for each rule $l \to r$). However, we have specific examples of this class of TRSs.

Example 3.10 *Let us consider the TRS $\mathcal{R}$:*

$\mathtt{first}(0, \mathtt{x}) \to []$

$\mathtt{first}(\mathtt{s}(\mathtt{x}), \mathtt{y} :: \mathtt{z}) \to \mathtt{y} :: \mathtt{first}(\mathtt{x}, \mathtt{z})$

The lhs's of this TRS do not constitute a strongly compatible set of terms (see Example 3.7). We have $\mu_{\mathcal{R}}^{com}(\mathtt{s}) = \mu_{\mathcal{R}}^{com}(::) = \emptyset$ and $\mu_{\mathcal{R}}^{com}(\mathtt{first}) = \{1, 2\}$. This TRS is not strongly replacing-independent due to the first rule. It is not left-normal due to the second rule. However, it is $\mu_{\mathcal{R}}^{com}$-left-normal.

If $\mathcal{R}$ is μ-left-normal, and $\mu' \sqsubseteq \mu$, then $\mathcal{R}$ is μ'-left-normal. This is immediate, since $O^{\mu'}(l) \subseteq O^\mu(l)$ for all $l \in L(\mathcal{R})$. If we take $\mu = \mu_\top$, we obtain the usual definition of left-normal TRS. Therefore, every left-normal TRS is μ-left-normal w.r.t. any replacement map μ (since $\mu \sqsubseteq \mu_\top$). If $\mu = \mu_\bot$, then any TRS is μ-left-normal, because, for all *lhs* l, $O^{\mu_\bot}(l) = \{\epsilon\}$, and $\epsilon \in O_\Sigma(l)$ (because $l \notin V$). Thus, we take $u_l = \epsilon$. As we show below, the good properties arise when $\mu_{\mathcal{R}}^{com} \sqsubseteq \mu$.

4 Context-sensitive rewriting and needed rewriting

A *needed redex* in a term t is a redex which must be reduced (either itself or some descendant) in any normalizing derivation starting from t [4, 7].

Since for general, orthogonal TRSs, needed redexes are not computable, the notion of *necessary set of redexes* by Sekar and Ramakrishnan [14] gives a meaningful notion of neededness for almost orthogonal TRSs. A necessary set of redexes is a set of redexes such that, at least one of the redexes in this set, or some descendant, must always be reduced in each normalizing derivation. For orthogonal, constructor-based TRSs, they give an algorithm to compute necessary sets of redexes, thus defining a computable (parallel) normalization procedure.

Since *csr* is complete w.r.t. root-normalization of terms (Theorem 3.2) but not w.r.t. normalization of terms (Example 3.5), *needed* rewriting is not completely adequate for characterizing the *cs*-computations. The notion of *root-needed* computation has also been analyzed in the literature [5, 12]. We follow the formalization of Middeldorp [12] to develop our results. A redex in a term t is root-needed, if it is contracted, itself or a descendant, in every rewrite sequence from t to a root-stable form. Since root-stable terms are an intermediate step to reach a normal form, every root-needed redex is also needed. Any non-root-stable term has a root-needed redex. Root-needed redexes in maximal non-root-stable subterms of a term are needed. The notion of necessary set of redexes extends to root-necessary set of redexes in the obvious way. A strategy is hyper root-normalizing if, given a term t having a root-stable form, there are no rewrite sequences starting from t which contain infinitely many root-needed steps. Repeated contraction of root-necessary sets of redexes is said *root-necessary reduction*.

Theorem 4.1 ([12]) *Root-necessary reduction is hyper root-normalizing for almost orthogonal TRSs.*

Since a root-needed redex is a particular case of a root-necessary set of redexes, we have the following immediate consequence.

Theorem 4.2 ([12]) *Root-needed reduction is hyper root-normalizing for orthogonal TRSs.*

4.1 Root-stable neededness of context-sensitive computations

In this section, we compare the context-sensitive computations with root-needed reductions. In the sequel, we usually identify redexes in a term with its occurrences. Ideally, if $\mathcal{I}^r_\mathcal{R}(t)$ is the set of occurrences of root-needed redexes of a term t, then we would like to have $\mathcal{I}^r_\mathcal{R}(t) = O^\mu_\mathcal{R}(t)$ for some replacement map μ. Of course, this is very difficult to obtain, as the replacement restrictions imposed by means of a replacement map μ are very simple. However, we show that under some conditions, we can extract a subset of replacing redexes $I \subseteq O^\mu_\mathcal{R}(t)$ which is contained in $\mathcal{I}^r_\mathcal{R}(t)$ or, at least, which is a root-necessary set of redexes. Hence, it is possible to use the (simple) replacement restrictions to obtain more refined computations (i.e., being more *root-needed*).

Our first result corresponds to Theorem 4.3 in [12]: *'In an orthogonal TRS, any non-root-stable term has a root-needed redex'.*

Theorem 4.3 *Let $\mathcal{R}$ be an orthogonal TRS and μ be such that $\mu^{com}_\mathcal{R} \sqsubseteq \mu$. Every non-root-stable term has a μ-replacing root-needed redex.*

Theorem 4.3 means that, if we consider a replacement map μ such that $\mu^{com}_\mathcal{R} \sqsubseteq \mu$, then by restricting the reductions to μ-replacing occurrences we do *not* lose the possibility of reducing root-needed redexes.

Theorem 4.4 *Let $\mathcal{R}$ be an orthogonal TRS, μ be such that $\mu^{com}_\mathcal{R} \sqsubseteq \mu$ and t be a non-root-stable term. Then, minimal$(O^\mu_\mathcal{R}(t))$ is a root-necessary set of redexes.*

This result improves the use of replacement restrictions by Maranget [11] to achieve optimal derivations by using parallel rewriting in a graph reduction framework. Due to the need to work in a graph reduction framework, Maranget restricts himself to a smaller class of orthogonal TRSs, for which $Var^{\mu}(r) \subseteq Var^{\mu}(l)$ and $\widetilde{Var^{\mu}}(r) \subseteq \widetilde{Var^{\mu}}(l)$ for all rules $l \to r$ in the TRS. For instance, the **if**-rules in Example 3.1 only satisfy these restrictions if $\mu(\mathtt{if}) = \{1, 2, 3\}$, i.e., no replacement restrictions are imposed. Thus, our results on neededness of restricted reductions are more general.

In strongly replacing-independent TRSs, given a term t, the ordered set $(O_{\mathcal{R}}^{\mu_{\mathcal{R}}^{com}}(t), \leq)$ is *flat*. This is due to the following fact.

Proposition 4.5 *Let $\mathcal{R}$ be an almost non-ambiguous, strongly replacing independent TRS and t be a term. Then, $minimal(O_{\mathcal{R}}^{\mu_{\mathcal{R}}^{com}}(t)) = maximal(O_{\mathcal{R}}^{\mu_{\mathcal{R}}^{com}}(t)) = O_{\mathcal{R}}^{\mu_{\mathcal{R}}^{com}}(t)$.*

Let us consider the derivation in Example 3.3. It is easy to verify that, in each step, the reduced redex is the only one which can be considered by *csr* to perform reductions[3]. When considering orthogonal, strongly replacing-independent TRSs, we get a surprising result: any replacing redex is a root-needed redex.

Theorem 4.6 *Let $\mathcal{R}$ be an orthogonal, strongly replacing-independent TRS. Let t be a non-root-stable term. Then, $O_{\mathcal{R}}^{\mu_{\mathcal{R}}^{com}}(t)$ is a set of root-needed redexes.*

We note that this means that, for every term t, $O_{\mathcal{R}}^{\mu_{\mathcal{R}}^{com}}(t)$ is a set of *needed* redexes. For instance, the derivation in Example 3.3 is (root-)needed reduction. However, there are root-needed redexes which are not replacing.

Example 4.7 *Let us consider the strongly replacing-independent TRS:*

$\mathsf{g(a, x)} \to \mathsf{x}$ $\qquad\qquad\qquad$ $\mathsf{b} \to \mathsf{a}$

and the whole set of root-normalizing derivations for $\mathsf{g(a, b)}$*:*

1) $\mathsf{g(a, \underline{b})} \to \underline{\mathsf{g(a, a)}} \to \mathsf{a}$

2) $\underline{\mathsf{g(a, b)}} \to \underline{\mathsf{b}} \to \mathsf{a}$

As we can show, redex b *at the occurrence* 2 *of* $\mathsf{g(a, b)}$ *is root-needed. However,* 2 *is not a replacing occurrence.*

Thus, even in strongly replacing-independent TRS, we cannot obtain $\mathcal{I}_{\mathcal{R}}^{r}(t) = O_{\mathcal{R}}^{\mu}(t)$. Theorem 4.6 shows that it is possible to perform root-needed reduction in parallel. This makes Kennaway's claim in [5] unaccurate: *in an orthogonal TRS, no term can have more than one strongly root-needed redex.* Kennaway argues that this justifies the existence of a 'conflict' between call by need and parallelism. Our notion of strongly replacing-independent TRSs reveals that this conflict depends on the election of the computable approximation to root-needed redexes (strongly root-needed redexes[4] in [5]). For instance, by considering $\mathcal{R}$

[3] This is an extreme case of Proposition 4.5: $O_{\mathcal{R}}^{\mu_{\mathcal{R}}^{com}}(t)$ is a singleton

[4] In a recent work, Durand and Middeldorp [3] have shown some inconsistencies in Kennaway's approximation to root-neededness.

as in Example 3.1, the term $t = \mathtt{sel}(0+0, \mathtt{from}(0))$ is not root-stable, and we have $O_{\mathcal{R}}^{\mu_{\mathcal{R}}^{com}}(t) = \{1,2\}$. By Theorem 4.6, 1 and 2 are occurrences of root-needed redexes. Thus, they can both be reduced in parallel.

We can still characterize root-needed redexes by means of replacement restrictions in the class of μ-left-normal TRSs.

Theorem 4.8 *Let $\mathcal{R}$ be an orthogonal TRS. Let μ be such that $\mu_{\mathcal{R}}^{com} \sqsubseteq \mu$ and $\mathcal{R}$ is μ-left-normal. Let t be a non-root-stable term. Then $min_{\leq_L}(O_{\mathcal{R}}^{\mu}(t))$ is a root-needed redex.*

5 Strategies in context-sensitive rewriting

A sequential rewriting strategy is a function $\mathbb{F}_{\mathcal{R}} : \mathcal{T}(\Sigma, V) \to \mathcal{T}(\Sigma, V)$ such that $\mathbb{F}_{\mathcal{R}}(t) = t$ if t is a normal form (i.e., $O_{\mathcal{R}}(t) = \emptyset$), and $t \to_{\mathcal{R}} \mathbb{F}_{\mathcal{R}}(t)$ otherwise (for parallel strategies $t \to_{\mathcal{R}}^{+} \mathbb{F}_{\mathcal{R}}(t)$) [6].

We drop the suffix $\mathcal{R}$ when no confusion arises. Also, we write $t \to_{\mathbb{F}} s$ instead of $t \to_{\mathcal{R}} \mathbb{F}_{\mathcal{R}}(t)$ if $s = \mathbb{F}_{\mathcal{R}}(t)$. The result of applying a sequential strategy $\mathbb{F}$ for a given TRS $\mathcal{R} = (\Sigma, R)$ can be split into two components: $\mathbb{P} : \mathcal{T}(\Sigma, V) \to \mathbb{N}^* \cup \{\Box\}$ which selects the redex occurrence which should be reduced, and $\mathbb{R} : \mathcal{T}(\Sigma, V) \to R$ which selects the rule which must be applied (see [1]). Then, $\mathbb{P}(t) = \Box$ iff t is a normal form.

If $u = \mathbb{P}(t) \neq \Box$, then $\mathbb{F}(t) = t[\sigma(r)]_u$ where $t|_u = \sigma(l)$, and $l \to r = \mathbb{R}(t)$. Sometimes, $\mathbb{P}$ can be further broken down as follows: $\mathbb{P} = \widehat{\mathbb{P}} \circ O_{\mathcal{R}}$ where $\widehat{\mathbb{P}} : \mathcal{P}(\mathbb{N}^*) \to \mathbb{N}^* \cup \{\Box\}$ selects an occurrence from a non empty set of redex occurrences ($\widehat{\mathbb{P}}(\emptyset) = \Box$, and $\widehat{\mathbb{P}}(U) \subseteq U$ for any $U \in \mathcal{P}(\mathbb{N}^*)$), and $O_{\mathcal{R}} : \mathcal{T}(\Sigma, V) \to \mathcal{P}(\mathbb{N}^*)$ is the usual function which gives the redex occurrences of a term t. Similar considerations can be made for parallel strategies.

For instance, let us consider the following well-known rewriting strategies [6]. We show the decomposition $\mathbb{P} = \widehat{\mathbb{P}} \circ O_{\mathcal{R}}$ for each strategy.

1. The *leftmost-innermost* strategy ($\mathbb{F}_{li}$) reduces the leftmost of the innermost redexes: $\mathbb{P}_{li}(t) = min_{\leq_L}(maximal_{\leq}(O_{\mathcal{R}}(t)))$.
2. The *parallel-innermost* strategy ($\mathbb{F}_{pi}$) simultaneously reduces all innermost redexes: $\mathbb{P}_{pi}(t) = maximal_{\leq}(O_{\mathcal{R}}(t))$.
3. The *leftmost-outermost* strategy ($\mathbb{F}_{lo}$) reduces the leftmost of the outermost redexes: $\mathbb{P}_{lo}(t) = min_{\leq_L}(minimal_{\leq}(O_{\mathcal{R}}(t))) = min_{\leq_L}(O_{\mathcal{R}}(t))$.
4. The *parallel-outermost* strategy ($\mathbb{F}_{po}$) reduces all outermost redexes: $\mathbb{P}_{po}(t) = minimal_{\leq}(O_{\mathcal{R}}(t))$.
5. The *full substitution rule* ($\mathbb{F}_{fs}$): simultaneously reduces all redexes (only defined for orthogonal TRSs): $\mathbb{P}_{fs}(t) = O_{\mathcal{R}}(t)$.

Note that, in the previous strategies, the question of *what* rule applies to a selected redex is left open. In non-ambiguous TRSs this is not a problem, since only one rule per redex applies ($\mathbb{R}$ is given by $\mathbb{P}$).

A rewriting strategy $\mathbb{F}$ for a TRS $\mathcal{R}$ is *normalizing* if, for each t having a normal form, the sequence $(\mathbb{F}^n(t) \mid n \geq 0)$ contains a normal form. For orthogonal

TRSs, results on normalization by means of the previous strategies are due to O'Donnell [13] (see also [6]): $\mathbb{F}_{li}$ and $\mathbb{F}_{pi}$ are normalizing iff the TRS is terminating. $\mathbb{F}_{lo}$ is normalizing for left-normal TRSs. $\mathbb{F}_{po}$ and $\mathbb{F}_{fs}$ are normalizing.

5.1 Context-sensitive strategies and restricted strategies

The notion of context-sensitive strategy or μ-strategy $\mathbb{F}_{\mathcal{R}(\mu)}$ is analogous to the standard notion as defined above: $\mathbb{F}_{\mathcal{R}(\mu)}(t) = t$ if t is a μ-normal form (i.e., $O^\mu_{\mathcal{R}}(t) = \emptyset$) and $t \hookrightarrow_{\mathcal{R}(\mu)} \mathbb{F}_{\mathcal{R}(\mu)}(t)$, otherwise, ($t \hookrightarrow^+_{\mathcal{R}(\mu)} \mathbb{F}_{\mathcal{R}(\mu)}(t)$ for parallel μ-strategies). Given a strategy $\mathbb{F}$, and a replacement map μ, we define the associated μ-restricted μ-strategy.

Definition 5.1 (μ-restriction of a rewriting strategy) *Let $\mathcal{R} = (\Sigma, R)$ be an orthogonal TRS, and μ be a Σ-map. Let $\mathbb{F}$ be a rewriting strategy with components $\mathbb{P}$, $\mathbb{R}$. Let $\mathbb{P} = \widehat{\mathbb{P}} \circ O_{\mathcal{R}}$. The μ-restriction of $\mathbb{F}$ is the μ-strategy $\mathbb{F}^\mu$ having components $\mathbb{P}^\mu = \widehat{\mathbb{P}} \circ O^\mu_{\mathcal{R}}$ and $\mathbb{R}^\mu$, where $\mathbb{R}^\mu$ is (uniquely) determined by the redexes selected by $\mathbb{P}^\mu$.*

For the leftmost-outermost, parallel-innermost, ... rewriting strategies, we obtain the corresponding μ-restricted μ-strategies by considering the *μ-replacing* redexes in a term (and only these ones). We just take $O^\mu_{\mathcal{R}}(t)$ instead of $O_{\mathcal{R}}(t)$ in the previous expressions for $\mathbb{P}_{li}, \ldots, \mathbb{P}_{fs}$, thus giving $\mathbb{P}^\mu_{li}, \ldots, \mathbb{P}^\mu_{fs}$, for the corresponding μ-restricted μ-strategies $\mathbb{F}^\mu_{li}, \ldots, \mathbb{F}^\mu_{fs}$.

We analyze the properties of μ-restricted μ-strategies $\mathbb{F}^\mu_{li}, \ldots, \mathbb{F}^\mu_{fs}$ concerning root-normalization. In the next section, we discuss normalization. The notion of root-normalizing strategy is analogous to normalizing strategies. We note the very special situation which arises with strongly replacing-independent TRSs:

Theorem 5.2 *Let $\mathcal{R}$ be an orthogonal, strongly replacing-independent TRS. Then, every $\mu^{com}_{\mathcal{R}}$-strategy $\mathbb{F}_{\mathcal{R}(\mu^{com}_{\mathcal{R}})}$ is hyper root-normalizing.*

In particular, when considering orthogonal, strongly replacing-independent TRSs, Proposition 4.5 entails that innermost and outermost $\mu^{com}_{\mathcal{R}}$-strategies collapse into a single class of *cs*-strategies.

The restriction of parallel-outermost and full substitution strategies are also root-normalizing.

Theorem 5.3 *Let $\mathcal{R}$ be an orthogonal TRS, and μ be such that $\mu^{com}_{\mathcal{R}} \sqsubseteq \mu$. Then, $\mathbb{F}^\mu_{po}$ and $\mathbb{F}^\mu_{fs}$ are hyper root-normalizing.*

Note that, since in the μ-restricted μ-strategies we consider a lesser set of redexes (because $minimal(O^\mu_{\mathcal{R}}(t)) \subseteq minimal(O_{\mathcal{R}}(t))$ and $O^\mu_{\mathcal{R}}(t) \subseteq O_{\mathcal{R}}(t)$), we obtain some advantages w.r.t. the corresponding parallel strategies.

Theorem 5.4 *Let $\mathcal{R}$ be an orthogonal TRS, and μ be such that $\mu^{com}_{\mathcal{R}} \sqsubseteq \mu$ and $\mathcal{R}$ is μ-left-normal. Then $\mathbb{F}^\mu_{lo}$ is hyper root-normalizing.*

Example 5.5 *Let us consider the $\mu_{\mathcal{R}}^{com}$-left-normal TRS $\mathcal{R}$:*

$\mathtt{g(f(a),f(x))} \to \mathtt{a}$ $\qquad\qquad$ $\mathtt{b} \to \mathtt{b}$

$\mathtt{h(x,a,f(y))} \to \mathtt{a}$

where $\mu_{\mathcal{R}}^{com}(\mathtt{f}) = \{1\}$, $\mu_{\mathcal{R}}^{com}(\mathtt{h}) = \{2,3\}$, and $\mu_{\mathcal{R}}^{com}(\mathtt{g}) = \{1,2\}$. We have the leftmost-outermost infinite derivation:

$$\mathtt{g(f(h(\underline{b},h(x,a,f(y)),f(y))),f(b))} \to \mathtt{g(f(h(\underline{b},h(x,a,f(y)),f(y))),f(b))} \to \cdots$$

However, the corresponding $\mu_{\mathcal{R}}^{com}$-restricted leftmost-outermost derivation is:

$$\mathtt{g(f(h(b,\underline{h(x,a,f(y))},f(y))),f(b))} \hookrightarrow \mathtt{g(f(\underline{h(b,a,f(y))}),f(b))}$$
$$\hookrightarrow \underline{\mathtt{g(f(a),f(b))}} \hookrightarrow \mathtt{a}$$

which does root-normalize the term. However, we cannot use any *$\mu_{\mathcal{R}}^{com}$-restricted $\mu_{\mathcal{R}}^{com}$-strategy. For instance, the 'rightmost' $\mu_{\mathcal{R}}^{com}$-reduction:*

$$\mathtt{g(f(h(b,h(x,a,f(y)),f(y))),f(\underline{b}))} \hookrightarrow \mathtt{g(f(h(b,h(x,a,f(y)),f(y))),f(\underline{b}))} \hookrightarrow \cdots$$

is infinite.

When we consider left-normal TRSs, there is no difference between the leftmost-outermost strategy and the restricted version. This is because they select exactly the same occurrences for reductions.

Proposition 5.6 *Let $\mathcal{R}$ be a left-normal TRS, μ be such that $\mu_{\mathcal{R}}^{com} \sqsubseteq \mu$ and t be a non-root-stable term. Then, $\mathbb{P}_{lo}(t) = \mathbb{P}_{lo}^{\mu}(t)$.*

5.2 Normalization with context-sensitive strategies

In this section, we discuss the use of a μ-strategy $\mathbb{F}_{\mathcal{R}(\mu)}$ to *normalize* terms. We know that, in general, *csr* is not able to compute normal forms, but only μ-normal forms. However, we have the following possibilities:

1. $\mathbb{F}_{\mathcal{R}(\mu)}$ is root-normalizing. Then, we can use it to obtain a root-stable form s of a term t and recursively apply it to the immediate subterms of s [5, 12]. We call this, *normalization via root-normalization*. The problem is that, in general, it is undecidable whether a term is root-stable or not.
2. $\mathbb{F}_{\mathcal{R}(\mu)}$ is μ-normalizing. Then, we can use it to obtain a μ-normal form s of a term t. Then, we recursively apply the μ-strategy to maximal non-replacing subterms of s. We call this, *normalization via μ-normalization*. We only need to provide some additional machinery to perform the 'jumps' into non-replacing parts of μ-normal forms (since this is not pure *csr*).
3. $\mathbb{F}_{\mathcal{R}(\mu)}$ is μ-normalizing, and the μ-normal form of t is a normal form (for instance, a value). Then, we can use $\mathbb{F}_{\mathcal{R}(\mu)}$ with no further refinements (*direct normalization*).

The first possibility is fairly discussed in [12]. In Section 5.1, we have characterized some root-normalizing cs-strategies. However, as stated in [12], not every root-normalizing strategy is normalizing and vice-versa. We must restrict ourselves to *context-free* root-normalizing strategies.

Definition 5.7 ([12]) *A sequential reduction strategy $\mathbb{F}$ is said to be context-free if for all root-stable terms $t = f(t_1, \ldots, t_i, \ldots, t_k)$ and $i \in \{1, \ldots, k\}$, such that $t \to_{\mathbb{F}} f(t_1, \ldots, t_i', \ldots, t_k)$, we have $t_i \to_{\mathbb{F}} t_i'$.*

Almost all strategies in the literature are context-free. The restricted *cs*-strategies in the previous section also are. We refer the reader to [12] for further details.

Concerning normalization via μ-normalization, a normalizing strategy is able to compute a normal form of a *weakly normalizing* term t. If we want to use a μ-normalizing μ-strategy $\mathbb{F}_{\mathcal{R}(\mu)}$ to obtain the normal form $\bar{t}$ of t, via a μ-normal form s, we must first ensure that the weakly normalizing term t is weakly μ-normalizing. Then, the μ-normalizing μ-strategy will compute s. In contrast to termination (see [9]), weak normalization is *not* preserved by *csr*.

Example 5.8 *Let us consider the (nonterminating) TRS*

$\mathtt{f}(\mathtt{x},\mathtt{a}) \to \mathtt{a} \qquad \mathtt{g}(\mathtt{a}) \to \mathtt{a} \qquad \mathtt{b} \to \mathtt{b}$

If we take $\mu(\mathtt{f}) = \{1\}$ *and* $\mu(\mathtt{g}) = \emptyset$, *then:*

1. *The term* $t = \mathtt{f}(\mathtt{b},\mathtt{g}(\mathtt{a}))$ *is weakly normalizing:* $\mathtt{f}(\mathtt{b},\underline{\mathtt{g}(\mathtt{a})}) \to \underline{\mathtt{f}(\mathtt{b},\mathtt{a})} \to \mathtt{a}$. *However,* t *is not weakly* μ*-normalizing, as there is only the following infinite reduction sequence:* $\mathtt{f}(\underline{\mathtt{b}},\mathtt{g}(\mathtt{a})) \hookrightarrow \mathtt{f}(\underline{\mathtt{b}},\mathtt{g}(\mathtt{a})) \hookrightarrow \cdots$.
2. *The term* $t = \mathtt{g}(\mathtt{b})$ *is weakly* μ*-normalizing (it is a* μ*-normal form), but* t *is not weakly normalizing:* $\mathtt{g}(\underline{\mathtt{b}}) \to \mathtt{g}(\underline{\mathtt{b}}) \to \cdots$.

However, when we work with the canonical replacement map (or greater), we have the following.

Theorem 5.9 *Let* $\mathcal{R}$ *be an almost orthogonal TRS and* μ *be such that* $\mu_{\mathcal{R}}^{com} \sqsubseteq \mu$. *If* t *is weakly normalizing, then* t *is weakly* μ*-normalizing.*

The next point is how to define the μ-normalizing μ-strategy $\mathbb{F}_{\mathcal{R}(\mu)}$. The connection between root-normalizing and μ-normalizing μ-strategies is also immediate. In fact, the proof is almost the same as Theorem 6.4 in [12] by considering the replacement restrictions.

Theorem 5.10 *Let* $\mathcal{R}$ *be a confluent TRS. A context-free root-normalizing* μ*-strategy is* μ*-normalizing.*

Since the restricted *cs*-strategies analyzed in the previous section are context-free, an easy consequence of Theorem 5.10 and Theorem 5.3 is that, for orthogonal TRSs, $\mathbb{F}_{po}^{\mu}$ and $\mathbb{F}_{fs}^{\mu}$ are μ-normalizing whenever $\mu_{\mathcal{R}}^{com} \sqsubseteq \mu$.

Theorem 4.6 says that any $\mu_{\mathcal{R}}^{com}$-reduction of a non-root-stable term in orthogonal, strongly replacing-independent TRSs only takes root-needed redexes. Thus, reductions to root-stable form performed by any $\mu_{\mathcal{R}}^{com}$-strategy in such TRSs are root-needed. Since root-needed reduction is trivially context-free (see [12]), Theorem 5.10 and Theorem 5.2 reveal that every root-normalizing $\mu_{\mathcal{R}}^{com}$-strategy is $\mu_{\mathcal{R}}^{com}$-normalizing for orthogonal, strongly replacing-independent TRSs. We have the following immediate consequence.

Theorem 5.11 *An orthogonal, strongly replacing-independent TRS* $\mathcal{R}$ *is* $\mu_{\mathcal{R}}^{com}$*-terminating iff it is weakly* $\mu_{\mathcal{R}}^{com}$*-normalizing.*

Finally, if $\mu_{\mathcal{R}}^{com} \sqsubseteq \mu$, by Theorem 5.10 and Theorem 5.4, we know that $\mathbb{F}_{lo}^{\mu}$ is μ-normalizing for orthogonal μ-left-normal TRSs.

Jumping into maximal non-replacing subterms of a μ-normal form is safe because replacing subterms of μ-normal forms are μ-normal forms and, provided that $\mu_{\mathcal{R}}^{com} \sqsubseteq \mu$, every μ-normal form is root-stable (see [8]).

For the last normalization procedure, whenever the normal form of a term is a value, we can use *csr* to compute it (Theorem 3.4). Now we are more concrete: we can use context-sensitive strategies to compute it.

Theorem 5.12 *Let $\mathcal{R} = (\Sigma, R) = (\mathcal{F} \uplus \mathcal{C}, R)$ be a confluent, left linear TRS. Let $\mathcal{B} \subseteq \mathcal{C}$ and $\delta \in \mathcal{T}(\mathcal{B}, V)$. Let μ be a Σ-map such that $\mu_{\mathcal{R}}^{\mathcal{B}} \sqsubseteq \mu$, and $\mathbb{F}_{\mathcal{R}(\mu)}$ be a μ-normalizing μ-strategy. Then $t \to^* \delta$ iff $t \hookrightarrow^*_{\mathbb{F}_{\mathcal{R}(\mu)}} \delta$.*

As opposed to Theorem 3.4, confluence is required in Theorem 5.12, because our strategies are deterministic. Otherwise, the value computed by $\mathbb{F}_{\mathcal{R}(\mu)}$ could be different from δ. Dealing with almost orthogonal TRSs, Theorem 5.9 shows that the computation of a normal form is consistent with the computation of a μ-normal form: if a term has a normal form, it also has a μ-normal form. Hence, if the input term has a normal form which is not a value, the μ-normalizing μ-strategy will stop (giving a μ-normal form). Thus, the computation is safe.

Even if we deal with *μ-terminating* TRSs [9, 16] the results in Section 4.1 ensure optimality of these *cs*-strategies in the sense that they reduce needed redexes. Since our optimality results concern $\mu_{\mathcal{R}}^{com}$ rather than $\mu_{\mathcal{R}}^{\mathcal{B}}$, we can lose optimality in context-sensitive reductions using $\mu_{\mathcal{R}}^{\mathcal{B}}$. To avoid this undesirable behavior, we have proposed a solution by using program transformations. They allow us to employ the results on neededness which are given in this paper to obtain complete evaluations which only consider needed redexes [10].

6 Conclusions and future work

We have given conditions to ensure the efficiency of computations using replacement maps greater than or equal to the canonical replacement map $\mu_{\mathcal{R}}^{com}$. We have also shown how to use the replacement restrictions to find out (root-)needed redexes. We have defined classes of TRSs, namely strongly replacing-independent and μ-left normal TRSs, for which this is very easy to achieve. We have introduced the notion of context-sensitive strategy. We have shown how to *restrict* a given rewriting strategy to obtain a *cs*-strategy. We have given conditions ensuring that the restricted *cs*-strategies obtained from the usual strategies preserve the good properties of the original ones. Restricted *cs*-strategies improve the behavior of the unrestricted ones by reducing the amount of wasteful computations or widening the class of TRSs for which the strategy is well-behaved. In this way, we obtain a suitable framework for the definition of normalizing strategies.

Completeness of *csr* concerns left-linear TRSs, rather than orthogonal ones (see [8]). A subject of future work could be to establish accurated approximations to root-needed and needed computations in a more general framework [3].

References

1. S. Antoy and A. Middeldorp. A Sequential Reduction Strategy. *Theoretical Computer Science*, 165(1):75-95, 1996.
2. N. Dershowitz and J.P. Jouannaud. Rewrite Systems. In J. van Leeuwen, editor, *Handbook of Theoretical Computer Science*, volume B: Formal Models and Semantics, pages 243-320. Elsevier, Amsterdam and The MIT Press, Cambridge, MA, 1990.
3. I. Durand and A. Middeldorp. Decidable Call by Need Computations in Term Rewriting (Extended Abstract). In *Proc. of CADE'97*, LNCS *to appear*.
4. G. Huet and J.J. Lévy. Computations in orthogonal term rewriting systems I, II. In J.L. Lassez and G. Plotkin, editors, *Computational logic: essays in honour of J. Alan Robinson*, pages 395-414 and 415-443. The MIT Press, Cambridge, MA, 1991.
5. R. Kennaway. A Conflict Between Call-By-Need Computation and Parallelism. In *Proc. of Workshop on Conditional and Typed Rewriting Systems, CTRS'94*, LNCS 968:247-261, Springer-Verlag, Berlin, 1994.
6. J.W. Klop. Term Rewriting Systems. In S. Abramsky, D.M. Gabbay and T.S.E. Maibaum. *Handbook of Logic in Computer Science*, volume 3, pages 1-116. Oxford University Press, 1992.
7. J.W. Klop and A. Middeldorp. Sequentiality in Orthogonal Term Rewriting Systems. *Journal of Symbolic Computation* 12:161-195, 1991.
8. S. Lucas. Context-sensitive computations in functional and functional logic programs. *Journal of Functional and Logic Programming*, 1997, *to appear*.
9. S. Lucas. Termination of Context-Sensitive Rewriting by Rewriting. In F. Meyer auf der Heide and B. Monien, editors, *Proc. of 23rd. International Colloquium on Automata, Languages and Programming, ICALP'96*, LNCS 1099:122-133, Springer-Verlag, Berlin, 1996.
10. S. Lucas. Transformations for Efficient Evaluations in Functional Programming. In H. Glasser and H. Kuchen, editors, *Proc. of 9th International Symposium on Programming Languages, Implementations, Logics, and Programs, PLILP'97*, LNCS *to appear*.
11. L. Maranget. Optimal Derivations in Weak Lambda-calculi and in Orthogonal Term Rewriting Systems In *Conference Record of the 18th ACM Symposium on Principles of Programming Languages*, pages 255-269, ACM Press, 1990.
12. A. Middeldorp. Call by Need Computations to Root-Stable Form. In *Conference Record of the 24th ACM Symposium on Principles of Programming Languages*, pages 94-105, 1997.
13. M.J. O'Donnell. Computing in Systems Described by Equations. LNCS 58, Springer-Verlag, Berlin, 1977.
14. R.C. Sekar and I.V. Ramakrishnan. Programming in Equational Logic: Beyond Strong Sequentiality. *Information and Computation* 104:78-109, 1993.
15. C. Reade. Elements of Functional Programming. Addison-Wesley Publishing Company, 1993.
16. H. Zantema. Termination of Context-Sensitive Rewriting. In H. Comon, editor, *Proc. of 8th International Conference on Rewriting Techniques and Applications, RTA'97*, LNCS 1232:172-186, Springer-Verlag, Berlin, 1997.

Conditional Term Graph Rewriting

Enno Ohlebusch

Technische Fakultät, University of Bielefeld,
P.O. Box 100131, 33501 Bielefeld, Germany
email: enno@TechFak.Uni-Bielefeld.DE

Abstract. For efficiency reasons, term rewriting is usually implemented by graph rewriting. It is known that graph rewriting is a sound and complete implementation of (almost) orthogonal term rewriting systems; see [BEG+87]. In this paper, we extend the result to properly oriented orthogonal conditional systems with strict equality. In these systems extra variables are allowed in conditions and right-hand sides of rules.

1 Introduction

Attempts to combine the functional and logic programming paradigms have recently been receiving increasing attention; see [Han94b] for an overview of the field. It has been argued in [Han95] that *strict equality* is the only sensible notion of equality for possibly nonterminating programs. In this paper, we adopt this point of view–so every functional logic program is regarded as an orthogonal conditional term rewriting system (CTRS) with strict equality. The standard operational semantics for functional (or equational) logic programming is conditional narrowing. It is well-known that extra variables in conditions (let alone right-hand sides) cause problems because narrowing may become incomplete or confluence may be lost. Therefore, many efforts have been made to characterize classes of confluent functional logic programs with extra variables for which narrowing is complete; see [Han95] for details. In [Han95], new interesting completeness results are provided. However, all of these results are standing on shaky ground. This is because all of them depend on the fact that conditional term graph rewriting is a sound and complete implementation of CTRSs with strict equality ([Han95], Theorem 3.5 and page 676: "Conditions 1 and 2 are necessary to extend Theorem 3.5 ..."). But the proof of this fact (given in [Han94a], Theorem 3.8) is incorrect. There is the following counterexample:

$$\mathcal{R} = \begin{cases} a \to x \Leftarrow g(x) {==} e & \\ g(b) \to e, & g(c) \to e \\ h(x) \to f(x,x), & f(b,c) \to d \end{cases}$$

Since $a \to_{\mathcal{R}} b$ and $a \to_{\mathcal{R}} c$ (consequently, the system is not confluent), it follows that $h(a) \to_{\mathcal{R}} f(a,a) \to^*_{\mathcal{R}} f(b,c) \to_{\mathcal{R}} d$. In the corresponding graph rewrite system, however, $f(a,a)$ does not reduce to $f(b,c)$; cf. [BEG+87], Example 5.4. It is the objective of this paper to prove that conditional term graph rewriting is a sound and complete implementation (w.r.t. the computation of normal forms) of properly oriented orthogonal CTRSs with strict equality (called functional CTRSs in what follows). Note that the above CTRS is not properly oriented. Aside from the mentioned reasons, our new result is interesting in its own right–simply because term rewriting is usually implemented by graph rewriting.

The remainder of the paper is organized as follows. In the next section, we recapitulate the basics of conditional term rewriting. In Section 3, functional CTRSs are introduced. Unfortunately, functional CTRSs do not satisfy the parallel moves lemma. In order to overcome this obstacle, we define a closely related "deterministic" reduction relation in which extra variables are instantiated by ground constructor terms only. We obtain as a consequence that functional CTRSs are level-confluent. This is not a new result–it is a special case of a theorem in [SMI95]. Our proof, however, is simpler than that in [SMI95]. Section 4 is dedicated to graph rewriting. We neither follow the approach of [BEG+87] nor that of [Plu93]. Instead, we use the term based model of [KO95] in which directed acyclic graphs correspond to well-marked terms. The first part of Section 4 is a mirror image of Section 3: it is shown that the graph rewrite relation of a functional CTRS has almost the same properties as the term rewrite relation. With the aid of the aforementioned results we finally achieve our principal result: graph rewriting is a sound and complete implementation of functional CTRSs. It should be possible to show that this result also holds for *almost orthogonal* systems. For space reasons, several proofs are omitted.

2 Preliminaries

The reader is assumed to be familiar with the basic concepts of term rewriting (which can be found in the surveys of Dershowitz & Jouannaud [DJ90] and Klop [Klo92], for instance). Here, we merely recall less common definitions and some basic facts concerning conditional term rewriting.

Let $(\mathcal{F}, \mathcal{R})$ be a term rewriting system (TRS). A function symbol $f \in \mathcal{F}$ is called a *defined symbol* if there is a rewrite rule $l \to r \in \mathcal{R}$ such that $l = f(t_1, \ldots, t_k)$ for some terms $t_1, \ldots, t_k$, otherwise it is called *constructor*. The set of defined symbols is denoted by $\mathcal{F}_\mathcal{D}$ while $\mathcal{F}_\mathcal{C}$ stands for the set of constructors. A *constructor term* is a term built from constructors and variables only. A non-overlapping left-linear TRS is called *orthogonal*. In an *almost orthogonal* TRS, the non-overlapping restriction is relaxed by allowing trivial overlays.

In a CTRS $(\mathcal{F}, \mathcal{R})$, rewrite rules have the form $l \to r \Leftarrow s_1 = t_1, \ldots, s_n = t_k$ with $l, r, s_1, \ldots, s_k,\ t_1, \ldots, t_k \in \mathcal{T}(\mathcal{F}, \mathcal{V})$. We frequently abbreviate the conditional part of the rewrite rule–the (possibly empty) sequence $s_1 = t_1, \ldots, s_k = t_k$–by c. If a rewrite rule has no conditions, we write $l \to r$. It is always required that l is not a variable. The $=$ symbol in the conditions can be interpreted in different ways, leading to different rewrite relations associated with $\mathcal{R}$. This paper deals with *oriented* CTRSs in which the equality signs are interpreted as reachability ($\to_\mathcal{R}^*$). Formally, the rewrite relation associated with an oriented CTRS $(\mathcal{F}, \mathcal{R})$ is the smallest relation that satisfies: $s \to_\mathcal{R} t$ if there exists a rewrite rule $l \to r \Leftarrow c$ in $\mathcal{R}$, a substitution $\sigma : \mathcal{V} \to \mathcal{T}(\mathcal{F}, \mathcal{V})$, and a context $C[\,]$ such that

$s = C[l\sigma], t = C[r\sigma]$, and $s_i\sigma \to_{\mathcal{R}}^* t_i\sigma$ for all $s_i = t_i$ in c. For every oriented CTRS $\mathcal{R}$, we inductively define TRSs $\mathcal{R}_n$, $n \in \mathbb{N}$, by:

$$\mathcal{R}_0 = \emptyset$$
$$\mathcal{R}_{n+1} = \{l\sigma \to r\sigma \mid l \to r \Leftarrow c \in \mathcal{R} \text{ and } s\sigma \to_{\mathcal{R}_n}^* t\sigma \text{ for all } s = t \text{ in } c\}.$$

Note that $\mathcal{R}_n \subseteq \mathcal{R}_{n+1}$ for all $n \in \mathbb{N}$. Furthermore, $s \to_{\mathcal{R}} t$ if and only if $s \to_{\mathcal{R}_n} t$ for some $n \in \mathbb{N}$. The *depth* of a rewrite step $s \to_{\mathcal{R}} t$ is defined to be the minimum n with $s \to_{\mathcal{R}_n} t$. A CTRS $\mathcal{R}$ is called *level-confluent* if every TRS $\mathcal{R}_n$ is confluent. As in [MH94], rewrite rules $l \to r \Leftarrow c$ will be classified according to the distribution of variables among l, r, and c, as follows:

type	requirement
1	$\mathcal{V}ar(r) \cup \mathcal{V}ar(c) \subseteq \mathcal{V}ar(l)$
2	$\mathcal{V}ar(r) \subseteq \mathcal{V}ar(l)$
3	$\mathcal{V}ar(r) \subseteq \mathcal{V}ar(l) \cup \mathcal{V}ar(c)$
4	no restrictions

An n-CTRS contains only rewrite rules of type n. For every rule $l \to r \Leftarrow c$, we define $\mathcal{EV}ar(l \to r \Leftarrow c) = \mathcal{V}ar(r) \cup \mathcal{V}ar(c) \setminus \mathcal{V}ar(l)$. An *extra variable* in $l \to r \Leftarrow c$ is a variable $x \in \mathcal{EV}ar(l \to r \Leftarrow c)$. Thus a 1-CTRS has no extra variables, a 2-CTRS has no extra variables in right-hand sides of rules, and a 3-CTRS may contain extra variables in right-hand sides of rules provided that these also occur in the corresponding conditional part.

In the sequel, we need a result owing to Staples [Sta75]. An abstract reduction system (ARS) $\mathcal{A}_2 = (A, \to_2)$ is called a *refinement* of another ARS $\mathcal{A}_1 = (A, \to_1)$ if $\to_1 \subseteq \to_2^*$. Such a refinement is called *compatible* if for all $a \to_2^* b$, there is a $c \in A$ such that $a \to_1^* c$ and $b \to_1^* c$. Staples' result states that a compatible refinement $\mathcal{A}_2$ of $\mathcal{A}_1$ is confluent if and only if $\mathcal{A}_1$ is confluent. In fact, we also need the following generalization of this result. Let $\mathcal{A}_1 = (A, \to_1)$ and $\mathcal{A}_2 = (A, \to_2)$ be ARSs. Let $\sim$ be an equivalence relation on A such that $\to_1 \subseteq \to_2^*$ and, for all $a \to_2^* b$, there are $c, d \in A$ such that $a \to_1^* c$, $b \to_1^* d$, and $c \sim d$. Let $i \in \{1, 2\}$. If $\mathcal{A}_i$ is confluent modulo $\sim$ (i.e., for all $c \;{}_i^*\!\leftarrow a \sim b \to_i^* d$, there are $e, f \in A$ such that $c \to_i^* e \sim f \;{}_i^*\!\leftarrow d$) and, for all $a \sim b \to_{3-i}^* c$, there is a $d \in A$ such that $a \to_{3-i}^* d \sim c$, then $\mathcal{A}_{3-i}$ is confluent modulo $\sim$.

3 Functional CTRSs

The unconditional TRS obtained from a CTRS $\mathcal{R}$ by omitting the conditions in its rewrite rules is denoted by $\mathcal{R}_u$.[1] For a CTRS $\mathcal{R}$, notions like left-linearity, (almost) orthogonality, and constructor term are defined via the TRS $\mathcal{R}_u$. A *normal* CTRS $\mathcal{R}$ is an oriented CTRS whose rules $l \to r \Leftarrow s_1 = t_1, \ldots, s_n = t_k$ are subject to the additional constraint that every t_j is a ground normal form with respect to $\mathcal{R}_u$. Orthogonal normal 2-CTRS satisfy the so-called parallel moves lemma. Thus they are (level-) confluent. We next briefly recall this result achieved by Bergstra and Klop [BK86]; see also Suzuki *et al.* [SMI95].

[1] Note that $\mathcal{R}_u$ may contain rules $l \to r$ with $\mathcal{V}ar(r) \not\subseteq \mathcal{V}ar(l)$.

Definition 1. Let $A : s \rightarrow_{[p, l \rightarrow r \Leftarrow c]} t$ be a rewrite step in a CTRS $\mathcal{R}$ and let $q \in \mathcal{P}os(s)$. The set $q \backslash A$ of *descendants* of q in t is defined by:

$$q \backslash A = \begin{cases} \{q\} & \text{if } q < p \text{ or } q \parallel p, \\ \{p \cdot p_3 \cdot p_2 \mid r_{|p_3} = l_{|p_1}\} & \text{if } q = p \cdot p_1 \cdot p_2 \text{ with } p_1 \in \mathcal{VP}os(l) \\ \emptyset & \text{otherwise.} \end{cases}$$

If $Q \subseteq \mathcal{P}os(s)$, then $Q \backslash A$ denotes the set $\bigcup_{q \in Q} q \backslash A$. The notion of descendant is extended to rewrite sequences in the obvious way.

Definition 2. Let $\mathcal{R}$ be a CTRS. We write $s \dashv\!\!\!\!\!\!\rightarrow_{\mathcal{R}_n} t$ if t can be obtained from s by contracting a set of pairwise disjoint redexes in s by $\mathcal{R}_n$. We write $s \dashv\!\!\!\!\!\!\rightarrow t$ if $s \dashv\!\!\!\!\!\!\rightarrow_{\mathcal{R}_n} t$ for some $n \in \mathbb{N}$. The minimum such n is called the depth of $s \dashv\!\!\!\!\!\!\rightarrow t$. The relation $\dashv\!\!\!\!\!\!\rightarrow$ is called *parallel rewriting*.

The parallel moves lemma for orthogonal normal 2-CTRS now reads as follows.

Lemma 3. *Let $\mathcal{R}$ be an orthogonal normal 2-CTRS. If $t \dashv\!\!\!\!\!\!\rightarrow_{\mathcal{R}_m} t_1$ and $t \dashv\!\!\!\!\!\!\rightarrow_{\mathcal{R}_n} t_2$, then there is a term t_3 such that $t_1 \dashv\!\!\!\!\!\!\rightarrow_{\mathcal{R}_n} t_3$ and $t_2 \dashv\!\!\!\!\!\!\rightarrow_{\mathcal{R}_m} t_3$. Moreover, the redexes contracted in $t_1 \dashv\!\!\!\!\!\!\rightarrow_{\mathcal{R}_n} t_3$ ($t_2 \dashv\!\!\!\!\!\!\rightarrow_{\mathcal{R}_m} t_3$) are the descendants in t_1 (t_2) of the redexes contracted in $t \dashv\!\!\!\!\!\!\rightarrow_{\mathcal{R}_n} t_2$ ($t \dashv\!\!\!\!\!\!\rightarrow_{\mathcal{R}_m} t_1$).*

In this paper, we are interested in CTRSs with strict equality. In such systems, the equality signs in the conditional part of a rule are interpreted as "the terms are reducible to a same ground constructor term in $\mathcal{R}$".

Definition 4. A 3-CTRS *with strict equality* is a 3-CTRS $(\mathcal{F} \uplus \mathcal{F}_{eq}, \mathcal{R} \uplus \mathcal{R}_{eq})$ which satisfies ($\uplus$ denotes the disjoint union of sets):

1. $\mathcal{F}_{eq} = \{==, \wedge, true, false\}$, where $\wedge$ is assumed to be right-associative.
2. The TRS $\mathcal{R}_{eq}$ consists of the rules:

$$\begin{array}{rcll} c == c & \rightarrow & true & \text{for all constants } c \in \mathcal{F}_\mathcal{C} \\ c(x_1, \ldots, x_n) == c(y_1, \ldots, y_n) & \rightarrow & \bigwedge_{i=1}^{n} (x_i == y_i) & \text{for all } n\text{-ary } c \in \mathcal{F}_\mathcal{C} \\ c(x_1, \ldots, x_n) == d(y_1, \ldots, y_m) & \rightarrow & false & \text{for all } c, d \in \mathcal{F}_\mathcal{C}, c \neq d \\ true \wedge x & \rightarrow & x & \\ false \wedge x & \rightarrow & false & \end{array}$$

3. Every rule in $\mathcal{R}$ has the form $l \rightarrow r \Leftarrow (s_1 == t_1) = true, \ldots, (s_k == t_k) = true$, where $l, r, s_1, \ldots, s_k, t_1, \ldots, t_k \in \mathcal{T}(\mathcal{F}, \mathcal{V})$.
4. The rewrite relation $\rightarrow_\mathcal{R}$ is defined by $\rightarrow_\mathcal{R} = \bigcup_{n \geq 0} \rightarrow_{\mathcal{R}_n}$, where $\rightarrow_{\mathcal{R}_0} = \emptyset$ and, for $n > 0$, $s \rightarrow_{\mathcal{R}_n} t$ if and only if there is a rule $l \rightarrow r \Leftarrow c$ in $\mathcal{R}$, a substitution $\sigma : \mathcal{V} \rightarrow \mathcal{T}(\mathcal{F}, \mathcal{V})$ with $\mathcal{D}(\sigma) = \mathcal{V}ar(l \rightarrow r \Leftarrow c)$, and a context $C[\,]$ such that $s = C[l\sigma]$, $t = C[r\sigma]$, and $(s_i\sigma == t_i\sigma) \rightarrow^*_{\mathcal{R}_{n-1} \cup \mathcal{R}_{eq}} true$ for all $(s_i == t_i) = true$ in c.

In the sequel, we simply write a rewrite rule as $l \rightarrow r \Leftarrow s_1 == t_1, \ldots, s_k == t_k$. When we speak of a CTRS $\mathcal{R}$ with strict equality, we tacitly assume that $\mathcal{R}$ is extended with $\mathcal{R}_{eq}$. The next proposition shows that the definition above specifies the desired behavior of a CTRS with strict equality; cf. [AEH94].

Proposition 5. *Let $\mathcal{R}$ be a 3-CTRS with strict equality. The following statements are equivalent for all terms s and t in $\mathcal{T}(\mathcal{F},\mathcal{V})$:*

1. *$s{=}{=}t$ is reducible to true in $\mathcal{R} \uplus \mathcal{R}_{eq}$.*
2. *s and t are reducible to a same ground constructor term in $\mathcal{R}$.*

Definition 6. A 3-CTRS $\mathcal{R}$ with strict equality is called *properly oriented* (cf. [SMI95]) if, for all $l \to r \Leftarrow s_1{=}{=}t_1, \ldots, s_k{=}{=}t_k$ in $\mathcal{R}$,

1. every t_j is a linear constructor term, and
2. $\mathcal{V}ar(s_i) \subseteq \mathcal{V}ar(l) \cup \bigcup_{j=1}^{i-1} \mathcal{V}ar(t_j)$.

A *functional* CTRS is a properly oriented orthogonal 3-CTRS with strict equality.[2]

The functional CTRS below computes the Fibonacci numbers (cf. [Klo92]).

$$\mathcal{R}_{fib} = \begin{cases} plus(0,x) & \to x \\ plus(s(x),y) & \to s(plus(x,y)) \\ fib(0) & \to pair(0,s(0)) \\ fib(s(x)) & \to pair(z, plus(y,z)) \Leftarrow fib(x){=}{=}pair(y,z) \end{cases}$$

Unfortunately, functional CTRSs do not satisfy the parallel moves lemma as witnessed by the following simple example taken from [SMI95].

$$\mathcal{R} = \begin{cases} f(x) \to y \Leftarrow x{=}{=}y \\ a \to b \\ b \to c \end{cases}$$

Then $f(a) \mathrel{+\!\!\!\!\!\!\Rightarrow}_{\mathcal{R}_2} a$ and $f(a) \mathrel{+\!\!\!\!\!\!\Rightarrow}_{\mathcal{R}_2} c$ but not $a \mathrel{+\!\!\!\!\!\!\Rightarrow}_{\mathcal{R}_2} c$.

We next introduce a special "deterministic" rewrite relation $\to_{\mathcal{R}^d}$ which is closely related to $\to_{\mathcal{R}}$ (the only difference is that in $\to_{\mathcal{R}^d}$ extra variables cannot be instantiated by non ground constructors terms).

Definition 7. Let $\mathcal{R}$ be a functional CTRS. Let $\to_{\mathcal{R}_0^d} = \emptyset$ and for $n > 0$ define $s \to_{\mathcal{R}_n^d} t$ if and only if there exists a rewrite rule $l \to r \Leftarrow c$ in $\mathcal{R}$, a substitution $\sigma : \mathcal{V} \to \mathcal{T}(\mathcal{F},\mathcal{V})$, and a context $C[\,]$ such that $s = C[l\sigma], t = C[r\sigma]$, $(s_i\sigma{=}{=}t_i\sigma) \to^*_{\mathcal{R}_{n-1}^d \cup \mathcal{R}_{eq}} true$ for all $s_i{=}{=}t_i$ in c, and $x\sigma$ is a ground constructor term for every extra variable x in $l \to r \Leftarrow c$. Finally, define $\to_{\mathcal{R}^d} = \bigcup_{n \geq 0} \to_{\mathcal{R}_n^d}$.

It is easy to prove that $s \to_{\mathcal{R}_n^d} t$ implies $s \to_{\mathcal{R}_n} t$ but not vice versa. The first statement of the next lemma shows that $\to_{\mathcal{R}^d}$ is deterministic in the sense that the contractum of a redex is uniquely determined. Furthermore, in contrast to $\to_{\mathcal{R}}$, the relation $\to_{\mathcal{R}^d}$ satisfies the parallel moves lemma. Because of the first statement of Lemma 8, there is a strong resemblance between the proof of the second statement and that of Lemma 3 (given in [BK86]).

[2] Note that Hanus [Han95] defines this notion differently. He calls a CTRS $\mathcal{R}$ functional if (1) $\mathcal{R}$ is normal, (2) $\mathcal{R}_u$ is almost orthogonal, and (3) $\to_{\mathcal{R}}$ is confluent.

Lemma 8. *Let $\mathcal{R}$ be functional. For all $m, n \in \mathbb{N}$, the following holds:*

1. *If $s = l_1\sigma_1 \to_{\mathcal{R}^d_m} r_1\sigma_1$ and $s = l_2\sigma_2 \to_{\mathcal{R}^d_n} r_2\sigma_2$, then the applied rewrite rules coincide and $\sigma_1 = \sigma_2$. In other words, if s is a redex, then there is a unique rewrite rule $l \to r \Leftarrow c \in \mathcal{R}$ and a unique substitution $\sigma : \mathcal{V} \to \mathcal{T}(\mathcal{F}, \mathcal{V})$ such that $s = l\sigma \to_{\mathcal{R}^d} r\sigma$.*
2. *If $t \mathrel{+\!\!\!\!\!\twoheadrightarrow}_{\mathcal{R}^d_m} t_1$ and $t \mathrel{+\!\!\!\!\!\twoheadrightarrow}_{\mathcal{R}^d_n} t_2$, then there is a term t_3 such that $t_1 \mathrel{+\!\!\!\!\!\twoheadrightarrow}_{\mathcal{R}^d_n} t_3$ and $t_2 \mathrel{+\!\!\!\!\!\twoheadrightarrow}_{\mathcal{R}^d_m} t_3$. Moreover, the redexes contracted in $t_1 \mathrel{+\!\!\!\!\!\twoheadrightarrow}_{\mathcal{R}^d_n} t_3$ ($t_2 \mathrel{+\!\!\!\!\!\twoheadrightarrow}_{\mathcal{R}^d_m} t_3$) are the descendants in t_1 (t_2) of the redexes contracted in $t \mathrel{+\!\!\!\!\!\twoheadrightarrow}_{\mathcal{R}^d_n} t_2$ ($t \mathrel{+\!\!\!\!\!\twoheadrightarrow}_{\mathcal{R}^d_m} t_1$).*

Proof. The proof proceeds by induction on $m + n$. The base case $m + n = 0$ holds vacuously. Suppose the lemma holds for all m' and n' with $m' + n' < k$. In the induction step, we have to prove that the lemma holds for all m and n with $m + n = k$. Observe that the inductive hypothesis implies the validity of the diagrams in Figure 1, where $m' + n' < k$.

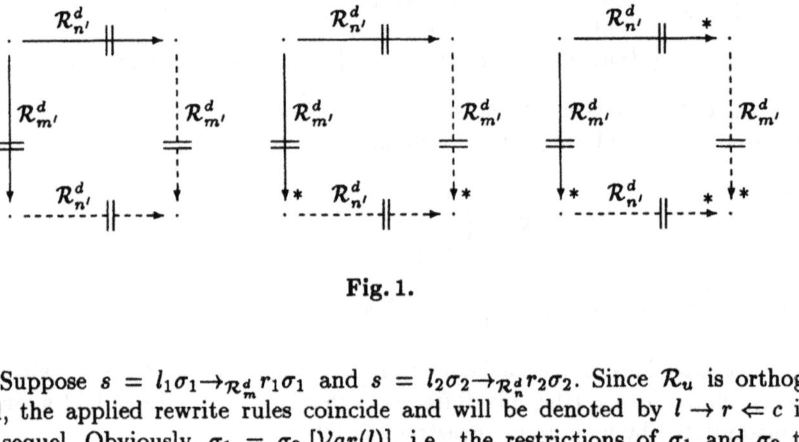

Fig. 1.

(1) Suppose $s = l_1\sigma_1 \to_{\mathcal{R}^d_m} r_1\sigma_1$ and $s = l_2\sigma_2 \to_{\mathcal{R}^d_n} r_2\sigma_2$. Since $\mathcal{R}_u$ is orthogonal, the applied rewrite rules coincide and will be denoted by $l \to r \Leftarrow c$ in the sequel. Obviously, $\sigma_1 = \sigma_2\ [\mathcal{V}ar(l)]$, i.e., the restrictions of σ_1 and σ_2 to $\mathcal{V}ar(l)$ coincide. It remains to show $\sigma_1 = \sigma_2\ [\mathcal{EV}ar(l \to r \Leftarrow c)]$. We show by induction on i that $\sigma_1 = \sigma_2\ [\mathcal{V}ar(l) \cup \bigcup_{j=1}^{i} \mathcal{V}ar(t_j)]$. If $i = 0$, then $\sigma_1 = \sigma_2\ [\mathcal{V}ar(l)]$. Let $i > 0$. According to the inductive hypothesis, $\sigma_1 = \sigma_2\ [\mathcal{V}ar(l) \cup \bigcup_{j=1}^{i-1} \mathcal{V}ar(t_j)]$. Since $\mathcal{V}ar(s_i) \subseteq \mathcal{V}ar(l) \cup \bigcup_{j=1}^{i-1} \mathcal{V}ar(t_j)$, it is sufficient to show $\sigma_1 = \sigma_2\ [\mathcal{V}ar(t_i)]$. Now $(s_i\sigma_1 == t_i\sigma_1) \to^*_{\mathcal{R}^d_{m-1}} true$ and $(s_i\sigma_2 == t_i\sigma_2) \to^*_{\mathcal{R}^d_{n-1}} true$ imply, by Proposition 5, that there exist ground constructor terms u_1 and u_2 such that $s_i\sigma_1 \to^*_{\mathcal{R}^d_{m-1}} u_1 \;{}_{\mathcal{R}^d_{m-1}}^{*}\!\!\leftarrow t_i\sigma_1$ and $s_i\sigma_2 \to^*_{\mathcal{R}^d_{n-1}} u_2 \;{}_{\mathcal{R}^d_{n-1}}^{*}\!\!\leftarrow t_i\sigma_2$. It is an immediate consequence of $s_i\sigma_1 = s_i\sigma_2$, $s_i\sigma_1 \mathrel{+\!\!\!\!\!\twoheadrightarrow}^*_{\mathcal{R}^d_{m-1}} u_1$, $s_i\sigma_2 \mathrel{+\!\!\!\!\!\twoheadrightarrow}^*_{\mathcal{R}^d_{n-1}} u_2$, and the inductive hypothesis (on k) that the two ground normal forms u_1 and u_2 coincide. Hence $t_i\sigma_1 \to^*_{\mathcal{R}^d_{m-1}} u_1 \;{}_{\mathcal{R}^d_{n-1}}^{*}\!\!\leftarrow t_i\sigma_2$. Thus, for all variables $x \in \mathcal{V}ar(t_i) \setminus \mathcal{V}ar(l) \cup \bigcup_{j=1}^{i-1} \mathcal{V}ar(t_j)$, it follows from the fact that t_i is a linear constructor term that $x\sigma_1 \to^*_{\mathcal{R}^d_{m-1}} u_x \;{}_{\mathcal{R}^d_{n-1}}^{*}\!\!\leftarrow x\sigma_2$ for some subterm u_x of u_1. Finally, since u_x is a ground constructor term and, by definition of $\to_{\mathcal{R}^d}$, for every $x \in \mathcal{EV}ar(l \to r \Leftarrow c)$, $x\sigma_1$

and $x\sigma_2$ are ground constructor terms, we infer $x\sigma_1 = u_x = x\sigma_2$.
(2) Since parallel reduction contracts pairwise disjoint redexes, it is sufficient to prove the lemma for the case where both $t \mathrel{+\!\!\!\!\!\rightarrow}_{\mathcal{R}^d_m} t_1$ and $t \mathrel{+\!\!\!\!\!\rightarrow}_{\mathcal{R}^d_n} t_2$ consist of a single $\rightarrow_{\mathcal{R}^d}$ step. In other words, we may assume $t \rightarrow_{\mathcal{R}^d_m} t_1$ and $t \rightarrow_{\mathcal{R}^d_n} t_2$. Furthermore, because $\rightarrow_{\mathcal{R}^d}$ is deterministic, the only interesting case is that where t is a redex, say $t = l\sigma \rightarrow_{\mathcal{R}^d_m} r\sigma = t_1$ for some rule $l \rightarrow r \Leftarrow c \in \mathcal{R}$, containing a proper subredex s which is contracted to s' in the step $t \rightarrow_{\mathcal{R}^d_n} t_2$.

Since $\mathcal{R}_u$ is orthogonal, there is a variable $x \in \mathcal{V}ar(l)$ such that s is a subterm of $x\sigma$. So $x\sigma = C[s]$ for some context $C[\,]$. Let q be the position in t such that $t|_q = s$. Consequently, for every descendant q' of q in t_1, we have $t_1|_{q'} = s$. Define $t_3 = t_1[q' \leftarrow s' \mid q' \in q\backslash t \rightarrow_{\mathcal{R}^d_m} t_1]$. Clearly, $t_1 \mathrel{+\!\!\!\!\!\rightarrow}_{\mathcal{R}^d_n} t_3$.

It remains to show $t_2 \mathrel{+\!\!\!\!\!\rightarrow}_{\mathcal{R}^d_m} t_3$. To this end, let us consider $t = l\sigma \rightarrow_{\mathcal{R}^d_m} r\sigma = t_1$ again. By definition of $\mathrel{+\!\!\!\!\!\rightarrow}_{\mathcal{R}^d_m}$, there exist ground constructor terms u_i such that $s_i\sigma \mathrel{+\!\!\!\!\!\rightarrow}^*_{\mathcal{R}^d_{m-1}} u_i$ and $t_i\sigma \mathrel{+\!\!\!\!\!\rightarrow}^*_{\mathcal{R}^d_{m-1}} u_i$ for all $s_i{=\!=}t_i$ in c. Define σ' by $y\sigma = y\sigma'$ for all $y \neq x$ and $x\sigma' = C[s']$. We show $s_i\sigma' \mathrel{+\!\!\!\!\!\rightarrow}^*_{\mathcal{R}^d_{m-1}} u_i$ and $t_i\sigma' \mathrel{+\!\!\!\!\!\rightarrow}^*_{\mathcal{R}^d_{m-1}} u_i$. It then follows that $t_2 = t[q \leftarrow s'] = l\sigma' \rightarrow_{\mathcal{R}^d_m} r\sigma' = t_3$. Since $s_i\sigma \mathrel{+\!\!\!\!\!\rightarrow}^*_{\mathcal{R}^d_n} s_i\sigma'$, $s_i\sigma \mathrel{+\!\!\!\!\!\rightarrow}^*_{\mathcal{R}^d_{m-1}} u_i$, and u_i is a normal form, it follows from the inductive hypothesis that $s_i\sigma' \mathrel{+\!\!\!\!\!\rightarrow}^*_{\mathcal{R}^d_{m-1}} u_i$. Analogously, we obtain $t_i\sigma' \mathrel{+\!\!\!\!\!\rightarrow}^*_{\mathcal{R}^d_{m-1}} u_i$.

Corollary 9. *$\rightarrow_{\mathcal{R}^d}$ is level-confluent (i.e., for every $n \in \mathbb{N}$, $\rightarrow_{\mathcal{R}^d_n}$ is confluent).*

Proof. Immediate consequence of Lemma 8. (Show that for every divergence $t_1 \; {}^*_{\mathcal{R}^d_n}\!\!\leftarrow t \rightarrow^*_{\mathcal{R}^d_n} t_2$ of length k, there is a valley $t_1 \mathrel{+\!\!\!\!\!\rightarrow}^*_{\mathcal{R}^d_n} t_3 \; {}^*_{\mathcal{R}^d_n}\!\!\leftarrow\!\!\!\!\!+ \; t_2$ of length k.)

Theorem 10. *Every functional CTRS $\mathcal{R}$ is level-confluent.*

Proof. It follows from $\rightarrow_{\mathcal{R}^d_n} \subseteq \rightarrow_{\mathcal{R}_n}$ and Proposition 11 that $\rightarrow_{\mathcal{R}_n}$ is a compatible refinement of $\rightarrow_{\mathcal{R}^d_n}$. Hence, by the aforementioned result of Staples [Sta75], $\rightarrow_{\mathcal{R}_n}$ is confluent if and only if $\rightarrow_{\mathcal{R}^d_n}$ is confluent.

As a matter of fact, Theorem 10 is a special case of a theorem shown in [SMI95]. The proof techniques, however, are different. Suzuki *et al.* [SMI95] showed their result by using an extended parallel rewriting relation.

Proposition 11. *If $s \rightarrow^*_{\mathcal{R}_n} t$, then there is a term u s.t. $s \rightarrow^*_{\mathcal{R}^d_n} u$ and $t \rightarrow^*_{\mathcal{R}^d_n} u$.*

Proof. We proceed by induction on the depth n of $s \rightarrow^*_{\mathcal{R}} t$. The proposition holds vacuously for $n = 0$. So let $n > 0$. We further proceed by induction on the length k of the reduction sequence $s \rightarrow^*_{\mathcal{R}_n} t$. Again, the case $k = 0$ holds vacuously. Suppose the claim is true for k. In order to show it for $k + 1$, we consider $s = C[l\sigma] \rightarrow_{\mathcal{R}_n} C[r\sigma] = t' \rightarrow^k_{\mathcal{R}_n} t$. It follows from the inductive hypothesis that there is a term u' such that $t' \rightarrow^*_{\mathcal{R}^d_n} u'$ and $t \rightarrow^*_{\mathcal{R}^d_n} u'$. Now if $\mathcal{EV}ar(l \rightarrow r \Leftarrow c) = \emptyset$, then $s \rightarrow_{\mathcal{R}^d_n} t'$ and the claim follows. Suppose $\mathcal{EV}ar(l \rightarrow r \Leftarrow c) \neq \emptyset$ and let $x \in \mathcal{EV}ar(l \rightarrow r \Leftarrow c)$. Then $x \in \mathcal{V}ar(t_j)$ for some $s_j{=\!=}t_j$ in c. Since $s \rightarrow_{\mathcal{R}_n} t'$, there is a ground constructor term u_j such that $s_j\sigma \rightarrow^*_{\mathcal{R}_{n-1}} u_j \; {}^*_{\mathcal{R}_{n-1}}\!\!\leftarrow t_j\sigma$. By the inductive hypothesis on n and the fact that u_j is a normal form, we conclude $s_j\sigma \rightarrow^*_{\mathcal{R}^d_{n-1}} u_j \;{}^*_{\mathcal{R}^d_{n-1}}\!\leftarrow t_j\sigma$. It follows that $x\sigma \rightarrow^*_{\mathcal{R}^d_{n-1}} u_x$ for some ground constructor subterm u_x of u_j because u_j is a ground constructor term and t_j is a constructor term. Note that u_x is unique because $\rightarrow_{\mathcal{R}^d_{n-1}}$ is confluent ($\rightarrow_{\mathcal{R}^d}$ is level-confluent by Corollary 9). Define σ' by $x\sigma' = u_x$ for every $x \in \mathcal{EV}ar(l \rightarrow r \Leftarrow c)$ and $y\sigma' = y\sigma$ otherwise. Observe that $z\sigma \rightarrow^*_{\mathcal{R}^d_{n-1}} z\sigma'$ for every variable $z \in \mathcal{D}(\sigma)$. Let $s' = C[r\sigma']$. According to the above, $t' \rightarrow^*_{\mathcal{R}^d_{n-1}} s'$. Observe that also $s \rightarrow_{\mathcal{R}^d_n} s'$ because $s_j\sigma' \rightarrow^*_{\mathcal{R}^d_{n-1}} u_j \;{}^*_{\mathcal{R}^d_{n-1}}\!\leftarrow t_j\sigma'$ for every $s_j{=}{=}t_j$ in c (it is a consequence of $s_j\sigma \rightarrow^*_{\mathcal{R}^d_{n-1}} u_j$, $s_j\sigma \rightarrow^*_{\mathcal{R}^d_{n-1}} s_j\sigma'$ and confluence of $\rightarrow_{\mathcal{R}^d_{n-1}}$ that $s_j\sigma' \rightarrow^*_{\mathcal{R}^d_{n-1}} u_j$). It now follows from confluence of $\rightarrow_{\mathcal{R}^d_n}$ in conjunction with $t' \rightarrow^*_{\mathcal{R}^d_{n-1}} s'$ and $t' \rightarrow^*_{\mathcal{R}^d_n} u'$ that s' and u' have a common reduct u w.r.t. $\rightarrow_{\mathcal{R}^d_n}$. Clearly, u is a common reduct of s and t w.r.t. $\rightarrow_{\mathcal{R}^d_n}$ as well.

Lemma 12. *Let $\mathcal{R}$ be a functional CTRS. Then, for every $n \geq 0$, the sets of normal forms $NF(\rightarrow_{\mathcal{R}_n})$ and $NF(\rightarrow_{\mathcal{R}^d_n})$ coincide.*

Proof. Obviously, $NF(\rightarrow_{\mathcal{R}_n}) \subseteq NF(\rightarrow_{\mathcal{R}^d_n})$ because $\rightarrow_{\mathcal{R}^d_n} \subseteq \rightarrow_{\mathcal{R}_n}$. We prove $NF(\rightarrow_{\mathcal{R}^d_n}) \subseteq NF(\rightarrow_{\mathcal{R}_n})$ indirectly. To this end, suppose there is a term $s \in NF(\rightarrow_{\mathcal{R}^d_n})$ but $s \notin NF(\rightarrow_{\mathcal{R}_n})$. Since s is not a normal form w.r.t. $\rightarrow_{\mathcal{R}_n}$, there is a rule $l \rightarrow r \Leftarrow c \in \mathcal{R}$, a context $C[\,]$ and a substitution σ such that $s = C[l\sigma] \rightarrow_{\mathcal{R}_n} C[r\sigma]$. In particular, for every $s_j{=}{=}t_j$ in c, there is a ground constructor term u_j such that $s_j\sigma \rightarrow^*_{\mathcal{R}_{n-1}} u_j \;{}^*_{\mathcal{R}_{n-1}}\!\leftarrow t_j\sigma$. It follows as in the proof of Proposition 11 that $s_j\sigma' \rightarrow^*_{\mathcal{R}^d_{n-1}} u_j \;{}^*_{\mathcal{R}^d_{n-1}}\!\leftarrow t_j\sigma'$. Hence $s = C[l\sigma] = C[l\sigma'] \rightarrow_{\mathcal{R}^d_n} C[r\sigma']$. This is a contradiction to $s \in NF(\rightarrow_{\mathcal{R}^d_n})$.

Term rewriting is mainly concerned with computing normal forms. Our results indicate that, from a computational point of view, it is more reasonable to work with the deterministic rewrite relation rather than the ordinary rewrite relation.

4 Conditional Term Graph Rewriting

In this section, we use the term based approach of [KO95] to term graph rewriting rather than those of [BEG+87] or [Plu93] (although the other approaches are more graphic). Doing so, it is possible to completely argue within the framework of term rewriting and to avoid concepts from different fields. Note that the first part of Section 4 is a mirror image of Section 3, where graph rewriting replaces term rewriting. We first recapitulate some basic notions from [KO95].

Let M be a countably infinite set of objects called *marks*. Let $\mathcal{F}^* = \{f^\mu \mid f \in \mathcal{F}, \mu \in M\}$ be the set of *marked* function symbols. For all $f^\mu \in \mathcal{F}^*$, the arity of f^μ coincides with that of f. Moreover, we define $symbol(f^\mu) = f$ and $mark(f^\mu) = \mu$. In the sequel we use natural numbers as marks. The elements of $\mathcal{T}^* = \mathcal{T}(\mathcal{F}^*, \mathcal{V})$ are called *marked* terms. Note that variables are not marked. The set $\mathcal{T}^*_w$ of *well-marked terms* over $\mathcal{F}^*$ is the subset of $\mathcal{T}^*$ such that

$t \in \mathcal{T}_w^*$ if and only if, for every pair (t_1, t_2) of subterms of t, $mark(root(t_1)) = mark(root(t_2))$ implies $t_1 = t_2$. For example, the term $plus^0(0^1, 0^1)$ is well-marked but $plus^1(0^1, 0^1)$ is not. Well-marked terms exactly correspond to directed acyclic graphs; the reader is referred to [KO95] for details. In contrast to [KO95], we are solely interested in well-marked terms. Thus, throughout the whole paper, marked stands for well-marked. Two subterms t_1 and t_2 of a marked term t are shared in t if $t_1 = t_2$; e.g. 0^1 and 0^1 are shared in $plus^0(0^1, 0^1)$. The notions *marked substitution* and *marked context* are defined in the obvious way.

Definition 13. If t is a marked term, then $e(t)$ denotes the term obtained from t by erasing all marks. Two marked terms s and t are called *equivalent* ($s \sim t$) if and only if s and t are isomorphic as dags; to be precise: (i) $e(s) = e(t)$ and (ii) for every pair of marks μ and ν for which there is a position $p \in \mathcal{P}os(s) = \mathcal{P}os(t)$ with $mark(s|_p) = \mu$ and $mark(t|_p) = \nu$, we have $\{q \in \mathcal{P}os(s) \mid mark(s|_q) = \mu\} = \{q \in \mathcal{P}os(t) \mid mark(t|_q) = \nu\}$. Two marked substitutions σ_1 and σ_2 are *equivalent* if $x\sigma_1 \sim x\sigma_2$ for every variable x.

For instance, $plus^0(0^1, 0^1) \sim plus^0(0^2, 0^2)$ but $plus^0(0^1, 0^1) \not\sim plus^0(0^1, 0^2)$. On the other hand, $e(plus^0(0^1, 0^1)) = e(plus^0(0^1, 0^2))$. Observe that the equivalence relation $\sim$ defined above differs from a similar one in [KO95] which requires (i) only. In the sequel, the marks of a term s are called *fresh* w.r.t. another marked term t if no marks occurring in t do also occur in s.

Definition 14. Let $\mathcal{R}$ be a left-linear 3-CTRS. A rule $l^* \to r^* \Leftarrow c^*$ is a *marked version* of a rule $l \to r \Leftarrow c$ in $\mathcal{R}$ if $e(l^*) = l$, $e(r^*) = r$, and $e(c^*) = c$.

Since we are solely interested in left-linear CTRSs, we extend the definition of [BEG+87] for left-linear unconditional term graph rewriting to the conditional case. As a technical consequence, we don't have to mark variables. So variables are maximally shared. On the other hand, by using fresh and mutually distinct marks for the right-hand side and the conditional part of a rewrite rule, we adopt a "minimal structure sharing scheme" (different structure sharing schemes are discussed in [KO95]). In our opinion, these choices are very natural.

Definition 15. Let $\mathcal{R}$ be a left-linear 3-CTRS with strict equality. Let s and t be marked terms. Let $\Rightarrow_{\mathcal{R}_0} = \emptyset$ and for $n > 0$, define $s \Rightarrow_{\mathcal{R}_n} t$ if there exists a marked version $l^* \to r^* \Leftarrow c^*$ of a rewrite rule $l \to r \Leftarrow c$ from $\mathcal{R}$, a marked substitution σ and a marked context $C[, \ldots,]$ such that

- $s = C[l^*\sigma, \ldots, l^*\sigma]$ and $t = C[r^*\sigma, \ldots, r^*\sigma]$,
- $l^*\sigma$ is not a subterm of $C[, \ldots,]$,
- for every $s_i == t_i$ in c^*, we have $(s_i\sigma == t_i\sigma) \Rightarrow^*_{\mathcal{R}_{n-1} \cup \mathcal{R}_{eq}} true^*$, where $true^*$ is a marked version of *true*.
- all marks on function symbols in r^*, c^*, and $x\sigma$ (for every extra variable x in $l \to r \Leftarrow c$) are mutually distinct and fresh w.r.t. s.

We call $\Rightarrow_{\mathcal{R}} = \bigcup_{n \geq 0} \Rightarrow_{\mathcal{R}_n}$ *noncopying* or *graph* rewrite relation w.r.t. $\mathcal{R}$.

$l^*\sigma$ is called the *contracted marked redex* in s. We use the notation $s \Rightarrow_{\mathcal{R}_n}^{l^*\sigma} t$ in order to specify the contracted marked redex. Note that all shared subterms $l^*\sigma$ are replaced simultaneously by $r^*\sigma$. Observe moreover that whenever $s \Rightarrow_{\mathcal{R}} t_1$ and $s \Rightarrow_{\mathcal{R}} t_2$ by reducing the same marked redex, then $t_1 \sim t_2$ ($t_1 = t_2$ does not hold in general because the introduced fresh marks may differ).

In the following, $\mathcal{R}$ denotes a functional 3-CTRS unless stated otherwise.

Proposition 16. *The following statements are equivalent for all $s, t \in \mathcal{T}_w^*$:*

1. $(s{=}{=}t) \Rightarrow_{\mathcal{R}\cup\mathcal{R}_{eq}}^* true^*$
2. *There exist marked ground constructor terms u and v such that $s \Rightarrow_{\mathcal{R}}^* u$, $t \Rightarrow_{\mathcal{R}}^* v$, and $e(u) = e(v)$.*[3]

Definition 17. The *deterministic* noncopying reduction relation $\Rightarrow_{\mathcal{R}^d}$ is defined analogous to $\Rightarrow_{\mathcal{R}}$: in a $\Rightarrow_{\mathcal{R}_n^d}$ rewrite step, it is additionally required that $x\sigma$ is a marked ground constructor term for every extra variable x in $l \to r \Leftarrow c$.

In order to illustrate how graph rewriting works, let $\mathcal{R}$ be the functional CTRS $\mathcal{R}_{fib}$ from Section 3 augmented by the rewrite rules $double(x) \to plus(x,x)$ and $snd(pair(x,y)) \to y$. There is the $\Rightarrow_{\mathcal{R}}$ (in fact, $\Rightarrow_{\mathcal{R}^d}$) reduction sequence:

$$\begin{aligned} double^0(snd^1(fib^2(s^3(0^4)))) &\Rightarrow_{\mathcal{R}} plus^5(snd^1(fib^2(s^3(0^4))), snd^1(fib^2(s^3(0^4)))) \\ &\Rightarrow_{\mathcal{R}} plus^5(snd^1(t), snd^1(t)) \\ &\Rightarrow_{\mathcal{R}} plus^5(plus^{12}(0^8, s^9(0^{10})), plus^{12}(0^8, s^9(0^{10}))) \\ &\Rightarrow_{\mathcal{R}} plus^5(s^9(0^{10}), s^9(0^{10})) \end{aligned}$$

where t denotes the marked term $pair^{11}(s^9(0^{10}), plus^{12}(0^8, s^9(0^{10})))$, because $fib^6(0^4) \Rightarrow_{\mathcal{R}} pair^7(0^8, s^9(0^{10}))$.

Lemma 18. *Let $\Rightarrow$ denote $\Rightarrow_{\mathcal{R}_n^d}$ or $\Rightarrow_{\mathcal{R}_n}$. If $s \sim t \Rightarrow^* u$, where the noncopying reduction of t to u consists of k steps, then there is a marked term v such that $s \Rightarrow^* v \sim u$, where s reduces to v in k steps.*

Proof. We show the lemma for $k = 1$, the whole claim then follows by induction. Suppose $s \sim t \Rightarrow^{l^*\sigma} u$. We may write $t = C[l^*\sigma, \ldots, l^*\sigma]$, where $l^*\sigma$ is not a subterm of the marked context $C[, \ldots,]$. Then $u = C[r^*\sigma, \ldots, r^*\sigma]$. Since $s \sim t$, s may be written as $s = \bar{C}[\bar{l}^*\bar{\sigma}, \ldots, \bar{l}^*\bar{\sigma}]$, where $\bar{l}^*\bar{\sigma}$ is not a subterm of $\bar{C}[, \ldots,]$ and $C[, \ldots,] \sim \bar{C}[, \ldots,]$. Note that $C[l^*\sigma, \ldots, l^*\sigma] \sim \bar{C}[\bar{l}^*\bar{\sigma}, \ldots, \bar{l}^*\bar{\sigma}]$ implies $e(x\sigma) \sim e(x\bar{\sigma})$ as well as $x\sigma = y\sigma$ if and only if $x\bar{\sigma} = y\bar{\sigma}$ for all $x, y \in \mathcal{V}ar(l)$. Let $\bar{l}^* \to \bar{r}^* \Leftarrow \bar{c}^*$ be a marked version of $l \to r \Leftarrow c$ such that all marks on $\bar{r}^*$ and $\bar{c}^*$ are fresh w.r.t. s and mutually distinct. For every extra variable x in $l \to r \Leftarrow c$ let $x\bar{\sigma}$ be a marked version of $e(x\sigma)$ such that all marks are mutually distinct and fresh w.r.t. s, $\bar{r}^*$ and $\bar{c}^*$. It is fairly simple to prove that $\bar{l}^*\bar{\sigma} \Rightarrow \bar{r}^*\bar{\sigma}$. Thus $s \Rightarrow v = \bar{C}[\bar{r}^*\bar{\sigma}, \ldots, \bar{r}^*\bar{\sigma}]$. It follows from $C[l^*\sigma, \ldots, l^*\sigma] \sim \bar{C}[\bar{l}^*\bar{\sigma}, \ldots, \bar{l}^*\bar{\sigma}]$, the properties of σ and $\bar{\sigma}$, and the fact that both r^* and $\bar{r}^*$ are freshly marked that $u \sim v$.

[3] Note that $u \sim v$ is not required.

The next lemma shows that the deterministic graph rewrite relation is subcommutative (cf. [Klo92]) modulo $\sim$.

Lemma 19. *For all $m, n \in \mathbb{N}$, the following statements hold:*

1. *If $s = l_1^* \sigma_1 \Rightarrow_{\mathcal{R}_m^d} r_1^* \sigma_1$ and $s = l_2^* \sigma_2 \Rightarrow_{\mathcal{R}_n^d} r_2^* \sigma_2$, then (i) $l_1^* \to r_1^* \Leftarrow c_1^*$ and $l_2^* \to r_2^* \Leftarrow c_2^*$ are marked versions of the same rewrite rule $l \to r \Leftarrow c \in \mathcal{R}$, (ii) $\sigma_1 \sim \sigma_2$, and (iii) $r_1^* \sigma_1 \sim r_2^* \sigma_2$.*
2. *If $s \Rightarrow_{\mathcal{R}_m^d}^{l_1^* \sigma_1} s_1$, $t \Rightarrow_{\mathcal{R}_n^d}^{l_2^* \sigma_2} t_1$, and $s \sim t$, then there are marked terms s_2 and t_2 such that (i) $s_1 \Rightarrow_{\mathcal{R}_n^d}^{l_2^* \sigma_2} s_2$ or $s_1 = s_2$, (ii) $t_1 \Rightarrow_{\mathcal{R}_m^d}^{l_1^* \sigma_1} t_2$ or $t_1 = t_2$, and (iii) $s_2 \sim t_2$.*

Proof. The proof is similar to that of Lemma 8. Again, we proceed by induction on $m + n$. The base case $m + n = 0$ holds vacuously. Suppose the lemma holds for all m' and n' with $m' + n' < k$. In the induction step, we have to prove that the lemma holds for all m and n with $m + n = k$. By using Lemma 18, it is not difficult to prove that the inductive hypothesis implies the validity of the diagrams in Figure 2, where $m' + n' < k$ and $\to$ stands for $\Rightarrow$.

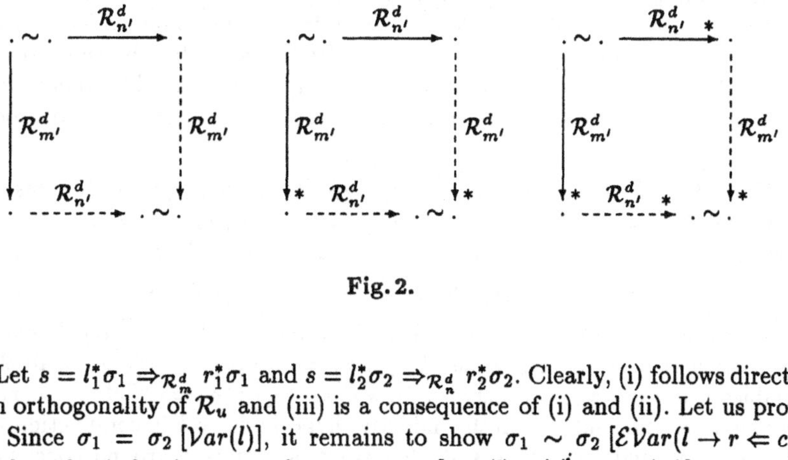

Fig. 2.

(1) Let $s = l_1^* \sigma_1 \Rightarrow_{\mathcal{R}_m^d} r_1^* \sigma_1$ and $s = l_2^* \sigma_2 \Rightarrow_{\mathcal{R}_n^d} r_2^* \sigma_2$. Clearly, (i) follows directly from orthogonality of $\mathcal{R}_u$ and (iii) is a consequence of (i) and (ii). Let us prove (ii). Since $\sigma_1 = \sigma_2\ [\mathcal{V}ar(l)]$, it remains to show $\sigma_1 \sim \sigma_2\ [\mathcal{EV}ar(l \to r \Leftarrow c)]$. We show by induction on i that $\sigma_1 \sim \sigma_2\ [\mathcal{V}ar(l) \cup \bigcup_{j=1}^{i} \mathcal{V}ar(t_j)]$. If $i = 0$, then $\sigma_1 = \sigma_2\ [\mathcal{V}ar(l)]$. So let $i > 0$. According to the inductive hypothesis, $\sigma_1 \sim \sigma_2\ [\mathcal{V}ar(l) \cup \bigcup_{j=1}^{i-1} \mathcal{V}ar(t_j)]$. Since $\mathcal{V}ar(s_i) \subseteq \mathcal{V}ar(l) \cup \bigcup_{j=1}^{i-1} \mathcal{V}ar(t_j)$, it is sufficient to show $\sigma_1 \sim \sigma_2\ [\mathcal{V}ar(t_i)]$. There are marked ground constructor terms u_1, u_2, v_1, v_2 such that $s_i \sigma_1 \Rightarrow_{\mathcal{R}_{m-1}^d}^* u_1$, $t_i \sigma_1 \Rightarrow_{\mathcal{R}_{m-1}^d}^* u_2$, where $e(u_1) = e(u_2)$, and $s_i \sigma_2 \Rightarrow_{\mathcal{R}_{n-1}^d}^* v_1$, $t_i \sigma_2 \Rightarrow_{\mathcal{R}_{n-1}^d}^* v_2$, where $e(v_1) = e(v_2)$. It now follows from the inductive hypothesis on k in combination with $s_i \sigma_1 \sim s_i \sigma_2$ that $u_1 \sim v_1$. Thus $e(u_2) = e(u_1) = e(v_1) = e(v_2)$. As in the proof of Lemma 8, for every extra variable x, there are marked ground constructor terms u_x and v_x such that $x\sigma_1 = u_x$, $x\sigma_2 = v_x$, and $e(u_x) = e(v_x)$. Since the marks on $x\sigma_1$ and $x\sigma_2$ are fresh and mutually distinct, we finally derive $u_x \sim v_x$.

(2) By Lemma 18, it is sufficient to prove that if $t \Rightarrow_{\mathcal{R}_m^d}^{l_1^*\sigma_1} s_1$ and $t \Rightarrow_{\mathcal{R}_n^d}^{l_2^*\sigma_2} t_1$, then (i) $s_1 \Rightarrow_{\mathcal{R}_n^d}^{l_2^*\sigma_2} s_2$ or $s_1 = s_2$, (ii) $t_1 \Rightarrow_{\mathcal{R}_m^d}^{l_1^*\sigma_1} t_2$ or $t_1 = t_2$, and (iii) $s_2 \sim t_2$ for some marked terms s_2 and t_2. We distinguish three cases:

(a) $l_1^*\sigma_1 = l_2^*\sigma_2$,
(b) $l_1^*\sigma_1$ is neither a subterm of $l_2^*\sigma_2$ nor conversely,
(c) $l_1^*\sigma_1$ is a proper subterm of $l_2^*\sigma_2$.

(a) With the aid of (1), this follows easily.
(b) The proof is analogous to Proposition 3.19, (1), case 1 in [KO95].
(c) We proceed in analogy to Proposition 3.19, (1), case 2 in [KO95]. We have

$$t = C[l_1^*\sigma_1, \ldots, l_2^*\sigma_2] = C[l_1^*\sigma_1, \ldots, C'[l_1^*\sigma_1, \ldots, l_1^*\sigma_1]]$$

where $l_2^*\sigma_2 = C'[l_1^*\sigma_1, \ldots, l_1^*\sigma_1]$, and $l_1^*\sigma_1$ is neither a subterm of $C[, \ldots,]$ nor of $C'[, \ldots,]$. Hence

$$s_1 = C[r_1^*\sigma_1, \ldots, C'[r_1^*\sigma_1, \ldots, r_1^*\sigma_1]]$$

$$t_1 = C[l_1^*\sigma_1, \ldots, r_2^*\sigma_2] = C[l_1^*\sigma_1, \ldots, C''[l_1^*\sigma_1, \ldots, l_1^*\sigma_1]$$

for some context $C''[, \ldots,]$ which does not contain $l_1^*\sigma_1$. Observe that no occurrence of $C'[r_1^*\sigma_1, \ldots, r_1^*\sigma_1]$ occurs in s_1 aside from those obtained by contracting the marked redex $l_1^*\sigma_1$ because we use fresh marks. By the same reason, $C[, \ldots, C''[, \ldots,]]$ does not contain $l_1^*\sigma_1$. Now if $l_1^*\sigma_1$ is not a subterm of t_1, then let $t_2 = t_1$. Otherwise define $t_2 = C[r_1^*\sigma_1, \ldots, C''[r_1^*\sigma_1, \ldots, r_1^*\sigma_1]]$ and observe that $t_1 \Rightarrow_{\mathcal{R}_m^d}^{l_1^*\sigma_1} t_2$.

We next show that $C'[r_1^*\sigma_1, \ldots, r_1^*\sigma_1] \Rightarrow_{\mathcal{R}_n^d} C''[r_1^*\sigma_1, \ldots, r_1^*\sigma_1]$. To this end, recall that $l_2^*\sigma_2 = C'[l_1^*\sigma_1, \ldots, l_1^*\sigma_1] \Rightarrow_{\mathcal{R}_n^d} r_2^*\sigma_2$. Thus, for every $s_i{=}{=}t_i$ in c_2^*, there exist marked ground constructor terms u_i and v_i such that $s_i\sigma_2 \Rightarrow_{\mathcal{R}_{n-1}^d}^* u_i$, $t_i\sigma_2 \Rightarrow_{\mathcal{R}_{n-1}^d}^* v_i$, and $e(u_i) = e(v_i)$. Since $\mathcal{R}_u$ is orthogonal, for every occurrence of $l_1^*\sigma_1$, there is a variable $x \in \mathcal{V}ar(l)$ such that $x\sigma_2 = C_x[l_1^*\sigma_1, \ldots, l_1^*\sigma_1]$ contains this particular occurrence. Define σ_2' by $x\sigma_2' = C_x[r_1^*\sigma_1, \ldots, r_1^*\sigma_1]$ for all those variables x and $y\sigma_2' = y\sigma_2$ otherwise. Now $l_2^*\sigma_2' \Rightarrow_{\mathcal{R}_n^d} r_2^*\sigma_2' = C''[r_1^*\sigma_1, \ldots, r_1^*\sigma_1]$. In order to see this, infer from the inductive hypothesis on k in conjunction with $s_i\sigma_2 \Rightarrow_{\mathcal{R}_{n-1}^d}^* u_i$ and $s_i\sigma_2 \Rightarrow_{\mathcal{R}_m^d} s_i\sigma_2'$ that there is a marked ground constructor term u_i' such that $s_i\sigma_2' \Rightarrow_{\mathcal{R}_{n-1}^d}^* u_i'$ and $u_i \sim u_i'$. Analogously, there is a marked ground constructor term v_i' such that $t_i\sigma_2' \Rightarrow_{\mathcal{R}_{n-1}^d}^* v_i'$, and $v_i \sim v_i'$. Hence the claim follows from $e(u_i') = e(u_i) = e(v_i) = e(v_i')$. This concludes the proof.

Corollary 20. *For every $n \in \mathbb{N}$, $\Rightarrow_{\mathcal{R}_n^d}$ is confluent modulo $\sim$.*

Theorem 21. *For every $n \in \mathbb{N}$, $\Rightarrow_{\mathcal{R}_n}$ is confluent modulo $\sim$.*

Proof. Because of $\Rightarrow_{\mathcal{R}_n^d} \subseteq \Rightarrow_{\mathcal{R}_n}$, Proposition 22, and Lemma 18, we conclude by the generalization of Staples' result (see Section 2) that $\Rightarrow_{\mathcal{R}_n}$ is confluent if and only if $\Rightarrow_{\mathcal{R}_n^d}$ is confluent.

Proposition 22. *If $s \Rightarrow^*_{\mathcal{R}_n} t$, then there are marked terms u and v such that $s \Rightarrow^*_{\mathcal{R}^d_n} u$, $t \Rightarrow^*_{\mathcal{R}^d_n} v$, and $u \sim v$.*

Lemma 23. *For every $n \in \mathbb{N}$, the sets $NF(\Rightarrow_{\mathcal{R}_n})$ and $NF(\Rightarrow_{\mathcal{R}^d_n})$ coincide.*

It is our next goal to show that, for every functional CTRS, $(\mathcal{T}^*_w, \Rightarrow_{\mathcal{R}})$ is a sound and complete implementation of $(\mathcal{T}(\mathcal{F},\mathcal{V}), \rightarrow_{\mathcal{R}})$ in the sense of Barendregt *et al.* [BEG+87]. To this end, we prove that the Gross-Knuth reduction strategy is normalizing (for unconditional orthogonal TRSs, this was shown in [O'D77]).

Definition 24. For every $n \in \mathbb{N}$, the Gross-Knuth reduction strategy w.r.t. $\rightarrow_{\mathcal{R}^d_n}$ is defined as follows: Take all the redexes in a term $s \in \mathcal{T}(\mathcal{F},\mathcal{V})$ and reduce them from innermost to outermost, producing t (notation $s \rightarrow^{GK}_{\mathcal{R}^d_n} t$).[4] Repeat the process with t and so on.

Theorem 25. *The Gross-Knuth reduction strategy is normalizing, i.e., if s has a normal form w.r.t. $\rightarrow_{\mathcal{R}^d_n}$, then every $\rightarrow^{GK}_{\mathcal{R}^d_n}$ reduction sequence is finite.*

Proof. The proof is *verbatim* the same as O'Donnell's proof for unconditional orthogonal TRSs and not repeated here; for details see [O'D77], Chapter V.

In contrast to the unconditional case, the Gross-Knuth strategy is not computable for CTRSs. The Gross-Knuth reduction strategy w.r.t. $\Rightarrow_{\mathcal{R}^d_n}$ is defined in analogy to Definition 24. It is fairly simple to see, that the reduct t is unique modulo $\sim$. It can be shown as above that $\Rightarrow^{GK}_{\mathcal{R}^d_n}$ is normalizing as well.

Definition 26. Let $\Rightarrow$ and $\rightarrow$ be binary relations on $\mathcal{T}^*_w$ and $\mathcal{T}(\mathcal{F},\mathcal{V})$, respectively. $(\mathcal{T}^*_w, \Rightarrow)$ is called a *sound implementation* of $(\mathcal{T}(\mathcal{F},\mathcal{V}), \rightarrow)$ if $s \Rightarrow^* t \in NF(\Rightarrow)$ implies $e(s) \rightarrow^* e(t) \in NF(\rightarrow)$. On the other hand, $(\mathcal{T}^*_w, \Rightarrow)$ is called a *complete implementation* of $(\mathcal{T}(\mathcal{F},\mathcal{V}), \rightarrow)$ if, for all marked terms s, $e(s) \rightarrow^* u \in NF(\rightarrow)$ implies the existence of a marked term t such that $s \Rightarrow^* t \in NF(\Rightarrow)$ and $e(t) = u$.

Proposition 27. $\Rightarrow_{\mathcal{R}^d_n}$ *is a sound and complete implementation of* $\rightarrow_{\mathcal{R}^d_n}$.

Proof. As usual, we use induction on n. The case $n = 0$ holds, so let $n > 0$ and suppose $\Rightarrow_{\mathcal{R}^d_{n-1}}$ is a sound and complete implementation of $\rightarrow_{\mathcal{R}^d_{n-1}}$. We show the following three statements from which the proposition immediately follows.

1. $\forall s,t \in \mathcal{T}^*_w$: if $s \Rightarrow^*_{\mathcal{R}^d_n} t$, then $e(s) \rightarrow^*_{\mathcal{R}^d_n} e(t)$.
2. $\forall t \in \mathcal{T}^*_w$: $t \in NF(\Rightarrow_{\mathcal{R}^d_n})$ if and only if $e(t) \in NF(\rightarrow_{\mathcal{R}^d_n})$.
3. $\forall s \in \mathcal{T}^*_w$: if $e(s) \rightarrow^*_{\mathcal{R}^d_n} u \in NF(\rightarrow_{\mathcal{R}^d_n})$, then there is a term $t \in \mathcal{T}^*_w$ such that $s \Rightarrow^*_{\mathcal{R}^d_n} t$ and $e(t) = u$.

[4] In fact, Gross-Knuth reduction is usually defined by: contract all redexes simultaneously. Then, however, one has to prove that the result is unequivocal. Although this is not very difficult, in the simpler definition above this is immediately clear by Lemma 8 (2).

(1) We proceed by induction on the length k of $s \Rightarrow^*_{\mathcal{R}^d} t$. The base case $k = 0$ clearly holds. Thus consider $s \Rightarrow^{l^*\sigma}_{\mathcal{R}^d_n} t' \Rightarrow^k_{\mathcal{R}^d_n} t$. According to the inductive hypothesis, $e(t') \rightarrow^*_{\mathcal{R}^d_n} e(t)$. Since $s \Rightarrow^{l^*\sigma}_{\mathcal{R}^d_n} t'$, we have $s = C[l^*\sigma, \ldots, l^*\sigma]$, $l^*\sigma$ is not a subterm of $C[, \ldots,]$, $t' = C[r^*\sigma, \ldots, r^*\sigma]$, and, for every $s_i == t_i$ in c^*, there are marked ground constructor terms u_i and v_i such that $s_i\sigma \Rightarrow^*_{\mathcal{R}^d_{n-1}} u_i$, $t_i\sigma \Rightarrow^*_{\mathcal{R}^d_{n-1}} v_i$, and $e(u_i) = e(v_i)$. Let $\tau = e(\sigma)$, i.e., $x\tau = e(x\sigma)$ for all $x \in \mathcal{D}(\sigma)$. By the inductive hypothesis on n, $e(s_i)\tau \rightarrow^*_{\mathcal{R}^d_{n-1}} e(u_i) = e(v_i) \;{}^*_{\mathcal{R}^d_{n-1}}\!\!\leftarrow e(t_i)\tau$. Hence $l\tau \rightarrow_{\mathcal{R}^d_n} r\tau$ and $e(s) \rightarrow^*_{\mathcal{R}^d_n} e(t)$.

(2) The *if* direction is easily shown. For an indirect proof of the *only if* direction, suppose $e(t) \notin NF(\rightarrow_{\mathcal{R}^d_n})$, i.e., $e(t) = C[l\sigma] \rightarrow_{\mathcal{R}^d_n} C[r\sigma]$, where, for every $s_i == t_i$ in c^*, $s_i\sigma \rightarrow^*_{\mathcal{R}^d_{n-1}} u_i$ and $t_i\sigma \rightarrow^*_{\mathcal{R}^d_{n-1}} u_i$ for some ground constructor term u_i. It is relatively easy to show that there is a marked version $l^* \rightarrow r^* \Leftarrow c^*$ of $l \rightarrow r \Leftarrow c$, a marked context $C^*[, \ldots,]$, and a marked substitution σ^* such that $t = C^*[l^*\sigma^*, \ldots, l^*\sigma^*]$ and $l^*\sigma^*$ is not a subterm of $C^*[, \ldots,]$. Since $e(s_i^*\sigma^*) = s_i\sigma$ and $e(t_i^*\sigma^*) = t_i\sigma$, it follows from the fact that $\Rightarrow_{\mathcal{R}^d_{n-1}}$ is a complete implementation of $\rightarrow_{\mathcal{R}^d_{n-1}}$ that there exist marked terms v_i^* and w_i^* such that $s_i^*\sigma^* \Rightarrow^*_{\mathcal{R}^d_{n-1}} v_i^* \in NF(\Rightarrow_{\mathcal{R}^d_{n-1}})$, $t_i^*\sigma^* \Rightarrow^*_{\mathcal{R}^d_{n-1}} w_i^* \in NF(\Rightarrow_{\mathcal{R}^d_{n-1}})$, and $e(v_i^*) = u_i = e(w_i^*)$. The latter particularly implies that v_i^* and w_i^* are marked ground constructor terms. Therefore, $t \notin NF(\Rightarrow_{\mathcal{R}^d_n})$, a contradiction.

(3) Consider

$$s \Rightarrow^{GK}_{\mathcal{R}^d_n} t_1 \Rightarrow^{GK}_{\mathcal{R}^d_n} t_2 \Rightarrow^{GK}_{\mathcal{R}^d_n} \cdots$$

Since $s' \Rightarrow^{GK}_{\mathcal{R}^d_n} t'$ obviously implies $e(s') \rightarrow^{GK}_{\mathcal{R}^d_n} e(t')$, we also have

$$e(s) \rightarrow^{GK}_{\mathcal{R}^d_n} e(t_1) \rightarrow^{GK}_{\mathcal{R}^d_n} e(t_2) \rightarrow^{GK}_{\mathcal{R}^d_n} \cdots$$

The latter sequence terminates with some $e(t_j) \in NF(\rightarrow_{\mathcal{R}^d_n})$ since the Gross-Knuth reduction strategy is normalizing. Moreover, $e(t_j) = u$ because $\rightarrow_{\mathcal{R}^d_n}$ is confluent. Thus t_j is the marked term we are looking for.

Theorem 28. $\Rightarrow_{\mathcal{R}_n}$ *is a sound and complete implementation of* $\rightarrow_{\mathcal{R}_n}$.

Proof. Again, we use induction on n to show:

1. $\forall s, t \in \mathcal{T}^*_w$: if $s \Rightarrow^*_{\mathcal{R}_n} t$, then $e(s) \rightarrow^*_{\mathcal{R}_n} e(t)$.
2. $\forall t \in \mathcal{T}^*_w$: $t \in NF(\Rightarrow_{\mathcal{R}_n})$ if and only if $e(t) \in NF(\rightarrow_{\mathcal{R}_n})$.
3. $\forall s \in \mathcal{T}^*_w$: if $e(s) \rightarrow^*_{\mathcal{R}_n} u \in NF(\rightarrow_{\mathcal{R}_n})$, then there is a term $t \in \mathcal{T}^*_w$ such that $s \Rightarrow^*_{\mathcal{R}_n} t$ and $e(t) = u$.

(1) The proof is the same as in Proposition 27.
(2) Follows from Proposition 27 in conjunction with Lemmata 12 and 23.
(3) By Proposition 11, there is a term v such that $e(s) \rightarrow^*_{\mathcal{R}^d_n} v$ and $u \rightarrow^*_{\mathcal{R}^d_n} v$. Since u is a normal form, we derive $u = v$ and thus $e(s) \rightarrow^*_{\mathcal{R}^d_n} u \in NF(\rightarrow_{\mathcal{R}^d_n})$. According to Proposition 27, there exists a marked term t such that $s \Rightarrow^*_{\mathcal{R}^d_n} t$ and $e(t) = u$. Hence $\Rightarrow^*_{\mathcal{R}^d_n} \subseteq \Rightarrow^*_{\mathcal{R}_n}$ concludes the proof.

Theorem 29. *$\Rightarrow_{\mathcal{R}}$ is a sound and complete implementation of $\rightarrow_{\mathcal{R}}$.*

Proof. It is fairly simple to prove soundness. In order to show completeness, we have to prove that for all marked terms s, $e(s) \rightarrow^*_{\mathcal{R}} u \in NF(\rightarrow_{\mathcal{R}})$ implies the existence of a marked term t such that $s \Rightarrow^*_{\mathcal{R}} t \in NF(\Rightarrow_{\mathcal{R}})$ and $e(t) = u$. Let n be the depth of $e(s) \rightarrow^*_{\mathcal{R}} u$. Now by Theorem 28, there is a term $t \in \mathcal{T}^*_w$ such that $s \Rightarrow^*_{\mathcal{R}_n} t \in NF(\Rightarrow_{\mathcal{R}_n})$ and $e(t) = u$. It is easy to prove that $t \in NF(\Rightarrow_{\mathcal{R}})$.

References

[AEH94] S. Antoy, R. Echahed, and M. Hanus. A Needed Narrowing Strategy. In *Proc. 21st ACM Symposium on Principles of Programming Languages*, pages 268–279, 1994.

[BEG+87] H.P. Barendregt, M.C.J.D. van Eekelen, J.R.W. Glauert, J.R. Kennaway, M.J. Plasmeijer, and M.R. Sleep. Term graph rewriting. In *Proc. Parallel Architectures and Languages Europe*, pages 141–158. LNCS **259**, 1987.

[BK86] J.A. Bergstra and J.W. Klop. Conditional Rewrite Rules: Confluence and Termination. *Journal of Computer and System Sciences* **32***(3)*, pages 323–362, 1986.

[DJ90] N. Dershowitz and J.-P. Jouannaud. Rewrite Systems. In J. van Leeuwen, editor, *Handbook of Theoretical Computer Science*, volume B, chapter 6. Elsevier – The MIT Press, 1990.

[Han94a] M. Hanus. On Extra Variables in (Equational) Logic Programming. Technical Report MPI-I-94-246, Max-Plank-Institut für Informatik, 1994.

[Han94b] M. Hanus. The Integration of Functions into Logic Programming: From Theory to Practice. *The Journal of Logic Programming* **19,20**, pages 583–628, 1994.

[Han95] M. Hanus. On Extra Variables in (Equational) Logic Programming. In *Proceedings of the 12th International Conference on Logic Programming*, pages 665–679. MIT Press, 1995.

[Klo92] J.W. Klop. Term Rewriting Systems. In S. Abramsky, D. Gabbay, and T. Maibaum, editors, *Handbook of Logic in Computer Science*, volume 2, pages 1–116. Oxford University Press, 1992.

[KO95] M. Kurihara and A. Ohuchi. Modularity in Noncopying Term Rewriting. *Theoretical Computer Science* **152**, pages 139–169, 1995.

[MH94] A. Middeldorp and E. Hamoen. Completeness Results for Basic Narrowing. *Applicable Algebra in Engineering, Communication and Computing* **5**, pages 213–253, 1994.

[O'D77] M.J. O'Donnell. *Computing in Systems Described by Equations.* LNCS **58**, 1977.

[Plu93] D. Plump. *Evaluation of Functional Expressions by Hypergraph Rewriting.* PhD thesis, Universität Bremen, 1993.

[SMI95] T. Suzuki, A. Middeldorp, and T. Ida. Level-Confluence of Conditional Rewrite Systems with Extra Variables in Right-Hand Sides. In *Proceedings of the 6th International Conference on Rewriting Techniques and Applications*, pages 179–193. LNCS **914**, 1995.

[Sta75] J. Staples. Church-Rosser Theorems for Replacement Systems. In J. Crosley, editor, *Algebra and Logic*, pages 291–307. Lecture Notes in Mathematics **450**, 1975.

Lazy Narrowing with Parametric Order Sorted Types*

J.M. Almendros-Jiménez, A. Gil-Luezas

Dpto. Sistemas Informáticos y Programación
Fac. Matemáticas, Univ. Complutense, Madrid, Spain
email:{jesusmal,anagil}@eucmos.sim.ucm.es

Abstract. Recently, a model theoretic semantics for lazy functional programming combining *parametric* and *inclusion* polymorphism has been proposed in [2]. The aim of the present work is to provide the previous one with the incorporation of a typed lazy narrowing calculus for goal solving which combines *lazy unification*, *sharing* and *type checking* at run-time. Furthermore, we state soundness and completeness results of the goal solving procedure w.r.t. the typed rewriting calculi presented in [2] which were proved to be also sound and complete w.r.t. the notion of model in [2]. Thus, all theoretical results described there are also preserved in this framework.

1 Introduction

The combination of different declarative paradigms (specially functional and logic) has been widely investigated during the last decade (see [14] for a survey). As a consequence of such research, several well-known functional logic languages such as BABEL or K-LEAF arose, combining lazy evaluation with unification and using *lazy narrowing* as goal solving mechanism.

Another interesting line of research has been (and currently is) the incorporation of type systems to declarative languages. As examples we have the language ML [16] and the works [17] and [12] which provide *parametric polymorphism* (so called static type systems) to logic and functional logic programming respectively. Other languages, like the equational one OBJ3 use instead *inclusion polymorphism* [9] (so called dynamic type systems) increasing the representation facilities by allowing subdivide the universe of discourse flexibly. The combination of both kinds of polymorphism has also been treated in literature. As a matter of fact, we have the works [8, 20] referring to functional programming and [21], [13], [15], [4, 5] related to logic programming. The type systems of these languages offer advantages from the traditional programming (static consistence at compile-time, avoidance of non meaningful expressions, explicit data structures and better structured programs) growing its importance with the size of the program. An additional advantage in functional logic programming is that computations on types can reduce otherwise necessary *reductions*, sometimes greatly increasing the speed of the computation by avoiding *backtracking* and providing more compact intensional answers.

* This research has been partially supported by the the Spanish National Project TIC95-0433-C03-01 "CPD".

Recently a model theoretic semantics for lazy functional programming with parametric order-sorted types was presented in [2]. In such work, the authors show how to integrate parametric and inclusion polymorphism in a functional logic language similar to BABEL or K-LEAF. Such work includes typed rewriting calculi (proved to be equivalent) and a notion of model, proving soundness and completeness of the rewriting calculi w.r.t. models and existence of free models for well-typed programs. However, no goal solving mechanism is presented. The aim of the present paper is to extend the previous work with the incorporation of a typed lazy narrowing calculus for goal solving (TLNC for short) which combines lazy unification with sharing in the line of untyped goal solving procedures [18, 11] and type-checking at run-time. We state results of completeness and soundness of TLNC w.r.t the typed rewriting calculi presented in [2]. As a consequence all theoretical results presented in [2] are also preserved here.

As far as we know, this is the first time both polymorphisms are integrated in such a language. The novelty and difficulty of this integration consist of types must be lazily checked at run-time (due to inclusion polymorphism and lazy functions). This is not the case, for example, in typed logic programming where only types for terms are checked during the unification process. However checking types at run-time allows optimizations in the use of higher-order variables, as was pointed out in [19].

Our language is constructor-based and programs are sets of rewriting rules for functions, with a conditional part including type and data conditions. In the above mentioned declarative languages, type conditions refer to types of data variables (environments) involved in the rule. In our case this is not enough; we need that each rule contains type conditions not only to variables but also to expressions. However, some of these type conditions can be checked statically [1] and thus they can be removed at compile time reducing the dynamic type checking.

The rest of the paper is organized as follows: Sect. 2 defines polymorphic signatures, programs and the typed rewriting calculus (TRC for short) presented in [2] which is closer to the operational semantics presented in Sect. 3. This section also shows a little but illustrative programming example. Section 3 describes a typed lazy narrowing calculus for goal solving, giving the main ideas behind the goal solving mechanism rather than all technical requirements for proving soundness and completeness. The paper finishes drawing up some conclusions.

2 The Programming Language

Both parametric and inclusion polymorphisms are expressed in our language by using polymorphic signatures Σ which consist of:

- *a type specification* containing a ranked set of polymorphic type constructors, partially ordered by $\leq$. For instance, the type specification:

$$\begin{array}{ll} opnat, nat \leq int & \\ posint, zero \leq nat & elist(\alpha), nelist(\alpha) \leq list(\alpha) \\ negint, zero \leq opnat & etree(\alpha), netree(\alpha) \leq tree(\alpha) \end{array}$$

defines subsorts relation for integer numbers, and specifies the generic empty list and nonempty lists of type α as subsorts of generic lists of type α. Similarly for trees.

Following [15], type specifications are lower quasi-lattice (i.e., every lower bounded set of type constructors has infimum) order sorted relations $\leq$ where only type constructors of the same arity can be compared. Remark that this last condition forces $elist(\alpha)$ and $etree(\alpha)$ to be unary. Accordingly, data constructors *nil* and *empty* for sorts $elist(\alpha)$ and $etree(\alpha)$ respectively will also be unary. However, this facilitates the search of types fulfilling a set of type constraints [8]. Notice that the lower quasi-lattice condition ensures also the existence of supremum for upper bounded sets of types.

Types $\tau, \tau', \ldots$ are built up from type constructors $(K, L, \ldots)$ and type variables $(\alpha, \beta, \ldots)$, and they can be compared by extending the order $\leq$ to type constructors. For instance, $nelist(elist(\alpha)) \leq list(list(\alpha))$

- *a set of type declarations* for data constructors (CON) and functions (FUN). As an example:

$$
\begin{array}{ll}
0 : zero & \\
suc : nat \rightarrow posint & pred : opnat \rightarrow negint \\
nil : elist(\alpha) & cons : \alpha \rightarrow list(\alpha) \rightarrow nelist(\alpha) \\
empty : etree(\alpha) & node : tree(\alpha) \rightarrow \alpha \rightarrow tree(\alpha) \rightarrow netree(\alpha) \\
head : nelist(\alpha) \rightarrow \alpha & tail : nelist(\alpha) \rightarrow list(\alpha) \\
root : netree(\alpha) \rightarrow \alpha & left, right : netree(\alpha) \rightarrow tree(\alpha)
\end{array}
$$

is a set of data constructor declarations (0, *suc*, *pred* for integers, *nil*, *cons* for lists and *empty*, *node* for trees) together with some usual operations for dealing with lists (*head* and *tail*) and trees (*root*, *left* and *right*).

Data constructor declarations $c : \tau_1 \ldots \tau_n \rightarrow \tau_0$ satisfy that K in $\tau_0 = K(\overline{\alpha})$ is minimal w.r.t. $\leq$ (i.e., no data constructors for non minimal types are allowed) and no type variable occurs more than once in τ_0 (i.e., declarations are as general as possible).

In contrast to functions, data constructor declarations satisfy the so-called *transparency property* which expresses that every type variable in τ_i must occur in τ_0. Declarations with extra type variables in τ_0 can be completed by adding the extra variables as new arguments in the declaration. Such new arguments, called *fictitious* are needed to ensure the existence of *least type* for well-typed terms, as it was pointed out in [13]. For instance, $nil : elist(\alpha)$ is completed to $nil : \alpha \rightarrow elist(\alpha)$. In the following, we assume that every such declaration has been automatically completed in this way at compile-time by using fresh data variables (see [1] for details).

Type declarations can be instantiated by applying type substitutions ρ. For example, $cons : list(bool) \rightarrow list(list(bool)) \rightarrow nelist(list(bool))$ is an instance given by $[\alpha/list(bool)]$, where *bool* is the type for booleans.

Expressions $e, e', \ldots$ are built up from data constructor and function symbols and data variables $(X, Y, \ldots)$. *Terms* $t, t', \ldots$ can be defined similarly but without using function symbols.

Programs consist of a polymorphic signature Σ and a set of non-overlapping conditional constructor based rewriting rules defining the behaviour of function symbols. For instance, a higher-order function filtering those elements of a list (we use Prolog's syntax for lists) satisfying a given property, can be declared as $\mathit{filter} : (\alpha \to \mathit{bool}) \to \mathit{list}(\alpha) \to \mathit{list}(\alpha)$ and defined by the rules:

$\mathit{filter}\ P\ [\,] := [\,] \Leftarrow P : \alpha \to \mathit{bool}$
$\mathit{filter}\ P\ [X|L] := [X|\mathit{filter}\ P\ L] \Leftarrow (P\ X) == \mathit{true} \Box P : \alpha \to \mathit{bool}, X : \alpha, L : \mathit{list}(\alpha)$
$\mathit{filter}\ P\ [X|L] := \mathit{filter}\ P\ L \Leftarrow (P\ X) == \mathit{false} \Box P : \alpha \to \mathit{bool}, X : \alpha, L : \mathit{list}(\alpha)$

Formally, a program rule has the form:

$$f\ t_1 \ldots t_n := r \Leftarrow C_D \Box C_T$$

where the body r of the rule is an expression, and the rule condition is composed of a set of data (C_D) and type (C_T) conditions. The elements of C_D are strict equalities $l == r$ between expressions (which regards two expressions as equal iff they have the same constructor normal form [10]) whereas the elements of C_T are type conditions $e : \tau$. Furthermore, (i) the tuple $(t_1, \ldots, t_n)$ of terms is linear (i.e., no variable occurs more than once), and (ii) data variables of r must occur in the head $f(t_1, \ldots, t_n)$ of the rule. Remark that (ii) does not exclude the existence of extra variables in the rule condition. (i) and (ii) together with non-overlapping natural conditions [10] ensure the functionality of definitions.

Static well-typedness: The well-definedness of the semantics of a typed program requires that it satisfies the following notion of *static well-typedness* (SW for short). A program rule is said static well-typed if $(\Sigma, C_T) \vdash_{SW} t_i : \tau_i, r : \tau_0$ and there are types σ_j such that $(\Sigma, C_T) \vdash_{SW} l_j : \sigma_j, r_j : \sigma_j$, for every strict equation $l_j == r_j \in C_D$, where $f : \tau_1 \ldots \tau_n \to \tau_0 \in \mathit{FUN}$, and $(\Sigma, C_T) \vdash_{SW} e : \tau$ is defined by:

(a) $e : \tau' \in C_T$ and $\tau' \leq \tau$;
(b) $e \equiv h\ e_1 \ldots e_n$, $\tau_0 \leq \tau$ and $(\Sigma, C_T) \vdash_{SW} e_i : \tau_i$, $1 \leq i \leq n$, for an instance $\tau_1 \ldots \tau_n \to \tau_0$ of the type declaration σ of $h : \sigma \in \mathit{CON} \cup \mathit{FUN}$.

In all declarative typed languages commented in the introduction, well-typedness of a rule is ensured by taking environments V instead of condition sets C_T. An environment V (for a rule) is a set of type conditions for data variables (occurring in the rule) such that every data variable does not occur more than once in V. However, environments are not strong enough to guarantee the well-typedness of rules in our language. For instance, the function $\mathit{second} : \mathit{nelist}(\alpha) \to \alpha$ defined by

$$\mathit{second}\ X := \mathit{head}(\mathit{tail}\ X) \Leftarrow X : \mathit{nelist}(\alpha), \mathit{tail}\ X : \mathit{nelist}(\alpha)$$

needs the condition $\mathit{tail}\ X : \mathit{nelist}(\alpha)$ to ensure the existence of a second element in the list, and this can not be concluded by using only conditions on data variables. In any case, combining data and type conditions in program rules offers a wider range of possibilities for writing programs.

Remark that at compile-time, some type conditions in C_T can be checked statically [1] and thus they can be removed at compile time reducing the dynamic type checking.

We finish this section by showing the expressiveness of our language through an example. Consider the following type relations:

$$\begin{array}{l} technician, artist \leq person \\ doctor, comp\_scientist, architect \leq technician \\ sculptor, painter, musician \leq artist \end{array}$$

with the related database:

$$\begin{array}{ll} john, michael : doctor & frank : comp\_scientist \\ thomas, margaret : architect & richard, marie : sculptor \\ robert, nathalie : painter & david : musician \end{array}$$

We define relationships by:

$$\begin{array}{ll} father : person \rightarrow person & mother : person \rightarrow person \\ father\ michael := john & mother\ michael := margaret \\ father\ nathalie := frank & mother\ nathalie := marie \\ father\ david := michael... & mother\ david := nathalie... \end{array}$$

Then the family tree of a person is given by a function $fam\_tree : person \rightarrow netree(person)$ defined by:

$$fam\_tree\ X := node\ (fam\_tree\ father\ X)\ X\ (fam\_tree\ mother\ X) \Leftarrow X : person$$

For traversing a tree, the function $flatten : list(tree(\alpha)) \rightarrow list(\alpha)$ –producing the list of the node values in a forest by breadth-first searching – can be defined as follows:

$$\begin{array}{l} flatten\ [\,] := [\,] \\ flatten\ [T|R] := [(root\ T)|flatten\ (append\ R\ [(left\ T), (right\ T)])] \\ \qquad\qquad \Leftarrow T : netree(\alpha), R : list(tree(\alpha)) \\ flatten\ [T|R] := flatten\ R \Leftarrow T : etree(\alpha), R : list(tree(\alpha)) \end{array}$$

Types can be used to define functions by analyzing cases according to the type of the arguments. For instance, $same\_kind : person \rightarrow person \rightarrow bool$ defined by:

$$\begin{array}{l} same\_kind\ X\ Y := true \Leftarrow X : artist, Y : artist \\ same\_kind\ X\ Y := true \Leftarrow X : technician, Y : technician \\ same\_kind\ X\ Y := false \Leftarrow X : artist, Y : technician \\ same\_kind\ X\ Y := false \Leftarrow X : technician, Y : artist \end{array}$$

Pattern matching could be also used, but we obtain evident improvements if types for arguments have many constructors (as *technician* and *artist*). Now, let $exists : (\alpha \rightarrow bool) \rightarrow list(\alpha) \rightarrow bool$ be a function checking if there is some element in a list satisfying a property:

$$\begin{array}{l} exists\ P\ L := true \Leftarrow filter\ P\ L : nelist(\alpha), P : \alpha \rightarrow bool, L : list(\alpha) \\ exists\ P\ L := false \Leftarrow filter\ P\ L : elist(\alpha), P : \alpha \rightarrow bool, L : list(\alpha) \end{array}$$

In our language, queries have the same structure as the conditional part of a well-typed program rule. For instance, we can ask "people" having an ancestor of the same kind:

$$exists\ (same\_kind\ X)\ (flatten\ [fam\_tree\ X]) == true \Box X : person$$

Remark that we benefit from the laziness of the language evaluating the family tree only as far as the answer *true* is found. The same can be said not only for data but also for types.

We also can ask artists whose parents are technicians, by the query

$$\Box father\ X : technician, mother\ X : technician, X : artist$$

Finally, for the query

$$same\_kind\ X\ Y == Z \Box X : artist, Y : person, Z : bool$$

we can use the type of data variables for deducing intensional answers as $Y : artist, Z = true$ or $Y : technician, Z = false$.

2.1 A Typed Rewriting Calculus

The semantics of the language is presented by means of a Typed Rewriting Calculus (in short *TRC*) in which formulas φ are derived from a program P and an environment V (denoted by $(P, V) \vdash_{TR} \varphi$). In [2] the soundness and completeness of *TRC* w.r.t. the denotational and declarative semantics was proved. *TRC* focuses on top-down proofs for formulas, hence it is closer to the operational semantics of the language. For the sake of simplicity, in the rest of the paper we restrict the presentation to first-order, but all our results could be extended to higher-order in the line of applicative systems [19, 10].

Basically, we incorporate a new kind of formulas –for type conditions– to those untyped rewriting calculi presented in [11]. Thus, the calculus introduces derivation rules for establishing the type of an expression and forces expressions involved in the formulas to be well-typed, in contrast to untyped calculi where equalities involving ill-typed expressions (e.g. $head([0, true]) == 0$) can be derived. A sound and complete untyped operational semantics computing ill-typed solutions might be fatal in a large application.

To model the behaviour of non-strict or partial functions, we introduce in the signature the data constructor $\bot : \alpha \to \alpha$ denoting the undefined value. So, our typed calculus provides meaning to non-strict equalities $e \rhd t$ –which represents that the *partial* (i.e. possibly containing $\bot$) term t approximates the value of e (i.e. e is reduced or lazily unified to the partial term t)–, strict equalities $l == r$ –which will be derived by reducing both sides to the same *total* (i.e. without occurrences of $\bot$) term– and type conditions $e : \sigma$ –which semantically define the well-typedness of an expression.

TRC is composed of the rules below, where $[P]$ is the set of program rules instances of the form $f(\bar{t})\theta := r\theta \Leftarrow C_D\theta \Box C_T\theta\rho$, for any data substitution θ and type substitution ρ.

Bottom $\dfrac{e, t : \tau}{e \rhd \bot\ (t)}$ Reflexivity $\dfrac{}{t \rhd t}$ if t is a variable or $t : \tau \in CON$

Decomposition $\dfrac{e_i \rhd t_i, t_i : \tau_i}{c(e_1, \ldots, e_n) \rhd c(t_1, \ldots, t_n)}$ if $c : \tau \in CON$ and $\tau_1..\tau_n \to \tau_0$ is an instance of τ

Reduction I $\dfrac{e_i \rhd t_i, C_D, C_T, r \rhd t}{f(e_1, \ldots, e_n) \rhd t}$ if $f(t_1, \ldots, t_n) := r \Leftarrow C_D \Box C_T \in [P]$ and $t \not\equiv \bot\ (t')$

Strict Equality $\dfrac{l \rhd t, r \rhd t}{l == r}$ if t is a total term

Note that, besides the type conditions introduced by **Reduction I**, new type conditions are also added by **Decomposition** and **Bottom** rules in order to avoid ill-typed equations can be proved. Fictitious arguments are also needed for this; otherwise, an equality as $tail([david]) == tail([true])$ could be derived by approximating both sides to nil.

Type assumption $\dfrac{\sigma \leq \tau}{X : \tau}$ if $X : \sigma \in V$

Type declaration $\dfrac{e_i : \sigma_i, \sigma_0 \leq \tau}{h(e_1, .., e_n) : \tau}$ if $h : \sigma \in CON \cup FUN$ and $\sigma_1..\sigma_n \rightarrow \sigma_0$ is an instance of σ

Reduction II $\dfrac{e_i \rhd t_i, C_D, C_T, r : \tau}{f(e_1, .., e_n) : \tau}$ if $f(t_1, .., t_n) := r \Leftarrow C_D \Box C_T \in [P]$

Note that, to derive $e \rhd t$, the head normal form of e is required in order to lazily unify it with the partial term t. For instance, in the context of the declarations

$tail : nelist(\alpha) \rightarrow list(\alpha)$ $\qquad tail([X|Xs]) := Xs \Leftarrow X : \alpha, Xs : list(\alpha)$
$from : nat \rightarrow nelist(nat)$ $\qquad from(N) := [N|from(suc(N))] \Leftarrow N : nat$

we have

$$\frac{[suc(0)|from(suc(suc(0)))] \rhd [suc(0)| \perp]}{tail(from(0)) \rhd [suc(0)| \perp]}$$

However, for deriving $f(\bar{e}) : \tau$, consulting the type declaration of f can be enough, and so the head normal form of $f(\bar{e})$ is not required. For instance, $from(0) : nelist(nat)$ is tested without any evaluation, however $tail(from(0)) : nelist(nat)$ needs the lazy reduction of the expression, since

$$\frac{from(suc(0)) : nelist(nat)}{tail(from(0)) : nelist(nat)}$$

Finally, note that the combination of data and type reduction rules in the calculus avoids ill-typedness of the equations. An equation is *TRC-well-typed* if there exists a *TRC*-provable common type for both sides of the equation. It can be proved that the *TRC*-derivable equalities are *TRC*-well typed by using the static well-typedness of program rules. For example, $head([0, true]) == 0$ is not *TRC*-provable: any possible derivation fails when the type condition C_T of $head([X|X_s]) := X \Leftarrow X : \alpha, X_s : list(\alpha)$ is tried to be proved.

The static well-typedness of program rules also ensures the following suitable property of program rules:

Proposition 1. *Let P be a SW-program, $f(\bar{t})\theta := r\theta \Leftarrow C_D\theta \Box C_T\theta\rho \in [P]$ and $f : \tau_1 \ldots \tau_n \rightarrow \tau_0 \in FUN$. If $(P, V) \vdash_{TR} C_T\theta\rho$ then $(P, V) \vdash_{TR} t_i\theta : \tau_i\rho$, $(P, V) \vdash_{TR} r\theta : \tau_0\rho$ and every $l == r \in C_D\theta$ is TRC-well-typed.*

3 A Typed Lazy Narrowing Calculus

To provide our language with operational semantics, we outline in what way an untyped lazy narrowing calculus for goal-solving similar to those presented in [18, 11], can be adapted to a typed one. Assuming that goals for these untyped narrowing calculi are finite multisets $\mathcal{C}$ of data constraints, we need to add type conditions to them and to combine data and type conditions solving. Such type conditions enable to add failure transformation rules which can be used to prune unsuccessful derivations at an early stage.

Informally, a solution for a goal $\mathcal{C}$ is composed of an environment V, a data substitution θ and a type substitution ρ in such a way that θ is well-typed w.r.t. V (i.e. if $X : \tau \in V$ then $(P, V) \vdash_{TR} X\theta : \tau$), and $(P, V) \vdash_{TR} \mathcal{C}\theta\rho$.

As usual, our typed lazy narrowing calculus consists of a set of rules which transform goals $\mathcal{C} \bullet\!\!\rightarrow^{Tr} \mathcal{C}'$ or produce failure, by means of a transformation rule Tr. A successful derivation $\mathcal{C} \bullet\!\!\rightarrow^{*} \mathcal{C}'$ is a sequence of applications of transformation rules such that $\mathcal{C}'$ is in solved form (i.e. $\bullet\!\!\rightarrow$-irreducible) and represents a solution for $\mathcal{C}'$ (and so also for $\mathcal{C}$). Hence, we will show how to specify a solution (V, θ, ρ) from a solved goal.

Although an initial goal $\mathcal{C}$ (a query) is as a well-typed rule condition, during the transformation process, $\mathcal{C}$ will also contain statements $e \rhd t$ and $\tau \leq \tau'$, whose meaning was already given in TRC. Besides, new kinds of statements are added to, in case of success, represent the solution; specifically, $X = t$ and $\alpha = \tau$ for θ and ρ respectively, and $Y : \alpha_Y$ for V, associating a type variable α_Y to each data variable Y in $\mathcal{C}$.

Goals: A goal $\mathcal{C}$ is given by $(\mathcal{S} \Box \mathcal{N})$, where:

- the solved part $\mathcal{S}$ is of the form $Y_1 : \sigma_1, \ldots, Y_m : \sigma_m, X_1 = t_1, \ldots, X_n = t_n, \alpha_1 = \tau_1, \ldots, \alpha_k = \tau_k$, where Y_i (respect. X_i and α_i) are all pairwise distinct
- the non-solved part $\mathcal{N}$ is of the form $e_1 \rhd s_1, \ldots, e_p \rhd s_p, l_1 == r_1, \ldots, l_t == r_t, e_1 : \tau_1, \ldots, e_l : \tau_l, \tau_1 \leq \tau_1', \ldots, \tau_h \leq \tau_h'$

and it must satisfy some technical properties peculiar to untyped calculi for achieving the effect of lazy evaluation with sharing, during goal solving (cfr. [11]). Additionally, there must be a condition $X : \alpha_X$ for each data variable X in $\mathcal{C}$ in order to compute V. Moreover, goals must satisfy the *well-typedness* property for ensuring the well-typedness of goal solutions. Such property states that the satisfiability of the type conditions in $\mathcal{C}$ implies that all expressions in $\mathcal{C}$ are well-typed[2]. Remark that queries are goals, and transformation rules will be defined in such a way that goals are transformed into new goals.

Solutions: The definition of solution must cover the case of intermediate goals of a computation, and so we are interested in tuples (V, θ, ρ) verifying the following *adequateness* properties:

---

[2] Since goals also represent intermediate steps of the transformation process, the satisfiability of the type conditions in $\mathcal{C}$ does not imply the well-typedness of the equalities. This will be the case only when equations have been solved.

- θ and ρ are idempotent substitutions.
- θ may maps variables occurring in right-hand sides of non strict equalities (so called *produced* variables) onto partial terms. Partial data substitutions are needed to solve non strict equalities $e\theta \rhd t\theta$.
- $V \supseteq \{X : \alpha_X\rho \mid X \in Dom(\theta) \cup dvar(\mathcal{C})\}$, where $dvar(\mathcal{C})$ stands for the set of data variables occurring in $\mathcal{C}$. Remark that variables α_X are introduced to calculate V.
- $X\theta : \alpha_X\rho$ is TRC-provable from V, i.e. solutions must be well-typed.

A solution for a goal $\mathcal{C} = (\mathcal{S}\Box\mathcal{N})$ is a tuple (V, θ, ρ) verifying the above adequateness properties along with:

- $Y : \sigma\rho \in V$ for all $Y : \sigma \in \mathcal{S}$, $X\theta \equiv t\theta$ for all $X = t \in \mathcal{S}$, $\alpha\rho \equiv \tau\rho$ for all $\alpha = \tau \in \mathcal{S}$ if $\alpha \not\equiv \alpha_X$, $\alpha_X\rho \geq \tau\rho$, if $X \in Dom(\theta)$, and $\alpha_X\rho \leq \tau\rho$, if $X \notin Dom(\theta)$.
- $\mathcal{N}\theta\rho$ is TRC-provable from V.

We denote by $Sol(\mathcal{C})$ to the set of solutions of $\mathcal{C}$.

Solved goals: A solved goal has the form $(\mathcal{S}\Box\emptyset)$, is $\bullet\!\!\rightarrow$-irreducible and defines a solution (V, θ, ρ) for it, given by:

- $V = \{Y : \sigma \mid Y : \sigma \in \mathcal{S}\}$
- $\theta = \{X/t \mid X = t \in \mathcal{S}\}$
- $\rho = \{\alpha/\tau \mid \alpha = \tau \in \mathcal{S}\}$

The adequateness properties of this solution follow from the technical requirements that goals must fulfill.

In any solution, the environment V contains annotations $X : \tau$ for variables $X \in Dom(\theta)$ and for free variables. The former represents the type of $X\theta$ and so lesser types are more general. The latter means that X can range over values of type τ and so greater types are more general. Formally, if (V', θ', ρ') is well-typed and there are a data substitution ψ and a type substitution μ such that $(P, V') \vdash_{TR} X\psi : \tau\mu$, for every $X : \tau \in V$, $\theta' = \theta\psi$, $V\mu \leq V'[Dom(\theta)], V'[\backslash Dom(\theta)] \leq V\mu$ and $\rho\mu = \rho'[\backslash\alpha_X]$[3] then (V', θ', ρ') is also a solution (i.e. (V, θ, ρ) is *more general than* (that is *subsumes*) (V', θ', ρ')). For instance, for the query

$$\emptyset\Box X == second([0, suc(Y)]), X : int, Y : nat, X : \alpha_X, Y : \alpha_Y$$

we obtain the answer (solved goal)

$$X = suc(Y), X : posint, Y : nat, \alpha_X = posint, \alpha_Y = nat\Box\emptyset$$

which defines a more general solution than

$$X = suc(Y), X : nat, Y : posint, \alpha_X = nat, \alpha_Y = posint.$$

[3] $\leq$ is straightforwardly extended to environments and substitutions. $\phi[S]$ (respect. $\phi[\backslash S]$) is the restriction of ϕ to elements of S (respect. the complement of S).

3.1 Transformation Rules

The well-typedness of goals and program rules guarantees that data expressions involved in the process are well-typed whenever type conditions be solved. But when a fresh variant of a program rule $f(\bar{t}) := r \Leftarrow C_D \Box C_T$ with new variables $Y_1, \ldots, Y_m$ is applied by means of the transformation rule[4]:

(ONE) *Outermost Narrowing in Equalities*

$$\mathcal{S}\Box f(e_1 \ldots e_n) \approx e, \mathcal{N} \bullet\!\!\rightarrow \mathcal{S}\Box e_1 \rhd t_1, \ldots, e_n \rhd t_n, C_D, C_T, r \approx e, \\ Y_1 : \alpha_{Y_1}, \ldots, Y_m : \alpha_{Y_m}, \mathcal{N}$$

the types of t_i and e_i ,$1 \leq i \leq n$, may be incompatible even though the lazy unification $e_i \rhd t_i$ succeeds. For instance, applying the rule

$$same\_kind(Z, T) := false \Leftarrow Z : artist, T : technician$$

to the goal $same\_kind(X, Y) == Z \Box X : technician, Y : artist, Z : bool$, the pattern unification $X \rhd Z, Y \rhd T$ succeeds, but the types *technician* and *artist* of X and Z respectively (analogously for Y and T) are incompatible.

To check compatibility of these types, the transformation rules that bind, imitate or eliminate variables are modified w.r.t. untyped ones presented in [11] as follows:

(BD) *Binding*

$$\mathcal{S}\Box X \approx t, X : \alpha_X, \mathcal{N} \bullet\!\!\rightarrow X = t, X : \alpha_X, \mathcal{S}[X/t]\Box \underline{t : \alpha_X}, \mathcal{N}[X/t]$$

(IM) *Imitation*

$$\mathcal{S}\Box X \approx c(\bar{e}), X : \alpha_X, \mathcal{N} \bullet\!\!\rightarrow X = c(\bar{X}), X : \alpha_X, \mathcal{S}[X/c(\bar{X})]\Box X_1 \approx e_1, \ldots, \\ X_n \approx e_n, \underline{c(\bar{X}) : \alpha_X}, X_1 : \alpha_{X_1}, \ldots, X_n : \alpha_{X_n}, \mathcal{N}[X/c(\bar{X})]$$

(EVE) *Eager Variable Elimination*

$$\mathcal{S}\Box e \rhd X, X : \alpha_X, \mathcal{N} \bullet\!\!\rightarrow \mathcal{S}\Box \underline{e : \alpha_X}, \mathcal{N}$$

where the underlined type conditions force the type compatibility. So, in the previous example, applying (BD) to $X \rhd Z$, the condition Z : *artist* would be added to the goal, producing failure together with Z : *technician* (analogously for Y and T). The type conditions that these three rules add along with the constructor decomposition rules are enough to ensure the type compatibility in the unification process.

The linearity of left hand-sides of program rules along with applicability conditions for the transformation rules avoid the occur check in non-strict equations. However for strict equations of the form $X == e$, rules (BD) and (IM) must fail whenever X occurs in a "safe way" (that will be defined later) in e.

Identity and decomposition rules are the same than the untyped case:

(ID) *Identity*

$$\mathcal{S}\Box X == X, \mathcal{N} \bullet\!\!\rightarrow \mathcal{S}\Box \mathcal{N}$$

[4] We use $\approx$ for representing both $\rhd$ and $==$.

(DC) *Decomposition*

$$\mathcal{S}\Box c(\bar{a}) \approx c(\bar{b}), \mathcal{N} \bullet\!\!\rightarrow \mathcal{S}\Box a_1 \approx b_1 \ldots a_n \approx b_n, \mathcal{N}$$

It is not needed to modify these rules because of the well-typedness of goals. For example, if C contains $suc(true) == suc(true)$ then it must contain either $suc(true) : \tau$, for some τ, or $true : nat$. In both cases, the transformation process will produce failure. On the other hand, for disagreement equations $c(\bar{a}) \approx d(\bar{b})$ a failure is produced.

Additionally to previous adaptations, rules for solving type conditions are also needed. Such rules are:

(DA) *Data Variable*

$$\mathcal{S}\Box X : \tau, \mathcal{N} \bullet\!\!\rightarrow \mathcal{S}\Box \alpha_X \leq \tau, \mathcal{N}$$

(SV) *Solved Variable*

$$\mathcal{S}\Box X : \alpha_X, \mathcal{N} \bullet\!\!\rightarrow X : \alpha_X, \mathcal{S}\Box\mathcal{N} \quad \text{if } X \notin dvar(\mathcal{N})$$

The type conditions $c(\bar{e}) : \tau$ must fulfill the type declaration of c. For instance, $suc(e) : nat$ is obtained from $e : nat$ and $posint \leq nat$. However, for equations $f(\bar{e}) : \tau$, the type declaration of f could not be enough. For instance, the type condition $head([suc(0), 0]) : nat$ can be solved directly from the type declaration of $head$, whereas $head([suc(0), 0]) : posint$ requires narrowing in order to be solved.

(LTC) *Lazy Type Checking*

$$\mathcal{S}\Box h(e_1, \ldots, e_n) : \tau, \mathcal{N} \bullet\!\!\rightarrow \mathcal{S}\Box e_1 : \tau_1, \ldots, e_n : \tau_n, \tau_0 \leq \tau, \mathcal{N}$$

where $h : \sigma \in CON \cup FUN$ and $\tau_1 \ldots \tau_n \rightarrow \tau_0$ is a fresh variant of σ.

(ONTC) *Outermost Narrowing in Type Conditions*

$$\mathcal{S}\Box f(e_1, \ldots, e_n) : \tau, \mathcal{N} \bullet\!\!\rightarrow \mathcal{S}\Box e_1 \rhd t_1, \ldots, e_n \rhd t_n, C_D, C_T, r : \tau, Y_1 : \alpha_{Y_1}, \ldots, Y_m : \alpha_{Y_m}, \mathcal{N}$$

where $f(\bar{t}) := r \Leftarrow C_D \Box C_T$ is a fresh variant of a program rule with new variables $Y_1, \ldots, Y_m$.

Finally, rules for solving structural subtype conditions, in the line of [4, 8] have to be considered:

(DCT) *Decomposition of types*

$$\mathcal{S}\Box K(\bar{\tau}) \leq L(\bar{\sigma}), \mathcal{N} \bullet\!\!\rightarrow \mathcal{S}\Box \tau_1 \leq \sigma_1, \ldots, \tau_n \leq \sigma_n, \mathcal{N}$$

if $K \leq L$ and failure, otherwise.

(TS) *Trivial Subtype*

$$\mathcal{S}\Box \alpha \leq \alpha, \mathcal{N} \bullet\!\!\rightarrow \mathcal{S}\Box\mathcal{N}$$

Before binding a type variable α, the number of conditions involving α is reduced as much as possible according to the quasi-lattice property of $\leq$, checking simultaneously the consistence of the conditions at hand.

(IN) *Infimum*

$$\mathcal{S}\Box\alpha \leq K(\bar{\tau}), \alpha \leq L(\bar{\sigma}), \mathcal{N} \bullet\!\!\rightarrow \mathcal{S}\Box\alpha \leq I(\bar{\alpha}), \alpha_1 \leq \tau_1, \ldots, \alpha_n \leq \tau_n, \alpha_1 \leq \sigma_1, \ldots, \alpha_n \leq \sigma_n, \mathcal{N}$$

if I is the infimum for K and L and failure, otherwise.

A similar rule (SP) exists for the supremum.

To bind a variable α_X, X has to be solved (i.e., $X \notin dvar(\mathcal{N})$) since otherwise X could be bound to a term t and then $t : \alpha_X$ would be added to the goal.

On the other hand, a type variable α can occur more than once in the goal, even if the previous rules could not be applied. For instance, in the conditions $\alpha \leq nat, \alpha \leq \beta, \beta \leq posint$, the appropriate value for α depends on that for β. Thus for solving these conditions, the possible values for type variables must be enumerated. The search space could be reduced by introducing additional rules as transitivity.

(MI) *Matching I*

$$\mathcal{S}\Box\alpha \leq L(\tau_1, \ldots, \tau_n), \mathcal{N} \bullet\!\!\rightarrow \alpha = K(\alpha_1, \ldots, \alpha_n), \mathcal{S}\rho\Box\alpha_1 \leq \tau_1, \ldots, \alpha_n \leq \tau_n\mathcal{N}\rho$$

where $K \leq L$ and $\rho = \{\alpha / K(\alpha_1, \ldots, \alpha_n)\}$.

(MII) *Matching II*

$$\mathcal{S}\Box\alpha \leq \beta, \mathcal{N} \bullet\!\!\rightarrow \alpha = \beta, \mathcal{S}\rho\Box\mathcal{N}\rho$$

where $\rho = \{\alpha/\beta\}$.

(MIII) *Matching III*

$$\mathcal{S}\Box\alpha \leq \beta, \mathcal{N} \bullet\!\!\rightarrow \alpha = K(\alpha_1, \ldots, \alpha_n), \beta = L(\beta_1, \ldots, \beta_n), \mathcal{S}\rho\Box \alpha_1 \leq \beta_1, \ldots, \alpha_n \leq \beta_n, \mathcal{N}\rho$$

where $K \leq L$ and $\rho = \{\alpha/K(\alpha_1, \ldots, \alpha_n), \beta/L(\beta_1, \ldots, \beta_n)\}$.

3.2 Soundness and Completeness

A detailed version of the just presented calculus (*TLNC* for short), including the syntactical applicability conditions for the transformation rules, can be found in [3] where it is proved the soundness and completeness of *TLNC* w.r.t. *TRC*. *TLNC* has been developed from the presented ones in [10] and in [11] (the latter for non-deterministic lazy functions). Remark that these results also hold for model-theoretic semantics presented in [2], where we prove the adequateness of both semantics, model-theoretic and proof.

For the sake of simplicity, instead of the syntactical conditions required to get a lazy, sound and complete operational semantics, we give the main ideas behind the goal solving mechanism. Such syntactical conditions in general allow that rules for solving data constraints and type conditions can be applied indistinctly. It is out of the scope of this paper to specify a concrete strategy giving rise to an efficient solving mechanism. Of course, *failure rules* must be applied as soon as possible and those highly non-deterministic, as *Matching*-rules, should be delayed.

For solving data constraints, firstly the non-strict equations $e \rhd t$ in $\mathcal{C}$ must be handled. Given an equation $e \rhd X$ in $\mathcal{C}$:

- if X does not occur elsewhere (except in $X : \alpha_X$), then (EVE) is applied. In consequence the reduction of e is not performed according to the non-strict semantics. However, in order to keep the well-typedness property, $e : \alpha_X$ must be introduced in C, which could require the reduction of e
- if X is demanded (that is, X occurs as a side of a strict equation), then either (IM) or (ONE) must be applied
- if X is not demanded, then (BD) is applied if e is a term; otherwise, $e \rhd X$ is delayed until the application of the transformation rules to the rest of the goal demands or allows to eliminate X.

If the right hand-side of $e \rhd t$ is not a variable, then either (BD), (DC) or (ONE) is applied.

For the resolution of strict equations, we must apply (ONE) in order to get head normal forms, that is, until either (DC) can be applied or a variable is obtained as a hand-side. In this last case, either a delayed equation can be activated, or (ID), (IM) or (BD) can be applied, checking (except for (ID)) that the equation $X == c(\bar{e})$ verifies that $X \notin svar(c(\bar{e}))$ ($svar(e)$ stands for the set of "safe" variables, i.e. variables occurring in e in some position which is not in the scope of a function symbol).

Note that any variable X can only be bound to a term t, since otherwise sharing would not be achieved. From an implementation point of view, *sharing* [6] of expressions in data and type conditions turns out to be essential for the avoidance of many redundant reductions.

With respect to type conditions, we need *don't know* choice in the application of (LTC) and (ONTC), so a *strong* completeness result can not be ensured (in the sense of [11]). If we apply (ONTC) before (LTC) unnecessary reductions could be produced in contrast to the lazy nature of our language (that allows infinite data). However, to apply (LTC) is not always enough to solve the type condition. Therefore, a lazy computation must try (LTC) before (ONTC).

Formally, a type condition $e : \sigma$ in a goal C is *demanded* by $(V, \theta, \rho) \in Sol(C)$ if $e\theta = f(e_1, .., e_n)$ and every TRC-proof for $e\theta : \sigma\rho$ of minimal length begins with the application of the TRC-rule Reduction II. And we say that a transformation rule Tr is *lazily applicable* to C w.r.t. $(V, \theta, \rho) \in Sol(C)$, if Tr is applicable to C and:

- if $Tr =$ (ONTC) then there exists $e : \tau \in C$ demanded by (V, θ, ρ)
- if $Tr =$ (LTC) then there exists $e : \tau \in C$ not demanded by (V, θ, ρ).

Type conditions $e : \tau$ demanded by a solution, require narrowing e for checking its type. In the proof of completeness the distinction between demanded and not demanded type conditions provides information about the branch containing the solution.

Theorem 2 Soundness. *Let C be a query and suppose that $C \bullet\!\!\rightarrow^* SS$, where SS is solved. Then every solution defined by SS is a solution of C.*

Theorem 3 Completeness. *Let C be a query and suppose that $(V, \theta, \rho) \in Sol(C)$. Then there exist a solved goal SS and a solution (V', θ', ρ') defined by SS such that $C \bullet\!\!\rightarrow^* SS$ and (V', θ', ρ') is more general than (V, θ, ρ).*

Proof Idea: Given a non solved goal C and assuming that $(V, \theta, \rho) \in Sol(C)$ then we prove that:

- there exists a transformation rule lazily applicable to C
- if Tr is a transformation rule lazily applicable to C then there exist a goal C' and a solution $(V', \theta', \rho') \in Sol(C')$ such that:
  - $C \bullet\!\!\rightarrow^{Tr} C'$.
  - (V', θ', ρ') is more general than (V, θ, ρ)
  - $\{\{(P, V') \vdash_{TR} C'\theta'\rho'\}\} < \{\{(P, V) \vdash_{TR} C\theta\rho\}\}$, where $<$ is a *well-founded ordering* over multisets of proofs [7]. □

4 Conclusions

In [2], rewriting calculi for lazy functional logic programming combining parametric and inclusion polymorphism were presented. Such rewriting calculi were proved to be sound and complete w.r.t. the model theoretic semantics also defined there. In the current paper we have provided [2] with a goal solving mechanism combining ideas of untyped lazy narrowing [18, 11] with type checking at run-time. We have stated results of soundness and completeness of the described goal solving mechanism w.r.t. the semantics in [2]. Type checking at run-time allows to reduce the search tree, compute more compact intensional answers and optimizations in the use of higher-order variables. However, to profit from all advantages of dynamic type checking, a strategy minimizing the run time of type conditions is required. Currently, we are working in the development of such a strategy and checking its behaviour in practice.

Acknowledgments: We would like to thank A. Gavilanes-Franco for his contribution to the development of this work.

References

1. J.M. Almendros-Jiménez. *Type Inference and Checking for Polymorphic Order-Sorted Typed Functional Logic Programs*, Procs. Joint Conference in Declarative Programming APPIA-GULP-PRODE'96, pp. 439-450, 1996.
2. J.M. Almendros-Jiménez, A. Gavilanes-Franco, A. Gil-Luezas. *Algebraic Semantics for Functional Logic Programs with Polymorphic Order-Sorted Types*, Procs. ALP'96, Springer LNCS 1139, pp. 299-313, 1996.
3. J.M.Almendros-Jiménez, A. Gil-Luezas. *Lazy Narrowing with Polymorphic Order-Sorted Types (Extended Version)*, Technical Report 30/96 DIA. Universidad Complutense. Madrid. 1996. Available in `http://mozart.mat.ucm.es`.
4. C. Beierle. *Type Inferencing for Polymorphic Order-Sorted Logic Programs*, Procs. ICLP'95, The MIT Press, pp. 765-779, 1995.
5. C.Beierle. *Concepts, Implementation and Applications of a Typed Logic Programming Language*, Logic Programming: Formal Methods and Practical Applications. C. Beierle and L. Plümer Eds. Elsevier Science, pp. 139-167, 1995.
6. P.H. Cheong. L. Fribourg. *Implementation of Narrowing: The Prolog-Based Approach*, In K.R. Apt, J.W. Bakker, J.J.M.M. Rutten, Eds. Logic Programming languages: Constraints, Functions and Objects. pp. 1-20. The MIT Press. 1993.

7. N. Dershowitz, A. Manna. *Proving Termination with Multisets Orderings*, Communications of the ACM 22(8), pp. 465-476, 1979.
8. Y. Fuh, P. Mishra. *Type Inference with Subtypes*, Theoretical Computer Science 73, pp. 155-175, 1990.
9. J.A. Goguen, J. Meseguer. *Order Sorted Algebra I: Equational deduction for Multiple Inheritance, Overloading, Exceptions and Partial Operations*, Theoretical Computer Science 105, pp. 217-273, 1992.
10. J.C. González-Moreno, T. Hortalá-González, M. Rodríguez Artalejo. *On the Completeness of Narrowing as the Operational Semantics of Functional Logic Programming*, Procs. CSL'92, Springer LNCS 702, pp. 216-230, 1993.
11. J.C. González-Moreno, T. Hortalá-González, F. López-Fraguas, M. Rodríguez-Artalejo. *A Rewriting Logic for Declarative Programming*, Procs. ESOP'96, Springer LNCS 1058, pp. 156-172, 1996.
12. M. Hanus. *A Functional and Logic Language with Polymorphic Types*, Procs. Int. Symp. on Design and Implementation of Symbolic Computation Systems, Springer LNCS 429, pp. 215-224, 1990.
13. M. Hanus. *Parametric Order-Sorted Types in Logic Programming*, Procs. TAPSOFT'91, Springer LNCS 494, pp. 181-200, 1991.
14. M. Hanus. *The Integration of Functions into Logic Programming: A Survey*, Journal of Logic Programming (19,20), Special issue "Ten Years of Logic Programming", pp. 583-628, 1994.
15. P.M. Hill, R.W. Topor. *A Semantics for Typed Logic Programming*, Chapter 1, Types in Logic Programming, Logic Programming Series, Frank Pfenning Editor, The MIT Press, pp. 1-58, 1992.
16. R. Milner. *A Theory of Type Polymorphism in Programming*, Journal of Computer and System Sciences, 17(3), pp. 348-375, 1978.
Logic Programming with Functions and Predicates: The Language BABEL, Journal of Logic Programming 12, pp. 191-223, 1992.
17. A. Mycroft, R.A. O'Keefe. *A Polymorphic Type System for Prolog*, Artificial Intelligence 23, pp. 295-307, 1984.
18. A. Middeldorp, S. Okui. *Deterministic Lazy Narrowing*, Procs. Fuji International Workshop on Functional and Logic Programming, World Scientific, pp. 104-118, 1995.
19. K. Nakahara, A. Middeldorp, T. Ida. *A Complete Narrowing Calculus for Higher-Order Functional Logic Programming*, Procs. PLILP'95, Springer LNCS 982, pp. 97-114, 1995.
20. G.S. Smith. *Principal Type Schemes for Functional Programs with Overloading and Subtyping*, Science of Computer Programming 23, pp. 197-226, 1994.
21. G. Smolka. *Logic Programming over Polymorphically Order-Sorted Types*, PhD thesis, Universität Kaiserslautern, Germany, 1989.

Termination of Algebraic Type Systems: The Syntactic Approach

Gilles Barthe and Femke van Raamsdonk *

CWI
P.O. Box 94079, 1090 GB Amsterdam
The Netherlands
{gilles,femke}@cwi.nl

1 Introduction

Combinations of type theory and rewriting are of obvious interest for the study of higher-order programming and program transformation with algebraic data types specifications; somewhat more recently, they also found applications in proof-checking. A natural question in this field concerns the termination or strong normalisation of such systems and is as follows: given a terminating type system T and a terminating rewriting system R, is the combination of T and R terminating? It is not surprising that this question has already received considerable attention, see for instance [1, 2, 4, 7, 11, 12, 15–17, 19, 24]. However, the situation is in our opinion not yet satisfactory, since most of the proofs of termination of a combination of a type theory and a rewriting system consist basically in redoing the proof of termination of the type theory. Ideally, one would like to have a modular *proof* of these modularity *results*, i.e. a proof that *uses but does not re-prove* the facts that the type theory and the term rewriting system are terminating.

The question we embark on is hence to develop general methods that permit to derive termination of the combination of a type theory and a rewriting system from termination of those systems separately. We make the question precise in the framework of algebraic type systems [7] which combine pure type systems and term rewriting systems. The advantage of this setting is its generality; for instance the combination of the calculus of constructions with a term rewriting system, as defined e.g. in [4], is an algebraic type system.

The first method we present is called *termination by translation*. An algebraic type system $\mathcal{A}$ is terminating if there exists a map into a terminating algebraic type system $\mathcal{A}'$ such that derivable judgements in $\mathcal{A}$ are mapped to derivable judgements in $\mathcal{A}'$ and rewrite steps in $\mathcal{A}$ are mapped to non-empty rewrite sequences in $\mathcal{A}'$. This technique, which is well-known in type theory, is an elaboration of termination by translation in first-order term rewriting. Despite its extreme simplicity, it permits to obtain, in a very easy way, useful termination results for algebraic type systems.

* A part of this work has been carried out while the second author was at INRIA Sophia Antipolis, France, on a grant of the HCM Cooperation Network EXPRESS.

The second method, which we call *termination by stability*, has not only useful applications but is also interesting in itself. The method is inspired from [16] where Dougherty considers untyped λ-calculus with β-reduction in combination with a first-order, single-sorted, term rewriting system $\mathcal{R}$. In particular, Dougherty shows that the union of $\rightarrow_\beta$ and $\rightarrow_\mathcal{R}$ is terminating on a suitably defined subset $\mathsf{Stable}(\mathcal{R})$ of the set of β-strongly normalising terms. Elements of $\mathsf{Stable}(\mathcal{R})$ are called stable terms, after which the method is named. Our interest in Dougherty's method lies in the fact that termination of the combined reduction relation is *reduced* to termination of its components, i.e. β-reduction and $\mathcal{R}$-reduction. In Section 3, we extend Dougherty's method to algebraic type systems.

In Section 5, we apply the two methods to find easy proofs of well-known results. For example, we give easy proofs of termination for the combination of higher-order λ-calculus $\lambda\omega$ and a terminating term rewriting system. Furthermore, we derive from the two methods a number of new results:

- The combination of higher-order λ-calculus, $\lambda\omega$, with $\beta\eta$-reduction and a terminating term rewriting system is terminating.
- Under certain mild conditions, the combination of a terminating pure type system and a terminating non-collapsing term rewriting system is terminating. As a corollary, we obtain that the combination of a pure type system and a ground rewriting system is terminating, under some mild conditions.

Our methods are flexible and robust. Firstly, they apply to several notions of reductions such as β-reduction, η-reduction, and, we claim, η-expansion. Secondly, they carry over to variations of algebraic type systems such as type-assignment systems, domain-free pure type systems or pure type systems with Π-conversion. Thirdly, the method scales up when other type constructions, such as the ones for products and sums, are considered.

Moreover, our methods are simple. They can be carried out in a weak system of arithmetic. This is the case since we *reduce* termination of an algebraic type system to that of a pure type system and *do not prove* the latter, which of course may require a strong system of arithmetic.

Finally, our methods are informative. In particular, they shed some light on the logical status of algebraic type systems. For example, a simple application of derivation-preserving translations shows that the internal logic of an algebraic type system cannot distinguish between two distinct closed algebraic terms.

Related work. The problem of termination for combinations of λ-calculus and term rewriting systems has already received considerable attention in higher-order rewriting but here we limit ourselves to termination results for algebraic type systems.

One of the first termination results for algebraic type systems is due to Breazu-Tannen and Gallier. In [12], they prove that the combination of the polymorphic λ-calculus –system F– with the curried version of a terminating first-order term rewriting system is terminating. The proof makes use of the 'candidats de reductibilité' and, for an essential part, consists in redoing the proof of termination for system F.

The combination of polymorphic λ-calculus with higher-order term rewriting is studied by Jouannaud and Okada in [19]. Using a computability argument, they show that provided some conditions on the form of the rewrite rules are satisfied, the combination of the polymorphic λ-calculus and a terminating higher-order rewriting system is again terminating. This result is generalized by Barbanera, Fernández and Geuvers in a series of papers first to intersection type systems, then to higher-order λ-calculus and finally to the so-called algebraic λ-cube [1, 3, 4]. Termination of the algebraic λ-cube is proved along the lines of [18] by using a computability predicate and two reduction preserving translations.

In [7], Barthe and Geuvers introduce the notion of algebraic type system and provide a general criterion for termination of an algebraic type system. The criterion is proved by a model construction based on saturated sets –so it re-does the termination proof for the corresponding pure type system. Unfortunately, the criterion requires the algebraic type system to have the subject reduction property, a severe restriction in the current state of knowledge. The problem is partially overcome in [9] where Barthe and Melliès use a labelled syntax to prove termination and subject reduction of algebraic type systems. However, the approach is complicated and requires to redo the proof of termination of the underlying pure type system.

Using a completely different approach, van de Pol shows in [24] termination of the combination of simply typed λ-calculus and the curried version of a terminating first-order term rewriting system. This result is obtained in the framework of higher-order rewriting systems, so in particular simply typed λ-calculus is coded as a higher-order rewriting system. The proof consists of extending a termination model of the term rewriting system to a termination model for simply typed λ-calculus.

Finally, several authors have recently considered algebraic type systems with η-expansion [14, 15]. In a nutshell, two techniques are used to prove termination: reducibility candidates and simulation of η-expansion. The first one is not modular, since it involves doing the termination proof again. The second one consists in defining a translation from legal terms to legal terms so that every infinite reduction sequence with η-expansions is translated into an infinite reduction sequence without η-expansions. This approach is in a sense orthogonal to ours as we translate an infinite reduction with algebraic reduction steps into an infinite reduction sequence without algebraic reduction steps. It turns out that our approach yields shorter and conceptually simpler proofs.

Organisation of the paper. The paper is organised as follows: in Section 2, we introduce the framework of algebraic type systems. Section 3 presents the techniques of termination by translation and termination by stability. In Section 4 we consider algebraic rewriting of algebraic pure type systems. Section 5 contains several applications of the two techniques, yielding new proofs of old results as well as new results. We conclude in Section 6.

2 Algebraic Type Systems

In this section we present the definition of an algebraic type system as the combination of a pure type system and a typed term rewriting system. First we recall the definition of a pure type system and give a suitable definition of a typed term rewriting system.

2.1 Pure Type Systems

Pure type systems were introduced by Berardi and by Terlouw as a general framework to define and study typed λ-calculi. The definition we present is a slight modification of the one given in [5].

Definition 1. A pure type system $\mathcal{S}$ is specified by a triple (U, TA, TR) with

1. U a set of *universes*,
2. $TA \subseteq U \times U$ a set of *typing axioms*,
3. $TR \subseteq U \times U \times U$ is a set of *typing rules*.

We assume a set V of *variables*, written as $x, y, z, \ldots$. The set of *pseudo-terms* of a pure type system $\mathcal{S} = (U, TA, TR)$ is defined by

$$T ::= V \mid U \mid \Pi V : T.T \mid \lambda V : T.T \mid TT$$

An *environment* is an ordered list of pairs of the form $x : A$ with $x \in V$ and $A \in T$. A *judgement* is a triple of the form $\Gamma \vdash M : A$ with Γ an environment and M, A pseudo-terms. Intuitively, a judgement assigns in a given environment a type to a term. The meaningful judgements of a pure type system are defined by means of a set of rules. One of these rules, the conversion rule, makes use of a rewrite relation on the set of pseudo-terms of the pure type system. For the sake of uniformity, we present the rules parametrised over the rewrite relation used in the conversion rule. A judgement then takes the form $\Gamma \vdash_{\mathcal{C}} M : A$, where $\mathcal{C}$ is the rewrite relation used in the conversion rule.

Definition 2. Let $\rightarrow_{\mathcal{C}}$ be a rewrite relation on the set of pseudo-terms of a pure type system $\mathcal{S} = (U, TA, TR)$.

1. A judgement $\Gamma \vdash_{\mathcal{C}} M : A$ is said to be *derivable* if it can be derived using the rules given in Table 1.
2. A pseudo-term M is said to be $\mathcal{C}$*-legal* if for some Γ and some A the judgement $\Gamma \vdash_{\mathcal{C}} M : A$ is derivable. The set of $\mathcal{C}$-legal terms of the pure type system $\mathcal{S}$ is denoted by $\mathcal{L}(\mathcal{S}, \mathcal{C})$.

If we simply state $\Gamma \vdash_{\mathcal{C}} M : A$, we mean that $\Gamma \vdash_{\mathcal{C}} M : A$ is a derivable judgement.

The most important rewrite relation on the set of pseudo-terms of a pure type system is the β-reduction relation, denoted by $\rightarrow_\beta$, which is defined as the compatible closure of

$$(\lambda x : A.M)N \rightarrow M[x := N]$$

axiom	$\dfrac{}{\vdash_C c : s}$	if $(c, s) \in TA$
start	$\dfrac{\Gamma \vdash_C A : s}{\Gamma, x : A \vdash_C x : A}$	if $x \notin \Gamma$, $x \in V$
weakening	$\dfrac{\Gamma \vdash_C M : A \quad \Gamma \vdash_C B : s}{\Gamma, x : B \vdash_C M : A}$	if $x \notin \Gamma$, $x \in V$
product	$\dfrac{\Gamma \vdash_C A : s_1 \quad \Gamma, x : A \vdash_C B : s_2}{\Gamma \vdash_C \Pi x : A.B : s_3}$	if $(s_1, s_2, s_3) \in TR$
application	$\dfrac{\Gamma \vdash_C M : \Pi x : A.B \quad \Gamma \vdash_C N : A}{\Gamma \vdash_C M\ N : B[x := M]}$	
abstraction	$\dfrac{\Gamma, x : A \vdash_C M : B \quad \Gamma \vdash_C (\Pi x : A.B) : s}{\Gamma \vdash_C \lambda x : A.M : \Pi x : A.B}$	
conversion	$\dfrac{\Gamma \vdash_C u : A \quad \Gamma \vdash_C B : s}{\Gamma \vdash_C u : B}$	if $A \downarrow_C B$

Table 1. PURE TYPE SYSTEMS

Often one considers the set of β-legal terms of a pure type system, equipped with the β-reduction relation, that is, the rewriting system $(\mathcal{L}(\mathcal{S}, \beta), \rightarrow_\beta)$.

An important example of pure type system is the calculus of constructions, defined by Coquand and Huet in [13]. Barendregt presents in [5] a fine-grain analysis of the calculus of constructions in terms of the λ-cube, a cube consisting of eight pure type systems. They all have $\{\star, \Box\}$ as the set of universes, and $\star : \Box$ as only typing axiom. Their sets of typing rules are as follows (here (s_1, s_2) abbreviates (s_1, s_2, s_2)):

$\lambda\rightarrow$	$: (\star, \star)$	λP	$: (\star, \star), (\star, \Box)$
$\lambda 2$	$: (\star, \star), (\Box, \star)$	$\lambda P2$	$: (\star, \star), (\Box, \star), (\star, \Box)$
$\lambda \underline{\omega}$	$: (\star, \star), (\Box, \Box)$	$\lambda P\underline{\omega}$	$: (\star, \star), (\Box, \Box), (\star, \Box)$
$\lambda \omega$	$: (\star, \star), (\Box, \star), (\Box, \Box)$	$\lambda P\omega$	$: (\star, \star), (\Box, \star), (\Box, \Box), (\star, \Box)$

Most of the systems of the λ-cube are of independent interest and appear in the literature, often in a variant form, see [5] for references. The calculus of constructions, $\lambda P\omega$, is the most complex system of the cube.

Morphisms of Pure Type Systems. Morphisms of pure type systems are maps between the sets of universes which preserve typing axioms and typing rules.

Definition 3. Let $\mathcal{A} = (U, TA, TR)$ and $\mathcal{A}' = (U', TA', TR')$ be pure type systems. A pure type system morphism between $\mathcal{A}$ and $\mathcal{A}'$ is a mapping

$$\phi : U \rightarrow U'$$

such that:

1. if $(u_1, u_2) \in TA$, then $(\phi(u_1), \phi(u_2)) \in TA'$,
2. if $(u_1, u_2, u_3) \in TR$, then $(\phi(u_1), \phi(u_2), \phi(u_3)) \in TR'$.

For a pure type morphism ϕ as in the previous definition, we write $\phi : \mathcal{A} \rightarrow \mathcal{A}'$ by a slight abuse of notation, also to denote the homomorphic extension of ϕ mapping pseudo-terms of $\mathcal{S}$ to pseudo-terms of $\mathcal{S}'$. A morphism as defined in this way is only concerned with the signature of a pure type system. If one is interested in a morphism that maps $\mathcal{C}$-legal terms in $\mathcal{S}$ to $\mathcal{C}'$-legal terms in $\mathcal{S}'$, then we should require in addition that $M \downarrow_{\mathcal{C}} N$ in $\mathcal{S}$ implies $\phi(M) \downarrow_{\mathcal{C}'} \phi(N)$ in $\mathcal{S}'$. Then it follows that $\mathcal{C}$-legal terms are mapped to $\mathcal{C}'$-legal terms by a straightforward induction on derivations.

2.2 Typed Term Rewriting Systems

In this subsection, we define typed term rewriting systems in such a way that they can be conveniently combined with pure type systems. We use the following notion of sorted signature.

Definition 4.

1. Let S be a set. An *algebraic type over* S is an expression of the form

$$s_1 \times \ldots \times s_n \rightarrow s$$

   with $n \geq 0$ and $s_1, \ldots, s_n, s \in S$. We write s instead of $\rightarrow s$.
2. A *sorted signature* is a pair (S, F) consisting of a set of sorts, written as $s, s', \ldots$, and a set of function symbols, written as $f, g, \ldots$, such that every function symbol $f \in F$ has a unique algebraic type over S.

Note that we simply assume every function symbol to have an algebraic type; we don't consider explicitly a function assigning algebraic types to function symbols. If a function symbol f has an algebraic type $s_1 \times \ldots \times s_n \rightarrow s$, then n is said to be the *arity* of f. The arity of a symbol f is denoted by $\mathsf{ar}(f)$.

In order to define terms, we assume a set V of *variables*, written as $x, y, z, \ldots$. We define an *environment* as an ordered list of type declarations of the form $x : s$, with $x \in V$ and s a sort. We say that a variable x is *declared* in Γ if $x : s \in \Gamma$ for some s and we assume that variables are declared at most once.

Definition 5. An expression M is a *typed algebraic term* (also simply called a *term*) over a sorted signature (S, F) if $\Gamma \vdash M : s$ is derivable for some environment Γ and sort s, using the rules given in Table 2.

$\overline{\Gamma, x : s \vdash x : s}$	if $s \in S$
$\dfrac{\Gamma \vdash M_1 : s_1 \quad \dots \quad \Gamma \vdash M_n : s_n}{\Gamma \vdash f(M_1, \dots, M_n) : s}$	if $f : s_1 \times \dots \times s_n \to s$

Table 2. TYPED ALGEBRAIC TERMS OVER (S, F)

Rewrite rules of a typed term rewriting system are defined as follows. Here $var(M)$ denotes the set of variables occurring in M.

Definition 6. Let (S, F) be a sorted signature. A *rewrite rule over* (S, F) is a pair of terms over (S, F), written as $l \to r$, such that

1. for every environment Γ, we have $\Gamma \vdash l : A$ implies $\Gamma \vdash r : A$,
2. $l \notin V$,
3. $var(r) \subseteq var(l)$.

Now we have collected all ingredients for the definition of a typed term rewriting system.

Definition 7. A *typed term rewriting system* $\mathcal{R}$ is specified by a pair $((S, F), R)$ with

1. (S, F) a sorted signature,
2. R a set of rewrite rules over (S, F).

The *rewrite relation* $\to_{\mathcal{R}}$ of a typed term rewriting system $\mathcal{R} = ((S, F), R)$ is defined as follows. We have $M \to_{\mathcal{R}} N$ if M is a typed algebraic term and there is a context $C[\bullet]$, a substitution θ and a rewrite rule $l \to r \in R$ such that $M = C[l\theta]$ and $N = C[r\theta]$. Here a context is a term with a unique occurrence of a special constant $\bullet$, and $C[M]$ denotes the result of replacing $\bullet$ in $C[\bullet]$ by M. Substitutions are supposed to preserve the typing.

We will assume the reader to be familiar with well-known properties of (untyped) term rewriting system, which can be found in [22, 23]. In the following, we will often simply say 'term rewriting system' instead of 'typed term rewriting system'.

Morphisms of Sorted Signatures. In the sequel, we shall use mappings that preserve the structure of sorted signatures. These mappings are defined as follows.

Definition 8. Let (S, F) and (S', F') be sorted signatures. A sorted signature morphism between (S, F) and (S', F') is a pair of mappings $\psi = (\psi_1, \psi_2)$ with

$$\psi_1 : S \to S'$$
$$\psi_2 : F \to F'$$

such that for every $f : s_1 \times \dots \times s_n \to s$ in (S, F), we have $\psi_2(f) : \psi_1(s_1) \times \dots \times \psi_1(s_n) \to \psi_1(s)$ in (S', R').

2.3 Algebraic Type Systems

The definition we present in this subsection is equivalent to the one given in [9] and inspired from [4, 7]. An algebraic type system is a combination of a pure type system and a typed term rewriting system. In order to define the combination, we need to specify how sorts are embedded into universes. This is the purpose of the embedding axioms EA below.

Definition 9. An *algebraic type system* is specified by a triple $\mathcal{S} +_{EA} \mathcal{R}$ consisting of

1. a pure type system $\mathcal{S} = (U, TA, TR)$,
2. a typed term rewriting system $\mathcal{R} = ((S, F), R)$,
3. a set of embedding axioms $EA \subseteq S \times U$ such that for every $s \in S$ there exists a $u \in U$ such that $(s, u) \in EA$.

In the sequel, we let $\mathsf{codom}(EA)$ denote the set of $u \in U$ such that there exists an $s \in S$ with $(s, u) \in EA$. Usually, e.g. in the algebraic λ-cube, $\mathsf{codom}(EA)$ is a singleton, but it is not necessarily desirable that all sorts live in the same universe. For instance, one could have a typed term rewriting system with sorts nat for natural numbers and ord for ordinals, and relate them to universes set and class in a pure type system by declaring $\mathsf{nat} : \mathsf{set}$ and $\mathsf{ord} : \mathsf{class}$.

In the remainder of this subsection consider an algebraic type system $\mathcal{A} = \mathcal{S} +_{EA} \mathcal{R}$ with $\mathcal{S} = (U, TA, TR)$ and $\mathcal{R} = ((S, F), R)$.

Definition 10.

1. The set T of *pseudo-terms* of $\mathcal{A}$ is defined as follows:
$$T ::= V \mid U \mid S \mid \Pi V : T.T \mid \lambda V : T.T \mid TT \mid f(T, \ldots, T)$$
where $f \in F$ and the arity of f is respected.
2. The rules used to form derivable judgements of $\mathcal{A}$ are parametrised over a rewrite relation $\rightarrow_{\mathcal{C}}$ on the set of pseudo-terms of $\mathcal{A}$. They are given in Table 3.
3. A pseudo-term M is said to be a *$\mathcal{C}$-legal term* if there exist an environment Γ and a pseudo-term A such that $\Gamma \vdash_{\mathcal{C}} M : A$ is a derivable judgement. The set of $\mathcal{C}$-legal terms is denoted by $\mathcal{L}(\mathcal{A}, \mathcal{C})$.

Traditionally, the rewrite relation considered for algebraic type systems is the union of β-reduction with algebraic reduction. It is defined as follows.

Definition 11.

1. The β-rewrite relation $\rightarrow_\beta$ is defined as the compatible closure of

$$(\lambda x : A.M)N \rightarrow M[x := N]$$

2. The algebraic rewrite relation $\rightarrow_\mathcal{R}$ is defined by $M \rightarrow_\mathcal{R} N$ if there exists a context $C[\bullet]$, a substitution θ and a rewrite rule $l \rightarrow r$ such that $M = C[l\theta]$ and $N = C[r\theta]$.

axiom	$\dfrac{}{\vdash_C s : s'}$	if $(s, s') \in TA \cup EA$
start	$\dfrac{\Gamma \vdash_C A : s}{\Gamma, x : A \vdash_C x : A}$	if $x \notin \Gamma$, $x \in V$
weakening	$\dfrac{\Gamma \vdash_C t : A \quad \Gamma \vdash_C B : s}{\Gamma, x : B \vdash_C t : A}$	if $x \notin \Gamma$, $x \in V$
product	$\dfrac{\Gamma \vdash_C A : s_1 \quad \Gamma, x : A \vdash_C B : s_2}{\Gamma \vdash_C \Pi x : A.B : s_3}$	if $(s_1, s_2, s_3) \in TR$
application	$\dfrac{\Gamma \vdash_C t : \Pi x : A.B \quad \Gamma \vdash_C u : A}{\Gamma \vdash_C t\ u : B[u/x]}$	
abstraction	$\dfrac{\Gamma, x : A \vdash_C t : B \quad \Gamma \vdash_C (\Pi x : A.B) : s}{\Gamma \vdash_C \lambda x : A.t : \Pi x : A.B}$	
function	$\dfrac{\Gamma \vdash_C M_1 : \sigma_1 \quad \ldots \quad \Gamma \vdash_C M_n : \sigma_n}{\Gamma \vdash_C f(M_1, \ldots, M_n) : \tau}$	if $f : \sigma_1 \times \ldots \times \sigma_n \rightarrow \tau$
conversion	$\dfrac{\Gamma \vdash_C u : A \quad \Gamma \vdash_C B : s}{\Gamma \vdash_C u : B}$	if $A \downarrow_C B$

Table 3. ALGEBRAIC PURE TYPE SYSTEMS

3. The rewrite relation $\rightarrow_{mix}$ is defined as $\rightarrow_{mix} = \rightarrow_\beta \cup \rightarrow_\mathcal{R}$.

In the sequel, we will make use of the following well-known definition.

Definition 12. Let $\rightarrow_C$ and $\rightarrow_D$ be rewrite relations on the set of pseudo-terms of $\mathcal{A}$. Then $\mathcal{L}(\mathcal{A}, C)$ is said to *have the subject reduction property for* $\rightarrow_D$ is for every $M \in \mathcal{L}(\mathcal{A}, C)$ we have that $\Gamma \vdash_C M : A$ and $M \rightarrow_D N$ implies $\Gamma \vdash_C N : A$.

Morphisms of Algebraic Type Systems. We define a morphism between algebraic type systems as a pair consisting of a morphism of pure type systems and a morphism of signatures.

Definition 13. Let $\mathcal{A} = \mathcal{S} +_{EA} \mathcal{R}$ and $\mathcal{A}' = \mathcal{S}' +_{EA'} \mathcal{R}'$ be algebraic type systems. An algebraic type system morphism between $\mathcal{A}$ and $\mathcal{A}'$ is a pair of mappings $\phi + \psi$ such that

1. $\phi : \mathcal{S} \rightarrow \mathcal{S}'$ is a pure type systems morphism,
2. $\psi = (\psi_1, \psi_2) : (S, F) \rightarrow (S', F')$ is a sorted signature morphism,
3. if $(s, u) \in EA$, then $(\psi_1(s), \phi(u)) \in EA'$.

Every morphism $\phi + \psi$ of algebraic type systems from $\mathcal{A}$ to $\mathcal{A}'$ can be extended homomorphically into a map from the set of $\mathcal{A}$-pseudo-terms into the set of $\mathcal{A}'$-pseudo-terms. By abuse of notation, we denote this map by $\phi + \psi$.

3 Techniques

In this section we present two techniques that can be used to derive termination of an algebraic type system $\mathcal{A} = \mathcal{S} +_{EA} \mathcal{R}$ from termination of $\mathcal{S}$ and $\mathcal{R}$. First we briefly comment on which problems occur.

A first problem is caused by the fact that an algebraic type system might have more terms than its underlying pure type system because of the conversion rule. So if $\mathcal{A} = \mathcal{S} +_{EA} \mathcal{R}$, then $\mathcal{L}(\mathcal{A}, mix)$ is not necessarily contained in $\mathcal{L}(\mathcal{S}, \beta)$. As a consequence, we cannot immediately conclude termination of $\rightarrow_\beta$ on $\mathcal{L}(\mathcal{A}, mix)$ from termination of $\rightarrow_\beta$ on $\mathcal{L}(\mathcal{S}, \beta)$.

Second, a well-known result originally due to Klop [21] (see also [11]) states that the rewrite relation $\rightarrow_{mix}$ is not necessarily confluent on the set of pseudo-terms of an algebraic type system. As a consequence, the traditional proof of subject reduction of $\mathcal{L}(\mathcal{A}, mix)$ for $\rightarrow_\beta$ breaks down [4, 9].

A third problem is how to infer termination of $\rightarrow_\mathcal{R}$ on some set of terms of an algebraic type system from termination of $\mathcal{R}$. This is discussed in Section 4.

3.1 Termination by Translation

A well-known technique to show termination of a rewriting system $(A_1, \rightarrow_1)$ is to map it into a terminating rewriting system $(A_2, \rightarrow_2)$ such that one step in the former corresponds to at least one step in the latter. In this subsection, we extend this technique to the case of algebraic type systems. Then the mapping should not only preserve the rewrite relation but should also map a derivable judgement to a derivable judgement. We have the following result; its proof is very easy and is omitted.

Proposition 14. *Let $\mathcal{A} = \mathcal{S} +_{EA} \mathcal{R}$ and $\mathcal{A}' = \mathcal{S}' +_{EA'} \mathcal{R}'$ be algebraic type systems. Let $\rightarrow_{\mathcal{C}}, \rightarrow_{\mathcal{D}}$ be rewrite relations on the set of pseudo-terms of $\mathcal{A}$ and let $\rightarrow_{\mathcal{C}'}, \rightarrow_{\mathcal{D}'}$ be rewrite relations on the set of pseudo-terms of $\mathcal{A}'$. Let $\phi + \psi : \mathcal{A} \rightarrow \mathcal{A}'$ be a morphism of algebraic type systems.*

1. *Suppose that for all pseudo-terms M and N in $\mathcal{A}$, we have*
   (a) $M \downarrow_{\mathcal{C}} N$ implies $(\phi + \psi)(M) \downarrow_{\mathcal{C}'} (\phi + \psi)(N)$,
   (b) $M \rightarrow_{\mathcal{D}} N$ implies $(\phi + \psi)(M) \rightarrow^{+}_{\mathcal{D}'} (\phi + \psi)(N)$.
   Then termination of $(\mathcal{L}(\mathcal{A}', \mathcal{C}'), \rightarrow_{\mathcal{D}'})$ implies termination of $(\mathcal{L}(\mathcal{A}, \mathcal{C}), \rightarrow_{\mathcal{D}})$.
2. *If in addition we have that for all pseudo-terms M and N in $\mathcal{A}$, $M \rightarrow_{\mathcal{E}} N$ implies $(\phi + \psi)(M) \rightarrow^{*}_{\mathcal{E}'} (\phi + \psi)(N)$, for a rewrite relation $\rightarrow_{\mathcal{E}}$ on the set of pseudo-terms of $\mathcal{A}$ and a rewrite relation $\rightarrow_{\mathcal{E}'}$ on the set of pseudo-terms of $\mathcal{A}'$, then we have that termination of $\mathcal{D}'$ relative to $\mathcal{E}'$ on $\mathcal{L}(\mathcal{A}', \mathcal{C}')$ implies termination of $\mathcal{D}$ relative to $\mathcal{E}$ on $\mathcal{L}(\mathcal{A}, \mathcal{C})$*

We stress that one of the purposes of the present paper is not to show that termination by translation is a technique to infer termination, because this is of course well-known, but to show that Proposition 14 has useful applications.

3.2 Termination by Stability

In this subsection we present a second technique to infer termination of an algebraic type system: termination by stability. The principle of this technique is due to Dougherty. He shows in [16] that termination of $\rightarrow_{\beta} \cup \rightarrow_{\mathcal{R}}$ follows from termination of $\rightarrow_{\beta}$ and termination of $\rightarrow_{\mathcal{R}}$, provided that we restrict attention to a set of *stable terms*. Stability is in fact an abstract form of typing, and Dougherty's result is obtained for untyped λ-calculus. In this subsection we adapt Dougherty's result to the case of algebraic type systems. Instead of making use of a generalisation of the notion of stability, adapted to the case of algebraic type systems, we will make use of a similar notion which we call *preservation of sorts*. It is defined as follows.

Definition 15. Let $\mathcal{A} = \mathcal{S} +_{EA} \mathcal{R}$ be an algebraic type system and let $\rightarrow_{\mathcal{C}}$ be a rewrite relation on the set of pseudo-terms of $\mathcal{A}$.

1. Two pseudo-terms M and N are said to be *$\mathcal{C}$-legally convertible* if there is an environment Γ and a sequence of terms $P_1, \ldots, P_n$ such that $\Gamma \vdash_{\mathcal{C}} P_i : s$ for every $i \in \{1, \ldots, n\}$ and
$$M \downarrow_{\mathcal{C}} P_1 \downarrow_{\mathcal{C}} \ldots \downarrow_{\mathcal{C}} P_n \downarrow_{\mathcal{C}} N.$$
2. $\mathcal{L}(\mathcal{A}, \mathcal{C})$ has *preservation of sorts* if no two sorts are $\mathcal{C}$-legally convertible and no sort is $\mathcal{C}$-legally convertible with a pseudo-term of the form $\Pi x : A.B$.

Preservation of sorts plays a rôle similar to arity-checking in [16]. In [4], it is proved that an algebraic type system obtained by a λ-calculus from the λ-cube with a term rewriting system enjoys preservation of sorts.

Preservation of sorts is used to show that algebraic reduction preserves β-normal forms.

Lemma 16. *Let $A = S +_{EA} R$ be an algebraic type system that has preservation of sorts. Let M be a β-normal form with $M \to_R M'$. Then M' is a β-normal form as well.*

Proof. First, let $l \to r$ be a rewrite rule of R and suppose that $l\theta$ is in β-normal form. We show that $r\theta$ is in β-normal form as well. To start with, since r consists only of function symbols of R and variables, there are no β-redexes in the r-part of $r\theta$. Further, there are no β-redexes in the θ-part of $r\theta$, since all variables occurring in r occur also in l and $l\theta$ is supposed to be in β-normal form. Finally, there are no β-redexes 'on the border between r and θ' in $r\theta$, since no sort s is β-convertible to a term of the form $\Pi y : A.B$, so neither l nor r has a subterm of the form xP.

Then we can proceed by induction on $C[\bullet]$ to prove that $C[l\theta]$ is in β-normal form implies that $C[r\theta]$ is in β-normal form. In the induction also preservation of types is used.

In the proof of the main result of this section, Theorem 19, we make use of a lemma concerning reduction diagrams. In these diagrams, we make use of complete developments of the set of all β-redexes in a term. The result of performing such a complete development in a term M is defined inductively as follows.

Definition 17. The term M^* is inductively defined as follows.

1. $(aM_1 \ldots M_n)^* = aM_1^* \ldots M_n^*$ with $a \in V \cup U \cup S$ and $n \geq 0$,
2. $(\lambda x : P.M)^* = \lambda x : P^*.M^*$,
3. $(\Pi x : P.Q)^* = \Pi x : P^*.Q^*$,
4. $((\lambda x : Q.M)NP_1 \ldots P_n)^* = M^*[x := N^*]P_1^* \ldots P_n^*$ with $n \geq 0$,
5. $f(M_1, \ldots, M_n)^* = f(M_1^*, \ldots, M_n^*)$ with $n \geq 0$.

We will make use of the following diagrams.

Lemma 18. *1. If $M \to_\beta N$, then $M^* \to_\beta^* N^*$. In a diagram:*

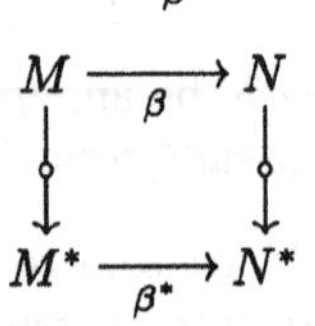

$$
\begin{array}{ccc}
M & \xrightarrow{\beta} & N \\
\downarrow & & \downarrow \\
M^* & \xrightarrow{\beta^*} & N^*
\end{array}
$$

2. If $M \to_R N$, then $M \to_R^* N^*$. In a diagram:

$$
\begin{array}{ccc}
M & \xrightarrow{R} & N \\
\downarrow & & \downarrow \\
M^* & \xrightarrow{R^*} & N^*
\end{array}
$$

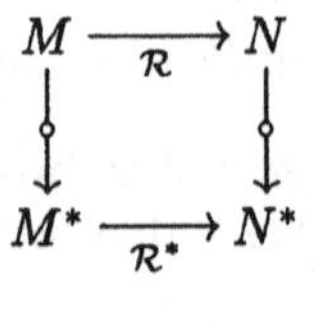

If the step $M \to_{\mathcal{R}} N$ takes place at position ϵ, then $M' = N'$.

Now we present the theorem which is the core of the termination by stability method.

Theorem 19. *Let $\mathcal{A} = \mathcal{S} +_{EA} \mathcal{R}$ be an algebraic type system. Suppose that*

1. *$\mathcal{L}(\mathcal{A}, \mathcal{C})$ has the subject reduction property for $\to_{mix}$,*
2. *$\mathcal{L}(\mathcal{A}, \mathcal{C})$ has preservation of sorts*
3. *$(\mathcal{L}(\mathcal{A}, \mathcal{C}), \to_\beta)$ is terminating,*
4. *$(\mathcal{L}(\mathcal{A}, \mathcal{C}), \to_{\mathcal{R}})$ is terminating.*

Then $(\mathcal{L}(\mathcal{A}, \mathcal{C}), \to_{mix})$ is terminating.

Proof. Let $M \in \mathcal{L}(\mathcal{A}, \mathcal{C})$. We prove that M is terminating with respect to $\to_{mix}$ by induction on the maximal length of a β-rewrite sequence starting in M, denoted by $\mathsf{maxred}_\beta(M)$.

1. $\mathsf{maxred}_\beta(M) = 0$. Let σ be a rewrite sequence starting in M. By Lemma 16 σ is of the form
$$\sigma : M = M_0 \to_{\mathcal{R}} M_1 \to_{\mathcal{R}} M_2 \to_{\mathcal{R}} \cdots.$$
By hypothesis 4, σ is finite.
2. $\mathsf{maxred}_\beta(M) > 0$. We proceed by induction on M, only the two difficult cases are treated here.
   (a) $M = (\lambda x : A.P)QQ_1 \ldots Q_n$ with $n \geq 0$. Let $\sigma : M = M_0 \to_{mix} M_1 \to_{mix} M_2 \to_{mix} \cdots$ be a rewrite sequence starting in M. Two cases are distinguished.
      i. Every term in σ is of the form $(\lambda x : A'.P')Q'Q'_1 \ldots Q'_n$ with $A \to^*_{mix} A', P \to^*_{mix} P', Q \to^*_{mix} Q', Q_i \to^*_{mix} Q'_i$. Then σ is finite by the induction hypothesis on M.
      ii. There is a k such that $M_k = (\lambda x : A'.P')Q'Q'_1 \ldots Q'_m$ and $M_{k+1} = P'[x := Q']Q'_1 \ldots Q'_m$. Now M_{k+1} is a *mix*-reduct of $M' = P[x := Q]Q_1 \ldots Q_m$. By the induction hypothesis on $\mathsf{maxred}_\beta(M)$, M' is terminating and hence σ is finite.
   (b) $M = f(M_1, \ldots, M_n)$. Let $\sigma : M = M_0 \to_{mix} M_1 \to_{mix} M_2 \to_{mix} \cdots$ be a rewrite sequence starting in M. Using Lemma 18 we build a rewrite sequence σ^* starting in M^* as follows:
$$\begin{array}{lccccccc} \sigma : & M_0 & \xrightarrow[mix]{} & M_1 & \xrightarrow[mix]{} & M_2 & \xrightarrow[mix]{} & \cdots \\ & \downarrow & & \downarrow & & \downarrow & & \\ \sigma^* & M_0^* & \xrightarrow[mix]{} & M_1^* & \xrightarrow[mix]{} & M_2^* & \xrightarrow[mix]{} & \cdots \end{array}$$
   Since clearly $\mathsf{maxred}_\beta(M^*) < \mathsf{maxred}_\beta(M)$ if M is not in β-normal form, the induction hypothesis on $\mathsf{maxred}_\beta(M)$ yields that σ^* must be finite. Therefore, there is a k such that for every $l \geq k$ every redex contracted in $M_l \to_{mix} M_{l+1}$ is in a subterm Q_1 of a subterm $(\lambda x : B.Q_0)Q_1$ of M_l. The subterm $(\lambda x : A.Q_0)Q_1$ is a subterm of a reduct of a subterm of M and hence by the induction hypothesis terminating.

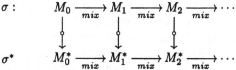

Note that we need preservation of sorts in order to be able to apply Lemma 16. Further, we use the properties that a subterm of a term in $\mathcal{L}(\mathcal{A},\mathcal{C})$ is in $\mathcal{L}(\mathcal{A},\mathcal{C})$ and that a $\rightarrow_{mix}$-reduct of a term in $\mathcal{L}(\mathcal{A},\mathcal{C})$ is in $\mathcal{L}(\mathcal{A},\mathcal{C})$. Indeed, subject reduction of $\mathcal{L}(\mathcal{A},\mathcal{C})$ for $\rightarrow_{mix}$ is crucial.

4 Algebraic Reduction

In order to show termination of $(\mathcal{L}(\mathcal{A}, mix), \rightarrow_{mix})$ for some algebraic type system $\mathcal{A} = \mathcal{S} +_{EA} \mathcal{R}$, we need to show in particular that $\rightarrow_{\mathcal{R}}$ is terminating on $\mathcal{L}(\mathcal{A}, mix)$. As already mentioned in the introduction, this is not guaranteed by termination of $\mathcal{R}$ only. In this section we present two results concerning termination of $\rightarrow_{\mathcal{R}}$ on some set of terms in an algebraic type system.

If a typed term rewriting system $\mathcal{R}$ is terminating, then it is not necessarily the case that its untyped version $\mathcal{E}(\mathcal{R})$, which is obtained by erasing all information concerning the sorts, is terminating. A counterexample is for instance an adaptation of the counterexample by Toyama, showing that termination is not a modular property of term rewriting system, see [25]. Now the difficulties can simply be avoided by considering term rewriting systems that are persistently terminating. A typed term rewriting system $\mathcal{R}$ is said to be ***persistently terminating*** is its untyped version $\mathcal{E}(\mathcal{R})$ is also terminating.

It is quite easy to see that if a term rewriting system $\mathcal{R}$ is persistently terminating, meaning that also $\mathcal{E}(\mathcal{R})$ is terminating, then $\rightarrow_{\mathcal{R}}$ is terminating on the set of pseudo-terms of an algebraic type system of the form $\mathcal{A} = \mathcal{S} +_{EA} \mathcal{R}$, as follows. We assume that the single sorted term rewriting system $\mathcal{E}(\mathcal{R})$ is terminating. Now we extend the signature of $\mathcal{E}(\mathcal{R})$ with fresh symbols δ of arity 0, and $\underline{\Pi}$, $\underline{\lambda}$, Appl of arity 2. Note that this extension $\mathcal{E}(\mathcal{R})'$ is still terminating. All pseudo-terms of an algebraic type system $\mathcal{A} = \mathcal{S} +_{EA} \mathcal{R}$ can be mapped to terms of the only sort of $\mathcal{E}(\mathcal{R})$, say s, by means of the following mapping:

$$\begin{aligned}
|a| &= \delta && \text{for } a \in V \cup U \cup S \\
|M\ N| &= \mathsf{App}(|M|, |N|) \\
|\lambda x : A.M| &= \underline{\lambda}(|A|, |M|) \\
|\Pi x : A.B| &= \underline{\Pi}(|A|, |B|) \\
|f(t_1, \ldots, t_n)| &= f(|t_1|, \ldots, |t_n|) && \text{if } f \in F \text{ and } \mathsf{ar}(f) = n
\end{aligned}$$

Since this mapping preserves the one-step rewrite relation, it follows that $\rightarrow_{\mathcal{R}}$ is terminating on the set of pseudo-terms.

Now the question is which terminating term rewriting systems are persistently terminating. An answer to this question is given by Zantema, who shows in [25] that termination is a persistent property both for non-collapsing and for non-duplicating term rewriting systems. Using the observation above, we have the following corollary of Zantema's result. It will be used in Section 5 to show that under certain conditions the combination of a terminating pure type system and a terminating and non-collapsing term rewriting system is terminating.

Theorem 20. *Let $\mathcal{A} = \mathcal{S} +_{EA} \mathcal{R}$ be an algebraic type system such that:*

1. $\mathcal{R}$ is terminating,
2. $\mathcal{R}$ is either non-collapsing or non-duplicating.

Then $\rightarrow_{\mathcal{R}}$ is terminating on the set of pseudo-terms of $\mathcal{A}$.

Another way to obtain termination of $\rightarrow_{\mathcal{R}}$ on some set of terms of an algebraic type system $\mathcal{A} = \mathcal{S} +_{EA} \mathcal{R}$ is by instead of imposing restrictions on $\mathcal{R}$ imposing restrictions on $\mathcal{A}$. Using the techniques sketched above, the following result can be obtained; for lack of space the proof is omitted.

Theorem 21. *Let $\mathcal{A} = \mathcal{S} +_{EA} \mathcal{R}$ be an algebraic type system such that*

1. $\mathcal{L}(\mathcal{A}, C)$ has preservation of sorts,
2. $\mathcal{L}(\mathcal{A}, C)$ has the subject reduction property for $\rightarrow_{\mathcal{R}}$,
3. $\mathcal{R}$ is terminating.

Then $(\mathcal{L}(\mathcal{A}, C), \rightarrow_{\mathcal{R}})$ is terminating.

This result will be used in Section 5 in order to show that the combination of a terminating pure type system without dependent types and a terminating term rewriting system is terminating.

5 Applications

In this section we apply the methods presented in Section 3 to several situations of interest.

5.1 Non-dependent Algebraic Type Systems

In this subsection we consider a restricted class of algebraic type systems where only β-reduction, not *mix*-reduction, is used in the conversion rule. So the set of legal terms we consider is of the form $\mathcal{L}(\mathcal{A}, \beta)$. If we have that the set of legal terms $\mathcal{L}(\mathcal{A}, \beta)$ has the subject reduction property for $\rightarrow_{\mathcal{R}}$, then the termination by stability method can be presented in a somewhat simpler form. This is expressed in the following proposition.

Proposition 22. *Let $\mathcal{A} = \mathcal{S} +_{EA} \mathcal{R}$ be an algebraic type system and suppose that:*

1. $\mathcal{L}(\mathcal{A}, \beta)$ has the subject reduction property for $\rightarrow_{\mathcal{R}}$,
2. $(\mathcal{L}(\mathcal{S}, \beta), \rightarrow_{\beta})$ is terminating,
3. $\mathcal{R}$ is terminating.

Then $(\mathcal{L}(\mathcal{A}, \beta), \rightarrow_{mix})$ is terminating.

Proof. First, since $\mathcal{L}(\mathcal{S}, \beta)$ has the subject reduction property for $\rightarrow_{\beta}$, it follows easily that $\mathcal{L}(\mathcal{A}, \beta)$ has the subject reduction property for $\rightarrow_{\beta}$. Because moreover we have by hypothesis that $\mathcal{L}(\mathcal{A}, \beta)$ has the subject reduction property for $\rightarrow_{\mathcal{R}}$, we can conclude that $\mathcal{L}(\mathcal{A}, \beta)$ has the subject reduction property for $\rightarrow_{mix}$. Second, $\mathcal{L}(\mathcal{A}, \beta)$ has preservation of sorts. Third, termination of $(\mathcal{L}(\mathcal{A}, \beta), \rightarrow_{\beta})$ follows from termination of $(\mathcal{L}(\mathcal{S}, \beta), \rightarrow_{\beta})$. Fourth, we have by Theorem 21 that $(\mathcal{L}(\mathcal{A}, \beta), \rightarrow_{\mathcal{R}})$ is terminating.

Hence we can by Theorem 19 conclude that $(\mathcal{L}(\mathcal{A}, \beta), \rightarrow_{mix})$ is terminating.

Non-dependent λ-calculi. We obtain a useful corollary of Proposition 22 by applying it to the case that the pure type system of the algebraic type system is a λ-calculus with non-dependent types, for instance a λ-calculus in the left plane of the λ-cube, and all sorts are declared to live in $\star$.

Corollary 23. *Let $\mathcal{A} = \mathcal{S} +_{EA} \mathcal{R}$ be an algebraic type system such that:*

1. *$\mathcal{S}$ is $\lambda \rightarrow$, $\lambda 2$ or $\lambda\omega$,*
2. $\mathsf{codom}(EA) = \{\star\}$,
3. *$\mathcal{R}$ is terminating.*

Then $(\mathcal{L}(\mathcal{A}, \beta), \rightarrow_{mix})$ is terminating.

Proof. Let $\mathcal{S}$ be $\lambda \rightarrow$, $\lambda 2$ or $\lambda\omega$. It can be shown that $\Gamma \vdash_\beta l\theta : A$ implies $\Gamma \vdash_\beta r\theta : A$. Then, since there are no rewrite steps in the types, and we have $s : \star$ for every sort s, we can show by induction on the context that $\Gamma \vdash_\beta C[l\theta] : A$ implies $\Gamma \vdash_\beta C[r\theta] : A$. This yields that $\mathcal{L}(\mathcal{A}, \beta)$ has the subject reduction property for $\rightarrow_\mathcal{R}$. termination of $(\mathcal{L}(\mathcal{A}, \beta), \rightarrow_\beta)$ follows from termination of $(\mathcal{L}(\mathcal{S}, \beta), \rightarrow_\beta)$. We can conclude by Proposition 22 that $(\mathcal{L}(\mathcal{A}, \beta), \rightarrow_{mix})$ is terminating.

η. An inspection of the proof of Corollary 23 yields that we have the same result for the combination of a λ-calculus in the left plane of the cube with $\beta\eta$-reduction, and a terminating term rewriting system. The η-reduction relation, denoted by $\rightarrow_\eta$, is defined as the smallest compatible closure of

$$\lambda x : A.Mx \rightarrow M$$

with the side-condition that x has no free occurrence in M. If $\mathcal{A} = \mathcal{S} +_{EA} \mathcal{R}$, then we denote by $\rightarrow_{mix_\eta}$ the rewrite relation $\rightarrow_\beta \cup \rightarrow_\eta \cup \rightarrow_\mathcal{R}$. We have the following result.

Corollary 24. *Let $\mathcal{A} = \mathcal{S} +_{EA} \mathcal{R}$ be an algebraic type system such that:*

1. *$\mathcal{S}$ is $\lambda \rightarrow$, $\lambda 2$ or $\lambda\omega$,*
2. $\mathsf{codom}(EA) = \{\star\}$,
3. *$\mathcal{R}$ is terminating.*

Then $(\mathcal{L}(\mathcal{A}, \beta\eta), \rightarrow_{mix_\eta})$ is terminating.

For $\lambda \rightarrow$ and $\lambda 2$, a similar result for the union of β-reduction, η-expansion and algebraic reduction can be obtained.

5.2 Non-collapsing Term Rewrite Rules

In this subsection we consider combinations of a pure type system and term rewriting system without collapsing rules. Throughout this section, we assume an algebraic type system $\mathcal{A} = \mathcal{S} +_{EA} \mathcal{R}$ with $\mathcal{R}$ a non-collapsing term rewriting system. Recall that a rewrite rule is said to be collapsing if it is of the form $l \rightarrow x$

with $x \in V$. We will suppose that for every sort s in a term rewriting system there is a distinguished constant c_s of sort s. This is not a serious restriction.

We denote by $\mathcal{R}'$ the term rewriting system $\mathcal{R}$ extended with a rewrite rule

$$f(x_1, \ldots, x_n) \to c_s$$

for every function symbol $f : s_1 \times \ldots \times s_n \to s$ in $\mathcal{R}$. Further, we denote by $\to_{mix'}$ the rewrite relation $\to_\beta \cup \to_{\mathcal{R}'}$ which is defined on the set of pseudo-terms of $\mathcal{A}$ and on the set of pseudo-terms of $\mathcal{S} +_{EA} \mathcal{R}'$.

Now the termination by stability method can be presented in a slightly more simple way. For the proof, we need $(\mathcal{L}(\mathcal{A}, mix'), \to_\beta)$ to be terminating. This follows from termination of $(\mathcal{L}(\mathcal{S}, \beta), \to_\beta)$ by the termination by translation method, provided that $\mathcal{S}$ has enough axioms and enough products, which can be enforced in a rather crude way by requiring $\mathcal{A}$ to be regular, a property that is defined as follows.

Definition 25. An algebraic type system $\mathcal{A} = \mathcal{S} +_{EA} \mathcal{R}$ is said to be *regular* if the following two conditions are satisfied:

1. Universes are connected, that is: for every $u \in U$ there exists $u' \in U$ such that either $(u, u') \in TA$ or $(u', u) \in TA$.
2. Universes which contain an algebraic sort have products, that is: for all $s_1, s_2 \in \mathsf{codom}(EA)$ there exists $s_3 \in \mathsf{codom}(EA)$ such that $(s_1, s_2, s_3) \in TR$.

Regularity is closely related to the notion of fullness for pure type systems. We have the following result.

Proposition 26. *Let $\mathcal{A} = \mathcal{S} +_{EA} \mathcal{R}$ be an algebraic type system such that:*

1. $\mathcal{S}$ is regular,
2. $(\mathcal{L}(\mathcal{S}, \beta), \to_\beta)$ is terminating,
3. $\mathcal{R}$ is non-collapsing,
4. $\mathcal{R}$ is terminating.

Then $(\mathcal{L}(\mathcal{A}, mix), \to_{mix})$ is terminating.

Proof. Let $\mathcal{A} = \mathcal{S} +_{EA} \mathcal{R}$ be an algebraic type system and assume that $\mathcal{R}$ is a non-collapsing term rewriting system. We can show that the rewrite relation $\to_{mix'}$ is confluent on the set of pseudo-terms of $\mathcal{A}$, by projecting a rewrite sequence to one where the algebraic part is replaced by constants c_s. As a consequence, we obtain that $\mathcal{L}(\mathcal{A}, mix')$ has the subject reduction property for $\to_{mix}$, and that $\mathcal{L}(\mathcal{A}, mix')$ has preservation of sorts.

Since $\mathcal{R}$ is terminating and non-collapsing, we have by Theorem 20 that the rewrite relation $\to_{\mathcal{R}}$ is terminating on the set of pseudo-terms of $\mathcal{A}$.

Using regularity, we can show using similar techniques to the one presented in [8], that termination of $(\mathcal{L}(\mathcal{S}, \beta), \to_\beta)$ implies termination of $(\mathcal{L}(\mathcal{A}, mix'), \to_\beta)$.

It then follows by Theorem 19 that $(\mathcal{L}(\mathcal{A}, mix'), \to_{mix})$ is terminating. Hence also the subsystem $(\mathcal{L}(\mathcal{A}, mix), \to_{mix})$ is terminating.

Ground Rewriting. Proposition 26 can be applied to the case where we consider the ground rewriting relation (the rewrite relation restricted to terms without variables) of an arbitrary terminating rewriting system, since the ground rewriting relation can be considered as generated by the infinitely many ground instances of the rewrite rules. A ground instance of a rewrite rule is clearly a non-collapsing rewrite rule. If $\mathcal{A} = \mathcal{S} +_{EA} \mathcal{R}$ is an algebraic type system, then we denote by $\rightarrow_{\mathcal{R}_g}$ the ground rewrite relation of $\mathcal{R}$, and by $\rightarrow_{mix_g}$ the rewrite relation $\rightarrow_\beta \cup \rightarrow_{\mathcal{R}_g}$. We have the following corollary of Proposition 26.

Corollary 27. *Let $\mathcal{A} = \mathcal{S} +_{EA} \mathcal{R}$ be an algebraic type system such that:*

1. *$\mathcal{S}$ is regular,*
2. *$(\mathcal{L}(\mathcal{S}, \beta), \rightarrow_\beta)$ is terminating,*
3. *$\mathcal{R}$ is terminating on ground terms.*

Then $(\mathcal{L}(\mathcal{A}, mix_g), \rightarrow_{mix_g})$ is terminating.

η. Again, the results presented in this subsection can easily be adapted to the case of an algebraic type system with $\beta\eta$-reduction.

5.3 Non-duplicating Term Rewrite Rules

If we consider an algebraic type system $\mathcal{A} = \mathcal{S} +_{EA} \mathcal{R}$ such that $\mathcal{R}$ is non-duplicating, then termination by translation may be applied to obtain several results. Indeed, we can define for every algebraic type system 'universal' algebraic type system such that β-strong normalisation of the latter imply *mix*-strong normalisation of the latter. Then, using termination of translation and postponement techniques, one can prove, provided $\mathcal{R}$ is terminating and non-duplicating, that termination of $\rightarrow_\beta$ in the 'universal' algebraic type system implies termination of $\rightarrow_{mix}$ in $\mathcal{A}$.

This illustrates that, despite its extreme simplicity, Proposition 14 can take us quite some way in the study of termination for algebraic type systems.

6 Concluding Remarks

We have developed purely syntactic methods to prove termination of algebraic type systems. Although we do not establish termination as a modular property of algebraic type systems, our methods yield simple proofs of well-known results as well as new results. Moreover they lead to a better understanding of the interaction between a type system and a rewriting system. In addition, the methods developed in this paper, especially termination by stability, may also be adapted to yield similar results for confluence, extending the 'confluence by stability' result in [16].

The most outstanding question left unanswered is termination of β-reduction for 'universal' algebraic type systems. A positive answer to that question would be a definite step towards modular proofs of strong normalization for algebraic type systems. It would also be interesting to see whether our methods can be adapted to algebraic type systems with higher-order term rewriting à la Jouannaud-Okada [19] or to typed λ-calculi with pattern matching [20].

Finally, the technique of derivation-preserving translations reveals the impossibility of distinguishing in the internal logic of the algebraic type system between two closed algebraic terms of the same type. This is clearly a weakness of algebraic type systems for dependent type theories. Some possible ways to fix this are described in [6, 20] and [10].

Acknowledgements. The diagrams in this paper are designed using the package Xy-pic of Kristoffer H. Rose. We thank the referees for their help in improving the presentation of the paper.

References

1. F. Barbanera and M. Fernández. Combining first and higher order rewrite systems with type assignment systems. In M.Bezem and J.-F. Groote, editors, *Proceedings of TLCA'93*, volume 664 of *Lecture Notes in Computer Science*, pages 60–74. Springer-Verlag, 1993.
2. F. Barbanera and M. Fernández. Modularity of termination and confluence in combinations of rewrite systems with λ_ω. In A. Lingas, R. Karlsson, and S. Karlsson, editors, *Proceedings of ICALP'93*, volume 700 of *Lecture Notes in Computer Science*, pages 657–668. Springer-Verlag, 1993.
3. F. Barbanera and M. Fernández. Intersection type assignment systems with higher-order algebraic rewriting. *Theoretical Computer Science*, 170(1–2):173–207, 15 December 1996.
4. F. Barbanera, M. Fernández, and H. Geuvers. Modularity of strong normalisation and confluence in the algebraic λ-cube. In *Proceedings of LICS'94*, pages 406–415. IEEE Computer Society Press, 1994.
5. H. Barendregt. Lambda calculi with types. In S. Abramsky, D. M. Gabbay, and T.S.E. Maibaum, editors, *Handbook of Logic in Computer Science*, pages 117–309. Oxford Science Publications, 1992. Volume 2.
6. G. Barthe and H. Geuvers. Congruence types. In H. Kleine Buening, editor, *Proceedings of CSL'95*, volume 1092 of *Lecture Notes in Computer Science*, pages 36–51. Springer-Verlag, 1996.
7. G. Barthe and H. Geuvers. Modular properties of algebraic type systems. In G. Dowek, J. Heering, K. Meinke, and B. Möller, editors, *Proceedings of HOA'95*, volume 1074 of *Lecture Notes in Computer Science*, pages 37–56. Springer-Verlag, 1996.
8. G. Barthe, J. Hatcliff, and M.H. Sørensen. Weak Normalization implies Strong Normalization in Generalized Non-Dependent Pure Type Systems. Draft, 1997.
9. G. Barthe and P.-A. Melliès. On the subject reduction property for algebraic type systems. Proceedings of CSL'96. To appear as LNCS, 1996.
10. G. Barthe, M. Ruys, and H. Barendregt. A two-level approach towards lean proof-checking. In S. Berardi and M. Coppo, editors, *Proceedings of TYPES'95*, volume 1158 of *Lecture Notes in Computer Science*, pages 16–35. Springer-Verlag, 1996.

11. V. Breazu-Tannen. Combining algebra and higher-order types. In *Proceedings of LICS'88*, pages 82–90. IEEE Computer Society Press, 1988.
12. V. Breazu-Tannen and J. Gallier. Polymorphic rewriting conserves algebraic strong normalisation. *Theoretical Computer Science*, 83:3–28, 1990.
13. T. Coquand and G. Huet. The Calculus of Constructions. *Information and Computation*, 76(2/3):95–120, February/March 1988.
14. R. Di Cosmo. A brief history of rewriting with extensionality. In F. Kamareddine, editor, *International Summer School on Type Theory and Term Rewriting, Glasgow, September 1996*. Kluwer, 199x. To appear.
15. R. Di Cosmo and D. Kesner. Combining algebraic rewriting, extensional lambda calculi, and fixpoints. *Theoretical Computer Science*, 169(2):201–220, 5 December 1996.
16. D. Dougherty. Adding algebraic rewriting to the untyped lambda calculus. *Information and Computation*, 101:251–267, 1992.
17. M. Fernandez. *Modèles de calcul multiparadigmes fondés sur la réécriture*. PhD thesis, Université Paris-Sud Orsay, 1993.
18. H. Geuvers and M.-J. Nederhof. A modular proof of strong normalisation for the Calculus of Constructions. *Journal of Functional Programming*, 1:155–189, 1991.
19. J.-P. Jouannaud and M. Okada. Executable higher-order algebraic specification languages. In *Proceedings of LICS'91*, pages 350–361. IEEE Computer Society Press, 1991.
20. J.-P. Jouannaud and M. Okada. Abstract data type systems. *Theoretical Computer Science*, 173(2):349–391, 1997.
21. J.W. Klop. *Combinatory reduction systems*. Number 127 in Mathematical Centre Tracts. CWI, 1980.
22. J.W. Klop. Term-rewriting systems. In S. Abramsky, D. M. Gabbay, and T.S.E. Maibaum, editors, *Handbook of Logic in Computer Science*, pages 1–116. Oxford Science Publications, 1992. Volume 2.
23. K. Meinke and J.V. Tucker, editors. *Many sorted logic and its applications*. John Wiley and Sons, 1993.
24. J. van de Pol. *Termination of higher-order rewrite systems*. PhD thesis, University of Utrecht, 1996.
25. H. Zantema. Termination of term rewriting: Interpretation and type elimination. *Journal of Symbolic Computation*, 17(1):23–50, January 1994.

Proof Net Semantics of Proof Search Computation

Luís Caires and Luís Monteiro
{lcaires,lm}@di.fct.unl.pt

Departamento de Informática - Universidade Nova de Lisboa
2825 Monte da Caparica, Portugal

Abstract. We present a sound and complete compositional semantics, structured around certain abstractions of proof nets, for proof-search computation in a linear logic-based language. The model captures the interaction of agents in terms of the actions they engage into and of the dynamic creation of names. The model is adequate for reasoning about a notion of operational equivalence. We will also suggest how a partial order semantics can be derived from the present approach.

1 Introduction

The "proof-search as computation" paradigm, where computational behaviour is extracted from the execution of goal-directed proof-search algorithms for some logic, has received much attention in recent years. The general concept of goal-directed proof search was explained in [16] by the notion of uniform-proof in cut-free sequent calculi for variants of intuitionistic logic, and also by the related notion of focused proof [1] in the more general setting of classical linear logic. Several programming and specification languages were proposed in this setting, either emphasising the deductive (theorem proving or meta-level reasoning) aspects (Forum [15]), or what we might call the reductive ones (for instance, ACL [13]) which are of a more operational nature and inspired by the interpretation of "formulas" as "agents" [14, 13].

In [6] we presented $\mathcal{L}_\pi$, a simple language that supports the reduction and state-oriented style of specification of process calculi without compromising the relational style of specification typical of logic programming. In particular we have shown that both the π-calculus with choice and the logic of (first-order) hereditary Harrop formulas can be adequately encoded into $\mathcal{L}_\pi$. $\mathcal{L}_\pi$ is actually a fragment of classical linear logic, and we argued that the study of its semantics can lead to a better understanding of the relations between proof-search and concurrency. For instance, the proposed transition system semantics clearly distinguishes static (structural congruence) from dynamic (reduction) aspects of proof-search, and shows how these are related to the notions of asynchronous and synchronous proof segments in focused proofs. In [6] we suggested that $\mathcal{L}_\pi$ was designed having in mind that connectives express global interaction patterns, not just proof-search directives; this paper attempts to make precise that remark by defining a compositional semantics for $\mathcal{L}_\pi$ that captures the role of agents *inside proofs* - a proof being a certain successfully completed computation. The interpretation is developed in terms of certain abstractions of proof nets and captures the interaction of agents in terms of the actions they engage into, the dynamic creation of names and the phenomenon of scope extrusion represented by the use of universal quantification [14]. The semantics can also be shown adequate for reasoning about a certain notion of operational equivalence. We will also show that a causality model can be derived from the present approach and relate them to a true concurrent semantics in the form a higher dimensional transition system.

We now explain, from an intuitive viewpoint, the main ideas behind the model. In this preliminary motivation, we assume some familiarity with proof nets for linear logic. In the context of a proof, a $\mathcal{L}_\pi$ agent interacts with the rest of the proof in which it occurs, what might be seen as the environment. These interactions may be local, in the sense that other interactions occurring in the same proof evolve independently or, on the contrary, there might be some causal dependencies involved. These dependencies become clearer if we look at a proof net (instead of at the sequent calculus proof) for a $\mathcal{L}_\pi$ agent as a picture of a particular computation. This observation also suggests an interpretation of agents in terms of their roles inside proof-nets, the main idea being to assign to each agent P a set of proof-structures, each one with a distinguished conclusion P that exhaust the possible behaviours of P inside proofs. What kind of proof structures shall we consider?

Let us consider a proof net π with several conclusions Δ, among them P. Starting from the occurrence P, if we follow the structural order up in the proof net, making some arbitrary choice of premise at intermediary links, we will necessarily arrive at some axiom-link connecting some atomic formulas a and $a^\perp$. Now, either both a and $a^\perp$ are hereditary premises of P or this is not the case. In the first case, the axiom-link can be seen as standing for an internal interaction of P (like a silent action in CCS). In the other case, the axiom-link is also signalling an interaction between complementary messages: however one is originated by P, while the other is caused by the environment. The set of such atomic occurrences at the borderline between the substructure of the proof net rooted at P and the rest of the proof can then be seen as a characterisation of the behaviour of P inside π (let us call ports to those atomic occurrences and a slice to such substructure).

This is but a partial characterisation, for it does not take into account the internal structure of the slice; this structure also constrains its possible contexts of occurrence inside a complete proof. For instance, in the proof structure of Fig.1 (a) we can connect (with axiom links) either a_2 to $a_1^\perp$ (indexes are used to distinguish different occurrences of the same formula) or b_1 to $b_2^\perp$ but not both because in that case the resulting proof structure is not a proof net (there is no sequent calculus proof of $\vdash a^\perp \otimes b, b^\perp \otimes a$). This can be detected by the existence of a cyclic Danos-Regnier (D-R) graph [10], and interpreted intuitively as a violation of causality: P $(a^\perp \otimes b)$ receives from Q $(b^\perp \otimes a)$ a message a that was caused by the sending by P of a message b to Q (this corresponds to a "deadlocked" proof structure in the sense of [2]). Now, we can capture these internal dependencies by a symmetric binary relation $\approx$ between ports such that $a \approx b$ iff there is a path in some D-R graph (a causal chain) connecting a and b.

In the present example, we should have $a_1^\perp \approx b_1$ and $b_2^\perp \approx a_2$. Therefore, since $a_1^\perp \not\approx a_2$ we can connect $a_1^\perp$ and a_2 by an axiom link and get the proof structure where $b_1 \approx b_2^\perp$. But then b_1, cannot be connected to $b_2^\perp$. When quantifiers are considered, dependencies related to occurrences of eigenvariables also arise and the situation gets a little more complex; we illustrate this point with a very simple example. Consider the slice in Fig.1 (b), where the variable $\check{u}$ is an input parameter and $\hat{y}$ is an output parameter. Here, the eigenvariable $\hat{y}$ is classified as an output parameter since its $\forall$-link belongs to the slice. For $\check{u}$, we have the opposite situation (a similar situation takes place in π-calculus when the notions of bound output $\overline{x}(y)$ and bound input $x(y)$ actions must be introduced). Now, if we try to match $b(\hat{y})$ with $b(\check{u})^\perp$ by inputting $\hat{y}$ into $\check{u}$ we immediately get a cycle in the D-R graph. So having $b(\hat{y}) \not\approx b(\check{u})^\perp$ is not enough and we must capture also dependencies among variables, in this example $\hat{x} \approx \check{u}$.

Since proof structures are too concrete syntactic objects for the present purpose, slices and the theory of proof nets will be used only indirectly to develop an "algebra" of interfaces. Therefore, in the interpretation we propose, the denotation $[\![P]\!]$ of a term P consists of a set of triples of the form $(\!|n; m; \approx|\!)$ (interfaces), each one characterising a certain slice $\mathcal{S}$ of P, where n is a set of names involved, m is the multiset of its ports and $\approx$ is a binary relation on $m \cup n$ that describes certain paths in the D-R graphs of $\mathcal{S}$.

The paper is organised as follows: after a brief introduction to $\mathcal{L}_\pi$ in Section 2, in Section 3 we briefly review some notions related to proof-nets in linear logic. After defining the concepts of slice and interface in Section 4 we present in Section 5 the semantics and state its correctness. In the closing Sections 6 and 7 we develop some applications of the model, namely a study of a notion of operational equivalence and an interpretation of causality towards a true concurrent model.

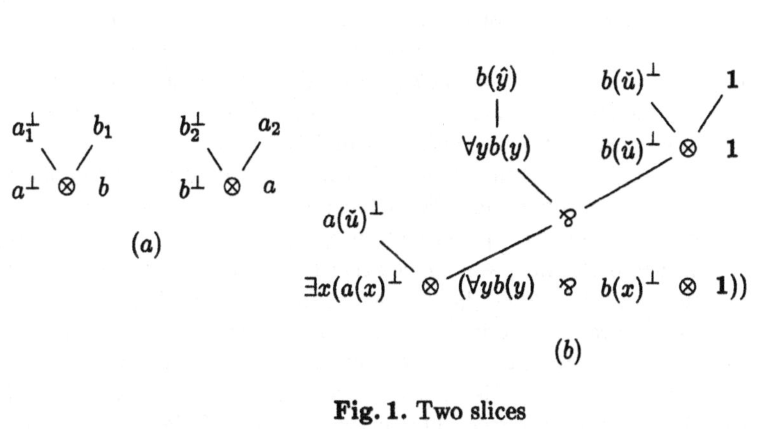

Fig. 1. Two slices

2 Language

We briefly review here the language and operational semantics of $\mathcal{L}_\pi$, see [6, 7] for further details and properties.

Given a denumerable set $\mathcal{V}$ of variables (or names), the set $\mathcal{T}$ of terms is defined inductively as follows: variables are terms, if x is a variable and $t_1, \cdots, t_n$ are terms then $x(t_1, \cdots, t_n)$ is also a term (with head x). Denote by $\mathcal{T}(\Sigma)$ the set of terms whose variables belong to Σ. We will also use $\tilde{x}$, $\tilde{y}$ ... for lists of distinct variables. The notation $\tilde{t}$ stands for a sequence $(t_1, \cdots, t_n)$ of terms or a multiset of terms, depending on the context.

The abstract syntax of raw agents is given by

$$\begin{aligned} P &::= \mathbf{0} \mid P|P \mid \nu x P \mid G \mid !G \mid \tilde{x} \triangleright P \bullet P \\ G &::= a \mid \tilde{x} \triangleright \tilde{a}.P \mid G + G \end{aligned}$$

where x range over $\mathcal{V}$ and a over $\mathcal{T}$. $a \in \mathcal{T}$ can be seen as an elementary message(like $\overline{x}y$ in the asynchronous π-calculus). Parallel composition $|$, choice $+$, replication $!$, restriction ν and inaction $\mathbf{0}$ have essentially the same meaning as in π-calculus. Both νx and $\tilde{x} \triangleright$ are binding prefixes; consider defined a relation $\equiv_\alpha$ of α-equivalence that identifies agents modulo (the names of) their bound variables. To explain input prefix and testing agents we need to introduce substitutions, that is, partial functions from $\mathcal{V}$ to $\mathcal{T}$ with a finite domain; substitutions act on terms and agents as expected. The input prefix agent $\tilde{x} \triangleright \tilde{a}.P$ waits for a message $\tilde{b}$ (a multiset of terms) and then behaves like $\sigma(P)$, if there is a substitution σ with domain $\tilde{x}$ such that $\sigma(\tilde{a}) = \tilde{b}$; $\tilde{b}$ is consumed atomically. The testing agent $\tilde{x} \triangleright Q \bullet P$ behaves like $\sigma(P)$ if the test $\sigma(Q)$ succeeds for some substitution σ with domain $\tilde{x}$. Roughly, a test $\sigma(Q)$ succeeds if there is a computation sequence starting with $\sigma(Q)$ and reaching a success state (defined below). Note that if some variable in the domain of a substitution σ occurs in the head of a subterm of t then $\sigma(t)$ is undefined. To prevent undefined substitutions, we "type" free variables as *rigid*, that is, variables that occur at heads of subterms, and cannot ever be substituted for, and *flexible* (the remaining free variables). The system of Fig.2 considers these distinctions and refines the above syntax of $\mathcal{L}_\pi$. In all judgements, Σ is a set of variables; rigid variables x are tagged as $\hat{x}$. When writing Σ, x we assume $x \notin \Sigma$. We define P to be a Σ-term whenever $\Sigma \blacktriangleright P$ is provable in the system of Fig.2 (the meaning of the auxiliary judgements $\blacktriangleright_g$ - guarded agents -, $\downarrow$ - flexible term -, $\uparrow$ - rigid term and $:$ - sequence of terms - should be clear. $\updownarrow t$ means either $\uparrow t$ or $\downarrow t$).

The concurrent operational semantics of $\mathcal{L}_\pi$ can be presented by the labelled transition system specification in Fig.3. We define structural congruence $\cong$ as the smallest congruence relation over agents containing $\equiv_\alpha$ such that $|$ is associative, commutative and has $\mathbf{0}$ for unit, $+$ is associative and commutative, and closed under the equations $\nu x(P|Q) \cong \nu x P|Q$ if x is not free in Q and $!P|\tilde{x} \triangleright G \bullet R \cong$ $!P|\tilde{x} \triangleright (G|!P) \bullet R$ if $\tilde{x}$ are not free in P. An action α (in labels) is a multiset of terms tagged, as either input action (a) or output action $(\overline{a})$. On complementary actions a and $\overline{b}$ we define synchronisation $a/b = a - b$ if $a \supseteq b$ and $a/b = \overline{b - a}$ if $b \supseteq a$ (where $-$ is multiset difference). On actions α and β of identical polarity,

$$\frac{\Sigma \updownarrow t_1 \cdots \Sigma \updownarrow t_n}{\Sigma : \tilde{t}} \quad \frac{\Sigma : \tilde{t} \ \hat{x} \in \Sigma}{\Sigma \uparrow x\tilde{t}} \quad \frac{x \in \Sigma}{\Sigma \downarrow x} \quad \frac{\Sigma, \hat{x} \blacktriangleright P}{\Sigma \blacktriangleright \nu x P}$$

$$\frac{\Sigma, \tilde{x} \blacktriangleright P \quad \Sigma, \tilde{x} \blacktriangleright Q}{\Sigma \blacktriangleright \tilde{x} \rhd P \bullet Q} \quad \Sigma \blacktriangleright 0 \quad \frac{\Sigma \blacktriangleright_g G}{\Sigma \blacktriangleright !G} \quad \frac{\Sigma \blacktriangleright P \ \Sigma \blacktriangleright Q}{\Sigma \blacktriangleright P|Q} \quad \frac{\Sigma \blacktriangleright_g P}{\Sigma \blacktriangleright P}$$

$$\frac{\Sigma, \tilde{x} \blacktriangleright P \quad \Sigma, \tilde{x} \uparrow a_1 \cdots \Sigma, \tilde{x} \uparrow a_n}{\Sigma \blacktriangleright_g \tilde{x} \rhd \tilde{a}.P} \text{ if } \tilde{x} \subset FV(\tilde{a}) \quad \frac{\Sigma \uparrow x\tilde{t}}{\Sigma \blacktriangleright_g x\tilde{t}} \quad \frac{\Sigma \blacktriangleright_g P \ \ \Sigma \blacktriangleright_g Q}{\Sigma \blacktriangleright_g P + Q}$$

Fig. 2. Syntax of Agents

we define composition $\alpha\beta$ as just the multiset union of the underlying multisets tagged with that same polarity of α and β. The $\surd$ (success state) represents any agent $\cong$-congruent with an agent of the form $\nu\tilde{x}(\mathbf{0}, !\mathbf{P})$. Now, agents are interpreted as formulas of linear logic (*CLLmix*, see Appendix) as follows

$$\begin{array}{llll} \ulcorner \mathbf{0} \urcorner \mapsto & \mathbf{1} & \ulcorner a \urcorner \mapsto & a \\ \ulcorner P|Q \urcorner \mapsto & \ulcorner P \urcorner \invamp \ulcorner Q \urcorner & \ulcorner \nu x P \urcorner \mapsto & \forall x \ulcorner P \urcorner \\ \ulcorner P + Q \urcorner \mapsto & \ulcorner P \urcorner \oplus \ulcorner Q \urcorner & \ulcorner \tilde{x} \rhd P \bullet Q \urcorner \mapsto & \exists \tilde{x}(! \ulcorner P \urcorner \otimes \ulcorner Q \urcorner) \\ \ulcorner !C \urcorner \mapsto & ?\ulcorner C \urcorner \invamp \mathbf{1} & \ulcorner \tilde{x} \rhd \tilde{a}.P \urcorner \mapsto & \exists \tilde{x}(a_1^\perp \otimes \cdots \otimes a_n^\perp \otimes \ulcorner P \urcorner) \end{array}$$

It can then be proved that the system $\mathcal{L}\pi_\rightarrow$ defines linear logic provability in the following sense

Theorem 1 *Let $\Sigma \blacktriangleright P$. Then $\Sigma; P \stackrel{*}{\rightarrow} \surd$ iff $\Sigma \vdash \ulcorner P \urcorner$ is provable in CLLmix.*

In [6] an analogous fact was presented for *CLL* without the rule of MIX. However, this formulation follows from several results therein and a slight simplification of the encoding of agents in *CLLmix* (just replace ?**1** by **1**). This shift is an improvement, since the modelling of independent computations is done in a more natural way. Thus, from now on by linear logic we mean *CLLmix*.

$$[\cong] \ \frac{P \cong P' \quad \tilde{v}; P' \rightarrow Q' \quad Q' \cong Q}{\tilde{v}; P \rightarrow Q}$$

$$[o] \ \tilde{v}; a \stackrel{\bar{a}}{\rightarrow} \mathbf{0} \qquad [i] \ \tilde{v}; \tilde{x} \rhd \tilde{a}.P \stackrel{\sigma(a)}{\rightarrow} \sigma(P) \qquad [\nu] \ \frac{\tilde{v}, x; P \rightarrow P'}{\tilde{v}; \nu x P \rightarrow \nu x P'}$$

$$[s] \ \frac{\tilde{v}; P \stackrel{\alpha}{\rightarrow} P'}{\tilde{v}; P|Q \stackrel{\alpha}{\rightarrow} P'|Q} \qquad [|] \ \frac{\tilde{v}; P \stackrel{\alpha}{\rightarrow} P' \quad \tilde{v}; Q \stackrel{\beta}{\rightarrow} Q'}{\tilde{v}; P|Q \stackrel{\alpha\beta}{\rightarrow} P'|Q'} \qquad [\tau] \ \frac{\tilde{v}; P \stackrel{\alpha}{\rightarrow} P' \quad \tilde{v}; Q \stackrel{\bar{\beta}}{\rightarrow} Q'}{\tilde{v}; P|Q \stackrel{\alpha/\beta}{\rightarrow} P'|Q'}$$

$$[\bullet] \ \frac{\tilde{v}; \sigma(P) \stackrel{*}{\rightarrow} \surd}{\tilde{v}; \tilde{x} \rhd P \bullet Q \rightarrow \sigma(Q)} \qquad [+] \ \frac{\tilde{v}; P \stackrel{\alpha}{\rightarrow} P'}{\tilde{v}; P + Q \stackrel{\alpha}{\rightarrow} P'} \qquad [!] \ \frac{\tilde{v}; !P|P \stackrel{\alpha}{\rightarrow} P'}{\tilde{v}; !P \stackrel{\alpha}{\rightarrow} P'}$$

Fig. 3. The labelled transition system specification $\mathcal{L}\pi_\rightarrow$.

3 Proof Nets

Here we review proof nets, some related notions and introduce notation.

Proof structures are graphs built from *nodes* (possibly underlined formula occurrences), *links* and *boxes*. A link connect a number of nodes, divided into its *premises* and *conclusions*. A node is a premise of at most one link and the conclusion of precisely one link. A node that is not a premise of any link is a *conclusion* of the proof structure. Axiom-links connect two complementary atomic formulas a and $a^{\perp}$. One-links connect to just one occurrence of **1**. $⅋$-(respectively $\otimes$-) links connect three nodes: the conclusion $a ⅋ b$ (resp. $a \otimes b$) and the two premises (a and by b). $\oplus_l$- ($\oplus_r$-) links connect its premise A to its conclusion $A \oplus B$ ($B \oplus A$). ?-links connect the conclusion $?A$ and the $n \geq 0$ premises either of the form A or $\underline{?A}$ (underlined formulas correspond to the discharged formulas of [11]). $\forall$-links connect its premise $A[x/e]$ to its conclusion $\forall x A$. The variable e does not occur free in the conclusion; it is the *eigenvariable* of the link. $\exists$-links connect its premise $A[x/t]$ to its conclusion $\exists x A$, where t is a term. We will always assume that a proof structure π satisfies the following properties [3, 4]: for each $\forall$-link L in π there is a specific eigenvariable e_L. No eigenvariable occurs free in a conclusion of π. Every node in π with a free occurrence of e_L belongs to a e_L-thread that ends in the premise of L, where a x-thread is a sequence of adjacent nodes $A_1 \cdots A_n$ in π (that is a path) such that $A_i \neq A_j$ (as nodes in the net) and $x \in FV(A_i)$. We will also say that A is x-linked to B is there is a x-thread from A to B and call the x-span of A to the set of nodes x-linked to A. Note that every maximal eL-thread starting in the premise P of a $\forall$-link L must end either in P or in the premise of some $\exists$-link. The set of these $\exists$-links is the *existential border* of e_L. Finally, boxes encapsulate proof structures with conclusions labelled by C and $?P_1 \cdots ?P_n$ and have conclusions $!C$ and $\underline{?P_1} \cdots \underline{?P_n}$ ($n \geq 0$). We will handle boxes at an atomic level treating them as generalised axioms. Also, in order to obtain an uniform treatment of both types of axioms we adopt a non standard notation for !-boxes, as follows. For each provable sequent of the form $?P_1, \ldots, ?P_n, !C$ we consider a !-link with premises $\underline{?P_1{}^{\perp}}, \ldots, \underline{?P_n{}^{\perp}}$ and conclusion $!C$, and allow axiom-links to connect pairs of nodes labelled by $\underline{?P}$ and $?\underline{P^{\perp}}$. We will then write boxes like the one on the left as shown on the right.

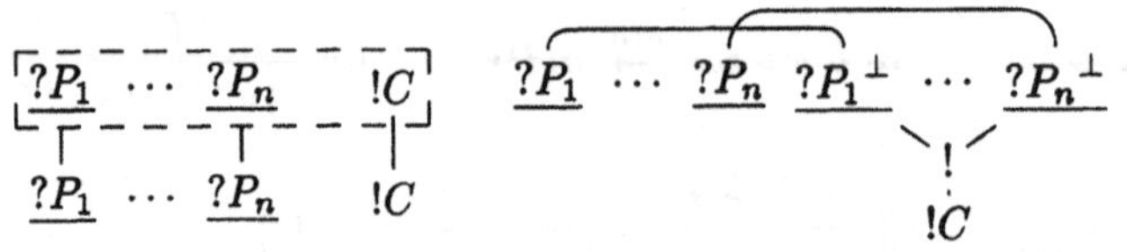

Note that !-links are just convenience to simplify some forthcoming definitions; a !-link together with some ?-type axioms is just a shorthand for a proof box.

There is a criterium to decide whether a proof structure comes from a sequent calculus derivation and is therefore a proof net [10, 4, 11, 3]. A *switching* for a proof structure is an assignment (i) to each of its $⅋$-links of a choice between one of its two premises, (ii) to each of its ?-links of a choice between one of its

n premises, and (iii) to each of its $\forall$-links of a choice between its premise or any node in the existential border of their eigenvariable. The Danos-Reignier (D-R) graph induced by a switching is obtained by keeping the nodes of the proof structure and the connections established by axiom, $\oplus$-, $\exists$- and $\otimes$-links, while for each $⅋$-link, ?-link and $\forall$-link the conclusion is connected to the premise selected by the switching. A proof structure is a proof net if and only if the D-R graph induced by any switching is acyclic (Danos-Regnier Criterium). By a D-R path we mean a path in a D-R graph.

4 Slices and Interfaces

As suggested in Section 1, a term P of $\mathcal{L}_\pi$ will be modelled by a set of abstractions of certain substructures of proof nets herein called slices. We start by defining

Definition 1 *(Span and Pre-Span) Given a proof net π with a formula occurrence P, a pre-span (span) $\mathcal{S}_P$ in π of P is defined as a substructure of π with nodes the set of all hereditary premises of P in π and links (a) all non-axiom links with an hereditary premise of P for conclusion (b) some (all) axiom-links $a_1 \sqcap a_2{}^\perp$ of π such that both a_1 and $a_2{}^\perp$ are hereditary premises of P.*

We will call *ports* to the occurrences of formulas of the span that are not conclusions of any link in the span. Ports are the interaction points of the span of a term with the rest of the proof that is, the external environment. Spans interact also by exporting and importing names (eigenvariables) to and from the environment; the following notions capture aspects of this fact.

Definition 2 *($\forall/\exists$-cells) Let $\mathcal{S}_P$ be a pre-span of P in π, x a eigenvariable of π occurring in some port α of $\mathcal{S}_P$, $\mathcal{U}$ the x-span of α inside $\mathcal{S}_P$ and $P \notin \mathcal{U}$. If $\mathcal{U}$ contains the $\forall$-link of x then $\mathcal{U}$ is a $\forall_x$-cell of $\mathcal{S}$, else $\mathcal{U}$ is a $\exists_x$-cell of $\mathcal{S}$.*

Definition 3 *(Slices and their parameters) Given a proof net π with a formula occurrence P, a pre-slice $\mathcal{S}_P$ of P is obtained from a pre-span $\mathcal{S}$ of P by replacing in each $(\forall/\exists)_{x_i}$-Cell of $\mathcal{S}$ every occurrence of x_i by a fresh and distinct variable u_i. These u_i will be called* parameters *of the pre-slice. Parameters of $\exists$-cells will be called* existential *and* universal *otherwise. $\mathcal{S}_P$ is a slice when $\mathcal{S}$ is a span.*

Parameters never occur free in the conclusion of the slice. In a slice $\mathcal{S}$, if a variable x occurs free both in its conclusion C and in some port α then there is a x-thread from C to α inside $\mathcal{S}$. In fact, suppose that there is no such x-thread. Then, since C does not belong to the x-span of α, x must be the parameter of some $(\forall/\exists)$-Cell of $\mathcal{S}$. But no parameter can occur free in the conclusion of the slice. A universal parameter never occurs in the head of an atomic port, for this would require an existentially quantified variable in the head of term somewhere and the syntax of $\mathcal{L}_\pi$ does not allow that.

Note that if π is a proof net with a single conclusion C then the slice of C in π is π itself. Likewise, if a slice of C in a proof net π has no ports then it is disconnected from the rest of π, and therefore must be a proof net itself. Every pre-slice $\mathcal{S}$ of A in π can be extended (in the sense that $\mathcal{S}$ is a substructure of $\mathcal{S}'$) to a slice $\mathcal{S}'$ of A, just by considering additional axiom links. Spans can be defined independently of their embedding inside proof nets as follows. A span is defined just like a proof structure with a single conclusion and satisfying the D-R criterium, except that we do not insist that a formula occurrence must be the conclusion of a link if that formula is a terminal formula. These formula occurrences are precisely the ports of the span. Such a span can give rise to a slice by identifying its $(\forall/\exists)$-cells with distinct parameters as specified in Definition 3. Note that given a slice of $\mathcal{S}$ of P so defined, we can always build a proof net π of with P among its conclusions such that $\mathcal{S}$ is the slice of P in π in the sense of Definitions 1 and 3. Slices have an internal structure that is not completely relevant to its composability as part of a larger proof net. Thus slices will be characterised by *interfaces.*

Definition 4 *(Interface) An interface is a triple* $(\!|n; m; \approx|\!)$ *where* m *is a finite multiset of signed terms,* n *is a finite set of signed names which occur in some terms of* m*, and* $\approx$ *is a symmetric binary relation (the path relation) on* $n \cup m$*. The set of all interfaces will be noted* $\mathcal{I}$*.*

Intuitively, an interface $(\!|n; m; \approx|\!)$ characterises a particular computation of a term, abstracting away from the internal structure of the slice it characterises. In particular, n contains denotations for the new names that are generated internally and also for those created by the environment, but read by the process at hand. This names have no "a priori" identity, and behave like bound variables inside the slice. So, names in n will actually be tagged as positive ($\hat{x}$) or negative ($\check{x}$) depending on being created inside the computation and exported to the environment or new names created outside and imported from the environment. By convention, we will also note positive elements of m (say ?P) by $\hat{?P}$, and negative elements (say $a^{\perp}$) by $\check{a}$. The symmetric relation $\approx$ characterises the interdependence among the ports and names, more precisely, the existence of certain paths in the D-R graphs of the slice. The rôle of $\approx$ is to constrain the possible interactions among ports of a set of slices. Note that $\approx$ relate formula *occurrences* (as nodes in the structure). Since names in an interface represent eigenvariables of the proof net, proof nets (and thus also slices) that only differ in the names of its eigenvariables should not be distinguished, we define an equivalence relation $\equiv_\alpha$ on interfaces by $(\!|n; m; \approx|\!) \equiv_\alpha (\!|n'; m'; \approx'|\!)$ iff there is a sign preserving bijection $\psi : n \mapsto n'$ such that $m' = \psi(m)$ and $\psi(x) \approx' \psi(y)$ iff $x \approx y$. From now on we will implicitly work with $\mathcal{I}/\equiv_\alpha$.

Definition 5 *(Characterisation of Slices) An interface* $\gamma = (\!|n; m; \approx|\!)$ *characterises a slice* $\mathcal{S}$ *of a proof net* π *if and only if*

1. There is a bijection φ *between* n *and the parameters of* $\mathcal{S}$ *such that* $x \in n$ *is positive iff* $\varphi(x)$ *is universal.*

2. m *is obtained from the multiset of terms at the atomic border of* $\mathcal{S}$ *by replacing every parameter* x *of* $\mathcal{S}$ *by* $\varphi(x)$*.*

3. $\approx$ *is the smallest symmetric binary relation on* $n \cup m$ *such that for all* $a, b \in m$ *and* $\hat{x}, \check{x}, \hat{y} \in n$*,*

3a) $a \approx b$ iff there is a D-R path in $\mathcal{S}$ connecting a and b.

3b) $\hat{x} \approx a$ iff there is a D-R path in $\mathcal{S}$ connecting a to the conclusion of the $\forall$-link with eigenvariable $\varphi(x)$.

3c) $\check{x} \approx a$ iff there is a D-R path in $\mathcal{S}$ connecting a and the premise of an $\exists_t$-link such that $\varphi(x)$ occurs free in t.

3d) $\check{x} \approx \hat{y}$ iff there is a D-R path in $\mathcal{S}$ connecting the premise of an $\exists_t$-link such that $\varphi(x)$ occurs free in t to the conclusion of the $\forall$-link with eigenvar $\varphi(y)$.

By "to the conclusion of the $\forall$-link" we mean entering by the structural path, not by an edge created by a switching for the link. Note that the characterisation relation is well defined in the sense that if $\mathcal{S}$ is a slice of π such that γ characterises $\mathcal{S}$ and $\gamma \equiv_\alpha \gamma'$ then γ' characterises $\mathcal{S}'$. Condition *3a*) on $\approx$ insures that $\approx$ can be used to check whether ports a and $b \equiv a^\perp$ can be linked together by an axiom-link: if $a \approx b$, linking a and b would produce a cyclic D-R graph in the slice. Condition 3*d*) has a close motivation, connected with scope extrusion, and is is related to the following property of proof structures in $\mathcal{L}_\pi$.

Lemma 1 *Let π be a $\mathcal{L}_\pi$ proof structure with a cyclic D-R path γ induced by an edge δ connecting the conclusion $\forall xA$ of a $\forall$-link to the premise $B[y/t]$ of some $\exists$-link. Then γ has the form*

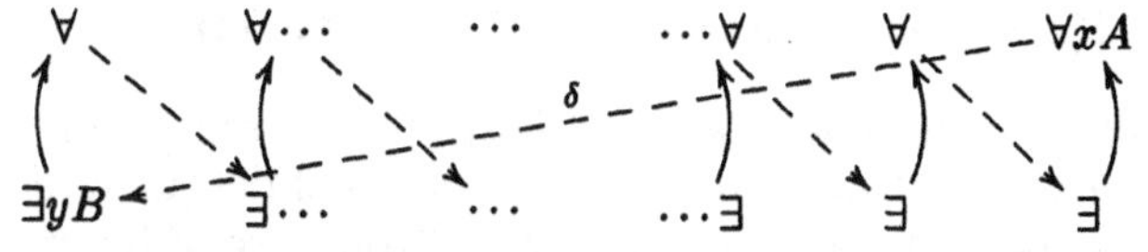

where dashed arrows stand for single edges induced by $\forall$ switches (among them δ) and solid arrows for acyclic paths not including such kind of edges.

Proof. (Sketch) By a diagram chase in π. Starting from any link in the structure we see that once we start going down (that is from premises to conclusions) one can never arrive at a $\forall$-link from the conclusion as is the case in γ. So we must go up from $\exists yB$ until $\forall xA$ is reached, crossing zero or more edges induced by $\forall$ switchings, and always choosing the upgoing edge in the path. ∎

Intuitively, the existential parameter $\check{y}$ of some $\exists$-Cell can be identified to the universal parameter $\hat{x}$ of a $\forall$-Cell only if $\hat{x} \not\approx \check{y}$. Otherwise, the new edges induced by the $\forall$ switch on the link with eigenvariable $\hat{x}$ will immediately lead to a cycle in the D-R graph. Conversely, doing such identification of parameters on an acyclic slice is always safe if $\hat{x} \not\approx \check{y}$, for if a cycle is induced, it must have the form above, that is, we should have $\hat{x} \approx \check{y}$. More precisely, using Lemma 1, we can prove

Lemma 2 *Let $\mathcal{S}$ be a pre-span. If there are an $\exists_x$-cell $\mathcal{E}$ and a $\forall_y$-cell in $\mathcal{S}$, and there is no D-R path, from a $\exists$-link in $\mathcal{E}$ such that x occurs free in its premise but not in its conclusion, to the conclusion on the $\forall$-link with eigenvariable y, then by substituting y for x in $\mathcal{E}$ we obtain a pre-span $\mathcal{S}'$.*

5 Denotation

Before presenting the interpretation of agents, we must define some operations on interfaces. These operations induce characterisations of certain pre-slices in terms of their components. First, let $\circ$ denote the empty interface $(\!|;;|\!)$. If $\alpha \equiv (\!|n;m;\approx|\!)$ and $\beta \equiv (\!|n';m';\approx'|\!)$ are interfaces, we write $\alpha \oplus \beta$ for $(\!|n \oplus n';m \oplus m';\approx \oplus \approx'|\!)$, where $\oplus$ stands for disjoint union. If α and β characterise the slices of P and Q in a proof where P and Q are linked by a $\wp$-link, then the pre-slice of $P \wp Q$ which considers no cross axiom (eg. axiom linking an hereditary premise of P to an hereditary premise of Q) is characterised by $\alpha \oplus \beta$; note that $(\mathcal{I}/\equiv_\alpha, \oplus, \circ)$ is a commutative monoid. In the context of $\mathcal{L}_\pi$ proofs one of the premises A and P of each $\otimes$-link (say A) is always connected to an axiom link. So if $\alpha = (\!|;m;\approx|\!)$ characterises the slice of A and β the slice of P then $\alpha \otimes_L \beta$ defined by $(\!|n';m \oplus m';\rho|\!)$ where $\rho = \approx \oplus \approx' \oplus \{(x,y) : x \in m, y \in m' \oplus n'\}$ characterises the slice with conclusion $A \otimes P$. Note that $\alpha \otimes_L \circ = \circ \otimes_L \alpha = \alpha$.

Let $\mathcal{S}$ be a slice of $\forall x A$ and $\mathcal{P}$ the slice of its premise $A[x/e]$ characterised by $\alpha = (\!|n;m;\approx|\!)$. If e occurs free in some element of m then $(\!|n \oplus \{\hat{u}\};m[e/\hat{u}];\approx|\!)$ characterises $\mathcal{S}$, otherwise α also characterises $\mathcal{S}$. This motivates the following definition

$$\begin{aligned}\forall_x \varphi = &\{(\!|n,\hat{u};m[x/\hat{u}];\approx|\!) : (\!|n;m;\approx|\!) \in \varphi \ \& \ x \in m \ \& \ x \notin hds(m)\}\\ \cup &\{(\!|n;m;\approx|\!) : (\!|n;m;\approx|\!) \in \varphi \ \& \ x \text{ not free in } m\}\end{aligned}$$

where φ is a set of interfaces, $\hat{u} \notin n$ and $hds(m)$ is the set of names that occur in the heads of atomic elements of m or in the heads of the guards of non atomic elements of m. Let $\mathcal{S}$ be a slice of $\exists x A$ and $\mathcal{P}$ the slice of its premise $A[x/t]$ characterised by $\alpha = (\!|n;m;\approx|\!)$. For each variable y that occurs in t, is not free in $\exists x A$, and occurs in some element of m corresponds a $\exists_y$-cell of $\mathcal{S}$. So define

$$\begin{aligned}\exists_{\tilde{y}} \varphi = &\{(\!|n \oplus \tilde{\check{u}};m[\tilde{y}/\tilde{\check{u}}];\approx'|\!) : (\!|n;m;\approx|\!) \in \varphi\}\\ \cup &\{(\!|n;m;\approx|\!) : (\!|n;m;\approx|\!) \in \varphi \ \& \ y \text{ not free in } m\}\end{aligned}$$

where $\approx' = \approx \oplus \{(\check{u},\hat{x}) : \hat{x} \in n \ \& \ \check{u} \in \tilde{\check{u}}\}$, $\tilde{\check{u}} \notin n$ and φ is a set of interfaces. We will also need some simple operations on path relations that capture the effect of adding or removing certain edges to a D-R graph, something crucial to model parallel composition. *Removal:* If L is a set of signed names or a multiset of signed terms then $\approx/L = \{(x,y) \in \approx : x,y \notin L\}$. *Connection* captures the effect of connecting two ports of a slice with an axiom link: if a, c are signed terms then $\approx[a \bowtie c] = \approx/\{a,c\} \cup \{(x,y) : x \approx a \ \& \ c \approx y\}$. *Fusion* captures the effect of merging two distinct $\exists$-cells: $\approx[\check{x} \bowtie \check{y}] = \approx/\{\check{x}\} \cup \{(\check{y},k) | \check{x} \approx k\}$. *Extrusion* captures the effect of merging a $\exists$-cell to a $\forall$-cell: $\approx[\check{x} \bowtie \hat{y}] = \approx/\{\check{x}\} \cup \{(a,b) | a \approx \hat{y} \ \& \ \check{x} \approx b\}$. Note that we always take implicitly the symmetric closure of path relations.

To model parallel composition we define a binary relation $\mapsto$ on $\mathcal{I}$ that characterises the effect of linking with an axiom-link two (complementary) ports of a pre-slice. That is, $\alpha \mapsto \beta$ iff α and β characterise two pre-slices of the same slice and β differs from α by considering one additional axiom link. Before the link

$$
\begin{array}{ll}
[\![\Sigma \blacktriangleright \mathbf{0}]\!]_\Sigma & = \{\circ\} \\
[\![\Sigma \blacktriangleright a]\!]_\Sigma & = \{(\!|\,; a; |\!)\} \\
[\![\Sigma \blacktriangleright P + Q]\!]_\Sigma & = [\![\Sigma \blacktriangleright P]\!]_\Sigma \cup [\![\Sigma \blacktriangleright Q]\!]_\Sigma \\
[\![\Sigma \blacktriangleright \tilde{x} \triangleright \alpha.P]\!]_\Sigma & = \cup_{t \in \mathcal{T}(\Sigma,\tilde{y})} \exists_{\tilde{y}} ([\![\Sigma, \tilde{y} \rhd \alpha[\tilde{x}/\tilde{t}]]\!]_{\Sigma,\tilde{y}} \otimes_L [\![\Sigma, \tilde{y} \blacktriangleright P[\tilde{x}/\tilde{t}]]\!]_{\Sigma,\tilde{y}}) \\
[\![\Sigma \blacktriangleright \tilde{x} \triangleright C \bullet P]\!]_\Sigma & = \cup_{t \in \mathcal{T}(\Sigma,\tilde{y})} \exists_{y} ([\![\Sigma, \tilde{y} \rhd C[\tilde{x}/\tilde{t}]]\!]_{\Sigma,\tilde{y}} \otimes_L [\![\Sigma, \tilde{y} \blacktriangleright P[\tilde{x}/\tilde{t}]]\!]_{\Sigma,\tilde{y}}) \\
[\![\Sigma \blacktriangleright \nu x P]\!]_\Sigma & = \forall_c [\![\Sigma, c \blacktriangleright P[x/c]]\!]_{\Sigma,c} \\
[\![\Sigma \blacktriangleright P|Q]\!]_\Sigma & = \{\gamma : \alpha \oplus \beta \succ \gamma \;\&\; \alpha \in [\![\Sigma \blacktriangleright P]\!]_\Sigma \;\&\; \beta \in [\![\Sigma \blacktriangleright Q]\!]_\Sigma\} \\
[\![\Sigma \blacktriangleright !P]\!]_\Sigma & = \{\gamma : \alpha_1 \oplus \cdots \oplus \alpha_n \succ \gamma \\
& \quad \& \; (\alpha_i \in [\![\Sigma \blacktriangleright P]\!]_\Sigma \text{ or } \alpha_i = (\!|\,; ?\hat{P}; |\!))\} \\
[\![\Sigma \rhd \alpha]\!]_\Sigma & = \{(\!|\,; \breve{\alpha}; (\alpha \times \alpha) - \mathrm{id}_\alpha |\!)\} \\
[\![\Sigma \rhd P]\!]_\Sigma & = \{(\!|\breve{\tilde{u}}; m[y/u]; (m \times m) - \mathrm{id}_m |\!) : \Sigma, \tilde{y} \vdash ?\Delta, P \\
& \quad \& \; m = ?\breve{\Delta} \;\&\; \tilde{y} \in FV(\Delta)\}
\end{array}
$$

Fig. 4. Denotation of $\mathcal{L}_\pi$ terms.

can be placed, the ports may have to be matched by renaming some parameters occurring on them. To that end we define the following notions. A substitution σ is *strict* for a and b if has for domain the set of negative names that occur in a and b, if $Dom(\sigma) \cap Im(\sigma) = \emptyset$ and if whenever $\sigma(x) = w \neq x$ then (i) $x \in a$ implies $w \in b$ and $w \notin a$ (ii) $x \in b$ implies $w \in a$ and $w \notin b$. A substitution $[\breve{x}/w]$ is *admissible* from $\approx$ to $\approx'$ if $\breve{x} \not\approx w$ and $\approx' = \approx [\breve{x} \bowtie w]$. A strict substitution (sequence) $\sigma = [\breve{x}_0/w_0] \cdots [\breve{x}_n/w_n]$ is admissible from $\approx_0$ to $\approx_{n+1}$ if $[\breve{x}_i/w_i]$ is admissible from $\approx_i$ to $\approx_{i+1}$. Intuitively, if σ is admissible from $\approx$ to $\approx'$ then its application on a slice with paths characterised by $\approx$ does not induce any cyclic D-R paths. We now define $\Mapsto$ as the least binary relation on $\mathcal{I}$ such that

$$(\!| n; m \oplus \{\hat{a}, \check{c}\}; \approx |\!) \Mapsto (\!| n'; \sigma(m); \approx' [\hat{a} \bowtie \check{c}] |\!) \text{ if } \hat{a} \not\approx' \check{c} \text{ and } \sigma(a) = \sigma(c) \qquad (1)$$

where σ is strict for a and b and admissible from $\approx$ to $\approx'$ and n' is the restriction of n to the names that still occur in $\sigma(m)$. Finally, take $\succ$ to be the transitive closure of $\Mapsto$. Using these basic operations and relations we can now present the full definition for the semantics of $\mathcal{L}_\pi$. A valid process term $\Sigma \blacktriangleright P$ with $\Sigma = \hat{x_1}, \hat{x_2}, \ldots, \hat{x_n}$ will be interpreted as a function $[\![\Sigma \blacktriangleright P]\!] : \mathcal{V}^n \to \wp(\mathcal{I})$. In Fig. 4 we define $[\![\Sigma \blacktriangleright P]\!]$ compositionally by induction on its "typing" derivation (note that, assuming that a term is well-formed, we write also $\blacktriangleright$ for $\blacktriangleright_g$) and start by stating a completeness property of the interpretation.

Proposition 1 *Let $\Sigma \blacktriangleright P$ be valid and let $S_{\ulcorner P \urcorner}$ be a slice of $\ulcorner P \urcorner$ in a proof net π. Then there is $\gamma \in [\![\Sigma \blacktriangleright P]\!]_\Sigma$ such that γ characterises $S_{\ulcorner P \urcorner}$ in π.*

Proof. (Sketch) See [8] for proof of this and following results. By induction on the structure of P. The case of a parallel composition $P ⅋ Q$ requires showing the existence of an strict and admissible substitution that matches the conclusions of every cross axiom between the slices of P and Q. The cases when P is of the form $!Q$ or $\tilde{x} \triangleright C \bullet Q$ are handled in a way similar to respectively $P|Q$ and $\tilde{x} \triangleright \alpha.Q$. For instance, for $\tilde{x} \triangleright C \bullet Q$ we must verify that each $\gamma \in [\![\Sigma \rhd C]\!]_\Sigma$ characterises the slice of any !-link with conclusion C. ■

Proposition 2 *Let* $\Sigma \blacktriangleright P$. *If* $\Sigma \vdash \ulcorner P \urcorner$ *is provable then* $\circ \in [\![\Sigma \blacktriangleright P]\!]_\Sigma$.

Proof. Since $\Sigma \vdash \ulcorner P \urcorner$ there is a proof net π with conclusion P. The slice of P in π is π itself, π is characterised by $\circ$ and the result follows from Proposition 1. ■

We now state soundness of the denotation function.

Proposition 3 *Let* $\Sigma \blacktriangleright P$ *be valid. If* $\gamma \in [\![\Sigma \blacktriangleright P]\!]_\Sigma$ *then* γ *characterises a slice of* P.

Proof. (Sketch) By induction on the structure of P, we will construct a slice in its direct proof context, cf. remarks in Section 4. Again, the more complex case is parallel composition, which we sketch here: If P has the form $Q|R$ then $\alpha \oplus \beta \succ \gamma$ for some $\alpha \in [\![\Sigma \blacktriangleright Q]\!]_\Sigma$ and $\beta \in [\![\Sigma \blacktriangleright R]\!]_\Sigma$. Clearly $\alpha \oplus \beta$ characterises the slice of $Q \parr R$ obtained by connecting by a $\parr$-link the slices of Q and R provided by the I.H. after renaming apart their parameters. Now, we can prove that if $\delta \mapsto \delta'$ as in (1) and δ characterises some slice $\mathcal{S}_\delta$ of F then δ' also characterises some slice $\mathcal{S}_{\delta'}$ of F. Using Lemma 2 and the fact that $\sigma = [\check{x}_1/w_1] \cdots [\check{x}_n/w_n]$ is a strict and admissible substitution from $\approx$ to $\approx'$ we can show that by replacing in each $\exists_{\varphi(\check{x}_i)}$-cell of $\mathcal{S}_\delta$ the existential parameter $\varphi(\check{x}_i)$ by the parameter $\varphi(w_i)$ or variable w_i a pre-span $\mathcal{U}$ is obtained such that $\check{a} \approx' \hat{c}$ iff there is a D-R path in $\mathcal{U}$ between $\check{a}$ and $\hat{c}$. So, since $\sigma(a) = \sigma(c)$ we can link the ports corresponding to $\sigma(a)^\perp$ and $\sigma(c)$ using an axiom link without introducing any cyclic D-R path. Finally, note that $\delta' = (\!|n; \sigma(m); \approx' [\check{a} \bowtie \hat{c}]|\!)$ indeed characterises $\mathcal{S}_{\delta'}$. ■

Proposition 4 *Let* $\Sigma \blacktriangleright P$. *If* $\circ \in [\![\Sigma \blacktriangleright P]\!]_\Sigma$ *then* $\Sigma \vdash \ulcorner P \urcorner$ *is provable.*

Proof. Since $\circ \in [\![\Sigma \blacktriangleright P]\!]_\Sigma$ by Proposition 3 there is a slice with conclusion P and no ports, that is, a proof net with conclusion P. ■

6 A notion of operational equivalence

In this section, we show that the semantics presented in the previous section, although not fully abstract, is adequate for reasoning about operational equivalence of $\mathcal{L}_\pi$ programs w.r.t the following notion of observability.

Definition 6 *Two agents* P *and* Q *are operationally equivalent (written* $P \sim Q$*) iff for all unary contexts* $C[-]$ *of* $\mathcal{L}_\pi$ *there is a proof of* $\vdash C[P]$ *if and only if there is a proof of* $\vdash C[Q]$.

Note that any notion of operational equivalence for $\mathcal{L}_\pi$ agents must be stronger than the present one due to the presence of the testing agent and Theorem 1.

Lemma 3 *(Context Lemma) Let $\Sigma, \tilde{x} \blacktriangleright P|Q$. For all $C[-]$ such that $\Sigma \blacktriangleright C[P]|C[Q]$ we have that $\Sigma \vdash C[P]$ implies $\Sigma \vdash C[Q]$ if for all Σ', $\tilde{t} \in \mathcal{T}(\Sigma')$ and $\Sigma' \blacktriangleright \Delta$, $\Sigma' \vdash P[\tilde{x}/\tilde{t}], \Delta$ implies $\Sigma' \vdash Q[\tilde{x}/\tilde{t}], \Delta$.*

Proof. By induction on the sequent calculus proof of $\Sigma' \vdash C[P], \Delta$. The need for the substitution arises because of the rule for the existential quantifier. ∎

Proposition 5 *If $[\![\Sigma, \tilde{x} \blacktriangleright P]\!]_{\Sigma,\tilde{x}} \subseteq [\![\Sigma, \tilde{x} \blacktriangleright Q]\!]_{\Sigma,\tilde{x}}$ then for all Σ', $\Sigma' \blacktriangleright \Delta$ and $\tilde{t} \in \mathcal{T}$, $\Sigma' \vdash \Delta, P[\tilde{x}/\tilde{t}]$ implies $\Sigma' \vdash \Delta, Q[\tilde{x}/\tilde{t}]$.*

Proof. By Prop. 2 and Prop. 4 using compositionally of $[\![\cdot]\!]$ wrt. $|$. ∎

Using Lemma 3 and Proposition 5 we conclude

Proposition 6 *(Adequacy) If $[\![\Sigma \blacktriangleright P]\!]_\Sigma \subseteq [\![\Sigma \blacktriangleright Q]\!]_\Sigma$ then for all $C[-]$ and Σ' such that $\Sigma' \blacktriangleright C[P]|C[Q]$, $\Sigma' \vdash C[P]$ implies $\Sigma' \vdash C[Q]$.*

All $\sim$-equations expressing principles of structural congruence can be proved valid in the present model. For example, the commutative monoid laws for $|$ follows from $(\mathcal{I}/\equiv_\alpha, \oplus, \circ)$ being a commutative monoid and some elementary properties of $\mapsto$. We illustrate the method with a couple of trivial examples

Proposition 7 *The following are valid: (a) $[\![\nu x x.P]\!] = \emptyset$. (b) $\nu x(x|x.0) \sim 0$.*

Proof. (a) Let $(\!|n; m; \approx|\!) \in [\![x.P]\!]$. Since $m = \{x\} \oplus m'$ and $x \in hds(m)$, $[\![\nu x x.P]\!]$ is empty. (b) $[\![x]\!] = \{(\!|; \hat{x}; |\!)\}$ and $[\![x.0]\!] = \{(\!|; \check{x}; |\!)\}$. Thus $\gamma \in [\![x|x.0]\!]$ iff $\alpha = (\!|; \hat{x}, \check{x}; |\!) \succ \gamma$. So $\gamma = \circ$ or $\gamma = \alpha$ and $x \in hds(\gamma)$. Then $[\![\nu x(x|x.0)]\!] = \{\circ\}$ ∎

7 Capturing Causality

In this section, we sketch how a notion of causality and a more direct relation to the transition system semantics can be obtained from the proof-net model described. The basic observation is that if we orient the symmetric path relation $\approx$ we obtain a partial order $\sqsubseteq$ in such a way that the essential properties of $\approx$ are kept and the order by which elementary actions are performed and names generated is also captured. For simplicity sake, we will restrict the present discussion to a subset of $\mathcal{L}_\pi$ without value passing (the propositional fragment). In the first place, note that, if $(\!|n; m; \approx|\!)$ characterises some slice, never is the case that $\hat{a} \approx \hat{b}$ for some $\hat{a}, \hat{b} \in m$ (both positive!). On the other hand, it might be that $\check{a} \approx \check{b}$, even if this information is useless, since $\check{a}$ and $\check{b}$, being of the same polarity, will never interact through an axiom-link. So, we could restrict the definition of $\approx$ in such a way that $a \approx b$ only if a and b are of opposite polarity. Another observation is that, if $\check{a} \approx \hat{b}$ then the path in the slice from the port $\check{a}$ to the port $\hat{b}$ climbs up the structural order, this is because a path can only arrive at a positive atom passing through the conclusion to a premise $\wp$-link. Now, the structural order is related to the sequentialization of proof-nets, since in the sequentialization theorem [11], links are always removed at the conclusions. The sequentalisation of a proof net is also related to the order by which sequent calculus rules are applied when a uniform proof-search procedure is applied.

So, if we retain $\breve{a} \sqsubseteq \breve{b}$ when $\breve{b}$ occurs above $\breve{a}$ in the structural order, we can interpret $\sqsubseteq$ as a partial order of events (nodes) labelled by terminal formulas. For example, for some $(\!|; m; \sqsubseteq|\!) \in [\![b.(c|a.P)]\!]$ we have $\breve{b} \sqsubseteq \hat{c}$ and $\breve{b} \sqsubseteq \breve{a}$.

In this setting, we can directly define a transition relation on interfaces by

Definition 7 *Let* $(\!|; m \oplus n; \sqsubseteq|\!) \xrightarrow{n} (\!|; m; \sqsubseteq/n|\!)$ *iff* $n \subset Min_{\sqsubseteq}(m)$ *where* $Min_{\sqsubseteq}(m) = \{x \in m : \nexists y \in m(y \neq x \;\&\; y \sqsubseteq x)\}$.

For the propositional fragment of $\mathcal{L}_\pi$ and a suitable transition system specification conservative over $\mathcal{L}\pi_{\rightarrow}$, we can then show the following result

Proposition 8 $\Sigma; P \xrightarrow{\tau^*\alpha} Q \xrightarrow{\beta^*} \surd$ *if and only if there is* $\gamma \in [\![\Sigma \blacktriangleright P]\!]_\Sigma$ *such that* $\gamma \xrightarrow{\alpha} \delta$ *and* $\delta \in [\![\Sigma \blacktriangleright Q]\!]_\Sigma$.

Above, by β^* we mean a sequence $\xrightarrow{\tau^*}\xrightarrow{\beta_1}\xrightarrow{\tau^*}\xrightarrow{\beta_2} \cdots$. An interesting aspect of this interpretation is that it is not contrived, in the sense that it does not result from an internalisation of the operational semantics as given by the labelled transition system (using, for example, a kind of expansion law), but results from a natural analysis of causality in proof-nets related to some standard proof-theoretic results, like the sequentialization theorem and the token-games of [2]. Moreover, since in $\mathcal{L}\pi_{\rightarrow}$, actions are multisets of terminal formulas, we are approximating true concurrency by means of a higher-dimensional transition system [9]. Extending this results to the full language constitutes work in progress.

8 Related Work and Conclusion

In the present paper, we presented a compositional semantics for a concurrent programming language based in linear logic organised around the theory of proof nets. Proof nets have been used to represent concurrent processes in the "proofs-as-processes" perspective, where computation corresponds to cut-elimination [5]. Here, we view a proof-net as a description of a particular (terminated) computation, and model a process as a set of pieces of proof nets herein called slices. The causal interpretation of Section 7 is connected to the token-games of [2] and has similar aims as those of [12] although adopting a different approach.

Acknowledgements To the anonymous referees for their useful comments and Project ESCOLA PRAXIS/2/2.1/MAT/46/94 for partially supporting this work.

Appendix. Sequent Calculus for CLLmix

$$\Sigma \vdash A, A^{\perp} \qquad \Sigma \vdash \mathbf{1} \qquad \frac{\Sigma \vdash A, \Delta \quad \Sigma \vdash B, \Gamma}{\Sigma \vdash A \otimes B, \Delta, \Gamma} \qquad \frac{\Sigma \vdash A, B, \Delta}{\Sigma \vdash A \parr B, \Delta}$$

$$\frac{\Sigma \vdash \underline{?A}, \cdots, \underline{?A}, A, \cdots, A, \Delta}{\Sigma \vdash ?A, \Delta} \qquad \frac{\Sigma \vdash A, ?\Delta}{\Sigma \vdash !A, \underline{?\Delta}} \qquad \frac{\Sigma, x \vdash A, \Delta}{\Sigma \vdash \forall x A, \Delta}$$

$$\frac{\Sigma \vdash \Delta \quad \Sigma \vdash \Gamma}{\Sigma \vdash \Delta, \Gamma} \qquad \frac{\Sigma \vdash A[x/t], \Delta}{\Sigma \vdash \exists x A, \Delta} \qquad \frac{\Sigma \vdash A}{\Sigma \vdash A \oplus B} \qquad \frac{\Sigma \vdash B}{\Sigma \vdash A \oplus B}$$

References

1. J-M. Andreoli. Logic programming with focusing proofs in linear logic. *J. of Logic and Computation*, 2(3):297–347, 1992.
2. Andrea Asperti. Causal dependencies in multiplicative linear logic with MIX. *Mathematical Structures in Computer Science*, 5(3):351–380, September 1995.
3. G. Bellin. Subnets of proof-nets in multiplicative linear logic with MIX. In *Mathematical Structures in Computer Science, to appear*, 1996. Available at ftp://ftp.logique.jussieu.fr/pub/distrib/bellin/mix.ps.gz.
4. G. Bellin and J.. van de Wiele. Empires and kingdoms in MLL. In J.-Y. Girard, Y. Lafont, and L. Regnier, editors, *Advances in Linear Logic*, pages 249–270. Cambridge University Press, 1995. London Mathematical Society Lecture Note Series 222, Proceedings of the 1993 Workshop on Linear Logic, Cornell Univesity, Ithaca.
5. Gianluigi Bellin and Philip Scott. On the π-calculus and linear logic. *Theoretical Computer Science*, 135:11–65, 1994. Also published as LFCS report ECS-LFCS-92-232, Laboratory for Foundations of Computer Science, Department of Computer Science, University of Edinburgh, UK.
6. L. Caires. A language for the logical specification of processes and relations. In Michael Hanus, editor, *Proceedings of the Algebraic and Logic Programming International Conference*, 1996.
7. L. Caires. A language for the logical specification of processes and relations. Technical Report 6.96, Universidade Nova de Lisboa, Faculdade de Ciências e Tecnologia,Departamento de Informática, 1996. Available at http://www-ctp.di.fct.unl.pt/~lcaires/writings/lpi6.96.ps.gz.
8. L. Caires and L. Monteiro. Proof net semantics of $\mathcal{L}_\pi$. Technical report, Universidade Nova de Lisboa, Faculdade de Ciências e Tecnologia,Departamento de Informática, 1997. Available at http://www-ctp.di.fct.unl.pt/~lcaires/writings/.
9. G. L. Cattani and V. Sassone. Higher dimensional transition systems. In *Proceedings of the Eleventh Annual IEEE Symposium on Logic in Computer Science*, pages 55–62. IEEE Computer Society Press, 1996.
10. Vincent Danos and Laurent Regnier. The structure of multiplicatives. *Archive for Mathematical Logic*, 26, 1989.
11. Jean-Yves Girard. Proof-nets: The parallel syntax for proof-theory. In P. Agliano and A. Ursini, editors, *Logic and Algebra*. Marcel Dekker, New York, 1996.
12. Alessio Guglielmi. *Abstract Logic Programming in Linear Logic—Independence and Causality in a First Order Calculus*. PhD thesis, Università di Pisa, 1996.
13. N. Kobayashi and A. Yonezawa. Asynchronous communication model based on linear logic. *Formal Aspects of Computing*, 7(2):113–149, 1995.
14. D. Miller. The π-calculus as a theory in linear logic: preliminary results. In E. Lamma and P. Mello, editors, *Proc. of the Workshop on Extensions of Logic Programming*, pages 242–264, 1992.
15. D. Miller. Forum: A multiple-conclusion specification logic. *Theoretical Computer Science*, 165(1):201–232, 30 September 1996.
16. D. Miller, G. Nadathur, F. Pfenning, and A. Scedrov. Uniform proof as a foundation for logic programming. *Annals of Pure and Applied Logic*, (51):125–157, 1991.

Explicit Substitutions for the λΔ-Calculus *

Gilles Barthe[1] Fairouz Kamareddine[2] Alejandro Ríos[2]

[1] CWI, P.O. Box 94079, 1090 GB Amsterdam, the Netherlands, email gilles@cwi.nl
[2] University of Glasgow, Department of Computing Science, 17 Lilybank Gardens, Glasgow G12 8QQ, Scotland, UK, email {fairouz,rios}@dcs.gla.ac.uk

Abstract. *The $\lambda\Delta$-calculus is a λ-calculus with a control-like operator whose reduction rules are closely related to normalisation procedures in classical logic. We introduce $\lambda\Delta$exp, an explicit substitution calculus for $\lambda\Delta$, and study its properties. In particular, we show that $\lambda\Delta$exp preserves strong normalisation, which provides us with the first example –moreover a very natural one indeed– of explicit substitution calculus which is not structure-preserving and has the preservation of strong normalisation property. One particular application of this result is to prove that the simply typed version of $\lambda\Delta$exp is strongly normalising.*
In addition, we show that Plotkin's call-by-name continuation-passing style translation may be extended to $\lambda\Delta$exp and that the extended translation preserves typing. This seems to be the first study of CPS translations for calculi of explicit substitutions.

1 Introduction

Explicit substitutions were introduced by Abadi, Cardelli, Curien and Lévy in [1] as a bridge between λ-calculus and its implementation. The fundamental idea behind explicit substitutions is simple: in order to provide a full account of the computations involved in computing a λ-term, one must describe a method to compute substitutions. Since the seminal work of Abadi, Cardelli, Curien and Lévy, explicit substitutions have developed into a subject of their own, finding further applications e.g. in proof-search [29], unification [11], representation of incomplete proofs [23, 21] and proof theory [16].

In this paper, we generalise some of the results on explicit substitutions for λ-calculi to classical λ-calculi, i.e. λ-calculi with control-like structures. More precisely, we consider a specific calculus with a control-like operator, called $\lambda\Delta$ [28], and define its explicit substitution variant $\lambda\Delta$exp. Then we prove that the $\lambda\Delta$exp enjoys some important properties:

- $\lambda\Delta$exp preserves strong normalisation, i.e. every strongly normalising $\lambda\Delta$-term is strongly normalising with respect to the reduction relation of $\lambda\Delta$exp;
- the simply typed $\lambda\Delta$exp calculus is strongly normalizing;

* This work is supported by NWO and the British council under UK/Dutch joint scientific research project JRP240 and EPSRC grant GR/K 25014.

- $\lambda\Delta$exp may be translated to λexp –a named explicit λ-calculus– using an extension of the continuation-passing style translation;
- the CPS translation maps simply typable $\lambda\Delta$exp-terms to simply typable λexp-terms and generalises Kolmogorov's double-negation translation.

The motivation for this work is three-fold:

1. control-like operators play a crucial role in functional programming languages, such as LISP [30], SML [2], Scheme [12], etc. We will only be able to claim that explicit substitutions provide a bridge between higher-order rewriting systems and their implementation if the theory of explicit substitutions can be extended –among other– to control-like operators;
2. control-like operators and explicit substitutions both have applications in theorem proving and proof theory. (See e.g. [24] for applications of control-like operators in theorem proving and [5, 14, 24] for applications of control-like operator in proof theory.) The former are used in classical theorem proving and the latter to represent incomplete proofs. By studying explicit substitutions with control operators, we lay the foundations for a classical theorem prover with the ability to handle incomplete proofs and for a classical proof theory based on explicit substitutions.
3. control-like operators fundamentally differ from λ-calculus in that they are not structure-preserving in the sense of [9]. Hence the results of [9] do not apply. Yet we will show that the decency method [7] can be adapted to our setting. This constitutes the first study of explicit substitutions for non-structure-preserving calculi and suggests the possibility of extending the results of [9] to a large and useful class of combinatory rewrite systems.

Organisation of the paper In Section 2, we introduce the $\lambda\Delta$-calculus and state some of its properties. In Section 3, we extend the $\lambda\Delta$-calculus with explicit substitutions. In Section 4, we establish the confluence and preservation of strong normalisation (PSN) of the $\lambda\Delta$exp-calculus. We use the interpretation method [15] to show confluence and the decency method to establish PSN [7]. We also show that the structure preserving method of [9] does not apply to the $\lambda\Delta$exp-calculus. In Section 5 we introduce the simply typed version of $\lambda\Delta$exp and show that it has the desirable properties such as subject reduction and strong normalisation. In Section 6, we present the first study of CPS-translations for calculi of explicit substitutions by providing a CPS-translation for $\lambda\Delta$exp and showing its soundness. In Section 7, we discuss related work. We conclude in Section 8.

Prerequisites and terminology We assume some basic familiarity with λ-calculus [4] and abstract rewriting [19]. We let $\lhd$ denote the subterm relation and $\rightarrow_R$ denote the compatible closure of a relation R –compatibility is defined as usual. The transitive and reflexive-transitive closures of $\rightarrow_R$ are denoted by $\twoheadrightarrow^+_R$ and $\twoheadrightarrow_R$ respectively. Finally, we let $\mathsf{SN}(R)$ denote the set of strongly normalising terms w.r.t. $\rightarrow_R$.

2 The $\lambda\Delta$-calculus

Control operators are programming constructs which allow the programmer to have more direct control over the evaluation of a program. In the late 80's, Griffin [14] observed that control operators could be simply typed by the classical axiom of double negation. After Griffin's discovery, there has been a great interest λ-calculi with control-like structures. The $\lambda\Delta$-calculus is such calculus. More precisely, the $\lambda\Delta$-calculus is an extension of the λ-calculus with a binding double negation operator Δ whose computational behavior is closely related to normalisation procedures for classical natural deduction [27] (and of course to reduction rules for control operators).

The following definition is taken from [28].

Definition 1

1. *The set T of (pure) terms is given by the abstract syntax:*

$$T = V \mid TT \mid \lambda V.T \mid \Delta V.T \qquad \text{with } V = \{x_n : n \in \mathbb{N}\}$$

where λ and Δ are binding operators.

2. *Meta-substitution $.[./.]$, free and bound variables are defined as usual. We let* $\mathsf{FV}(a)$ *and* $\mathsf{BV}(a)$ *denote respectively the sets of free and bound variables of a term a.*
3. *β-reduction $\rightarrow_\beta$ is defined as the compatible closure of*

$$(\lambda x.a)\, b \quad \rightarrow_\beta \quad a[b/x]$$

4. *μ-reduction $\rightarrow_\mu$ is defined as $\rightarrow_{\mu_1} \cup \rightarrow_{\mu_2} \cup \rightarrow_{\mu_3}$ where μ_i-reduction for $1 \le i \le 3$ is defined to be the compatible closure of the corresponding i-rule:*

$$\begin{array}{lll} (\Delta x.a)\, b & \rightarrow_{\mu_1} \Delta y.a[\lambda w.y\ (w\ b)/x] & \text{if } y, w \notin \mathsf{FV}(b), y \neq w \\ \Delta x.x\ a & \rightarrow_{\mu_2} a & \text{if } x \notin \mathsf{FV}(a) \\ \Delta x.x\ (\Delta y.x\ a) & \rightarrow_{\mu_3} a & \text{if } x, y \notin \mathsf{FV}(a) \end{array}$$

5. $\rightarrow_{\beta\mu} = \rightarrow_\beta \cup \rightarrow_\mu$.

For motivations and explanations of the Δ-operator, we refer the reader to [28]. We shall briefly mention however that the rule μ_1 is what makes the Δ-operator into a control one. Note that μ_1, does not destroy the control nature of the term. After application, a Δ-term remains a Δ-term. μ_2 acts like an η-rule and together with μ_3 allows to define a catch and throw mechanism.

We let $x, y, z, w, \ldots$ range over V and $a, b, c, \ldots$ range over T and $\mathcal{O}$ to range over $\{\lambda, \Delta\}$. For the sake of hygiene, we consider terms modulo α-conversion –generalised over Δ– and assume Barendregt's variable convention [4].

The following proposition is taken from [28].

Proposition 2 *$\rightarrow_{\beta\mu}$ is confluent (CR).*

Finally, we define the norm $\beta\mu$-norm $\beta\mu(a)$ of a pure term a as the maximal number of $\beta\mu$-reduction steps in a reduction starting from a. It is finite if $a \in \mathsf{SN}(\beta\mu)$ and infinite otherwise. The norm of a term will be used in Section 4.

3 The $\lambda\Delta$exp-calculus

The $\lambda\Delta$exp-calculus is a named calculus of explicit substitutions for $\lambda\Delta$.

Definition 3

1. *The set T^e of terms of the $\lambda\Delta$exp-calculus is given by the abstract syntax:*

$$T^e = V \mid T^eT^e \mid \lambda V.T^e \mid \Delta V.T^e \mid T^e[V := T^e] \quad \textit{with } V = \{x_n : n \in \mathbb{N}.\}$$

where λ, Δ, $.[. := .]$ are binding operators. Free and bound variables are defined in the obvious way.

2. *$\underline{\beta}$-reduction $\rightarrow_{\underline{\beta}}$ is defined as the compatible closure of*

$$(\lambda x.a)\, b \quad \rightarrow_{\underline{\beta}} \quad a[x := b]$$

3. *$\underline{\mu}$-reduction $\rightarrow_{\underline{\mu}}$ is defined as $\rightarrow_{\underline{\mu_1}} \cup \rightarrow_{\underline{\mu_2}} \cup \rightarrow_{\underline{\mu_3}}$ where $\underline{\mu_i}$-reduction for $1 \leq i \leq 3$ is defined to be the compatible closure of the corresponding i-rule:*

$$\begin{array}{lll} (\Delta x.a)\, b & \rightarrow_{\underline{\mu_1}} \Delta y.a[x := \lambda w.y\, (w\, b)] & \textit{if } y, w \notin \mathsf{FV}(b), y \neq w \\ \Delta x.x\, a & \rightarrow_{\underline{\mu_2}} a & \textit{if } x \notin \mathsf{FV}(a) \\ \Delta x.x\, (\Delta y.x\, a) & \rightarrow_{\underline{\mu_3}} a & \textit{if } x, y \notin \mathsf{FV}(a) \end{array}$$

4. *σ-reduction $\rightarrow_\sigma$ is defined as the compatible closure of*

$$\begin{array}{lll} x[x := b] & \rightarrow_\sigma b & \\ y[x := b] & \rightarrow_\sigma y & \textit{if } x \neq y \\ (a\, a')[x := b] & \rightarrow_\sigma (a[x := b])\, (a'[x := b]) & \\ (Oy.a)[x := b] & \rightarrow_\sigma Oy.(a[x := b]) & \textit{if } y \notin \mathsf{FV}(b) \end{array}$$

5. $\rightarrow_{\underline{\beta\mu\sigma}} = \rightarrow_{\underline{\beta}} \cup \rightarrow_{\underline{\mu}} \cup \rightarrow_\sigma$ *and* $\rightarrow_{\underline{\beta\mu_i}} = \rightarrow_{\underline{\beta}} \cup \rightarrow_{\underline{\mu_i}}$ *for* $1 \leq i \leq 3$.

Again we let $a, b, c, \ldots$ range over T^e. The variable convention, α-conversion, meta-substitution, *etc* are generalised in the obvious way. In particular,

$$\mathsf{FV}(a[x := b]) = \mathsf{FV}(b) \cup (\mathsf{FV}(a) \setminus \{x\})$$

Definition 4 *The set $\sigma\mathsf{FV}(a)$ of* **substitutable free variables** *of a term a is defined inductively as follows:*

$$\begin{aligned} \sigma\mathsf{FV}(x) &= \{x\} \\ \sigma\mathsf{FV}(ab) &= \sigma\mathsf{FV}(a) \cup \sigma\mathsf{FV}(b) \\ \sigma\mathsf{FV}(Ox.a) &= \sigma\mathsf{FV}(a) \setminus \{x\} \\ \sigma\mathsf{FV}(a[x := b]) &= \begin{cases} \sigma\mathsf{FV}(a) & \textit{if } x \notin \mathsf{FV}(a) \\ (\sigma\mathsf{FV}(a) \setminus \{x\}) \cup \sigma\mathsf{FV}(b) & \textit{if } x \in \mathsf{FV}(a) \end{cases} \end{aligned}$$

We conclude this section by noting that $\lambda\Delta$exp contains λexp as a subcalculus. The latter is a named explicit λ-calculus, called λx in [8], and obtained from $\lambda\Delta$exp by leaving out Δ.

4 Confluence and preservation of Strong Normalisation

In this section, we show that the $\lambda\Delta$exp-calculus enjoys confluence and preservation of strong normalisation.

4.1 Confluence

Confluence is proved as usual, using the interpretation method of [10, 15].

Lemma 5 *Let $a, b \in T^e$. The following holds:*

1. *$\to_\sigma$ is SN and CR. Hence, every term $c \in T^e$ has a unique σ-normal form, denoted $\sigma(c)$.*
2. *$\sigma(ab) = \sigma(a)\sigma(b)$, $\sigma(\lambda x.a) = \lambda x.\sigma(a)$, $\sigma(\Delta x.a) = \Delta x.\sigma(a)$, $\sigma(a[x := b]) = \sigma(a)[\sigma(b)/x]$.*
3. *Projection: If $a \twoheadrightarrow_{\beta\underline{\mu}\sigma} b$ then $\sigma(a) \twoheadrightarrow_{\beta\mu} \sigma(b)$.*
4. *Simulation: for pure terms a, b, if $a \to_{\beta\mu} b$ then $a \twoheadrightarrow^+_{\beta\underline{\mu}\sigma} b$.*

Proof: Analogous to the proofs of the corresponding results for λexp [8]. We just remark that the function used to prove SN should be here extended with $h(\Delta x.a) = h(a) + 1$. □

Theorem 6 *The $\lambda\Delta$exp-calculus is confluent.*

Proof: If $a \twoheadrightarrow_{\beta\underline{\mu}\sigma} b_1$ and $a \twoheadrightarrow_{\beta\underline{\mu}\sigma} b_2$ then by Lemma 5, $\sigma(a) \twoheadrightarrow_{\beta\mu} \sigma(b_i)$, for $i \in \{1, 2\}$. By CR of $\lambda\Delta$, there exists c such that $\sigma(b_i) \twoheadrightarrow_{\beta\mu} c$, and by Lemma 5 $\sigma(b_i) \twoheadrightarrow_{\beta\underline{\mu}\sigma} c$. Hence, $b_i \twoheadrightarrow_{\beta\underline{\mu}\sigma} c$. □

4.2 Preservation of strong normalisation

Every term is $\beta\underline{\mu}\sigma$-strongly normalising if the σ-normal forms of its subterms are $\beta\mu$-strongly normalising.

Lemma 7 *If $a \in \mathsf{SN}(\beta\underline{\mu}\sigma)$ and $b \lhd a$, then $\sigma(b) \in \mathsf{SN}(\beta\mu)$.*

Proof: If $\sigma(b) \notin \mathsf{SN}(\beta\mu)$, then $b \notin \mathsf{SN}(\beta\underline{\mu}\sigma)$ as $b \twoheadrightarrow_\sigma \sigma(b)$ and we use Lemma 5.4. Absurd as $b \lhd a$ and $a \in \mathsf{SN}(\beta\underline{\mu}\sigma)$. □

Corollary 8 *If a is a pure term such that $a \in \mathsf{SN}(\beta\underline{\mu}\sigma)$, then $a \in \mathsf{SN}(\beta\mu)$.*

Proof: If a is pure, $\sigma(a) = a$. □

In other words, $\mathsf{SN}(\beta\underline{\mu}\sigma) \cap T \subseteq \mathsf{SN}(\beta\mu)$. The question arises if the converse holds, i.e. whether $\mathsf{SN}(\beta\mu) \subseteq \mathsf{SN}(\beta\underline{\mu}\sigma)$.

Definition 9

1. *A term* $a \in T$ *obeys the* preservation of strong normalisation *(PSN) property if* $a \in \mathsf{SN}(\beta\mu) \Longrightarrow a \in \mathsf{SN}(\underline{\beta\mu\sigma})$.
2. *A term* $a \in T^{e}$ *obeys the* generalised preservation of strong normalisation *(GPSN) property if* $(\forall b \triangleleft a.\sigma(b) \in \mathsf{SN}(\beta\mu)) \Longrightarrow a \in \mathsf{SN}(\underline{\beta\mu\sigma})$.

The GPSN property is a mild generalization of the PSN property.[3] In our view, the GPSN property is more fundamental than the PSN property for two reasons:

1. the GPSN property applies to all terms, not only the pure ones;
2. for most typed λ-calculi with explicit substitutions, strong normalisation is an immediate consequence of the GPSN property and of strong normalisation of the standard calculus without explicit substitutions.

We shall prove that the $\lambda\Delta$exp-calculus has the GPSN property using the decency technique of [7] –the technique was introduced to prove that λexp has the PSN property. First, we start with some technical definitions.

Definition 10

1. *A substitution item* $[x := b]$ *is* superfluous *in* a *if* $x \notin \sigma\mathsf{FV}(c)$ *for every* $c[x := b] \triangleleft a$.
2. *A reduction* $a \rightarrow_{\underline{\beta\mu\sigma}} b$ *is* superfluous *if the contracted redex in* a *occurs in a superfluous substitution item* $[x := d]$.

Superfluous reduction plays a role similar to the internal reduction notions of [6, 18] –but the two notions are different from each other. The following is a refinement of Lemma 5.

Lemma 11 *If* $a \rightarrow_{\underline{\beta\mu}} b$ *is not superfluous, then* $\sigma(a) \twoheadrightarrow^{+}_{\beta\mu} \sigma(b)$.

Proof: By induction on the structure of a. □

The following definition of *decent* term is central to the GPSN proof. Note that every $a \in \mathsf{SN}(\underline{\beta\mu\sigma})$ is decent and every decent term is decent of order n.

Definition 12

1. *A term* a *is called* decent *if for every* $[x := b]$ *in* a, $b \in \mathsf{SN}(\underline{\beta\mu\sigma})$.
2. *A term* a *is called* decent of order n *if for every* $[x := b]$ *in* a, $b \in \mathsf{SN}(\underline{\beta\mu\sigma})$ *or* $\beta\mu(\sigma(b)) < n$.

Finally, the following notion of *ancestor* gives a full characterisation of how a substitution item might have been generated. This notion aims to achieve similar conditions to those used in the backtracking lemmas of [6, 18] in the minimal derivation method. Note that we use ")a" to denote an application item. For example, in $(\lambda x.a)b$ the application item is $)b$.[4]

Definition 13 *For a reduction* $a \twoheadrightarrow_{\underline{\beta\mu\sigma}} a'$, *we define the notion of* the ancestor *of a substitution item in* a' *as follows:*

[3] It is easy to show that a pure term obeys PSN iff it obeys GPSN.

[4] One can even go further as in [17] by calling λx the λ item but this is not needed here.

1. *If* $a \rightarrow_{\underline{\beta\mu\sigma}} a'$ *and* $b = b'$ *or if* $b \rightarrow_{\underline{\beta\mu\sigma}} b'$ *and* $a = a'$ *then the substitution item* $[x := b']$ *in* $a'[x := b']$ *has ancestor* $[x := b]$ *in* $a[x := b]$.
2. *In the following reductions, the first underlined item (which may be an application written "$)$.") is ancestor of the second underlined (substitution) item:*

$$
\begin{array}{ll}
(bc)\underline{[x := a]} & \rightarrow_{\underline{\beta\mu\sigma}} (b\underline{[x := a]})c[x := a] \\
(bc)\underline{[x := a]} & \rightarrow_{\underline{\beta\mu\sigma}} (b[x := a])c\underline{[x := a]} \\
(\mathcal{O}y.b)\underline{[x := a]} & \rightarrow_{\underline{\beta\mu\sigma}} \mathcal{O}y.b\underline{[x := a]} \\
((\lambda x.b\underline{)a}) & \rightarrow_{\underline{\beta\mu\sigma}} b\underline{[x := a]} \\
((\Delta x.a\underline{)b}) & \rightarrow_{\underline{\beta\mu\sigma}} \Delta y.a\underline{[x := \lambda w.y(wb)]}
\end{array}
$$

3. *The ancestor relation behaves as expected in the confrontation with σ-reductions; i.e., if* $\xi[x := a]$ *is a context in which* $[x := a]$ *appears, then:*

$$
\begin{array}{ll}
(\lambda y.b)\xi\underline{[x := a]} & \rightarrow_{\underline{\beta\mu\sigma}} b[y := \xi\underline{[x := a]}] \\
(\Delta y.b)\xi\underline{[x := a]} & \rightarrow_{\underline{\beta\mu\sigma}} \Delta z.b[y := \lambda w.z(w\xi\underline{[x := a]})] \\
(\lambda y.\xi\underline{[x := a]})b & \rightarrow_{\underline{\beta\mu\sigma}} \xi\underline{[x := a]}[y := b] \\
(\Delta y.\xi\underline{[x := a]})b & \rightarrow_{\underline{\beta\mu\sigma}} \Delta z.\xi\underline{[x := a]}[y := \lambda w.z(wb)] \\
(\mathcal{O}y.\xi\underline{[x := a]})[z := b] & \rightarrow_{\underline{\beta\mu\sigma}} \mathcal{O}y.\xi\underline{[x := a]}[z := b] \\
(\mathcal{O}y.b)[z := \xi\underline{[x := a]}] & \rightarrow_{\underline{\beta\mu\sigma}} \mathcal{O}y.b[z := \xi\underline{[x := a]}] \\
(bc)[z := \xi\underline{[x := a]}] & \rightarrow_{\underline{\beta\mu\sigma}} b[z := \xi\underline{[x := a]}]c[z := \xi\underline{[x := a]}] \\
(b\xi\underline{[x := a]})[y := c] & \rightarrow_{\underline{\beta\mu\sigma}} b[y := c]\xi\underline{[x := a]}[y := c] \\
(\xi\underline{[x := a]}b)[y := c] & \rightarrow_{\underline{\beta\mu\sigma}} \xi\underline{[x := a]}[y := c]b[y := c]
\end{array}
$$

4. *The ancestor relation is compatible; e.g.: if* $a \rightarrow_{\underline{\beta\mu\sigma}} a'$ *where* $[x := b']$ *in* a' *has ancestor* $[x := b]$ *resp.,* $)b$ *in* a, *and if* $c \rightarrow_{\underline{\beta\mu\sigma}} c'$ *then* $[x := b']$ *in* $a'c'$ *has ancestor* $[x := b]$ *resp.,* $)b$ *in* ac.

The following lemma is similar to bactracking in the minimal derivation method of [6, 18].

Lemma 14 *If* $a \rightarrow_{\underline{\beta\mu\sigma}} a'$ *and* $[x := b']$ *is in* a', *then one of the following holds:*

1. *Exactly one* $[x := b]$ *in* a *is an ancestor of* $[x := b']$ *in* a' *and* $b \twoheadrightarrow_{\underline{\beta\mu\sigma}} b'$.
2. $[x := b']$ *has an application item* $)b$ *as ancestor with* $b = b'$ *or* $b' = \lambda w.y(wb)$ *for some* $y, w \notin \mathsf{FV}(b)$ *and* $y \neq w$.

Proof: By induction on the structure of a. □

The following technical lemma is informative about the subterms b of a term a that are not part of substitution items $[y := d]$ in a. It says that for any such b, performing some meta-substitutions on $\sigma(b)$ results in a subterm of $\sigma(a)$.

Lemma 15

1. *If* $b \triangleleft a$ *and* b *is not a part of* d *for some* $[y := d]$ *in* a, *then* $\exists m, x_1, \ldots x_m, c_1, \ldots c_m$ *such that* $\sigma(b)[c_1/x_1][c_2/x_2]\ldots[c_m/x_m]$ *is a subterm of* $\sigma(a)$.
2. *If* $(\mathcal{O}x.b)c \triangleleft a$ *which is not part of* d *for any* $[y := d]$ *in* a, *and if* $\sigma(a) \in \mathsf{SN}(\beta\mu)$ *then* $\beta\mu(\sigma(c)) < \beta\mu(\sigma(a))$.

Proof: 1: By induction on the structure of a. 2: By 1 and Lemma 5, there exists $c_i, x_i, 1 \le i \le m$ such that $(Ox.\sigma(b))\sigma(c)[c_1/x_1]\ldots[c_m/x_m] \lhd \sigma(a)$. Hence $\beta\mu(((Ox.\sigma(b))\sigma(c))) \le \beta\mu(\sigma(a))$. It follows that $\beta\mu(\sigma(c)) < \beta\mu(\sigma(a))$. □

The following lemma is the key to proving GPSN. It says that any $\underline{\beta\mu\sigma}$-reduct a' of a decent term a whose σ-normal form has no infinite $\beta\mu$-derivations, is itself decent and its σ-normal form has no infinite $\beta\mu$-derivations.

Lemma 16 *If a is a decent term s.t. $\sigma(a) \in \mathsf{SN}(\beta\mu)$ and $a \twoheadrightarrow_{\underline{\beta\mu}\sigma} a'$, then a' is decent of order $\beta\mu(\sigma(a))$.*

Proof: By induction on the number of reduction steps in $a \twoheadrightarrow_{\underline{\beta\mu}\sigma} a'$.

- For the base case, as a is decent, a is decent of order $\beta\mu(\sigma(a))$.
- For the induction step, assume $a \twoheadrightarrow_{\underline{\beta\mu}\sigma} a'' \to_{\underline{\beta\mu}\sigma} a'$. By IH, a'' is decent of order $\beta\mu(\sigma(a))$. Let $[x := b]$ in a'. We must show that $b \in \mathsf{SN}(\underline{\beta\mu}\sigma)$ or $\beta\mu(\sigma(b)) < \beta\mu(\sigma(a))$.
  The ancestor of $[x := b]$ in a'' is either:
  1. $[x := b']$ in a'' where $b' \twoheadrightarrow_{\underline{\beta\mu}\sigma} b$
  2. $)b$ in a'' and $(\lambda x.c)b \to_{\underline{\beta\mu}\sigma} c[x := b]$ is the contracted redex in $a'' \to_{\underline{\beta\mu}\sigma} a'$.
  3. $)b'$ in a'' where $(\Delta x.c)b' \to_{\underline{\beta\mu}\sigma} c[x := \lambda w.y(wb')]$ is the contracted redex in $a'' \to_{\underline{\beta\mu}\sigma} a'$ and $b = \lambda w.y(wb')$.

Case 1 As a'' is decent of order $\beta\mu(\sigma(a))$, then either $b' \in \mathsf{SN}(\underline{\beta\mu}\sigma)$ or $\beta\mu(\sigma(b')) < \beta\mu(\sigma(a))$. Hence, $b \in \mathsf{SN}(\underline{\beta\mu}\sigma)$ or $\beta\mu(\sigma(b)) \le \beta\mu(\sigma(b')) < \beta\mu(\sigma(a))$ using Lemma 5.

Case 2 If $)b$ is not part of d for some $[y := d]$ in a'', then by Lemma 15, as $\beta\mu(\sigma(a'')) < \infty$, $\beta\mu(\sigma(b)) < \beta\mu(\sigma(a'')) \le \beta\mu(\sigma(a))$ by Lemma 5. If $)b$ is part of d for some $[y := d]$ in a'', then we may assume that there is no $[z := e]$ such that $)b$ is part of e and $[z := e]$ is part of d. Then as a'' is decent, either $d \in \mathsf{SN}(\underline{\beta\mu}\sigma)$ or $\beta\mu(\sigma(d)) < \beta\mu(\sigma(a''))$. If $d \in \mathsf{SN}(\underline{\beta\mu}\sigma)$ then $b \in \mathsf{SN}(\underline{\beta\mu}\sigma)$. If $\beta\mu(\sigma(d)) < \beta\mu(\sigma(a'')) \le \beta\mu(\sigma(a))$ then as $(\lambda x.c)b$ is not part of some $[z := e]$ in d, we get by Lemma 15 that $\beta\mu(\mu\sigma(b)) < \beta\mu(\mu\sigma(d))$. Hence, $\beta\mu(\mu\sigma(b)) < \beta\mu(\mu\sigma(a))$.

Case 3 Similar to the second but note that $\beta\mu(\sigma(\lambda w.y(wb'))) = \beta\mu(\mu\sigma(b'))$ by Lemma 5, and $b' \in \mathsf{SN}(\underline{\beta\mu}\sigma)$ iff $\lambda w.y(wb') \in \mathsf{SN}(\underline{\beta\mu}\sigma)$. □

Finally, we show that every decent term whose σ-normal form is $\beta\mu$-strongly normalising is itself $\underline{\beta\mu}\sigma$-strongly normalising:

Theorem 17 *If a is a decent term and $\sigma(a) \in \mathsf{SN}(\beta\mu)$, then $a \in \mathsf{SN}(\underline{\beta\mu}\sigma)$.*

Proof: By strong induction on $\beta\mu(\sigma(a)) < \infty$ (note that $\sigma(a) \in \mathsf{SN}(\beta\mu)$). By Lemma 16, $\forall a'$, if $a \twoheadrightarrow_{\underline{\beta\mu}\sigma} a'$, then a' is decent of order $\beta\mu(\sigma(a))$.

Assume a has an infinite derivation. We shall derive a contradiction. As σ is SN (Lemma 5), this derivation can be written as

$$a \twoheadrightarrow_\sigma b_1 \to_{\underline{\beta\mu}} c_1 \twoheadrightarrow_\sigma b_2 \to_{\underline{\beta\mu}} c_2 \ldots$$

Again by Lemma 5, $\sigma(a) = \sigma(b_1) \twoheadrightarrow_{\beta\mu} \sigma(c_1) \twoheadrightarrow_{\beta\mu} \sigma(c_2) \twoheadrightarrow_{\beta\mu} \cdots$.
By Lemma 11 and the fact that $\beta\mu(\sigma(a)) < \infty$, only finitely many of the reductions $b_m \rightarrow_{\underline{\beta\mu}} c_m$ are not superfluous –otherwise, we will have an infinite $\beta\mu$-derivation starting at $\sigma(a)$ which is impossible since $\beta\mu(\sigma(a)) < \infty$. So let $b_M \rightarrow_{\underline{\beta\mu}} c_M$ be the last non-superfluous $\rightarrow_{\underline{\beta\mu}}$-reduction and define h_2 as follows:

$$h_2(x) = 1 \qquad h_2(ab) = h_2(a) + h_2(b) + 1$$

$$h_2(Ox.b) = h_2(b) + 1 \qquad h_2(a[x := b]) = \begin{cases} h_2(a).(h_2(b) + 2) & \text{if } x \in \sigma\mathsf{FV}(b) \\ 2h_2(a) & \text{otherwise} \end{cases}$$

It is easy to prove by induction on the structure of terms that:

- If $a \rightarrow_{\underline{\beta\mu\sigma}} b$ is superfluous then $h_2(a) = h_2(b)$;
- If $a \rightarrow_{\mu_2\mu_3} b$ is not superfluous then $h_2(a) > h_2(b)$;
- If $a \rightarrow_{\sigma} b$ is not superfluous then $h_2(a) > h_2(b)$.

Now, $\exists N > M$ such that $\forall n \geq N$, $h_2(c_n) = h_2(c_N)$, as $\forall n > M$, $b_n \rightarrow_{\underline{\beta\mu_1}} c_n$ is superfluous. Hence, $h_2(b_n) = h_2(c_n)$. Moreover, $h_2(d) < \infty$ for any term d.

Next, look at the part of the derivation: $c_N \twoheadrightarrow_{\sigma} b_{N+1} \rightarrow_{\underline{\beta\mu}} c_{N+1} \twoheadrightarrow_{\sigma} \cdots$.
We know that in this derivation, all $\underline{\beta\mu}$-reduction steps are superfluous. As $\forall n \geq N$, $h_2(c_n) = h_2(c_N) = h_2(b_n) = h_2(b_{n+1})$, it must be also the case that $c_n \twoheadrightarrow_{\sigma} b_{n+1}$ is superfluous for all $n \geq N$, otherwise, $h_2(c_n) > h_2(b_{n+1})$, contradiction.

Hence, one $[x := d]$ in c_N has an infinite $\underline{\beta\mu\sigma}$-derivation. Otherwise, there wouldn't be an infinite $\underline{\beta\mu\sigma}$-derivation starting at c_N, contradicting infinity of $c_N \twoheadrightarrow_{\sigma} b_{N+1} \rightarrow_{\underline{\beta\mu}} c_{N+1} \cdots$.
Now, take one innermost $[x := d]$ in c_N which has an infinite $\underline{\beta\mu\sigma}$-derivation. Then d is decent. As c_N is a $\underline{\beta\mu\sigma}$-reduct of a, then c_N is decent of order $\beta\mu(\sigma(a))$ by Lemma 16. Moreover, $\beta\mu(\sigma(d)) < \beta\mu(\sigma(a))$.

Hence, by IH, we get that $d \in \mathsf{SN}(\underline{\beta\mu\sigma})$. Absurd. □

Now, the proof of GPSN is immediate:

Theorem 18 (Generalised Preservation of Strong Normalisation) *Let $a \in \mathcal{T}^e$, if every subterm b of a satisfies $\sigma(b) \in \mathsf{SN}(\beta\mu)$, then $a \in \mathsf{SN}(\underline{\beta\mu\sigma})$.*

Proof: By induction on the structure of a. As a is a subterm of a, then $\sigma(a) \in \mathsf{SN}(\beta\mu)$. If $[x := b]$ is a substitution item in a, then the IH holds for b and $b \in \mathsf{SN}(\underline{\beta\mu\sigma})$ and hence a is decent. So by Theorem 17, $a \in \mathsf{SN}(\underline{\beta\mu\sigma})$. □

5 A type-assignment for $\lambda\Delta$exp

In [28], a classical type-assignment system for $\lambda\Delta$ is presented. The type-assignment system is simply typed, with a specific type $\perp$ standing for absurdity. Δ is typed with double negation.

Definition 19

1. *The set of types is given by the abstract syntax:* $\mathcal{T} = \perp \mid \mathcal{T} \rightarrow \mathcal{T}$

2. A variable declaration is a pair $x : A$ where $x \in V$ and $A \in \mathcal{T}$.
3. A context is a finite list of declarations $\Gamma = x_1 : A_1, \ldots, x_n : A_n$ such that $i \neq j \Rightarrow x_i \neq x_j$. If $\Gamma = x_1 : A_1, \ldots, x_n : A_n$ is a context, $B \in \mathcal{T}$ and x does not occur in Γ, then $\Gamma, x : B$ is used to denote the context $x_1 : A_1, \ldots, x_n : A_n, x : B$.
4. The set of contexts is denoted by $\mathcal{C}$.
5. The derivability relation $\vdash_{\beta\mu} \subseteq \mathcal{C} \times \mathcal{T} \times \mathcal{T}$ is defined as follows (using the standard notation):

$$(var)\quad \frac{}{\Gamma \vdash_{\beta\mu} x : A}\ \text{if } (x : A) \in \Gamma \qquad (\lambda)\quad \frac{\Gamma, x : A \vdash_{\beta\mu} a : B}{\Gamma \vdash_{\beta\mu} \lambda x.a : A \rightarrow B}$$

$$(ap)\quad \frac{\Gamma \vdash_{\beta\mu} a : A \rightarrow B \quad \Gamma \vdash_{\beta\mu} b : A}{\Gamma \vdash_{\beta\mu} a\, b : B} \qquad (\Delta)\quad \frac{\Gamma, x : A \rightarrow \bot \vdash_{\beta\mu} a : \bot}{\Gamma \vdash_{\beta\mu} \Delta x.a : A}$$

6. The derivability relation $\vdash_{\underline{\beta\mu\sigma}} \subseteq \mathcal{C} \times \mathcal{T}^{s} \times \mathcal{T}$ is defined by the above rules and the new rule:

$$(subst)\qquad \frac{\Gamma, x : A \vdash_{\underline{\beta\mu\sigma}} a : B \quad \Gamma \vdash_{\underline{\beta\mu\sigma}} b : A}{\Gamma \vdash_{\underline{\beta\mu\sigma}} a[x := b] : B}$$

The following lemma establishes three basic properties of the type system:

Lemma 20

1. *Subject Reduction: if $\Gamma \vdash_{\underline{\beta\mu\sigma}} a : A$ and $a \rightarrow_{\underline{\beta\mu\sigma}} b$, then $\Gamma \vdash_{\underline{\beta\mu\sigma}} b : A$.*
2. *Conservativity: if $\Gamma \vdash_{\underline{\beta\mu\sigma}} a : A$ then $\Gamma \vdash_{\beta\mu} \sigma(a) : A$.*
3. *Closure under subterms: every subterm of a well-typed term is well-typed.*

Proof: By an easy induction on the derivation of $\Gamma \vdash_{\underline{\beta\mu\sigma}} a : A$. □

The following proposition establishes that the simply typed version of $\lambda\Delta$exp is SN. Its proof is simple thanks to the generalised PSN.

Proposition 21

1. *If $\Gamma \vdash_{\beta\mu} a : A$, then $a \in \mathsf{SN}(\beta\mu)$.*
2. *If $\Gamma \vdash_{\underline{\beta\mu\sigma}} a : A$, then $a \in \mathsf{SN}(\underline{\beta\mu\sigma})$.*

Proof: 1: proved in [28]. 2: assume a is a term of minimal length such that $\Gamma \vdash_{\underline{\beta\mu\sigma}} a : A$ and $a \notin \mathsf{SN}(\underline{\beta\mu\sigma})$. By Lemma 20.2 and 1 above, $\sigma(a) \in \mathsf{SN}(\beta\mu)$. By GPSN (Theorem 18), a must therefore contain a strict subterm b such that $\sigma(b) \notin \mathsf{SN}(\beta\mu)$. By Lemma 4, $\rightarrow_{\beta\mu} \subseteq \twoheadrightarrow_{\underline{\beta\mu\sigma}}$, hence it follows that $\sigma(b) \notin \mathsf{SN}(\underline{\beta\mu\sigma})$ and so $b \notin \mathsf{SN}(\underline{\beta\mu\sigma})$. By Lemma 20.3, b is a well-typed term. This contradicts the minimality of a. □

6 CPS translation

Continuation-passing style (CPS) translation is a standard compilation technique. Its properties have been thoroughly studied in the context of pure and typed λ-calculus, see for example [26, 22]. In this section, we extend these results to the $\lambda\Delta$exp-calculus. To our knowledge, it is the first study of CPS translations for calculi of explicit substitutions.

Definition 22 *The CPS translation* $\underline{\cdot}$ *takes as input a* $\lambda\Delta$exp*-term and returns as output a* λexp*-term. It is defined as follows:*

1. CPS translation on terms:

$$\begin{aligned}
\underline{x} &= \lambda k.\, x\, k \\
\underline{\lambda x.\, M} &= \lambda k.\, k\, (\lambda x.\, \underline{M}) \\
\underline{M_1\, M_2} &= \lambda k.\, \underline{M_1}\, (\lambda y.\, y\, \underline{M_2}\, k) \\
\underline{\Delta x.\, M} &= \lambda k.\, \underline{M}[x := \lambda h.\, h\, \lambda j.\, \lambda i.\, i\, (j\, k)]\lambda z.\, z \\
\underline{M[x := N]} &= \underline{M}[x := \underline{N}]
\end{aligned}$$

2. CPS translations on types:

$$\begin{aligned}
(\!|\alpha|\!) &= \neg\neg\alpha \\
(\!|A \to B|\!) &= \neg\neg((\!|A|\!) \to (\!|B|\!))
\end{aligned}$$

where $\neg A \equiv A \to \bot$ *for some fixed type* $\bot$.

The translation is an extension of Plotkin's call-by-name translation for the untyped λ-calculus. When considered as a translation on typed terms, the translation corresponds to Kolmogorov's double-negation translation. Also note that the explicit CPS translation yields a CPS translation $\underline{\underline{\cdot}}$ from pure $\lambda\Delta$-terms to pure λ-terms in the obvious way; this translation is proved correct in [5].

Theorem 23 (Correctness of CPS translation)

1. For every two terms M, N,

$$M =_{\beta\mu\sigma} N \quad \Rightarrow \quad \underline{M} =_{\beta\sigma} \underline{N}$$

2. For every judgement (Γ, M, A),

$$\Gamma \vdash_{\lambda\mu\mathsf{exp}} M : A \quad \Rightarrow \quad (\!|\Gamma|\!) \vdash_{\lambda\mathsf{exp}} \underline{M} : (\!|A|\!)$$

Proof. The first item is proved in three steps:

1. prove by induction on the structure of the terms that for every term a,

$$\underline{\sigma(b)}[\underline{\sigma(c)}/x] \quad \twoheadrightarrow_{\beta\sigma} \quad \underline{\sigma(b)[\sigma(c)/x]}$$

2. prove that for every term a, we have $\underline{a} \twoheadrightarrow_{\beta\sigma} \underline{\sigma(a)}$. We treat the case where $a \equiv b[x := c]$. We have

$$\begin{aligned}
\underline{a} &\twoheadrightarrow_{\beta\sigma} \underline{\sigma(b)}[x := \underline{\sigma(c)}] && \text{by I.H.} \\
&\twoheadrightarrow_{\beta\sigma} \underline{\sigma(b)}[\underline{\sigma(c)}/x] \\
&\twoheadrightarrow_{\beta\sigma} \underline{\sigma(b)[\sigma(c)/x]} \\
&\equiv \underline{\sigma(b[x := c])}
\end{aligned}$$

3. use the interpretation method, the correctness of $\underline{\underline{\cdot}}$ and the fact that $\underline{a} \twoheadrightarrow_{\underline{\beta}\sigma} \underline{\underline{a}}$ to conclude.

$$
\begin{aligned}
M =_{\underline{\beta\mu}\sigma} N &\Rightarrow \sigma(M) =_{\beta\mu} \sigma(N) \\
&\Rightarrow \underline{\underline{\sigma(M)}} =_{\beta} \underline{\underline{\sigma(N)}} \\
&\Rightarrow \underline{\sigma(M)} =_{\underline{\beta}\sigma} \underline{\sigma(N)} \\
&\Rightarrow \underline{M} =_{\underline{\beta}\sigma} \underline{N}
\end{aligned}
$$

For the second item, proceed by induction on the structure of derivations.

The above theorem proves that the CPS translation preserves equalities. One may consider whether the CPS translation preserves reductions. Unfortunately, $\underline{\cdot}$ does not.

Lemma 24 *Let a and b be $\lambda\Delta$exp-terms.*

1. $a \rightarrow_{\underline{\beta}\sigma} b \quad \Rightarrow \quad \underline{a} \twoheadrightarrow^{+}_{\underline{\beta}\sigma} \underline{b}$
2. $a \rightarrow_{\underline{\mu}} b \quad \Rightarrow \quad \underline{a} =_{\underline{\beta}\sigma} \underline{b}$

Proof. Show that for every term a, we have $\lambda k.\underline{a}\ k \twoheadrightarrow_{\lambda\mathrm{exp}} \underline{a}$. Then proceed by induction on the structure of the terms.

In the $\lambda\Delta$-calculus, it is possible to obtain a reduction-preserving translation by defining an optimized CPS-translation which performs some so-called administrative reductions. This reduction correspondence may be used for example to deduce strong normalisation of the $\lambda\Delta$-calculus from strong normalisation of the simply typed λ-calculus [5].

The question arises whether such an optimized CPS translation may be used to prove PSN for $\lambda\Delta$exp. In calculi on explicit substitutions, it is however not possible to obtain such a reduction-preserving translation unless some form of composition of substitutions is assumed:

$$
a[x := b][y := c] \quad \rightarrow \quad a[x := b[y := c]] \quad \text{if } y \notin FV(a) \qquad (*)
$$

The above rule is needed in order to obtain an optimized CPS translation which is not too optimizing. Indeed, assume that we want to find optimizations c_1 and c_2 s.t.

$$
\begin{aligned}
\underline{(\Delta x.\, a)\ b} &\twoheadrightarrow_{\lambda\mathrm{exp}} c_1 \\
\underline{\Delta y.\, a[x := \lambda w.y\ (w\ b)]} &\twoheadrightarrow_{\lambda\mathrm{exp}} c_2 \\
c_1 &\twoheadrightarrow_{\lambda\mathrm{exp}} c_2
\end{aligned}
$$

In the current calculus, we have to perform too many steps to find such a c_1. We have:

$$
\begin{aligned}
\underline{(\Delta x.\, a)\ b} &\equiv \lambda k.(\lambda k'.\underline{a}[x := \lambda h.h\ \lambda j.\lambda i.i\ (j\ k')]\ \lambda z.z)\ \lambda j.j\ \underline{b}\ k \\
&\twoheadrightarrow \lambda k.\underline{a}[x := \lambda h.h\ \lambda j.\lambda i.i\ (j\ k')][k' := \lambda j.j\ \underline{b}\ k]\ \lambda z.z
\end{aligned}
$$

If we want to proceed further without reducing the substitution items, then some form of composition of substitutions, as indicated above, is necessary. Unfortunately, the rule $(*)$ breaks PSN, as shown in [8]. It remains open whether one can find a restriction of (∗) which does not break PSN and which allows to obtain a reduction correspondence for CPS.

Remark: it may be possible to obtain a reduction-preserving translation by using meta-substitution instead of explicit substitution in the definition of the CPS translation for Δ-abstractions. However, we consider that a CPS translation between calculi of explicit substitutions should use explicit substitution rather than meta-substitution.

7 Related work

7.1 On preservation of strong normalisation

In a recent paper [9], Bloo and Rose describe how to construct an explicit substitution CRS from an arbitrary CRS.[5] Moreover they show that PSN holds for a restricted class of CRSs, which they call structure-preserving. Unfortunately, PSN for the $\lambda\Delta$exp-calculus cannot be derived from [9]. Indeed, the first μ-rewrite rule is written in the CRS framework as $(\mu x.X(x))\ Y \rightarrow \mu y.X(\lambda w.y\ (w\ Y))$. The condition of structure-preserving requires the argument $\lambda w.y\ (w\ Y)$ of the meta-application in the right-hand side to be a subterm of the left-hand side. Obviously this is not the case.

Independently of [9], Bloo and Geuvers have developed a technique based on recursive path ordering (RPO) to prove PSN for various calculi of explicit substitutions. As was pointed to us by Roel Bloo, the RPO technique may be used to prove PSN for $\lambda\Delta$exp. Finally, the minimal derivation technique of [6, 18] may be used to prove PSN of $\lambda\Delta$exp.

7.2 On explicit substitutions for control-like operators

Audebaud and Pym, Ritter and Wallen have studied calculi of explicit substitutions for another classical λ-calculus, namely Parigot's $\lambda\mu$-calculus [25]. Audebaud's calculus [3] of explicit substitutions is an explicit substitution calculus with de Bruijn indices and composition of substitutions –in the spirit of $\lambda\sigma$– whereas Pym, Ritter and Wallen's $\lambda\mu\epsilon$ [29] calculus is a named explicit substitution calculus without composition of substitutions –in the spirit of λexp.

In [3], the system presented is shown to be confluent on open terms. Confluence on open terms is not however a question that is usually studied in calculi written with named variables (such as the $\lambda\Delta$exp).

In [29], it is shown by a computability predicate argument that simply typable $\lambda\mu\epsilon$-terms are strongly normalising. Their result and ours do not imply each other in neither way. Yet we are confident that the GPSN proof of this paper may be adapted to $\lambda\mu\epsilon$. The advantage of GPSN is that it implies strong normalisation of the simply-typed, polymorphic, higher-order $\lambda\mu\epsilon$-calculus.

[5] The theory of Combinatory Reduction Systems was developed by J.W. Klop [20].

8 Conclusion

We have introduced a calculus of explicit substitutions $\lambda\Delta$exp for the calculus $\lambda\Delta$ and proved various properties of the calculus.

On the one hand, we showed that $\lambda\Delta$exp has the GPSN property. To our knowledge, $\lambda\Delta$exp is the first calculus of explicit substitutions which has the PSN property and is not structure-preserving. Its study suggests that one may be able to prove PSN for a class of CRSs substantially bigger than the class of structure-preserving CRSs.

On the other hand, we showed that Plotkin's call-by-name CPS translation can be extended to the $\lambda\Delta$exp in such a way that typing is preserved. Studying CPS translations for calculi of explicit substitutions seems to be an interesting subject, which we plan to investigate in greater depth.

Our choice of the $\lambda\Delta$-calculus rather than other calculi of control-like operators is based on the fact that the $\lambda\Delta$-calculus is the simplest (and most restrictive) control calculus. It is an open question to study explicit substitutions for non-local control operators such as Felleisen's $\mathcal{C}$ [13]. Interestingly, expliciting such calculi will require an explicit handling of contexts. This subject is left for future work.

Finally, it remains to exploit the results of this paper in classical theorem-proving and proof theory and other applications mentioned in the introduction. An implementation of a proof/type checker based on $\lambda\Delta$exp is currently being developed at Glasgow.

Acknowledgements We are grateful for Roel Bloo for his observation that the RPO method of [8] does apply to $\lambda\Delta$exp. The first author would also like to thank John Hatcliff and Morten Heine Sørensen for discussions on classical λ-calculi.

References

1. M. Abadi, L. Cardelli, P.-L. Curien, and J.-J. Lévy. Explicit Substitutions. *Journal of Functional Programming*, 1(4):375–416, 1991.
2. A. W. Appel. *Compiling with Continuations*. Cambridge University Press, 1992.
3. P. Audebaud. Explicit substitutions for the $\lambda\mu$-calculus. Technical Report RR94-26, Ecole Normal Superieure de Lyon, 1994.
4. H. Barendregt. *The Lambda Calculus : Its Syntax and Semantics*. North Holland, 1984.
5. G. Barthe, J. Hatcliff, and M.H. Sørensen. A notion of classical pure type system. In *Proceedings of MFPS'97*, volume 6 of *Electronic Notes in Theoretical Computer Science*, 1997. To appear.
6. Z. Benaissa, D. Briaud, P. Lescanne, and J. Rouyer-Degli. λv, a calculus of explicit substitutions which preserves strong normalisation. *Journal of Functional Programming*, 6(5), 1996.
7. R. Bloo. Preservation of Strong Normalisation for Explicit Substitution. Technical Report CS-95-08, Department of Mathematics and Computing Science, Eindhoven University of Technology, 1995.
8. R. Bloo and H. Geuvers. Explicit substitution: On the edge of strong normalisation. Technical Report CS-96-10, Department of Mathematics and Computing Science, Eindhoven University of Technology, 1996.

9. R. Bloo and K. Rose. Combinatory reduction systems with explicit substitutions that preserve strong normalisation. In H. Ganzinger, editor, *RTA '96*, volume 1103 of *Lecture Notes in Computer Science*. Springer-Verlag, 1996.
10. P.-L. Curien, T. Hardin, and J.-J. Lévy. Confluence properties of weak and strong calculi of explicit substitutions. *Journal of the ACM*, 43(2):362–397, March 1996.
11. G. Dowek, T. Hardin, and C. Kirchner. Higher-order unification via explicit substitutions. In *Proceedings of the Tenth Annual Symposium on Logic in Computer Science*, pages 366–374. IEEE Computer Society Press, 1995.
12. R.K. Dybvig. *The Scheme Programming Language*. Prentice-Hall, 1987.
13. M. Felleisen, D.P. Friedman, E. Kohlbecker, and B. F. Duba. A syntactic theory of sequential control. *Theoretical Computer Science*, 52(3):205–237, 1987.
14. T.G. Griffin. A formulae-as-types notion of control. In *Principles of Programming Languages*, pages 47–58. ACM Press, 1990.
15. T. Hardin. Confluence Results for the Pure Strong Categorical Logic CCL : λ-calculi as Subsystems of CCL. *Theoretical Computer Science*, 65(2):291–342, 1989.
16. H. Herbelin. *Elimination des coupures dans les sequents qu'on calcule*. PhD thesis, Université de Paris 7, 1994.
17. F. Kamareddine and R. P. Nederpelt. A useful λ-notation. *Theoretical Computer Science*, 155:85–109, 1996.
18. F. Kamareddine and A. Ríos. A λ-calculus à la de Bruijn with explicit substitutions. Proceedings of PLILP'95. *Lecture Notes in Computer Science*, 982:45–62, 1995.
19. J.-W. Klop. Term rewriting systems. *Handbook of Logic in Computer Science*, II, 1992.
20. J.-W. Klop, V. van Oostrom, and F. van Raamsdonk. Combinatory reduction systems: Introduction and survey. *Theoretical Computer Science*, 121:279–308, 1993.
21. L. Magnusson. *The implementation of ALF: a proof editor based on Martin-Löf's monomorphic type theory with explicit substitution*. PhD thesis, Department of Computer Science, Chalmers University, 1994.
22. A.R. Meyer and M. Wand. Continuation semantics in typed lambda-calculi (summary). In R. Parikh, editor, *Logics of Programs*, volume 193 of *Lecture Notes in Computer Science*, pages 219–224. Springer-Verlag, 1985.
23. C. Muños. Proof representation in type theory: State of the art. XXII Latinamerican Conference of Informatics CLEI Panel 96, June 3–7, 1996, Santafé de Bogotá, Colombia, April 1996.
24. C. Murthy. *Extracting Constructive Contents from Classical Proofs*. PhD thesis, Cornell University, 1990.
25. M. Parigot. $\lambda\mu$-calculus: An algorithmic interpretation of classical natural deduction. In *International Conference on Logic Programming and Automated Reasoning*, volume 624 of *Lecture Notes in Computer Science*, pages 190–201. Springer-Verlag, 1992.
26. G. Plotkin. Call-by-name, call-by-value and the λ-calculus. *Theoretical Computer Science*, 1(2):125–159, December 1975.
27. D. Prawitz. *Natural Deduction: A proof theoretical study*. Almquist & Wiksell, 1965.
28. N.J. Rehof and M.H. Sørensen. The λ_Δ calculus. In M. Hagiya and J. Mitchell, editors, *Theoretical Aspects of Computer Software*, volume 789 of *Lecture Notes in Computer Science*, pages 516–542. Springer-Verlag, 1994.
29. E. Ritter, D. Pym, and L. A. Wallen. On the intuitionistic force of classical search. In P. Miglioli, U. Moscato, D. Mundici, and M. Ornaghi, editors, *Procedings of TABLEAU'96*, volume 1071 of *Lecture Notes in Artificial Intelligence*, pages 295–311. Springer Verlag, 1996.
30. G. L. Steele. *Common Lisp: The Language*. Digital Press, Bedford, MA, 1984.

A Left-Linear Variant of λσ

César A. Muñoz H.

INRIA Rocquencourt
B.P. 105
78153 Le Chesnay Cedex, France
E-mail: Cesar.Munoz@inria.fr
Tel: (33) 1 39 63 51 57, Fax: (33) 1 39 63 53 30

Abstract. In this paper we consider λ-calculi of explicit substitutions that admit open expressions, i.e. expressions with meta-variables. In particular, we propose a variant of the $\lambda\sigma$-calculus that we call $\lambda_{\mathcal{L}}$. For this calculus and its simply-typed version, we study its meta-theoretical properties. The $\lambda_{\mathcal{L}}$-calculus enjoys the same general characteristics as $\lambda\sigma$, i.e. a simple and finitary first-order presentation, confluent on expressions with meta-variables of terms and weakly normalizing on typed expressions. Moreover, $\lambda_{\mathcal{L}}$ does not have the non-left-linear surjective pairing rule of $\lambda\sigma$ which raises technical problems in some frameworks.

1 Introduction

There are several versions of λ-calculi of explicit substitutions (see, among others, [1, 20, 14, 2, 21, 3, 17, 25, 6]). All these calculi implement β-reductions by means of a lazy mechanism of reduction of substitutions.

In typed λ-calculi, the explicit substitutions have been proposed as a framework for higher-order unification [4, 5, 19], or for representation of incomplete proofs [22, 26]. In these approaches, terms with holes are represented by open terms, i.e. terms with meta-variables.

In order to consider open terms, most of the calculi of explicit substitutions have a strong drawback: non-confluence on terms with meta-variables. Confluence and weak normalization are sufficient to decide equivalence of terms. Hence, these two properties seem to be desirable in any extension of λ-calculi of explicit substitutions with meta-variables.

The $\lambda\sigma$-calculus[1] is one of the most popular calculus of explicit substitutions. It is a first-order rewrite system with two sorts of expressions: terms and substitutions. In this calculus, free and bound variables are represented by de Bruijn's indices, and hence, λ-terms correspond to ground $\lambda\sigma$-terms without substitutions. The $\lambda\sigma$-calculus is not confluent on general open terms [3]. However, it is confluent if we consider expressions with meta-variables of terms but no meta-variables of substitutions [32]. These expressions are usually called *semi-open* expressions.

Compared with other confluent calculi on semi-open expressions (e.g. $\lambda_{\Uparrow}$ [3], λ_{S_e} [14] or λ_{ζ} [25]), the $\lambda\sigma$-calculus is a finitary first-order system (λ_{S_e} is not),

[1] In this paper we use $\lambda\sigma$ to designate the locally confluent calculus proposed in [1].

it allows composition and simultaneous substitutions (λ_ζ does not), and it is compatible with the extensional η-rule ($\lambda_\Uparrow$ is not).

The composition operator was introduced in $\lambda\sigma$ to solve a critical pair, and so, to gain local confluence. Composition of substitutions introduces simultaneous substitutions that happens to be useful for several purposes. For example, the modeling of closures of an abstract machine [12] or the pruning of search space in unification algorithms [4, 5, 19]. Also, this feature improves the substitution mechanism by allowing parallel substitutions of variables. An interesting discussion about composition of substitutions in λ-calculus can be found in [29].

However, composition of substitutions and simultaneous substitutions are responsible of the following non-left-linear rule in $\lambda\sigma$: $\mathbf{1}[S]\cdot(\uparrow\circ S) \xrightarrow{\text{(SCons)}} S$. Informally, if we interpret S as a list, $\mathbf{1}$ as the head function and $\uparrow$ as the tail function, then this rule corresponds to the surjective-pairing rule. The (SCons)-rule is impractical for many reasons. We have shown in [27] that $\lambda\sigma$ may loses the subject reduction property in a dependent type system due to (SCons). But also, independently, Nadathur [30] has remarked that this non-left-linear rule is difficult to handle in implementations. In fact, he shows that (SCons) is admissible in $\lambda\sigma$ when we consider semi-open terms and the following scheme of rule: $\mathbf{1}[\uparrow^n]\cdot\uparrow^{n+1} \xrightarrow{\text{(SCons)}} \uparrow^n$, where $\uparrow^n$ is a notation for $\overbrace{\uparrow\circ\ldots\circ\uparrow}^{n\text{-times}}$.

Following this idea, we propose a calculus of explicit substitutions that enjoys the same general features as $\lambda\sigma$, i.e. a simple and finitary first-order presentation, confluent on expressions with meta-variables of terms and weakly normalizing on typed terms. But, in contrast to $\lambda\sigma$, the new calculus does not have the (SCons)-rule which raises technical problems in some frameworks.

The rest of the paper is organized as follows. In Section 2 we present the $\lambda_\mathcal{L}$-calculus. The confluence property of $\lambda_\mathcal{L}$ is show in Section 3. In Section 4 we study the simply-typed version of $\lambda_\mathcal{L}$. In Section 5 we prove that $\lambda_\mathcal{L}$ is weakly normalizing on typed expressions. Last section summarizes the main contributions of this work.

2 $\lambda_\mathcal{L}$-Calculus

The finitary presentation of the scheme suggested by Nadathur is gained by the introduction of a sort to represent natural numbers and with an adequate set of rewrite rules to compute with them.

Well formed expressions in $\lambda_\mathcal{L}$ are defined by the following grammar:[2]

$$\begin{array}{lll} \textbf{Naturals} & n & ::= 0 \mid Suc(n) \\ \textbf{Terms} & M,N & ::= \mathbf{1} \mid \lambda M \mid (M\ N) \mid M[S] \\ \textbf{Substitutions} & S,T & ::= \uparrow^n \mid M\cdot S \mid S\circ T \end{array}$$

[2] In previous manuscripts ([28, 27]) the name of the calculus was λ_ϕ, but we have changed to $\lambda_\mathcal{L}$ in order to avoid confusion with the $\lambda\phi$-calculus proposed by Lescanne in [20].

The $\lambda_{\mathcal{L}}$-calculus is given by the rewrite system in Fig. 1.

$(\lambda M N)$	$\longrightarrow$	$M[N \cdot \uparrow^0]$	(Beta)
$(\lambda M)[S]$	$\longrightarrow$	$\lambda M[\mathbf{1} \cdot (S \circ \uparrow^{Suc(0)})]$	(Lambda)
$(M\ N)[S]$	$\longrightarrow$	$M[S]\ N[S]$	(App)
$M[S][T]$	$\longrightarrow$	$M[S \circ T]$	(Clos)
$\mathbf{1}[M \cdot S]$	$\longrightarrow$	M	(VarCons)
$M[\uparrow^0]$	$\longrightarrow$	M	(Id)
$(M \cdot S) \circ T$	$\longrightarrow$	$M[T] \cdot (S \circ T)$	(Map)
$\uparrow^0 \circ S$	$\longrightarrow$	S	(IdS)
$\uparrow^{Suc(n)} \circ (M \cdot S)$	$\longrightarrow$	$\uparrow^n \circ S$	(ShiftCons)
$\uparrow^{Suc(n)} \circ \uparrow^m$	$\longrightarrow$	$\uparrow^n \circ \uparrow^{Suc(m)}$	(ShiftShift)
$\mathbf{1} \cdot \uparrow^{Suc(0)}$	$\longrightarrow$	$\uparrow^0$	(Shift0)
$\mathbf{1}[\uparrow^n] \cdot \uparrow^{Suc(n)}$	$\longrightarrow$	$\uparrow^n$	(ShiftS)

Fig. 1. The rewrite system $\lambda_{\mathcal{L}}$

A first remark is that $\lambda_{\mathcal{L}}$ gathers, in its syntax, some notations that are frequently used to speak informally of $\lambda\sigma$. For example, the substitutions *id* and $\overbrace{\uparrow \circ \ldots \circ \uparrow}^{n+1}$ of $\lambda\sigma$, correspond respectively to $\uparrow^0$ and $\uparrow^{Suc(n)}$ in $\lambda_{\mathcal{L}}$. In the same way, the de Bruijn's indices $\underline{1}$ and $\underline{n+1}$ are represented respectively by $\mathbf{1}$ and $\mathbf{1}[\uparrow^n]$ in $\lambda_{\mathcal{L}}$. Thus, the scheme of rule suggested by Nadathur can be written as a first-order (and finitary) rule.

The sub-system $\mathcal{L}$ is obtained by dropping (Beta) from $\lambda_{\mathcal{L}}$.

Proposition 1. *$\mathcal{L}$ is terminating.*

Proof. In [36] this property has been proved by using the *semantic labelling* method (cf. [35]). An alternative proof is proposed in [28]. □

The rewrite system $\mathcal{L}$ is not confluent, not even locally confluent, on open expressions. We can check mechanically, for example using the RRL system [16], that $\mathcal{L}$ has the following critical pairs:

- **(Id-Clos).** $M[S] \xleftarrow{\mathcal{L}^+} M[S][\uparrow^0] \xrightarrow{\mathcal{L}^+} M[S \circ \uparrow^0]$.
- **(Clos-Clos).** $M[(S \circ T) \circ T'] \xleftarrow{\mathcal{L}^+} M[S][T][T'] \xrightarrow{\mathcal{L}^+} M[S \circ (T \circ T')]$.
- **(Shift0-Map).** $S \xleftarrow{\mathcal{L}^+} (\mathbf{1} \cdot \uparrow^{Suc(0)}) \circ S \xrightarrow{\mathcal{L}} \mathbf{1}[S] \cdot (\uparrow^{Suc(0)} \circ S)$.
- **(ShiftS-Map).** $\uparrow^n \circ S \xleftarrow{\mathcal{L}} (\mathbf{1}[\uparrow^n] \cdot \uparrow^{Suc(n)}) \circ S \xrightarrow{\mathcal{L}^+} \mathbf{1}[\uparrow^n \circ S] \cdot (\uparrow^{Suc(n)} \circ S)$.

– **(Lambda-Clos).** $\lambda M[\mathbf{1} \cdot ((S \circ \uparrow^{Suc(0)}) \circ (\mathbf{1} \cdot (T \circ \uparrow^{Suc(0)})))] \xleftarrow{\mathcal{L}^+}$ $(\lambda M)[S][T] \xrightarrow{\mathcal{L}^+} \lambda M[\mathbf{1} \cdot ((S \circ T) \circ \uparrow^{Suc(0)})]$.

If we consider (Beta), then we have additionally the following critical pair with (App):

$$M[N[S] \cdot S] \xleftarrow{\lambda_{\mathcal{L}}^+} (\lambda M\ N)[S] \xrightarrow{\lambda_{\mathcal{L}}^+} M[N[S] \cdot ((S \circ \uparrow^{Suc(0)}) \circ (N \cdot \uparrow^0))]$$

The following lemma proves that these critical pairs are joinable on the set of expressions that contain meta-variables of terms, but no meta-variables of substitutions or naturals, i.e. on semi-open expressions. Due to space limitation, we only sketch the proof of the main properties. For detailed proofs, see the extended version of this paper [28].

Proposition 2. *The critical pairs of $\lambda_{\mathcal{L}}$ are $\mathcal{L}$-joinable on semi-open expressions.*

Proof. For any any critical pair we reduce substitutions to $\mathcal{L}$-normal forms. Next, we proceed by structural induction on $\mathcal{L}$-normal substitutions. □

In the general case, local ground confluence cannot be mechanically verified [15]. However, the Critical Pair's lemma [13], i.e. a rewrite system is confluent if its critical pairs are joinable, holds also for ground expressions (cf. [15]): a rewrite system is *ground confluent* if its critical pairs are *ground joinable*. The Critical Pair's Lemma is not true for general many-sorted systems, but in [33] it has been proved that it holds if for every rule $l \longrightarrow r$, the sort of l and the sort of r are the same.

Proposition 3. *$\mathcal{L}$ is locally confluent on semi-open expressions.*

Proof. Notice that the $\lambda_{\mathcal{L}}$-calculus has three sorts of expressions: Naturals, Substitutions and Terms, but only meta-variables of terms are admitted. We must extend the Critical Pair's lemma to semi-open expressions. We check that $\mathcal{L}$ is a sort compatible system, i.e. terms reduce to terms and substitutions reduce to substitutions. Now, the proof follows straightforwardly the proofs in [33, 15]. Notice that if two expressions are joinable, then they are in particular joinable in semi-open expressions. Hence, it suffices to concentrate on those critical pairs that are not joinable on open terms, and we conclude with Proposition 2. □

Theorem 4. *$\mathcal{L}$ is confluent on semi-open expressions.*

Proof. By Proposition 1, $\mathcal{L}$ is terminating and by Proposition 3, $\mathcal{L}$ is locally confluent, so by Newman's Lemma, $\mathcal{L}$ is confluent. □

Corollary 5. *$\mathcal{L}$-normal forms of semi-open expressions always exist, and they are unique. We denote by $x\downarrow_{\mathcal{L}}$ the $\mathcal{L}$-normal form of x.*

Remark: The non-linearity of $\lambda_{\mathcal{L}}$ due to (ShiftS) is only apparent since the term with a double occurrence in this rule can be considered as a constant in the set of semi-open expressions. In particular, there are not reduction rules for natural numbers.

3 Confluence

An useful technique to prove confluence in calculi of explicit substitutions is the *interpretation method* [11, 17]. Although the interpretation method can be used to prove confluence on terms with meta-variables (cf. [32]), we prefer to use a technique that was coined in [34]: the Yokouchi-Hikita's Lemma. This lemma seems to be suitable for left-linear calculi of explicit substitutions [3, 31, 25].

Lemma 6 Yokouchi-Hikita's Lemma. *Let R and S be two relations defined on a set X such that: 1. R is confluent and terminating, 2. S is strongly confluent and 3. S and R commute in the following way, for any $x, y, z \in X$, if $x \xrightarrow{R} y$ and $x \xrightarrow{S} z$, then there exists $w \in X$ such that $y \xrightarrow{R^*SR^*} w$ and $z \xrightarrow{R^*} w$, i.e. the following diagram holds:*

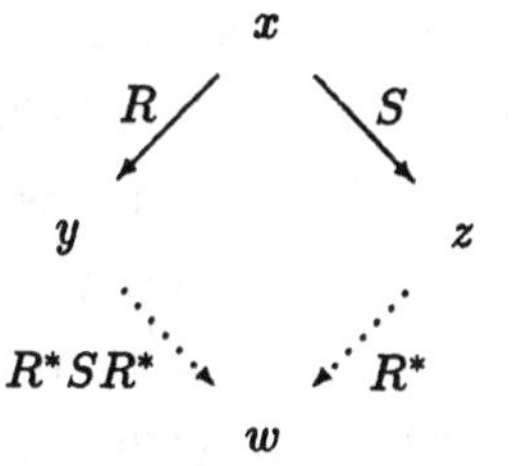

Then the relation R^*SR^* is confluent.

Proof. See [3]. □

We take the set of semi-open expressions as X, $\mathcal{L}$ as R and $B_{\|}$ as S, where $B_{\|}$ is the parallelization of (Beta) defined by:

$$\frac{}{x \longrightarrow x}\ (\text{Refl}_{\|}) \qquad \frac{M \longrightarrow N}{\lambda M \longrightarrow \lambda N}\ (\text{Lambda}_{\|})$$

$$\frac{M \longrightarrow M' \qquad N \longrightarrow N'}{M\ N \longrightarrow M'\ N'}\ (\text{App}_{\|}) \qquad \frac{M \longrightarrow N \qquad S \longrightarrow T}{M[S] \longrightarrow N[T]}\ (\text{Clos}_{\|})$$

$$\frac{M \longrightarrow N \qquad S \longrightarrow T}{M \cdot S \longrightarrow N \cdot T}\ (\text{Cons}_{\|}) \qquad \frac{S \longrightarrow S' \qquad T \longrightarrow T'}{S \circ T \longrightarrow S' \circ T'}\ (\text{Comp}_{\|})$$

$$\frac{M \longrightarrow M' \qquad N \longrightarrow N'}{(\lambda M\ N) \longrightarrow M'[N' \cdot \uparrow^0]}\ (\text{Beta}_{\|})$$

Proposition 7. *On semi-open expressions, $\mathcal{L}$ and $B_{\|}$ satisfy the conditions of Lemma 6. Therefore, $\mathcal{L}^* B_{\|} \mathcal{L}^*$ is confluent.*

Proof. (1) By Proposition 1 and Theorem 4, $\mathcal{L}$ is terminating and confluent on semi-open expressions. (2) $B_{\|}$ is strongly confluent, since (Beta) by itself is a left linear system with no critical pairs (cf. [13]). (3) Assume that an arbitrary expression x reduces in one $\mathcal{L}$-step to y, and in one $B_{\|}$-step to z. We prove, by induction on the depth of the $\mathcal{L}$-redex reduced in x, that there exists w such that $y \xrightarrow{\mathcal{L}^* B_{\|} \mathcal{L}^*} w$ and $z \xrightarrow{\mathcal{L}^*} w$. At the base case x is a $\mathcal{L}$-redex:

- (App). There are two cases:
  - $x = (M\ N)[S] \xrightarrow{\text{(App)}} (M[S]\ N[S]) = y$ and $(M\ N)[S] \xrightarrow{B_{\|}} (M'\ N')[S'] = z$, with $M \xrightarrow{B_{\|}} M'$, $N \xrightarrow{B_{\|}} N'$ and $S \xrightarrow{B_{\|}} S'$. By definition of $B_{\|}$, $(M[S]\ N[S]) \xrightarrow{B_{\|}} (M'[S']\ N'[S']) = w$. But also, $(M'\ N')[S'] \xrightarrow{\text{(App)}} (M'[S']\ N'[S']) = w$.
  - $x = (\lambda M\ N)[S] \xrightarrow{\text{(App)}} ((\lambda M)[S]\ N[S]) = y$ and $(\lambda M\ N)[S] \xrightarrow{B_{\|}} M'[N' \cdot \uparrow^0][S'] = z$, with $M \xrightarrow{B_{\|}} M'$, $N \xrightarrow{B_{\|}} N'$ and $S \xrightarrow{B_{\|}} S'$. Let $\hat{S}'$ the $\mathcal{L}$-normal form of S' (Corollary 5). Then, $y = ((\lambda M)[S]\ N[S]) \xrightarrow{\text{(Lambda)}} (\lambda M[\mathbf{1} \cdot (S \circ \uparrow^{Suc(0)})]\ N[S]) \xrightarrow{B_{\|}} M'[\mathbf{1} \cdot (S' \circ \uparrow^{Suc(0)})][N'[S'] \cdot \uparrow^0] \xrightarrow{\mathcal{L}^*} M'[N'[\hat{S}'] \cdot \hat{S}']$. But also, $M'[N' \cdot \uparrow^0][S'] \xrightarrow{\mathcal{L}^*} M'[N'[\hat{S}'] \cdot \hat{S}']$. This case is the only interesting one.
- (Lambda). $x = (\lambda M)[S] \xrightarrow{\text{(Lambda)}} \lambda M[\mathbf{1} \cdot (S \circ \uparrow^{Suc(0)})] = y$ and $x = (\lambda M)[S] \xrightarrow{B_{\|}} (\lambda M')[S'] = z$, with $M \xrightarrow{B_{\|}} M'$ and $S \xrightarrow{B_{\|}} S'$. By definition of $B_{\|}$, $\lambda M[\mathbf{1} \cdot (S \circ \uparrow^{Suc(0)})] \xrightarrow{B_{\|}} \lambda M'[\mathbf{1} \cdot (S' \circ \uparrow^{Suc(0)})] = w$. But also, $(\lambda M')[S'] \xrightarrow{\text{(Lambda)}} \lambda M'[\mathbf{1} \cdot (S' \circ \uparrow^{Suc(0)})] = w$.
- The other cases are similar to the previous one.

At the induction step we solve with the induction hypothesis. □

Theorem 8 Confluence. *$\lambda_{\mathcal{L}}$ is confluent on semi-open expressions.*

Proof. Notice that $\lambda_{\mathcal{L}} \subseteq \mathcal{L}^* B_{\|} \mathcal{L}^* \subseteq \lambda_{\mathcal{L}}{}^*$. If $x \xrightarrow{\lambda_{\mathcal{L}}{}^*} y$ and $x \xrightarrow{\lambda_{\mathcal{L}}{}^*} z$, then by Proposition 7, there exists w such that $y \xrightarrow{(\mathcal{L}^* B_{\|} \mathcal{L}^*)^*} w$ and $z \xrightarrow{(\mathcal{L}^* B_{\|} \mathcal{L}^*)^*} w$. So, $y \xrightarrow{\lambda_{\mathcal{L}}{}^*} w$ and $z \xrightarrow{\lambda_{\mathcal{L}}{}^*} w$. □

4 The simply-typed version

We consider a simple type theory, where types are generated from a set of basic types $a, b, \ldots$ and the arrow ($\rightarrow$) type constructor. The simple type system we propose is inspired in that of $\lambda\sigma$ [1].

Like the simply-typed λ-calculus in de Bruijn's notation, typing contexts (of free variables) are structured as lists of types. The grammar of types and contexts is:

$$
\begin{array}{lll}
\textbf{Types} & A, B & ::= a, b, \ldots \mid A \rightarrow B \\
\textbf{Contexts}\ \Gamma & & ::= nil \mid A.\Gamma
\end{array}
$$

Typed terms differ from untyped ones only in abstraction expressions. We prefer a *Church style* notation where types of binder variables appear explicitly in the syntax.

$$\textbf{Terms}\ M, N \ ::= \ \ldots \mid \lambda_A.M \mid \ldots$$

The $\lambda_{\mathcal{L}}$-calculus is modified according to this new syntax of abstractions. However, it is not difficult to see that properties of Section 2 and 3 are preserved.

Typing assertions have one of the following forms:

- $\Gamma \vdash M : A$, the term M has type A in the context Γ.
- $\Gamma \vdash S \triangleright \Delta$, the substitution S has type Δ in the context Γ.

$$\frac{}{A.\Gamma \vdash \mathbf{1} : A}\ (\mathrm{Var}) \qquad\qquad \frac{A.\Gamma \vdash M : B}{\Gamma \vdash \lambda_A.M : A \to B}\ (\mathrm{Abs})$$

$$\frac{\Gamma \vdash M : A \to B \quad \Gamma \vdash N : A}{\Gamma \vdash (M\ N) : B}\ (\mathrm{Appl}) \qquad \frac{\Gamma \vdash S \triangleright \Delta \quad \Delta \vdash M : A}{\Gamma \vdash M[S] : A}\ (\mathrm{Clos})$$

$$\frac{}{\Gamma \vdash \uparrow^{0} \triangleright \Gamma}\ (\mathrm{Id}) \qquad\qquad \frac{\Gamma \vdash \uparrow^{n} \triangleright \Delta}{A.\Gamma \vdash \uparrow^{Suc(n)} \triangleright \Delta}\ (\mathrm{Shift})$$

$$\frac{\Gamma \vdash S \triangleright \Delta' \quad \Delta' \vdash T \triangleright \Delta}{\Gamma \vdash T \circ S \triangleright \Delta}\ (\mathrm{Comp}) \qquad \frac{\Gamma \vdash M : A \quad \Gamma \vdash S \triangleright \Delta}{\Gamma \vdash M \cdot S \triangleright A.\Delta}\ (\mathrm{Cons})$$

Each meta-variable is typed in a unique context by a unique type (c.f. [4, 22]):

$$\frac{}{\Gamma_X \vdash X : A_X}\ (\mathrm{Meta}_X)$$

Example 1.

1. This is a type derivation of $A.nil \vdash \lambda_B.(X\ \mathbf{1}[\uparrow^{Suc(0)}]) : B \to C$.

$$\dfrac{\dfrac{\dfrac{}{B.A.nil \vdash X : A \to C}\ (\mathrm{Meta}_X) \quad \dfrac{\dfrac{\dfrac{}{A.nil \vdash \uparrow^{0} \triangleright A.nil}\ (\mathrm{Id})}{B.A.nil \vdash \uparrow^{Suc(0)} \triangleright A.nil}\ (\mathrm{Shift}) \quad \dfrac{}{A.nil \vdash \mathbf{1} : A}\ (\mathrm{Var})}{B.A.nil \vdash \mathbf{1}[\uparrow^{Suc(0)}] : A}\ (\mathrm{Clos})}{B.A.nil \vdash (X\ \mathbf{1}[\uparrow^{Suc(0)}]) : C}\ (\mathrm{Appl})}{A.nil \vdash \lambda_B.(X\ \mathbf{1}[\uparrow^{Suc(0)}]) : B \to C}\ (\mathrm{Abs})$$

2. The term $(\lambda_A.X\ X)$ is not well-typed in any context. Notice that in the following derivation:

$$\dfrac{\dfrac{\dfrac{\ldots}{A.\Gamma \vdash X : A}}{\Gamma \vdash \lambda_A.X : A \to A}\ (\mathrm{Abs}) \qquad \dfrac{\ldots}{\Gamma \vdash X : A}}{\Gamma \vdash (\lambda_A.X\ X) : A \to A}\ (\mathrm{Appl})$$

the meta-variable X must be typed in two different contexts: $A.\Gamma$ and Γ.

3. Let X be a meta-variable such that $\Gamma \vdash X : A$. In this example, we take the index $\underline{2}$ as a notation for $\mathbf{1}[\uparrow^{Suc(0)}]$. We have the valid typing judgment: $\Gamma \vdash (\lambda_A.\lambda_B.\underline{2}\ X) : B \to A$. We obtain by $\lambda_{\mathcal{L}}$-reduction:

$$(\lambda_A.\lambda_B.\underline{2}\ X) \xrightarrow{\text{(Beta)}} (\lambda_B.\underline{2})[X \cdot \uparrow^0] \xrightarrow{\lambda_{\mathcal{L}}^*} \lambda_B.X[\uparrow^{Suc(0)}]$$

Also, we can verify that $\Gamma \vdash \lambda_B.X[\uparrow^{Suc(0)}] : B \to A$.

Notice that the type system is syntax directed, i.e. there is one rule for each constructor of terms and substitutions. Using this fact, we can prove easily that for a given context, the type of an expression is unique (*type uniqueness' lemma*).

Lemma 9 Type Uniqueness.

1. *If* $\Gamma_1 \vdash M : A_1$ *and* $\Gamma_2 \vdash M : A_2$, *then* $A_1 = A_2$.
2. *If* $\Gamma_1 \vdash S \triangleright \Delta_1$ *and* $\Gamma_2 \vdash S \triangleright \Delta_2$, *then* $\Delta_1 = \Delta_2$.

Proof. We proceed by simultaneous structural induction on M and S. □

Example 1(3) suggests that typing is preserved under $\lambda_{\mathcal{L}}$-reductions. This property is known as *subject reduction*.

Theorem 10 Subject Reduction. *Let* x *and* y *be such that* $x \xrightarrow{\lambda_{\mathcal{L}}^*} y$, *then*

- *if* x *is a term and* $\Gamma \vdash x : A$, *then* $\Gamma \vdash y : A$, *and*
- *if* x *is a substitution and* $\Gamma \vdash x \triangleright \Delta$, *then* $\Gamma \vdash y \triangleright \Delta$.

Proof. We show that typing is preserved for one-step reductions (i.e. $\xrightarrow{\lambda_{\mathcal{L}}}$), and then it is also for its reflexive and transitive closure (i.e. $\xrightarrow{\lambda_{\mathcal{L}}^*}$). Let $x \xrightarrow{\lambda_{\mathcal{L}}} y$ be a one-step reduction, we proceed by induction on the depth of the redex reduced in x. At the initial case x is reduced at the top level, and we prove that every rule preserves typing. At the induction step we resolve with induction hypothesis. □

In the $\lambda_{\mathcal{L}}$-system, just as in $\lambda\sigma$, instantiation of meta-variables and typing commute. This property guarantees the soundness of instantiation of meta-variables in the unification algorithm [4, 5, 19], or in the refinements steps of incomplete proofs [26].

Lemma 11 Instantiation Soundness. *Let* N *be a term such that* $\Gamma_X \vdash N : A_X$, *where* Γ_X *and* A_x *are respectively the unique context and unique type of a meta-variable* X. *Then,*

1. *if* $\Delta \vdash M : B$, *then* $\Delta \vdash M\{X \mapsto N\} : B$, *and*
2. *if* $\Delta \vdash S \triangleright \Delta'$, *then* $\Delta \vdash S\{X \mapsto N\} \triangleright \Delta'$,

where $x\{X \mapsto N\}$ *is a notation for the remplacement of meta-variable* X *by* N *in the expression* x *without take care of possible capture of free variables.*

Proof. We reason by induction on type derivation. □

5 Weak Normalization

Strong normalization on typed terms does not hold for $\lambda_{\mathcal{L}}$. In fact, Melliès shows in [23] that his counter-example for preservation of strong normalization in the $\lambda\sigma$-calculus [24], can be adapted to systems without associativity of composition (as $\lambda_{\mathcal{L}}$), and even if we give priority to the rules (ShiftCons) and (VarCons).

In λ-calculi of explicit substitutions that implement one-step semantic of β-reduction —i.e. if M, N are pure terms[3] and $M \xrightarrow{\beta} N$, then $M \xrightarrow{\text{(Beta)}} M'$ where N is the substitution-normal form of M'— as $\lambda\sigma$, $\lambda_{\Uparrow}$ and $\lambda_{\mathcal{L}}$, weak normalization on typed pure terms follows directly from strong normalization of typed λ-calculus. When we consider semi-open expressions, it arises an additional difficulty: the presence of meta-variables and substitutions on normal forms. Notice that the set of normal forms of semi-open expressions is not include in the set of pure terms, e.g. the term $X[\uparrow^{Suc(0)}]$ is a $\lambda_{\mathcal{L}}$-normal form, but it is not pure.

For the simply-typed version of $\lambda\sigma$ (with meta-variables), Goubault-Larreq [10] proposes a clever translation from $\lambda\sigma$-terms into a family of λ-terms. In this approach, weak normalization is deduced from strong normalization of the simply-typed λ-calculus. That proof is adapted to a second-order type system without dependent types in [9].

In this section, we prove that $\lambda_{\mathcal{L}}$ is weakly normalizing on typed expressions. In particular, we show that the reduction of (Beta) followed by a $\mathcal{L}$-normalization is strongly normalizing on typed expressions. The proof we provide can be adapted to $\lambda\sigma$ in a straightforward way. This gives an alternative proof to that developed by Goubault-Larreq. Our proof is based on that proposed by Geuvers for the Calculus of Construction [7]. The technique that we use is extended to a dependent type system with explicit substitutions in [27].

The general idea of the proof is to give an interpretation for each type into a set of terms satisfying certain closure properties (these sets are called *saturated* sets). Terms are also interpreted by functions called *valuations*. In our proof, valuations are just particular explicit substitutions. We prove that if M is a $\mathcal{L}$-normal form and $\Gamma \vdash M : A$, then for any valuation S of M, the substitution normal form of $M[S]$, i.e. $(M[S])\downarrow_{\mathcal{L}}$, is included in the interpretation of A, denoted $[\![A]\!]$. The identity substitution is a valuation of any term, thus, in particular, $(M[\uparrow^0])\downarrow_{\mathcal{L}} = M \in [\![A]\!]$. The closure properties of $[\![A]\!]$ are sufficient to conclude that M is weakly normalizing.

We define $\mathcal{NF}_{\mathcal{L}}$ as the set that contains all the $\mathcal{L}$-normal forms of semi-open expressions.

Definition 12. Let $x, y \in \mathcal{NF}_{\mathcal{L}}$, we say that x *$\beta_{\mathcal{L}}$-converts* to y, noted by $x \xrightarrow{\beta_{\mathcal{L}}} y$, if and only if $x \xrightarrow{\text{(Beta)}} w$ and $y = w\downarrow_{\mathcal{L}}$.

We denote by $\mathcal{SN}$ the set of $\beta_{\mathcal{L}}$-strongly normalizing expressions of $\mathcal{NF}_{\mathcal{L}}$.

Definition 13. Let M be in $\mathcal{NF}_{\mathcal{L}}$, M is *neutral* if it does not have the form $\lambda_A.N$. The set of neutral terms is denoted by $\mathcal{NT}$.

[3] A pure term is a ground term which does not contain substitutions.

Definition 14. A set of terms $\Lambda \subseteq \mathcal{NF}_{\mathcal{L}}$ is *saturated* if

1. $\Lambda \subseteq \mathcal{SN}$.
2. If $M \in \Lambda$ and $M \xrightarrow{\beta_{\mathcal{L}}} M'$, then $M' \in \Lambda$.
3. If $M \in \mathcal{NT}$, and whenever we reduce a $\beta_{\mathcal{L}}$-redex of M we obtain a term $M' \in \Lambda$, then $M \in \Lambda$.

The set of saturated sets is denoted by **SAT**.

From Def. 14(3):

Remark 15. Let $M \in \mathcal{NT}$ such that M is a $\beta_{\mathcal{L}}$-normal form. For any $\Lambda \in$ **SAT**, $M \in \Lambda$.

Lemma 16. $\mathcal{SN} \in$ **SAT**.

Proof. We verify easily the following conditions.

1. $\mathcal{SN} \subseteq \mathcal{SN}$.
2. If $M \in \mathcal{SN}$ and $M \xrightarrow{\beta_{\mathcal{L}}} M'$, then $M' \in \mathcal{SN}$.
3. If $M \in \mathcal{NT}$, and whenever we reduce a $\beta_{\mathcal{L}}$-redex of M we obtain a term $M' \in \mathcal{SN}$, then $M \in \mathcal{SN}$.

□

Definition 17. Let $\Lambda, \Lambda' \in$ **SAT**, we define the set

$$\Lambda \to \Lambda' = \{M \in \mathcal{NF}_{\mathcal{L}} \mid \forall N \in \Lambda \ : \ (M\ N) \in \Lambda'\}$$

Lemma 18. **SAT** *is closed under function spaces, i.e. if* $\Lambda, \Lambda' \in$ **SAT**, *then* $\Lambda \to \Lambda' \in$ **SAT**.

Proof. We show:

1. $\Lambda \to \Lambda' \subseteq \mathcal{SN}$.
   Let $M \in \Lambda \to \Lambda'$, by Def. 17 and Def. 14(1), $(M\ N) \in \Lambda' \subseteq \mathcal{SN}$ for all $N \in \Lambda$. Thus, $M \in \mathcal{SN}$.
2. If $M \in \Lambda \to \Lambda'$ and $M \xrightarrow{\beta_{\mathcal{L}}} M'$, then $M' \in \Lambda \to \Lambda'$.
   Let $N \in \Lambda$, we show that $(M'\ N) \in \Lambda'$. By hypothesis, $(M\ N) \xrightarrow{\beta_{\mathcal{L}}} (M'\ N)$, and $(M\ N) \in \Lambda'$. Thus, by Def. 14(2), $(M'\ N) \in \Lambda'$.
3. If $M \in \mathcal{NT}$, and whenever we reduce a $\beta_{\mathcal{L}}$-redex of M we obtain a term $M' \in \Lambda \to \Lambda'$, then $M \in \Lambda \to \Lambda'$.
   Let $N \in \Lambda$, we show that $(M\ N) \in \Lambda'$. Since $(M\ N) \in \mathcal{NT}$, then by Def. 14(3), it suffices to prove that if $(M\ N) \xrightarrow{\beta_{\mathcal{L}}} M''$, then $M'' \in \Lambda'$. We have $N \in \Lambda \subseteq \mathcal{SN}$, so we can reason by induction on $\nu(N)$[4]. In one step $(M\ N)$ $\beta_{\mathcal{L}}$-reduces to:

[4] "If x is strongly normalizing, $\nu(x)$ is a number which bounds the length of every normalization sequence beginning with x" [8].

- $(M' \ N)$, with $M \xrightarrow{\beta_{\mathcal{L}}} M'$. By hypothesis, $M' \in \Lambda \to \Lambda'$ and $N \in \Lambda$, thus $(M' \ N) \in \Lambda'$.
- $(M \ N')$, with $N \xrightarrow{\beta_{\mathcal{L}}} N'$. By Def. 14(2), $N' \in \Lambda$, and $\nu(N') < \nu(N)$, so by induction hypothesis, $(M \ N') \in \Lambda'$.
- There is no other possibility since $M \in \mathcal{NT}$.

□

Definition 19. The *type interpretation function* is defined inductively on types as follows:

$$\begin{array}{lcll} [\![\iota]\!] & = & \mathcal{SN} & \text{if } \iota \text{ is a basic type} \\ [\![A \to B]\!] & = & [\![A]\!] \to [\![B]\!] & \end{array}$$

Remark 20. By Lemma 18, for any type A, $[\![A]\!] \in \mathbf{SAT}$.

Lemma 21. *Let $M, S \in \mathcal{NF}_{\mathcal{L}}$, for any substitution T*

1. *if $M \xrightarrow{\beta_{\mathcal{L}}} M'$, then $(M[T])\downarrow_{\mathcal{L}} \xrightarrow{\beta_{\mathcal{L}}} (M'[T])\downarrow_{\mathcal{L}}$, and*
2. *if $S \xrightarrow{\beta_{\mathcal{L}}} S'$, then $(S \circ T)\downarrow_{\mathcal{L}} \xrightarrow{\beta_{\mathcal{L}}} (S'[T])\downarrow_{\mathcal{L}}$.*

Proof. We reason by simultaneous structural induction on M and S. □

Corollary 22. *Let $M, S \in \mathcal{NF}_{\mathcal{L}}$, for any substitution T*

1. *if $(M[T])\downarrow_{\mathcal{L}} \in \mathcal{SN}$, then $M \in \mathcal{SN}$, and*
2. *if $(S \circ T)\downarrow_{\mathcal{L}} \in \mathcal{SN}$, then $S \in \mathcal{SN}$.*

Lemma 23. *Let $M \in \mathcal{NF}_{\mathcal{L}}$, if for all $N \in [\![A]\!]$, $(M[N \cdot \uparrow^0])\downarrow_{\mathcal{L}} \in [\![B]\!]$, then $\lambda_A.M \in [\![A]\!] \to [\![B]\!]$.*

Proof. Let $N \in [\![A]\!]$, we show that $(\lambda_A.M \ N) \in [\![B]\!]$. Since $(\lambda_A.M \ N) \in \mathcal{NT}$, it suffices to prove that if $(\lambda_A.M \ N) \xrightarrow{\beta_{\mathcal{L}}} M''$, then $M'' \in [\![B]\!]$. We have $(M[N \cdot \uparrow^0])\downarrow_{\mathcal{L}} \in [\![B]\!] \subseteq \mathcal{SN}$, so by Corollary 22, $M \in \mathcal{SN}$; and by hypothesis, $N \in [\![A]\!] \subseteq \mathcal{SN}$. Thus, we can reason by induction on $\nu(M) + \nu(N)$. In one step $(\lambda_A.M \ N)$ $\beta_{\mathcal{L}}$-reduces to:

- $(M[N \cdot \uparrow^0])\downarrow_{\mathcal{L}}$. By hypothesis, $(M[N \cdot \uparrow^0])\downarrow_{\mathcal{L}} \in [\![B]\!]$.
- $(\lambda_A.M' \ N)$, with $M \xrightarrow{\beta_{\mathcal{L}}} M'$. By Lemma 21, $(M[N \cdot \uparrow^0])\downarrow_{\mathcal{L}} \xrightarrow{\beta_{\mathcal{L}}} (M'[N \cdot \uparrow^0])\downarrow_{\mathcal{L}}$. Since, $(M[N \cdot \uparrow^0])\downarrow_{\mathcal{L}} \in [\![B]\!]$, we have by Def. 14(2), $(M'[N \cdot \uparrow^0])\downarrow_{\mathcal{L}} \in [\![B]\!]$. But also, $\nu(M') < \nu(M)$, so by induction hypothesis, $(\lambda_A.M' \ N) \in [\![B]\!]$.
- $(\lambda_A.M \ N')$, with $N \xrightarrow{\beta_{\mathcal{L}}} N'$. By Def. 14(2), $N' \in [\![A]\!]$, so by hypothesis, $(M[N' \cdot \uparrow^0])\downarrow_{\mathcal{L}} \in [\![B]\!]$. But also, $\nu(N') < \nu(N)$, so by induction hypothesis, $(\lambda_A.M \ N') \in [\![B]\!]$.

□

Lemma 24. *For any $\Lambda \in \mathbf{SAT}$, substitution $S \in \mathcal{SN}$, and meta-variable X, $(X[S])\downarrow_{\mathcal{L}} \in \Lambda$.*

Proof. Let $M = (X[S])\downarrow_{\mathcal{L}}$, we reason by induction on $\nu(S)$. M is neutral, then by Def. 14(3), it suffices to consider the reductions of M.

- $M \xrightarrow{\beta_{\mathcal{L}}} X$. By Remark 15, $X \in \Lambda$.
- $M \xrightarrow{\beta_{\mathcal{L}}} X[S']$, with $S \xrightarrow{\beta_{\mathcal{L}}} S'$. By hypothesis, $S' \in \mathcal{SN}$ and $\nu(S') < \nu(S)$, so by induction hypothesis, $(X[S'])\downarrow_{\mathcal{L}} = X[S'] \in \Lambda$.

In every case, M $\beta_{\mathcal{L}}$-reduces into terms in Λ, thus by Def. 14(3), $(X[S])\downarrow_{\mathcal{L}} \in \Lambda$. □

Definition 25. The *valuations* of Γ, noted by $[\![\Gamma]\!]$, is a set of substitutions in $\mathcal{NF}_{\mathcal{L}}$ defined inductively on Γ as follows:

$$\begin{array}{lcl} [\![nil]\!] & = & \{\uparrow^n \mid \text{for any natural } n\} \\ [\![A.\Gamma']\!] & = & [\![nil]\!] \cup \{M \cdot S \in \mathcal{NF}_{\mathcal{L}} \mid M \in [\![A]\!], S \in [\![\Gamma']\!]\} \end{array}$$

Notice that if $M \in [\![A]\!]$ and $S \in [\![\Gamma]\!]$, then $M \cdot S$ is not necessarily in $[\![A.\Gamma]\!]$ (since $M \cdot S$ may not be in $\mathcal{NF}_{\mathcal{L}}$). However, we verify easily the following property.

Remark 26. If $M \in [\![A]\!]$ and $S \in [\![\Gamma]\!]$, then $(M \cdot S)\downarrow_{\mathcal{L}} \in [\![A.\Gamma]\!]$.

Lemma 27. *For any Γ, $[\![\Gamma]\!] \subseteq \mathcal{SN}$.*

Proof. We prove by structural induction on S that if $S \in [\![\Gamma]\!]$, then $S \in \mathcal{SN}$.

- $S = \uparrow^n$. In this case S is a $\beta_{\mathcal{L}}$-normal form, then the conclusion is trivial.
- $S = M \cdot T$. By Def. 25, $\Gamma = A.\Gamma'$, $T \in [\![\Gamma']\!]$ and $M \in [\![A]\!] \subseteq \mathcal{SN}$. By induction hypothesis, $T \in \mathcal{SN}$. We prove by induction on $\nu(M) + \nu(T)$ that $M \cdot T \in \mathcal{SN}$ (notice that $M \cdot T \in \mathcal{NF}_{\mathcal{L}}$).

Definition 28. Let $M, S \in \mathcal{NF}_{\mathcal{L}}$, we define

1. Γ satisfies that M is of type A, noted by $\Gamma \models M : A$, if and only if $(M[T])\downarrow_{\mathcal{L}} \in [\![A]\!]$ for any $T \in [\![\Gamma]\!]$.
2. Γ satisfies that S is of type Δ, noted by $\Gamma \models S \triangleright \Delta$, if and only if $(S \circ T)\downarrow_{\mathcal{L}} \in [\![\Delta]\!]$ for any $T \in [\![\Gamma]\!]$.

Proposition 29 Soundness of $\models$.

1. If $\Gamma \vdash M : A$, then $\Gamma \models M : A$,
2. If $\Gamma \vdash S \triangleright \Delta$, then $\Gamma \models S \triangleright \Delta$.

Proof. By simultaneous induction on derivations $\Gamma \vdash M : A$ and $\Gamma \vdash S \triangleright \Delta$. The last applied rule is:

- (Var). In this case, $M = \mathbf{1}$ and $\Gamma = A.\Gamma'$. Let $T \in [\![\Gamma]\!]$, there are three cases:
  - $T = \uparrow^0$. Therefore, $(\mathbf{1}[T])\downarrow_{\mathcal{L}} = \mathbf{1}$. But also, $\mathbf{1}$ is a neutral $\beta_{\mathcal{L}}$-normal form, then by Remark 15, $\mathbf{1} \in [\![A]\!]$.

- $T = \uparrow^{Suc(n)}$. Therefore, $(\mathbf{1}[T])\downarrow_{\mathcal{L}} = \mathbf{1}[\uparrow^{Suc(n)}]$. But also, $\mathbf{1}[\uparrow^{Suc(n)}]$ is a neutral $\beta_{\mathcal{L}}$-normal form, then by Remark 15, $\mathbf{1}[\uparrow^{Suc(n)}] \in [\![A]\!]$.
- $T = M' \cdot S'$. Therefore, $(\mathbf{1}[T])\downarrow_{\mathcal{L}} = M'$. By Def. 25 and hypothesis $\Gamma = A.\Gamma'$, we have that $M \in [\![A]\!]$.

– (Clos). In this case $M = M'[S']$, $\Gamma \vdash S \triangleright \Delta$, and $\Delta \vdash M' : A$. We reason by cases analysis on M' and S'.
  - $M' = \mathbf{1}$ and $S' = \uparrow^{Suc(n)}$. Let $T \in [\![\Gamma]\!]$, by induction hypothesis, $(\uparrow^{Suc(n)} \circ T)\downarrow_{\mathcal{L}} \in [\![\Delta]\!]$. Notice that $(\mathbf{1}[\uparrow^{Suc(n)}][T])\downarrow_{\mathcal{L}} = (\mathbf{1}[\uparrow^{Suc(n)} \circ T])\downarrow_{\mathcal{L}}$ $= (\mathbf{1}[(\uparrow^{Suc(n)} \circ T)\downarrow_{\mathcal{L}}])\downarrow_{\mathcal{L}}$. By induction hypothesis, $(\mathbf{1}[(\uparrow^{Suc(n)} \circ T)\downarrow_{\mathcal{L}}])\downarrow_{\mathcal{L}} \in [\![A]\!]$, and thus, $(\mathbf{1}[\uparrow^{Suc(n)}][T])\downarrow_{\mathcal{L}} \in [\![A]\!]$.
  - $M = X$ (X is a meta-variable). Let $T \in [\![\Gamma]\!]$, by induction hypothesis, $(S' \circ T)\downarrow_{\mathcal{L}} \in [\![\Delta]\!]$. Notice that $(X[S'][T])\downarrow_{\mathcal{L}} = (X[S' \circ T])\downarrow_{\mathcal{L}} = (X[(S' \circ T)\downarrow_{\mathcal{L}}])\downarrow_{\mathcal{L}}$. By induction hypothesis, $(X[(S' \circ T)\downarrow_{\mathcal{L}}])\downarrow_{\mathcal{L}} \in [\![A]\!]$, and thus, $(X[S'][T])\downarrow_{\mathcal{L}} \in [\![A]\!]$.

– (Meta$_X$). In this case $M = X$ (X is a meta-variable). Let $T \in [\![\Gamma]\!]$, there are two cases:
  - $T = \uparrow^0$. Therefore, $(X[T])\downarrow_{\mathcal{L}} = X$. But also, X is a neutral $\beta_{\mathcal{L}}$-normal form, then by Remark 15, $X \in [\![A]\!]$.
  - $T \neq \uparrow^0$. Therefore, $(X[T])\downarrow_{\mathcal{L}} = X[T]$. By Lemma 27, $T \in \mathcal{SN}$, then by Lemma 24, $X[T] \in [\![A]\!]$.

– (Abs). In this case $M = \lambda_{A_1}.M_1$, $A_1.\Gamma \vdash M_1 : B_1$, and $A = A_1 \rightarrow B_1$. By Def. 19, $[\![A]\!] = [\![A_1 \rightarrow B_1]\!] = [\![A_1]\!] \rightarrow [\![B_1]\!]$. Let $T \in [\![\Gamma]\!]$ and $\Uparrow(T)$ be a notation for $\mathbf{1} \cdot (T \circ \uparrow^{Suc(0)})$. We have $((\lambda_{A_1}.M_1)[T])\downarrow_{\mathcal{L}} = \lambda_{A_1}.(M_1[\Uparrow(T)])\downarrow_{\mathcal{L}}$. By Lemma 23, it suffices to prove that for any $N \in [\![A_1]\!]$, $((M_1[\Uparrow(T)])\downarrow_{\mathcal{L}}[N \cdot \uparrow^0])\downarrow_{\mathcal{L}} \in [\![B_1]\!]$. By hypothesis and Remark 26, $(N \cdot T)\downarrow_{\mathcal{L}} \in [\![A_1.\Gamma]\!]$, then by induction hypothesis, $(M[(N \cdot T)\downarrow_{\mathcal{L}}])\downarrow_{\mathcal{L}} = ((M_1[\Uparrow(T)])\downarrow_{\mathcal{L}}[N \cdot \uparrow^0])\downarrow_{\mathcal{L}} \in [\![B_1]\!]$.

– (App). In this case $M = (M_1\ N_1)$, $\Gamma \vdash M_1 : B \rightarrow A$ and $\Gamma \vdash N_1 : B$. Let $T \in [\![\Gamma]\!]$, so we have, $((M_1\ N_1)[T])\downarrow_{\mathcal{L}} = ((M_1[T])\downarrow_{\mathcal{L}}\ (N_1[T])\downarrow_{\mathcal{L}})$. By induction hypothesis, $(M_1[T])\downarrow_{\mathcal{L}} \in [\![B \rightarrow A]\!] = [\![B]\!] \rightarrow [\![A]\!]$ and $(N_1[T])\downarrow_{\mathcal{L}} \in [\![B]\!]$. Hence, $((M_1\ N_1)[T])\downarrow_{\mathcal{L}} \in [\![A]\!]$.

– (Id), (Shift). In this case $S = \uparrow^n$. We prove by structural induction on n and T that if $T \in [\![\Gamma]\!]$ and $\Gamma \vdash \uparrow^n \triangleright \Delta$, then $(\uparrow^n \circ T)\downarrow_{\mathcal{L}} \in [\![\Delta]\!]$.

– (Cons). In this case $S = M' \cdot S'$, $\Gamma \vdash M' : A'$, $\Gamma \vdash S' \triangleright \Delta'$ and $A'.\Delta' = \Delta$. Let $T \in [\![\Gamma]\!]$, so we have, $(S \circ T)\downarrow_{\mathcal{L}} = ((M'[T])\downarrow_{\mathcal{L}} \cdot (S' \circ T)\downarrow_{\mathcal{L}})\downarrow_{\mathcal{L}}$. By induction hypothesis, $(M'[T])\downarrow_{\mathcal{L}} \in [\![A']\!]$ and $(S' \circ T)\downarrow_{\mathcal{L}} \in [\![\Delta']\!]$. From Remark 26 we conclude that $((M'[T])\downarrow_{\mathcal{L}} \cdot (S' \circ T)\downarrow_{\mathcal{L}})\downarrow_{\mathcal{L}} \in [\![\Delta]\!]$.

□

Theorem 30. *Let M, S be expressions in $\mathcal{NF}_{\mathcal{L}}$.*

1. *If $\Gamma \vdash M : A$, then $M \in \mathcal{SN}$.*
2. *If $\Gamma \vdash S \triangleright \Delta$, then $S \in \mathcal{SN}$.*

Proof. By Def. 25, $\uparrow^0 \in [\![\Gamma]\!]$. Hence,

1. By Proposition 29, $(M[\uparrow^0])\downarrow_{\mathcal{L}} = M \in [\![A]\!]$, and by Def. 14, $[\![A]\!] \subseteq \mathcal{SN}$.

2. By Proposition 29, $(S \circ \uparrow^0)\downarrow_{\mathcal{L}} = S \in [\![\Delta]\!]$, and by Lemma 27, $[\![\Delta]\!] \subseteq \mathcal{SN}$. □

Theorem 31. *If* $\Gamma \vdash M : A$ *and* $\Gamma \vdash S \rhd \Delta$, *then* M *and* S *are weakly normalizing, and thus* M *and* S *have* $\lambda_{\mathcal{L}}$*-normal forms.*

Proof. Let $N = M\downarrow_{\mathcal{L}}$ and $T = S\downarrow_{\mathcal{L}}$, the subject reduction property (Theorem 10) says that typing is preserved under reductions, hence $\Gamma \vdash N : A$ and $\Gamma \vdash T \rhd \Delta$. Therefore, by Theorem 30, N and T are both in $\mathcal{SN}$. Finally, remark that a $\beta_{\mathcal{L}}$-normal form in $\mathcal{NF}_{\mathcal{L}}$ is a $\lambda_{\mathcal{L}}$-normal form too. □

6 Conclusions

We have proposed a variant of $\lambda\sigma$, namely $\lambda_{\mathcal{L}}$. This calculus enjoys the same general properties of $\lambda\sigma$:

- a simple and finitary first-order rewrite system,
- confluent on terms with meta-variables,
- weakly terminating on typed terms and
- with composition of substitutions and simultaneous substitutions.

However, in contrast to $\lambda\sigma$, $\lambda_{\mathcal{L}}$ does not have the (SCons)-rule and so, it is left-linear in the sort of terms and substitutions.

Although $\lambda_{\mathcal{L}}$ was designed to allow meta-variables, it happens to be useful in the same framework where $\lambda\sigma$ is. In particular both calculi share the same description of normal forms. For example, the higher-order unification algorithm via explicit substitutions proposed in [4] can be expressed in $\lambda_{\mathcal{L}}$, almost without modifications. Moreover, since $\lambda_{\mathcal{L}}$ does not have the surjective pairing rule, it is useful for applications where this feature of $\lambda\sigma$ pose technical problems, for instance higher-order equational unification via explicit substitutions [19], or dependent type systems [27].

Another left-linear variant of $\lambda\sigma$ is the $\lambda_{\Uparrow}$-calculus [3]. The system $\lambda_{\Uparrow}$ is fully confluent on open terms, not only with meta-variables of terms but also with meta-variables of substitutions. However, $\lambda_{\Uparrow}$ is incompatible with the extensional rule (η) due to the fact that substitutions *id* and $\mathbf{1}\cdot\uparrow$ are not $\lambda_{\Uparrow}$-convertible. A key point in $\lambda_{\mathcal{L}}$ is the preservation of this extensional equivalence. The extensional version of $\lambda_{\mathcal{L}}$-calculus is confluent on ground terms as shown in [18], and we conjecture that it is also on semi-open expressions.

The $\lambda_{\mathcal{L}}$-calculus is extended to dependent types in [27] and work is in progress to use this calculus in a formulation of the Calculus of Inductive Constructions with explicit substitutions and open expressions.

Acknowledgments Many thanks to all persons contributing to this work, in particular to Gilles Dowek, Delia Kesner, Benjamin Werner, Bruno Barras, Gopalan Nadathur and the anonymous referees for their useful remarks and suggestions on the subject of this paper. The author is very grateful with Thomas Arts and Hans Zantema for their help with Proposition 1, in particular Hans Zantema send to me a proof of this proposition in a personal communication [36].

References

1. M. Abadi, L. Cardelli, P.-L. Curien, and J.-J. Lévy. Explicit substitution. *Journal of Functional Programming*, 1(4):375–416, 1991.
2. R. Bloo and K. H. Rose. Preservation of strong normalisation in named lambda calculi with explicit substitution and garbage collection. In *CSN-95: Computer Science in the Netherlands*, November 1995.
3. P.-L. Curien, T. Hardin, and J.-J. Lévy. Confluence properties of weak and strong calculi of explicit substitutions. *Journal of the ACM*, 43(2):362–397, March 1996.
4. G. Dowek, T. Hardin, and C. Kirchner. Higher-order unification via explicit substitutions (extended abstract). In *Proceedings, Tenth Annual IEEE Symposium on Logic in Computer Science*, pages 366–374, San Diego, California, 26–29 June 1995. IEEE Computer Society Press.
5. G. Dowek, T. Hardin, C. Kirchner, and F. Pfenning. Unification via explicit substitutions: The case of higher-order patterns. In M. Maher, editor, *Proceedings of the Joint International Conference and Symposium on Logic Programming*, Bonn, Germany, September 1996. MIT Press. To appear.
6. M. C. F. Ferreira, D. Kesner, and L. Puel. λ-calculi with explicit substitutions and composition which preserve β-strong normalization. *LNCS*, 1139, 1996.
7. H. Geuvers. A short and flexible proof of Strong Normalization for the Calculus of Constructions. In P. Dybjer and B. Nordström, editors, *Types for Proofs and Programs, International Workshop TYPES'94*, volume 996 of *LNCS*, pages 14–38, Båstad, Sweden, 1994. Springer.
8. J.-Y. Girard, P. Taylor, and Y. Lafont. *Proof and Types*. Cambridge University Press, 1989.
9. J. Goubault-Larrecq. A proof of weak termination of typed $\lambda\sigma$-calculi. Manuscript, 1997.
10. J. Goubault-Larrecq. Une preuve de terminaison faible du $\lambda\sigma$-calcul. Technical Report RR-3090, Unité de recherche INRIA-Rocquencourt, Janvier 1997.
11. T. Hardin. Confluence results for the Pure Strong Categorical Logic CCC: λ-calculi as subsystems of CCL. *Theoretical Computer Science*, 65(2):291–342, 1989.
12. T. Hardin, L. Maranget, and B. Pagano. Functional back-ends and compilers within the lambda-sigma calculus. In Thomas Johnsson, editor, *The Workshop on the Implementation of Functional Languages '95*. Bastad, Sweden, September 1995.
13. G. Huet. Confluent reductions: Abstract properties and applications to term rewriting systems. *J.A.C.M.*, 27(4), October 1980.
14. F. Kamareddine and A. Rios. A λ-calculus à la de Bruijn with explicit substitutions. In *PLILP*. LNCS, 1995.
15. D. Kapur, P. Narendran, and F. Otto. On ground-confluence of term rewriting systems. *Information and Computation*, 86(1):14–31, May 1990.
16. D. Kapur and H. Zhang. RRL: A rewrite rule laboratory-user's manual. Technical Report 89-03, Department of Computer Science, The University of Iowa, 1989.
17. D. Kesner. Confluence properties of extensional and non-extensional λ-calculi with explicit substitutions (extended abstract). In Harald Ganzinger, editor, *Proceedings of the 7th International Conference on Rewriting Techniques and Applications (RTA-96)*, volume 1103 of *LNCS*, pages 184–199, New Brunswick, NJ, USA, 1996. Springer-Verlag.
18. D. Kesner. Confluence of extensional and non-extensional λ-calculi with explicit substitutions. Preprint, 1997.

19. C. Kirchner and C. Ringeissen. Higher order equational unification via explicit substitutions. Preprint, 1996.
20. P. Lescanne. From $\lambda\sigma$ to $\lambda\upsilon$ a journey through calculi of explicit substitutions. In *Proceedings of the 21st Annual ACM SIGPLAN-SIGACT Symposium on Principles of Programming Languages*, pages 60–69, January 1994.
21. P. Lescanne and J. Rouyer-Degli. Explicit substitutions with de Bruijn's levels. In J. Hsiang, editor, *Rewriting Techniques and Applications*, volume 914 of *LNCS*, pages 294–308, Chapel Hill, North Carolina, 1995. Springer-Verlag.
22. L. Magnusson. *The Implementation of ALF—A Proof Editor Based on Martin-Löf's Monomorphic Type Theory with Explicit Substitution.* PhD thesis, Chalmers University of Technology and Göteborg University, January 1995.
23. P.-A. Melliès. Exemple de non terminaison forte dans un $\lambda\sigma$-calcul typé où la priorité serait donnée aux deux règles *shiftcons* et *varcons*, modulo lois de monoïde. Preprint, 1995.
24. P.-A. Melliès. Typed λ-calculi with explicit substitutions may not terminate. In *Typed Lambda Calculi and Applications*, number 902 in LNCS. Second International Conference TLCA'95, Springer-Verlag, 1995.
25. C. Muñoz. Confluence and preservation of strong normalisation in an explicit substitutions calculus (extended abstract). In *Proceedings, Eleven Annual IEEE Symposium on Logic in Computer Science*, New Brunswick, New Jersey, July 1996. IEEE Computer Society Press.
26. C. Muñoz. Proof representation in type theory: State of the art. In *Proceedings, XXII Latinamerican Conference of Informatics CLEI Panel 96*, Santafé de Bogotá, Colombia, June 1996.
27. C. Muñoz. Dependent types with explicit substitutions: A meta-theoretical development. Preprint electronically available at: `http://pauillac.inria.fr/~cesar/Papers/typ96.ps.gz`, 1997.
28. C. Muñoz. Meta-theoretical properties of λ_ϕ: A left-linear variant of $\lambda\sigma$. Technical Report RR-3107, Unité de recherche INRIA-Rocquencourt, Février 1997.
29. G. Nadathur. A fine-grained notation for lambda terms and its use in intensional operations. Technical Report TR-96-13, Department of Computer Science, University of Chicago, May 30 1996.
30. G. Nadathur. The (SCons) rule. Personal communication, 1996.
31. B. Pagano. Confluent extensions of $\lambda_\Uparrow$. Personal communication, 1996.
32. A. Ríos. *Contributions à l'étude de λ-calculs avec des substitutions explicites.* PhD thesis, U. Paris VII, 1993.
33. M. Schmidt-Schauss. *Computational aspects of an order-sorted logic with term declarations*, volume 395 of *Lecture Notes in Computer Science and Lecture Notes in Artificial Intelligence.* Springer-Verlag Inc., New York, NY, USA, 1989.
34. H. Yokouchi and T. Hikita. A rewriting system for categorical combinators with multiple arguments. *SIAM Journal on Computing*, 19(1):78–97, February 1990.
35. H. Zantema. Termination of term rewriting by semantic labelling. *Fundamenta Informaticae*, 24:89–105, 1995.
36. H. Zantema. Termination of ϕ and Π_ϕ by semantic labelling. Personal communication, 1996.

Perpetuality and Uniform Normalization

Zurab Khasidashvili and Mizuhito Ogawa

NTT Basic Research Laboratories
3-1 Morinosato-Wakamiya, Atsugi, Kanagawa, 243-01, Japan
{zurab,mizuhito}@theory.brl.ntt.co.jp

Abstract. We define a perpetual one-step reduction strategy which enables one to construct *minimal* (w.r.t. Lévy's ordering $\trianglelefteq$ on reductions) infinite reductions in Conditional Orthogonal Expression Reduction Systems. We use this strategy to derive two characterizations of *perpetual* redexes, i.e., redexes whose contractions retain the existence of infinite reductions. These characterizations generalize existing related criteria for perpetuality of redexes. We give a number of applications of our results, demonstrating their usefulness. In particular, we prove equivalence of weak and strong normalization (the *uniform normalization* property) for various restricted λ-calculi, which cannot be derived from previously known perpetuality criteria.

1 Introduction

The objective of this paper is to study sufficient conditions for *uniform normalization*, UN, of a term in an orthogonal (first or higher-order) rewrite system, and for the UN property of the rewrite system itself. Here a term is UN if either it does not have a normal form, or if any reduction eventually terminates in a normal form; the rewrite system is UN if every term is UN. Interest in criteria for UN arises, for example, in the proofs of strong normalization of typed λ-calculi, as it relates to the work on reducing strong normalization proofs to proving weak normalization [Ned73, Klo80, dVr87, dGr93, Kha94c]. Further, the question: 'Which classes of terms have the uniform normalization property?' is posed in [BI94] in connection with finding UN solutions to fixed point equations, and with representability of partial recursive functions by UN-terms only, in the λ-calculus.[1] The UN property is clearly useful as then all strategies are normalizing, and in particular, there is more room for optimality (cf. [GK96]).

It is easy to see that a rewriting system is UN iff all of its redexes are *perpetual*. These are redexes that reduce terms having an infinite reduction, which we call ∞-terms, to ∞-terms. Therefore, studying the UN property reduces to studying perpetuality of redexes. The latter has already been studied quite extensively in the literature. The classical results in this direction are *Church's Theorem* [CR36], stating that the λ_I-calculus is uniformly normalizing, and the *Conservation Theorem* of Barendregt et al [BBKV76, Bar84], stating that β_I-redexes are perpetual in the λ-calculus. Bergstra and Klop [BK82] give a sufficient and necessary criterion for perpetuality of β_K-redexes in every context. Klop [Klo80] generalized Church's Theorem to all non-erasing orthogonal Combinatory Reduction Systems (CRSs) by

[1] The UN property is called *strong normalization* in [BI94].

showing that the latter are UN, and Khasidashvili [Kha94c] generalized the Conservation Theorem to all orthogonal Expression Reduction Systems (ERSs) [Kha92], by proving that all non-erasing redexes are perpetual in orthogonal ERSs.

For orthogonal Term Rewriting Systems (OTRSs), a very powerful perpetuality criterion was obtained by Klop [Klo92] in terms of *critical* redexes. These are redexes that are not perpetual, i.e., reduce ∞-terms to strongly normalizable terms (*SN-terms*). Klop showed that any critical redex u must erase an argument possessing an infinite reduction. The later is not true for higher-order rewrite systems, because substitutions (from the outside) into the arguments of u may occur during rewrite steps, which may turn an SN argument of u into an ∞-term. However, we show that a critical redex u in a term t must necessarily erase a *potentially infinite* argument, i.e., an argument that would become an ∞-(sub)term after a number of (*passive*) steps in t. From this, we derive a criterion, called *safety*, of perpetuality of redexes in every context, similar to the perpetuality criterion of β_K-redexes [BK82]. These are the main results of this paper, and we will demonstrate their usefulness in applications.

We obtain our results in the framework of *Orthogonal (Context-sensitive) Conditional Expression reduction Systems* (OCERSs) [KO95]. CERS is a format for higher-order rewriting, or to be precise, second-order rewriting, which extends ERSs [Kha92] by allowing restrictions both on arguments of redexes and on the contexts in which the redexes can be contracted. Various interesting typed λ-calculi, including the simply typed λ-calculus and the system **F** [Bar92], can directly be encoded as OCERSs (see also [KOR93]); λ–calculi with specific reduction strategies (such as the call-by-value λ-calculus [Plo75]) can also be naturally encoded as OCERSs. ERSs are very close to the more familiar format of CRSs of Klop [Klo80], and we claim that all our results are valid for orthogonal CRSs as well (see [Raa96] for a detailed comparison of various forms of higher-order rewriting). However, using an example due to van Oostrom [Oos97], we will demonstrate that our results cannot be extended to higher-order rewriting systems where function variables can be bound [Wol93, Nip93, OR94], as they can exhibit pretty strange behaviour not characteristic of the λ-calculi.

In order to prove our perpetuality criteria, we first generalize the *constricting* (or *zoom-in*) perpetual strategy, independently discovered by Plaisted [Pla93], Sørensen [Sør95], Gramlich [Gra96], and Melliès [Mel96] (with small differences), from term rewriting and the λ-calculus to OCERSs. These strategies specify a construction of infinite reductions (whenever possible) such that all steps are performed in some smallest ∞-subterm. Our strategy is slightly more general than the above, and can be restricted so that the computation becomes constricting, and this allows for simple and concise proofs of our perpetuality criteria. We also show that constricting perpetual reductions are minimal w.r.t. Lévy's ordering on reductions in orthogonal rewriting systems [Lév80, HL91].

Despite the fact that our criteria are simple and intuitive, they appear to be strong tools in proving strong normalization from weak normalization in orthogonal (typed or type-free) rewrite systems. We will show that previously known related criteria [CR36, BBKV76, BK82, Klo80, Klo92, Kha94c] can be obtained as special cases. We will also derive the UN property for a number of variations of β-reductions [Plo75, dGr93, BI94, HL93], which cannot be derived from previously known perpetuality criteria, as immediate consequences of our criteria.

2 Conditional Expression Reduction Systems

In this section, we recall the basic theory of orthogonal Conditional Expression Reduction Systems, OCERSs, as developed in [KO95], and some results concerning *similarity* of redexes in OERSs from [Kha94c]. CERSs extend *Expression Reduction Systems* [Kha92], a formalism of higher-order (rather, second-order) rewriting close to *Combinatory Reduction Systems* [Klo80]. We refer to [Raa96] for an extensive survey of the relationship between various formats of higher-order rewriting, such as [Klo80, Kha92, Wol93, Nip93, OR94]. Restricted rewriting systems with substitutions were first studied in [Pkh77] and [Acz78]. We refer to [Klo92] for a survey of results concerning conditional TRSs.

Terms in CERSs are built from the alphabet like in the first order case. The symbols having binding power (like λ in λ-calculus or $\int$ in integrals) require some binding variables and terms as arguments, as specified by their arity. Scope indicators are used to specify which variables have binding power in which arguments. For example, a β-redex in the λ-calculus appears as $Ap(\lambda x\, t, s)$, where Ap is a function symbol of arity 2, and λ is an operator sign of arity $(1,1)$ and scope indicator (1). Integrals such as $\int_s^t f(x)\,dx$ can be represented as $\int x(s,t,f(x))$ using an operator sign $\int$ of arity $(1,3)$ and scope indicator (3).

Metaterms will be used to write rewrite rules. They are constructed from metavariables and meta-expressions for substitutions, called metasubstitutions. Instantiation of metavariables in metaterms yields terms. Metavariables play the role of variables in the TRS rules, and function variables in HRS and HORS rules [Nip93, OR94]. Differently from HRSs and HORSs, metavariables *cannot* be bound.

Definition 2.1 Let Σ be an *alphabet* comprising *variables*, denoted by x, y, z and *symbols* (*signs*). A symbol σ can be either a *function symbol* (*simple operator*) having an *arity* $n \in N$, or an *operator sign* (*quantifier sign*) having *arity* $(m,n) \in N \times N$. In the latter case σ needs to be supplied with m *binding* variables $x_1,\ldots,x_m$ to form the *quantifier* (*compound operator*) $\sigma x_1 \ldots x_m$. If σ is an operator sign it also has a *scope indicator* specifying, for each variable, in which of the n arguments it has binding power. *Terms* t, s, e, o are constructed from variables, function symbols and quantifiers in the usual first-order way, respecting (the second component of the) arities. A predicate AT on terms specifies which terms are *admissible*.

Metaterms are constructed like terms, but also allowing as basic constructions *metavariables* A, B, ... and *metasubstitutions* $(t_1/x_1,\ldots,t_n/x_n)t_0$, where each t_i is an arbitrary metaterm and the x_i have a binding effect in t_0. An *assignment* θ maps each metavariable to some term. The application of θ to a metaterm t is written $t\theta$ and is obtained from t by replacing metavariables with their values under θ, and by replacing metasubstitutions $(t_1/x_1,\ldots,t_n/x_n)t_0$, in right to left order, with the result of substitution of terms $t_1,\ldots,t_n$ for free occurrences of $x_1,\ldots,x_n$ in t_0.

The specification of a CERS consists of an alphabet (generating a set of terms possibly restricted by the predicate AT) as specified above and a set of rules (generating the rewrite relation possibly restricted by the predicates AA and AC) as specified below. The predicate AT can be used to express sorting and typing constraints, since sets of admissible terms allowed for arguments of an operator can be seen as terms of certain sorts or types.

The ERS syntax is very close to the syntax of the λ-calculus. For example, the β-rule is written as $Ap(\lambda xA, B) \rightarrow (B/x)A$, where A and B can be instantiated by any terms. The η-rule is written as $\lambda xAp(A, x) \rightarrow A$, where it is required that $x \notin A\theta$ for an assignment θ, otherwise an x occurring in $A\theta$ and therefore bound in $\lambda x(A\theta, x)$ would become free. A rule like $f(A) \rightarrow \exists x(A)$ is also allowed, but in that case the assignment θ with $x \in A\theta$ is not. Such a collision between free and bound variables cannot arise for restricted (by the condition (*) below, see Definition 2.2) assignments.

Definition 2.2 A rewrite rule is a (named) pair of metaterms $r : t \rightarrow s$, such that t and s do not contain free variables. We close the rules under assignments: $r\theta : t\theta \rightarrow s\theta$ if $r : t \rightarrow s$ and θ is an assignment. To avoid the capturing of free variables, this is restricted to assignments θ such that

(*) *each free variable occurring in a term $A\theta$ assigned to a metavariable A is either bound in the θ-instance of each occurrence of A in the rule or in none of them.*

The term $t\theta$ is then called a *redex* and $s\theta$ its *contractum*. We close under contexts $C[r\theta] : C[t\theta] \rightarrow C[s\theta]$, if $r\theta : t\theta \rightarrow s\theta$ and $C[\,]$ is a context (a term with one hole).

The rewrite relation thus obtained is the usual (unconditional, context-free) ERS-rewrite relation. If restrictions are put on assignments, via an *admissibility* predicate AA on rules and assignments, the rewrite relation will be called *conditional*. We call redexes that are instances of the same rule (i.e., with the same admissibility predicate) *weakly similar*. If restrictions are put on contexts, via a predicate AC on rules, assignments and contexts, the rewrite relation will be called *context-sensitive*.

A *CERS* R is a pair consisting of an alphabet and a set of rewrite rules, both possibly restricted.

Note that we allow metavariable-rules like $\eta^{-1} : A \rightarrow \lambda xAp(Ax)$ and metavariable-introduction-rules like $f(A) \rightarrow g(A, B)$, which are usually excluded a priori. This is only useful when the system is conditional.

Let $r : t \rightarrow s$ be a rule in a CERS R and let θ be admissible for r. Subterms of a redex $v = t\theta$ that correspond to the metavariables in t are the *arguments* of v, and the rest is the *pattern* of v (hence the binding variables of the quantifiers occurring in the pattern belong to the pattern too). Subterms of v rooted in the pattern are called the *pattern-subterms* of v.

Notation We use a, b, c, d for constants, t, s, e, o for terms and metaterms, u, v, w for redexes, and N, P, Q for reductions. We write $s \subseteq t$ if s is a subterm of t. A one-step reduction in which a redex $u \subseteq t$ is contracted is written as $t \xrightarrow{u} s$ or $t \rightarrow s$ or just u. We write $P : t \twoheadrightarrow s$ or $t \overset{P}{\twoheadrightarrow} s$ if P denotes a reduction (sequence) from t to s, write $P : t \twoheadrightarrow$ if P may be infinite, and write $P : t \twoheadrightarrow \infty$ if P is infinite (i.e, of the length ω). $P + Q$ denotes the concatenation of P and Q. $FV(t)$ denotes the set of free (i.e., unbound) variables of t.

Below, when we speak about terms and redexes, we will always mean admissible terms and admissible redexes, respectively.

2.1 Orthogonal CERSs

The idea of orthogonality is that contraction of a redex does not destroy other redexes (in whatever way), but rather leaves a number of their residuals. A prerequisite for the definition of residual is the notion of *descendant*, also called *trace*, allowing tracing of subterms during a reduction. Whereas this is pretty simple in the first-order case, ERSs may exhibit complex behaviour due to the possibility of nested metasubstitutions, thereby complicating the definition of descendants. However, it is a standard technique in higher-order rewriting [Klo80] to *decompose* or *refine* each rewrite step into two parts: a *TRS*-part replacing the left-hand side by the right-hand side without evaluating the (meta)substitutions and a *substitution*-part evaluating the delayed substitutions. To express substitution, we use the S-reduction rules

$$S^{n+1}x_1 \dots x_n A_1 \dots A_n A_0 \to (A_1/x_1, \dots, A_n/x_n)A_0, \quad n = 1, 2, \dots,$$

where S^{n+1} is the *operator sign of substitution* with arity $(n, n+1)$ and scope indicator $(n+1)$, and $x_1, \dots, x_n$ and $A_1, \dots, A_n, A_0$ are pairwise distinct variables and metavariables.[2] Thus S^{n+1} binds only in the last argument. The difference with β-rules is that S-reductions can only perform β-developments of λ-terms, so one can think of them as (simultaneous) let-expressions.

Thus the descendant relation of a rewrite step can be obtained by composing the descendant relation of the TRS-step and the descendant relations of the S-reduction steps. All known concepts of descendants agree in the cases when the subterm $s \subseteq t$ which is to be traced during a step $t \xrightarrow{u} o$ is in an argument of the contracted redex u, properly contains u, or does not overlap with it. The differences occur in the case when s is a pattern-subterm, in which case we define the contractum of u to be the descendant of s, while according to many (especially early) definitions, s does not have a u-descendant.

We will explain the concept with examples. Consider first a TRS-step $t = f(g(a)) \to b = s$ performed according to the rule $f(g(x)) \to b$. The descendant of both pattern-subterms $f(g(a))$ and $g(a)$ of t in s is b, and a does not have a descendant in s. The refinement of a β-step $t = Ap(\lambda x(Ap(x,x)), z) \to_\beta f(z) = e$ would be $t = Ap(\lambda x(Ap(x,x)), z) \to_{\beta_f} o = S^2 xzAp(x,x) \to_S f(z) = e$; the descendant of both t and $\lambda x(Ap(x,x))$ after the *TRS*-step is the contractum $S^2 xzAp(x,x)$, and the descendants of $Ap(x,x), z \subseteq t$ are respectively the subterms $Ap(x,x), z \subseteq o$; the descendant of both $o = S^2 xzAp(x,x)$ and $Ap(x,x)$ after the substitution step is the contractum e; the descendant of $z \subseteq o$, as well as of the bound occurrence of x in $Ap(x,x)$, is the occurrence of z in e.

Definition 2.3 Let $t \xrightarrow{u} s$ in a CERS R, let $v \subseteq t$ be an admissible redex, and let $w \in s$ be a u-descendant of v. We call w a *u-residual* of v if (a) the patterns of u and v do not overlap; (b) w is a redex weakly similar to v; and (c) w is admissible. (So u itself does not have *u-residuals* in s.) The notion of *residual* of redexes extends naturally to arbitrary reductions. A redex in s is called a *new* redex or a *created* redex if it is not a residual of a redex in t. The *ancestor* relation is converse to that of descendant, and the *predecessor* relation to that of residual.

[2] We assume that the CERS does not contain the symbols S^{n+1}.

Definition 2.4 ([KO95]) A CERS is called *orthogonal* (OCERS) if:

- the left-hand side of a rule is not a single metavariable,
- the left-hand side of a rule does not contain metasubstitutions, and its metavariables contain those of the right-hand side,
- all the descendants of an admissible redex u in a term t under the contraction of any other admissible redex $v \subseteq t$ are residuals of u.

The second condition ensures that rules exhibit deterministic behaviour when they can be applied. The last condition is the counterpart of the *subject reduction property* in typed λ-calculi [Bar92]. For example, consider the rules $a \to b$ and $f(A) \to A$ with admissible assignment $A\theta = a$. The descendant $f(b)$ of the redex $f(a)$ after contraction of a is not a redex since the assignment $A\theta = b$ is not admissible, hence the system is not orthogonal.

As in the case of the λ-calculus [Bar84], for any co-initial (i.e., with the same initial term) reductions P and Q, one can define in OCERSs the notion of *residual of P under Q*, written P/Q, due to Lévy [Lév80]. We write $P \trianglelefteq Q$ if $P/Q = \emptyset$ ($\trianglelefteq$ is the *Lévy-embedding* relation); P and Q are called *Lévy-equivalent*, *strongly-equivalent*, or *permutation-equivalent* (written $P \approx_L Q$) if $P \trianglelefteq Q$ and $Q \trianglelefteq P$. It follows easily from the definition of / that, for any (appropriate) P' and Q', $(P+P')/Q \approx_L P/Q + P'/(Q/P)$ and $P/(Q+Q') \approx_L (P/Q)/Q'$.

Theorem 2.5 (Strong Church-Rosser [KO95]) For any finite co-initial reductions P and Q in an OCERS, $P + (Q/P) \approx_L Q + (P/Q)$.

2.2 Similarity of redexes

The idea of *similarity* of redexes [Kha94] u and v is that u and v are weakly similar, i.e., match the same rewrite rule, and quantifiers in the pattern of u and v bind 'similarly' in the corresponding arguments. Consequently, for any pair of corresponding arguments of u and v, either both are erased after contraction of u and v, or none is. For example, recall that a β-redex $Ap(\lambda xt, s)$ is an *I-redex* if $x \in FV(t)$, and is a *K-redex* otherwise. Then, all I-redexes are similar, and so are all K-redexes, but no I-redex is similar to a K-redex.

We can write a CERS redex as $u = C[\overline{x_1}t_1, \ldots, \overline{x_n}t_n]$, where C is the pattern, $t_1, \ldots, t_n$ are the arguments, and $\overline{x_i} = \{x_{i_1}, \ldots, x_{i_{n_i}}\}$ is the subset of binding variables of C such that t_i is in the scope of an occurrence of each x_{i_j}, $i = 1, \ldots, n$. Let us call the maximal subsequence $j_1, \ldots, j_k$ of $1, \ldots, n$ such that $t_{j_1}, \ldots, t_{j_k}$ have u-descendants the *main sequence* of u or the *u-main sequence*, call $t_{j_1}, \ldots, t_{j_k}$ (u-)*main arguments*, and call the remaining arguments (u)-*erased*. Now the similarity of redexes can be defined as follows:

Definition 2.6 Let $u = C[\overline{x_1}t_1, \ldots, \overline{x_n}t_n]$ and $v = C[\overline{x_1}s_1, \ldots, \overline{x_n}s_n]$ be weakly similar. We call u and v *similar*, written $u \sim v$, if the main sequences of u and v coincide, and for any main argument t_i of u, $\overline{x_i} \cap FV(t_i) = \overline{x_i} \cap FV(s_i)$.

The following lemma, whose proof is similar to that of Lemma 3.3 in [Kha94c], shows that only pattern-bindings (i.e., bindings from inside the pattern) of free variables in *main* arguments of a redex are relevant for the erasure of its arguments. Below, θ will (besides denoting assignments) also denote substitutions assigning terms to variables; when we write $o' = o\theta$ for some substitution θ, we assume that no free variables of the substituted subterms become bound in o' (i.e., we rename bound variables in o when necessary).

Lemma 2.7 Let $u = C[\overline{x_1}t_1, \ldots, \overline{x_n}t_n]$ and $v = C[\overline{x_1}s_1, \ldots, \overline{x_n}s_n]$ be weakly similar redexes, and let for any main argument t_i of u, $\overline{x_i} \cap FV(t_i) = \overline{x_i} \cap FV(s_i)$. Then the main sequences of u and v coincide, and consequently, $u \sim v$. In particular, if $u = v\theta$, then $u \sim v$.

3 A Minimal Perpetual Strategy

In this section we generalize the constricting perpetual strategy [Pla93, Sør95, Gra96, Mel96] from TRSs and the λ-calculus to all OCERSs.

Let us first fix the terminology. Recall that a term t is called *weakly normalizable*, a *WN-term*, written $WN(t)$, if it is reducible to a *normal form*, i.e., a term without a redex. t is called *strongly normalizable*, an *SN-term*, written $SN(t)$, if it does not possess an infinite reduction. We call t an ∞*-term*, $\infty(t)$, if $\neg SN(t)$. Clearly, for any term t, $SN(t) \Rightarrow WN(t)$. If the converse is also true, then we call t *uniformly normalizable*, or a *UN-term*. So for UN-terms t, either t does not have a normal form, or all reductions from t eventually terminate. Correspondingly, a rewrite system R is called respectively WN, SN, or UN if so is any term in R.

Following [BK82, Klo92], we call a redex occurrence $u \subseteq t$ *perpetual* if $\infty(t) \Rightarrow \infty(s)$, where $t \xrightarrow{u} s$, and call u *critical* otherwise. Recall that a *perpetual strategy* is a function on terms which selects a perpetual redex in any ∞-term, and selects any redex (if any) otherwise [Bar84]. A redex (not an occurrence) is called *perpetual* iff its occurrence in any (admissible) context is perpetual.

Finally, let us recall the concept of *external* redexes [HL91]. These are redexes whose residuals or descendants can never occur in an argument of another redex. Any external redex is outermost, but not vice versa. (For example, consider the OTRS $R = \{f(x, g(y)) \rightarrow y, a \rightarrow g(b)\}$; then the first a in $f(a, a)$ is outermost but not external; the second a is external.) It is shown in [HL91] that any term not in normal form, in an OTRS, has an external redex; the same holds true for orthogonal ERSs [Kha94c], and similarly, for OCERSs as well.

Theorem 3.1 Any term not in normal form has an external redex, in an OCERS.

Definition 3.2 Let $P : t \twoheadrightarrow$ and $s \subseteq t$. We call P *internal* to s if it contracts redexes only in (the descendants of) s.

Definition 3.3 (1) Let $\infty(t)$, in an OCERS, and let $s \subseteq t$ be a smallest subterm of t such that $\infty(s)$ (i.e., $SN(e)$ for every proper subterm $e \subsetneq s$). We call s a *minimal perpetual subterm* of t, and call any external redex of s a *minimal perpetual redex* of t.

(2) Let F_m^∞ be a one-step strategy which contracts a minimal perpetual redex in t if $\infty(t)$, and contracts any redex otherwise. Then we call F_m^∞ a *minimal perpetual*

strategy. We call F_m^∞ *constricting* if for any F_m^∞-reduction $P : t_0 \xrightarrow{u_0} t_1 \xrightarrow{u_1} \ldots$ (i.e., constructed using F_m^∞), and for any i, $P_i^* : t_i \xrightarrow{u_i} t_{i+1} \xrightarrow{u_{i+1}} \ldots$ is internal to s_i, where $s_i \subseteq t_i$ is the minimal perpetual subterm containing u_i.

Note that F_m^∞ is not in general a computable strategy, as SN is undecidable already in orthogonal TRSs [Klo92].

Lemma 3.4 Let $\infty(t)$, let $s \subseteq t$ be a minimal perpetual subterm of t, and let $P : t \twoheadrightarrow \infty$ be internal to s. Then exactly one residual of any external redex u of s is contracted in P.

Proof. Let $t = C[s]$ and $s = C'[s_1, \ldots, u, \ldots, s_n]$, where C' consists of the symbols on the path from the top of s to u. If on the contrary P does not contract a residual of u, then every step of P takes place either in one of the s_i, or in the arguments of u (since u is external in s). Hence at least one of these subterms has an infinite reduction – a contradiction, since s is a minimal perpetual subterm. Since u is external, P cannot duplicate its residuals, hence P contracts exactly one residual of u.

Theorem 3.5 A minimal perpetual strategy F_m^∞ is a perpetual strategy, in an OCERS.

Proof. Suppose $\infty(t_0)$, let s_0 be a minimal perpetual subterm of t_0, and let $u \subseteq s_0$ be a minimal perpetuality redex. Let $P : t_0 \xrightarrow{u_0} t_1 \xrightarrow{u_1} t_2 \twoheadrightarrow \infty$ be internal to s_0. By Lemma 3.4, exactly one residual of u, say u_i, is contracted in P. Let $P_{i+1} : t_0 \xrightarrow{u_0} t_1 \xrightarrow{u_1} \ldots \xrightarrow{u_i} t_{i+1}$ and $P_{i+1}^* : t_{i+1} \xrightarrow{u_{i+1}} t_{i+2} \twoheadrightarrow \infty$ (i.e., $P : t_0 \xrightarrow{P_i} t_i \xrightarrow{u_i} t_{i+1} \xrightarrow{P_{i+1}^*}$). Then, by Theorem 2.5, $P = P_{i+1} + P_{i+1}^* \approx_L u + (P_i/u) + P_{i+1}^*$, i.e., u is a perpetual redex. Hence F_m^∞ is perpetual.

Definition 3.6 We call F_m^∞ the *leftmost* minimal perpetual strategy if in each term it contracts the leftmost minimal perpetual redex.[3]

Lemma 3.7 The leftmost minimal perpetual strategy is constricting, in an OCERS.

Proof. Let $P : t_0 \xrightarrow{u_0} t_1 \xrightarrow{u_1} t_2 \twoheadrightarrow \infty$ be a leftmost minimal perpetual reduction, and let $s_i \subseteq t_i$ be the leftmost minimal perpetual subterm of t_i. Since by Theorem 3.5 u_i is perpetual for the term s_i, the descendant of s_i is an ∞-term, hence contains s_{i+1}; and it is immediate that P is constricting.

Although we do not use it in the following, it is interesting to note that the constricting perpetual reductions are minimal w.r.t. Lévy's embedding relation $\trianglelefteq$, hence the name *minimal*.

The relations $\trianglelefteq, \approx_L$ and $/$ are extended to co-initial possibly infinite reductions N, N' as follows. $N \trianglelefteq N'$, or equivalently, $N/N' = \emptyset$ if, for any redex v contracted

[3] Sørensen's and Melliès' strategies correspond to our leftmost and constricting minimal perpetual strategies, respectively. Gramlich's and Plaisted's strategies are defined for non-orthogonal rewrite systems, and they do not specify the perpetual redexes as external redexes of a minimal perpetual subterm.

in N, say $N = N_1 + v + N_2$, $v/(N'/N_1) = \emptyset$; and $N \approx_L N'$ iff $N \trianglelefteq N'$ and $N' \trianglelefteq N$. Here, for any infinite P, $u/P = \emptyset$ if $u/P' = \emptyset$ for some finite initial part P' of P, and P/Q is only defined for finite Q, as the reduction whose initial parts are residuals of initial parts of P under Q.

Theorem 3.8 Let $P : t_0 \xrightarrow{u_0} t_1 \xrightarrow{u_1} t_2 \twoheadrightarrow \infty$ be a constricting minimal perpetual reduction and let $Q : t_0 \twoheadrightarrow \infty$ be any infinite reduction such that $Q \trianglelefteq P$. Then $Q \approx_L P$.

Proof. Since P is constricting, there is a minimal perpetual subterm $s_0 \subseteq t_0$ such that P is internal to s_0. Since $Q \trianglelefteq P$, Q is internal to s_0 as well. By the construction, u_0 is an external redex in s_0, and by Lemma 3.4 exactly one residual u' of u_0 is contracted in Q. So let $Q : t_0 \overset{Q_j}{\twoheadrightarrow} t'_j \xrightarrow{u'} t'_{j+1} \overset{Q^*_{j+1}}{\twoheadrightarrow} \infty$. Then $Q \approx_L u_0 + Q_j/u_0 + Q^*_{j+1}$, and obviously $u_0 \trianglelefteq Q$. Similarly, since P is constricting, for any finite initial part P' of P, $P' \trianglelefteq Q$, and therefore $P \trianglelefteq Q$. Thus $Q \approx_L P$.

4 Two Characterizations of Critical Redexes

In this section, we give a very intuitive characterization of critical redex occurrences for OCERSs, generalizing Klop's characterization of critical redex occurrences for OTRSs [Klo92], and derive from it a characterization of perpetual redexes similar to Bergstra and Klop's perpetuality criterion for β-redexes [BK82]. Our proofs are surprisingly simple, yet the results are rather general and useful in applications. We need three simple lemmas first.

Lemma 4.1 Let $t \xrightarrow{u} s$, let $o \subseteq t$ be either in an argument of u or not overlapping with u, and let $o' \subseteq s$ be a u-descendant of o. Then $o' = o\theta$ for some substitution θ. If moreover o is a redex, then so is o' and $o \sim o'$.

Proof. Since u can be decomposed as a TRS-step followed by a number of substitution steps, it is enough to consider the cases when u is a TRS step and when it is an S-reduction step. If u is a TRS-step, or is an S-reduction step and o is not in its last argument, then o and o' coincide, hence $o \sim o'$ when o is a redex. Otherwise, $o' = o\theta$ for some substitution θ, and if o is a redex, we have again $o \sim o'$ by orthogonality and Lemma 2.7 since free variables of the substituted subterms cannot be bound in $o\theta$ (by the variable convention).

Lemma 4.2 Let s be a minimal perpetual subterm of t, and let $P : t \twoheadrightarrow \infty$ be internal to s. Then P has the form $P = t \twoheadrightarrow o \xrightarrow{u} e \twoheadrightarrow \infty$, where u is the descendant of s in o (i.e., a descendant of s necessarily becomes a redex and is contracted in P).

Proof. If on the contrary P does not contract descendants of s, then infinitely many steps of P are contracted in at least one of the proper subterms of s, contradicting its minimality.

Lemma 4.3 Let $P = u + P'$ be a constricting minimal perpetual reduction starting from t, in an OCERS, and let u be in an argument o of a redex $v \subseteq t$. Then P is internal to o.

Proof. Let $s \subseteq t$ be the minimal perpetual subterm containing u. By definition of minimal perpetual reductions, u is an external redex of s, hence s does not contain v. Since P is constricting, it is internal to s, and we have by orthogonality and Lemma 4.2 that s cannot overlap with the pattern of v. The lemma follows.

Definition 4.4 (1) Let $P : t_0 \xrightarrow{u_0} t_1 \xrightarrow{u_1} \ldots \xrightarrow{u_{k-1}} t_k$, and let $s_0, s_1, \ldots, s_k$ be a chain of descendants of s_0 in along P (i.e, s_{i+1} is a u_i-descendant of $s_i \subseteq t_i$). Then, following [BK82], we call P *passive* w.r.t. $s_0, s_1, \ldots, s_k$ if the pattern of u_i does not overlap with s_i (s_i may be in an argument of u_i or be disjoint from u_i) for $0 \leq i < k$. In the latter case, we call s_k a *passive* descendant of s_0. By Lemma 4.1, $s_k = s\theta$ for some substitution θ. We call θ the *P-substitution* (w.r.t. $s_0, s_1, \ldots, s_k$), or a *passive substitution.*

(2) Let t be a term in an OCERS, and let $s \subseteq t$. We call s a *potentially infinite* subterm of t if s has a passive descendant s' (along some reduction starting from t) s.t. $\infty(s')$. (Thus $\infty(s\theta)$ for some passive substitution θ.)

Theorem 4.5 Let $\infty(t)$ and let $t \xrightarrow{v} s$ be a critical step, in an OCERS. Then v erases a potentially infinite argument o (thus $\infty(o\theta)$ for some passive substitution θ).

Proof. Let $P : t = t_0 \xrightarrow{u_0} t_1 \xrightarrow{u_1} t_2 \twoheadrightarrow \infty$ be a constricting minimal perpetual reduction, which exists by Theorem 3.5 and Lemma 3.7. Since v is critical, $SN(s)$, hence in particular P/v is finite. Let j be the minimal number such that $u_j/V_j = \emptyset$ and $u_j \notin V_j$, where $V_j = v/P_j$ and $P_j : t \twoheadrightarrow t_j$ is the initial part of P with j steps. (Below, V_j will denote both the corresponding set of residuals of v and its complete development.) By the Finite Developments theorem [KO95], no tail of P can contract only residuals of v; and since P/v is finite, such a j exists.

$$\begin{array}{ccccccccc} t = t_0 & \twoheadrightarrow & t_l & \twoheadrightarrow & t_j & \xrightarrow{u_j} & t_{j+1} & \twoheadrightarrow & P \\ v\downarrow & & V_l\downarrow & & V_j\downarrow & & \downarrow & & \\ s = s_0 & \twoheadrightarrow & s_l & \twoheadrightarrow & s_j & \underset{\emptyset}{\twoheadrightarrow} & s_{j+1} & \underset{\emptyset}{\twoheadrightarrow} & P/v \end{array}$$

Since $u_j/V_j = \emptyset$ and $u_j \notin V_j$, there is a redex $v' \in V_j$ whose residual is contracted in V_j and erases (the residuals of) u_j. Since V_j consists of (possibly nested) residuals of a single redex $v \subseteq t_0$, the quantifiers in the pattern of v' cannot bind variables inside arguments of other redexes in V_j. Therefore v' is similar to its residual contracted in V_j by Lemma 2.7, and hence $u_j/v' = \emptyset$, implying that v' erases its argument o', say m-th from the left, containing u_j. By Lemma 4.3, the tail $P_j^* : t_j \twoheadrightarrow \infty$ of P is internal to o'.

Let $v_i \subseteq t_i$ be the predecessors of v' along P_j (so $v_0 = v$ and $v_j = v'$; note that a redex can have at most one predecessor), and let o_i be the m-th argument of v_i (thus $o' = o_j$). Note that $u_i \neq v_i$ since v_i has residuals. Let l be the minimal number such that u_l is in an argument of v_l (such an l exists as u_j is in an argument of v_j). Then all the remaining steps of P are in the same argument of v_l by Lemma 4.3, and it must be the m-th argument o_l of v_l (thus $\infty(o_l)$); but v' erases its m-th argument, implying by Lemma 2.7 that v_l also erases its m-th argument o_l. Further, by the choice of l, no steps of P are contracted inside v_i for $0 \leq i < l$, thus v_l is a passive descendent of v, and o_l is a passive descendant of o_0. Hence, by Lemma 4.1 $v \sim v_l$. Thus v erases a potentially infinite argument o_0 (since $\infty(o_l)$), and we are done.

Note in the above theorem that if the OCERS is an OTRSs, a potentially infinite argument is actually an ∞-term (since passive descendants are all identical), implying Klop's perpetuality lemma [Klo92]. O'Donnell's [O'Do77] lemma, stating that any term from which an innermost reduction is normalizing is strongly normalizable, is an immediate consequence of Klop's Lemma.

Corollary 4.6 Any redex whose erased arguments are closed SN-terms is perpetual, in OCERSs.

Proof. Immediate, as closed SN-terms cannot be potentially infinite subterms.

Note that Theorem 4.5 implies a general (although not computable) perpetual strategy: simply reduce a redex which does not erase a potentially infinite subterm. It is easy to check that the (maximal) perpetual strategies of Barendregt et al [BBKV76, Bar84] and de Vrijer [dVr87], and in general, the *limit* perpetual strategy of Khasidashvili [Kha94b, Kha94c], are special cases, as these strategies contract redexes whose arguments are in normal form, and no (sub)terms can be substituted in the descendants of these arguments. The minimal perpetual strategy, and hence the perpetual strategies of [Sør95, Mel96], are also special cases of the above general perpetual strategy.

We conclude this section with a characterization of perpetuality of erasing redexes, similar to the perpetuality criterion of β_K-redexes in [BK82].

Below, a substitution θ will be called SN iff $SN(x\theta)$ for every variable x.

Definition 4.7 We call a redex u *safe* (respectively, *SN-safe*) if either it is non-erasing, or else it is erasing and for any (resp. SN-) substitution θ, if $u\theta$ erases an ∞-argument, then the contractum of $u\theta$ is an ∞-term. (Note that, by Lemma 2.7, u is erasing iff $u\theta$ is, for any θ.)

Lemma 4.8 Let $\infty(t)$ and $s = t\theta$, in an OCERS. Then $\infty(s)$.

Proof. We prove that any infinite reduction $P : t\xrightarrow{u_0}t_1\xrightarrow{u_1}t_2 \twoheadrightarrow \infty$ can be simulated by some $Q : s = t\theta\xrightarrow{w_0}t_1\theta\xrightarrow{w_1}t_2\theta \twoheadrightarrow \infty$. it is enough to show that $t\xrightarrow{u}o$ implies $s = t\theta\xrightarrow{w}o\theta$ for some $w \subseteq s$, and to consider only the cases when u is a TRS-step or an S-reduction step. The first case is immediate, and the second follows from the Church-Rosser property for S-reductions.

Theorem 4.9 Any safe redex v, in an OCERS R, is perpetual.

Proof. Assume on the contrary that there is a context $C[]$ such that $t = C[v] \rightarrow s$ is a critical step. Let l be the minimal number such that, for some constricting minimal perpetual reduction $P : t = t_0\xrightarrow{u_0}t_1\xrightarrow{u_1}t_2 \twoheadrightarrow \infty$, the tail $P_l^* : t_l \twoheadrightarrow \infty$ of P is in an erased argument of a residual of v. Such an l exists by the proof of Theorem 4.5 (in the notation of that theorem, P_l^* is in an erased argument of $v_l \subseteq t_l$). Let v_l be the outermost among redexes in t_l which contain u_l (and therefore, whole P_l^*) in an erased argument, o_l, say m-th from the left (thus $\infty(o_l)$). By the proof of

Theorem 4.5, the m-th argument o of v is v-erased, $o_l = o\theta$, and $v_l = v\theta$ for some passive substitution θ.

We want to prove that the safety of v implies $\infty(s_l)$, hence $\infty(s)$, contradicting the assumption that $t \xrightarrow{v} s$ is critical (see the diagram for Theorem 4.5). By the Finite Developments theorem, we can assume that s_l is obtained from t_l by contracting (some of) the redexes in V_l in the following order: (a) contract redexes in V_l disjoint from v_l; (b) contract redexes in V_l that are in the main arguments of v_l; (c) contract the residual v_l^* of v_l; (d) contract the remaining redexes, i.e., those containing v_l in a main (by the choice of v_l) argument. Since the parts (a) and (b) do not effect o_l, v_l^* erases an ∞-argument. (Recall from the proof of Theorem 4.5 that redexes in V_l are similar to their residuals contracted in any development of V_l.) Since $v_l = v\theta$ and redexes in (b) are in the substitution part of v_l, $v_l^* = v\theta^*$ for some substitution θ^*, hence its contractum e is infinite by safety of v. By the choice of v_l, e has a descendant e' in s_l after the part (d), and by Lemma 4.1, $e' = e\theta'$ for some substitution θ'. By Lemma 4.8, $\infty(e)$ implies $\infty(e')$, hence $\infty(s_l)$ – a contradiction.

5 Applications

We now give a number of applications of our perpetuality criteria, demonstrating their usefulness and powerfulness. Below, in some of the examples, we will use the conventional λ-calculus notation [Bar84]; and by the *argument* of a β-redex $(\lambda x.s)o$ we will mean its second argument o.

5.1 The restricted orthogonal λ-calculi

Let us call *orthogonal restricted λ-calculi* (ORLC) the calculi that are obtained from the λ-calculus by restricting the β-rule (by some conditions on arguments and contexts) and that are orthogonal CERSs. Examples include the λ_I-calculus, the call-by-value λ-calculus [Plo75], as well as a large class of typed λ-calculi.

If R is an ORLC, then in the proofs of Theorem 4.5 and Theorem 4.9, the P_l-substitution (and in general, any passive substitution along a constricting perpetual reduction) is SN. This can be proved similarly to [BK82] (see Proposition 2.8), since, in the terminology of [BK82] and the notation of Theorem 4.5 and Theorem 4.9:

- P_l is SN-substituting (meaning that the arguments of contracted β-redexes are SN). This is immediate from the minimality of P_l, and
- P_l is *simple* (meaning that no subterms can be substituted in the substituted, during the previous steps, subterms). This follows immediately from externality, w.r.t. the chosen minimal perpetual subterm, of minimal perpetual redexes (P_l is standard).

Hence, we have the following two corollaries, of which the latter is a mere extension of Bergstra-Klop criterion [BK82] (in the case of β-redexes, the converse statement is much easier to prove, see [BK82]).

Corollary 5.1 Let $\infty(t)$ and let $t \xrightarrow{v} s$ be a critical step, in an ORLC. Then v erases a potentially infinite argument o such that $\infty(o\theta)$ for some passive SN-substitution θ.

Corollary 5.2 Any SN-safe redex v, in an ORLC, is perpetual.

Note that these corollaries are not valid for OCERSs in general since, unlike ORLC, passive substitutions along constricting perpetual reductions need not be SN in OCERSs: Let $R = S \cup \{\sigma x AB \to Sx\omega(A/x)B, E(x) \to a\}$ where $\omega = \lambda x.Ap(x,x)$. Then the step $\sigma x Ap(x,x)E(x) \to \sigma x Ap(x,x)a$ is SN-safe (as it only erases a variable), but is critical as can be seen from the following diagram, of which the bottom part is the only reduction starting from $\sigma x Ap(x,x)a$:

$$\begin{array}{ccccccccc}
\sigma x Ap(x,x)E(x) & \xrightarrow[\sigma]{} & SxwE(Ap(x,x)) & \xrightarrow[S]{} & E(Ap(w,w)) & \xrightarrow[\beta]{} & E(Ap(w,w)) & \xrightarrow[\beta]{} & \\
E\downarrow & & E\downarrow & & E\downarrow & & E\downarrow & & \\
\sigma x Ap(x,x)a & \xrightarrow[\sigma]{} & Sxwa & \xrightarrow[S]{} & a & \twoheadrightarrow_{\emptyset} & a & \twoheadrightarrow_{\emptyset} &
\end{array}$$

5.2 Plotkin's call-by-value λ-calculus

Plotkin [Plo75] introduced the *call-by-value* λ-calculus, λ_V, which restricts the usual λ-calculus by allowing the contraction of redexes whose arguments are *values*, i.e., either abstractions $\lambda x.t$ or variables (we assume that there are no δ-rules in the calculus). Let the *lazy* call-by-value λ-calculus λ_{LV} be obtained from λ_V by allowing only call-by-value redexes that are not in the scope of a λ-occurrence (λ_{LV} is enough for computing values in λ_V, see Corollary 1 in [Plo75]). Then it follows from Corollary 5.1, as well as from Corollary 5.2, that any λ_{LV}-redex is perpetual, hence λ_{LV} is UN. Indeed, let $v = (\lambda x.s)o$ be a λ_{LV}-redex. Then, if o is a variable, then it is immediate that v cannot be critical, and if o is an abstraction, any of its instances is an abstraction too, hence is a λ_{LV}-normal form. This is not surprising, however, as λ_{LV}-redexes are disjoint,[4] and there is no duplication or erasure of (admissible) redexes.

5.3 De Groote's β_{IS}-reduction

De Groote [dGr93] introduced β_S-reduction on λ-terms by the following rule: β_S : $(((\lambda x.M)N)O) \to ((\lambda x.(MO)N)$, where $x \notin FV(M,O)$. He proved that the β_{IS}-calculus is uniformly normalizing. Clearly, this is an immediate corollary of Theorem 4.5 as the β_S- and β_I-rules are non-erasing (note that these rules do not conflict because of the conditions on bound variables). Using this result, the author proves strong normalization of a number of typed λ-calculi.

5.4 Böhm &Intrigila's λ-δ_k-calculus

Böhm and Intrigila [BI94] introduced the λ-δ_k-calculus in order to study UN solutions to fixed point equations, in the λη-calculus. Since the K-redexes are the source of failure of the UN property in the λ(η)-calculus, they define a 'restricted K

---

[4] if u, v are redexes in a term t and $u = (\lambda x.e)o$, then $v \notin e$ because of the main λ of u, and $v \notin o$ since o is either a variable or an abstraction; orthogonality of λ_{LV} follows from a similar argument.

combinator' δ_K by the following rule: $\delta_K AB \to A$, where B can be instantiated to closed λ-δ_k-normal forms (possibly containing δ_K constants; such a reduction is still well defined). λ-δ_k-terms are λ_I-terms with the constant δ_K. The authors show that the λ-δ_k-calculus has the UN property. This result follows from Corollary 4.6 only if the η-rule is dropped. However, Klop shows in [Klo80] that η-redexes are perpetual, and we hope that our results can be generalized to weakly-orthogonal CERSs (and thus cover the η-rule since η-redexes are non-erasing) using van Oostrom and van Raamsdonk's technique for simulating $\beta\eta$ reductions with β-reductions [OR94].

5.5 Honsell &Lenisa's β_{N^o}-calculus

Honsell and Lenisa [HL93] define a similar reduction, β_{N^o}-reduction, on λ-terms by the following rule: β_{N^o} : $(\lambda x.A)B \to (B/x)A$, where B can be instantiated to a closed β-normal form. We have immediately from Corollary 4.6 that β_{N^o} is UN. Note however that the later does not follow (at least, without an extra argument) from Bergstra and Klop's characterization of perpetual β_K-redexes [BK82] as $\beta_{N^o} \subset \beta$ but not conversely. (If t has an infinite β_{N^o}-reduction and $t \xrightarrow{u} s$ is a β_{N^o}-step, then the Bergstra-Klop criterion implies existence of an infinite β-*reduction* starting from s, not existence of an infinite β_{N^o}-reduction.)

6 Concluding Remarks

We have obtained two criteria for perpetuality of redexes in orthogonal CERSs, and demonstrated their usefulness in applications. We claim that our results are also valid for Klop's orthogonal *substructure* CRSs [KOR93].

However, they cannot be generalized (at least, directly) to orthogonal *Pattern Rewrite Systems* (OPRSs) [Nip93], as witnessed by the following example due to van Oostrom [Oos97]. It shows that already the Conservation Theorem fails for OPRSs (i.e., non-erasing steps need not be perpetual): Let $R = \{g(M.N.X(x.M(x), N)) \to_g X(x.I, \Omega),\ @(\lambda(x.M(x)), N) \to_\beta M(N)\}$ where $\Omega = @(\lambda(x.xx), \lambda(x.xx))$. Then $g(M.N.@(\lambda(x.M(x)), N)) \to_\beta g(M.N.M(N))$ is non-erasing but critical, as can be seen from the following diagram, of which the bottom part is the only reduction starting from $g(M.N.M(N))$. Such strange behavior arises because of λ_K-reduction steps in the substitution calculus, which are invisible in a PRS reduction step.

$$
\begin{array}{ccccccc}
g(M.N.@(\lambda(x.M(x)), N)) & \underset{g}{\longrightarrow} & @(\lambda(x.I), \Omega) & \overset{\Omega}{\underset{\beta}{\longrightarrow}} & @(\lambda(x.I), \Omega) & \overset{\Omega}{\underset{\beta}{\longrightarrow}} & \cdots \\
\beta\downarrow & & \beta\downarrow & & \beta\downarrow & & \\
g(M.N.M(N)) & \underset{g}{\longrightarrow} & I & \underset{\emptyset}{\longrightarrow} & I & \underset{\emptyset}{\longrightarrow} & \cdots
\end{array}
$$

Acknowledgments We thank Vincent van Oostrom for useful comments, and for the counterexample.

References

[Acz78] Aczel P. A general Church-Rosser theorem. Preprint, University of Manchester, 1978.

[Bar84] Barendregt H. P. The Lambda Calculus, its Syntax and Semantics. North-Holland, 1984.

[Bar92] Barendregt H. P. Lambda calculi with types. In: Handbook of Logic in Computer Science, vol. 2, S. Abramsky, D. Gabbay, and T. Maibaum eds. Oxford University Press, 1992, p. 117-309.

[BBKV76] Barendregt H. P., Bergstra J., Klop J. W., Volken H. Some notes on lambda-reduction, In: Degrees, reductions, and representability in the lambda calculus. Preprint no. 22, University of Utrecht, Department of mathematics, 1976, p. 13-53.

[BK82] Bergstra J. A., Klop J. W. Strong normalization and perpetual reductions in the Lambda Calculus. J. of Information Processing and Cybernetics, 18:403-417, 1982.

[BI94] Böhm C., Intrigila B. The Ant-Lion paradigm for strong normalization. Information and Computation, 114(1):30-49, 1994.

[CR36] Church A., Rosser, J. B. Some Properties of Conversion. Transactions of the American Mathematical Society, 39:472-482, 1936.

[GK96] Glauert J. R. W., Khasidashvili Z. Minimal relative normalization in orthogonal expression reduction systems. In Proc. of the 16th International Conference on Foundations of Software Technology and Theoretical Computer Science, FST&TCS'96, Springer LNCS, vol. 1180, V. Chandru, ed. 1996, p. 238-249.

[Gra96] Gramlich B. Termination and confluence properties of structured Rewrite Systems. Ph.D. Thesis, Kaiserslautern University, 1996.

[dGr93] De Groote P. The conservation theorem revisited. In: Proc. of the 1st International Conference on Typed Lambda Calculi and Applications. Springer LNCS, vol. 664, M. Bezem, J. F. Groote, eds. Utrecht, 1993, p. 163-178.

[HL93] Honsell F., Lenisa M. Some results on the full abstraction problem for restricted lambda calculi. In Proc. of the 18th International Symposium on Mathematical Foundations of Computer Science, MFCS'93, Springer LNCS, vol. 711, A. M. Borzyszkowski, S. Sokolowski, eds. 1993, p. 84-104.

[HL91] Huet G., Lévy J.-J. Computations in Orthogonal Rewriting Systems. In: Computational Logic, Essays in Honor of Alan Robinson, J.-L. Lassez and G. Plotkin, eds. MIT Press, 1991, p. 394-443.

[Kha92] Khasidashvili Z. The Church-Rosser theorem in Orthogonal Combinatory Reduction Systems. Report 1825, INRIA Rocquencourt, 1992.

[Kha94] Khasidashvili Z. On higher order recursive program schemes. In: Proc. of the 19th International Colloquium on Trees in Algebra and Programming, CAAP'94, Springer LNCS, vol. 787, S. Tison, ed. Edinburgh, 1994, p. 172-186.

[Kha94b] Khasidashvili Z. Perpetuality and strong normalization in orthogonal term rewriting systems. In: Proc. of 11th Symposium on Theoretical Aspects of Computer Science, STACS'94, Springer LNCS, vol. 775, P. Enjalbert, E. W. Mayr, and K. W. Wagner, eds. Caen, 1994, p. 163-174.

[Kha94c] Khasidashvili Z. The longest perpetual reductions in orthogonal expression reduction systems. In: Proc. of the 3rd International Conference on Logical Foundations of Computer Science, LFCS'94, Springer LNCS, vol. 813, Nerode A., Matiyasevich Yu. V. eds. 1994. p. 191-203.

[KO95] Khasidashvili Z, van Oostrom V. Context-sensitive conditional expression reduction systems. In proc. of the International Workshop on Graph Rewriting and Computation, SEGRAGRA'95. In Electronic Notes in Computer Science, A. Corradini, U. Montanari, eds. Elsevier Science B.V., August, 1995, p. 141-150.

[Klo80] Klop J. W. Combinatory Reduction Systems. Mathematical Centre Tracts n. 127, CWI, Amsterdam, 1980.

[Klo92] Klop J. W. Term Rewriting Systems. In: Handbook of Logic in Computer Science, vol. 2, S. Abramsky, D. Gabbay, and T. Maibaum eds. Oxford University Press, 1992, p. 1-116.

[KOR93] Klop J. W., van Oostrom V., van Raamsdonk F. Combinatory reduction systems: introduction and survey. In: To Corrado Böhm, Special issue of Theoretical Computer Science, 121:279-308, 1993.

[Lév80] Lévy J.-J. Optimal reductions in the Lambda-calculus. In: To H. B. Curry: Essays on Combinatory Logic, Lambda-calculus and Formalism, Hindley J. R., Seldin J. P. eds, Academic Press, 1980, p. 159-192.

[Mel96] Melliès P.-A. Description Abstraite des Systèmes de Réécriture. Thèse de l'Université Paris 7, 1996.

[Ned73] Nederpelt R. P. Strong Normalization for a typed lambda-calculus with lambda structured types. Ph.D. Thesis, Eindhoven, 1973.

[Nip93] Nipkow T. Orthogonal higher-order rewrite systems are confluent. In: Proc. of the 1st International Conference on Typed Lambda Calculus and Applications, TLCA'93, Springer LNCS, vol. 664, Bezem M., Groote J.F., eds. Utrecht, 1993, p. 306-317.

[O'Do77] O'Donnell M. J. Computing in systems described by equations. Springer LNCS, vol. 58, 1977.

[Oos94] Van Oostrom V. Confluence for Abstract and Higher-Order Rewriting. Ph.D. Thesis, Free University, Amsterdam, 1994.

[Oos97] Van Oostrom V. Personal communication, 1997.

[OR94] Van Oostrom V., van Raamsdonk F. Weak orthogonality implies confluence: the higher-order case. In: Proc. of the 3rd International Conference on Logical Foundations of Computer Science, LFCS'94, Springer LNCS, vol. 813, Nerode A., Matiyasevich Yu. V. eds. 1994. p. 379-392.

[Pkh77] Pkhakadze Sh. Some problems of the Notation Theory (in Russian). Proceedings of I. Vekua Institute of Applied Mathematics of Tbilisi State University, Tbilisi, 1977.

[Pla93] Plaisted D. A. Polynomial time termination and constraint satisfaction tests. In: Proc. of the 5th International Conference on Rewriting Techniques and Applications, RTA'93, Springer LNCS, vol. 690, C. Kirchner, ed. 1993, p. 405-420.

[Plo75] Plotkin G. Call-by-name, call-by-value and the λ-calculus. Theoretical Computer Science, 1:125-159, 1975.

[Raa96] Van Raamsdonk F. Confluence and normalisation for higher-order rewriting. Ph.D. Thesis, Free University, Amsterdam, 1996.

[Sør95] Sørensen M. H. Properties of infinite reduction paths in untyped λ-calculus. In: Proc. of Tbilisi Symposium on Logic, Language and Computation, TSLLC'95. Selected papers. J. Ginzburg, Z. Khasidashvili, J.J. Lévy, C. Vogel, E. Vallduví, eds. SiLLI publications, CSLI, Stanford, 1997. To appear.

[dVr87] De Vrijer R. C. Surjective pairing and strong normalization: two themes in lambda calculus. Ph.D. Thesis, Amsterdam, 1987.

[Wol93] Wolfram D. The causal theory of types. Cambridge Tracts in Theoretical Computer Science, vol. 21, Cambridge University Press, 1993.

Model Generation with Existentially Quantified Variables and Constraints

Slim Abdennadher and Heribert Schütz

Universität München, Institut für Informatik, Oettingenstr. 67, D-80538 München
{Slim.Abdennadher|Heribert.Schuetz}@informatik.uni-muenchen.de

Abstract. In this paper we present the CPUHR-tableau calculus, a modification of positive unit hyperresolution (PUHR) tableaux, the calculus underlying the model generator and theorem prover Satchmo. In addition to clausal first order logic, CPUHR tableaux are able to manipulate existentially quantified variables without Skolemization, and they allow to attach constraints to these variables as in constraint logic programming. This extension allows to handle efficiently many realistic model generation problems that cannot be handled by model generators for clausal theories such as PUHR tableaux. In this paper we deal with CPUHR tableaux only for formulas without function symbols other than constants.

1 Introduction

In the last years in the automated deduction community there has been increasing interest in *model generation*, that is, in methods for automatic construction of interpretations that satisfy a given theory. This research direction complements the traditional direction of *theorem proving*. In the area of (disjunctive) logic programming forward-chaining methods typically correspond to model generation while backward-chaining methods correspond to (refutational) theorem proving.

Satchmo [11] has been an early approach to automated model generation. It has originally been developed as a tool for checking the consistency of integrity constraints in relational databases: If Satchmo can generate a (Herbrand) model for a set of integrity constraints, then the integrity constraints are consistent, and can therefore be satisfied by some database instance.

Example 1. Consider, for example, this set of integrity constraints for a database with relations for employees, projects, and assignment of employees to projects:

- Every employee is assigned to at least one project.
- Every project has at least one assigned employee.
- If an employee is assigned to a project, then the employee and the project must exist in the respective relations.

In addition we know that mary is an employee. These conditions can be written as formulas[1]

$$\begin{gathered}\mathtt{employee(E)} \rightarrow \exists \mathtt{P}\ \mathtt{assigned(E,P)} \\ \mathtt{project(P)} \rightarrow \exists \mathtt{E}\ \mathtt{assigned(E,P)} \\ \mathtt{assigned(E,P)} \rightarrow \mathtt{employee(E)} \\ \mathtt{assigned(E,P)} \rightarrow \mathtt{project(P)} \\ \mathtt{employee(mary)}\end{gathered}$$

which are implicitly universally closed.

The first and the second formula in this example contain existentially quantified variables. The third and the fourth formula are "referential integrity constraints", a kind of integrity constraints that appear frequently in relational databases. They would require existential variables as well if we had not restricted **employee** and **project** to a single argument for the sake of simplicity.

Satchmo expects its input to be given in clausal form. So the existentially quantified variables have to be Skolemized:

$$\begin{gathered}\mathtt{employee(E)} \rightarrow \mathtt{assigned(E,f(E))} \\ \mathtt{project(P)} \rightarrow \mathtt{assigned(g(P),P)}\end{gathered}$$

Unfortunately Satchmo does not terminate when applied to the Skolemized clause set because it enumerates the infinite Herbrand model

$$\begin{aligned}\{&\mathtt{employee(mary)}, \mathtt{assigned(mary,f(mary))}, \\ &\mathtt{project(f(mary))}, \mathtt{assigned(g(f(mary)),f(mary))}, \\ &\mathtt{employee(g(f(mary)))}, \mathtt{assigned(g(f(mary))),f(g(f(mary)))))}, \\ &\ldots\}.\end{aligned}$$

In this paper we present CPUHR tableaux, a modification of positive unit hyper resolution (PUHR) tableaux [2], the calculus underlying Satchmo. CPUHR tableaux do not require Skolemization of existential variables. Therefore CPUHR tableaux terminate for many applications where PUHR tableaux do not terminate when applied to the respective Skolemized theory. For the theory in Example 1 the finite set

$$\{\mathtt{employee(mary)}, \mathtt{assigned(mary,P)}, \mathtt{project(P)}\}$$

of atoms is generated, which contains a variable P. Every ground instantiation of P leads to a finite Herbrand model of the theory. This result has the additional advantage that it is closer to the problem specification than a model containing Skolem functions.

CPUHR tableaux allow also to attach constraints[2] to the existentially quantified variables (which explains the "C" in the name). Intuitively, constraints

[1] We adopt the Prolog convention that variable names start with capital letters and predicate and constant symbols start with lowercase letters.

[2] Note that by "constraints" we understand constraints in the sense of constraint logic programming, unless we explicitly speak of "integrity constraints" for databases.

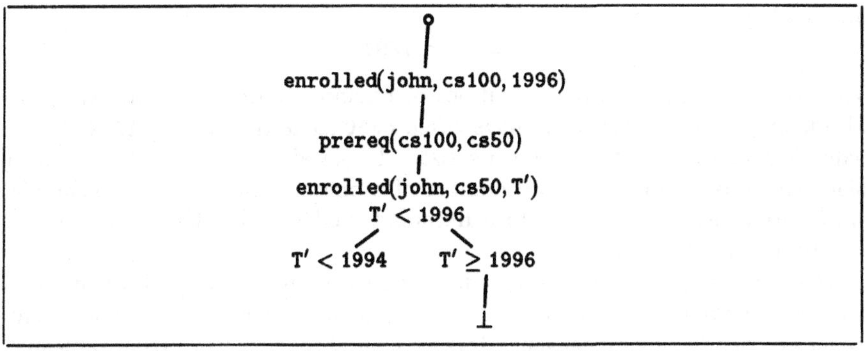

Fig. 1. The tableau generated for Example 2

represent elementary restrictions for and relationships between variables, for example equality or order relationships. They are checked and simplified by a constraint solver that implements a predefined constraint theory.

Example 2. Consider the following informations that we have about a university and a student: If a student S is enrolled in a course C at some time T and C has another course C′ as a prerequisite, then S must also be enrolled in C′ at some time T′ before T. john has only taken courses before 1994 and from 1996 onward. He has taken course cs100 in 1996. cs100 has prerequisite cs50.

1. $\mathtt{enrolled(S, C, T)} \wedge \mathtt{prereq(C, C')} \rightarrow \exists \mathtt{T'}(\mathtt{enrolled(S, C', T')} \wedge \mathtt{T'} < \mathtt{T})$
2. $\mathtt{enrolled(john, C, T)} \rightarrow \mathtt{T} < \mathtt{1994} \vee \mathtt{T} \geq \mathtt{1996}$
3. enrolled(john, cs100, 1996)
4. prereq(cs100, cs50)

Here "$<$" and "$\geq$" are constraint symbols known to the constraint solver.

The tableau generated for this theory is given in Figure 1. First, we introduce facts 3 and 4 from the theory. An instance of rule 1 is activated and we introduce enrolled(john, cs50, T′) and $\mathtt{T'} < \mathtt{1996}$. This activates an instance of rule 2 and we distinguish two cases corresponding to the disjuncts on the right hand side of the implication. In the right case we get a contradiction between two constraints ($\mathtt{T'} < \mathtt{1996}$ and $\mathtt{T'} \geq \mathtt{1996}$) and the branch is closed. We mark this by the symbol "$\perp$".

In the left case no rule application can add new information. For example, rule 2 is not activated by facts 3 and 4 because T would be instantiated to 1996, which would result in a tautology since "$\mathtt{1996} \geq \mathtt{1996}$" is trivially true. The constraint solver collects, combines, and simplifies the constraints in the branch and we get a set of atoms

$$A = \{\mathtt{enrolled(john, cs100, 1996)}, \mathtt{prereq(cs100, cs50)}, \\ \mathtt{enrolled(john, cs50, T')}\}$$

and a set of constraints

$$C = \{\mathtt{T}' < \mathtt{1994}\}.$$

We have found out that the conditions of Example 2 are consistent. We have also found out that **john** must have taken **cs50** some time before **1994**. Every valuation for the variable $\mathtt{T}'$ which satisfies C can also be applied to A, which leads (together with an infinite number of atoms for the constraint symbols, which are of no interest here) to a Herbrand model of the theory (and of the constraint theory, of course).

The extension of clausal first order logic by existential variables and constraints allows to handle efficiently many realistic model generation problems that cannot be handled by model generators for clausal theories like PUHR tableaux. Still, one goal in the design of the CPUHR-tableau calculus was to keep much of the "light-weight" flavour of Satchmo and PUHR tableaux, which make their use in (disjunctive) logic programming and deductive databases attractive.

In this paper we deal with CPUHR tableaux only for formulas without function symbols other than constants. Note that this restriction is not as hard as it would be in the absence of existential variables, since (a) we do not need Skolem functions and (b) we will adopt the constraint logic programming approach that a constraint theory does not mainly define properties of functions (constants in our case) by means of equations. We rather leave constants uninterpreted and let the constraint theory define certain predicates.

The paper is organized as follows. The next section gives some definitions and notations which will be used throughout the paper. Section 3 presents the CPUHR-tableau calculus. In section 4 we give soundness and completeness properties for model generation. Section 5 discusses related work. We summarize our contribution and point out some directions for further research in section 6.

2 Preliminaries

We expect the reader to have some basic understanding of logic, tableau calculi, and constraint solving. For the sake of clarity we nevertheless give definitions for some of the notions used in this paper.

We use two disjoint sorts of predicate symbols: *constraint predicates* and *free predicates*. Intuitively, constraint predicates are defined by some constraint theory and handled by an appropriate constraint solver, while free predicates are defined by a user-supplied theory. The CPUHR-tableau calculus tries to compute appropriate interpretations for the free predicates. We call an atomic formula with a constraint predicate an *atomic constraint* and an atomic formula with a free predicate an *atom*.

Throughout the paper we expect some constraint theory CT to be given which has the following properties:

- CT is consistent.
- CT is *ground complete*, that is, for every ground atomic constraint c either $CT \models c$ or $CT \models \neg c$.

- CT does not contain any free predicates.
- CT defines among other constraint predicates equality ("=") and disequality ("≠") as syntactic equality and disequality, using for example Clark's axiomatization.
- There is a constraint solver that implements CT.

Because of the consistence and the ground completeness CT has a single Herbrand model

$$CM := \{c \mid CT \models c\}$$

in the sublanguage without free predicates. As usual, we identify a Herbrand model with the set of ground atomic formulas it satisfies.

We use the notation "$\{v_1 \mapsto t_1, \ldots, v_n \mapsto t_n\}$" for substitutions, which means that the variables $v_1, \ldots, v_n$ are mapped to the terms $t_1, \ldots, t_n$, resp.

For an interpretation I and a variable valuation (sometimes also called "variable assignment") θ we denote the fact that the formula or set of formulas F is satisfied by I and θ as "$I, \theta \models F$". The fact that a closed formula is satisfied by an interpretation I is denoted as "$I \models F$". By "$I, \theta \not\models F$" or "$I \not\models F$" we mean that F is not satisfied by I and θ or by I.

3 The CPUHR-Tableau Calculus

3.1 Syntax

The CPUHR-tableau calculus deals with closed first-order formulas of a certain type, which we call "rules", and it manipulates tableaux of a certain form.

Definition 3. A *rule* is a closed formula of the form

$$\forall \overline{X}(b_1 \wedge \cdots \wedge b_l \rightarrow \exists \overline{Y}(h_1 \vee \cdots \vee h_m \vee c_1 \vee \cdots \vee c_n)),$$

where every b_i and every h_j is an atom, and every c_k is an atomic constraint.

We call the left and right side of the implication the *body* and the *head* of the rule, respectively. We write empty conjunctions and disjunctions as $\top$ and $\bot$, respectively. A rule with an empty body is represented just by its head.

A rule has to satisfy a *range-restriction* condition: Every free variable in the head appears also in the body.

A *specification* is a set of rules.

For brevity we do not write the universal quantifiers in examples, rules are implicitly universally closed.

Example 4. Since conjunctions may not occur in rule heads, we replace condition 1 of Example 2 by the three rules

$$\mathtt{enrolled(S, C, T)} \wedge \mathtt{prereq(C, C')} \rightarrow \exists \mathtt{T'}\,\mathtt{aux(S, C', T', T)}$$
$$\mathtt{aux(S, C', T', T)} \rightarrow \mathtt{enrolled(S, C', T')}$$
$$\mathtt{aux(S, C', T', T)} \rightarrow \mathtt{T'} < \mathtt{T}$$

using an auxiliary predicate **aux**.

For the rest of the paper we assume that some specification S is given, for which we are generating models.

We have used the traditional tree representation of a tableau in Figure 1 with open and closed branches. In the formal presentation of the calculus a tableau is given as the set of "open" branches of the tree representation. "Closing" a branch means to remove it from the set. In the representation of branches we separate the atoms and atomic constraints that appear along the corresponding open branch of the tree:

Definition 5. A *branch* is a pair (A, C) where A is a set of atoms, C is a set of atomic constraints. A *CPUHR tableau* is a set of branches.

In contrast to PUHR tableaux, where a branch represents a single Herbrand interpretation, a branch of a CPUHR tableau represents a set of Herbrand interpretations because the variables in the branch are implicitly existentially quantified:

Definition 6. We say that branch (A, C) of a tableau represents the set

$$\mathit{Int}(A,C) := \{A\theta \cup CM \mid \theta \text{ is a valuation for the variables in } A \text{ and } C \text{ such that } CM, \theta \models C\}$$

of Herbrand interpretations and that a tableau represents the set

$$\mathit{Int}(T) := \bigcup_{(A,C)\in T} \mathit{Int}(A,C)$$

of Herbrand interpretations.

A formula is *satisfied* by a branch (A, C) if it is satisfied by every interpretation in $\mathit{Int}(A, C)$. It is *violated* by a branch if it is not satisfied by the branch.

Note that $\mathit{Int}(\emptyset) = \emptyset$ and $\mathit{Int}(\{(\emptyset, \emptyset)\}) = \mathit{Int}(\emptyset, \emptyset) = CM$.

3.2 The Inference Rule

CPUHR tableaux for a given specification S are constructed as follows:

- The *initial* tableau $\{(\emptyset, \emptyset)\}$ is a CPUHR tableau for S.
- Further CPUHR tableaux for S are constructed by the following inference rule:

$$\frac{\begin{array}{c} T \text{ is a CPUHR tableau for } S \\ (A,C) \in T \\ E \text{ is a tuple of atoms in } A \\ R \in S \\ R \text{ is applicable to } E \text{ and } (A,C) \end{array}}{T \setminus \{(A,C)\} \cup \mathit{expand}(A,C,E,R) \text{ is a CPUHR tableau for } S}$$

All the complexity of the inference rule is hidden in the notion of applicability and the function *expand*, which are described in detail below. The inference rule is a combination of the PUHR rule and the splitting rule given by Bry and Yahya [2] extended to the more powerful specifications that can be handled by CPUHR tableaux.

In the rest of the paper we will assume that the variables in R are renamed in such a way that no variable in R appears in A or C and that no variable is quantified both universally and existentially in R.

Expansion. The expansion *expand*(A, C, E, R) of a branch (A, C) with a given rule R and electrons[3] E consists of three steps:

- $\exists$-unification of the rule body with the electrons,
- splitting of the branch according to the disjunction in the rule head, and
- normalization of the constraints.

We explain these steps before we show how they are combined by the definition of the function *expand*.

$\exists$-Unification. We have to "unify" the body of R with the tuple of electrons E. The type of unification that we need is, however, different from the usual unification in resolution calculi because the variables in the electrons are quantified existentially rather than universally. Furthermore note that the electrons may share variables. We call the modified unification ***$\exists$-unification***.

As an introductory example consider the rule $\mathtt{p(Z,Z)} \rightarrow \mathtt{q(Z)}$ and the branch $(\{\mathtt{p(X,a)}\}, \emptyset)$. The branch represents the Herbrand interpretations $\{\mathtt{p(c,a)}\}$ for arbitrary constants $\mathtt{c}$. Only for those interpretations where $\mathtt{c}$ equals $\mathtt{a}$, the rule should be applied. Therefore we distinguish two cases by the constraints "$\mathtt{X} = \mathtt{a}$" and "$\mathtt{X} \neq \mathtt{a}$". In the latter case the rule cannot be applied, while in the former case an instance of the rule should be applied where $\mathtt{Z}$ is instantiated to $\mathtt{a}$.

The $\exists$-unification will in general return a set of solutions rather than a single one. Every solution is a pair (σ, D) where σ is a substitution for the universal variables or "*fail*" and D is a set of atomic constraints. Intuitively, σ is an appropriate instantiation for the universal variables of the rule for those interpretations in *Int*(A, C) that satisfy D.

The $\exists$-unification proceeds as follows:

- We first check whether the tuple E of electrons has the same number of components as there are atoms in the rule body and whether the predicate symbols and arities of the body atoms coincide with the predicate symbols and arities of the corresponding electrons. If this is not the case, then the $\exists$-unification fails unconditionally (i.e., for every interpretation in *Int*(A, C)) and we return

$$\mathit{ex\_unify}(\mathit{body}(R), E) := \{(\mathit{fail}, \emptyset)\}.$$

[3] As usual in hyperresolution, *electrons* are the "peripheral" formulas involved in a hyperresolution step, that is, all the formulas except for the "central" formula R.

- Otherwise we define a set of equations

$$G := \{t = t' \mid t \text{ is an argument of a body atom and } t' \text{ is the corresponding argument of the corresponding electron.}\}$$

- Every universal variable from the body of R appears on the left hand side of at least one equation in G. We (nondeterministically) choose exactly one equation for every such variable. The chosen equations define a substitution σ for the universal variables. Let G' be the set of remaining equations of G, that is, the equations without universal variables and the equations with universal variables that have not been chosen for σ.
- We now apply σ to G'. The equations in $G'\sigma$ do not contain universal variables any more, but there may be existential variables. We have to deal with those interpretations that satisfy $G'\sigma$ and with those that violate some equation in $G'\sigma$. Therefore we return a solution for each of these cases:

$$\begin{aligned} &\mathit{ex\_unify}(\mathit{body}(R), E) := \\ &\qquad \{(\sigma, G'\sigma)\} \cup \{(\mathit{fail}, \{t \neq t'\}) \mid G'\sigma \text{ contains an equation } t = t'.\} \end{aligned}$$

Note that for every variable valuation θ there is some solution (σ, D) in the result of the $\exists$-unification (possibly with $\sigma = \mathit{fail}$) such that D is satisfied by CM and θ.

A set D of constraints in a solution returned by the $\exists$-unification function may be inconsistent or inconsistent with the old constraints in C. Then we might omit the respective solution, but we leave this to the normalization step below.

Example 7. Let R be rule 1 of Example 4 with renamed variables

$$\texttt{enrolled(A,B,C)} \land \texttt{prereq(B,D)} \rightarrow \exists \texttt{E aux(A,D,E,C)},$$

and let E be the pair (`enrolled(john,C1,T)`, `prereq(C2,C1)`) of electrons, which means that at some unknown time `T` the student `john` has taken some unknown course `C1`, which is a prerequisite for some other unknown course `C2`. The $\exists$-unification algorithm computes the following values:

$$\begin{aligned} G &= \{\texttt{A} = \texttt{john}, \texttt{B} = \texttt{C1}, \texttt{C} = \texttt{T}, \texttt{B} = \texttt{C2}, \texttt{D} = \texttt{C1}\} \\ \sigma &= \{\texttt{A} \mapsto \texttt{john}, \texttt{B} \mapsto \texttt{C1}, \texttt{C} \mapsto \texttt{T}, \texttt{D} \mapsto \texttt{C1}\} \\ G' &= \{\texttt{B} = \texttt{C2}\} \\ G'\sigma &= \{\texttt{C1} = \texttt{C2}\} \\ \mathit{ex\_unify}(\mathit{body}(R), E) &= \{(\sigma, \{\texttt{C1} = \texttt{C2}\}), (\mathit{fail}, \{\texttt{C1} \neq \texttt{C2}\})\} \end{aligned}$$

We expect that frequently G' is empty or contains only trivially valid equations as in the following example, so that the possible branching that will be introduced by the $\exists$-unification step (see below) will not matter too much.

Example 8. Let R be rule 2 of Example 2 with renamed variables

$$\mathtt{enrolled(john, A, B)} \rightarrow \mathtt{B} < \mathtt{1994} \vee \mathtt{B} \geq \mathtt{1996},$$

and let E be the electron $\mathtt{enrolled(john, cs30, T)}$. Then the $\exists$-unification algorithm computes

$$\begin{aligned} G &= \{\mathtt{john} = \mathtt{john}, \mathtt{A} = \mathtt{cs30}, \mathtt{B} = \mathtt{T}\} \\ \sigma &= \{\mathtt{A} \mapsto \mathtt{cs30}, \mathtt{B} \mapsto \mathtt{T}\} \\ G' &= \{\mathtt{john} = \mathtt{john}\} \\ \mathit{ex\_unify}(\mathit{body}(R), E) &= \{(\sigma, \{\mathtt{john} = \mathtt{john}\}), (\mathit{fail}, \{\mathtt{john} \neq \mathtt{john}\})\} \end{aligned}$$

Splitting. To apply a rule head $\exists \overline{Y}(h_1 \vee \cdots \vee h_m \vee c_1 \vee \cdots \vee c_n)$ in a branch (A, C) we

- split the branch into one branch for every disjunct in the rule head and
- add the disjuncts to the corresponding new branches after applying the substitution σ that has been obtained in the $\exists$-unification step.

This is formalized by the function

$$\begin{aligned} &\mathit{split}(A, C, \exists \overline{Y}(h_1 \vee \cdots \vee h_m \vee c_1 \vee \cdots \vee c_n), \sigma) := \\ &\quad (A \cup \{h_1\sigma\}, C), \cdots, (A \cup \{h_m\sigma\}, C), (A, C \cup \{c_1\sigma\}), \cdots, (A, C \cup \{c_n\sigma\})\}. \end{aligned}$$

Note that the variables $\overline{Y}$ do not occur in (A, C) and that they are not affected by σ because of the variable renaming mentioned at the beginning of Section 3.2. Note also that the branch is closed if the head is the empty disjunction $\perp$.

Example 9. For the rule head and the substitution σ from Example 8 and the branch $(A, C) = (\{\mathtt{enrolled(john, cs30, T)}\}, \{\mathtt{T} \leq \mathtt{1996}, \mathtt{john} = \mathtt{john}\})$ the splitting step generates

$$\begin{aligned} \mathit{split}(A, C, \mathtt{B} < \mathtt{1994} \vee \mathtt{B} \geq \mathtt{1996}, \sigma) = \{&(A, \{\mathtt{T} \leq \mathtt{1996}, \mathtt{john} = \mathtt{john}, \mathtt{T} < \mathtt{1994}\}), \\ &(A, \{\mathtt{T} \leq \mathtt{1996}, \mathtt{john} = \mathtt{john}, \mathtt{T} \geq \mathtt{1996}\})\} \end{aligned}$$

Constraint Normalization. We call the constraint solver to close or simplify a tableau branch (A, C):

- The branch is closed if no variable valuation satisfies C together with CM, that is, if $CM \not\models \exists C$.
- Otherwise the branch may be simplified. Let $\overline{X}$ be the common variables of A and C and let $\overline{Y}$ be the local variables of C, that is, those variables that do not appear in A. The constraint solver converts C, X, and Y into a substitution ν for the variables $\overline{X}$ and a set of constraints C' with local variables $\overline{Y'}$ such that

$$CM \models \forall \overline{X}(\exists \overline{Y} \bigwedge C \leftrightarrow \overline{X} = \overline{X}\nu \wedge \exists \overline{Y'} \bigwedge C') \tag{1}$$

  Here "$\overline{X} = \overline{X}\nu$" stands for a conjunction of equations where every variable in $\overline{X}$ is identified with the term to which it is mapped by ν. We typically expect that C' is the same as C or in some way simpler than C.

This leads to the normalization function

$$normalize(A, C) := \begin{cases} \emptyset & \text{if } CM \not\models \exists C \\ \{(A\nu, C')\} & \text{where } \nu \text{ and } C' \text{ satisfy (1), if } CM \models \exists C. \end{cases}$$

Example 10. Consider the branches generated in Example 9. In the first branch the constraint solver might simplify the constraints to "$\mathtt{T} = \mathtt{1996}$" and *normalize* propagates this equality to the atom of the branch:

$$normalize(\{\mathtt{enrolled}(\mathtt{john}, \mathtt{cs30}, \mathtt{T})\}, \{\mathtt{T} \leq \mathtt{1996}, \mathtt{T} \geq \mathtt{1996}\}) = \{(\{\mathtt{enrolled}(\mathtt{john}, \mathtt{cs30}, \mathtt{1996})\}, \emptyset)\}$$

In the second branch the constraint solver typically removes the redundant constraint "$\mathtt{T} \leq \mathtt{1996}$":

$$normalize(\{\mathtt{enrolled}(\mathtt{john}, \mathtt{cs30}, \mathtt{T})\}, \{\mathtt{T} \leq \mathtt{1996}, \mathtt{T} < \mathtt{1994}\}) = \{(\{\mathtt{enrolled}(\mathtt{john}, \mathtt{cs30}, \mathtt{T})\}, \{\mathtt{T} < \mathtt{1994}\})\}$$

Combination of the Expansion Steps. To expand a branch (A, C) with electrons E and rule R we proceed as follows:

- We split (A, C) into one branch for every member (σ, D) of the result of the $\exists$-unification of E and the body of R. We add the constraints in D to the respective branch.
- For a subbranch $(A, C \cup D)$ for which the $\exists$-unification has been successful (i.e., $\sigma \neq fail$) the corresponding instance of the head of R is applied, which means that the subbranch is split and extended again.
- Finally every branch is normalized, which may close some branches.

To formalize the fact that splitting may only be performed if the $\exists$-unification succeeds, we define an auxiliary function *split'*:

$$split'(A, C, H, \sigma) = \begin{cases} \{(A, C)\} & \text{if } \sigma = fail \\ split(A, C, H, \sigma) & \text{otherwise} \end{cases}$$

Now we can define *expand* formally:

$$expand(A, C, E, R) = \{(A'', C'') \mid \text{There is a } \sigma\text{, which is a substitution or "}fail\text{", sets } D \text{ and } C' \text{ of atomic constraints, and a set } A' \text{ of atoms such that } (\sigma, D) \in ex\_unify(body(R), E) \text{ and } (A', C') \in split'(A, C \cup D, head(R), \sigma) \text{ and } (A'', C'') \in normalize(A', C')\}$$

Note that there are two possible reasons for branch splitting: Branch splitting can be enforced "implicitly" by the $\exists$-unification and "explicitly" by a disjunctive rule head. There are also two possible reasons for closing a branch: A rule head may be the empty disjunction (i.e., $\perp$) and an introduced constraint may be inconsistent with other constraints.

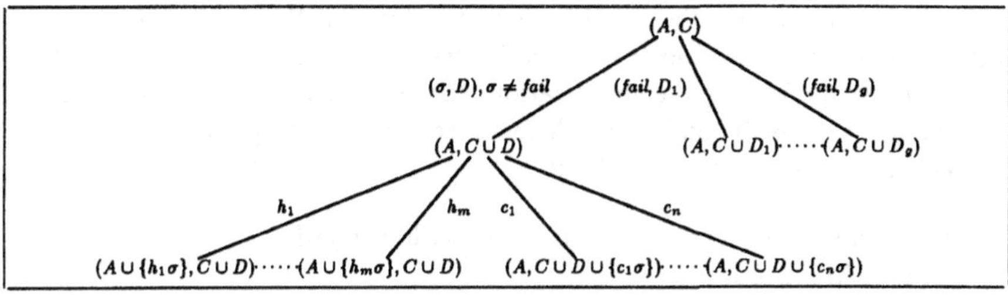

Fig. 2. The branching performed by *ex_unify* and *split*

Figure 2 gives an overview of the branching performed by the ∃-unification and splitting steps in the case that one solution of the ∃-unification is successful. The normalization step, which would follow every leaf, has been omitted in the figure.

Example 11. Consider the branch (A, C) from Example 9 and the rule R and the electron E from Example 8. Then according to those examples and Example 10 we get

$$\begin{aligned} \mathit{expand}(A, C, E, R) = \{&(\{\mathtt{enrolled(john, cs30, 1996)}\}, \emptyset), \\ &(\{\mathtt{enrolled(john, cs30, T)}\}, \{\mathtt{T < 1994}\})\} \end{aligned}$$

Applicability. It is possible that $\mathit{expand}(A, C, E, R)$ does not really "apply" the rule $R := \forall\overline{X}(b_1 \wedge \cdots \wedge b_l \rightarrow \exists\overline{Y}(h_1 \vee \cdots \vee h_m \vee c_1 \vee \cdots \vee c_n))$:

- If the ∃-unification step fails unconditionally (i.e., $\mathit{ex\_unify}(\mathit{body}(R), E) = \{(\mathit{fail}, \emptyset)\}$), then *split'* does not lead to a modification of the branch (A, C).
- If the ∃-unification succeeds for some constraints D (i.e., $\mathit{ex\_unify}(\mathit{body}(R), E)$ contains a solution (σ, D) with $\sigma \neq \mathit{fail}$) but D is not consistent with C (i.e., $CM \not\models \exists \bigwedge(C \cup D)$), then formally *split'* does apply R, but all the generated branches will be closed by the normalization step.

Furthermore there are cases where R is applied but it does not really add information:

- If the splitting step generates a branch $(A \cup \{h_j\sigma\}, C \cup D)$ where A already contains an atom subsuming $h_j\sigma$, then this branch is essentially the same as the input $(A, C \cup D)$ to the splitting step. Here an atom *subsumes* $h_j\sigma$ if one can instantiate the existential variables $\overline{Y}$ in such a way that $h_j\sigma$ is instantiated to the atom.
- If the splitting step generates a branch $(A, C \cup D \cup \{c_k\sigma\})$ where $c_k\sigma$ is already entailed by $C \cup D$ (i.e., $CM \models \forall(\bigwedge(C \cup D) \rightarrow \exists\overline{Y} c_k\sigma)$, then this branch is essentially also the same as the input $(A, C \cup D)$ to the splitting step.

In all these cases the rule R or the relevant instance of R (i.e., after application of the substitution σ) is already satisfied before the inference step. Since our goal is to generate models for the specification, that is, to satisfy all rules, we avoid such inference steps. Therefore we define that a rule R is applicable to a tuple E of electrons and a branch (A, C) if

- there is a $(\sigma, D) \in \mathit{ex\_unify}(\mathit{body}(R), E)$ with $\sigma \neq \mathit{fail}$,
- $CM \models \exists \bigwedge(C \cup D)$,
- $h_j\sigma\tau \notin A$ for every atom h_j in $\mathit{head}(R)$ and every substitution τ for the variables $\overline{Y}$, and
- $CM \not\models \forall(\bigwedge(C \cup D) \rightarrow \exists\overline{Y} c_k\sigma)$ for every atomic constraint c_k in $\mathit{head}(R)$.

An important effect of this condition is that it avoids trivial nontermination of the calculus by repeated application of a rule to the same electrons.

Example 12. Consider the second of the two branches generated in Example 11 and the rule R and the electron E from Example 8:

$$\begin{aligned}(A, C) = (\{&\mathtt{enrolled(john, cs100, 1996)}, \mathtt{prereq(cs100, cs50)},\\ &\mathtt{aux(john, cs50, T', 1996)}\},\\ &\emptyset).\end{aligned}$$

The first rule of Example 4 is not applicable to the electrons (**enrolled(john, cs100, 1996), prereq(cs100, cs50)**) and the branch (A, C) because **aux(john, cs50, T'', 1996)** is subsumed by the branch.

The second rule of Example 2 is not applicable to the electron **enrolled(john, cs100, 1996)** and the branch (A, C) because the constraint $\mathtt{1996} \geq \mathtt{1996}$ is trivially entailed by any set of constraints.

The following lemma essentially says that the applicability condition is not too restrictive for model generation, because a rule can be applied to a branch if it is not (yet) satisfied by the branch.

Lemma 13. *Let R be a rule that is violated by a branch (A, C). Then there is a tuple E of electrons in A such that R is applicable to E and (A, C).*

Proof. (Sketch) Let R be

$$\forall\overline{X}(b_1 \wedge \cdots \wedge b_l \rightarrow \exists\overline{Y}(h_1 \vee \cdots \vee h_m \vee c_1 \vee \cdots \vee c_n)).$$

There is an interpretation $I \in \mathit{Int}(A, C)$ with $I \not\models R$. So there must be a valuation ρ for the variables $\overline{X}$ with

- $I, \rho \models b_i$ for $1 \leq i \leq l$,
- $I, \rho \not\models \exists\overline{Y} h_j$ for $1 \leq j \leq m$, and
- $I, \rho \not\models \exists\overline{Y} c_k$ for $1 \leq k \leq n$.

According to the definition of $Int(A, C)$ there must be a valuation θ for the variables in (A, C) such that $I = A\theta \cup CM$ and $CM, \theta \models C$.

From the first property given for ρ we can conclude that the $b_i\rho$ occur in I and, since they are atoms rather than constraints, that there are atoms $a_i \in A$ such that $b_i\rho = a_i\theta$. We choose $E := (a_1, \ldots, a_l)$. This choice and the properties of ρ and θ ensure that the four conditions for the applicability of R to E and (A, C) hold. □

4 Soundness and Completeness

We now show that CPUHR tableaux have some desirable properties for model generation.

Definition 14. A branch (A, C) is *saturated* if there is no rule $R \in S$ and no tuple E of electrons in A such that R is applicable to E and (A, C). A tableau is *saturated* if its elements are saturated.[4]

Now the following theorem is an immediate consequence of Lemma 13:

Theorem 15 (Model Soundness). *Let T be a saturated tableau for a specification S and let I be a Herbrand interpretation in $Int(T)$. Then I is a model of S.*

Note that it is not obvious whether it is always possible to construct a saturated tableau. Since saturation means that no rule is applicable, we can simply try to apply all applicable rules with a fair strategy until no more rule can be applied. This works in many cases, but a proof that this will always terminate eventually would have to pose additional requirements on the constraint theory CT.

Theorem 16 (Weak Model Completeness). *Let T be a tableau for the specification S and let M be a Herbrand model of S and CT. Then there is an interpretation $I \in Int(T)$ such that $I \subseteq M$.*

Proof. (By induction on the derivation of T.)

For the initial tableau $\{(\emptyset, \emptyset)\}$ we choose $I := \emptyset \in \{\emptyset\} = Int(\{(\emptyset, \emptyset)\})$, which is trivially a subset of M.

Now let T be a tableau with an interpretation $I \in Int(T)$ with $I \subseteq M$ and let T' be derived by an inference step from T. We show that there is an interpretation $I' \in Int(T')$ with $I' \subseteq M$ (ignoring the constraint normalization steps because they obviously do not change the set of represented interpretations):

I is represented by some branch (A, C) of T. If this is not the branch that is expanded in the step from T to T', then (A, C) is also a branch of T'. In this case we choose $I' := I$ and are done.

[4] Saturation depends like applicability on the given specification and the constraint theory.

Otherwise T' contains the branches *expand*(A, C, E, R) for some electrons E in A and some rule R in S. There is a valuation θ for the variables in (A, C) such that $I = A\theta \cup CM$ and $CM, \theta \models C$. For one of the pairs (σ, D) returned by the $\exists$-unification the constraints D are also satisfied by CM and θ. It follows that $I \in Int(A, C \cup D)$.

If the corresponding σ is "*fail*", then T' contains the branch $(A, C \cup D)$. In this case we also choose $I' := I$ and are done.

Otherwise, if the corresponding σ is not "*fail*", then the body atoms of $R\sigma\theta$ (R with the universal variables instantiated according to $\sigma\theta$) are equal to the corresponding electrons a_i after application of θ. Since the electrons appear in A, the atoms $a_i\theta$ appear in I and therefore in M.

Since M is a model of the specification, it also satisfies R and also $R\sigma\theta$. According to the previous considerations it satisfies the body of $R\sigma\theta$ and therefore also the head. So there is a valuation θ' that maps the variables in A and C in the same way as θ and the existential variables in R in such a way that $h_j\sigma\theta' \in M$ for some head atom h_j of R or $c_k\sigma\theta' \in M$ for some head constraint c_k of R.

In the former case we choose $I' := A\theta' \cup \{h_j\sigma\theta'\} \cup CM$. We have $I' = I \cup \{h_j\sigma\theta'\} \subseteq M$ and $I' \in Int(A \cup \{h_j\sigma\}, C \cup D)$, where $(A \cup \{h_j\sigma\}, C \cup D)$ is a branch of T'.

In the latter case we choose $I' := A\theta' \cup CM$. We have $I' = I \subseteq M$ and $I' \in Int(A, C \cup D \cup \{c_k\sigma\})$, where $(A, C \cup D \cup \{c_k\sigma\})$ is a branch of T'. □

We call this theorem "weak" because it does not say that every Herbrand model can be constructed, but only that for every Herbrand model a subset can be constructed. This is not a problem, since we usually want to construct minimal rather than arbitrary Herbrand models. With saturated tableaux we get the following completeness result for minimal Herbrand models:

Theorem 17 (Minimal Model Completeness). *Let T be a saturated tableau for the specification S, and let M be a minimal Herbrand model of $S \cup CT$. Then $M \in Int(T)$.*

Proof. By Theorem 16, there is an Interpretation $I \in Int(T)$ such that $I \subseteq M$. Since T is saturated, by Theorem 15 I is a model of S, and since I interprets constraints in the same way as CM, it is a model of CT. Since M is a minimal model of $S \cup CT$ it follows that $I = M$. □

5 Related Work

Without special care, Skolem functions for existentially quantified variables frequently lead to an explosion of the generated models. The introduction of Skolem constants at runtime by the δ-rule of tableau calculi [13] has a similar effect. This behaviour can sometimes be avoided

- either by a modification of the δ-rule as proposed in [3,1], and in [8] under the name δ^*-rule, which tries to reuse old constants before a new constant is introduced,[5] or
- by mapping different ground terms to a single member of the universe (according to an equational theory), which means that a non-Herbrand model is generated.

In CPUHR tableaux existential variables are not Skolemized at all. Furthermore we have made the choice that the constraint theory implemented by the constraint solver essentially defines the interpretations of predicates rather than that of function symbols.

This allows to use a fixed Herbrand domain. We think that for many applications (e.g. database applications, where the set of objects in the real world is fixed) such a domain is most appropriate and allows easy modelling. (Still, different applications might prefer different approaches and some of the three approaches above could be mapped to other ones.)

Kirchner discusses in [9] the use of constraints in automated deduction. She presents three approaches dealing with constraints: Expression of strategies using constraints, schematization of complex unification problems through constraints and the incorporation of built-in theories in a deduction process. The work described in the present paper gives another advantage of the use of constraints especially in model generation: CPUHR-tableau calculus allows to handle efficiently many realistic problems that cannot be handled by model generators for clausal theories like PUHR tableaux.

Other approaches for model generation involving constraints in the literature work with equational constraints:

- Satchmo has been extended to handle equations in rule heads [6]. Equations are added to an equational theory for the current branch at runtime.
- Caferra et al. [5,4] use equality and disequality constraints for model generation. Both their calculus and their use of constraints is quite different to ours: It attaches constraints to universally rather than to existentially quantified variables, and it is mainly based on resolution rather than tableaux.

Constraint Handling Rules (CHR, [7]) is a high-level language for the implementation of constraint solvers. One type of rules in CHR, the "propagation rules" can be augmented by disjunction and are then similar to the rules handled in this paper.

The operational semantics of these rules differs, however, from CPUHR tableaux: Instead of $\exists$-unification it just uses matching.[6] This does never lead to branching or impose new constraints on the existential variables. Furthermore, the mechanism that avoids repeated application of a rule to the same electrons is not comparable to the one used in CPUHR tableaux.

---

[5] Similar techniques have been used in extensions of Satchmo [6].

[6] In our terminology: Unification succeeds only if G' is already satisfied.

CHR can be used for the implementation of CPUHR tableaux. In fact the idea of combining features of CHR and Satchmo have led to the work presented in this paper.

6 Conclusion and Future Work

In this paper, we have outlined two extensions to the PUHR-tableau calculus. In addition to clausal first order logic, CPUHR tableaux are able to manipulate existentially quantified variables without Skolemization, and they allow to attach constraints to these variables as in constraint logic programming. We have also given certain soundness and completeness properties of the CPUHR-tableau calculus with respect to model generation.

The CPUHR-tableau calculus terminates in many cases where the PUHR-tableau calculus does not terminate when applied to the respective Skolemized specification. Therefore the extensions allow to handle efficiently many realistic model generation problems that cannot be handled by model generators for clausal theories like PUHR tableaux.

Following the considerations in the previous section, our approach to dealing with existential variables and constraints may also be interesting for tableau calculi other than PUHR tableaux.

Our approach can be seen as an extension of disjunctive logic programming with forward chaining [10] by constraints. The requirements for a constraint solver are essentially the same as those posed by traditional constraint logic programming systems with backward chaining.

Interesting directions for future work include

- integration of function symbols in the language,
- optimization possibilities that arise with constraint solvers that can handle certain disjunctions of constraints without case splitting,
- efficient implementation of the calculus, possibly based on constraint handling rules [7] or on the compiling implementation of Satchmo [12],
- determination of properties of constraint theories that guarantee that saturated tableaux can be generated or at least approximated, and
- a description of the first-order theories that can be transformed into specifications for CPUHR tableaux (as in Example 4) and the development of transformation algorithms.

Acknowledgements

We thank Thom Frühwirth for helpful comments on an earlier draft of this paper. The support for the second author by the Bayerischer Habilitations-Förderpreis is appreciated.

References

1. F. Bry and R. Manthey. Checking consistency of database constraints: A logical basis. In *12th Int. Conf. on Very Large Data Bases (VLDB)*, Kyoto, Japan, 1986.
2. F. Bry and A. Yahya. Minimal model generation with positive unit hyper-resolution tableaux. In *5th Workshop on Theorem Proving with Tableaux and Related Methods*, Springer LNAI, 1996.
3. F. Bry. Proving finite satisfiability of deductive databases. In *Proc. of the Conference Logic and Computer Science*, Karlsruhe, Germany, 1987. Springer-Verlag.
4. R. Caferra and N. Peltier. Model building and interactive theory discovery. In *4th Workshop on Theorem Proving with Analytic Tableaux and Related Methods 95*, Springer LNAI 918, pages 154–168, 1995.
5. R. Caferra and N. Zabel. Extending resolution for model construction. In *Logics in AI: European Workshop JELIA '90*, Springer LNAI 478, pages 153–169, 1991.
6. M. Denecker and D. De Schreye. On the duality of abduction and model generation in a framework for model generation with equality. *Journal of Theoretical Computer Science*, 1994.
7. T. Frühwirth. Constraint handling rules. In A. Podelski, editor, *Constraint Programming: Basics and Trends*, LNCS 910. Springer-Verlag, 1995.
8. J. Hintikka. Model minimization – an alternative to circumscription. *Journal of Automated Reasoning*, 4(1):1–14, Mar. 1988.
9. H. Kirchner. On the use of constraints in automated deduction. In A. Podelski, editor, *Constraint Programming: Basics and Trends*, LNCS 910. Springer, 1995. (Châtillon-sur-Seine Spring School, France, May 1994).
10. J. Lobo, J. Minker, and A. Rajasekar. *Foundations of Disjunctive Logic Programming*. MIT Press, 1992.
11. R. Manthey and F. Bry. SATCHMO: A theorem prover implemented in Prolog. In *9th Int. Conf. on Automated Deduction (CADE)*, Springer LNCS 310, pages 415–434, 1988.
12. H. Schütz and T. Geisler. Efficient model generation through compilation. In M. McRobbie and J. Slaney, editors, *Proceedings of the 13th International Conference on Automated Deduction*, number 1104 in Lecture Notes in Artificial Intelligence, pages 433–447. Springer-Verlag, 1996.
13. R. Smullyan. *First-Order Logic*. Springer-Verlag, 1968.

Optimal Left-to-Right Pattern-Matching Automata

Nadia Nedjah*, Colin D. Walter and Stephen E. Eldridge

Computation Dept., UMIST, PO. Box 88, Manchester M60 1QD, UK.
{nn, cdw, see} @sna.co.umist.ac.uk www.co.umist.ac.uk

Abstract

We propose a practical technique to compile pattern-matching for prioritised overlapping patterns in equational languages into a minimal, deterministic, left-to-right, matching automaton. First, we present a method for constructing a tree matching automaton for such patterns. This allows pattern-matching to be performed without any backtracking. Space requirements are reduced by using a directed acyclic graph (*dag*) automaton that shares all the isomorphic subautomata which are duplicated in the tree automaton. We design an efficient method to identify such subautomata and avoid duplicating their construction while generating the dag automaton. We conclude with some easily computed bounds on the size of the automata, thereby improving on previously known equivalent bounds for the tree automaton.

Keywords: Term rewriting system, pattern-matching, tree automaton, dag automaton.

1. Introduction

The key technical problems in implementing equational computations as reduction sequences are finding redexes, choosing which redex to reduce at each step and performing the reduction. The first stage is often called *pattern-matching* and this can be achieved as in lexical analysis by using a finite automaton. In order to avoid backtracking over symbols already read, extra patterns are added. These correspond to overlaps in the prefixes of original patterns. In this paper, we focus on avoiding the duplication of subautomata caused by the repetition of pattern suffixes when these new patterns are added. This results in a more efficient pattern-matcher. Consequently, we also obtain much improved bounds on the size of the recognising automaton.

A simple-minded way of pattern-matching is to try each rule sequentially until a left-hand side is matched or the whole pattern set is exhausted. However, this method may consume considerable effort unnecessarily. Usually, patterns are pre-processed to produce an intermediate representation allowing the matching to be performed more efficiently. One such representation consists of a matching automaton [3, 4, 7].

Here we concentrate on another method of building minimal (with respect to size), deterministic (i.e. no backtracking), matching automata for prioritised, overlapping patterns. First, a method for generating a deterministic tree matching automaton for a given pattern set is described. Although the generated automaton is efficient since it avoids symbol re-examination, it can only achieve this at the cost of increased space. As we shall see, the main reason for the increase in space requirements is the duplication of functionally identical or isomorphic subautomata in the tree-based automaton. However, the problem of directly constructing matching automata that do not duplicate such subautomata has not been previously described [2, 11]. We tackle

*Author sponsored by the British Council and the Algerian Ministry for High Education.

this next, describing a method that efficiently identifies equivalent states that would lead to identical subautomata and then constructing the equivalent reduced dag-based automaton. This is achieved without explicitly constructing the tree automaton first. Finally, we bound the size of the dag automaton using easily obtained parameters.

2. Notation and Definitions

In this section, we recall the notation and concepts that will be used in the rest of the paper. Symbols in a *term* are either function or variable symbols. The non-empty set of function symbols $F = \{a, b, f, g, ...\}$ is *ranked* i.e., every function symbol f in F has an *arity* which is the number of its arguments and is denoted $\#f$. A term is either a constant, a variable or has the form $ft_1t_2...t_{\#f}$ where each t_i, $1 \leq i \leq \#f$, is itself a term. We abbreviate terms by removing the usual parentheses and commas. This is unambiguous in our examples since the function arities will be kept unchanged throughout, namely $\#f = 4$, $\#g = \#h = 2$, $\#a = \#b = 0$. Variable occurrences are replaced by ω, a meta-symbol which is used since the actual symbols are irrelevant here. A term containing no variables is said to be a *ground* term. We generally assume that patterns are linear terms, i.e. each variable symbol can occur at most once in them. Pattern sets will be denoted by L and patterns by $\pi 1$, $\pi 2$, ..., or simply by π. A term t is said to be an *instance* of a pattern π if there is a *substitution* σ for the variables of π such that $t = \sigma\pi$.

Definition 2.1: A *position* in a term is a path specification which identifies a node in the parse tree of the term. Position is specified here using a list of positive integers. The empty list Λ denotes the position of the root of the parse tree and the position $p.k$ ($k \geq 1$) denotes the root of the kth argument of the function symbol at position p.

Positions of symbols in a term can be totally ordered according to the left-to-right order of the symbols in the term or the pre-order traversal of the parse tree. This ordering generalises to cases where the positions are of symbols in different terms because we can compare their integer lists lexicographically. So any set of positions can be put in left-to-right order.

Definition 2.2: A *matching item* is a triple $r{:}\alpha\bullet\beta$ where $\alpha\beta$ is a term and r is a *rule label*. The label identifies the origin of the term $\alpha\beta$ and hence, in a term rewriting system, the rewrite rule which has to be applied when $\alpha\beta$ is matched. The label is not written explicitly below except where necessary. The meta-symbol $\bullet$ is called the *matching dot*, α and β are called the *prefix* and *suffix* respectively, and the first symbol of β is called the *matching symbol*. The position of the matching dot is called the *matching position* and is identified with the position of the matching symbol. A *final* matching item is one of the form $\alpha\bullet$. It has a *final* matching position which we write as ∞.

Throughout this paper left-to-right traversal order is used. So the matching item $\bullet\beta$ represents the initial state prior to matching the pattern β. In general, the matching item $\alpha\bullet\beta$ denotes that the symbols in α have been matched and those in β have not yet been recognised. Finally, the matching item $\alpha\bullet$ is reached on successfully matching the whole pattern α.

Definition 2.3: A set of matching items in which all the items have the same prefix is called a *matching set*. A matching set in which all the items have an empty prefix is called an *initial* matching set whereas a matching set in which all the items have an empty suffix is called a *final* matching set. The *rule set* for a matching set is the set of labels appearing in its items.

Definition 2.4: For a set L of pattern suffixes and any symbol s, let $L\backslash s$ denote the set of pattern suffixes obtained by removing the initial symbol s from those members of L which commence with s. Then, for $f \in F$ define L_ω and L_f by:

$$L_\omega = L\backslash\omega$$

$$L_f = \begin{cases} L\backslash f \cup \omega^{\#\phi} L\backslash\omega & \text{if } L\backslash f = \varnothing \\ \varnothing & \text{otherwise} \end{cases}$$

where $\omega^{\#f}$ denotes a string of $\#f$ symbols ω. The *closure* $\overline{L}$ of a pattern set L is then defined recursively by Gräf [2] as follows:

$$\overline{L} = \begin{cases} L & \text{if } L = \{\varepsilon\} \text{ or } L = \varnothing \\ \bigcup\limits_{s\in F\cup\{\omega\}} s\,\overline{L_s} & \text{otherwise} \end{cases}$$

Roughly speaking, with two item suffixes of the form $f\alpha$ and $\omega\beta$ we always add the suffix $f\omega^{\#f}\beta$ in order to postpone by one more symbol the decision between these two patterns. Otherwise backtracking might be required to match $\omega\beta$ if input f leads to failure to match $f\alpha$.

3. Tree Matching Automata

In this section, we describe a practical and efficient method to construct a tree matching automaton for a prioritised overlapping pattern set. The pattern set L is converted into the above closed pattern set $\overline{L}$ while generating the matching automaton. In general, the construction technique described here is inspired by the LALR method used in YACC to generate parsers for LR-languages [1,5]. This has been used for many years to compile imperative languages. The pattern set to be compiled is considered as a set of right-hand sides of syntactic productions. However, there are no Shift-Reduce or Reduce-Reduce conflicts since we are only treating root matching of the input and the priority rule enables us to resolve multiple matches.

The pattern set compiles into a deterministic tree matching automaton which is represented by the 4-tuple $\langle S_0, S, S_\infty, \delta\rangle$ where S is the state set, $S_0 \in S$ is the initial state, $S_\infty \subseteq S$ is the final state set and δ is the state transition function. The states are labelled by matching sets which consist of original patterns whose prefixes match the current input prefix, together with extra instances of the patterns which are added to avoid backtracking in reading the input. In particular, the matching set for S_0 contains the initial matching items formed from the original patterns and labelled by the rules associated with them. Transitions are considered according to the symbol at the matching position, i.e. that immediately after the matching dot. For each symbol $s \in F\cup\{\omega\}$ and state with matching set M, a new state with matching set $\delta(M,s)$ is derived using the composition of the functions *accept* and *close* defined in Figure 3.1.

$$
\begin{aligned}
accept(M,s) &= \{r{:}\alpha s{\bullet}\beta \mid r{:}\alpha{\bullet}s\beta \in M\} \\
close(M) &= M \cup \{r{:}\alpha{\bullet}f\omega^{\#f}\mu \mid r{:}\alpha{\bullet}\omega\mu \in M \text{ and} \\
&\qquad \exists\, q{:}\alpha{\bullet}f\lambda \in M \text{ for some suffix } \lambda \text{ and } f \in F\} \\
\delta(M,s) &= close(\ accept(M,s)\ )
\end{aligned}
$$

Figure 3.1: *Automata Transition Function*

The items obtained by recognising the symbols in those patterns of M where s is the next symbol form the set $accept(M,s)$ which is called the *kernel* of $\delta(M,s)$. However, the set $\delta(M,s)$ may contain more items. The presence of two items $\alpha{\bullet}\omega\mu$ and $\alpha{\bullet}f\lambda$ in M creates a non-deterministic situation since the variable ω could be matched by a term having f as head symbol. The item $\alpha{\bullet}f\omega^{\#f}\mu$ is added to remove this non-determinism and avoid backtracking. The transition function thus implements simply the main step in the closure operation described by Gräf [2] and set out in the previous section. Hence the pattern set resulting from the automaton construction using the transition function of Figure 3.1 coincides with the closure operation of Definition 2.4. The item labels simply keep account of the originating pattern for when a successful match is achieved.

Non-determinism is worst where the input can end up matching the whole of two different patterns. Then we need a priority rule to determine which pattern to select.

Definition 3.2: A pattern set L is *overlapping* if there is a ground term that is an instance of at least two distinct patterns in L. Otherwise, L is *non-overlapping*.

Definition 3.3: A *priority rule* is a partial ordering on patterns such that if π_1 and π_2 are overlapping patterns then either π_1 has *higher* priority than π_2 or π_2 has *higher* priority than π_1.

When a final state is reached, if several rules have been successfully matched, then the priority rule is engaged to select the one of highest priority. Examples of priority rules are the *textual* and *specificity* priority rules. The textual rule is used in the majority of functional languages. Among the matched patterns, the rule chooses the pattern that appears first in the text. The specificity rule [6] can be used only if for any pair of overlapping patterns, one pattern is an instance of the other. The former pattern is said to be *more defined* than the latter. So among the matched patterns, the rule chooses the most defined pattern. Whatever rule is used, we will apply the word *match* only to the pattern of highest priority which is matched.

Definition 3.4: A term t *matches* a pattern $\pi \in L$ if, and only if, t is an instance of π and t is not an instance of any other pattern in L of higher priority than π.

Example 3.5: Let $L = \{faa\omega a, fga\omega aab, f\omega bbb\}$ be the pattern set of rules numbered 1, 2 and 3 respectively. The matching automaton for L is given in Figure 3.6. Each state is labelled with its matching set. Transitions corresponding to failures are omitted, and an ω-transition is only taken when there is no other available transition which accepts the current symbol. The automaton can be used to drive the pattern-matching process irrespective of the chosen term rewriting strategy.

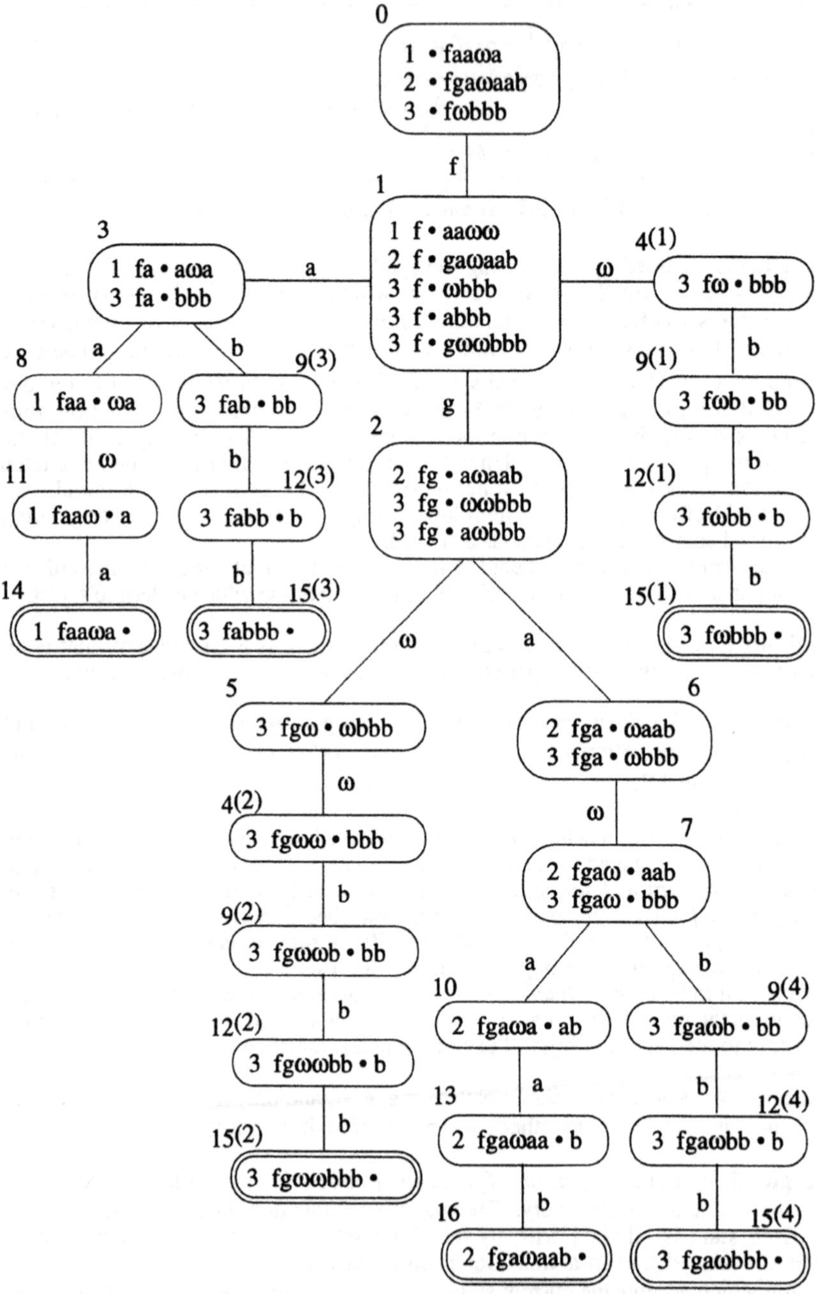

Figure 3.6: *Tree Automaton for* {1: *faaωa*, 2: *fgaωaab*, 3: *fωbbb*}.

4. Optimal Pattern-Matching Automata

The tree automaton described above is time efficient during operation because it avoids symbol re-examination. However, it achieves this at the cost of increased space requirements. The unexpanded automaton corresponding to the pattern set of Figure 3.6, and to which no patterns are added, is given in Figure 4.1. It is much smaller. There, *fabbb* is only recognised by backtracking from state 2 to state 1 and then taking the branch through state 4 instead. But in Figure 3.6 a branch recognising *fabbb* has been added to avoid backtracking, thereby duplicating the existing sub-branch which recognises the *bbb* in *fωbbb*. We can see similar duplication in several other branches of Figure 3.6; those identified by sharing the same main state numbers.

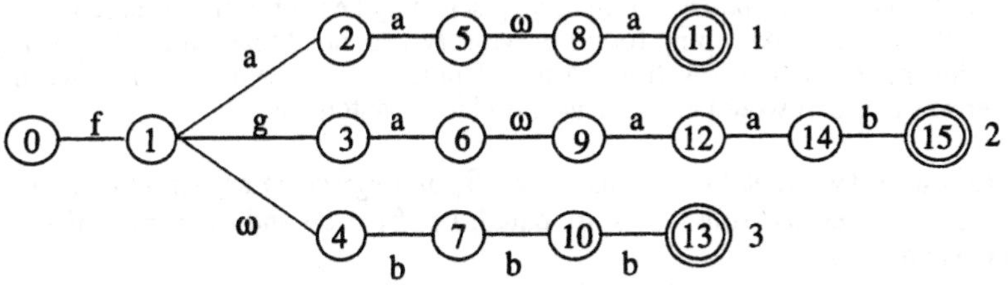

Figure 4.1: *Unexpanded Automaton for* {1: *faaωa*, 2: *fgaωaab*, 3: *fωbbb*}.

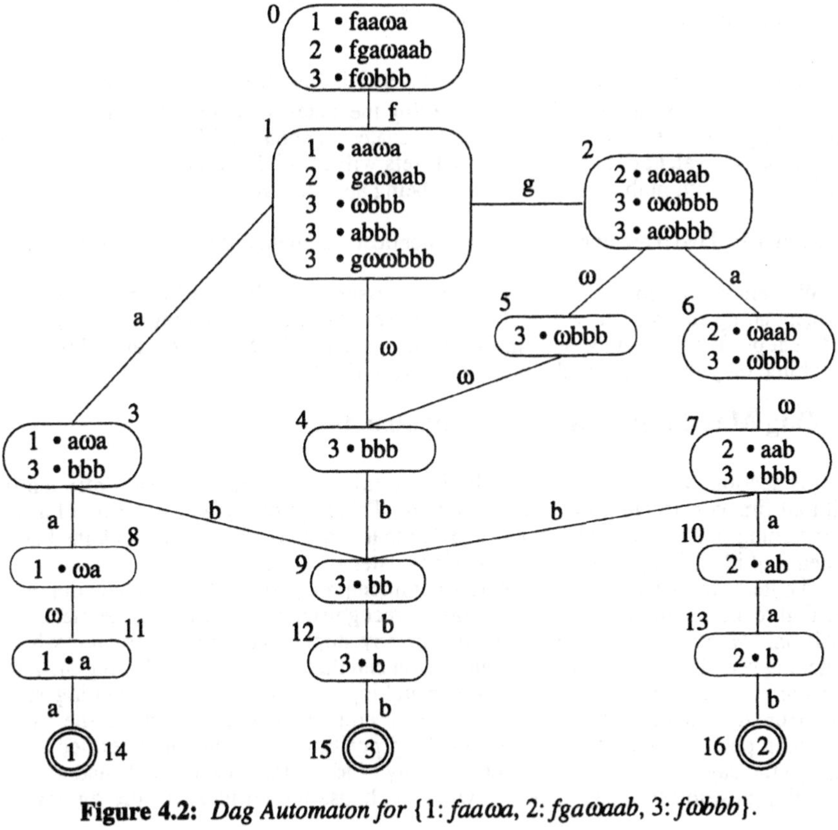

Figure 4.2: *Dag Automaton for* {1: *faaωa*, 2: *fgaωaab*, 3: *fωbbb*}.

By sharing duplicated branches, the tree automaton can be converted into an equivalent but smaller directed acyclic graph (*dag*) automaton. States which recognise the same inputs and assign the same rule numbers to them are functionally equivalent, and can be identified.. For instance, the dag automaton corresponding to Figure 3.6 is given in Figure 4.2. The number of states is thereby reduced from 27 to 17, leaving just one state more than in the non-deterministic machine of Figure 4.1.

The above example hides the complexity of recognising duplication where a number of suffixes are being recognised, not just one. The required dag automaton can be generated using finite state automaton minimisation techniques but this may require a lot of memory and time. The obvious alternative approach consists of using the matching sets to check new states for equality with existing ones while generating the automaton. In the case of equality, the new state is discarded and the existing one is shared. However, comparison of matching sets may be prohibitively expensive and it may well require bookkeeping for all previously generated matching sets. A major aim of this paper is to show how to avoid much of this work. First, we must characterise states that would generate isomorphic subautomata.

Definition 4.3: Two matching items $r_1{:}\alpha_1{\bullet}\beta_1$ and $r_2{:}\alpha_2{\bullet}\beta_2$ are *equivalent* if, and only if, the suffixes and rule labels are equal, i.e. $\beta_1 = \beta_2$ and $r_1 = r_2$. Otherwise, they are *inequivalent.*

Definition 4.4: Two matching sets M_1 and M_2 are *equivalent* if, and only if, to every item i in $M_1 \cup M_2$ there correspond items $i_1 \in M_1$ and $i_2 \in M_2$ which are equivalent to i. Otherwise, the sets are *inequivalent.*

For instance, in Figure 3.6 the matching sets labelling the states $9^{(1)}$ and $9^{(2)}$ are equivalent whereas the matching sets labelling the states 3 and $4^{(2)}$ are inequivalent. Clearly, equivalence is the right criterion for coalescing nodes of the tree automaton to obtain the equivalent dag automaton: such sets will certainly accept the same pattern suffixes and result in the same rewrite rule being applied. So,

Lemma 4.5: Two matching sets generate identical automata if they are equivalent.

We believe this equivalence is actually necessary as well as sufficient to combine corresponding states in the automaton. However, equivalent matching sets may have different prefixes, as can be seen in Figure 3.6. Since only the suffixes are relevant to matching, only they appear labelling the states in Figure 4.2.

5. Dag Matching Automaton Construction

In this section, we describe how to build the minimised dag automaton efficiently without first constructing the tree automaton. This requires the construction of a list of matching sets in a suitable order to ensure that every possible state is obtained, and a means of identifying potentially equivalent states.

The items in matching sets all share a common prefix before the matching dot (e.g. see Figure 3.6), namely the string of symbols recognised before reaching the matching position. Hence, the matching position of any item is an invariant of the whole matching set. The states of the tree automaton can therefore be ordered using the left-to-right total ordering on the common matching positions of their matching sets. Unfortunately, states which are functionally equivalent may not share the same matching position (see [8]). So the matching position is not uniquely defined for a state in the dag automaton. However, one way of assigning an acceptable and unique matching position to a dag state is always to choose the leftmost (or the rightmost) position of all the states which have been coalesced. This is done starting with the initial state and working downwards.

The dag automaton is constructed as in Algorithm 5.1. We iteratively construct the machine using a list l of matching sets in which the sets are ordered according to the matching position of the set. So the initial matching set is first and final matching sets come last. Each set in l is paired with its corresponding state in the automaton and a pointer is kept to the current position in the list l.

Algorithm 5.1: Initialise l to contain just the pair of the initial matching set and state, and set the current pointer to it. For the iterative step, let $\langle M,S\rangle$ be the current pair in l. For each symbol $s \in F\cup\{\omega\}$, compute the non-empty matching sets $\delta(M,s)$ as defined above. If there is no pair $\langle M',S'\rangle$ in l such that $\delta(M,s)$ is equivalent to M' then create a state S', add it to the automaton with a transition labelled s from S to S' and insert the pair $\langle\delta(M,s),S'\rangle$ into l according to the matching position of $\delta(M,s)$. Otherwise, i.e. when such a pair $\langle M',S'\rangle$ already exists in l, create a transition s from S to S'. Lastly, increment the pointer to the next matching set in l, if such exists, and repeat. The process halts when the end of the list l is reached.

The list l represents the equivalence classes of matching states where the assigned matching position is that of the representative which is generated first. In each new set which is generated, the position of the current matching set is incremented at least one place to the right. So new members of l are always inserted to the right of the current position. This ensures that all necessary transitions will eventually be generated without moving the pointer backwards in l. It is easy to see from the definition of the *close* function that added patterns cannot contain positions that were not in one of the original patterns. So l only contains sets with matching positions from a finite collection and, as each set can only generate a finite number of next states all of which are to the right, the total length of l is bounded and the algorithm must terminate.

The tree and dag automata clearly accept the same language and the automaton is minimal, in the sense that, by construction, none of the matching sets labelling the states in the automaton are equivalent. We now illustrate the algorithm.

Example 5.2: When applied to the pattern set of Example 3.5, the algorithm generates the same matching sets as in Figure 3.6, and we number the sets as there. It is clear from that figure that matching sets which are equivalent have been given the same number (with different bracketed subscripts for different occurrences) whereas inequivalent sets have different numbers. The left-to-right order by the matching position is given in Figure 5.3.

Matching position	List of states
Λ	0
1	1
1.1	2
1.2	5, 6
2	3, 4, 7
3	8, 9, 10
4	11, 12, 13
∞	14, 15, 16

Figure 5.3: *States of Figure 3.6 with their Matching Positions.*

One possible final list l which preserves this order is therefore given by reading it from top to bottom: (0, 1, 2, 5, 6, 3, 4, 7, 8, 9, 10, 11, 12, 13, 14, 15, 16). As each state in this list becomes the current state, it is readily seen that the new states it generates (as given by the transitions from the current state in Figure 3.6) are further along the list because their matching positions are further to the right. In fact, the states are numbered in order of creation in this list: State 0 generates state 1 which in turn generates states 2, 3 and 4. Then state 2 generates states 5 and 6 which are to the left of 3 and 4 and so are inserted before them. Next, state 5 generates a state which is found to be equivalent to 4, so that in the dag there will be a transition to state 4 from both states 1 and 5. The process continues until the final states 14, 15 and 16 are reached (one for each initial pattern) when the algorithm terminates and the dag automaton of Figure 4.2 is obtained.

6. Checking for Equivalence

In this section, we show how matching sets can frequently be discriminated easily so that the cost of checking for equivalence is reduced. However, in some cases, comparison of suffixes in the matching sets cannot be avoided. We look at three properties to help achieve this. One is the set of rules represented by patterns in the matching set, another is the matching position and the third is a state *weight* function wt. The first and last yield the same values for equivalent states. We must extend the arity notation $\#f$ to include variable symbols and ω which are all considered to be like constants and so of arity 0 i.e, $\#\omega = 0$.

Definition 6.1: The weight wt of a string of function and variable symbols s_i is:

$$wt(s_1 \dots s_n) = 1 + \sum_{i=1}^{n} (\#s_i - 1) \qquad \text{for } n \geq 0$$

and the weight of a matching item $\alpha{\bullet}\beta$ is defined as the weight of its prefix, viz. $wt(\alpha{\bullet}\beta) = wt(\alpha)$.

The following properties are readily verified (e.g. part (iii) by structural induction):

Lemma 6.2:

(i) $wt(\varepsilon) = 1$ i.e., the weight of the empty string is 1.

(ii) $wt(\alpha_1\alpha_2 \dots \alpha_n) = 1 + \sum_{i=1}^{n}(wt(\alpha_i) - 1)$ for any n strings $\alpha_1, \alpha_2, \dots, \alpha_n$.

(iii) $wt(t) = 0$ for any term t.

(iv) $wt(\alpha{\bullet}\beta) = n$ if $\beta = t_1 \dots t_n$ is a string of n terms.

(v) $wt(\sigma(\alpha)) = wt(\alpha)$ for any string α and substitution σ.

Using the arities as given previously to our example function symbols, we have for example:

$$wt(fag{\bullet}\omega aab) = 1 + (\#f-1) + (\#a-1) + (\#g-1) = 1 + 3 - 1 + 1 = 4$$
$$wt(fafab{\bullet}\omega aab) = 1 + (\#f-1) + (\#a-1) + (\#f-1) + (\#a-1) + (\#b-1) = 4$$

So the weight obtained is indeed the number of individual subterms after the matching dot. As symbol strings or as sequences of terms, these suffixes are identical although their parent patterns have different structures. For a matching item $\alpha{\bullet}\beta$, β is always a sequence of terms and so the weight function represents the number of terms in the suffix that have not yet been checked. This is the number of disconnected subtrees left after deleting the prefix nodes from the parse tree of the original term.

Since the prefix is an invariant of a matching set M, so is the weight and we can safely write $wt(M)$ for the common weight of any item in M. By (iv), the weight is determined uniquely from any suffix. So, as equivalent sets have the same suffix sets, the weight of a matching set is an invariant of its equivalence class. Equivalent matching sets must also have the same subsets of rules represented in their patterns.

Lemma 6.3: Equivalent matching sets have the same weights and rule set.

In Figure 4.2, all inequivalent matching sets are distinguished by the use of either the weight function or the rule set. Thus the criteria are useful in practice. However, they will clearly not be sufficient in general. In the opposite direction, it is also sometimes easy to establish equivalence. Combining these with the matching position, we have the following very useful result which enables the direct checking of equivalence to be avoided entirely in Example 3.5.

Theorem 6.4: Matching sets that share a common matching position, weight and rule set are equivalent.

Proof: It suffices to show the kernels of the matching sets are equivalent, since then the function *close* will add equivalent items to both sets. Let M_1 and M_2 be two matching sets that share the same weight, rule set and common matching position p. Let $i_1 = r{:}\alpha_1{\bullet}\beta_1$ and $i_2 = r{:}\alpha_2{\bullet}\beta_2$ be any two items associated with the same rule in their respectively kernels. The definitions of *accept* and *close* guarantee that the suffixes consist of a suffix of the original pattern π_r of the rule preceded by a number of copies of ω. To identify this suffix, let p' be the maximal prefix of the position p corresponding to a symbol in π_r. This is either the whole of p or is the position of a variable symbol ω. Either way, substitutions made by *close* for variables before p' in either i_1 or i_2 have already been fully passed in the prefix, and no substitution has yet been made for any variable further on in π_r. So if β is the suffix of π_r that starts at p' then the items i_1 and i_2 must have the form $\alpha_1{\bullet}\omega^{n_1}\beta$ and $\alpha_2{\bullet}\omega^{n_2}\beta$ for some $n_1, n_2 \geq 0$. Since M_1 and M_2 have equal weight, we have $wt(\alpha_1) = wt(\alpha_2)$. So $n_1 = n_2$ by Lemma 6.2(iv) and i_1 and i_2 are equivalent. We conclude that M_1 and M_2 are equivalent.

Although matching sets that share these three properties are equivalent, the matching positions of equivalent matching sets are not necessarily identical. An example can be found elsewhere (see [8]). Finally, we observe what weights and matching positions are possible:

Theorem 6.5: The weight and matching position of any matching set are the same as those of some matching item consisting of an original pattern with a matching dot.

Proof: From the definition of *close*, every symbol in an added pattern has the same position as a symbol in some pattern of the generating set. When that position becomes the matching position in the two corresponding patterns, the resulting items will have the same weight. By induction, these positions and weights must occur in the original pattern set.

7. Complexity

In this last main section, we evaluate the space complexity of the dag automaton by giving an upper bound for its size in terms of the number of patterns and symbols in the original pattern set. The bound established considerably improves Gräf's bound [2]. The *height* of a tree or dag automaton is the maximum distance from its root to a final state. The *breadth* of a tree automaton is the number of its final states, which is the size of the closure $\overline{L}$. Gräf bounds the size of the tree automaton by showing that

$$height(A_{tree}) \leq \sum_{\pi \in L} |\pi| \quad \text{and} \quad breadth(A_{tree}) \leq \prod_{\pi \in L} (|\pi|+1)$$

and then using the fact that the automaton size is less than the product of its breadth and height. We need a generalisation of breadth which is applicable to the dag automata here. We choose a rightmost matching position for each dag state so that positions move rightwards along every path. The following definition depends on this choice and so is not an invariant:

Definition 7.1: The *breadth* of a dag automaton is the maximum number of matching sets having the same matching position.

This wider definition of breadth coincides with the one for tree automata because:

Lemma 7.2: The maximum number of matching sets with the same matching position in a *tree* automaton is always the number of final matching sets, i.e. its breadth as a tree.

Proof: Along any branch from initial to final state of the *tree* automaton, the matching positions are all distinct because each state has a position to the right of its parent. Hence, for every occurrence of a given position in the tree, there is at least one occurrence of a final position at the end of the branch. Thus, there are at least as many final states as states with any given matching position.

Lemma 7.3: If A_{dag} is the dag automaton corresponding to the tree automaton A_{tree} then

$$breadth(A_{dag}) \leq breadth(A_{tree}) \quad \text{and} \quad height(A_{dag}) = height(A_{tree}).$$

Proof: The breadth inequality arises because every state in the dag corresponds to some state in the tree automaton that has the same assigned position. Also, the height of the dag and tree automata must coincide since the former has no cycles and so paths in the tree cannot become shorter in the dag.

The size of the tree automaton is bounded above by the product of its height and breadth. The nearest equivalent result for dag automata is that its size is bounded by the product of the number of different matching positions and its breadth. In the following, the bound on the breadth of the dag automaton is much better than that above for the tree automaton, and the bound for the number of positions essentially duplicates the height bound for the tree automaton. So immediately we have a much better overall bound on the size of the dag automaton than that given by Gräf for the tree automaton.

Lemma 7.4: If at least one pattern has 2 or more symbols, then the breadth of the dag automaton for a pattern set L is bounded above by $\left(2^{|L|}-1\right)\left(Max_{\pi \in L}|\pi|-1\right)$ where $|\pi|$ is the length of pattern π and $|L|$ is the size (cardinality) of L.

Proof: There is only one state, the initial one, which has the initial position and there are exactly $|L|$ states which have the final position, one for each pattern of L. So the breadth bound holds for them. Otherwise assume that the breadth is determined by a non-initial, non-final position. By Theorem 6.4, the maximum number of inequivalent states with the same matching position is bounded by the product of the number of different possible weights and the number of different possible rule sets. The rule set for any state could be any non-empty subset of L, of which there are $2^{|L|}-1$. So it remains to show that $Max_{\pi\in L}|\pi|-1$ is an upper bound on the number of possible weights. Using Theorem 6.5, the weight of a state is the weight of a prefix of a rule in L. This is the number of terms that could appear in its suffix. As we ignore initial and final positions, the weight is bounded below by 1 and above by one less than the number of symbols in the suffix, and hence by the length of the pattern minus 1. So up to at most $Max_{\pi\in L}|\pi|-1$ different weights are possible.

Lemma 7.5: The height of the minimised dag for a pattern set L is bounded above by $2-|L|+\sum_{\pi\in L}|\pi|$ and the number of its distinct positions is bounded by above $1+\sum_{\pi\in L}|\pi|$.

Proof: Along a path from the initial node to a final node, the positions are all distinct, each child having a position to the right of its parent, with each position appearing in some pattern of L. The number of non-initial, non-final positions counting multiplicities is $\sum_{\pi\in L}(|\pi|-1)$. Adding $1+|L|$ to this gives an upper bound on the total number of distinct positions, whereas adding 2 gives an upper bound on the height of the dag.

Combining the methods of proof for these two results above yields a very much better bound on dag automaton size than simply taking the product of breadth and number of positions. Our main conclusion about the space efficiency of the dag automaton described here is the following:

Theorem 7.6: The size of the dag automaton for a pattern set L is bounded above by:

$$1+|L|+(2^{|L|}-1)\left(\sum_{\pi\in L}(|\pi|-1)\right).$$

Proof: The number of states in the minimised dag automaton is $1+|L|$ plus the number of non-initial, non-final states in the dag. By Theorem 6.4, we just need to count the number of possible (*weight*, *position*) pairs, and multiply by the bound $2^{|L|}-1$ on the number of different possible rule sets. By Theorem 6.5, every (*weight*, *position*) pair of interest is given by a non-initial symbol position in an original pattern. So the number of such pairs is bounded by the number of such symbols, i.e. by $\sum_{\pi\in L}(|\pi|-1)$.

The above bound is easily computable with no internal knowledge of the patterns. However, if we have more specific information about subsets of rules starting with given function symbols, then the following improved bound may be applicable:

Corollary 7.7: The size of the dag automaton for a pattern set L is bounded above by:

$$1 + |L| + \sum_{f\in F^*}\left(1 + (2^{|L\backslash f|}-1)\left(\sum_{\pi\in L\backslash f}(|\pi|-1) \right) \right) + \delta\left(Max_{\pi\in L}|\pi|-2 \right)$$

where $L\backslash f$ is as in Definition 2.4, F^* is the subset of function symbols which appear as first symbols in L, and $\delta = 1$ if ω is a pattern of L and L has a pattern of length at least 3, and $\delta = 0$ otherwise.

Proof: Assume, first of all, that ω is not itself a pattern in L. So $L = \bigcup_{f\in F^*} f\,L\backslash f$ and $|L| = \sum_{f\in F}|L\backslash f|$. Then, after the initial state, the automaton splits into disjoint subautomata A_f which are entered according to the symbol f read first. Thus the size of the automaton is bounded by the number $1+|L|$ of initial and final states, plus 1 for the initial state of each A_f plus the number of non-initial, non-final states in each A_f. The rule set available for each state in A_f is restricted to a subset of those in $L\backslash f$ and the (*weight*, *position*) pairs of states must correspond to symbol positions in patterns of $L\backslash f$. So we can apply Theorem 7.6 to bound A_f in terms of $L\backslash f$ and so obtain the result. Now assume that ω is the initial symbol of a pattern. Then it is actually the whole pattern, so A_ω would consist of a single final state. The *close* function would add patterns to each A_f so that failure to match a pattern of $fL\backslash f$ would result in passing directly to a sequence of states which recognises all remaining input symbols and terminates at the final state of A_ω. For convenience, we will count this sequence of states as part of A_ω. Then, apart from extra transitions, the only difference the pattern ω makes is to add A_ω, which has at most $Max_{\pi\in L}|\pi|-2$ non-final states.

8. Conclusion

First, we described a practical method that compiles a set of prioritised overlapping patterns into an equivalent deterministic automaton which does not need backtracking to announce a match. Re-examination of symbols while matching terms is completely avoided. The matching automaton can be used to drive the pattern-matching process with any rewriting strategy.

In the main body of the paper, we described a method to generate an equivalent minimised dag matching automaton very efficiently without constructing the tree automaton first. We directly built the dag-based automaton by identifying the states of the tree-based automaton that would generate identical subautomata. By using the dag-based automata we can implement left-to-right pattern-matchers that avoid symbol re-examination without much increase in the space requirements.

Some useful functions were described for distinguishing inequivalent states when building the dag automaton. A theorem which guarantees equivalence in terms of several simple criteria was then applied to establish improved upper bounds on the size of the dag automaton in terms of just the number of patterns and symbols in the original pattern set. These considerably improve Gräf's previous bounds for the tree automaton.

References

[1] Aho, A.V., Sethi, R. and Ulmann, J.D., Compilers: Principles, Techniques and Tools, Addison-Wesley Publishing Company, 1986.

[2] Gräf, A., "Left-to-Right Pattern-Matching", in *Proc. Rewriting Techniques and Applications*, Lecture Notes in Computer Science, Vol. 488, pp. 323-334, Springer Verlag, 1991.

[3] Hoffman, C.M. and O'Donnell, M.J., "Pattern-Matching in Trees", *Journal of the ACM*, Vol 29, pp. 68-95, January 1982.

[4] Hoffman, C.M., O'Donnell, M.J. and Strandh, R. "Programming with Equations", *Software, Practice and Experience*, Vol. 15, No. 12, pp. 1185-1204, December 1985.

[5] Johnson, S. C., *Yacc - Yet Another Compiler Compiler*, Computing Science Technical Report 32, AT&T Laboratories, Murray Hill, N. J., 1975.

[6] Kennaway, J. R., "The Specificity Rule for Lazy Pattern Matching in Ambiguous Term Rewriting Systems", *Proc. 3rd European Symposium on Programming*, Lecture Notes in Computer Science, Vol. 432, pp. 256-270, Springer -Verlag, 1990.

[7] Knuth, D.E., Morris, J. and Pratt, V., "Fast Pattern-Matching in Strings", *SIAM Journal on Computing*, Vol. 6, No. 2, pp. 323-350, 1977.

[8] Nedjah, N., *Pattern-Matching Automata for Efficient Evaluation in Equational Programming*, Ph.D. Thesis, UMIST, Manchester, UK, 1997.

[9] Nedjah, N., Walter, C.D. and Eldridge, S.E., *Efficient Automaton-Driven Pattern-Matching for Equational Programs*, Technical Report, Computation Dept., UMIST, Manchester, UK, 1996.

[10] O'Donnell, M.J., Equational Logic as a Programming Language, The MIT Press, 1985.

[11] Sekar, R.C., Ramesh, R. and Ramakrishnan, I.V., "Adaptive Pattern Matching", *SIAM Journal on Computing*, Vol. 24, No. 5, pp. 1207-1234, December 1995.

Lecture Notes in Computer Science

For information about Vols. 1–1229

please contact your bookseller or Springer-Verlag

Vol. 1230: J. Duncan, G. Gindi (Eds.), Information Processing in Medical Imaging. Proceedings, 1997. XVI, 557 pages. 1997.

Vol. 1231: M. Bertran, T. Rus (Eds.), Transformation-Based Reactive Systems Development. Proceedings, 1997. XI, 431 pages. 1997.

Vol. 1232: H. Comon (Ed.), Rewriting Techniques and Applications. Proceedings, 1997. XI, 339 pages. 1997.

Vol. 1233: W. Fumy (Ed.), Advances in Cryptology — EUROCRYPT '97. Proceedings, 1997. XI, 509 pages. 1997.

Vol 1234: S. Adian, A. Nerode (Eds.), Logical Foundations of Computer Science. Proceedings, 1997. IX, 431 pages. 1997.

Vol. 1235: R. Conradi (Ed.), Software Configuration Management. Proceedings, 1997. VIII, 234 pages. 1997.

Vol. 1236: E. Maier, M. Mast, S. LuperFoy (Eds.), Dialogue Processing in Spoken Language Systems. Proceedings, 1996. VIII, 220 pages. 1997. (Subseries LNAI).

Vol. 1238: A. Mullery, M. Besson, M. Campolargo, R. Gobbi, R. Reed (Eds.), Intelligence in Services and Networks: Technology for Cooperative Competition. Proceedings, 1997. XII, 480 pages. 1997.

Vol. 1239: D. Sehr, U. Banerjee, D. Gelernter, A. Nicolau, D. Padua (Eds.), Languages and Compilers for Parallel Computing. Proceedings, 1996. XIII, 612 pages. 1997.

Vol. 1240: J. Mira, R. Moreno-Díaz, J. Cabestany (Eds.), Biological and Artificial Computation: From Neuroscience to Technology. Proceedings, 1997. XXI, 1401 pages. 1997.

Vol. 1241: M. Akşit, S. Matsuoka (Eds.), ECOOP'97 – Object-Oriented Programming. Proceedings, 1997. XI, 531 pages. 1997.

Vol. 1242: S. Fdida, M. Morganti (Eds.), Multimedia Applications, Services and Techniques – ECMAST '97. Proceedings, 1997. XIV, 772 pages. 1997.

Vol. 1243: A. Mazurkiewicz, J. Winkowski (Eds.), CONCUR'97: Concurrency Theory. Proceedings, 1997. VIII, 421 pages. 1997.

Vol. 1244: D. M. Gabbay, R. Kruse, A. Nonnengart, H.J. Ohlbach (Eds.), Qualitative and Quantitative Practical Reasoning. Proceedings, 1997. X, 621 pages. 1997. (Subseries LNAI).

Vol. 1245: M. Calzarossa, R. Marie, B. Plateau, G. Rubino (Eds.), Computer Performance Evaluation. Proceedings, 1997. VIII, 231 pages. 1997.

Vol. 1246: S. Tucker Taft, R. A. Duff (Eds.), Ada 95 Reference Manual. XXII, 526 pages. 1997.

Vol. 1247: J. Barnes (Ed.), Ada 95 Rationale. XVI, 458 pages. 1997.

Vol. 1248: P. Azéma, G. Balbo (Eds.), Application and Theory of Petri Nets 1997. Proceedings, 1997. VIII, 467 pages. 1997.

Vol. 1249: W. McCune (Ed.), Automated Deduction – CADE-14. Proceedings, 1997. XIV, 462 pages. 1997. (Subseries LNAI).

Vol. 1250: A. Olivé, J.A. Pastor (Eds.), Advanced Information Systems Engineering. Proceedings, 1997. XI, 451 pages. 1997.

Vol. 1251: K. Hardy, J. Briggs (Eds.), Reliable Software Technologies – Ada-Europe '97. Proceedings, 1997. VIII, 293 pages. 1997.

Vol. 1252: B. ter Haar Romeny, L. Florack, J. Koenderink, M. Viergever (Eds.), Scale-Space Theory in Computer Vision. Proceedings, 1997. IX, 365 pages. 1997.

Vol. 1253: G. Bilardi, A. Ferreira, R. Lüling, J. Rolim (Eds.), Solving Irregularly Structured Problems in Parallel. Proceedings, 1997. X, 287 pages. 1997.

Vol. 1254: O. Grumberg (Ed.), Computer Aided Verification. Proceedings, 1997. XI, 486 pages. 1997.

Vol. 1255: T. Mora, H. Mattson (Eds.), Applied Algebra, Algebraic Algorithms and Error-Correcting Codes. Proceedings, 1997. X, 353 pages. 1997.

Vol. 1256: P. Degano, R. Gorrieri, A. Marchetti-Spaccamela (Eds.), Automata, Languages and Programming. Proceedings, 1997. XVI, 862 pages. 1997.

Vol. 1258: D. van Dalen, M. Bezem (Eds.), Computer Science Logic. Proceedings, 1996. VIII, 473 pages. 1997.

Vol. 1259: T. Higuchi, M. Iwata, W. Liu (Eds.), Evolvable Systems: From Biology to Hardware. Proceedings, 1996. XI, 484 pages. 1997.

Vol. 1260: D. Raymond, D. Wood, S. Yu (Eds.), Automata Implementation. Proceedings, 1996. VIII, 189 pages. 1997.

Vol. 1261: J. Mycielski, G. Rozenberg, A. Salomaa (Eds.), Structures in Logic and Computer Science. X, 371 pages. 1997.

Vol. 1262: M. Scholl, A. Voisard (Eds.), Advances in Spatial Databases. Proceedings, 1997. XI, 379 pages. 1997.

Vol. 1263: J. Komorowski, J. Zytkow (Eds.), Principles of Data Mining and Knowledge Discovery. Proceedings, 1997. IX, 397 pages. 1997. (Subseries LNAI).

Vol. 1264: A. Apostolico, J. Hein (Eds.), Combinatorial Pattern Matching. Proceedings, 1997. VIII, 277 pages. 1997.

Vol. 1265: J. Dix, U. Furbach, A. Nerode (Eds.), Logic Programming and Nonmonotonic Reasoning. Proceedings, 1997. X, 453 pages. 1997. (Subseries LNAI).

Vol. 1266: D.B. Leake, E. Plaza (Eds.), Case-Based Reasoning Research and Development. Proceedings, 1997. XIII, 648 pages. 1997 (Subseries LNAI).